KINtop Studies in Early Cinema – volume 4
series editors: Frank Kessler, Sabine Lenk, Martin Loiperdinger

The Komedi Bioscoop:
Early Cinema in Colonial Indonesia

For Jonathan and Aviv

KINtop. Studies in Early Cinema

KINtop Studies in Early Cinema expands the efforts to promote historical research and theoretical reflection on the emergence of moving pictures undertaken by the internationally acclaimed *KINtop* yearbook (published in German from 1992–2006). It brings a collection of anthologies and monographs in English by internationally renowned authors as well as young scholars. The scope of the series ranges from studies on the formative years of the emerging medium of animated photographs to research on the institutionalisation of cinema in the years up to the First World War. Books in this series will also explore the many facets of 19th and early 20th century visual culture as well as initiatives to preserve and present this cinematographic heritage. Early cinema has become one of the most dynamic fields of scholarly research in cinema studies worldwide, and this series aims to provide an international platform for new insights and fresh discoveries in this thriving area.

Series editors: Frank Kessler, Sabine Lenk, Martin Loiperdinger

The Komedi Bioscoop: Early Cinema in Colonial Indonesia

Dafna Ruppin

British Library Cataloguing in Publication Data

The Komedi Bioscoop: Early Cinema in Colonial Indonesia

Series: KINtop Studies in Early Cinema – volume 4

A catalogue entry for this book is available from the British Library

ISBN: 9780 86196 723 0 (Paperback)

Published by
John Libbey Publishing Ltd, 3 Leicester Road, New Barnet, Herts EN5 5EW, United Kingdom
e-mail: john.libbey@orange.fr; web site: www.johnlibbey.com

Distributed worldwide by **Indiana University Press**,
Herman B Wells Library – 350, 1320 E. 10th St., Bloomington, IN 47405, USA.
www.iupress.indiana.edu

© 2016 Copyright John Libbey Publishing Ltd. All rights reserved.
Unauthorised duplication contravenes applicable laws.

Printed and bound in the United States of America.

Contents

Foreword	xi
Glossary and Notes on Language, Spelling and Currency	xiii
Prologue	xv
Introduction	1
Historical Context: The Late Colonial State in Indonesia	7
Current State of Research on Early Cinema in Colonial Indonesia	11
Time Frame, Geographical Scope and Sources	13
Engaging with Modernity	16
Trade Networks and Turn-of-the-Century Intermedial Entertainment Landscape	23
Indies Spectators and Spectatorial Positions: An Overview	32
Chapter Outline	38

PART I   Emerging Networks of Entertainment

Chapter 1   Trials and Tribulations of Early Travelling Shows, 1896–1898   43
    1.1 Introduction of Animated Photography: Harley's Kinetoscope, 1896   44
    1.2 "Truly Scientific Entertainment": Talbot's Scenimatograph, 1896–1897   49
    1.3 Moving Pictures Incorporated into Other Entertainment Forms   64
    1.4 Conclusion   81

Chapter 2   The Dutch Come into the Picture   83
    2.1 The Dutch Subsidiary of the American Biograph   84
    2.2 The American Biograph as Java Biorama   94
    2.3 The Java Cineograph Company   105
    2.4 Conclusion   115

Chapter 3   *Komedi Bioscoop*, *Indische* Films and the Localisation of Film Exhibition   117
    3.1 Manifestations of the *Indische* in Local Popular Culture   120
    3.2 Abdulally Esoofally   124
    3.3 The Netherlands Indies Biograph Company   145
    3.4 Conclusion   177

PART II	Local Cinema Cultures	
Chapter 4	**Surabaya: Queen City of Moving Picture Venues**	**183**
4.1	Canvas and Bamboo Tents at Pasar Besar	189
4.2	Tax and Legislation of Public Amusements in Surabaya	194
4.3	The Plague and the Plight of Cinema Shows, 1910–1911	196
4.4	Building Plans in 1910s	197
4.5	Constructing Cinema Palaces: C. J. Umbgrove's East-Java Bioscope, 1913	199
4.6	Public Education or School for Crime: Local Censorship Initiatives, 1912	209
4.7	Conclusion	213
Chapter 5	**Batavia: Capital of Chinese Cinema Venues**	**215**
5.1	Venues for Early Shows	222
5.2	Municipal Power and Taxation	225
5.3	Permanent Venues	235
5.4	Conclusion	260
Chapter 6	**Semarang: The Battleground over the Permanent Fairground Town**	**263**
6.1	Early Shows at Semarang Theatre	266
6.2	Weather and Hygiene: "The rain is a sworn enemy of the cinema tent"	268
6.3	Controlling the "permanent fairground": Permits and Public Amusements Tax	270
6.4	Municipal Council Resists "Cinema Fever"	274
6.5	Plans for a New Multi-Purpose Semarang Theatre Building	278
6.6	The Semarang International Colonial Exhibition, 1914	279
6.7	Conclusion	286
Chapter 7	**Medan: The Making and Breaking of a Monopoly**	**289**
7.1	Direct Current: The Arrival of Moving Pictures in Medan	294
7.2	Tent Shows on the Esplanade	296
7.3	Restaurant Shows and Screenings at Plantations	299
7.4	Municipal Cinema Theatre and Medan's Cinema Monopoly: The Case of the Orange Bioscope	302
7.5	End of Medan's Cinema Monopoly	311
7.6	Conclusion	315

Concluding Remarks — 317

Bibliography — 326

Appendix Local Views as Screened by Exhibitors — 339

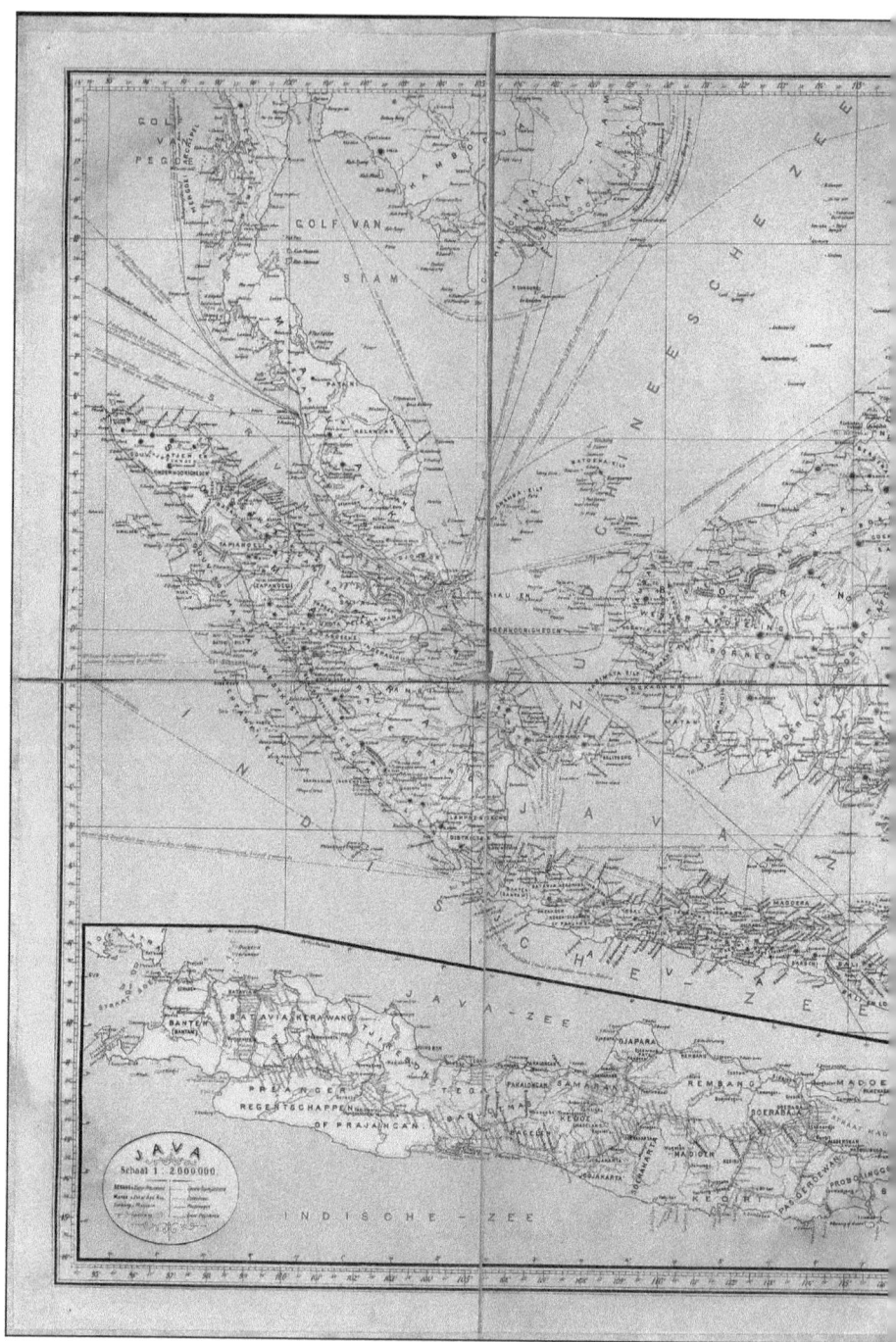

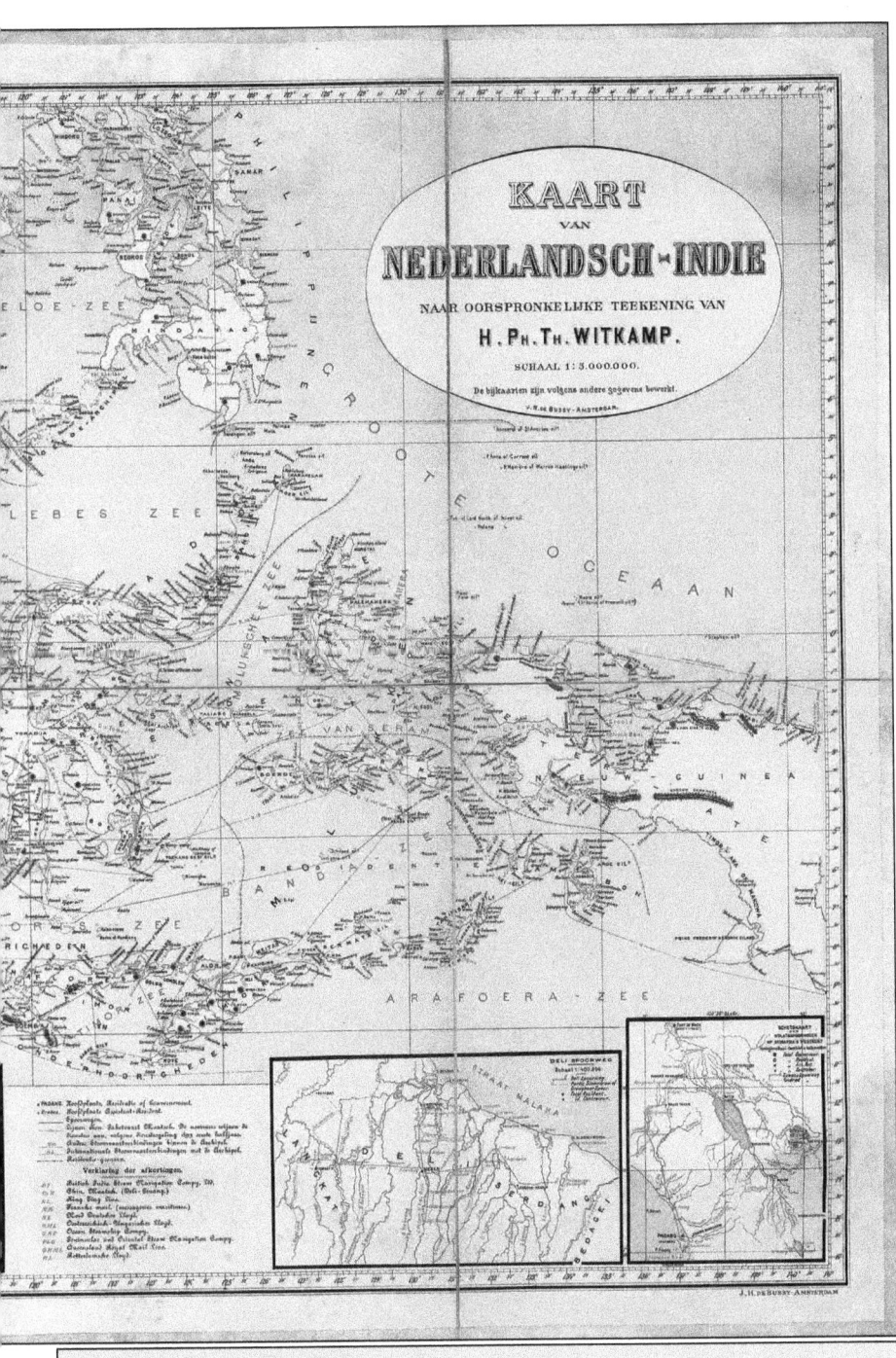

Frontispiece: Map of the Netherlands Indies, ca. 1893, showing railway lines and steamship connections. [Courtesy of the University of Texas Libraries, The University of Texas at Austin (source: http://www.lib.utexas.edu/maps/historical/nederlandsch_indie_1893.jpg)]

Foreword

This book is an outcome of my PhD research conducted at the Research Institute for Cultural Inquiry (ICON) at Utrecht University. It formed part of the research project "The Nation and Its Other: The Emergence of Modern Popular Imagery and Representations", which was funded by the Netherlands Organisation for Scientific Research (NWO) Cultural Dynamics programme. It would not have been accomplished without the support of scholars, friends, family, librarians and archivists. While these few lines cannot be sufficient to convey my gratitude, I hope to here nevertheless express my deep thanks to all those who have made it possible to set off on this adventure.

I would like to thank my PhD supervisors, Frank Kessler and André van der Velden, for their constant guidance, advice, encouragement and kindness. Frank's wide knowledge of film history and much beyond provided boundless inspiration and, on a more practical level, plenty of leads to references and sources strewn throughout the length and breadth of this work. André's persistent and thoughtful questioning helped me gain control of the research path which, at times, threatened to endlessly *schlep* me around.

Many thanks are due to the members of my PhD committee: Joris van Eijnatten, Sonja de Leeuw, Martin Loiperdinger, Henk Schulte Nordholt, and William Uricchio. They have provided valuable input and insightful comments at various stages of this writing process.

A special thank you to Sabine Lenk, whose close reading and editorial feedback were absolutely vital in transforming the PhD thesis into the current book version. Her constructive input and eye for detail have been greatly appreciated.

John Libbey's professionalism, support, and enduring patience have greatly facilitated the final stages of bringing this work to print. Thank you to Matthew Cohen who took the time to counsel and share from his vast knowledge of popular entertainment in the region. His advice on the painstaking process of collecting and organising the source materials has been instrumental in facilitating a smooth writing experience.

Judith Thissen's active support and involvement during the research process helped me to explore further options and to discount the craziness of studying (yet) another language in order to be able to conduct this research. I thank you immensely.

Many hours were spent in solitude at various libraries, yet I always felt I had a fellow traveller in Nadi Tofighian. Nadi generously shared his own findings, conducted detailed discussions over long Skype calls, and provided valuable comments. I am deeply indebted to him.

I have benefited from discussions with various colleagues and scholars from different institutions over the course of this research. I wish to thank Rommy Albers, Ben Arps, Soeluh van den Berg, Louise Bethlehem, Marieke Bloembergen, Stephen Bottomore, Sarah Dellmann, Karel Dibbets, Claire Dupré la Tour, Wolfgang Fuhrmann, Alison Griffiths, Stephen Putnam Hughes, Judith Keilbach, Peter Keppy, Jeffrey Klenotich, Nico de Klerk, Rotem Kowner, Paul Kusters, Richard Maltby, Paul S. Moore, Mette Peters, Bambang Purwanto, Lisabona Rahman, Sandeep Ray, Emjay Rechsteiner, Jeroen Salman, Orlow Seunke, Rianne Siebenga, Suryadi, Heather Sutherland, Fenneke Sysling, Eric Tagliacozzo, and Klaas de Zwaan.

The staff members of libraries and archives consulted during this research are too numerous to name here. Librarians and archivists often went out of their way to make sure I had access to materials. I would like to especially thank the staff of the microfilm collection at the PNRI in Jakarta who, beyond putting up with my poor skills in Indonesian, also endured my presence long past the reading room's opening hours over the course of three intensive months. Thank you also for producing the scans from several Malay newspapers reprinted here. Scans from Dutch newspapers were retrieved from the Delpher online database. Images from the KITLV heritage collection (now, part of Leiden University Library) and from the KIT photograph collection in Amsterdam are reproduced here as well. Many thanks also to Scott Merrillees for permitting the reproduction of several postcards from his private collection.

My Jakarta team played a key role in making me feel welcome in an utterly new environment. I wish to thank Rodel M. Briones, Pak Bimo, Tito Imanda, Ekky Imanjaya, Nayla Majestya, Dror Ziulkowski. A special thank you to Forum Lenteng's Hafiz Rancajale, Otty Widasari, Mahardika Yudha, and Yuki Aditya for their ongoing support of this research. Their recognition of this work's importance to Indonesian film heritage has provided great encouragement and motivation throughout the course of this project. Forum Lenteng's financial contribution to this publication is gratefully acknowledged.

While all translations from Dutch and Malay are my own, I could not have done it without some help. I would like to thank Klaas and André for their assistance with the Dutch texts, and Bram Hendrawan and Suryadi for their help with the Malay texts. Any errors in translation, or possible faults at identifying a company or newspaper source, are my own.

Finally, my family has always provided unbounded love and support and encouraged me to follow my dreams, wherever they may take me. I love you.

Aix-en-Provence, April 2016.

Glossary and Notes on Language, Spelling and Currency

Glossary

alun alun	Central town square. Also spelled aloen aloen
bangsawan	Generic name for Malay-language popular theatre originating from colonial Malaysia. Shares similarities with *komedi stambul*
dalang	Puppet master of Javanese shadow play (*wayang kulit*)
gambar hidup	Living pictures (direct translation of the Dutch form at the time, *levende beelden*). Also spelled *gambar hidoep*
gamelan	Traditional ensemble music on Java and Bali, mostly involving percussion instruments
Indisch or *Indische*	Dutch term meaning something "of the Indies" but also used to refer to hybrid European-Indonesian practices, such as in literature or performance arts, but also dress and food
Indo	A Eurasian of mixed Indonesian and European descent
kampung	Malay word for a rural village, but can also denote traditional neighbourhoods, typically inhabited by non-Europeans, within an urban setting. Also spelled *kampong*
komedi	Commercial entertainment, such as *komedi stambul* (genre of popular Malay opera), *komedi kuda* (circus, literally "horse show")
nyai	An informal native wife or concubine. Also spelled *njai*
pasar	A market or bazaar. Also used in *pasar malam* (night fair) or *Pasar Gambir* (Gambir Fair, held in Batavia annually as of 1906 to celebrate the birthday of Queen Wilhelmina)
peranakan	A term used to refer to Indies-born Chinese, as opposed to *totok*
priyayi	Indonesian native elite class
ronggeng	Popular Malay folk-dance
sekaten	A Javanese traditional week-long celebration marking the birth of the Islamic prophet Muhammad
stadstuin	City gardens
topeng	Masked-dance performance with *gamelan* accompaniment
totok	Colloquial term for residents of the Netherlands Indies who were not born in the Indies, either European or Chinese

tuan	A prefix equivalent to "sir" or "mister" in reference to a European man. Also spelled *toean*
tukang	Craftsman, possessing or displaying expert knowledge
warung	A small shop, kiosk or café-restaurant, either mobile or fixed. Also spelled *warong* or *waroeng*
wayang	General term for traditional theatre, as in *wayang kulit* (Javanese shadow puppet theatre) and *wayang wong* or *wayang orang* (traditional dance drama with live actors) with *gamelan* accompaniment

Notes on Language, Spelling and Currency

The Dutch and Malay language sources consulted in this research predate standardisation of vernacular Malay as Indonesian, as well as of the Dutch post-Second World War spelling reform. In this book, I have used modern spelling for place names (for instance, "Surabaya" rather than "Soerabaia" or "Soerabaja"). In cases of Dutch newspapers using a Malay word or Malay newspapers using a Dutch word, I have chosen to keep the spelling as appeared in the original source.

In his book on the Komedie Stamboel, Matthew Cohen uses spelling to differentiate between the Komedie Stamboel, referring to the specific troupe under investigation in his study, which was established in Surabaya in 1891, and *komedi stambul* in reference to the genre of Malay popular opera. I have retained this differentiation throughout this book.

The currency used on Java was the Dutch guilder. The currency symbol f refers to florins, which is interchangeable with guilder, and was commonly used in advertisements of the day. Before the currency reform of 1907–1909, the currency used on Sumatra in the period under investigation was the Mexican dollar.

Prologue

26 August 1904, Bandung – then a little mountain town – in a state of uproar. This was usually the case when a bamboo shed or circus tent was set up on the Pieterspark-Plein (where the complex of the Java Bank now stands).

But on that 26 August something special was about to occur, if to judge by the posters on the walls and trees with catchy inscriptions like: "Never before shown in the Indies!" "Dreams which have now become reality!" "Go see it, go see it!"

The area surrounding the large bamboo shed was very quickly occupied by numerous stall keepers selling syrup, satay, soto and other delicious goodies.

One hour before the start there was already such an overwhelming crowd, that it was difficult for people to get to the ticket box office.

At 7 pm the show would begin. Boong Indri, his younger brother Tjo and the Vink brothers also stood with hearts beating hard, staring at the posters by the ticket box office (far too generous a term for it, really), when suddenly Mr. Frühling, a well-known figure in Bandung, threw a question at them: "Hey lads, can you whistle?"

Boong Indri answered: "Whistle? But sir, what kid cannot whistle, what a question". "Yes, but", repeated Mr. F., "I mean if you can whistle the 'Katjang goreng March,' the 'Bandung waltz,' the 'Satay-polka' (very popular tunes at the time, which on every festive occasion were played back by the ronzebons of Kang Ismael [a band of Indonesians with Western instruments])".

"There is nothing to it, sir", we said. "Very well then", said Mr. F. "I have a nice proposition for you, come along with me behind the ticket box office".

Now just a short sketch of Mr. Frühling. A German by birth, a wrestler, and the only pianist in Bandung, i.e. he could sort of thrum on the piano but could not read music, even if the notes were as big as watchtowers. Yet, he did not lack in musicality; namely, feeling that the rhythm in music is based on a beat in multiples of four. "So lads", he said, "you obviously want to go to this film screening, hè? Listen then, you can enter for free, if you are willing to work with me". Our curiosity ran high!

"There are", he continued, "as you know, three films on the programme:
a. The man with dog vision,
b. A street in Mecca and
c. The circulatory system of a frog.

Well, upon the first a waltz is played. I then play four beats: 1 oom-pah pah, 2 oom-pah pah, 3 oom-pah pah, 4 oom-pah pah and then you launch with the Bandung waltz, get it?" We answered in unison, "Yes, sir!"

"With the second film", Mr. F. continued, "a march is heard. I then play four beats again: oom-pah, oom-pah, oom-pah, oom-pah, and then you come in with the 'Katjang goreng March', got it?"

We: "Yes, sir!"

"For the third film", said the German, "we can do the 'Satay-polka,' also in march tempo, but slower!"

After a rehearsal behind the ticket box office, which went very smoothly, the wrestler said, "Boys, you may come in, go stand next to the piano, the show is about to begin in a few minutes!"

The piano – owned by Mr. F. – stood on the grass at the back of the "hall". It seemed strange to us that the bamboo benches in the front were for the indigenous population, while the rear was reserved for Europeans. Unlike any other theatre, where the best seats were always in the front.

The shed was completely full. People flocked especially to sit as close as possible to the white screen, thinking that you could see best from there. It was indeed a novelty...

Just before the start, a violent clamour came from the piano!

When opening the piano lid at the top – aimed at enhancing the sound to the outside – a serpent suddenly thrust its head up and drew out its tongue at us innocent whistlers... We stood as if transfixed to the ground in terror. Not so our burly pianist. Without disclosing himself, he quickly and with lightning speed raised his right arm into the air and with a flat hand gave the snake what was then called a "blow" [oppattatter], so that its first performance was also to be its last. The head was crushed into pieces against the piano wall.

We hardly recovered from the first fright, when the clatter of the projection device provided us with another shock. The hall was suddenly dark and we read on the white screen: "the man with dog vision".

The pianist: "Attention lads!" Then the four beat oom-pah-pah and we nicely launched into the "Bandung waltz". But... what was unfolding there on the screen in front of our eyes (a long-haired man, like a gorilla, smoking a kind of "Churchill cigar" and soon became nauseous) gripped us to such an extent that we forgot our work and the melodious strike.

The piano-slayer furiously: "Whistle! Whistlle[!]" He immediately poked me in the back and instinctively I passed it on to my companions. But no one knew where to begin... The German hissed at us, "Don't do that again, you hear!"

Luckily, this reproach was drowned out by the booing in the "hall" when the smoking gorilla on the screen began vomiting. A short break between the 1st and 2nd films came as a relief. We had to prepare for the "Katjang goreng march", which would also be preceded by four beats: oom-pah, oom-pah.

Then began the familiar clatter again, and we were once again in the dark. After four beats of oom-pah we again sprang in perfectly, but then there was suddenly a great confusion in the front ranks among the Indonesians. What was going on?

The film, "A street in Mecca", began with the approach of a haji from afar. Coming closer, the picture gradually grew to a frightening monster so the Indonesians were seized with great fear in the front rows and soon started running among loud cries: "djoeriek, djoeriek!" (a ghost, a ghost!) Within a few minutes the cinema was almost empty because many Europeans, who thought that a fire had broken out, also took flight.

The great commotion was a welcomed opportunity for Boong Indri and his comrades to make a run for it...

"My First Cinema Screening" by Boong Indri.
From Tong Tong. Het Enige Indische Blad in Nederland 1, no. 2
(30 July 1958): 2.

Introduction

In March of 1897 a reporter from Bandung, the city in Central Java referred to in Boong Indri's account and soon to be nicknamed the Paris of Java, thanks to its tree-lined boulevards and fountains, offered the following survey of the local popular entertainment scene:

> Bandung cannot complain of the inconveniences of an isolated life, which many inland cities in Java have reason to. Travelling artists and impresarios occasionally come here to give shows and spectacles of amusements in various fields, whose debuts first appear and are proofed in Batavia – the 'pick of the bunch.' [...] Among the above spectacles are many that one will never get to see in a Dutch provincial town. Where has one in the rural provinces seen a Scenimatograph at work, as Mr. Talbot has shown us here on the 24th?[1]

This may have been a correct estimate on the journalist's part. Although the first Lumière films were screened in Amsterdam already in March 1896, and while moving pictures were further popularised across the Netherlands at fairgrounds and in vaudeville shows over the next few years, film-going on a large scale never really took off before the First World War, compared to other European countries.[2] Consequently, the Dutch were neither primary exporters nor producers of moving pictures in the Netherlands Indies (present-day Indonesia) in the early days of cinema. Nevertheless, as this research has found, moving pictures were introduced and commercialised in the Indies thanks to the efforts of *other* entrepreneurs of myriad nationalities and ethnicities, almost in parallel with these processes in the West.[3] A decade later, in 1907, there were reportedly 35 companies touring Java alone, holding shows up to three times

---

1   "Nederlandsch-Indië", *Java-Bode* (29 March 1897). Unless otherwise stated, all translations from Dutch and Malay are my own.

2   See Ivo Blom, *Jean Desmet and the Early Dutch Film Trade* (Amsterdam: Amsterdam University Press, 2003), 37; André van der Velden and Judith Thissen, "Spectacles of Conspicuous Consumption: Picture Palaces, War Profiteers and the Social Dynamics of Moviegoing in the Netherlands, 1914–1922", *Film History* 22 (2010): 453–462.

3   A similar trend was also apparent in modern transport and communications, where "the first commercial prototypes appeared in Europe or North America, but it was seldom long before they appeared in Asia" (Howard Dick and Peter J. Rimmer, *Cities, Transport and Communications: The Integration of Southeast Asia since 1850* (Houndmills: Palgrave Macmillan, 2003), 41). See further the section on Trade Networks and Turn-of-the-Century Intermedial Entertainment Landscape.

a day in bamboo tents accommodating thousands of spectators.[4] By the early 1910s, brick and stone cinema houses were constructed in cities and towns across the archipelago. "Even Malang", a Surabayan newspaper incredulously reported in 1912, "was soon to be enriched with a *modern* cinema theatre".[5]

Up until this research, it was generally believed that the Netherlands Indies in the period preceding the First World War was only a market where old, degraded film copies from the Netherlands could be shipped off to, and where the history of film essentially began in the 1920s, when Indonesians became involved in filmmaking.[6] Even people in the Netherlands at the time would have been surprised to learn of cinema's popularity and well-developed infrastructure in the Indies, as a 1913 report in the Amsterdam-based trade weekly *De Kinematograaf* claimed.[7] However, as the article continued:

> To the connoisseur of conditions in the Indies, this fact may seem less strange, since the path of the cinema there was already fully paved in advance. The yonder living Europeans and also the natives had hitherto little pleasure to taste, as the circumstances linked to the establishment and installation of an entertainment venue always carry with them the danger of not being profitable and usually the enterprise even results in failure. The cinema, however, quickly and easily obtained a foothold, and where once only dull tents stood with the ringing name "Cinema Theatre", it has now elevated itself to proud palaces, which conform to the most *modern* demands. Europeans and natives have become the loyal visitors of the Photoplay [*Lichtbeelden*] Theatre, and the Chinese, the Malays and the Javanese are already fanatic about your cinema darlings and "World Stars".[8]

This research traces the emergence of a local culture of movie-going in the Netherlands Indies (particularly on Java and Sumatra), covering the time period from the earliest commercial screenings identified in this research in 1896 until the outbreak of the First World War in 1914. By drawing on a variety of primary sources, namely, Dutch- and Malay-language newspapers, government documents, travelogues, guidebooks, and archival maps and photographs held in libraries and archives in the Netherlands and in Indonesia, it strives to portray the "conditions in the Indies" that enabled early cinema to "quickly and easily [obtain] a foothold".[9] The chapters that follow map out the introduction of the new technology by independent touring exhibitors, the constitution of a market for moving picture shows, the embedding of moving picture exhibition within the local popular entertainment scene, and the Dutch colonial authorities' efforts to control film consumption and distribution. Finally, as moving picture technologies and the venues built to accommodate them were closely identified by contemporary commentators with concepts such as "modern", "novelty" and "progress", this study considers what kinds of en-

4 "Bioscoopconcurrentie", *Nieuwe Soerabaja Courant* (16 August 1907).
5 "Nieuwe bioscooploods", *Nieuwe Soerabaja Courant* (10 April 1912), emphasis added.
6 See further discussion in the section on Current State of Research on Early Cinema in Colonial Indonesia.
7 "Het Bioscooptheater in onzen Oost", *De Kinematograaf* 1, no. 35 (1913): 254.
8 Ibid., emphasis added.
9 Ibid.

gagements with modernity the nascent practice of cinema-going was able to offer spectators in colonial Indonesia.

The research approach of this study is in line with the "new cinema history", a methodology which since the 1990s has shifted the focus in the writing of cinema history "[...] away from the content of films to consider their circulation and consumption, and to examine the cinema as a site of social and cultural exchange".[10] According to Richard Maltby, our attention as cinema historians should shine a spotlight on intermediary figures who may be embodied in "[...] the small businessmen who acted as cultural brokers, navigators and translators of the middle ground constructing a creolised culture out of their community's encounters with the mediated external world".[11] The following chapters will thus highlight the work of local and travelling exhibitors, managers, agents, and cinematographers in introducing and popularising moving images in colonial Indonesia. Furthermore, in an effort to look "beyond the idea of the movie theatre as a closed space where people are immersed in darkness and where they are submerged as figures constructed by the cinematic apparatus or by particular film texts or genres", this empirical study considers movie-going "as a social act performed by people of flesh and blood, who actively engage with movies and with other people, firmly situated within specific social, cultural, historical and spatial confines".[12] Focusing on the cinema as a social institution, in which technology, race and colonialism converged, moving picture venues in the Indies are perceived here as liminal spaces in which daily interactions across boundaries could occur within colonial Indonesia's multi-ethnic and increasingly polarized colonial society.

In a traditional approach to writing film history from the perspective of production, the gradated institutionalisation of cinema as a medium has been described by André Gaudreault and Philippe Marion as a successive process: "from the *appearance* of a technological process – that of the apparatus that records moving images – to the *emergence* of 'moving pictures', or the establishment of diverse procedures which endow the process with the status of an apparatus, to the *constitution* of an established medium".[13] This schema serves here as a useful starting point, yet the specific conditions under which this process occurs when studying exhibition make it necessary to refine the framework. The emphasis on the "birth" of cinema, even in the more

---

10   Richard Maltby, "New Cinema Histories", in Richard Maltby, Philippe Meers and Daniel Biltereyst (eds.), *Explorations in New Cinema History: Approaches and Case Studies* (Oxford: Wiley-Blackwell, 2011), 3–40, here 3.

11   Richard Maltby, "On the Prospect of Writing Cinema History from Below", *Tijdschrift voor Mediageschiedenis* 9, no. 2 (2006): 91.

12   Daniel Biltereyst, Richard Maltby and Philippe Meers, "Cinema, Audiences and Modernity: An Introduction", in Daniel Biltereyst, Richard Maltby and Philippe Meers (eds.), *Cinema, Audiences and Modernity: New Perspectives on European Cinema History* (London: Routledge, 2012), 1–16, here 2.

13   André Gaudreault and Philippe Marion, "A medium is always born twice...", *Early Popular Visual Culture* 3, no. 1 (2005): 5.

attenuated model of Gaudreault and Marion's "second birth", is absorbed in a series of firsts: the inventors of the different devices are associated with the technology's appearance, the emergence of established procedures is linked to the first camera operators, and the first film directors are responsible for the constitution of the medium.[14] The history of production, for all its claims to universality, therefore habitually locates all of the above procedures as occurring in the West, mostly in France, Britain, and the United States. A history of exhibition and reception, resembling what historian of technology David Edgerton calls a "history of technology-in-use", can help us broaden this traditional geography of cinema to include places where the technology of moving images was distributed and consumed.[15] A "use-based history of technology", Edgerton claims, "[...] gives us a [global] history of technology engaged with all the world's population, which is mostly poor, non-white and half female".[16] A history of early movie-going in colonial Indonesia thus unveils an aspect of spectators' everyday life experience and, in the process, enables us to question traditional schemes of the diffusion of technology, globalisation and modernity.

The graphic portrayal of a boy's first moving picture show in Bandung in 1904, quoted in full in the Prologue and written by an *Indische*[17] man under the pen name Boong Indri about half a century after the fact, touches on some of the questions that we will be concerned with throughout the chapters that follow.[18] Among them: Who were the entrepreneurs behind the exhibition, distribution and production of moving images in the Netherlands Indies? What other popular entertainment forms were they in competition with over spectators' attention and money? Who were the spectators who patronised moving picture shows? How did exhibitors advertise their shows? What films made up their programmes? What musical accompaniment was provided during (and in-between) films? What food and beverages were on offer inside and outside exhibition venues? Where did such performances take place – geographically (in major cities, small towns, or rural areas) and venue-wise (in canvas tents, converted buildings, bamboo tents, purpose-built cinema theatres, etc.)? What were the seating arrangements in these venues? What kinds of interactions took place between exhibitors and their audiences, and between different spectators seated in various ranks?

At the same time, while this striking story/memoir captures some of the particular subtleties of the early screening situation in the Indies, this retro-

14   Ibid.

15   David Edgerton, *The Shock of the Old: Technology and global history since 1900* (London: Profile Books, 2008 [2006]), xi.

16   Ibid., xiii.

17   From a family of mixed European and Indonesian descent. A Eurasian child would have been recognized by the colonial state as Dutch or, rather "European", if acknowledged by his or her Dutch/European father.

18   It remains unclear to what extent Boong Indri's story is memoir or fiction, but it appears to switch between these registers. It is most likely a spiced-up version of an actual movie-going experience in the Indies.

spective account published in *Tong-Tong*, a Dutch-language magazine printed in The Hague and devoted to *Indisch* culture and society, serves as a reminder that we must treat sources with caution and scrutiny.[19] For it is not only infused with what Edward Said identifies as an "Orientalist" discourse, imagining the Indonesian "Natives" as inferior or childlike and positing them as irrational "Others" to the rational "European" spectators, but it is also permeated with precisely the kinds of ideas about the early movie-going experience that are being questioned by the new cinema history.[20] Thus, the enduring myth of spectators in the West running away from the screen at the sight of an arriving train, itself the product of a similar racial imaginary that reduced these spectators "to a state usually attributed to savages in their primal encounter with the advanced technology of Western colonialists, howling and fleeing in impotent terror before the power of the machine", seeps into this depiction of Indonesian spectators, supposedly encountering the projection of moving images for the first time.[21] This establishing moment, contrasted by the author with the imminent danger of the serpent behind the scenes, is re-created here by using

---

19 Andrew Goss, "From *Tong-Tong* to Tempo Doeloe: Eurasian Memory Work and the Bracketing of Dutch Colonial History, 1957–1961", *Indonesia* 70 (October 2000): 25. *Tong-Tong*, published from 1958 until the 1970s, addressed a readership of repatriated "Eurasians and *Indisch* 'browned Netherlanders,'" those full-blooded Dutch who had come to feel at home in the colony", with a circulation of over ten thousand subscribers in 1960 (ibid., 25, italics in original).

20 According to Said, through the writings of "poets, novelists, philosophers, political theorists, economists, and imperial administrators", the West has constructed the "Orient" as a subordinate, uncivilised "Other" in contrast to the advanced, cultured "West" (Edward W. Said, *Orientalism* (New York: Vintage Books, 1979), 2). Many have followed up on Said's work, see for example: Homi K. Bhabha, *The Location of Culture* (London: Routledge, 1994); Mary Louise Pratt, *Imperial Eyes: Travel Writing and Transculturation* (London: Routledge, 1992); Anne McClintock, *Imperial Leather: Race, Gender, and Sexuality in the Colonial Contest* (London: Routledge, 1995). The great amount of critique it has garnered is probably just as attesting to how influential it has been since its publication, see Aijaz Ahmad, *In Theory: Classes, Nations, Literatures* (London: Verso, 1992); James Clifford, "On Orientalism", in *The Predicament of Culture: Twentieth Century Ethnography, Literature and Art* (Cambridge, MA: Harvard University Press, 1988), 255–276; Robert J. C. Young, *White Mythologies: Writing History and the West* (London: Verso, 1990).

21 Tom Gunning, "An Aesthetic of Astonishment: Early Film and the (In)Credulous Spectator", in Linda Williams (ed.), *Viewing Positions: Ways of Seeing Film* (New Brunswick: Rutgers University Press, 1995), 114–133, here 115. Race and class (and gender), according to McClintock, do not exist in isolation from each other, but rather "they come into existence *in and through* relation to each other – if in contradictory and conflictual ways" (McClintock, *Imperial Leather*, 5, italics in original). According to Tom Gunning, writing with an aesthetic concern, even if early audiences in the West reacted with "astonishment" to moving images, this was very much part of the "aesthetic of attraction" characteristic of early cinema and often encouraged by exhibitors, in which the spectator was to remain "aware of the act of looking, the excitement of curiosity and its fulfilment" (Gunning, "An Aesthetic of Astonishment", 121). From an empirical point of view, as Martin Loiperdinger convincingly demonstrates, the "moving images projected onto the screen with the Cinématographe Lumière could hardly be mistaken for reality" due to the heavy flickering effect produced during the projection, as well as the light intensity available at the time which would have very much limited the quality and size of the projected image (Martin Loiperdinger, "Lumière's Arrival of the Train: Cinema's Founding Myth", trans. Bernd Elzer, *The Moving Image* 4, no. 1 (Spring 2004): 96). Moreover, no contemporary "reports of panic among the audience" in Paris have been found, nor any police reports about any accidents that would have ensued considering the crowds and location (ibid., 94). "The reportedly reiterated anecdote that the contemporary audience felt physically threatened and therefore panicked", Loiperdinger concludes, "must be relegated to the realm of historical fantasy" (ibid., 96). See also Stephen Bottomore's elaborated consideration of reactions to the "train effect" in Stephen Bottomore, "The Panicking Audience?: Early Cinema and the 'Train Effect'", *Historical Journal of Film, Radio and Television* 19, no. 2 (1999): 177–216.

the image of a Haji pilgrim to Mecca approaching the camera as the source of indigenous spectators' trepidation.

However, just as the naivety of early Western audiences has since been questioned, this empirically-based historical study does not take Boong Indri's description of Indonesian spectators at face value. As an *Indisch* immigrant to the Netherlands trying to carve out a place for himself, part of his agenda in writing here was to differentiate himself (and his community) from the lower class of indigenous "Natives" he describes. To be sure, this research has not shored up any accounts of this kind of behaviour from Malay-language newspapers of the time. The only examples found in this research of frantic spectators actually rushing out of venues, further corroborated by local police reports, were in cases of real danger such as a fire breaking out and a stampede ensuing.[22] By comparison, a case of a python snake causing panic at a cinema house in Bandung, before members of the audience summarily beat it to death, was recorded in *Taman Sari* in 1911.[23] It is also worth noting that spectators in the Indies, especially in its urban centres, were often well-versed in earlier and contemporary forms of both Western and (commercial and traditional) indigenous entertainments pre-dating moving pictures, among them: circuses, magic shows, lantern slide projections, *bangsawan* and *komedi stambul* acts (both referring to forms of popular Malay opera) and Javanese *wayang kulit* (shadow-play), as will be further detailed below. In fact, many residents of Bandung, as the above quote from 1897 suggests, would have encountered moving image projection quite a few years before 1904. By interrogating such instances and unpacking the colonial discourses they invoke, the present research strives to complicate such simplistic conceptualisations of spectators in the Indies.[24]

This introduction aims to provide some historical context, as well as to define the concepts and themes that will be used throughout the following chapters, often drawn from various disciplines. The first part presents historical background on Dutch colonialism and the period of the late colonial state in Indonesia, in order to situate the chapters that follow in a broader historical context. The following two sections provide overviews of the current state of research on Indonesian cinema history, and of the geographical and chronological scope of this study. The fourth section discusses the term "modernity", which has been widely utilised in film studies, in research on Southeast Asia specifically and in postcolonial studies more generally. Its use here likewise demands examination and explanation.

22 Although, as Fuller-Seeley and Potamianos caution in the context of early film exhibition in rural America, "having not yet located evidence of such occurrences does not mean they never took place" (Kathryn H. Fuller-Seeley and George Potamianos, "Introduction: Researching and Writing the History of Local Moviegoing", in Kathryn H. Fuller-Seeley (ed.) *Hollywood in the Neighbourhood: Historical Case Studies of Local Moviegoing* (Berkeley: University of California Press, 2008), 3–19, here 7).

23 "Oelar di Bioscoop Bandoeng", *Taman Sari* (31 July 1911).

24 See also Nadi Tofighian's writing on Western technology and so-called "Native astonishment" in Nadi Tofighian, *Blurring the Colonial Binary: Turn-of-the-Century Transnational Entertainment in Southeast Asia*, PhD Dissertation (Stockholm University, 2013), 90–96.

Introduction

In the fifth section, the history of global trade networks in the Indies is considered alongside the flow of commercial entertainments conveyed via them. The transnational popular entertainment scene that preceded early cinema and also formed its immediate intermedial landscape, underestimated by the 1913 report from *De Kinematograaf*, will be highlighted here. As the reporter suggested, it would have surely been easier for an itinerant exhibitor – even with cumbersome equipment and film stock – to tour the archipelago, compared to a *komedi stambul* troupe with a cast and crew of fifty or more, or a circus with forty to seventy artists, on top of an entire menagerie.[25] Nevertheless, the availability of such earlier forms of indigenous and Western popular entertainments opened up the trade routes for film distributors and exhibitors, on the one hand, and made spectators from all levels of colonial society into potential movie-goers, on the other hand.

Finally, we turn our attention back to moving picture venues and their spectators. By way of a summary and in anticipation of things to come, the spectatorial positions and viewing conditions in the various seating areas are sketched out. The elasticity of the racial classifications in colonial society as they manifested themselves inside and outside the cinema space, as well as their intersection with other factors, such as class, gender, and religion, should be kept in mind. All of these factors, I would argue, may have played into who could occupy which spectator position in colonial Indonesia. This is followed by an outline of the chapters.

Historical Context: The Late Colonial State in Indonesia

The time frame under examination in this study (1896–1914) lies within the period generally referred to as the "late colonial state" (1880–1942).[26] Although the Dutch East India Company (*Verenigde Oostindische Compagnie*, VOC) was present in the archipelago since the early seventeenth century, a fully-fledged colonial state was only formed in the nineteenth century and early twentieth century. Following forced cultivation of government crops as of 1830, a scheme known as the Cultivation System (*Cultuurstelsel*), pressure from liberals and enterprises in the Netherlands led to an opening up of the Indies market to private entrepreneurs as of the 1870s.[27] This was facilitated by the opening of the Suez Canal in 1869 and the rapid introduction of steam shipping, which slashed the journey time between Europe and Asia to only few weeks.[28]

25 See Matthew Isaac Cohen, *The Komedie Stamboel: Popular Theatre in Colonial Indonesia, 1891–1903* (Leiden: KITLV Press, 2006), 1; Tofighian, *Blurring the Colonial Binary*, 122.

26 See Robert Cribb (ed.), *The Late Colonial State in Indonesia: Political and Economic Foundations of the Netherlands Indies 1880–1942* (Leiden: KITLV Press, 1994).

27 For more on the Cultivation System, also known as the Culture System, see J. S. Furnivall, *Netherlands India: A Study of Plural Economy* (Cambridge: Cambridge University Press, 2010 [1967]), 115–147. For an overview of the switch from the Cultivation System to the "liberal" period and their impacts on Indonesian society, see M. C. Ricklefs, *A History of Modern Indonesia since c. 1200*, Third Edition (Houndmills: Palgrave Macmillan, 2001 [1981]), 155–170.

28 See Jean Gelman Taylor, *Global Indonesia (Routledge Contemporary Southeast Asia Series)* (London: Routledge, 2013), 60.

Furthermore, the means of communications with the metropole was revolutionized by the advent of the telegraph. By 1872, within five or six years from the establishment of the first transatlantic link between Europe and the US, the main cities in Asia and Australia were also connected via telegraph with the centres of world economy in Europe and America.[29]

Yet, it is crucial to note that the Indonesian archipelago had a history of openness to things foreign – whether this meant trade in products, migration of peoples or religious beliefs – long before the VOC established its Asian base of operation in Batavia (present-day Jakarta) in 1619. As Henk Schulte Nordholt clarifies, "Indonesian societies have always been relatively open systems; influences from abroad and their local interpretations were part and parcel of the local cultures".[30] One of the most important global networks to be considered in the case of Indonesia is Islam, and the connections created with the world's Islamic community through the gradual conversion of the archipelago's inhabitants going back to the thirteenth century.[31] By the nineteenth century, while Islam continued to figure prominently in the daily lives of Indonesians, colonial rule, with its mechanised modes of transport, telegraph and steamship networks, was the harbinger of modern globalisation.[32]

Racial classification was one of the building blocks of the Dutch colonial administration. This meant that the different groups of the population – Europeans (*Europeanen*), "Natives" (*Inlanders*) and Foreign Orientals (*Vreemde Oosterlingen*) – were treated differently "[...] in legislation, judicial practice and executive policy".[33] It should therefore not surprise us that racial categories seeped into venues for consumption of popular entertainment, by way of segregated seating arrangements or separate entrance ways, as we shall see below. Dutch colonial society was stratified and classified by these racial categories, which determined one's place and prospects in society. The marker "Dutch" was in fact hardly used due to the fact that there was a wide variety of Europeans of other nationalities living and working in the colonies, and

---

29 See Dick et al., *Cities, Transport and Communications*, 38. Only the Philippines joined late, in May 1880.

30 Henk Schulte Nordholt, "Introduction", in Henk Schulte Nordholt (ed.), *Outward Appearances: Dressing State and Society in Indonesia* (Leiden: KITLV Press, 1997), 1–37, here 8–9.

31 See Taylor, *Global Indonesia*, 53–55. For a study of Islam and Islamic nationalism under Dutch rule in colonial Indonesia, see Michael Francis Laffan, *Islamic Nationhood and Colonial Indonesia: The umma below the winds* (London: RoutledgeCurzon, 2003). Islam must have been present in maritime Southeast Asia since the early Islamic era thanks to Muslim emissaries sent from Arabia to China during the time of the third Caliph of Islam, Uthman (644–56). While evidence of Islamization in the region goes back to the thirteenth century, as evidence in tombstone engravings bearing Muslim names, it was not widespread until the seventeenth century (see Ricklefs, *A History of Modern Indonesia*, 3–4). When the Dutch first landed in Indonesia, most inhabitants of the islands were not Muslim, but since the Dutch did not try to convert Indonesians to Christianity, the missionaries in the archipelago were rather Muslim who taught Islam (Taylor, *Global Indonesia*, 54).

32 Ibid., 8.

33 C. Fasseur, "Cornerstone and stumbling block: Racial classification and the late colonial state in Indonesia", in Robert Cribb (ed.), *The Late Colonial State in Indonesia: Political and Economic Foundations of the Netherlands Indies 1880–1942* (Leiden: KITLV Press, 1994), 31–56, here 31.

therefore "European" was preferred in official parlance.³⁴ In 1905, there were nearly 30,000,000 "Natives", 317,000 "Foreign Orientals" and about 65,000 "Europeans" living in Java and Madura, making Europeans merely 0.22 per cent of the total population, most of them residing in cities.³⁵

However, all these figures are misleading for various reasons. First, an undetermined number of those registered by the census as "European" were in fact of mixed parentage, in most cases born to an Indonesian mother and a European father. According to estimates around 1900, by the early twentieth century, 80 per cent of the Dutch population of the colony had been born in the tropics, and an unspecified but large majority of them would have been so-called mixed.³⁶ Nevertheless, it was around this time that the makeup of the "European" society in the colony was beginning to change. With the arrival of private entrepreneurs since the opening up of the market in the 1870s, and the influx of more women and families arriving from Europe around the turn-of-the-century, the "European" group was growing ever more exclusive.³⁷ Second, to add even more to the confusion, in 1899 the status of the Japanese was equated to that of "Europeans" following their defeat of the Chinese in the Sino-Japanese Wars. However, out of the one thousand or so Japanese living in the Indies, 80 per cent were women engaged as prostitutes or hairdressers.³⁸ Third, the category of "Foreign Orientals" represented mostly the Chinese, a term which was used to refer to Indies-born Chinese or to new immigrants from the Mainland, but was further applied to Arabs, Indians and other Southeast Asians. Finally, the category of "Native" covered the entire spectrum of indigenous-born Indonesians, which included a variety of ethnicities: Javanese, Madurese, Sundanese, Bugis, Dayaks, etc. Therefore, while the classification system was rigid, there was still some fluidity within and between the categories.

Around the turn of the century, the formation of a colonial state shifted into high gear. The Ethical Policy, proclaimed in 1901, intended to bring development and prosperity to the indigenous population of the Indies. Takashi Shiraishi identifies it as "The Modern Age" in the life of the colony:

---

34 See Kees van Dijk, *The Netherlands Indies and the Great War 1914–1918* (Leiden: KITLV Press, 2007), 17.

35 See Furnivall, *Netherlands India*, 347.

36 See Rudolf Mrázek, *Engineers of Happy Land: Technology and Nationalism in a Colony* (Princeton: Princeton University Press, 2002), 9. Among all the legally Dutch children born in the Indies, 40 per cent could not even speak Dutch (ibid.).

37 See Robert van Niel, *The Emergence of the Modern Indonesian Elite* (Dordrecht-Holland/Cinnaminson-U.S.A.: Foris Publications, 1984), 7–8. Immigration of European women (and children) was previously restricted by the VOC on a number of counts, from fears that they would encourage their husbands to make a quick profit and would want to repatriate immediately, to concerns that European children would become sick easily (see Ann Laura Stoler, *Carnal Knowledge and Imperial Power: Race and the Intimate in Colonial Rule* (Berkeley: University of California Press, 2002), 47). VOC employees were recruited as single men and encouraged to engage in concubinage with local women.

38 See Michael Laffan, "Tokyo as a shared Mecca of modernity: War echoes in the colonial Malay world", in Rotem Kowner (ed.), *The Impact of the Russo-Japanese War* (London: Routledge, 2007), 219–238, here 223.

The watchword of the new era was "progress." The words signifying progress – such as *vooruitgang* (advance), *opheffing* (uplifting), *ontwikkeling* (development), and *opvoeding* (upbringing) – embellished the language of the day together with *bevordering van welvaart* (promotion of welfare). [… Progress was understood as] progress to modernity, progress as evolution under Dutch tutelage […].[39]

The Ethical Policy placed an emphasis on Western-style education, which was necessary for the production of a skilled work force to sustain the colonial state as well as private business enterprises. It was further seen as a way "[...] to 'uplift' the natives and to guide them to modernity and to 'association between East and West'".[40] Agricultural technology (and the training it entailed) was also brought in to the colony as part of these efforts.[41] Another key term during this period was decentralisation: "[...] decentralisation from the Hague to Batavia, from Batavia to the regions, from the Dutch to the Indonesians".[42] The Governor General of the Indies was the highest authority figure in the colony, with the regional Residents, Assistant Residents and District Officers (or Controllers) below him. As of 1905, local Municipal Councils (*Gemeenteraad*) began to be set up in the main cities, thus adding more administrators on the local level.[43] These councils were comprised of Dutch, Indonesian and Chinese members, but in effect remained under Dutch control.

"By about 1910", Ricklefs writes, "the boundaries of the present state of Indonesia had been roughly drawn by colonial armed forces, at a great cost in lives, money, devastation, social cohesion and human dignity and freedom".[44] However, just as the islands of the Netherlands Indies were being stitched together under the colonial state, or perhaps very much in response to this, a budding Indonesian nationalist movement emerged. "Because colonialism so thoroughly disrupted indigenous society, the colonial state provided an unprecedented focus for the political aspirations of Indonesians; at the same time, the facilities provided directly or indirectly by the colonial state – especially

---

39 Takashi Shiraishi, *An Age in Motion: Popular Radicalism in Java, 1912–1926* (Ithaca: Cornell University Press, 1990), 27, italics in original.

40 Ibid., 28. As of 1893, two types of schools were introduced: one for the Indonesian elite class (*priyayi*) and the other – for children of the rest of the population, their numbers increasingly growing over the years. However, the language of instruction in both kinds of schools was Malay, which therefore limited the kind of positions their graduates could later occupy. Only in 1914 Dutch-language schools for "Natives" replaced the first type of schools (ibid., 28–29). However, "although Western-style education expanded substantially, the number of students was never great compared with the huge native population in the Indies, and the literate formed only a tiny proportion of the population" (ibid., 29).

41 See Suzanne Moon, *Technology and Ethical Idealism: A History of Development in the Netherlands East Indies* (Leiden: CNWS Publications, 2007). Efforts towards development and progress, especially in road and railway construction, obviously pre-dated the Ethical Policy and were part of the colonial project throughout the nineteenth century.

42 Ricklefs, *A History of Modern Indonesia*, 203.

43 Ibid. By 1939 there were 32 Municipal Councils, 19 of which were located on Java.

44 Ibid., 189. The People's Council (*Volksraad*), opened in 1918 as "a proto-parliament with limited powers" was also limited "because the Indies government held the final word and could even be overruled by the Ministry of the Colonies in The Hague, this council never represented more than a shadow of responsible government" (Elsbeth Locher-Scholten, *Women and the Colonial State: Essays on Gender and Modernity in the Netherlands Indies 1900–1942* (Amsterdam: Amsterdam University Press, 2000), 18).

education and various kinds of technology – gave Indonesians the practical and intellectual tools to assemble a broad national movement for independence."[45]

Current State of Research on Early Cinema in Colonial Indonesia

The writing of early cinema history in Indonesia has often been constricted by the shortage of surviving film materials. This was also my experience when visiting the film archive of the EYE Film Institute Netherlands in Amsterdam for the first time. The initial plan for this research was to focus on the representations of the Dutch colonies in Indonesia in moving images produced in the late nineteenth century up to 1910, and I went to the archive in order to get a sense of the materials available in their collection. To my great disappointment, I was informed that the earliest film of the Netherlands Indies that they have dates back to 1910, which is a stencil-coloured Pathé actuality film about the local sugar industry.[46] This is followed by a handful of films from 1912 onwards that are part of the collection of the Colonial Institute, documenting life in the colonies.[47] Moreover, serious doubt was expressed as to whether anybody had ever been there before with a film camera.

Up until recently, this region and period have received hardly any attention in studies of early cinema or of cinema history. The reason for this lack is two-fold. On the one hand, as Nico de Klerk points out, the traditional approach to national film history is production-driven, thus obscuring the experience of national audiences whose cinema-going experiences are comprised of nationally-produced films as well as international products.[48] Anthologies of early cinema history in general and of the history of cinema in Indonesia in particular therefore previously set the starting date for cinema in the region as December 1900 and merely gloss over the following couple of decades, usually dedicating a page or two to early cinema and quickly moving

---

45 Robert Cribb, "Introduction: The late colonial state in Indonesia", in Robert Cribb (ed.), *The Late Colonial State in Indonesia: Political and Economic Foundations of the Netherlands Indies 1880–1942* (Leiden: KITLV Press, 1994), 1–9, here 2.

46 The earliest film of the Netherlands Indies held in the collection of the EYE Film Institute is RÉCOLTE ET INDUSTRIE DE LA CANNE À SUCRE (Pathé Frères, 1910).

47 For more on the film collection of the Colonial Institute filmed by Dutch Captain J.C. Lamster, see Nico de Klerk, "'The Transport of Audiences': Making Cinema 'National'", in Richard Abel, Giorgio Bertellini and Rob King (eds.), *Early Cinema and the "National"* (New Barnet: John Libbey, 2008), 101–108; Janneke van Dijk, Jaap de Jonge and Nico de Klerk (eds.), *J. C. Lamster, een vroege filmer in Nederlands-Indië* (Amsterdam: KIT Publishers, 2010). See also two recently published and forthcoming dissertations which analyse early and later colonial films from the Netherlands Indies available at EYE Film Institute and the Netherlands Institute for Sound and Vision (Nederlands Instituut voor Beeld en Geluid) in Hilversum: Gerda Jansen Hendriks, *Een voorbeeldige kolonie: Nederlands-Indië in 50 jaar overheidsfilms, 1912–1962*, PhD Dissertation (University of Amsterdam, 2014); Sandeep Ray, *Celluloid Colony: The Inadvertent Ethnography in Propaganda Films from the Dutch East Indies (1912–1930)*, PhD Dissertation (National University of Singapore, 2015).

48 See Nico de Klerk, "Volgt het voorbeeld van John Wayne: Over onze grenzeloze nationale cinema", in Rommy Albers, Jan Baeke and Rob Zeeman (eds.), *Film in Nederland* (Gent/Amsterdam: Ludion/Filmmuseum, 2004), 414–421, here 415.

on to the 1920s, when Indonesians themselves, often Chinese Indonesians, became involved in narrative filmmaking.[49]

On the other hand, unlike other European colonial powers such as Britain or France, the Dutch were neither a filmmaking nor film-going nation, and consequently were not primary exporters or producers of moving pictures in colonial Indonesia in the early days of cinema.[50] Studies from the Dutch or Western perspectives have therefore similarly underplayed the significance of the Indies as a market for early film distribution and consumption, zooming in on the period of the mid-1910s, by which point the colony had supposedly become a "junk market" where inferior, second-hand prints could be shipped off to for their final on-screen runs.[51] Studies of social issues and film censorship in the Indies, written by Dutch and Indonesian scholars, have paid hardly any attention to the experiences of pre-First World War exhibitors.[52]

Nevertheless, this research has found that moving pictures were introduced and popularised in the Dutch colonies of the Netherlands Indies thanks to the efforts of other entrepreneurs of myriad nationalities and ethnicities, with the earliest accounted for screening given by a Batavia-based French photographer by the name Louis Talbot and his Scenimatograph in this capital city already

---

49   See S. M. Ardan, "Indonesia", trans. Raymond Edmondson, in Richard Abel (ed.), *Encyclopedia of Early Cinema* (London: Routledge, 2005), 320. Indonesian publications include: Taufik Abdullah, Misbach Yusa Biran and S. M. Ardan, *Film Indonesia. Bagian I (1900–1950)* (Jakarta: Perum Percetakan Negara Ri, 1993); H. M. Johan Tjasmadi, *100 tahun sejarah bioskop di Indonesia* (Bandung: Megindo Tunggal Sejahtera, 2008); Misbach Yusa Biran, *Sejarah Film 1900–1950: Bikin Film di Jawa* (Jakarta: Kommunitas Bambu, 2009). By their nature as comprehensive overviews of a long period of cinema history, these three latter titles mention the early period only briefly and focus on later periods in the history of production of Indonesian cinema. None of them deal with the period pre-1900.

50   For more on early colonial cinema in France, see Panivong Norindr, "Enlisting Early Cinema in the Service of 'la plus grande France'", in Richard Abel, Giorgio Bertellini and Rob King (eds.), *Early Cinema and the "National"* (New Barnet: John Libbey, 2008), 109–117. For imagery and early cinema in imperial Britain, see James R. Ryan, *Picturing Empire: Photography and the Visualization of the British Empire* (Chicago: The University of Chicago Press, 1998); John M. Mackenzie (ed.), *Imperialism and Popular Culture* (Manchester: Manchester University Press, 1986). For German use of early cinema for colonial propaganda, see Wolfgang Fuhrmann, *Imperial Projections. Screening the German Colonies* (New York, Oxford: Berghahn, 2015).

51   In his study of the Desmet collection, Ivo Blom has found that in "[...] 1913/14, Desmet regularly met with buyers of films who either lived and traded in the Dutch East Indies (modern Indonesia) or sold their films there. The demand in the East Indies for films was greater than in the Netherlands, as programmes there were changed twice a week, as opposed to just once in the Netherlands. Films which had completed all their runs in the Netherlands were sent to the Dutch East Indies, where they embarked upon a 'second run'. Needless to say, the quality of these prints left a lot to be desired." (Blom, *Jean Desmet*, 213). According to the *Bioscope*'s 'Special Foreign and Export Supplement' issues on 11 January and 12 July 1916, the "current junk markets were considered to be the West Indies, Dutch East Indies, Malay Peninsula and parts of South America" (Kristin Thompson, *Exporting Entertainment: America in the World Film Market, 1907–34* (London: BFI Publishing, 1985), 70).

52   See M. Sarief Arief, *Politik Film di Hindia Belanda* (Depok: Komunitas Bambu, 2010); Robert van den Berg, *Film en filmkeuring in Nederlands-Indië 1910–1925*, PhD Dissertation (Radboud University Nijmegen, 1988); Rob van den Berg, "De koloniale maatstaf: filmkeuring in Nederlands-Indië", *Jambatan: Tijdschrift voor de geschiedenis van Indonesië* 9, no. 3 (1991): 91–107; Soeluh van den Berg, "Notabele ingezetenen en goedwillende ambtenaren: De Nederlands-Indische filmkeuring, 1912–1942", in Soeluh van den Berg and René Witte (eds.), *Jaarboek Mediageschiedenis 4: Nederlands-Indië* (Amsterdam: Stichting Mediageschiedenis, 1992), 145–171; Tanete A. Pong Masak, *Le cinéma indonésien (1926–1967): Études d'Histoire Sociale*, PhD Dissertation (L'École des Hautes Études en Sciences Sociales, Paris, 1989).

Introduction

on 11 October 1896 (see Section 1.2).⁵³ The findings of Nadi Tofighian indicate that the first shows in the rest of the region all followed in 1897: Manila in January, Singapore in May, Bangkok in June and Taiping in December.⁵⁴ Tofighian's recently published PhD dissertation on transnational entertainment in Southeast Asia in the late nineteenth century and early twentieth century is the only other in-depth academic inquiry of early cinema in the region. Covering an impressively wide scope of regions in Southeast Asia, including Thailand, Vietnam and Cambodia, his writing focuses mostly on colonial Singapore and Malaysia. His research further helps to shed light on the situation in the Netherlands Indies up to 1907.⁵⁵

Time Frame, Geographical Scope and Sources

The time frame of this study runs from 1896 to 1914, allowing some flexibility in order to be able to provide information on earlier forms of entertainment as well as indications of future developments in the Indies movie-going scene and exhibition practices. Since it is generally recognized that the First World War greatly disrupted the international distribution of films, among other things, leading to changes in the way the industry was managed, it makes sense to let the current work run up to the outbreak of war. The period under discussion here further dictates the geographical scope of this work. The Outer Islands of the Netherlands Indies were finally being brought under the colonial state's control during the first decades of the twentieth century. The main focus of this research is thus limited to the islands already – more or less – under Dutch rule, namely, Java and Sumatra and, to a certain extent, Celebes (present-day Sulawesi).

The majority of newspapers consulted in this research are Dutch-language colonial newspapers held at the National Library of the Netherlands (Koninklijke Bibliotheek, KB) in The Hague. These naturally carry with them a certain bias that a contemporary researcher must try to take into account. I have also consulted newspapers in Malay (the forerunner of standardised Indonesian, or *bahasa Indonesia*) at the National Library of the Republic of Indonesia (Perpustakaan Nasional Republik Indonesia, PNRI) in Jakarta and at the Royal Institute of Southeast Asian and Caribbean Studies (Koninklijk Instituut voor Taal-, Land- en Volkenkunde, KITLV) in Leiden in order to counteract this partiality. Nevertheless, surviving copies from this period are far less comprehensive than the Dutch documents. At times newspapers clearly reported inaccurate information. For example: in September 1902 Mr. Nast came down

---

53   Advertisement, *Java-Bode* (9 October 1896). I would like to thank Nadi Tofighian for sharing his findings on Talbot's 1897 screenings in Surabaya with me, which enabled me to trace Talbot's activities back to 1896 and further unearth his tour route across the Indonesian archipelago.
54   See Tofighian, *Blurring the Colonial Binary*, 81.
55   For an overview of the historiography of cinema in Southeast Asia, see ibid., 41–45.

with cholera and even put his device and films for sale, but six days later reportedly passed away in hospital in Surabaya.[56] Nevertheless, about 6 months later, Nast miraculously returned from the dead with his Kinematograph.[57] I have therefore tried to consult as many newspapers as possible published in the same city, in Dutch and Malay, in order to diversify the material and be able to contrast and compare the information.

Moreover, it is important to remember that the Malay and Dutch newspapers would have been written by and for a certain class of society, and thus do not necessarily reflect popular or widespread opinion. Since the mid nineteenth century, Malay newspapers appeared in Romanised script, for the most part, and were modelled on Dutch and English publications and edited by European, Eurasian and Indies-born (*peranakan*) Chinese. They contained reports and notices of various lengths, covering current events from near and far, as well as Malay adaptations of stories, often appearing in serialised form.[58] In general, the readership for the Malay newspapers, originating from the major urban centres and distributed across Java, Sumatra and Celebes, consisted mostly of *peranakan* Chinese who were also leading tradesmen who advertised in such publications, native elite (*priyayi*) and Eurasian traders and officials.[59] By the 1890s, the average number of subscribers for a popular daily Malay newspaper was between 600 and 800.[60] For the sake of comparison, the Dutch-language daily *Het Nieuws van den Dag voor Nederlandsch-Indië* published in Batavia but distributed outside of the capital too, had about 1,000 copies in circulation in 1901.[61] Limited readership and circulation notwithstanding, the vast number of reports about and reviews of moving picture shows found in Dutch and Malay newspapers, even if a certain percentage of these represents sponsored content by exhibitors, indicates that movie-going was a noteworthy aspect of everyday life in urban colonial Indonesia.

Another problem of basing the research on newspaper material is that, while many of the large cities, such as Batavia and Surabaya, had more than one publication, not every town had its own newspaper. This means that the main cities of the Indies are over-represented in this study as information on smaller towns or rural areas is more difficult to come by. Moreover, even in the major cities not all shows would have been advertised in the newspapers, as I sometimes found only the review of a screening, without any advertisements. Thus, these exhibitors clearly had other ways of advertising their shows which are practically unobtainable to us. The only handbill I was physically able to

56 See "Onze Nieuwtjes", *Soerabaija-Courant* (3 September 1902).
57 See "Nederlandsch-Indië", *Soerabaiasch-Handelsblad* (4 April 1903).
58 See Henk Maier, "Explosions in Semarang: Reading Malay tales in 1895", *Bijdragen tot de Taal-, Land- en Volkenkunde (BKI)* 162, no. 1 (2006): 4.
59 Ahmat B. Adam, *The Vernacular Press and the Emergence of Modern Indonesian Consciousness (1855–1913)* (Ithaca: Cornell Southeast Asia Program, 1995), 33.
60 Ibid., 48.
61 Ibid., 48, footnote 53.

locate was for a cinema from Bandung at the library of the Royal Tropical Institute (Koninklijk Instituut voor de Tropen, KIT) in Amsterdam, identified in their catalogue as circa 1930, although I suspect it was most likely from a show given in the mid-1910s, based on the film titles.[62]

The information collected from newspapers includes: shipping information (arrival and departure of exhibitors, sometimes also arrival of films), advertisements (often include programme list, ticket prices, location), tour plans (especially if a manager was employed), permit requests submitted/granted/refused, reviews of the shows and film programmes, descriptions of the cinema space and audience, reports on cinema shows in other locations, general entertainment and leisure scene, information on urban development projects (clearing *kampung*, construction of shops, road development, transportation, electricity networks). This kind of data on moving picture shows (and other entertainments in the Indies) did not appear then under an "arts" or "culture" section of these newspapers. Instead, reports on moving picture shows pop up among the stream of daily news, police bulletins, letters to the editor, telegrams, advertisements, and just about anywhere over the pages of the newspapers. It is therefore inevitable that many references to moving picture shows have been missed in the process of leafing or scrolling through. This research has benefited immensely from the continually growing database of digitized newspapers by the KB in The Hague, in addition to the digitized Singapore and Australian newspapers, which enabled me to initially identify that there was a large amount of untapped material on the scope of early cinema in the Netherlands Indies and to further delve into non-digitized sources for the instances in which moving picture shows appeared. Nevertheless, most of the time of this research was spent pouring over the microfilm collections of several libraries, covering an estimated total of 55,000 meters of microfilm.

Other sources consulted include colonial government documents held at the National Archives of the Netherlands (NA) in The Hague and the National Archives of Indonesia (ANRI) in Jakarta. Instead of watching films at the EYE Netherlands Film Institute in Amsterdam, days were spent looking through trade journals, such as *De Kinematograaf*, which employed a correspondent in the Indies and was also distributed in the colonies. The Kroch Library at Cornell University housing the John M. Echols Collection on Southeast Asia allowed free roaming of boundless open bookshelves. Unfortunately, the KIT and KITLV libraries, whose rich collections of books, maps and photographic materials have also been consulted for this research, have regrettably closed their doors since then due to budget cuts and their collections have been relocated, mostly to the library of Leiden University.

---

62 "Programma [van de] Nederlandsch-Indische Electro Bioscoop in den Soloschen Schouwburg", ca. 1930, Koninklijk Instituut voor de Tropen, accessed on 2 February 2014, http://search.kit.nl/vivisimo/cgi-bin/query-meta.exe?v%3Aproject=kit-da&query=nederlandsch-indische+electro+bioscoop. Unfortunately, even though the document has been digitized, it appears to be no longer available online.

Engaging with Modernity

Contemporary commentators who were attending and writing in Dutch and Malay newspapers about their visits to moving picture shows in the Indies around the turn of the century often used words like "modern", "novelty" and "progress" to describe their experiences. Studying early movie-going in colonial Indonesia thus invites us to consider how spectators were engaging with modernity in these situations. Elsbeth Locher-Scholten, in her study of gender and modernity in the late colonial state of the Netherlands Indies, usefully differentiates between two kinds of discussions on modernity. The first is linked to the post-Renaissance and Enlightenment formulation of modernity as "the application of rationality, the development of capitalism and industrialisation, including concomitant long-term processes, such as urbanisation, consumerism and individualisation".[63] This is what Joel Kahn identifies as the objective stance of modernity in the works of social theorists along the "[...] Hegel/Marx/Weber tradition that sees modernity as an identifiable socio-historical process of transformation out there in the world, one that began in either the sixteenth or the eighteenth century western Europe" resulting in secularization and universalistic claims to rationalism.[64]

The second type of modernity, according to Locher-Scholten, "[...] refers to the longing in the late nineteenth and early twentieth centuries for progress, development and 'the modern' as well as the attraction of twentieth-century 'modern' objects like cars and telephones".[65] This is compatible with what Kahn sees as the subjective turn in revised notions of the classical narrative of Euro-American modernity in recent critical theory, which put "[...] modern subjectivity at the core of our understanding of what it is to be modern so that modernity becomes as much a state of mind as a set of objective historical processes. Modernity is now seen as inseparable from the modern imaginaries that make it possible."[66] As part of such critique, especially in the work of postcolonial studies, researchers are now finding "[...] evidence for the contemporary modernisation of the West and the non-West – in Russia, Japan, the Islamic world, China – evidence not of a single modernity subsequently indigenised as a consequence of 'westernisation' [or of "secondary" or "incomplete" modernities], but instead of parallel modernities [...] or multiple modernities".[67]

It should be noted that a wide debate about cinema in the context of turn-of-the-century modernity has preoccupied film researchers since the 1980s. Without going into all the nuances of the arguments, intermittently going back and forth on the matter over the years, I will try to briefly lay out some of the

---

63   Locher-Scholten, *Women and the Colonial State*, 32.
64   Joel S. Kahn, *Modernity and Exclusion* (London: SAGE Publications, 2001), 8.
65   Locher-Scholten, *Women and the Colonial State*, 32.
66   Kahn, *Modernity and Exclusion*, 11.
67   Ibid., 15.

Introduction

main issues at the heart of the debate. The so-called "modernity thesis", as summarised by Ben Singer, posits that "[...] the urban environment of modern capitalism brought about some kind of fundamental change in the human 'sensorium', creating a pervasive new 'mode of perception' which ultimately had a significant impact on the development of cinema, encouraging cinema to take shape in ways that mirrored the fragmentation and abruptness of urban experience".[68] Various scholars of early cinema have traditionally drawn on the work of Charles Baudelaire on the ephemeral experience of modern urban life, on Georg Simmel's writings on subjective attitudes in the face of the onslaught of stimuli in metropolitan settings, or on Walter Benjamin's work on the mode of perception of modern spectacles.[69] As one proponent of this "modernity thesis", Gunning's "aesthetic of astonishment", mentioned above, proposes that the pre-1908 "cinema of attractions" reflected the disjointed turn-of-the-century urban, industrialized sensorial state, and at the same time was a consequence of it.[70]

This "modernity thesis" has been heavily criticized and challenged, especially its suggestions of "changes in human perception brought about by the condition of modern life [and its] claims about the role played in this process by motion pictures".[71] David Bordwell, for example, contests the notion of a "radical pervasive change in ways of seeing" prompted by modern life, supposedly occurring in the West at some point between 1850 and 1920.[72] He further points out that not all early films reflected a culture of shock, thrills and fragmentation. "It is very likely that a wide variety of perceptual abilities is at work in any given period", Bordwell claims, casting doubt on any assumption of a single "mode of perception", or film style, for that matter, that define an era.[73] Joe Kember has similarly argued that advocates of the "modernity thesis" have tended to over-emphasise the "disempowering and alienating aspects of modernity", at the expense of other institutional practices that provide comfort

---

68 Ben Singer, *Melodrama and Modernity: Early Sensational Cinema and Its Contexts* (New York: Columbia University Press, 2001), 9. The term "modernity thesis" was coined by David Bordwell as part of his critique of this approach, see David Bordwell, *Figures Traced in Light: On Cinematic Staging* (Berkeley: University of California Press, 2005), 244–249.

69 Excerpts of the three texts all appear in Vanessa R. Schwartz and J.M. Przyblyski (eds.). *The Nineteenth-Century Visual Culture Reader* (New York: Routledge, 2004): Charles Baudelaire, "The Painter of Modern Life (1863)", 37–42; Georg Simmel, "The Metropolis and Mental Life (1903)", 51–55; Walter Benjamin, "The Work of Art in the Age of Mechanical Reproduction (1936)", 63–70. As Frank Kessler points outs, with more than seventy years separating the writings of Baudelaire and Benjamin, with Simmel lying somewhere in the middle, therein already lies a problem of what the concept of "modernity" precisely refers to in each of these texts (Frank Kessler, "Viewing Change, Changing Views: The 'History of Vision'-Debate", in Annemone Ligensa and Klaus Kreimeier (eds.), *Film 1900: Technology, Perception, Culture* (New Barnet: John Libbey, 2009), 23–35, here 28).

70 Tom Gunning. "An Aesthetic of Astonishment", 116.

71 Biltereyst et al., "Cinema, Audiences and Modernity", 4.

72 David Bordwell, *On the History of Film Style* (Cambridge, MA: Harvard University Press, 1997), 144.

73 Ibid., 143.

and relief to spectators.[74] The coupling of modernity and urbanity, according to Fuller-Seeley and Potamianos, has led to "[...] sweeping generalizations about the mass audience, the urban audience, the urban working-class audience, or the female or male audience".[75] This study, however, does not intend to grapple further with this debate since it identifies other issues at stake in the way cinema and modernity played out in the context of colonial Indonesia.[76] As Biltereyst, Maltby and Meers suggest, it embraces a more dynamic approach to the study of cinema and modernity, "[...] in which counter-forces or alternative traditions of modernity compete with hegemonic or culturally dominant forms of it".[77] This move towards "multiple modernities" has also been prevalent in studies of modernity in Southeast Asia, as indicated above, which have further questioned "the Western origin of the 'modern'".[78] Modernity in twentieth century colonial Indonesia, Locher-Scholten claims, "came from many more directions other than just the coloniser alone": it was influenced by "[...] American culture, Parisian fashion, Japanese examples and Islamic reforms in the Middle East and during the process took particular Indonesian expressions".[79] Residents of the Indies, according to Mrázek, were eager "[...] to attain modernity by technologies that were unabashedly frivolous, and by machineries that served primarily to produce an appearance and an amusement".[80] Studies of fashion, literature,

---

74   Joe Kember, *Marketing Modernity: Victorian Popular Shows and Early Cinema* (Exeter: University of Exeter Press, 2009), 16. By marketing cinema's capability to address the increasing speed of everyday life and the experience of modernity while creating institutional practices that were based on proximity and comfort (of the lecturer, other live performers, and of the connections to earlier forms of popular entertainment), early cinema stitched itself "into the fabric of everyday life, productively capitalising upon, but also introducing changes to, constructions of communication and self-identity that audiences cherished" (ibid., 212–213).

75   Fuller-Seeley et al., "Introduction", 8. In an article appearing in the same volume, Robert C. Allen calls to decentralise the emphasis on the metropolis by researching small-town and rural movie-going practices instead, and thus to defy the triangulation of cinema, modernity and the metropolis. See Robert C. Allen, "Decentering Historical Audience Studies. A Modest Proposal", in Kathryn H. Fuller-Seeley (ed.), *Hollywood in the Neighborhood: Case Studies of Local Moviegoing* (Berkeley: University of California Press, 2008), 20–33.

76   See Kessler for a more detailed outline and effort to unravel the rigid stance taken at times by proponents and adversaries of the "modernity thesis"/"history-of-vision" debate. Kessler proposes to make the case more explicit by reversing the perspective: "Instead of asking how the experience of modern (urban, mechanised, industrialised, fragmented etc.) life has impacted on cinema and, conversely, in what ways cinema affected the visual habits of its viewers, it might be easier to explore the various ways in which cinema taps into such experiences" (Kessler, "Viewing Change, Changing Views", 28).

77   Biltereyst et al, "Cinema, Audiences and Modernity", 5.

78   Locher-Scholten, *Women and the Colonial State*, 34. As Adrian Vickers points out, the conflation of "colonialism, modernity, and westernization" is a gross oversimplification of the interactions between the three (Adrian Vickers, "Modernity and Being *Moderen*: An Introduction", in Adrian Vickers (ed.), *Being Modern in Bali: Image and Change* (New Haven: Yale University Southeast Asia Studies, 1996), 1–36, here 9). He differentiates between an international discourse of "the modern", relating to the spread of capitalism and other Enlightenment notions and practices around the world, and what Balinese talk about as "*moderen*", used as "a trope for a whole series of historical transformations, from the level of the self to the level of state development" (ibid., 2–3, 5, italics in original).

79   Locher-Scholten, *Women and the Colonial State*, 34.

80   Mrázek, *Engineers of Happy Land*, 132.

Introduction

and popular culture in Southeast Asia indeed show that residents of this region "experimented with the new and modern just as early as Europeans did".[81]

Providing close readings of 1930s advertisements and school notices targeting the indigenous elite and middle classes, Henk Schulte Nordholt disconnects modernity from nationalism through the concept of "cultural citizenship".[82] He argues that, rather than a linear move, traditionally identified in writings on Indonesia from urbanisation, through the rise of indigenous middle classes and the spread of modernity towards nationalism, these individuals were more interested in modernity, or modern lifestyles. And while they were denied political power and many civil rights, through "educational programmes and commercial advertisements", members of the indigenous middle class were, nevertheless, "explicitly invited to abandon traditional habits and to become the new cultural citizens of the colony".[83] In the late colonial period, modernity could be acquired through the purchase of particular products or by conducting oneself in a certain way. Embracing a modern lifestyle, according to Schulte Nordholt, worked in turn to reinforce the interests of the colonial regime, especially since the majority of indigenous students who were the product of this system ended up working for the government.[84]

As Cohen writes about the Komedie Stamboel, it "[...] is typically represented as Indonesia's first 'modern' theatre, due to its intensive capitalization, its rational production system, and its flexible repertoire, as well as its genealogical position as the forerunner of both commercial theatre and 'art' drama" (*opera, tonil, sandiwara, drama, theater*).[85] In the introductory notes to his 2006 book on the Komedie Stamboel, Cohen identifies other turn-of-the-century "cultural form associated with modernity" requiring further research, including the phonograph and cinema.[86] Some of this work has since been explored. In Elizabeth Chandra's work on vernacular Chinese-Malay literature, modernity,

---

81 Bart Barendregt, "Sonic Histories in Southeast Asia", in Bart Barendregt (ed.), *Sonic Modernities in the Malay World: A History of Popular Music, Social Distinction and Novel Lifestyles (1930s–2000s)* (Leiden: Brill, 2014), 1–43, here 6.

82 See Henk Schulte Nordholt, "Modernity and middle classes in the Netherlands Indies: Cultivating cultural citizenship", in Susie Protschky (ed.), *Photography, Modernity and the Governed in Late-colonial Indonesia* (Amsterdam: Amsterdam University Press, 2015), 223–254; Henk Schulte Nordholt, "Modernity and Cultural Citizenship in the Netherlands Indies", *Journal of Southeast Asian Studies* 42, no. 3 (October 2011): 435–457.

83 Schulte Nordholt, "Modernity and middle classes in the Netherlands Indies", 228–229.

84 Ibid., 226.

85 Matthew Isaac Cohen, "On the Origins of the Komedi Stamboel: Popular Culture, Colonial Society, and the Parsi Theatre Movement", *Bijdragen tot de Taal-, Land- en Volkenkunde* 157, no. 2 (2001): 348–349, italics in original. Doris Jedamski writes that, by the 1920s, Miss Riboet's Orion and Dardanella Opera, heirs of the Komedie Stamboel, began to abandon plays taken from Western opera or from *Arabian Nights*, but rather drew theatrical inspiration from cinematic narratives and devices. This trend "can be interpreted as a sign of modernity and Westernization", Jedamski writes, "although it was primarily a response to the shortage of play scripts that still prevailed at the time" (Doris Jedamski, "... and then the lights went out: From Stamboel to Tonil – Theatre and the Transformation of Perceptions", *South East Asia Research* 16, no. 3 (2008): 498). It was rather "the drastic changes in the apparatus and its context that significantly point to the evolving [modern] *dispositif* of the theatre" (ibid.).

86 Cohen, *The Komedie Stamboel*, xiii.

conflated with the Malay notion of progress, is "seen as the progenitor of women's increasing autonomy and young people's diminishing morality in general" in early twentieth century novels.[87] The arrival of the phonograph in the Dutch East Indies has since been the subject of extensive research by Suryadi, who places the phonograph on the long list of Western technologies brought by Europeans to the colony for the purpose of development and modernisation.[88] The contributions to a recent volume of essays, *Sonic Modernities in the Malay World*, focus on "[...] the interplay between the production of popular music, shifting ideas of the modern and, in its aftermath, processes of social differentiation in twentieth-century Southeast Asia".[89]

Many studies of modernity in Southeast Asia thus appear to adhere to Frederick Cooper's approach to modernity, as explored in *Colonialism in Question*. Providing an overview and critique of the use of the term in postcolonial studies and the conceptual confusion that exists, he argues

> Scholars should not to try for a slightly better definition so that they can talk about modernity more clearly. They should instead listen to what is being said in the world. If modernity is what they hear, they should ask how it is being used and why; otherwise, shoehorning a political discourse into modern, antimodern, or postmodern discourses, or into 'their' modernity or 'ours,' is more distorting than revealing.[90]

"*Finding* a discourse of modernity", Cooper suggests, "could be a revealing demonstration".[91] Guided by this approach, if we examine the language used to describe moving pictures in contemporary reports in Dutch and Malay, we find several uses of "modernity" over time. Initially, at the stage of introduction of the technology, the Dutch texts describe it as an innovation or invention of "modern science" while the parallel advertisements in Malay label it as something that is "new" to people in the Indies, suggesting that modernity is

---

87   Elizabeth Chandra, "Women and Modernity: Reading the Femme Fatale in Early Twentieth-Century Indies Novels", *Indonesia* 92 (October 2011): 158.

88   See Suryadi, "The 'talking machine' comes to the Dutch East Indies: The arrival of Western media technology in Southeast Asia", in *Bijdragen tot de Taal-, Land en Volkenkunde (BKI)* 162, no. 2/3 (2006): 269–305. The introduction of the phonograph resembles that of moving picture technology, in the sense that Suryadi identifies different functions of its exhibition: as a new innovation, on the one hand, and as a tool for entertainment, on the other hand.

89   Barendregt, "Sonic Histories in Southeast Asia", 1. This book is one of the fruits of an NWO-funded research project, "Articulating Modernity: The Making of Popular Music in 20th Century Southeast Asia and the Rise of New Audiences", which is headed by Henk Schulte Nordholt. See also the work of Peter Keppy, who is one of the leading researchers of this project: Peter Keppy, "Southeast Asia in the Age of Jazz: Locating Popular Culture in the Colonial Philippines and Indonesia", *Journal of Southeast Asian Studies* 44, no. 3 (October 2013): 444–464.

90   Frederick Cooper, *Colonialism in Question: Theory, Knowledge, History* (Berkeley: University of California Press, 2005), 115. Cooper is particularly disparaging of writings on "colonial modernity", a concept which he claims "[...] reduces the conflicting strategies of colonization to a modernity perhaps never experienced by those being colonized, and gives insufficient weight to the ways in which colonized people sought – not entirely without success – to build lives in the crevices of colonial power, deflecting, appropriating, or reinterpreting the teachings and preachings thrust upon them" (ibid., 16).

91   Ibid., 131, italics in original.

identified in both cases as something novel and innovative.[92] It is derived from a new way of thinking and producing knowledge, namely, scientific thinking. Once the technology became more established, the topics of films began to be described as "modern", for instance: "modern films", "modern dramas", "the most modern courtroom drama", "a modern morality drama".[93] Modern is thus evoked in the sense of something contemporary, of our time, that does away with tradition, such as in the construct "spectacles to behold in the field of modern cinema", or in the use of the word "modern" in the name of moving picture companies, like Modern Bioscope or Apollo Modern Biograph.[94] Furthermore, cinema was sometimes described as a "modern learning source", with a positive value judgement.[95] To extend Schulte Nordholt's use of "cultural citizenship" to cinema spectators, moving pictures in this view were perceived as modern tools of "public education". And whereas elitist colonial schools were only accessible to a certain elite class of society, movie-going was available to individuals of all ages and from all levels of colonial society. It provided spectators an education in modern things, whether in the content of films representing modernisation, progress, industry, and urbanisation, or in the form of encountering the technology itself and of patronising the increasingly modern venues that housed them.

Nevertheless, while cinema would later be used in the service of colonial objectives, like education about hygiene, and although early exhibitors often tapped into the educational discourse of the Ethical Policy, moving pictures' pedagogical potential was largely unrealised by the colonial authorities in the period of this research.[96] Conversely, cinema was frequently, and with even more urgency, described as a source of negative influence in "the 'modern' manner".[97] Thieves in the big cities were allegedly being "modernised by the

---

92   Advertisement, *Java-Bode* (4 March 1897); Advertisement, *Bintang Barat* (8 March 1897). It is crucial to examine and compare the language used in Dutch and Malay texts. As Vickers warns the "modern/*moderen* involves processes of translation, finding similarities. In Indonesian the connected ideas of progress/*kemajuan*, development/*pembangunan* and individual achievement/*budi* – along with a series of linked terms – are in fact fundamentally different terms from their English versions, involving radically different perceptions" (Vickers, "Modernity and Being *Moderen*", 5, italics in original).

93   Advertisement, *Soerabaiasch-Handelsblad* (8 November 1910); "De zedelijkheid en de bioscoop", *Soerabaiasch-Handelsblad* (23 March 1914); Advertisement, *Het Nieuws van den Dag voor Nederlandsch-Indië* (15 June 1914); "Nederlandsch-Indië", *Soerabaiasch-Handelsblad* (1 December 1914).

94   "Cinéma-théâtre", *Java-Bode* (29 September 1908); "Kabar Hindia", *Taman Sari* (17 July 1908); Advertisement, *Soerabaiasch-Handelsblad* (30 March 1910).

95   "Cinematograaf en onderwijs", *De Locomotief* (2 October 1908).

96   See Eric A. Stein on 1930s hygiene promotion films in Java: Eric A. Stein, "Colonial Theatres of Proof: Representation and Laughter in 1930s Rockefeller Foundation Hygiene Cinema in Java", *Health & History* 8, no. 2 (2006): 14–44.

97   "De 'modern' manier", *Nieuwe Soerabaja Courant* (10 February 1910). Such anxieties about the corrupting power of cinema are reminiscent of parallel discussions in the West. According to Grieveson's work on film censorship in the United States in the early twentieth century, cinema as "a school for crime" was in fact a common trope, consequently making it "subject to increasingly intense public discussions and governmental interventions" (Lee Grieveson, *Policing Cinema: Movies and Censorship in Early-Twentieth-Century America* (Berkeley: University of California Press, 2004), 14). Moving pictures were often linked with legislative "discourses on youth, class, ethnicity, gender, urban unrest, and modernity" (ibid., 15).

cinema".[98] In the Malay press, instances of taking bad example from films showing the "progress of thieves" were usually described by a similarly ironic use of the word *kemajuan* (progress).[99] The connections drawn to crime and unrest made the need to police and control moving picture shows increasingly pertinent. The colonial authorities in this period thus did not appear to be interested in using moving pictures to serve their purposes. Rather than prescribing what spectators should see on screen, they would become gradually more obsessed with rules and regulations to limit the scope of the content on offer.

Finally, the most prevalent direct use of the word "modern" applies to the description of venues, thus introducing an aesthetic dimension, especially as cinemas became more permanent and built out of brick and stone in the early 1910s. A cinema theatre was judged to be modern if it met "modern demands", when it was "built in the modern style", as a "modern and beautifully finished stone cinema building", with a "modern décor" and "modern façade that befits [a] new cinema building", and with an interior arrangement that was "so modern and so comfortable" with the "highest modern furnishing" and "modern cinema installation".[100] Most of these mentions, not surprisingly, came out of Surabaya, which was the leader in modern cinema amenities. The "most modern of all" cinema buildings, according to *Bintang Soerabaia*, was the East Java Bioscope. Considering the fact that most Indonesians would not have been able to access nor even gain a glimpse of the more luxurious part of the cinema, such a statement is revealing of the way modernity was limited and controlled.[101]

---

98 "Kiekjes uit Rembang", *Bataviaasch Nieuwsblad* (15 January 1912). This kind of use of the word "progress" resembles Chandra's study of early twentieth century Chinese-Malay novels in which "progress" in the form of Western education of reading of Western novels has a negative moral effect on Chinese girls. "In these stories, the two menaces – Western education and fiction – are conflated and given common signifiers, 'progress' (*kemadjoean*) and 'modernity' (*moderen*)" (Chandra, "Women and Modernity", 162, italics in original).

99 "Roijal Bioscope", *Selompret Melajoe* (14 December 1905); "Mangambil tjonto dari gambar hidoep", *Pembrita Betawi* (10 December 1912).

100 "Cine-Lumen", *Java-Bode* (6 October 1910); "Schouwburgplannen", *Nieuwe Soerabaja Courant* (24 January 1912); "Nieuwe permanente bioscoop", *Nieuwe Soerabaja Courant* (15 January 1912); "De Elite bioscoop", *Bataviaasch Nieuwsblad* (3 July 1912); "Een bioscooptheater op Simpang", *Soerabaiasch-Handelsblad* (23 September 1912); "De 'Non Plus Ultra'-Bioscope", *Soerabaiasch-Handelsblad* (27 September 1912); Advertisement, *De Locomotief* (16 December 1912).

101 "Oost Java Bioscope", *Bintang Soerabaia* (13 November 1913). As Locher-Scholten argues, modernity never followed a straight course, but "[...] in the colonial context, it met with even more hesitation and ambivalence than in the West. It was hampered by colonial fears about the loss of Indonesian traditions and culture, which would endanger political tranquillity and ultimately Dutch sovereignty. It was thus a 'half-way' measure of 'gendered' and 'classed' colonial modernity, which Indonesian women experienced: night labour of rural women was regulated but not forbidden; servants were to be educated but kept at a safe distance; European fashion in the Indies did not refer to an Indonesian context but focused on Europe instead; political rights were something that was denied to women for a long time and would have been granted – had it not been for a strong opposition – to Dutch women only; monogamy should be introduced to a select group of the Indonesian elite, but was also meant to protect Dutch women, who might choose to marry Indonesian Muslim men" (Locher-Scholten, *Women and the Colonial State*, 34).

This quick exercise is helpful for efficiently ordering and providing a sweeping overview of the data collected in this research. It nevertheless leaves out other things new and innovative that contemporary commentators associated with the cinema or with the act of movie-going, such as the use of electricity, the ever-increasing speed of the trade networks used for shipping up-to-date films, costume and dress both on and off screen, and a general culture of going out.[102] All of these will be further delved into in the following chapters. Similarly to Locher-Scholten's study of women and modernity in the late colonial state, "modernity in its longing for progress and 'the modern'" is used here "as a narrative label" for organising the chapters that follow on the emergence of movie-going in colonial Indonesia.[103]

Trade Networks and Turn-of-the-Century Intermedial Entertainment Landscape

Since the 1980s, studies of early cinema, referring roughly to cinema before 1914–1915, have been preoccupied with examining the emergence of moving pictures in connection with their intermedial sphere.[104] This approach applies to studies such as Gaudreault and Marion's, mentioned above, which investigate the institutionalisation of the medium in connection with the various technologies and "cultural series" that preceded it.[105] It is further evoked in research that centres on the exhibition and consumption of early films which, as Joe Kember shows in the case of Victorian Britain, "[...] arrived within entertainments that already had fully developed exhibition and performance practices, and which had carefully cultivated the nuanced expertise audiences now habitually brought to their interpretation of moving pictures".[106]

The case of moving picture exhibition and consumption in the Netherlands Indies presents an especially intriguing case for the study of early cinema, considering the trade networks already set in place by the time moving image technology was in circulation as well as the amalgam of itinerant amusements on offer. In turn-of-the-century colonial Indonesia, railways built by the Dutch authorities connected plantations and mines in the hinterlands to port cities, thus facilitating internal and global trade while simultaneously enabling efficient deployment of colonial troops.[107] These "tools of empire", along with

---

102 See for instance, "Soerabaia op Zaterdagavond", *Soerabaiasch-Handelsblad* (4 July 1910).

103 Locher-Scholten, *Women and the Colonial State*, 32.

104 For more on the concept of intermediality in the study of early cinema, see the special issue of *Early Popular Visual Culture*, particularly the introduction: Andrew Shail, "Intermediality: Disciplinary flux or formalist retrenchment?", *Early Popular Visual Culture* 8, no. 1 (2010): 3–15.

105 Gaudreault et al., "A medium is always born twice…", 3–15. See also André Gaudreault, "The Culture Broth and the Froth of Cultures of So-called Early Cinema", in André Gaudreault, Nicolas Dulac and Santiago Hidalgo (eds.), *A Companion to Early Cinema* (Malden, MA/Oxford: Wiley-Blackwell, 2012), 15–31.

106 Kember, *Marketing Modernity*, 7. See also Andrew Shail, "'A distinct advance in society': Early cinema's 'proletarian public sphere' and isolated spectatorship in the UK, 1911–18", *Journal of British Cinema and Television* 3, no. 2 (2006): 210.

107 See Taylor, *Global Indonesia*, 35. See also Daniel R. Headrick, *The Tools of Empire: Technology and European Imperialism in the Nineteenth Century* (New York: Oxford University Press, 1981).

communication networks and newspapers, steam-shipping and electricity infrastructures, were also utilised by travelling exhibitors of moving pictures who were, like the rest of the *komedi*[108] enterprise in this sense, "parasitic of the colonial state".[109] According to Nadi Tofighian's further zoomed-out assessment of the entire region, Southeast Asia's system of trade and communication networks enabled "[...] to establish a circuit of transnational itinerant theatres, operas, circuses, vaudeville, and *bangsawan* groups. Early film exhibitors and film reels [merely] followed this circuit."[110]

Tofighian's findings further exemplify how early film distribution in Southeast Asia relied on global and local trade networks, dividing the market's development into roughly three phases.[111] During the first phase, from 1896 to 1903, itinerant exhibitors bought films directly from offices in Europe and the US and used this stock for their travelling shows. The second phase, beginning in 1904, is characterised by Tofighian as an "inter-Asian film trade", whereby corporations and commercial shops in the region began to trade in films, alongside their dealings in other products. The third stage began in August 1907, when Pathé Frères opened its subsidiary office in Singapore, distributing films across the entire region, before stationing an agent in the Indies as of 1908.[112] On top of these, local exhibitors, as we shall encounter here, were themselves offering film stock for sale or for exchange, to revitalise their selection of films.[113]

The Netherlands Indies was in fact at the forefront of modern modes of transportation in Southeast Asia and in the frontier of technology in this field on an international scale. Southeast Asia's first railway opened on Java in 1867 (at the same time as Japan), connecting the island's productive interior to the main north coast ports of Batavia, Semarang and Surabaya. Railways in other parts of Southeast Asia were not introduced before the 1880s and 1890s.[114] The first automobiles arrived in Java in 1894, Singapore in 1896, Bangkok in 1897, North Sumatra in 1902 and Rangoon in 1905.[115] Horse trams began operating in Batavia in 1869, followed by Manila (1881), Tokyo (1882) and Bangkok

---

108 *Komedi* was the Malay term for commercial entertainment, likely introduced in the Indies via French entertainment troupes (see Cohen, *The Komedie Stamboel*, 11). The term *komedi* would later be used in combination with the Dutch word *bioscoop* in order to refer to moving picture shows (see further in Chapter 3).

109 Ibid., 24.

110 Tofighian, *Blurring the Colonial Binary*, 61, italics in original. Also see Tofighian's second chapter, which is dedicated to "Distribution" (ibid., 111–147).

111 Ibid., 136.

112 Ibid. For more on Pathé Frères in the Indies see Section 5.3.1.

113 According to Blom, by 1914, firms such as Éclair opened agencies in the Netherlands Indies, enabling film dealers to acquire film programmes for an entire year directly from companies like Bison, Vitagraph and American Biograph (see Blom, *Jean Desmet*, 214). This research was not able to find much information from primary sources on film distribution in the Indies. More research into this important aspect of the local film culture is therefore required.

114 See Dick et al., *Cities, Transport and Communications*, 59–61.

115 Ibid., 66.

(1889), while the more comfortable and reliable steam tram followed in Batavia in 1882, Singapore (1885), Surabaya (1889) and Penang (1893).[116] An electric tram was running in Batavia in April 1899, three months before the first line in the Netherlands.[117]

The wide availability of these modes of transport was probably one of the draws of colonial Indonesia for touring entertainers, especially Java which exhibitors chose to tour either overland, along the railroad tracks, or hopping from one port city to the other via steamship connections. The distribution of such transportation technologies across the archipelago was nevertheless uneven, which played a role in the routes taken by such touring entrepreneurs and the audiences who had access to their shows. By 1900 Java had by far the most extensive railway coverage out of the islands under Dutch control, particularly in Central and East Java, "which was supplemented by a rapidly expanding narrow-gauge tramway network".[118] By 1909 this (mostly government-owned) substantial rail network ran a total length of 2,170 kilometres.[119] Railway-building on Sumatra, in comparison, did not even attempt to unite the whole island and basically served three separate regions.[120] The northern Sumatra network, begun at different ends in the 1880s, was finally completed only in 1916. Similarly the southern line was fully joined together only in 1927. Meanwhile a third, smaller network developed in West Sumatra from the 1880s. These three distinct networks were never linked, and it was left to road transport to accomplish the unification of the island.[121]

At the same time, as many touring exhibitors around the turn of the century discovered, travel and transportation modes were not always comfortable or reliable.[122] Trains could run late and often did not have a fixed schedule.[123] Thus, one entrepreneur who arrived ahead of time in Magelang, Central Java, in order to set up his venue, found out a week later that his films were still on their way from Malang, in East Java, and would not arrive in time for the

---

116 Ibid., 69.

117 Ibid., 70.

118 Ibid., 59, 61.

119 261 kilometres were privately owned, and the rest state owned (E. Wellenstein, "Means of Communication", in Arnold Wright (ed.), *Twentieth Century Impressions of Netherlands India: Its History, People, Commerce, Industries and Resources* (London: Lloyd's Greater Britain Publishing Company, 1909), 189–204, here 190).

120 See Anthony Reid, *An Indonesian Frontier: Acehnese & Other Histories of Sumatra* (Singapore: Singapore University Press, 2005), 29.

121 Ibid. Nevertheless, the big push for road construction was only in the 1920s. "The total length of State lines in Sumatra [in 1920s] measures 284 km. And 2050 km. of tramway line. The total length of the Deli Railway Company, a private enterprise, is 439 km" (ibid.).

122 In 1913, a moving pictures entrepreneur actually proposed to operate one train car on Javanese trains as a cinema for the pleasure of passengers, but his proposal was shot down, suggesting a bath car was more urgent in the tropics. "Een cinema- of een badwagen?", *Sumatra Post* (2 July 1913).

123 Only in 1909 the *Soerabaiasch-Handelsblad* was suggesting that it was time to introduce a fixed schedule for trams, similar to the Netherlands ("De Dienstregeling van Trams", *Soerabaiasch-Handelsblad* (12 June 1909)).

opening show.[124] Important pieces of luggage were at risk of going amiss during railway journeys, like one variety showman travelling with his Edison Bioscope, as well as an ape in a small cage that fell off the train on Sumatra.[125] Steamships were sometimes delayed for days, or even sunk while carrying equipment, as occurred to an exhibitor travelling from Surabaya to Makassar who did not even bother insuring his device and films.[126]

Another issue touring entertainers (and their spectators) had to reckon with was the tropical climate of the Indonesian archipelago.[127] The wet conditions were often blamed for the blurriness of the projection, inadequate lighting, or low audience attendance.[128] Other travelling entertainers, such as circus acts and *komedi stambul* troupes, faced similar difficulties in their tours of Java during the west monsoon season, roughly from November to March. In the northern part of Sumatra, by comparison, the rainiest month is August. "Many potential spectators will not go out at night during these months", Cohen muses over the *stambul* audience, and his reflections can equally be applied to potential cinema spectators. "The racket of pounding rain can diminish sound quality and audibility even in well-insulated theater buildings."[129] Some entertainment companies were inclined to step down during the monsoon months, but moving picture exhibitors were active all year round, possibly seeing this as an opportunity to make some money by stepping into the empty slot left by other performers. This would have been even more the case once more permanent venues were set up around 1907 and had to keep regular schedules.

Many travelling entertainers were represented by agents or managers, who would have presumably helped to plan the tour routes and arrive at the site earlier, to arrange the required permits ahead of time.[130] All touring entertainers had to apply for permits to offer their shows, but they were essentially free agents, roaming the archipelago via the transportation networks set up by the colonial authorities, advertising and promoting themselves by hanging posters, distributing handbills, and through advertisements and promotional content in the local newspapers, in Dutch and Malay.[131] In the nineteenth century, a

124 "Magelang", *De Locomotief* (22 September 1909).

125 Advertisement, *Sumatra Post* (27 July 1907).

126 "Uit Macassar", *Het Nieuws van den Dag voor Nederlandsch-Indië* (11 March 1911).

127 On the weather conditions of the archipelago, see C. Braak, "Climate of Netherlands India", in Wright (ed.), *Twentieth Century Impressions*, 303–308. The annual average of rainfall in West Java and Sulawesi and in the whole of Sumatra and Borneo, as measured in the first decade of the twentieth century, exceeded 2,000 mm, with some stations measuring at between 6,000 to 7,000 mm per annum (ibid., 304).

128 For instance: "De Kinematograaf", *Het Centrum* (5 July 1897); "Nederlandsch-Indië", *Bataviaasch Nieuwsblad* (5 December 1898); "Nederlandsch-Indië", *Bataviaasch Nieuwsblad* (18 May 1899).

129 Cohen, *The Komedie Stamboel*, 92.

130 See, for instance, the active role of agents and managers in the early phonograph exhibitions in Southeast Asia in Suryadi, "The 'talking machine' comes to the Dutch East Indies, 269–305.

131 The first vernacular newspapers in Malay appearing in the 1860s. For more on the vernacular press, see Adam, *The Vernacular Press*. The Malay print industry will be further expanded on in the section on Time Frame, Geographical Scope and Sources below and in Section 3.1.1.

Introduction

performing troupe of "Foreign Orientals", arriving from China, India or Malaya, was usually granted a six-month permit upon arrival at port, while "European" performers were able to obtain longer permits, sometimes even settling permanently in the Indies.[132] By the end of the nineteenth century, permits to perform and to set up a tent for shows were slightly more complicated to attain and had to be applied for separately in each region and town. At times this could wholly change the originally planned tour route of a company. This procedure became even more complex once the decentralisation scheme was underway as of 1905, leading to clashes between the various local administrations and the newly founded Municipal Councils. Control of the contents of moving picture shows was initially relatively lax, and left up to local police forces in each location. However, by the 1910s, and contrary to the decentralisation of most services, efforts to apply centralised control and censorship were in process.

Performing arts have a long history in the Indonesian archipelago and in the surrounding region, predating later varieties of commercial entertainments. Traditional performances include theatrical dance (*wayang wong* or *wayang orang*, literally, human *wayang*) and shadow play (*wayang kulit*). Both of these forms present adaptations drawn from the Indian epics, the *Mahabharata* and the *Ramayana*, in addition to Malay stories, presented by a puppeteer (*dalang*) with leather-made puppets in the case of *wayang kulit*, or with staged actors in the case of *wayang wong*.[133] The *wayang wong*, while originally a royal dance theatre sponsored by sultans and watched by the elite of Javanese and European society, also became a commercial art form in the 1890s, "[...] enacted in enclosed spaces by paid actors for ticket-purchasing spectators".[134] The *wayang kulit*, originating from the Javanese royal courts and accompanied by a *gamelan* ensemble, enables spectators to watch the show from both sides of the screen: either in front of the canvas, enjoying the shadow effect, or behind the screen, watching the *dalang* working the puppets.[135] While it is tempting to understand movie-going in colonial Indonesia within the framework of this earlier form of storytelling on a screen, it is crucial to remember that the *wayang kulit* is mostly performed as a folk tradition rather than for paying spectators. Thus, although early cinema shared certain elements with *wayang kulit* (for instance, the effect of light projected on a screen, the suspension of disbelief inherent to the viewing process, or even the arrangement of seats in certain venues), entrepreneurs of moving pictures had to cultivate an audience of paying

---

132 See Cohen, *The Komedie Stamboel*, 19.
133 See Jedamski, "... and then the lights went out", 486.
134 Cohen, "On the Origins of the Komedi Stamboel", 323. Commercial *wayang wong* also commented on the politics of the time, which were probably one of the reasons why the Resident of Batavia announced in 1890 that no more permits would be issued, soon followed by other cities in West Java.
135 According to Mrázek, most people on Java prefer to watch *wayang* from the "front", where they can see the work of the *dalang* and enjoy watching the performance aspect of the puppet show (see Jan Mrázek, *Phenomenology of a Puppet Theatre: Contemplations on the Art of Javanese Wayang Kulit* (Leiden: KITLV Press, 2005), 27). In traditional Western terms, it would appear that most spectators are seated backstage.

spectators in order to survive as a commercial entertainment form. The cultural practice of movie-going, or the act of consuming moving pictures, must therefore be located within the context of other turn-of-the-century commercial amusements.

Examining the predecessors to moving picture shows, which were also its direct competitors touring the local scene during the period in focus in this research, the relative independence of the early movie-going scene in the Netherlands Indies from the Netherlands itself becomes generally observable across the popular entertainment landscape of the nineteenth century. Among these itinerant acts were American magicians, British and Indian circus troupes, *soirées variées* featuring such acts as *féeries*, *tableaux vivants* or Chinese dancers, visiting and locally-grown *komedi stambul* or *bangsawan* companies, Japanese and Australian acrobats, and French and Austrian operetta performers.[136] And even if more Dutch performers, like Louis Bouwmeester or the Brondgeest ensemble, were travelling to the Netherlands Indies at the beginning of the twentieth century, with the hopes of making a fortune, it soon transpired that the less than satisfactory profits were not necessarily worth the risks involved, consisting of tough living conditions and tropical fevers suffered by their crews.[137] The Batavia cemetery was in fact infamously known among Western entertainers as "[...] 'The Actors' Graveyard', being so named because nearly every theatrical company which [went] there [left] someone behind".[138]

European dramaturgical influences, techniques and venues began to filter in with the arrival of colonial settlers, especially in the nineteenth century, introducing "[g]reasepaint, bright lights, wing-and-drop scenery, trapdoors and flies, box seats and stalls, tickets, posters, leaflets, and all the apparatus of theatre [...]".[139] By the mid-nineteenth century, non-Europeans began using "[...] European dramaturgical forms and theatrical technology to perform plays in their own languages and idioms".[140] The first such instance recorded in Southeast Asia was the Parsi Theatre, originating from the Parsi minority of Bombay and touring the Indies as of the 1880s. The repertoire of these commercial theatre troupes was incredibly mixed, appropriating and localising Sanskrit epics, Shakespearean plays, and stories from *The Thousand and One Nights*.[141] Stage effects were of primary concern to these troupes and producers "[...] often went to great lengths to obtain the latest in stage technologies".[142] In fact, many spectators in colonial Indonesia would have first been exposed

---

136 See Cohen's discussion of the nineteenth century entertainment scene in the Indies in Cohen, *The Komedie Stamboel*, 1–27

137 "Tooneelspelers in Indië", *Bataviaasch Nieuwsblad* (10 January 1905).

138 Carl Hertz, *A Modern Mystery Merchant: The Trials, Tricks and Travels of Carl Hertz, the Famous American Illusionist* (London: Hutchinson & Co., 1924), 168–9.

139 Cohen, *The Komedie Stamboel*, 4.

140 Ibid.

141 See Cohen, "On the Origins of the Komedie Stamboel", 316.

142 Ibid., 317.

to moving picture technology when the Victoria Parsi Theatrical Company included Cinematograph screenings on the programme during their tour of Java in June–December 1898.[143]

Komedi stambul and *bangsawan* refer to hybrid forms of popular Malay opera, drawing on local traditions while simultaneously influenced by Parsi Theatre, as well as European texts and stage techniques. Emerging in the late nineteenth century in the Indies and in British Malaya, respectively, travelling troupes crisscrossed the entire region with their shows, exchanging actors and managers, until they finally collapsed any real distinction between *stambul* and *bangsawan*.[144] The Komedie Stamboel, a local troupe established in Surabaya in 1891 with a mixed cast of "Natives", Indies-born Chinese and Eurasians, staged texts drawn from similar source materials as the Parsi Theatre.[145] By the early 1900s there were various such companies touring Java, performing mostly in tent-like structures, with repertoires comprised of stories from *The Thousand and One Night*, adaptations of local tales, such as *nyai*[146] stories, European fairy tales and operas, Shakespeare plays, and stories originating from Chinese legends. "Hardly any of the theatre troupes", Jedamski maintains, "made it to the firm stages of a big city theatre hall".[147]

According to Nadi Tofighian's extensive research of turn-of-the-century entertainment in Southeast Asia, the circus "was the benchmark against which other entertainment forms in Southeast Asia were compared, as it was very popular, particularly the menagerie and the hippodrome".[148] Known in Malay as *komedi kuda* (horse show) and initially holding irregular appearances on Java, by the end of the nineteenth century large troupes toured Java and the other islands of the archipelago more regularly, playing in tents that could seat thousands of spectators.[149] Circuses often included sideshows for which separate tickets were sold, and as of the late 1890s these sideshows may also have included moving pictures.[150] A stay of a few weeks in Batavia in 1905 could

---

143   See further on the Victoria Parsi Theatrical Company with its Cinematograph in Section 1.3.3.

144   See Tan Sooi Beng, *Bangsawan, A Social and Stylistic History of Popular Malay Opera* (Singapore: Oxford University Press, 1993), 16–18; Cohen, *The Komedie Stamboel*, 40–49; Matthew Isaac Cohen, "Border Crossings: Bangsawan in the Netherlands Indies in the Nineteenth and Early Twentieth Centuries", *Indonesia and the Malay World* 30, no. 87 (2002): 101–115.

145   In his book on the Komedie Stamboel, Cohen uses spelling to differentiate between the Komedie Stamboel, referring to the specific troupe under investigation in his study, which was established in Surabaya in 1891, and *komedi stambul* in reference to the genre of Malay popular opera (Cohen, *The Komedie Stamboel*, xiv). I have retained this differentiation throughout this book.

146   *Nyai* was the term used for an informal "Native" wife. For more on *Nyai* stories in literature, on stage and on film, see Section 3.2.4

147   Jedamski, "…and then the lights went out", 489.

148   Tofighian, *Blurring the Colonial Binary*, 50–51.

149   See Cohen, *The Komedie Stamboel*, 12. The Australian circus company FitzGerald Company, for example, toured the region with a giant tent seating 6,000 people (see Gillian Arrighi, "The Circus and Modernity: A Commitment to 'the Newer' and 'the Newest'", *Early Popular Visual Culture* 10, no. 2 (2012): 169; Tofighian, *Blurring the Colonial Binary*, 98).

150   On the Ripograph or Giant Cinematograph at Harmston's Circus, see Section 1.3.1

yield anything from 8,500 to 20,000 guilders for a circus company.[151] Itinerant circus companies were so popular that Matthew Cohen has found examples of people seeking advance payments or pawning valuable possessions in order to be able to buy a ticket for the circus.[152] The cinema would later be blamed as the motivation for such behaviour, as one employer from Buitenzorg (Bogor) in Central Java complained: "Employees ask for advance payment no longer because their father or mother passed away, – I had a stable boy who lost seven mothers, – but because they want to go to the bioscope".[153]

Other popular itinerant entertainers in Southeast Asia, according to Tofighian, were magicians and illusionists, with a total of about ten different stage magicians on tour in the region at the turn of the century.[154] Magicians, such as Georges Méliès, also played a vital role in early film production. According to the present research, several film titles which may be attributed to Méliès were even screened in the Indies by Louis Talbot's Scenimatograph as early as in 1897, after which Talbot continued his tour of Southeast Asia.[155] American magician Carl Hertz, who acquired an R. W. Paul device in London in 1896, performed his shows in the major port cities of Java during July and August 1898, sometimes combined with moving pictures.[156] Nevertheless, the "[...] fortune of magicians gradually declined with the advent of cinematic devices, and ten years after the earliest film exhibitions, magicians were advertising in newspapers for engagements".[157] They were now being hired as variety acts by cinema theatres across the region, including Surabaya's cinema palace of the East Java Bioscope.[158]

Optical and musical devices were exhibited before moving pictures, framed as technological innovations, illustrative or educational tools, or as forms of entertainment – a pattern which is also discernible in the later exhibition of moving pictures. The Edison Phonograph was first demonstrated on Java in May 1892 by Douglas Archibald, an exhibitor who claimed to have introduced the machine in England, Australia, New Zealand, Ceylon and India.[159] Four years later, the Phonograph was already used by Mr. Harley when exhibited in combination with Edison's Kinetoscope.[160] Magic lantern slides by prime producer Merkelbach and projection devices shipped by Ivens & Co. from the Netherlands were offered for sale, while itinerant showmen exhibited at hotels

---

151 See "Betawi 22 Juni 1905", *Taman Sari* (22 June 1905). A *komedi stambul* troupe managed by Mr. Hunter, also present around the same time, reportedly made 15,000 guilders. I have not found any indications of these companies' expenses.

152 See Cohen, *The Komedie Stamboel*, 12.

153 "Bioscoop-mani", *Het Nieuws van den Dag voor Nederlandsch-Indië* (12 October 1905).

154 See Tofighian, *Blurring the Colonial Binary*, 129–130.

155 For more on Talbot's Scenimatograph, see Section 1.2.

156 For more on Hertz's shows with the Cinematographe, see Section 1.3.4

157 Tofighian, *Blurring the Colonial Binary*, 130.

158 For more on the East Java Bioscope, see Section 4.5.

159 See Suryadi, "The 'talking machine' comes to the Dutch East Indies", 277.

160 For more on Harley and the Kinetoscope, see Section 1.1.

Introduction

and European Club houses (*Sociëteit*, colloquially referred to as *soos*), or offered their services for rent at private parties.[161] Lantern slides were also used as illustrative tools for lectures, and sometimes were featured in moving picture shows, to the disappointment of at least one spectator of the Biograph Pathé as part of a *variété* evening, who identified magic lantern slides as something shown at children's parties.[162] X-ray devices on display could reveal if a person were carrying a bullet instead of money in their wallet as part of an illustration of the new technology at the Club house, or as part of a magic show on the theatre stage.[163]

Additional attractions included steam carousels, which often popped up next to the tent of another public amusement like moving pictures, *stambul* or circus. In fact, the usage of steam boilers for moving picture companies was initially registered in annual government reports in combination with the usage for carousels, until the two categories were split up in the reports for 1906 as the number of boilers used by moving picture companies began to far outnumber that of carousels.[164] Waxwork museums offered beautiful stereoscopic plates alongside shocking anatomical exhibits.[165] Panoramas and panopticums depicting battle scenes from the Sino-Japanese War (August 1894 – April 1895) or the Boer War (October 1899 – May 1902), as well as city views like Athens, Constantinople, or even the 1889 Paris exposition, attracted hordes of visitors from all levels of society.[166]

There were also fairgrounds, similar to the European or Dutch traditions (*kermis*) which included attractions such as "The cannibals of Borneo", "The Miracle Lamp", "The living talking human head", the Kinematograph and Edison's Phonograph.[167] The *Pasar Malam* (night market) and annual *Pasar Gambir* (Gambir fair) were arts and crafts markets which featured similar fairground attractions, like dancers, swordsmen, *gamelan* music and moving picture shows, exhibited either in the open-air or in enclosed spaces. Local

161 Advertisement, *Deli Courant* (13 March 1897); Advertisement, *De Locomotief* (17 May 1910); Advertisement, *Java-Bode* (6 January 1898). Cees Ivens (1871–1941) took over his father's photography business in Nijmegen in 1894. He then opened more shops of *Het Nederlandsch Fototechnische Bureau C. A. P. Ivens & Co.* (C.A.P.I.) in Groningen, Amsterdam, and The Hague. His son, Joris Ivens (1898–1989), was a Dutch documentary filmmaker (Ansje van Beusekom, "Ivens, Cees A. P.", in Richard Abel (ed.), *Encyclopedia of Early Cinema* (London: Routledge, 2005), 342).

162 "Globetrotter", *Nieuwe Soerabaja Courant* (16 October 1908); Advertisement, *Het Nieuws van den Dag voor Nederlandsch-Indië* (28 December 1904); "Tournée Artistique", *Soerabaiasch-Handelsblad* (6 September 1905).

163 "Soerakarta 12 Augustus, 1898", *De Nieuwe Vorstenlanden* (12 August 1898); Advertisement, *Het Nieuws van den Dag voor Nederlandsch-Indië* (30 January 1907).

164 *Koloniaal Verslag* 1907–1908: Bijlage W, 2.

165 "One can view an interesting anatomical collection and simultaneously do a good deed", the *Java-Bode* commented on Mr. Silbermann's wax museum, which pledged to donate towards the Transvaal Fund ("Nederlandsch-Indië", *Java-Bode* (26 October 1899)).

166 Advertisement, *Deli Courant* (12 December 1896); "Verspreide Indische Berichten", *De Locomotief* (7 March 1900); Advertisement, *Soerabaija-Courant* (27 April 1896); Advertisement, *Semarangsche Courant* (30 September 1896).

167 "Kermis", *Het Centrum* (31 August 1898).

views of these celebrations were also captured by entrepreneurs of moving pictures on site, and subsequently exhibited to local audiences in the same city and across the archipelago.

Indies Spectators and Spectatorial Positions: An Overview

As Joe Kember argues for early cinema spectators in nineteenth century Britain, "[...] audiences already possessed expert knowledge concerning the longstanding market for novelty. They had learned this from decades of exposure to spectacular images, bizarre performances, and other commodifications of alterity on the fairground, in the lecture theatre, and elsewhere."[168] As shown above, spectators of moving pictures in the Indies would have come to moving picture shows with prior experience from other entertainments, both similar to and different from those of early movie-goers in the West. Spectatorship was in fact an everyday experience in turn-of-the-century urban colonial culture, with its open galleries that allowed "crowds of eavesdropping onlookers" to partake even in the most private spaces of the exclusive European Club houses.[169] "There was even a Dutch colonial word coined to describe the incidental audience members", Cohen writes. "They were known as *nontonners*, from the Batavia Malay word *nonton*, 'to go see a sight'."[170] In his extensive study of the Komedie Stamboel, and drawing on Tom Gunning's work on early cinema's "aesthetic of astonishment" as referenced here earlier, Cohen finds that spectators at the *komedi* were intended to react with "astonishment, rather than mystification":

> In European terms, komedi involved 'modern magic' and not 'sorcery'; in Malay terms, komedi was a cultural form of the *heran* and not the *aneh*. Heran was an attitude toward the world that encompassed confusion; surprise, astonishment, and amazement; and mystery and wonder. Appreciation of attractions presupposed a degree of sophistication, an ability to recognize and appreciate illusionism and technological prowess, and not confuse the wonders of the komedi stage with the genuine magic of spirit possession in hobbyhorse dancing [...].[171]

Stambul shows thus attracted avid and capable spectators comprised of "[...] drunken European men, middle-income Muslim families, Chinese store owners, prostitutes, sailors and soldiers, Eurasian clerks, and nearly everyone else".[172] The make-up of movie audiences was probably not very different, as moving pictures were rapidly moving out of the more elitist European venues in the form of European-style theatres or European Club houses used for the very first shows, and into canvas tents and later more fixed bamboo tents, which were often located in and around the main town or village square (*Alun Alun*).

168 Kember, *Marketing Modernity*, 212.
169 Cohen, *The Komedie Stamboel*, 6.
170 Ibid., italics in original.
171 Ibid., 12, italics in original.
172 Ibid., 1.

The plurality of ethnicities in the Indies, as sketched out above, was also represented in the mix of movie-goers, as well as of film exhibitors who were of various backgrounds, including American, Armenian, British, Chinese, Dutch, French, Indian, Japanese and Indonesian or Eurasian.[173] With such a rich melange of ethnicities and dialects, as well as high rates of illiteracy among spectators, a visual medium like moving pictures, combined with musical accompaniment – whether from a gramophone playing a Western, Chinese or Malay repertoire, a piano player or orchestrion,[174] a string orchestra or *gamelan* ensemble[175] – would have generally been suitable for a wide range of audiences.[176] Neither the language of intertitles nor of the texts spoken by the lecturer, if present, can be determined for all cases. Even if the nationality of an exhibitor is known, this does not guarantee the language he or she would have used. An exhibitor identified as English might have spoken German when screening French films, while an Armenian manager could translate German intertitles into English.[177]

In the 1890s, a household servant would have earned between 16 to 18 guilders per month, i.e. approximately 60 cents per day.[178] The daily wage of planters in the rural regions would have been 20 to 25 cents for men and 15 cents for women.[179] And while the earliest shows found in 1896 were priced at one or even two guilders per ticket, depending on the location of the show, by 1897 cheaper tickets were introduced at 50 cents and below, thus making moving picture shows more widely available to the entire population of the major Indies cities and even some smaller towns and rural areas. To put the ticket

173 In studying the history of early film distribution in the region, Tofighian problematizes Brian Larkin's concept of the "colonial sublime", by which Larkin refers to Western technology as used to amaze and assert the position of the coloniser over the colonised (Brian Larkin, *Signal and Noise: Media, Infrastructure, and Urban Culture in Nigeria* (Durham: Duke University Press, 2008), 35–40). Tofighian points out that, soon after the introduction of the technology, many of the exhibitors of moving pictures in Southeast Asia were in fact Asians themselves, thus putting into question "[...] the idea of the white man as the transmitter of technology and civilisation" (Tofighian, *Blurring the Colonial Binary*, 96).

174 First introduced in the early nineteenth century, an orchestrion is an automatic musical device playing from a perforated music roll and intended to sound like a band or orchestra. The pianola, a self-playing piano worked by the player controlling the pneumatic mechanism, was another popular option. According to Tofighian, "[...] piano was the most common live accompaniment to film exhibitions [in Southeast Asia], especially if the exhibition took place in the Town Hall rather than in a tent" (Tofighian, *Blurring the Colonial Binary*, 107). Although I have not found information on the accompanying music or instruments for every company, it is safe to assume that most, if not all, shows had some kind of musical accompaniment. Whenever this information was available, I have made a point of mentioning it in the discussion.

175 *Gamelan* is a traditional musical ensemble mostly made up of percussive instruments and popular on Java and Bali. It is often used to accompany dance or *wayang*.

176 "According to the 1920s census, the literacy rate of the natives in Java was still only 2.74 percent in the vernacular and 0.13 percent in Dutch. And yet, the number of literate people was substantial: 943,000 in native languages and 87,000 in Dutch" (Shiraishi, *An Age in Motion*, 19).

177 "Nederlandsch-Indië", *Advertentieblad voor Tegal en Omstreken* (11 December 1897); "De Chronofoon", *Soerabaiasch-Handelsblad* (20 July 1905).

178 See W. Basil Worsfold, *A Visit to Java. With An Account of The Founding of Singapore* (London: Richard Bentley and Son, 1893), 29.

179 See Arthur Keyser, *From Jungle to Java. The Trivial Impressions of a Short Excursion to Netherlands India* (Westminster: The Roxburghe Press, 1897), 75.

prices of moving picture shows into context, even at the early novelty stage admission was in the same price range as other entertainments on Java discussed in the previous section, such as magic shows (f0.50 to f1.50), panoramas (f0.25 cents to f1), and *tableaux vivants* (f0.25 cents to f2.50).[180] A visit to the circus would have usually cost f4 for first class seats, f2 for second class, f1 for a bench seat, and f0.50 in the gallery which was reserved for "Natives"[181] only – a pricing category which would be introduced by moving pictures exhibitors more regularly in the early 1900s.[182]

As of the turn of the century, tickets for moving picture shows were being offered in different pricing and seating categories, with the cheapest tickets, explicitly offered to "Natives", available at 25 cents and continually dropping throughout the following decades to 15, 10 and sometimes as cheap as 2 cents. Depending on the venue, seats for "Natives" would have been either in the upstairs gallery, right in front of the screen, in what became known as the *kambing* (literally, goat) class, or behind the screen. The latter layout would have been familiar to spectators in the Indies from the *wayang kulit*, as mentioned above. Having looked through tens of thousands of meters of Dutch and Malay newspapers on microfilm from five major colonial cities, from 1896 to 1918, I have come across plenty of evidence suggesting that this latter arrangement was widely employed throughout the entire period and in many venues across the archipelago.[183] It is not clear when exactly this practice was first introduced in moving picture tents nor when it was abandoned, but it was so widespread that even the luxurious cinema palace of the East Java Bioscope, built in 1913 to accommodate 750 "Europeans" and 400 "Natives", offered cheaper seats for "Native" spectators behind the screen.[184] This research has also found several venues specifically targeting "Native" spectators, which often practiced a gender-based separation of the movie audience, creating separation between male and female spectators. In some regions where Islam was more prominent, this appears to have occurred also in "mixed" cinemas, presumably enforced only in the section for "Natives".[185]

Sometimes separate tickets were also offered to "Foreign Orientals", yet,

---

180 Advertisement, *Java-Bode* (26 May 1897); Advertisement, *Semarang-Courant* (24 October 1896); Advertisement, *Soerabaija-Courant* (9 April 1897); Advertisement, *Soerabaija-Courant* (15 April 1897). The currency symbol f refers to florins, which is interchangeable with guilder.

181 The word "Native" here, always in quotation marks, will be used as a proxy for the original Dutch term *Inlander* used by exhibitors in their advertisements and in reports appearing in Dutch newspapers, government documents, etc.

182 Advertisement, *Soerabaija-Courant* (15 June 1896).

183 It was supposedly practiced in other parts in the region, according to Stephen Bottomore's entry on British Malaya in the *Encyclopedia of Early Cinema* (Stephen Bottomore, "Malaya", in Abel (ed.), *Encyclopedia of Early Cinema*, 590–591). However, Nadi Tofighian has told me in private communication that he has not found any such instances in his own research on Southeast Asia in this period. I take this as evidence that this practice was less prevalent outside the Netherlands Indies.

184 "Oost Java Handels Mij en Oost Java Bioscope", Soerabaiasch Nieuwsblad (10 November 1913). See further on the East Java Bioscope in Section 4.5 and for more examples of this practice in Section 2.3.2 and Section 3.2.5.

185 "Internationale Bioscope", *Deli-Courant* (6 August 1909).

significantly, tickets for "Europeans" always remained unmarked. The only instances advertisements addressed European spectators directly were to specify that "Europeans" would not be admitted to the section reserved for "Natives". So it appears that some "Europeans" had no qualms about sitting next to "Natives", as long as they could save a few cents in the process. This suggests that, at least to a certain extent, the practice denoted an economic or class-based differentiation rather than purely racial segregation. And while pricing categories clearly mirrored the racial mechanisms ingrained into colonial practice, it also shows that movie-going was available to all members of colonial society.[186] In fact, even those who could not afford a ticket often found a way to sneak inside the tent.

Around 1910, according to the account by a travelling exhibitor in the region published in the trade journal The Kinematograph, moving picture exhibitions were

> [...] held in large well-built tents of canvas or bamboo and matting – not circular, but long and narrow on the lines of a hall and with no posts to obstruct the view. The management seems to spare no expense in making their "houses" attractive and comfortable, and the approaches are richly carpeted [sic] and lined with banks of tropical plants. Most of them have their own electric light generators, and the entrances are a veritable blaze of light.[187]

Such venues, often described as a "semi-permanent tent" or even a "permanent tent", sometimes stood for years in the same spot while the companies exhibiting the films would rotate every few months, leading one to wonder how the notion of a fixed, purpose-built venue was applied in such cases.[188] In this context, it is worth noting that the Dutch word *"tent"* can refer to a canvas tent, in the English sense, or be used as a generic term denoting a non-permanent structure such as a shed or barn. It is also a colloquialism for referring to an establishment, in the same sense as the English term "joint" or "place". The term *"bamboetent"* used to describe many of the, more or less, permanent early moving picture venues in the Indies is thus rather effective at capturing the transient permanence of many of these structures. Spectators were able to purchase food and drink as well as cigarettes and rolling tobacco, whether in buffets provided by cinema entrepreneurs or in independent *warungs* (kiosks) just outside.

In light of the supposedly neat distribution of "European" and "Native" sections, it is difficult to estimate where the Chinese fit into this layout. Yet, since many of the owners of exhibition venues and film companies in the Indies were themselves Chinese, and given that many of the Chinese traders were the wealthiest residents of the colonies, we can safely assume that they were welcomed visitors in the cinemas and, presumably, would have been seated in

---

186 See also discussion in Charlotte Setijadi-Dunn and Thomas Barker, "Imagining 'Indonesia': Ethnic Chinese film producers in pre-independence cinema", *Asian Cinema* 21, no. 2 (2010): 7–24.

187 Harold G. Coulter, "The Kinematograph in the East", *The Kinematograph & Lantern Weekly* (4 February 1909): 1039. I would like to thank Rianne Siebenga for sharing this report with me.

188 "Een Nieuwe bioscoop", *Nieuwe Soerabaja Courant* (11 September 1908); "Nederlandsch-Indië", *Soerabaiasch-Handelsblad* (28 September 1908). See also Tofighian's discussion of this issue in Tofighian, *Blurring the Colonial Binary*, 97–98.

the so-called "European" section.[189] And while for several decades the Chinese were restricted in terms of travel and further subjected to strict zoning in urban areas by Dutch government regulation wishing to control their commercial activity, by 1904 such restrictions were significantly relaxed and mobility facilitated.[190] As mentioned above, sometimes separate tickets were offered to "Foreign Orientals", at times specifying Chinese and Arabs, in which case they would have probably been seated in second or third class on wooden stools or benches in front of the screen, while the fourth class for Natives would have been seated on the ground or bamboo mats behind the screen.

Another group that problematizes the layout of the space is the Indonesian native elite class. For instance, at a venue in Surabaya in 1909, the section for the "Native" class of spectators was split into two: one area was intended for the Indonesian elite while the other was for the "Native coolies", since the former did not wish to be seated next to the latter.[191] It is not clear whether in this case the sections for "Natives" were in the very front of the screen or behind it. In yet another example found in 1914 of a screening held for five to six thousand spectators in celebration of opening a new warehouse of a company in Central Java, the local "Native" rulers were seated next to the European company directors and their wives in front of the screen, while the masses of "little people" were behind the screen.[192] Furthermore, according to Rudolf Mrázek's interviews with members of the Indonesian elite class who grew up in Batavia in the 1920s and 1930s, one self-proclaimed movie-going buff talked about the first time his father took him to a movie theatre, when he was eight years old, and being seated in the prestigious box seat.[193] To push the point even further, when the local authorities in Medan decided to permit only "Europeans" to attend a newly arrived moving picture show, for fear of potential negative influence of the violent content on "Native" spectators, one of the newspapers clarified that "European" also included "Native" elites and Chinese traders.[194]

---

189 See further on the Chinese involvement in the local moving picture scene in Chapter 5.

190 The 1863 pass system (*passenstelsel*) regulations were at times upheld so strictly that in the late nineteenth century "it became necessary for Chinese to get new visas for every four days spent away from home. A pass was required for short trips, such as the one from Batavia to Meester Cornelis, only an hour's journey even in 1900" (Lea E. Williams, *Overseas Chinese Nationalism: The Genesis of the Pan-Chinese Movement in Indonesia, 1900–1916* (Glencoe: The Free Press, 1960), 30). Those travelling without a pass or with a fake document risked fines and imprisonment. As of 1904, travel passes were issued for a one-year period rather than a single journey (see Alexander Claver, *Dutch Commerce and Chinese Merchants in Java: Colonial Relationships in Trade and Finance, 1800–1942* (Leiden: Brill, 2014), 188).

191 "Vardon-bioscoop", *Nieuwe Soerabaja Courant* (10 September 1909).

192 "De Bioscoopramp te Boeloes", *Sumatra Post* (30 January 1914). During the show one of the films caught on fire, and although it was quickly put out, calls of "fire, fire" led people from the "Native" section of the audience to flee the venue. Fifty-eight children, sixteen women, and "one married man" were killed in the stampede on the spot and two others died of related injuries later (ibid.). The company holding the event in which the tragedy occurred offered the families of the deceased five guilders to cover the cost of the funeral and another five guilders per day for holding communal feasts (*slametan*) over the following days (ibid.).

193 See Rudolf Mrázek, *A Certain Age: Colonial Jakarta through the Memories of its Intellectuals* (Durham: Duke University Press, 2010), 118.

Introduction

Either way, it appears that, for the most part, if "Native" or Chinese spectators were able and willing to spend more money on a cinema ticket, they would not have been barred from entering other sections of the cinema.[195] As Cohen found, in the *komedi stambul*, whoever could afford to pay was able to sit wherever he (or she) chose.[196] In light of the population statistics and the number of seats in moving picture venues, we can assume that the situation was similar among cinema entrepreneurs out for a profit. On occasion, even cinemas that insisted that "Europeans" were not allowed in the section for "Natives", would enable them to sit there if the section for "Europeans" was full. Nevertheless, spectators were expected to be dressed in appropriate clothing. "Spectators sitting in the first-class section should not utter vulgarity, wear hitched-up sarongs, or put their feet up."[197] The question of clothing, in a society in which what you were wearing was one of the strongest identifiers of whom you were and where you gained access to, only became more complicated by the 1910s, as Indonesians took up low-level office posts and began to adopt European clothing to replace their traditional dress.[198] Finally, the "European" category is in fact the trickiest one to deconstruct, since we do not know the exact number of Eurasians in this class. Moreover, being "European" in the Indies did not necessarily denote that one was of a high economic or social status and colonial administrators, as Ann Stoler shows, had long been concerned about "poor whites" and "pauperism" in their territories.[199] The starting salary of a European assistant on a plantation in Sumatra in 1910, for instance, would have been 175 guilders in the first year. This sum, one newspaper noted, providing a full account of the projected spending of an assistant in one year, did not even leave employees with enough money to go to a movie.[200] Meanwhile, the growing number of poor Europeans aroused anxieties about maintaining the prestige of this group, leading the colonial authorities to encourage more women and families to emigrate from Europe to the colonies, in the hopes that this would help make the European community more "European".[201] Many film exhibitors tried to address these issues by offering a fifty per cent discount to soldiers below the rank of officer (and to children) for second and third class seats.

194 "De Bioscoop en de Inlanders", *Sumatra Post* (5 August 1909).
195 The only example found of restrictive policies was in the abovementioned case in Medan, where "Natives" were initially banned from attending the International Bioscope's shows. The policy was changed after a couple of shows, but the box seats were still off limits to "Native" spectators. "De Bioscoop en de Inlanders", *Sumatra Post* (7 August 1909). We can only assume that such restrictions were applied in other cases too. For more on the International Bioscope, see Section 7.3.
196 See Cohen, *The Komedie Stamboel*, 132.
197 Ibid.
198 See Mrázek, *Engineers of Happy Land*, 131. For more on the role and meaning of clothing in Indies society, see the various contributions in Schulte Nordholt (ed.), *Outward Appearances*.
199 See Ann L. Stoler, "Making Empire Respectable: The Politics of Race and Sexual Morality in 20th-Century Colonial Cultures", *American Ethnologist* 16, no. 4 (1989): 634–660.
200 "Assistenten-Salarissen", *Sumatra Post* (4 May 1910).
201 See Stoler, *Carnal Knowledge and Imperial Power*, 60–64.

Gender was therefore another category that played into cinema attendance. Women of either ethnic group were generally encouraged to attend with their partners, often by offering half price on the second ticket to a man attending with his spouse. Considering there were various arrangements of marriages across the racial line, one might expect that this led to further mixing at moving picture venues. Indonesian women who served as caretakers to European children were at times invited to attend children's programmes with their charges at a discount. It is not clear to what extent women of any group had the liberty to enter the cinema on their own. Nevertheless, considering several reports according to which Chinese women complained about harassment from cinema staff members, as well as the fact that cinemas targeting Muslim audiences were likely to offer gender-based separation, we can assume that some women attended the cinema unaccompanied.

The space for "Europeans" in cinemas was definitely the section in which exhibitors invested the most efforts and money in making it comfortable, inviting and "modern". For example, the interior of the Chinese-owned iron structure of the Sirene Bioscope in Surabaya had green-coloured wallpaper decoration in the section intended for Europeans and was equipped with electric lighting and excellent ventilation.[202] The Netherlands Indies Biograph Company apparently turned the trumpet of the gramophone used to accompany the show towards the more expensive seats in the tent.[203] And the upstairs *Balcon de luxe* of the East Java Bioscope provided a comfortable vantage point from which one had an unobstructed view of the screen and the audience in the hall, except for the "Native" spectators who were seated, once again, behind the screen.[204]

Chapter Outline

This book is divided into two parts comprised of a total of seven chapters which are arranged chronologically, although they do contain some overlaps due to the fact that several of the companies described were active over the course of a few years. The two parts differ somewhat in approach.[205] The first three

---

202 "De Irene-bioscoop" [sic], *Nieuwe Soerabaja Courant* (10 September 1909).

203 "De Chronofoon", *Soerabaiasch-Handelsblad* (20 July 1905). For more on the Netherlands Indies Biograph, see Section 3.3.

204 "Het nieuwe gebouw van de 'Oost-Java-bioscope' te Soerabaia", *Weekblad voor Indië* 34 (7 December 1913), 787.

205 Earlier versions of several chapters were previously presented in various forums. Parts of the Introduction were presented at the HoMER conferences in Prague in 2013 and in Milan in 2014. Parts of Chapter 1 were presented at Klub Kajian Film at the Jakarta Arts Institute (IKJ) and at the 7th Annual Southeast Asian Cinemas Conference in Singapore in 2012. Parts of Chapter 2 were presented at the Eighth International Seminar on the Origins and History of Cinema in 2011 at Girona and published in the conference proceedings. Portions of Chapter 4 were previously presented at the 8th Annual Southeast Asian Studies Graduate Student Conference at Cornell University and subsequently appeared in Dafna Ruppin, "From 'Crocodile City' to '*Ville Lumière*': Cinema Spaces on the Urban Landscape of Colonial Surabaya". *SOJOURN: Journal of Social Issues in Southeast Asia* vol. 29, no. 1 (2014): 1–30. They are reproduced here with permission of the journal. Thanks are due to the many commentators at these conferences, monthly film seminars, and Early Cinema Colloquia, as well as to the anonymous referees of the published work.

chapters making up Part I focus on the first decade of moving picture shows in the Netherlands Indies, roughly from 1896 to 1909. Since this period was shaped by the work of travelling showmen and women, the chapters trace the movements of itinerant moving picture exhibitors in the region, trying to piece together their tour routes, exhibition practices, film programmes and target audiences. The first chapter examines the introduction of the new technology in the Netherlands Indies by the various exhibitors of different nationalities and origins active from 1896 to 1898. We shall see that spectators in the Indies first encountered moving pictures either as an independent attraction, as in the case of Harley's Kinetoscope or Talbot's Scenimatograph, or in combination with other forms of popular entertainment, namely: as a side-show to the circus, or incorporated on stage into variety, magic or Parsi theatre shows.

Chapter 2 draws attention to the Dutch role in moving picture exhibition, whether through the activities of the Indies branch of the *Nederlandsche Biograaf- en Mutoscope Maatschappij*, the Dutch subsidiary of the American Mutoscope and Biograph Company, or through film contents which were of particular Dutch concern, such as: Queen Wilhelmina's investiture and marriage, as well as scenes from the Second Boer War (1899–1902) and the Russo-Japanese War (1904–1905). The latter two were represented on screen over the course of the conflicts (and sometimes also beyond) by several competing companies, including a Japanese Cinematograph, and drew the attention of European and non-European spectators to Dutch vulnerabilities in the region.

Chapter 3 identifies the period of 1903 to 1909 as the age of the *komedi bioscoop*, which was characterised by companies ever-more influenced by local forms of entertainment, in terms of the film content that they were programming or even producing, as well as in their exhibition and seating practices. The chapter introduces the term *Indisch/Indische*, meaning something that pertains to the Indies or Indies-like, as it came to be understood in the study of print culture (newspapers and literature) and performance studies (*stambul*), and applies this notion to the local moving picture industry in this period. It focuses on two main exhibition companies, both managed by culturally and ethnically intermediary figures: Indian showman Abdulally Esoofally's Royal Bioscope, and the Armenian-owned Netherlands Indies Biograph Company and its offshoot companies.

The last four chapters form Part II of this book, with each chapter focusing on one of the major port cities in Java and Sumatra: Surabaya (Chapter 4), Batavia (Chapter 5), Semarang (Chapter 6), and Medan (Chapter 7). The focus on these particular cities derives from the availability of sources, on the one hand, and from the fact that these four cities would later be singled out in the Bioscope Ordinance (*Bioscoopordonnantie*) of 1916 as hubs of cinema exhibition and film distribution to be closely monitored under the new censorship plan (for more on the Bioscope Ordinance, see Concluding Remarks). These modernising urban landscapes are used here as case studies for investigating overarching patterns of change in colonial society under the decentralisation scheme, which influenced both the undertakings of cinema entrepreneurs and the mobility of their spectators. Each chapter examines the particular conditions which exhibitors of moving pictures had to contend with, in the form of local legislation, urban planning and transportation, licensing and taxation, as well as control and censorship.

Focusing on the development of exhibition venues, which became more fixed as of 1907, each of the chapters in Part II first provides a local historical overview, briefly reviewing the early sites for moving picture shows, and proceeds to explore their growth over time: from canvas and bamboo tents, through iron constructs, to cinema palaces. Furthermore, each chapter highlights certain phenomena which became prominent in the selected locations. Surabaya was the largest city in the colony at the time and, as the home ground of the Komedie Stamboel in the nineteenth century, had the most developed popular entertainment scene. It was therefore soon crowned as the reigning leader in cinema amenities and comforts, and served as home to the first cinema studio in the Indies. Batavia, as the capital of the colony, came in at close second, much due to its highly developed transportation network that enabled spectators to move freely through the city even to locations which were initially considered remote. It also had a large Chinese community, which displayed a high level of involvement in the local moving picture scene, as entrepreneurs and spectators. Semarang, located in between Batavia and Surabaya, was a far more low-key site in terms of popular entertainment and thus serves as a productive contrast. It was nevertheless a centre of cultural life, with its Dutch-language newspaper *De Locomotief* which was read throughout Java and beyond, and holding the Semarang International Colonial Exhibition in 1914. Finally, Medan on Sumatra is the only non-Javanese city to be discussed in detail here. With the different conditions which led to its construction to begin with, surrounded by a large number of foreign-run tobacco, coffee and rubber plantations exploiting coolie workers imported from Java and Mainland China, as well as the nearby Aceh War waged for several decades, it provides an example of more controlled film exhibition as expressed in the cinema monopoly it created and in its establishment of a municipal cinema building.

As a final remark, coming into this research, I had some trepidations of my own about delving into this material which, being neither Dutch nor Indonesian, was foreign to me on at least these two levels. Yet, I came to realise in the process, that my double immersion as a researcher placed me in a similar position to that of the exhibitors I was chasing after, who were often neither Dutch nor Indonesian themselves. I therefore tried to make productive use of this condition, observing with delight and bewilderment the material unfolding before my eyes on the microfilm screen. It is hoped that the writing, emerging from the excitement of archival discoveries just as much as from the frustrations of impasses reached, has managed to capture and convey to the reader some of the thrills of new encounters and at times vexation with the developing technology experienced by early movie-goers in the Indies.

PART I

Emerging Networks of Entertainment

1

Trials and Tribulations of Early Travelling Shows, 1896–1898

This chapter focuses on the arrival of moving pictures in the Netherlands Indies, tracing the first years of moving picture shows in the archipelago by following up on the work of several of the itinerant showmen and women who toured the region between 1896 and 1898. It aims to sketch out the routes that these exhibitors took (locally and, wherever possible, in the region), their programming choices, their advertising and exhibition strategies, as well as their target audiences. It exposes the significant role played by local and travelling entertainers of various nationalities in the introduction and popularisation of moving pictures as part of the local popular entertainment scene. Highlighting the technical and operational difficulties encountered by these entrepreneurs along their journeys, this chapter provides a snapshot of the transition of these new technologies from scientific novelty to popular entertainment. As the two advertisements for Talbot's Scenimatograph shows in Batavia in March 1897 suggest, moving pictures were to be understood as the "most wonderful invention of Modern Science" experiencing "unrivalled success wherever it is shown", according to the Dutch text, and as a "new discovery" that attracts "crowded audiences everywhere" leaving many spectators "astonished" by this novelty, in the Malay version (see Figures 1–1 and 1–2).[206]

We begin with the initial introduction of moving pictures in 1896 in the form of Edison's Kinetoscope, before moving on to the first projections of animated photography. Similarly to the intermedial variety show tradition in the West at the time, most of the examples discussed here will be of moving picture shows incorporated into other forms of entertainment: the Ripograph as a side show for Harmston's Circus, Miss Meranda's variety programme including a sometimes risqué Kinematograph and Gramophone act, the Victoria Parsi Theatrical Company which incorporated a Cinematograph into some of its shows, and the American magician Carl Hertz who performed with an R. W. Paul device which he referred to as a Cinematographe.[207] Nevertheless, some

---

206 Advertisement, *Java-Bode* (4 March 1897); Advertisement, *Bintang Barat* (8 March 1897).

207 For an overview of early film programming in the West, see Richard Abel, "Early Film Programs: An Overture, Five Acts, and an Interlude", in André Gaudreault et al. (eds.) *A Companion to Early Cinema* (Malden, MA/Oxford: Wiley-Blackwell, 2012), 334–359.

The Komedi Bioscoop: Early Cinema in Colonial Indonesia

Figure 1–1. Advertisement for a Talbot Scenimatograph screening, *Java-Bode* (4 March 1897). Retrieved from Delpher on 5 October 2015, http://resolver.kb.nl/resolve?urn= ddd:010496056:mpeg21:a0040.

Figure 1–2. Advertisement for a Talbot Scenimatograph screening, *Bintang Barat* (8 March 1897). Scan courtesy of PNRI, Jakarta.

of the most intriguing findings relate to locally-based French photographer Louis Talbot, who not only gave what appear to be the first commercial projections of moving pictures in the Indies in October 1896, but also devoted his entire programme to animated photography. Moreover, Talbot was also the first to film and exhibit local views of colonial Indonesia to local audiences, as well as to spectators across Southeast Asia. The findings presented in this chapter will thus show that animated photography arrived in the Indonesian archipelago thanks to the efforts of independent entrepreneurs, revealing that early cinema was almost instantly a global phenomenon, not just in terms of views of faraway places screened to audiences in the West, but also in terms of film exhibition and local production in remote imperial outposts.

1.1 Introduction of Animated Photography: Harley's Kinetoscope, 1896

> *THE KINETOSCOPE AND PHONOGRAPH which are shown here by Mr. Harley at the theatre are worth a look. Yesterday afternoon we were given the opportunity to witness these wondrous inventions and we therefore recommend to everyone to go there. The Kinetoscope has two closets, a peephole fitted at the top with support for the forehead, so one leans against the hole with it. As soon as the electric battery is activated, the glass, which one looks through, becomes illuminated with an electric light in the closet. Mr. Harley gave us a detailed explanation about the operation, composition, etc. However, we find this too extensive to mention here.*
>
> "Onze Nieuwtjes", Semarang-Courant *(25 November 1896).*

News of the exhibition of Edison's Kinetoscope in Amsterdam appeared in Netherlands Indies newspapers already at the beginning of 1895, long before Mr. Harley, mentioned in the above quote, arrived there to exhibit the

1 – Trials and Tribulations of Early Travelling Shows, 1896–1898

Kinetoscope to residents of the archipelago.²⁰⁸ And while the *Semarang-Courant* was reluctant to elaborate on the technical details of the wondrous apparatus right before residents of Semarang were about to witness it for themselves for the first time in November 1896, readers of *De Locomotief*, another Semarang-based newspaper, were treated to a particularly detailed account of "Edison's New Invention" already in January 1896:

> Agents of the company for the operation of Edison's Kinetoscopes are currently to be found in all the great cities of Europe. These devices consist of a box with a peephole. If one looks through it, one can watch a fist fight, a duel, a dance solo, a declaration of love, a blacksmith working a hammer, a courtship scene, or the like. We have in effect a series of instant-photographs taken at a rate of 2760 per minute or 165000 per hour, which are later exhibited as living and moving objects. The images are projected at the same rate for the eye, and the illusion that one observes reality itself is deceptive. One perceives the movements naturally, as they occurred in reality.²⁰⁹

Edison was, by that point, a well-established brand name in the Indies, after a couple of decades of exhibitors touring the region with highly popular phonograph shows.²¹⁰ It is therefore not surprising that his new – successful and less successful – inventions were being covered in the daily press in Dutch and Malay, and eagerly awaited with much anticipation.

Mr. Harley, or Dr. or Prof. Harley according to his adopted stage name – a common practice at the time, in order to endow the show with more scientific prestige – arrived in Singapore with his wife and daughter from Calcutta on 8 May 1896.²¹¹ It appears that he then travelled to Penang, before coming back again to give shows in Singapore in July 1896, with reports endorsing him as "[…] a well known entertainer formerly at the Crystal Palace [in London…]. Besides Dr. Harley's troupe, which includes Miss Dagmar and the Magnetic Lady, and presents an illusionary and facial entertainment, the Doctor is showing Edison's latest kinetoscope, that clever invention which by a multitude of photographs gives the similitude of life and motion".²¹² Among the scenes available on the Kinetoscope, which were accompanied to the sounds of a phonograph, were: "'The Gaiety Girls' and 'the Two Macs' […,] 'The

---

208 "Wetenschappelijk Nieuws", *De Locomotief* (8 February 1895); "Wetenschappelijk Nieuws", *Java-Bode* (27 February 1895).

209 "Een Nieuwe Uitvinding van Edison", *De Locomotief* (4 January 1896). The technical description in the report matches Mannoni's account of the technology, see Laurent Mannoni, *Le grand art de la lumière et de l'ombre: archéologie du cinéma* (Paris: Nathan, 1994), 364.

210 For more on the arrival of the gramophone in the Netherlands Indies, see Suryadi, "The 'talking machine' comes to the Dutch East Indies", 269–305.

211 "Arrivals", *The Straits Times* (8 May 1896). According to Tofighian, based on Stephen Bottomore, Harley exhibited the Kinetoscope in Calcutta and likely elsewhere in the region from late 1895 (see Tofighian, *Blurring the Colonial Binary*, 69). Harley's Kinetoscope exhibition in Singapore in July 1896 was the earliest Kinetoscope exhibition found by Tofighian (ibid.).

212 Untitled, *The Singapore Free Press* (10 July 1896). A report in *De Locomotief* also mentions an Edison Kinetoscope exhibited in Penang in a report from early June 1896 ("Onze Buren", *De Locomotief* (1 June 1896)).

Butterfly Dance', 'A Fire Scene', 'A Blacksmith's Shop', 'A Cock Fight' and a 'Bathroom Scene' [...]".[213] At first, the Kinetoscope was exhibited at Messrs. W. Robinson's Music Warehouse on Battery Road, yet the shop's opening hours quickly proved to be limiting for potential customers of the Kinetoscope, and therefore shows were also offered every evening after the shop closed, up till 11 pm, at the Stamford Hotel, where presumably Harley was staying.[214]

However, by the time Harley was ready to pack up and continue his travels, either in British Malaya or onward to Java at the end of July, the tour was delayed as Harley was "[...] obliged to stay in Singapore for a few days on account of the sickness of one of his assistants".[215] Harley then advertised that he was "open to private engagements".[216]

> DR. HARLEY. CONJUROR, Ventriloquist and Facial Phenomenon, may be engaged for private Parties, Clubs &c, or for the Edison's [sic] wonder, Kinetoscope and Phonograph combined. The most amusing programme in the world. Terms and particulars, ROBINSON'S Music Store, Kinetoscopes on view Stamford Hotel.[217]

The sudden strike of illness, as we shall see throughout, was an eventuality that had to be expected by travelling entertainers in this region, and unfortunately could not be averted. So it appears that Harley brought the Kinetoscope as a side-attraction to his stage acts, which probably served as a source of extra income and something to fall back on when other problems arose, preventing the regular routine of the stage shows. Conversely, the stage shows and private engagements were able to cover up for any technical hitches that occurred with the device, as will be discussed below upon the continuation of his tour in Java.

It is not clear if Harley had any pre-scheduled tour engagements in Java or whether he intended to arrive there first and then make all the necessary plans. Some travelling showmen would have had previous knowledge of the technical facilities awaiting them, having previously toured the region with other entertainment options. Either way, by the time Harley finally arrived in Batavia in mid-August 1896, it appears that there were no available venues for his stage shows, and therefore only advertisements for the Kinetoscope appeared in the local newspapers:

> With permission from the Resident. Edison's greatest discovery, the "Kinetoscope" does for the eyes what the Phonograph does for the ears. It reproduces things that really happen. One sees people in motion, including Dancers, Forging at the blacksmith's, Cock-fighting, etc. The greatest miracle of

---

213 "The Kinetoscope", *The Singapore Free Press* (15 July 1896). Possible film titles: GAIETY GIRLS (1894), ANNABELLE BUTTERFLY DANCE (1894 or 1895), FIRE RESCUE SCENE (1894), NEW BLACKSMITH SHOP (1895) or BLACKSMITHING SCENE (1894), THE COCK FIGHT (1894), A BAR ROOM SCENE (1894). There is also an Edison film THE BARBERSHOP (1894), which might have been the "Bathroom scene" referred to in the newspaper (Charles Musser, *Edison Motion Pictures, 1896–1900. An Annotated Filmography* (Gemona: Le Giornate del Cinema Muto, 1997)).

214 Untitled, *The Singapore Free Press* (11 July 1896); "The Kinetoscope", *The Straits Times* (17 July 1896).

215 Advertisement, *The Singapore Free Press* (22 July 1896).

216 Ibid.

217 Advertisement, *The Straits Times* (22 July 1896).

1 – Trials and Tribulations of Early Travelling Shows, 1896–1898

Photography and Electricity. On view, Room No. 3 Hotel des Indes from 4 in the afternoon until 11 at night in the American bar of the Hotel des Indes, fee ƒ 1.- per person, children half price.[218]

Articles accompanying the advertisements displayed excitement that the Kinetoscope, "the entertaining viewing machine [*kijkkast*]" which "has greatly caught on everywhere", is finally available at the Hôtel des Indes and predicted that it was bound to attract much attention.[219] In the following days, detailed descriptions of the technology were included in the reports, possibly based on the explanations provided by Harley himself, who probably offered journalists to preview the Kinetoscope before opening to the public in order to promote his attractions.[220] Yet, his stay in Batavia was rather short-lived, and by 22 August the *Java-Bode* reported that only "today and tomorrow there is an opportunity to get acquainted with Edison's kinetoscope; on Monday the owner is leaving and is headed to the interior. When he returns, he will give a few performances at the theatre".[221]

From what this research was able to find, Harley continued to tour with the Kinetoscope and his stage shows, promoted in the Indies as the "Lucky Star Company", to Bandung in western Java, where he performed at the *Sociëteit Braga*, and to Solo (Surakarta) in Central Java, for shows at the *Sociëteit Harmonie*.[222] Since there are a few weeks left blank in between each newspaper report found in this research, it is likely to assume that he had other destinations on Java which, by that point, had a dense railway network (see further in the Introduction).

By November 1896, Harley reached eastern Java for shows in Surabaya, the major coastal and entertainment town in the region, where the Kinetoscope was placed at the Grimm Restaurant, located on one of the main junctions in the city's downtown area.[223] After about a week in Surabaya, he started making his way back to western Java via Semarang where the Kinetoscope was displayed at the Semarang Theatre.[224] And although journalists were very enthusiastic about the new invention, as we have seen in the build-up of expectations above, the general public in Semarang never got to see the Kinetoscope in

218 Advertisement, *Java-Bode* (19 August 1896). The language of the ad picks up on Edison's own description of his experimentation with the Kinematograph and Kinetoscope as "an instrument which does for the eye what the phonograph does for the ear" ("History of Edison Motion Pictures", Library of Congress, accessed 2 February 2016, http://www.loc.gov/collections/edison-company-motion-pictures-and-sound-recordings/articles-and-essays/history-of-edison-motion-pictures/).

219 "Nederlandsch-Indië", *Java-Bode* (17 August 1896).

220 "Verspreide Indische Berichten", *De Locomotief* (20 August 1896); "Nederlandsch-Indië", *Het Nieuw Bataviaasch Handelsblad* (22 August 1896). Tofighian has similarly found that the exhibition of the Kinetoscope was often preceded by a lecture, and that such technical descriptions were repeated in the Singapore press (see Tofighian, *Blurring the Colonial Binary*, 70).

221 "Nederlandsch-Indië", *Java-Bode* (22 August 1896).

222 "Nederlandsch-Indië", *Java-Bode* (12 September 1896); "Nederlandsch-Indië", *De Nieuwe Vorstenlanden* (9 October 1896).

223 Advertisement and "Onze Nieuwtjes", *Soerabaija-Courant* (5 November 1896).

224 Advertisement and "Kinetoscoop", *Semarang-Courant* (24 November 1896).

action due to the fact that the batteries ran out, and there was no possibility to re-charge them on the spot.[225] While a similar problem was reported during the earlier run in Singapore and was presumably resolved, since the Kinetoscope continued to be exhibited there for a few more weeks after concerns were raised about the inability to recharge the batteries locally, no such solution was to be found on Java.[226] This research has found that Harley's "Lucky Star Company" gave additional shows in Tegal and possibly in Cirebon, but has not found any further mentions of the Kinetoscope.[227]

Upon arrival back in Batavia and checking in to the Hotel Leroux at the beginning of January 1897, it appears that Harley finally gave up on his Kinetoscope endeavour and advertised it for sale, alongside a phonograph and other devices for performing magic tricks.[228] It is very likely that the device was bought by the Batavia Zoo, since the latter began advertising that a Kinetoscope accompanied by a "Graphophine" would be available for viewing on its premises as of early February.[229]

So far I have not touched upon the identity of the audience for Harley's Kinetoscope exhibitions. While Harley and his Kinetoscope were the first instance of exhibition of animated photography in the Netherlands Indies, it is safe to say that this was a rather elitist affair for a largely "European" audience.[230] The venues selected in each city – from hotels, through European-style theatres or club houses, to cafés – were not the usual haunts of "Native" spectators, other than perhaps members of the Indonesian elite class. At a price of one guilder per person (and 50 cents for children), even if each viewer was allowed a number of viewings of the device, this was a steep asking price, if we consider other entertainments the same money could buy at the time (see Introduction). Therefore, while the new technological invention certainly aroused curiosity, at least among the "European" community in the Indies, it is difficult to estimate how financially successful it was. Presumably, by the end of his tour Harley concluded that the trouble of lugging around the device and the technical difficulties of re-charging the batteries were not worth the hassle. The arrival of other devices for the projection of moving images, as will be discussed below, may have also contributed to the decision.

225 "De Kinetoscoop en Phonograaf", *Semarang-Courant* (25 November 1896); "Kinetoscoop", *De Locomotief* (25 November 1896).

226 "Edison's Kinetoscope. A Wonderful Machine", *The Straits Times* (13 July 1896).

227 "Nederlandsch-Indië", *Advertentieblad Tegal* (30 December 1896). Harley, his wife and daughter were on the passenger list from Cirebon to Batavia aboard the steamship *Carpentier*, on 29 December 1896 ("Schepen & Passagiers", *Semarang-Courant* (2 January 1897)).

228 Advertisement, *Java-Bode* (5 January 1897). The ad was repeated on 7 and 9 January.

229 Advertisement, *Java-Bode* and *Bataviaasch Nieuwsblad* (5 February 1897).

230 Compare to the initial audience of the first kinetoscope parlour in midtown Manhattan, which Musser identifies as middle class due to "a peek costing 5 ¢ and most patrons expected to see a series of five scenes" (Charles Musser, *Before the Nickelodeon: Edwin S. Porter and the Edison Manufacturing Company* (Berkeley: University of California Press, 1991), 42). One guilder in the 1890s was worth approximately US 40 cents (Cohen, *The Komedi Stamboel*, 393, endnote 36). Therefore, compared to five cents of the cost of the Kinetoscope in the US, consumers in the Indies paid eight times the price.

Finally, it should be noted that the discrete peepshow nature of the Kinetoscope's viewing experience may not have been well-suited to the Indies society which, according to Matthew Cohen, was "an open-gallery society", where people of all classes and ethnicities were constantly on the lookout for sites to explore and sights to absorb in the colonial cities, whether as paying viewers or as chance onlookers.[231] Moreover, the fact that the Kinetoscope had to be operated individually and further required viewers to lean their heads against the peephole, seems to have dictated a certain degree of exclusivity in the setup of its viewing spaces in order to accommodate new ideas about how colonial society should be managed. In a period of growing tensions around inter-racial mixing and with the arrival of more women from Europe to the colonies, the Kinetoscope entailed a risk of crossing boundaries of intimacy by the very tactile nature of the device. In the following sections of this chapter, we shall see how the setting of the Kinetoscope's exhibition differed from the experience of projecting moving images, which could be enjoyed by viewers of a multitude of ethnicities at the same time in venues that very easily created separation between the different classes of ticket purchasers.

1.2 "Truly Scientific Entertainment": Talbot's Scenimatograph, 1896–1897

1.2.1 A Fiery Start

The earliest commercial screening of projected animated photography found in this research was performed by an apparatus advertised as the Scenimatograph on Sunday, 11 October 1896.[232] The exhibitor, Louis Talbot, had been operating a photography studio in Batavia since 1894 and was apparently a well-regarded professional in the city.[233] In 1895, Talbot was even commissioned to photograph the portrait of the Governor General of the Indies.[234] Advertisements for the screening began appearing in the major Batavia newspapers only two days before the opening night at the Batavia Theatre (*Batavia Schouwburg*, also known as *komedie gebouw* or *rumah komedie*) located in the Chinatown district, scheduling two screenings: the first at 6.30 pm and the second at 7.30 pm (see Figures 1–3).[235] The advertisement announced: "[...] Animated photography! Science news. The biggest success in the whole of Europe [...] Do not miss it."[236] Ticket prices were fixed at one guilder per person.

231   Cohen, *The Komedie Stamboel*, 6.
232   The name of the device is spelled in various ways throughout the period (Scenimatograph, Scénimatographe, Scenimatograaf, etc.). I have chosen to use the spelling used in the English-language advertisements in the Singapore press for Talbot's screenings there in 1898.
233   Advertisement, *Java-Bode* (23 July 1894).
234   "Nederlandsch-Indië", *Java-Bode* (8 June 1895).
235   Advertisement, *Java-Bode* (9 October 1896). In the 1970s the Batavia Theatre operated as a (Chinese) cinema house (see "De Schouwburg", *Tong Tong. Het Enige Indische Blad in Nederland* 20, no. 5 (1 November 1975): 5). It continues to serve as a theatre today, and is now the Gedung Kesenian Jakarta, or Jakarta Art Building.
236   Advertisement, *Java-Bode* (9 October 1896).

> **Met toestemming van den Resident.**
>
> **Le Scénimatographe!**
>
> **Photographie Animée**
>
> **Wetenschappelijk Nieuws.**
>
> **Het grootste succès voor geheel Europa**
>
> ZONDAG 11 OCTOBER 1896,
>
> zullen er in den Schouwburg te Batavia gegeven worden
>
> **twee voorstellingen**
>
> De eerste om half zeven 's avonds.
> De tweede om half acht 's avonds.
> ENTRÉE f 1.— per voorstelling.
> **Verzuimt niet te gaan zien**
> Leest de recensies in de Europ. bladen.

Figure 1–3. Advertisement for the Scenimatograph, *Java-Bode* (9 October 1896). Retrieved from Delpher on 5 October 2015, http://resolver.kb.nl/resolve?urn=ddd:010496317:mpeg21:a0044.

An article in the *Java-Bode* one day before the screenings, further hyped up the expectations:

> This Sunday there will be something very surprising to see in the Theatre here, a scenimatograph, through which the results of the kinetograph can be transferred, so it is much easier and has far more benefits than when one must peer into the latter instrument. This invention by Edison was first shown at the Chicago World Fair and has since flourished around the world. What one sees, one might call plates in action. The performances are given at half past six and half past seven.[237]

Another newspaper, *Het Nieuw Bataviaasch Nieuwsblad*, further wrote:

> According to the forthcoming advertisement in this newspaper, performances of the scenimatograph will take place tomorrow evening at the Theatre here.
>
> With it photographic images of people and their natural movements are brought forth stretched out on canvas in *natural* size; hence also the name, animated photography, for this new application of science.
>
> For every picture one needs a 23 meter long strip which features 900 instantaneous photographic images in their different movements – all these 900 different photos, and enlarged to life size, are brought forth with amazing speed in just one minute, and that causes the truly striking optical illusion as if the person depicted is conjured up in real life and motion.

[237] "Nederlandsch-Indië", *Java-Bode* (10 October 1896).

1 – Trials and Tribulations of Early Travelling Shows, 1896–1898

Figure 1–4. Exterior of the Batavia Theatre, ca. 1890.
Courtesy of Leiden University Library, Image code 31883.

Figure 1–5. Interior of the Batavia Theatre, ca. 1890.
Courtesy of Leiden University Library, Image code 11691.

Many of our readers will have probably seen something similar recently under a different name in the Hotel des Indes. There they had to look down and watch a miniscule figure – very nice it must be said! in natural motion. – Here, however, one sits very comfortably in a chair at the theatre and [sees] the life-size images in natural motion. We have no doubt that this truly scientific entertainment will attract many spectators.[238]

Interestingly, both newspaper reports directly linked the new device with the Kinetoscope, which was on show in Batavia just six weeks earlier.[239] It is therefore not surprising that the first article identified Edison as the inventor of the technology, using his name to promote the new apparatus, and this trend continued in other publications. Nevertheless, the Scenimatograph was probably a machine of French origin, as later advertisements promoted the Scenimatograph as "[...] the only real and authentic French Apparatus in the East Indies".[240]

From the high cost of the entrance fee, and the choice of location for the show at the higher end European-style theatre, it is reasonable to assume that the Scenimatograph screenings were, once again, neither intended for, nor accessible to, most of the indigenous population. Built in 1821 as an artistic contribution of the military to the city, throughout the nineteenth century the Batavia Theatre hosted popular French and Italian operas, concerts, *tableaux vivants*, variety programmes, Parsi theatre shows, and moving pictures.[241] It offered box and parterre seats at more expensive prices and balcony seats which were priced at a lower cost (see Figures 1–4 and 1–5). While not directly stated in advertisements, this practice effectively separated between audience members along class and racial lines.[242] However, even when cheaper seats for the Scenimatograph shows were indeed offered at 50 cents, this would have still been beyond the purchasing power of most indigenous Indonesians (see discussion of pricing in the Introduction). Therefore, Talbot's audience was presumably mostly made up of European (many of them Eurasian) spectators, members of the Indonesian elite class, Chinese and Japanese spectators, and a handful of "Natives" (see further below).

Newspaper articles the day after the screening provide us with plenty of information on the events of the previous night. One reviewer for *Java-Bode* referred to the programme directly, having enjoyed the performance and films offered, yet complained about the flickering effect which was painful on the

---

238 "Nederlandsch-Indië", *Het Nieuw Bataviaasch Handelsblad* (10 October 1896), italics in original. These kinds of texts were likely public relations pieces written by the exhibitor or delivered to journalists in order to promote the show.

239 Advertisement, *Java-Bode* (19 August 1896).

240 Advertisement, *Het Nieuw Bataviaasch Nieuwsblad* (5 August 1897).

241 Susan Abeyasekere, *Jakarta: A History* (Singapore: Oxford University Press, 1989 [1987]), 55–56.

242 Visitors seated in the balcony were in fact not allowed to move down into the foyer, once spectators in the box and parterre were settled into their seats. The former were provided with a separate café in the upstairs floor, or had to step outside to *warung* on the street to get some refreshments ("Nederlandsch-Indië", *Het Nieuws van den Dag voor Nederlandsch-Indië* (14 September 1900)).

1 – Trials and Tribulations of Early Travelling Shows, 1896–1898

eyes and rendered the images unclear at times.[243] Several journalists reported that they enjoyed the films on the programme, which I suspect featured some Lumière titles based on their accounts of the line-up that included: scenes at the photographer, a quarrel between a French cabdriver and his passenger, views of squares in Paris and Vienna, and a serpentine dance.[244] Nevertheless, the real drama occurred after the second screening of the evening when, as reported in the *Bataviaasch Nieuwsblad*:

> By the collapse of a burning candle – carelessness of a native – the flames came into contact with the celluloid reels, [containing] series of thousands of photographic images on them, with the result being that they burned in an instant.[245]

Ironically enough, the only film that survived the fire was titled "Peasants burning dried grass".[246] Whether or not Talbot's "Native" employee was indeed at fault for this accident is obviously debatable, but in any case the shows clearly could not continue with only a single title on the programme.[247] "This is a great loss and disappointment", the journalist continued; however, he comforted his readers,

> [...] the exhibitor, who is a good photographer, and who has some blank celluloid rolls in his possession, hopes to redress the loss within about ten days with views of various parts of Batavia. If he manages to secure these, he will surely have much success. So, for instance, if he can produce such a recording of the arrival of a mail boat at Tanjung Priok, the departure of an express train from Koningsplein [Merdeka Square], music on the Waterlooplein [Lapangan Banteng], or other highly fast paced moments.[248]

---

243 "Nederlandsch-Indië", *Java-Bode* (12 October 1896). As Sabine Lenk has pointed out to me, vibrations could be caused by trembling or flickering. Trembling would refer to an unstable image, which does not stay steady in the same position due to the use of irregular perforation holes. Flickering means that the light intensity of the projection beam is constantly changing, or that one sees the change of images due to a projection speed which is too low.

244 Ibid. These may correspond to the Lumière film PHOTOGRAPHE (1895, Lumière catalogue No. 118). Another possibility would be a Joly-Normandin film recently restored in Switzerland with the given title "Le cocher et le mauvais payeur" from 1896 ("Le cocher et le mauvais payeur", Swiss Camera Museum, accessed on 2 February 2016, http://www.cameramuseum.ch/fr/N2071/le-cocher-et-le-mauvais-payeur.html). Or possibly another Lumière title DANSE SERPENTINE (1896, Lumière catalogue No. 765). Pathé Frères also had several scenes in Paris: PLACE DE LA BASTILLE, PLACE DE LA RÉPUBLIQUE, PLACE DE LA CONCORDE, PLACE DE L'OPÉRA, PLACE DE L'ÉTOILE (all from 1896). Méliès made PLACE DE L'OPÉRA, PLACE DU THÉÂTRE-FRANÇAIS and DANSE SERPENTINE before September 1896. The Lumière Cinématographe was only commercialised in 1897, and this research has not been able to tie Talbot directly to the Lumières. As Frank Kessler has suggested to me, Talbot may have gotten his films and camera-projector equipment from Joly-Normandin. Sabine Lenk has proposed that it might have been an R.W. Paul device sold by Paul in London.

245 "Nederlandsch-Indië", *Bataviaasch Nieuwsblad* (12 October 1896).

246 The newspaper identifies it as "Paysants brûlant seche" (ibid.). This may correspond to MAUVAISES HERBES (Lumière catalogue No. 64), BRÛLEUSE D'HERBES (Pathé Frères, 1896) or JARDINIER BRÛLANT DES HERBES (Méliès, 1896).

247 One might also question whether indeed such a fire ever occurred, considering burning prints of nitrate would have potentially led to a much greater explosion that would not have been manageable. In this case, the story of the burning candle was used to cover for another technical problem that prevented the shows from continuing.

248 "Nederlandsch-Indië", *Bataviaasch Nieuwsblad* (12 October 1896).

According to *Het Nieuw Bataviaasch Nieuwsblad*, Mr. Talbot had asked to inform the public that shows have been discontinued due to the accident, and that he now planned on "[...] making his own recordings of remarkable people and objects in motion here on site or in the vicinity, which can be used for new performances".[249] These responses show that journalists appreciated and understood the innovation of the new medium, highlighting its ability to capture motion, and even suggesting appropriate scenes to be filmed. And if the local audience was disappointed with these developments, one can only imagine how frustrated Talbot must have been.[250] While he apparently had blank celluloid strips with him, presumably with the intention of indeed capturing some local scenes, the circumstances certainly left him no choice in the matter and drove him to local production almost immediately.

Yet, his forecast of coming back for shows within about ten days was somewhat over-optimistic. Over the following decades, even more experienced cinematographers found the sensitive equipment difficult to handle in the hot and humid conditions. We can learn about some of the challenges from a later account from 1913, when a cinematographer by the name A. F. Neys wrote about his "Cinema experiences in the tropics" in a three-part series of articles in the Dutch trade weekly *De Kinematograaf*.[251] The first problem Neys encountered was packing the device to ensure that it was waterproof and protected against shocks. For this purpose, an armoured wooden box was devised, which was nevertheless discarded after a week as it turned out the wood attracted a lot of heat, creating a breeding box for mould. This led Neys to the conclusion that the equipment was better left in the open and constantly kept clean by one of his coolies.[252] Moreover, his first month of filming was disrupted by constant monsoon rains. Finally, most of the films made over the first couple of months were destroyed when he attempted to develop them, until he figured out a way to tackle this problem by climbing up a mountain every night, where the temperatures were cooler and the films could be washed in a natural stream and then dried in a specially-built bamboo hut.[253] Talbot presumably had a darkroom that he could work in, but one can assume that he met with other unexpected difficulties. For the next few months, we find no accounts of Talbot's whereabouts in the region.

---

249 "Voorstelling met de 'Scênimatographe'", *Het Nieuw Bataviaasch Handelsblad* (12 October 1896).

250 Talbot may have already been scheduled to travel onwards for shows in Semarang, according to a report that appeared in the *Semarang-Courant* at the end of September, pre-empting the arrival of a "cinématographe" within a couple of weeks' time ("Cinématographe", *Semarang-Courant* (30 September 1896)). There is no direct mention of Talbot, yet he is the only exhibitor found in this research prior to 1897. Furthermore, it seems that the highly anticipated instrument for the exhibition of "living pictures" never materialized in Semarang until April 1897, when Talbot finally arrived there (Advertisement, *De Locomotief* (29 March 1897)).

251 A. F. Neys, "Bioscopische ervaringen in de tropen", *De Kinematograaf* 31 (22 August 1913): 205; *De Kinematograaf* 32 (29 August 1913): 214–215; *De Kinematograaf* 33 (5 September 1913): 224–225.

252 A. F. Neys, "Bioscopische ervaringen in de tropen", *De Kinematograaf* 31 (22 August 1913): 205.

253 A. F. Neys, "Bioscopische ervaringen in de tropen", *De Kinematograaf* 32 (29 August 1913): 214.

1.2.2 Triumphant Return

The first advertisements upon Talbot's return to the scene appeared in several Batavia newspapers three days before the opening night at the Batavia Theatre on Sunday, 7 March 1897, in addition to another show on 9 March.[254] The advertisements read: "Reproduction of living photographs with the Scenimatograph by Mr. L. Talbot. The most wonderful invention of Modern Science. Unrivalled Success, wherever it is shown. Only two Performances."[255] An article running simultaneously in the *Bataviaasch Nieuwsblad* drew readers' attention to the upcoming performances, stressing that Talbot did not intend to give more than two shows, so everyone should make sure not to miss seeing his achievements with the Scenimatograph.[256] This seems to be a common occurrence, where only a couple of shows would have been initially scheduled and more added later, according to demand. It is the first time that Talbot's name was used in the advertisement to promote his performances. Another name appearing on the advertisement from now on was Mr. Von Geyer as the Scenimatograph's manager.[257] According to a report a few weeks later by the Batavia correspondent for *The Singapore Free Press*, "Mr. Von Geyer, who formerly visited Batavia with the Hungarian musician M. Ovide de Musin, has now joined Mr. Talbot".[258] The new manager probably introduced a new ticket pricing system: box or parterre for one guilder, gallery for 50 cents. This time, only one screening was scheduled per evening, at 7 pm. Advertisements continued to appear in the major Batavia newspapers every day, this time – in both the Dutch and Malay papers (see Figures 1–1 and 1–2).

Reports on the screening were published the day after the opening night, with rave reviews of the performance and especially the local views of the Netherlands Indies. According to a report in the Malay newspaper *Bintang Barat* the day after the first screening:

> Last night there was a magic picture show which surprised people at the *komedi* building in Pasar Baru, when all the seats were taken and a few people could not get seats. This is because the show is new.[259]

The *Java-Bode* wrote:

> It was packed and sweltering in the theatre, where Mr. Talbot performed with the Scenimatograph yesterday evening, but despite the heat, people were entertained by the excellent living photographs [*levende photografieën*] projected on a canvas. Aside for some Indies [*Indische*] scenes, on the street, in the countryside, a fight between a sergeant and four Acehnese and many others, people got to see a few European [scenes], with a serpentine dancer standing out especially. Mr. Talbot assured us that people in Europe do not get to watch better performances than

---

254 Advertisement, *Java-Bode* (4 March 1897).

255 Ibid.

256 "Nederlandsch-Indië", *Bataviaasch Nieuwsblad* (4 March 1897).

257 Von Geyer's name would later be linked to other travelling musicians in the East Indies, but I have not found him mentioned in connection with any other exhibitors of moving pictures.

258 "Batavia", *The Singapore Free Press* (5 April 1897).

259 "Betawie. 8 Maart 1897", *Bintang Barat* (8 March 1897), emphasis added.

these, that the vibrations are inevitable and that it is not possible to have the images swiftly follow each other. Whoever was in the theatre yesterday is sure to return on Tuesday, when a new programme will be screened, or at least strongly recommend to others not to miss it, as we are doing.[260]

According to information gathered from the Batavia newspapers and from reviews of later screenings in other towns, these local views included actualities, such as a tram in Rijswijk, bathing "Natives" and women washing clothes in the Kali river at Noordwijk, a scene from the Batavia Zoo, and the departure of a mail boat from Tanjung Priok. Another intriguing scene depicted a fight between a sergeant and four Acehnese, a topical film considering the contemporary Aceh War which had been raging in since the 1870s, news of which filled up the colonial newspapers on a daily basis.[261]

These films would later be included in Talbot's programme titled "Pictures from the Native Life", once he concluded his tour of Java and moved on to screenings in Singapore in January 1898.[262] As the review in the Singaporean press recounted: "The Javanese dancing girl is very good and better perhaps is the scene of a number of boys bathing in the Kali at Batavia, the water movement, and even the glisten of the sun on the moving bodies being shown. There are a number of films dealing with rehearsed scenes, an Attack on a sergeant in Aceh, Two's company and Three's none and a café scene."[263] The Aceh scene was probably indeed a staged film, according to descriptions of the film in various reviews in the Indies newspapers pointing to its fakeness.[264] The following account from *Semarang-Courant* is particularly revealing about this as a sort of trick film: "The plate [...] shows a sergeant who defends himself with a rifle against four Acehnese, putting down three, and finally suffers a wound to the head, but still has so much strength that he draws out his machete and slashes the head of the Acehnese, then rises and dresses his wounds".[265] It was often described as being received to loud applause and cheers from the audience and, at times, as the best film on the entire programme.[266]

260 "Nederlandsch-Indië", *Java-Bode* (8 March 1897).

261 While the Dutch hoped to annex Aceh, in northern Sumatra, under a treaty agreement with the Sultanate of Aceh, as they have achieved in other cases in the region, the fierce resistance by the Acehnese left the military option as the only way to bring it under colonial control. The Dutch bombarded and burned villages in their efforts of advancing, and although the Aceh War was declared over by the Dutch several times, the guerrilla resistance, which became dominated by religious leaders, continued and in the mind of many Acehnese never truly ended (Ricklefs, *A History of Modern Indonesia*, 187–188).

262 Advertisement, *The Singapore Free Press* (17 January 1898).

263 "The Scenimatograph", *The Singapore Free Press* (20 January 1898).

264 There are many examples of faked news films in early cinema; for further information on "fakes" see Bottomore on "fakes" made during the Greco-Turkish War, the Spanish-American War, and the Boer War: Stephen Bottomore, *Filming, Faking and Propaganda: The Origins of the War Film, 1897–1902*, PhD Dissertation (Utrecht University, 2007), Chapters 3, 6, and 10. The reception of "fakes", such as Méliès's Greco-Turkish War films, according to Bottomore, was "a mixed response. A few people might have believed that some of the films were genuine, especially if [...] the showmen proclaimed that they were so. Other viewers had doubts on the matter" (ibid., Chapter 3, 14).

265 "De Scenimatograaf", *Semarang-Courant* (7 April 1897).

266 "De Scenimatograaf", *Semarang-Courant* (5 April 1897).

1 – Trials and Tribulations of Early Travelling Shows, 1896–1898

On top of these local views, it seems that Talbot was able to get hold of a new stock of films from Europe. Another successful scene was one which presented a magician, described in the Bandung newspaper *De Preanger-Bode* as "[...] so realistic that one of the spectators very naively remarked that the audience now gets to see magic tricks for the same entrance fee".[267] Based on later reports of Talbot's Scenimatograph screenings in Singapore, this was "'Disappearance of a lady on the opera stage' as performed by Robert Houdin in Paris", which was quite probably the famous Méliès production, shown along with two other films that may be attributed to Méliès as well: "The Haunted House" and "A Nightmare".[268] Finally, another scene of a serpentine dancer in colour was shown, at least in Batavia, Bandung, Solo (Surakarta) and finally Semarang, where this particular film strip caught fire in the middle of a screening, with the dancer "[...] with her long dress hovering close to the source of the fire".[269] Audiences in Kudus, Pati, Juwana and Surabaya, which came up next on his tour of Java, unfortunately did not get a chance to watch this scene, which was otherwise extremely popular anywhere it was shown.

According to various newspaper reports from his second run of Batavia screenings, it seems that Talbot was experimenting with his display techniques. Thus, a couple of days after the first screening, on 9 March, he apparently played the films slightly faster than before because, the newspaper claimed, the packed venue became impatient and loud.[270] A few days later, having added more screenings due to the success of his first shows, Talbot changed the position of the projection unit: from behind the screen to the middle of the parterre.[271] Furthermore, Talbot and his manager Von Geyer were also testing out ways of reaching new audiences, popularizing the apparatus, and giving it a favourable reputation: from seeking permission to play at the military canteen, through screenings for Club houses, to screenings for the benefit of orphans – whether by offering to donate all net profits to orphan homes or by inviting orphans to attend free screenings.[272] Orphans who attended the show in Semarang were reportedly "just as amused as the audience" by the new attraction.[273]

The public relations machine generated by Von Geyer also included constant communication with the newspapers. Thus, a report in the *Java-Bode* appearing at the conclusion of Talbot's shows in Batavia in March 1897, detailed his

267 "Plaatselijk Nieuws", *De Preanger-Bode* (29 March 1897).
268 "To-day's Advertisements", *The Singapore Free Press* (17 January 1898). These titles may correspond to Méliès's ESCAMOTAGE D'UNE DAME AU THÉÂTRE ROBERT-HOUDIN (1896), LE MANOIR DU DIABLE (1896) or LE CHÂTEAU HANTÉ (1897), and LE CAUCHEMAR (1896).
269 "De Scenimatograaf", *Semarang-Courant* (7 April 1897).
270 "Nederlandsch-Indië", *Java-Bode* (10 March 1897).
271 "Nederlandsch-Indië", *Java-Bode* (15 March 1897).
272 "Scénimatograaf", *De Locomotief* (6 April 1897); Advertisement, *Bataviaasch Nieuwsblad* (16 July 1897); Advertisement, *Bataviaasch Nieuwsblad* (12 March 1897); "De Scenimatograaf", *Semarang-Courant* (5 April 1897); "Onze Nieuwtjes", *Soerabaija-Courant* (23 April 1897).
273 "De Scenimatograaf", *Semarang-Courant* (7 April 1897).

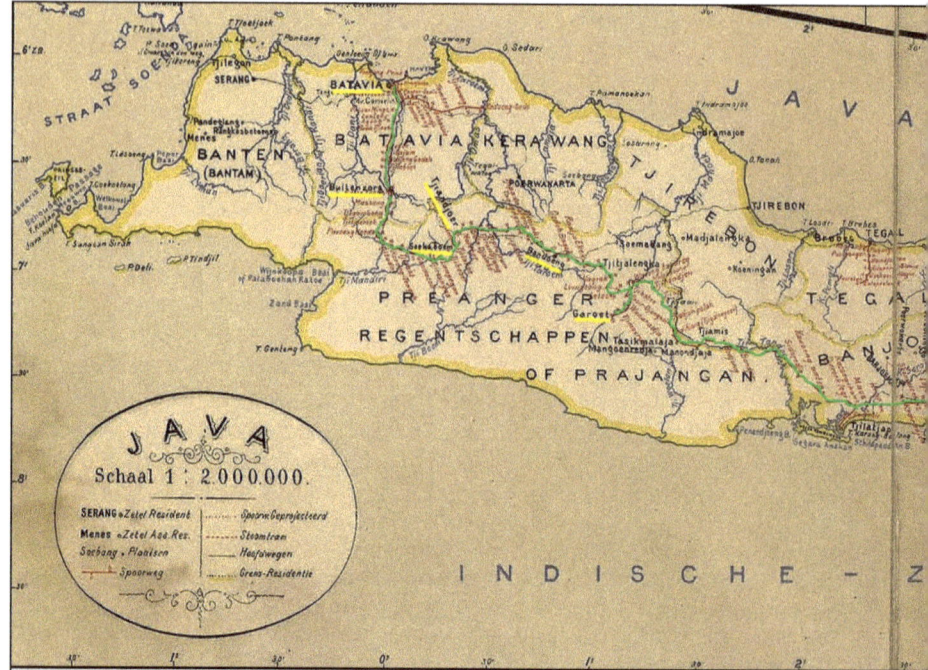

Figure 1–6. Talbot's projected tour route of Java marked in green (railway) and orange (road), with stated locations underlined in yellow. Another possibly easier way to get from Juwana to Surabaya would have be[en to] return to Semarang by train and hop on a steamer to Surabaya. Railway map adapted from Map of the Netherlands Indies, ca. 1893, Courtesy of the University of Texas Libraries, The University of Texas at A[ustin] (source: http://www.lib.utexas.edu/maps/historical/nederlandsch_indie_1893.jpg).

planned tour route: Buitenzorg (Bogor) on 21 March, Cianjur on 23 March, Bandung on 24 March, Sukabumi on 25 March, Garut on 26 March, Purworejo on 28 March, Yogyakarta on 29 March, Klaten on 31 March, Solo (Surakarta) on 1 April, Semarang on 4 April, as well as further destinations of which no prearranged dates were available yet, including Kudus, Pati, Juwana and Surabaya.[274] All these destinations could be reached by railway or narrow gauge tramway connection (see map as Figure 1–6).

1.2.3 Competition in Surabaya

By the time Talbot arrived for Scenimatograph shows in Surabaya in mid-April 1897, he suddenly found himself facing competition from another device advertised as the Kenotograph, on display in the Chinese quarter of the city. Local-grown and foreign popular entertainment companies passed through this port city with their shows throughout the nineteenth century (see further on Surabaya's popular entertainment scene in Chapter 4). No wonder then

---

[274] "Nederlandsch-Indië", *Java-Bode* (19 March 1897). This is by no means an exhaustive list. There may have been other shows, yet, since many other towns did not have newspapers and did not advertise or review the shows, it is difficult to sketch out a complete route.

1 – Trials and Tribulations of Early Travelling Shows, 1896–1898

that competition was fierce in Surabaya and audiences highly demanding. Announcing his first shows to be given on 20, 22 and 24 April at the Surabaya Theatre, Talbot's advertisements included a word of warning to the public: "Do not confuse with the announced kinetograph [sic], which is trying to deceive the public because of the great success that the Scenimatograph has garnered[...]".[275] These advertisements further stressed the success of the new technology in Europe, the US and Australia, drawing on an international appeal. On the same page, we find the advertisement for the Kenotograph, which rather highlighted the local aspects by mentioning that the electric lamp used for the screening was from the local firm Hekking.[276] Mr. J. van der Lelij, a jewellery tradesman by day, was signed as manager.[277]

A note should be made about their choices of venues, too. The venue for Talbot's shows was the Surabaya Theatre in the European settlement in the northwestern part of the city (see Figure 1–7). The European-style theatre at Komedieplein was "[...] completed in 1854 at a cost of 55,000 guilders and renovated in 1877 under the supervision of an actor from a touring French operetta company".[278] Throughout the nineteenth century, it played host to "[...] touring English music hall companies, stage magicians from India and

---

275 Advertisement, *Soerabaiasch-Handelsblad* (17 April 1897).

276 The firm Hekking was involved in various infrastructure in the Indies, including telephony, water, and electricity. Hekking & Co. would later become the Java Electricity Company (*Javasche Electriciteits Maatschappij*).

277 Ibid.

278 Cohen, *The Komedie Stamboel*, 35.

Figure 1–7. Surabaya Theatre, photo by G.C.T. van Dorp & Co., ca. 1910. Courtesy of Leiden University Library, Image code 1403788.

Italy, Italian opera, French troupes performing *opéra comique* and *opéra-bouffe*, and Australian burlesque outfits".[279] Meanwhile, the Kenotograph performed at Chinatown's Kapasan Theatre (*Komediegebouw*). Aside for the Kenotograph screenings, Kapasan Theatre, which was undergoing much construction and development work in the 1890s, would have also played host to *komedi stamboel* troupes, *féeries* and *tableaux vivants*. In many ways, the "[...] theatre rivaled the theatre of the Europeans at Komedieplein, with its spacious hall, double roof, fresh décor, good lighting, and ventilation".[280] The two venues catered to different audiences, as the prices of tickets to the moving picture shows that they presented makes clear. While Talbot offered his screenings at a steep cost of one guilder per ticket, with an additional 25 cents for reserved seating, the Kenotograph's prices varied: ƒ 1.50 for a booth seat, ƒ 1 for first class, 75 cents for second class, and 25 cents for third class.[281] It therefore appears likely that, whereas the Scenimatograph shows would have been attended mostly by "Europeans", Chinese and members of the Indonesian native elite, the audience at the Kenotograph would have been comprised of more varied class and ethnic backgrounds.

The first Scenimatograph screening was very well received, based on the next day's review in the *Soerabaiasch-Handelsblad*, claiming that praise for the device

279 Ibid., 35, emphasis added.

280 *Java-Bode* (15 February 1893), quoted in Cohen, *The Komedie Stamboel*, 72. The Victoria Parsi Theatre Company with its Cinematograph also performed at the Kapasan Theatre for a couple of months in late 1898 (Advertisement, *Soerabaija-Courant* (3 December 1898)). See further on the Victoria Parsi Theatre Company in Section 1.3.3.

281 Advertisement, *Soerabaija-Courant* (17 April 1897).

1 – Trials and Tribulations of Early Travelling Shows, 1896–1898

was not exaggerated and showing particular interest in the local views of Batavia.[282] Some criticism of the flickering, produced as a result of intermittent light and projection speed, was given, yet the invention was nevertheless deemed to be "superb".[283] This was a recurrent critique that Talbot was faced with in most towns he visited where I have found reviews of his shows, yet it was often as vehemently defended as it was criticized. See, for instance, this article from Semarang a few weeks earlier:

> Anyone who realizes what a Scenimatograph is and how it works cannot but speak of it with praise.
>
> Some, uninitiated of course, say the light is not constant and the images are not sharp enough. Nothing can be further than the truth, and thus less true, than this comment.
>
> The bright light of petroleum gas, which, like electric light makes a carbon tip glow, is as constant as possible and shaking necessarily has to take place because in over two minutes' time people get two thousand seven hundred different images on the canvas […].
>
> No, all these observations, which only come from ignorance, are incorrect, and it therefore remains an irrefutable truth that the Scenimatograph is a wonderful invention that we cannot admire enough.[284]

Another Surabaya newspaper recommended sitting at a further distance away from the screen in order to avoid the annoyance of the flickering.[285]

The screening of the Kenotograph in the Chinatown district of Surabaya the next day was similarly criticized for the flickering effect.[286] With its favourable entrance prices and its location in the Kapasan Theatre, home to the popular *komedi stambul*, one would expect that the audience of the Kenotograph would have been more mixed than Talbot's pricey Scenimatograph shows, which took place at the European-style theatre on Komedieplein.[287] Indeed, according to the review in *Soerabaiasch-Handelsblad*, both the "brown and yellow brother" attending the screening signalled with their cheers that the show was very much to their liking.[288] What films were being shown by the Kenotograph? According to the same article, the Kenotograph had ordered 24 films from Paris.[289] Another review from a screening the following week, this time at the exclusive Simpang Club (*Simpangsche Sociëteit*), claimed that while the Kenotograph films seemed initially less suitable, they were in fact brighter and better

---

282 "Nederlandsch-Indië", *Soerabaiasch-Handelsblad* (21 April 1897).

283 Ibid.

284 "De Scenimatograaf", *Semarang-Courant* (7 April 1897). Many of the technical details provided in this and other articles are often inaccurate, which suggests that correct information about the new technology was not spread widely enough for people in the Indies to be familiar with it, or that journalists misunderstood Talbot's explanations or misinterpreted what they had read in a European newspaper.

285 "Onze Nieuwtjes", *Soerabaija-Courant* (23 April 1897).

286 "Nederlandsch-Indië", *Soerabaiasch-Handelsblad* (22 April 1897).

287 See also Cohen's chapter on the Komedie Stamboel's establishing years in Surabaya (Cohen, *The Komedie Stamboel*, 28–85).

288 "Nederlandsch-Indië", *Soerabaiasch-Handelsblad* (22 April 1897).

289 Ibid.

than those that Mr. Talbot boasted of, but no descriptions of the films or indication of their titles were given.[290]

The *Soerabaiasch-Handelsblad* further reported that the Kenotograph and Scenimatograph were caught up in competition to the utmost extreme.[291] In what seems to be a desperate attempt to stamp out his competitor, Talbot reportedly reached an agreement to rent the Kapasan Theatre for fifteen days as of 25 April, in return for a hundred guilders per night.[292] Whether or not he was planning to hold shows there or simply wanted his competitors to be left without a proper venue remains unclear. In any case, the agent of the Kenotograph announced in response that, in such a case, he would place a tent outside the building and offer free shows during this period.[293] None of these hypothetical plans ever materialised.

After an apparently failed screening of the Scenimatograph on 25 April, when the device did not operate properly and spectators had to be given a refund, Talbot added a final show on 28 April at the Surabaya Theatre, this time charging only half a guilder as entrance fee.[294] This appears to have been his last show in Surabaya.

1.2.4 Departure from Java

After the rocky ride in Surabaya, Talbot started heading back to Batavia via more shows in Solo (Surakarta), Yogyakarta and Bandung.[295] Upon reaching Batavia again in mid-July 1897, we find advertisements for a couple of screenings at the Concordia Military Club (*Militaire Sociëteit Concordia*). In the advertisement published by the Club, members were asked to carefully observe the following rules of attendance: the first night's show would be available only to members and their children whose last name begins with letters between A and M, while the rest of the members were welcomed only for the following evening's show.[296] A couple of weeks later, on 7 and 8 August, Talbot gave what appear to be his last shows on Java, with advertisements pointing out that he was back at the Batavia Theatre by popular demand before his departure.[297] By that point, competition was growing from other devices now touring the archipelago, such as the Kenotograph mentioned above, the Ripograph or

---

290 "Onze Nieuwtjes", *Soerabaija-Courant* (29 April 1897).
291 "Nederlandsch-Indië", *Soerabaiasch-Handelsblad* (22 April 1897).
292 Ibid.
293 Ibid.
294 Advertisement and "Onze Nieuwtjes", *Soerabaija-Courant* (26 April 1897).
295 "Nederlandsch-Indië", *De Nieuwe Vorstenlanden* (7 May 1897); "Jogjakarta", *Mataram* (17 May 1897); "Nederlandsch-Indië", *De Preanger-Bode* (12 July 1897). Again, there may have been other shows since there is quite a large gap of a few weeks. The limits of basing the research on newspaper material are highlighted by the fact that in Bandung, for instance, no advertisements for the Scenimatograph were found – only reviews. Therefore, he must have had other ways of advertising shows, such as handbills or posters, which remain unobtainable to this researcher.
296 Advertisement, *Java-Bode* (16 July 1897); Advertisement, *Java-Bode* (17 July 1897).
297 Advertisement, *Bataviaasch Nieuwsblad* (6 August 1897).

1 – Trials and Tribulations of Early Travelling Shows, 1896–1898

Giant Cinematograph, and the Kinematograph (see further discussion of these devices in Section 1.3). No reviews or reports were found about Talbot's last shows in the local Batavia newspapers.

The next mention that this research has found of Talbot and his Scenimatograph is from the city of Medan on Sumatra. Talbot and his manager Von Geyer arrived there on board the steamship *Calypso* from Singapore on 16 November, presumably after some screenings in Singapore, since an article in the Medan newspaper *Deli Courant* mentions that the device had received good reviews in the newspapers in Java and the Straits Settlements.[298] After a couple of shows at the *Witte Sociëteit*, for an entrance price of ƒ 1.50 for adults and ƒ 1 for children, Talbot gave one more show at another Club house – this time in Binjai, just outside Medan.[299] Street views from Europe and scenes of life in Batavia were reportedly received to applause from the audience in Medan, and the journalist was especially mesmerised by the scene of an arriving train, making "one feel like one is in Europe again".[300] On 19 December, according to the records of passenger lists, "the Scenimatograph company" left Medan on board the steamship *Avagyee* headed for Penang.[301]

Talbot arrived back in Singapore only about a month later, where he played a couple of shows at the Adelphi Hall in mid-January of 1898.[302] Prices of admission were $1.00 for reserved seats, $0.50 for first class seats, $0.25 for second class seats, and children at half price for reserved or first class seats.[303] While his tour of Java ended on a somewhat sombre if not sour note, and after what seems to be a rather low-key visit in Sumatra, Talbot might have taken comfort in his wonderful reception in Singapore. In fact, he was so well-received in Singapore that one newspaper credited him with inventing the device, only to publish a correction the next day: "M. Talbot hastens to disclaim the honour, and to explain that he is the maker of most of the films he is now showing".[304] As mentioned above, the local views of the Indies found their way into his programme here and were very much appreciated by the local newspapers:

> The series of pictures now being shown by M. Talbot at the Adelphi Hall are much in advance of anything of the kind that has hitherto been seen here in Singapore, and are well worth going to see. In the first place the oxy-ether light is steady and good, and the apparatus runs smoothly. In the second place M. Talbot is himself

---

298 "De Scènimatograaf", *Deli Courant* (17 November 1897).

299 Advertisement, *Deli Courant* (17 November 1897); Advertisement, *Deli Courant* (24 November 1897). Note that the Scenimatograph ticket prices were advertised in guilders, although the currency on Sumatra at the time was still the Mexican dollar.

300 "De Scènimatograaf", *Deli Courant* (20 November 1897).

301 "Aangekomen en vertrokken passagiers", *Deli Courant* (22 December 1897).

302 Advertisement, *The Singapore Free Press* (17 January 1898).

303 The exchange rate between the Mexican dollar used in Sumatra and the guilder used on Java fluctuated during this period, but was around $0.7 per guilder (see Tofighian, *Blurring the Colonial Binary*, 60).

304 "The Scenimatograph", *The Straits Times* (18 January 1898); "The Scenimatograph", *The Straits Times* (19 January 1898).

a photographer and has taken many of the films shown. These distinctly appeal to a local audience.[305]

The last advertisement for the Scenimatograph in Singapore appeared on 24 January 1898 and Tofighian has found further shows in Siam (Thailand) in June of 1898, although without indication of the film programme offered.[306]

1.3 Moving Pictures Incorporated into Other Entertainment Forms

1.3.1 *The Ripograph or Giant Cinematograph at Harmston's Circus*

Another device which was touring the Indies shortly after Talbot's second run in 1897 was the Ripograph or Giant Cinematograph.[307] Owned by a Mr. D. H. R. Mores, the Ripograph arrived in Batavia at the end of May 1897 after performing in Penang, via a short layover and some shows in Singapore where it presented "[...] animated figures in motion taken by means of life photographs as for instance a street scene, or a charge of cavalry, or the like".[308] Mr. Tom J. Liddiard, the advance agent of the Ripograph, arrived in Singapore from Penang only to discover that the Town Hall was not presently available for rent, and therefore only a few shows were offered at the Adelphi Hall next to the Adelphi Hotel before heading off to Java, with the promise of returning to Singapore later for more shows.[309] The advertisements in Singapore, and later also in the Indies – in Dutch and Malay newspapers – boasted that the device was brought "[...] direct from Paris at a cost of over $10,000. The largest live pictures in the world. The greatest invention of the 19th century. Pictures of every day life with Life movements. See: The Charge of The Lancers; See: The Serpentine Dance, with coloured lime light effects; See: Li Hung-Chang in Paris. Lots of other marvellous living scenes."[310]

Nevertheless, the shows in Java did not get off to a good start either. While Liddiard arrived on board the steamship *De Carpentier* from Singapore a few days before the opening show, scheduled for Sunday, 30 May at the Batavia

---

305 "The Scenimatograph", *The Straits Times* (20 January 1898).

306 Advertisement, *The Singapore Free Press* (24 January 1898); see Tofighian, *Blurring the Colonial Binary*, 222.

307 The device was advertised as "Ripograaf of de Reusachtige Cinematograaf" in Dutch and "Repograaf atawa Cenematograaf jang paling besar" in Malay (Advertisement, *The Straits Times* (15 May 1897); Advertisement, *Bataviaasch Nieuwsblad* (29 May 1897); Advertisement, *Pembrita-Betawi* (29 May 1897)).

308 "The Ripograph", *The Straits Times* (10 May 1897). The earliest cinematographic exhibitions in Singapore were given by the Ripograph or Giant Cinematograph between 12 and 26 May 1897 "for a supposedly sophisticated audience at the refined Adelphi Hall" (Tofighian, *Blurring the Colonial Binary*, 74). In Singapore the Ripograph was presented in advertisements as the "new venture" of stage entertainer Arthur Sullivan; however, this research did not find any references to Sullivan in the Indies newspapers (Advertisement, *The Straits Times* (12 May 1897)). It is possible that the device was acquired from Sullivan by Mores.

309 "The Ripograph", *The Straits Times* (10 May 1897); Advertisement, *The Straits Times* (25 May 1897). The Australian Tom J. Liddiard had previously toured the region as an actor for the Stanley Opera Company, and later served as manager for Bijou Entertainers, Bijou Troubadours, and Liddiard's Lilliputians (see Tofighian, *Blurring the Colonial Binary*, 74–75).

310 Advertisement, *The Straits Times* (15 May 1897). Advertisements were found in *Java-Bode*, *Bataviaasch Nieuwsblad* and *Pembrita-Betawi*, the latter starting on 29 May 1897.

1 – Trials and Tribulations of Early Travelling Shows, 1896–1898

Theatre, several newspapers in Dutch and Malay reported that the ship carrying the equipment for the Ripograph show was delayed in Singapore, and therefore the opening had to be postponed.[311] It is always better to schedule the show a couple of days after the expected arrival date, *Het Nieuw Bataviaasch Handelsblad* advised, in order to avoid potentially disappointing the public "[...] which must be detrimental to the troupe".[312] New shows three times a day, at 6.30, 7.15 and 9.30pm, were scheduled for 1 June.[313] These appear to have been rather short programmes, which were typical of exhibitions of moving pictures in Batavia and Surabaya at the time. In these cities, which had multiple options for entertainment, spectators might have hopped from one attraction to another in a single evening.[314] And while the *Java-Bode* praised the show, stating that the "serpentine dance [with colour effects] alone is well worth the entrance fee", *Het Nieuw Bataviaasch Handelsblad* continued to be less enthusiastic, reporting that the attendance of the opening shows was low and that although various images were "fine and artfully finished", some of the numbers left much to be desired.[315] Nevertheless, the next day it appears that attendance improved, and even *Het Nieuw Bataviaasch Handelsblad* was willing to admit that the images were clearer and that the serpentine dancer with lime-light effect was "artistic and beautiful".[316]

The Ripograph did finally enjoy a successful run in Batavia, with screenings in various venues: from the Batavia Theatre, through the Batavia Zoo, to the Toko Cavadino.[317] The latter was considered at least by some to be better suited for the exhibition of moving pictures than the theatre, though without specifying any particular reasons for this claim.[318] Since the light intensity of such a device was probably quite weak, it might be that the smaller space, compared to the large theatre, produced a better image on screen. According to *Pembrita-Betawi*, "thousands of people" have seen the show at Pasar Baru (Batavia

311 "Aangekomen passagiers", *Het Nieuw Bataviaasch Handelsblad* (28 May 1897).
312 "Nederlandsch-Indië", *Het Nieuw Bataviaasch Handelsblad* (31 May 1897).
313 Advertisement, *Java-Bode* (1 June 1897).
314 According to Tofighian, there were, "in essence, two different ways of programming. One was to have a long programme lasting the whole evening; the other was having a short programme with several exhibitions per day" (Tofighian, *Blurring the Colonial Binary*, 104). The first alternative was common in smaller towns, like Medan, which can be attributed to the lack of other entertainments. By comparison, the American Biograph in Surabaya in September 1899 scheduled only one show per evening, from 7 pm to 8.30 pm, thus ending before the circus and opera performances were to start at 9 pm, reportedly robbing the latter entertainments of spectators ("Uit Soerabaja", *De Locomotief* (11 September 1899)). For more on the American Biograph, see Section 2.1.
315 "Nederlandsch-Indië", *Java-Bode* (2 June 1897); "Nederlandsch-Indië", *Het Nieuw Bataviaasch Handelsblad* (1 June 1897).
316 "Nederlandsch-Indië", *Het Nieuw Bataviaasch Handelsblad* (2 June 1897).
317 The restaurant and confectionary and pastry shop known as "Toko Cavadino" was established around 1863 by Conrad Alexander Willem Cavadino, who was previously "the innkeeper" at the Concordia Military Club. By the late 1860s or very early 1870s, the restaurant became the Hotel Cavadino, and the Toko Cavadino in front of the hotel served as the retail section selling candy, chocolate, cigars, wine, beer and liquor, among other goods. See Scott Merrillees, *Batavia in Nineteenth Century Photographs* (Richmond, Surrey: Curzon, 2000), 136.
318 "Nederlandsch-Indië", *Bataviaasch Nieuwsblad* (12 June 1897).

Figure 1–8. Combined advertisement for Harmston's Circus and the Ripograph, *Bintang Soerabaia* (18 June 1897). Scan courtesy of PNRI, Jakarta.

Figure 1–9. Advertisement for Harmston's circus, *Soerabaiasch-Handelsblad* (22 June 1897). Retrieved from Delpher on 5 October 2015, http://resolver.kb.nl/resolve?urn= ddd:011139708:mpeg21:a0012.

Theatre) and Toko Cavadino.[319] In preparation for its tour of Java, the Ripograph's owners were looking to recruit a pianist for the continued tour of Java, adding a notice at the bottom of their advertisements for the shows in Batavia:

319 "Betawie", *Pembrita-Betawi* (14 June 1897).

1 – Trials and Tribulations of Early Travelling Shows, 1896–1898

"Wanted: A Pianist gentleman who is willing to travel throughout Java with the Ripograph. Contact the owner D. H. R. Mores in person, Hotel Leroux."[320] The Ripograph indeed travelled across Java, arriving in Surabaya at the end of June.[321] Interestingly, for the shows in Surabaya and the rest of its tour of Java, the Ripograph appears to have launched collaboration with another successful entertainment enterprise touring Southeast Asia – Harmston's Circus (see Figures 1–8 and 1–9).[322] From now on, the Ripograph screenings were to be given in a side-tent on the premises of the circus, charging separate entrance prices for the circus shows and cinema screenings: one guilder per seat, half price for children, and 25 cents for "Natives".[323] Harmston's Circus was touring through the Netherlands Indies and the entire region from the 1890s through the 1930s.[324] According to Cohen, circuses in the region often originated from Australia, Europe or the United States, taking on more local features as they were touring in Asia, such as clowns who could speak Malay.[325] Harmston's African-American manager, Charles Barney Hicks, was especially skilled at advertising and promoting his entertainment companies and producing positive publicity.[326] The Ripograph's partnership with this popular circus would have therefore ensured the new attraction a well-oiled publicity machine and reputation of quality entertainment, links with experienced managers and directors in the region versed in the tour routes, permits and potential venues, and a mixed audience.

Curiously enough, throughout their whole stint with Harmston's Circus until the end of August, the Ripograph was advertised across Java in their joint

320   Advertisement, *Java-Bode* (2 June 1897).
321   Another device, not to be confused with the "Ripograph or Giant Cinematograph", which was advertised as the "Giant Cinematograph" (*Reusachtige Cinematograaf*), was exhibited at the same time by a Mr. Ribaud in Semarang ("Kinematograaf", *De Locomotief* (11 June 1897)). The shows given at the Semarang Theatre on Saturday and Sunday apparently attracted little attention from the public, and were criticized for the quality of the lighting as well as the poor size and clarity of the images ("Kinematograaf", *De Locomotief* (14 June 1897); "Kinematograaf", *Semarang-Courant* (14 June 1897)). A similar disappointment was registered when Ribaud continued for shows in Yogyakarta a couple of weeks later, about which the correspondent for *De Locomotief* wrote: "I would gladly believe that the cinematographe [*kinematograaf*] in Paris according to the programme [handbill] attracts thousands of visitors daily, but then what people get to see must be very different" ("Nederlandsch-Indië", *De Locomotief* (6 July 1897)). This research did not find any indication of the films on Ribaud's programme.
322   I have not found mention of any official agreement between the Ripograph and Harmston, yet some of the titles on Harmston's Ripograph tour repeat the independent Ripograph screenings: "Charge of the Lancers" and "Serpentine Dance" with coloured lime light effects, among others (Advertisement, *Soerabaija-Courant* (29 June 1897)). Additionally, another advertisement recaps the point of bringing the machine from Paris at a cost of $10,000. Advertisement, *De Preanger-Bode* (26 August 1897). On top of this, another name appearing on the shipping lists alongside Liddiard when travelling to Batavia was a man by the name of Hicks, who was likely Chas. B. Hicks, the manager of Harmston's Circus ("Aangekomen passagiers", *Het Nieuw Bataviaasch Handelsblad* (28 May 1897)). Harmston's Circus was also giving shows in Singapore at the same time as the Ripograph in May 1897, before travelling to Java (Advertisement, *The Straits Times* (12 May 1897)).
323   Advertisement, *Soerabaija-Courant* (23 June 1897).
324   See Cohen, *The Komedie Stamboel*, 18.
325   Ibid.
326   For more on Harmston's Circus and Charles Barney Hicks, see Tofighian, *Blurring the Colonial Binary*, 119–124.

advertisements as "The Ripograph and the giant Scenimatograph" (*De Ripograph en de reusachtig Scenimatograph*) in Dutch, or simply as "Ripograph-Scenimatograph" (*Ripograph-Scenimatograph*) in Malay.[327] A review of the first Ripograph screening in Surabaya praised the new apparatus:

> The scenimatograph or ripograph was first shown yesterday in a side-tent on the grounds of Harmston's Circus. The series are more extensive than what we got to see here a few weeks ago. One picture, the last one, shows a dancer who produces a worthy performance of Loi[e] Fuller's dance. Since this is in colour, it gives it a special vibrant effect.[328]

Talbot's Scenimatograph was therefore adopted and used as a reference point for the new technology. In a period when early cinema was still struggling over names and definitions, the Scenimatograph had risen to the stature of a recognisable brand name in colonial Indonesia. As their tour of Java progressed, the name Scenimatograph would travel to Blitar, Kediri, Mojokerto and Madiun, according to later advertisements which stated the planned dates and locations in East Java.[329]

By August 1897, Harmston's Circus and the Ripograph were back in Central Java. In their shows in Solo (Surakarta), Ripograph screenings were first offered at the Club building one day before the circus' opening, and then Ripograph films were exhibited in the pauses in between circus acts.[330] It is not clear whether the latter shows were still at the Club, or back on the circus grounds in a side-tent. Ticket prices appeared to change from one location to another, for instance, tickets in Benteng, presumably for "Native" spectators, cost only an extra 10 cents on top of the tickets for the circus shows, according to a report in *Selompret Melajoe*.[331] In Yogyakarta tickets advertised for "Javanese" were priced at 25 cents, while the only other ticket category was for "first class" seats at one guilder per person.[332] However, in Bandung, where screenings were again initially shown at the Concordia Club and then on the circus grounds, no cheap tickets were offered, with tickets priced at one guilder per person and 50 cents for children.[333]

All that being said, associating itself with Harmston's Circus was not necessarily a guarantee of box office success for the Ripograph. While circuses were one of the most popular amusements, they did occasionally run into serious competition from local forms of entertainment such as the *komedi stambul*. For

---

327 Advertisement, *Soerabaija-Courant* (17 June 1897); Advertisement, *Bintang Soerabaia* (18 June 1897).
328 "Onze Nieuwtjes", *Soerabaija-Courant* (23 June 1897).
329 Advertisement, *Soerabaiasch-Handelsblad* (27 July 1897).
330 "Nederlandsch-Indië", *De Nieuwe Vorstenlanden* (6 August 1897). In Surabaya, the Concordia Club provided tickets to its members for the last two shows of the Ripograph: the special children's programme and the regular evening programme ("Nederlandsch-Indië", *Soerabaiasch-Handelsblad* (11 July 1897)).
331 "Circus Harmston", *Selompret Melajoe* (17 August 1897).
332 Advertisement, *Het Centrum* (17 August 1897).
333 Advertisement, *De Preanger-Bode* (23 August 1897).

example, in 1893, Mahieu's Komedie Stamboel surpassed Harmston's Circus during their parallel runs in Semarang, leading Harmston's management to try to reach an agreement with Mahieu for the companies to alternate nights of performance, but Mahieu refused.[334]

Clashes between Harmston's and Chinese spectators continually flared up on various occasions. For example, in 1908, when the circus was preparing for shows in Blitar, an incident was reported in daily newspapers across Java wherein a Chinese was accidentally injured in the eye by a German employee while they were engaged in cleaning the tent for the upcoming shows. Yet a rumour soon spread that the Chinese man was killed by the German, backed up by reports in a Malay newspaper from Surabaya, leading the Chinese in Blitar and elsewhere in the archipelago to boycott Harmston's Circus.[335] Over the years, as the Chinese population of the Indies became more involved in the local moving picture scene – both as owners or exhibitors as well as movie-goers – their influence only became greater, and they did not have a problem with boycotting a certain venue if they felt that they were being mistreated (see further on the Chinese involvement in the exhibition and boycott of moving pictures in Chapter 5, especially Section 5.3.4).

1.3.2 Miss Meranda's Kinematograph and Gramophone

One of the most unusual exhibitors on the circuit at the time was a female entertainer referred to by the newspapers as Miss (or Madame) Meranda, who travelled in the region with a variety show made up of live performances, gramophone display, and a device advertised as a Kinematograph accompanied by a gramophone. Her shows drew much attention anywhere she travelled thanks to the all-female cast of acrobats, singers and dancers, as well as the allegedly *risqué* content of some of the films on show. Another exceptional aspect of Miss Meranda's shows was that she began her tour of the Indies in Celebes (present-day Sulawesi), rather than the most populated island of Java, where the previous exhibitors discussed here started their travels across the archipelago.

An article in the *Java-Bode* from July 1897 with the heading "Letters from Makassar" reported as follows:

> What you get to learn on such an occasion you folks know. Oh these marshals, how they sat there, with beaming, shiny faces, writhing with urgency to be seated in the front rows [...]. Madame Meranda, the owner of the Cinematograph and a few other things, was to give a representation only for the gentlemen, naturally

---

334 Cohen, *The Komedie Stamboel*, 156. Cohen proposes that Harmston's failure in this case partially derived from the fact that it prevented Chinese spectators from sitting in the fifty-cent seats, which were reserved for Muslims. "Chinese spectators reasoned that it would be better to spend one guilder and get a seat at the Komedie Stamboel than spend one guilder and sit in the bleachers at the circus" (ibid., 414, endnote 48).

335 "Harmston's Circus geboycot", *Soerabaiasch-Handelsblad* (9 October 1908).

for a mighty nice fee and what came from it... "nothing new", at least no picture or tune more than the day-time spectacles at best were given. Madame was in a stockinet, *voila tout!* [...] Oh dear, what a disappointment.[336]

While Miss Meranda apparently made good business in Makassar, after disappointing her audience, she reportedly boarded a steamship to Java as a fourth class passenger the next day, with the hopes of gaining more success there.[337]

Arriving in Surabaya at the end of July 1897, Miss Meranda's opening show on Saturday, 24 July was to take place in a building on Sociëteitstraat, formerly occupied by the Velodrome.[338] To add to the "attractiveness" of the "Kinematograph and Graphophone [sic]" show, she reportedly enhanced the programme with a few numbers on the "sweet sounding resonance zither", a seven-year-old acrobat by the stage name "Small Lilly" on her velocipede, and the acrobatic gymnast "Miss Virginia".[339] These were possibly her daughters, since a later report identifies them as a family of entertainers.[340] Yet the "main attraction of the evening", according to the advertisements, was the "[...] boudoir of a Parisian woman and the sensational scene *Enfin Seul!!* This scene is being shown every night of the past six months in all the capitals of Europe."[341] Doors were scheduled to open at 9 pm while the show was to begin at 9.30 pm. Despite the late start and controversial content, Miss Meranda was apparently still expecting a young crowd, since tickets were priced at two guilders per person, with a half-price discount for children below the age of ten. It is surprising that in light of these expensive ticket prices, especially in comparison with the Ripograph which had left Surabaya just a couple of weeks earlier, *Bintang Soerabaia* nevertheless mentioned that because "the prices are cheap surely many people will love this new stuff".[342] This makes one suspect that, although no actual advertisements for the show appeared in this (or any other) Malay newspaper, paid notices were inserted into the pages of the newspaper disguised as objective reporting. It is most likely that the high cost of tickets made these performances, once again, beyond the reach of most Indonesians.

The review of the first show in *Soerabaija-Courant* mentioned that Miss Meranda's Kinematograph was the fourth such device to visit Surabaya, thus supporting the findings presented here of three devices preceding her visit,

336 "Brieven uit Makassar", *Java-Bode* (23 July 1897). In Europe, as Sabine Lenk indicated to me, such films as shown by Miss Meranda were considered "pornographic" or at least immoral, and would have been shown in a special show for men.

337 Ibid.

338 "India Ollanda", *Bintang Soerabaia* (23 July 1897). In spite of this report promoting the show, no actual advertisements for the shows were found in the Malay newspapers.

339 "Ons Dagelijksch Nieuws", *Thieme's Nieuw Advertentieblad* (22 July 1897). There was often confusion with the names of devices at the time, so while the article refers to a "graphophone", the advertisements mentioned a "gramophone".

340 "Nederlandsch-Indië", *Advertentieblad Tegal* (11 December 1897).

341 Advertisement, *Soerabaija-Courant*, *Soerabaiasch-Handelsblad* and *Thieme's Nieuw Advertentieblad* (22 July 1897), emphasis added.

342 "India Ollanda", *Bintang Soerabaia* (23 July 1897).

1 – Trials and Tribulations of Early Travelling Shows, 1896–1898

namely: Talbot's Scenimatograph, Van der Lely's Kenotograph, and the Ripograph at Harmston's Circus.[343] Once again, the article evoked the Scenimatograph by stating that "[...] the scenimatographic images [...] were better than those that have been shown here until now".[344] The images, which were screened at the end of the night's programme, were identified as being of French origin further noting that, given their nationality, it should not be surprising to anyone that they were a bit *risqué*. A couple of "undressed scenes" were reportedly cut just in time.[345] Despite the supposed hype, the shows the next night had to begin later than scheduled due to low turnout, but at around 10 pm spectators were crowding the venue so "the exhibitor and star of the show Miss Meranda had reason to be satisfied".[346] *Soerabaiasch-Handelsblad* claimed the Kinematograph was very interesting and better than the device exhibited at Harmston's.[347] The living pictures, some of which were of an "intimate" nature, appealed to the gentlemen in the crowd, especially the bedroom scenes, in addition to the scenes of the three men playing a card game, which were better produced than anything they had seen before. Even the annoying flicker effect was hardly noticeable. However, the venue was deemed to be too small, too humble and impractical, thus compromising the acoustics. For the last two shows in Surabaya, on 28 and 29 July, Miss Meranda no longer advertised the extra acts on the programme, only highlighting the Kinematograph and gramophone.[348]

A few nights later, on Thursday and Friday, 5 and 6 August, Miss Meranda was already offering shows at the *Sociëteit Harmonie* in Solo (Surakarta), riding high on the positive reviews from Surabaya which were being quoted in the local newspaper *De Nieuwe Vorstenlanden*.[349] The article further recommended to avoid sitting too close to the gramophone, possibly because spectators flocked to the device out of curiosity, but found it too loud when in operation. Ticket prices were only slightly cheaper in Solo (Surakarta) at f 1.50 per person, and a half-price discount for children below ten years of age. The review of the following show drew comparisons with Talbot, claiming that Miss Meranda's Kinematograph was better than the Scenimatograph, even though the flickering was still annoying on the eye.[350] "A few of the images that were screened", it was noted, "were less suitable for women and children".[351]

---

343 "Onze Nieuwtjes", *Soerabaija-Courant* (26 July 1897).
344 Ibid.
345 Ibid.
346 "Ons Dagelijksch Nieuws", *Thieme's Nieuw Advertentieblad* (27 July 1897).
347 "Nederlandsch-Indië", *Soerabaiasch-Handelsblad* (27 July 1897).
348 Advertisement, *Soerabaiasch-Handelsblad* (28 July 1897); Advertisement, *Soerabaiasch-Handelsblad* (29 July 1897).
349 "Nederlandsch-Indië", *De Nieuwe Vorstenlanden* (2 August 1897).
350 "Nederlandsch-Indië", *De Nieuwe Vorstenlanden* (6 August 1897).
351 Ibid.

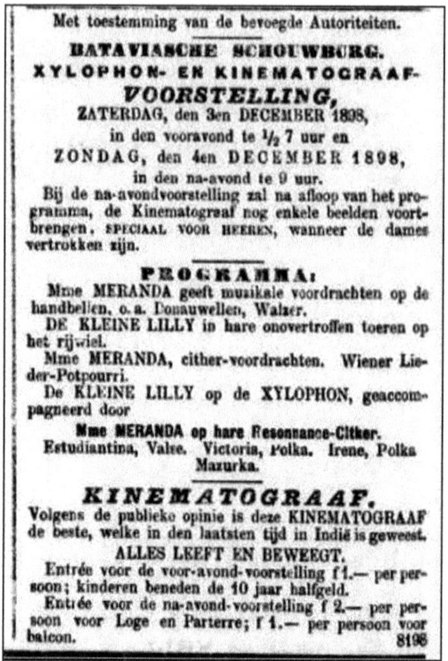
Met toestemming van de bevoegde Autoriteiten.

BATAVIASCHE SCHOUWBURG.

XYLOPHON- EN KINEMATOGRAAF-

VOORSTELLING,

ZATERDAG, den 3en DECEMBER 1898,

in den vooravond te ½ 7 uur en

ZONDAG, den 4en DECEMBER 1898,

in den na-avond te 9 uur.

Bij de na-avondvoorstelling zal na afloop van het programma, de Kinematograaf nog enkele beelden voortbrengen, SPECIAAL VOOR HEEREN, wanneer de dames vertrokken zijn.

PROGRAMMA:

Mme MERANDA geeft muzikale voordrachten op de handbellen, o. a. Donauwellen, Walzer.

DE KLEINE LILLY in hare onovertroffen toeren op het rijwiel.

Mme MERANDA, cither-voordrachten. Wiener Lieder-Potpourri.

De KLEINE LILLY op de XYLOPHON, geaccompagneerd door

Mme MERANDA op hare Resonnance-Cither.

Estudiantina, Valse. Victoria, Polka. Irene, Polka Mazurka.

KINEMATOGRAAF.

Volgens de publieke opinie is deze KINEMATOGRAAF de beste, welke in den laatsten tijd in Indië is geweest.

ALLES LEEFT EN BEWEEGT.

Entrée voor de voor-avond-voorstelling f 1.— per persoon; kinderen beneden de 10 jaar halfgeld.

Entrée voor de na-avond-voorstelling f 2.— per persoon voor Loge en Parterre; f 1.— per persoon voor balcon. 8196

Figure 1–10. Advertisement for Miss Meranda's Xylophone and Kinematograph, including a notice for a Gentlemen's programme, *Bataviaasch Nieuwsblad* (3 December 1898). Retrieved from Delpher on 5 October 2015, http://resolver.kb.nl/resolve?urn=ddd:011032259:mpeg21:a0031.

Having learned a lesson from the experience in Solo (Surakarta) perhaps, the shows in Semarang at the Semarang Theatre, on Sunday, 15 August, clearly distinguished between the programme suitable for the whole family and a gentlemen's only programme.[352] The venue also dictated a change in ticket pricing: box and stalls for two guilders per person, parterre for one guilder, and half-price discount for children and soldiers below the rank of officers. Following the performances of Little Lilly and her bicycle, Miss Meranda on the zither, the gramophone display and a short break, a few nice pictures were screened with the Kinematograph: "serpentine dancer, the card players and the man who with a brim of a hat produced all sorts of treats".[353] Once the performance was over at about eleven o'clock, "a sort of 'epilogue'" for "gentlemen only" was announced by someone in the audience, for which another 47.70 guilders were raised, which were subsequently donated "for the benefit of the poor".[354]

As Miss Meranda continued her journeys in Java, newspapers persisted in misidentifying the Kinematograph as a "Scenimatograph" and repeatedly found it to be better than the Ripograph.[355] It is not clear where exactly she travelled to after the shows in Solo (Surakarta), but presumably she performed in Yogyakarta, and by November was giving shows in western Java: in Bandung at the *Sociëteit Braga*, in Tegal, in Cirebon and finally in December in Batavia at *Sociëteit Amicitia*.[356] According to a report from *Advertentieblad Tegal* which was quoting a Yogyakarta newspaper, the shows in Cirebon brought in the respectable sum of 468 guilders from sales of tickets and photographs.[357] The

352 Advertisement, *De Locomotief* (13 August 1897).

353 "Kinematograaf en Graphophoon", *De Locomotief* (16 August 1897).

354 Ibid.

355 "Nederlandsch-Indië", *Preanger-Bode* (25 November 1897); "Nederlandsch-Indië", *Advertentieblad Tegal* (11 December 1897).

356 Ibid.; Advertisement, *Java-Bode* (11 December 1897).

357 "Nederlandsch-Indië", *Advertentieblad Tegal* (11 December 1897).

1 – Trials and Tribulations of Early Travelling Shows, 1896–1898

same report also claimed that Miss Meranda was in fact English and spoke to the Dutch public in German when announcing the ten-minute break in the programme.

After the shows in Batavia in December 1897, Miss Meranda presumably left Java. She did come back for a few shows in 1898 and 1899, this time – advertised as "Xylophone and Kinematograph" performances. It was still a variety show combined with film screenings, with extra scenes "especially for gentlemen" after the evening performance was done, "when the ladies have left" the hall (see Figure 1–10).[358] Among the scenes available in 1899 were: "Inauguration parade of H. M. Queen Wilhelmina", "The explosion of the 'Maine'" and "Naval Battle for Manila".[359] At this point, a report in *De Locomotief* identified the troupe as "the Nast family".[360] It is quite likely that there was a link to Mr. Nast, who later toured the Indies with a Kinematograph, including in Makassar.[361] In 1902, Nast got in trouble with the authorities in Surabaya for screening an inappropriate film (see further in Section 2.3.1). The last shows performed by Miss Meranda herself found in this research were given in Semarang in August 1899, and were once more criticised by *De Locomotief* for their inappropriate content which was nevertheless combined with more suitable scenes from Queen Wilhelmina's investiture (see further in Section 2.1.2).[362]

1.3.3 Victoria Parsi Theatrical Company and the Cinematograph

New theatre forms influenced by the encounter with Europe were beginning to emerge in South Asia around 1850. The Parsi community of Bombay, comprised of Zoroastrians who had arrived from Iran a millennium earlier, were one of the first to assume and adapt Western forms of theatre and operate drama performing companies.[363] Their programmes were based on Urdu and Hindi texts and incorporated Indian dance and music with European stage techniques.[364] Made up of Parsi and non-Parsi actors and performing to equally mixed audiences, Parsi theatre companies from Bombay and other parts of India "[...] synthesized elements of Asian and European origin, lending it a hybrid, middle-brow character".[365] Such troupes toured extensively throughout the subcontinent, and by the 1880s also reached the Netherlands Indies, where they proved to be instantly popular.[366]

358 Advertisement, *Bataviaasch Nieuwsblad* (30 November 1898).
359 Advertisement, *Soerabaiasch-Handelsblad* (31 May 1899).
360 "Alweer wat nieuws", *De Locomotief* (26 July 1898). Possible films on the programme: COMBAT NAVAL DEVANT MANILLE (Méliès, 1898), QUAIS DE LA HAVANE ET EXPLOSION DU CUIRASSÉ "MAINE" (Méliès, 1898).
361 "Makassar", *De Makassaar* (18 January 1901).
362 "Nederlandsch-Indië", *De Locomotief* (28 August 1899).
363 See Kathryn Hansen, *Stages of Life: Indian Theatre Autobiographies* (London: Anthem Press, 2011), 3.
364 See Cohen, *The Komedie Stamboel*, 42.
365 Hansen, *Stages of Life*, 3.
366 As Cohen argues, "Parsi theater primed Indonesian audiences for a theater using Western stage technology to present non-Western stories in a non-Western language" (Cohen, *The Komedie Stamboel*, 42).

The Victoria Parsi Theatrical Company was established in Bombay in 1868 by "influential Parsis".[367] In the 1880s the Company, now under the management of Khurshed Baliwala and consisting of ninety performers, performed in London during the Indian and Colonial Exhibition of 1885–1886, and later continued to tour Europe and the United States.[368] It later toured through Burma (Myanmar), the Straits Settlements, Java, Siam (Thailand) and Ceylon (Sri Lanka) in 1898 and 1899.[369] The Company was one of the most renowned theatrical troupes in Asia at the turn of the century, travelling widely with a large quantity of stage equipment, requiring ten train carts for transporting its equipment when on tour in Java.[370] Among the Victoria Parsi Theatre attractions were: "English-language songs, ballet dancers, magical scenic effects, and the cinematograph [...]. Actors regularly were wreathed with garlands at the end of much-applauded shows."[371]

In June 1898, an advance agent for the Victoria Parsi Theatrical Company by the name Mr. Van Katwijk was sent out from Batavia to Surabaya, to seek a permit for setting up a tent in Kapasan in July. However, the *Soerabaiasch-Handelsblad* estimated that the permit would be refused, since July coincided with the investiture celebrations of Queen Wilhelmina and the festival committee wanted free use of the site under question.[372] Yet, since the Surabaya authorities kept deferring the decision in regards to the permit, the company reportedly decided to debut in Batavia instead.[373] In the meantime, the Company itself remained in Singapore, where its shows combined stage acts based on stories from *A Thousand and One Nights*, such as "Gule-Bakavli or The Fairy Flower" and "Alibaba and Forty Thieves", alongside what was billed as "[...] the revival of The Cinematograph or Living Picture. More perfect than before. Under the management of a new artist from Jerico."[374] *The Straits Times* promoted it as "[...] an improved cinematograph display in the hands of an expert".[375]

The Victoria Parsi Theatrical Company finally gave its opening show in Batavia two months later, in a tent at Mangga Besar that was found to be clean, spacious and comfortably furnished.[376] And while the opening show took place in mid-August, the Cinematograph only re-joined the troupe in Batavia mid-September.[377] The "Theatre" was especially decorated and lit for the occasion,

367 "Nederlandsch-Indië", *Soerabaiasch-Handelsblad* (16 June 1898).
368 See Tofighian, *Blurring the Colonial Binary*, 91.
369 Ibid.
370 See Cohen, *The Komedie Stamboel*, 280.
371 Ibid.
372 "Nederlandsch-Indië", *Soerabaiasch-Handelsblad* (16 June 1898).
373 "India Ollanda", *Bintang Soerabaia* (22 June 1898); "Nederlandsch-Indië", *Soerabaiasch-Handelsblad* (21 June 1898).
374 Advertisement, *The Singapore Free Press* (18 July 1898).
375 "Parsee Theatre", *The Straits Times* (18 July 1898).
376 "Victoria Parsi Tooneelgezelschap", *Bataviaasch Nieuwsblad* (15 August 1898).
377 Advertisement, *Java-Bode* (12 September 1898).

1 – Trials and Tribulations of Early Travelling Shows, 1896–1898

with the Resident of Batavia and the Assistant Resident of Police and their wives in attendance.[378] A separate gala event was attended by Captain of the Chinese Tio Tek Ho, his family and other Chinese dignitaries.[379] Ticket prices for an evening's programme varied from ƒ 2, through ƒ 1, 50 cents, and down to 25 cents.[380]

The programmes were frequently changed and often referred to in the newspapers as *"soirée variée"*, including songs, dances, pantomimes, comedy scenes and screenings of the Cinematograph. However, soon after its arrival, by 21 September, the Cinematograph was already being offered for sale along with other theatre supplies, including "Mats, Bamboos and Chairs" and a phonograph – "everything in good condition".[381] The sales notice was repeated several times while the Cinematograph screenings continued until the last shows in Batavia at the beginning of October.[382] By the time the troupe finally arrived in Surabaya for shows in mid-November, there was no Cinematograph mentioned on the programme.[383] However, a couple of weeks later, Cinematograph screenings were included on the programme again.[384]

Newspapers in Surabaya, which as may be recalled had been eagerly awaiting the arrival of the Victoria Parsi Theatrical Company at least since June of that year, continued reporting about the plans and preparations. Speculations were raised about where the shows were to be given, and concerns were expressed that the troupe was by now too comfortably successful in Batavia.[385] Rumours had it that the troupe would probably arrive in Surabaya with considerably less actors, since some were stricken with nostalgia and had already made their way back to Singapore.[386] Work on the stage at the Kapasan Theatre finally started at the beginning of November, as members of the troupe already arrived while its luggage and equipment was still being transported via Semarang to Surabaya in ten train wagons.[387] *Soerabaiasch-Handelsblad* approved of the choice of venue, stating that the Kapasan Theatre was fitting also for a European audience and further provided a good buffet.[388]

The Victoria Parsi Theatre shows attracted not only the attention of the local press, but also the entertainment-seeking public. The opening show on 13

378 "Nederlandsch-Indië", *Java-Bode* (24 September 1898).
379 Advertisement, *Bataviaasch Nieuwsblad* (30 September 1898).
380 Advertisement, *Java-Bode* (14 September 1898). Gala show tickets were more expensive for the first two classes, at ƒ 2 and ƒ 1, respectively, but the cheapest tickets remained the same for the third and fourth classes.
381 Advertisement, *Java-Bode* (21 September 1898).
382 Advertisement, *Java-Bode* (3 October 1898).
383 Advertisement, *Soerabaiasch-Handelsblad* (9 November 1898).
384 Advertisement, *Soerabaiasch-Handelsblad* (3 December 1898).
385 "Nederlandsch-Indië", *Soerabaiasch-Handelsblad* (20 October 1898); "Nederlandsch-Indië", *Soerabaiasch-Handelsblad* (4 November 1898).
386 "Nederlandsch-Indië", *Soerabaiasch-Handelsblad* (4 November 1898).
387 "Nederlandsch-Indië", *Soerabaiasch-Handelsblad* (5 November 1898).
388 Ibid.

November, as well as shows on the following nights, were so packed that several other venues and entertainers who were performing in Surabaya at the time, such as the magician P. Bosakowski at the Surabaya Theatre, or a *stambul* company Komedie Bogor from Buitenzorg (Bogor) at *kampung* Sidodadi, were reportedly left without an audience for their shows.[389] According to Cohen, Mahieu's Komedie Stamboel changed its tour plans altogether in order to avoid competition with the Parsi theatre in Surabaya.[390]

The Victoria Parsi Theatre's programme, which was appreciated for its costumes and stage design, was generally deemed suitable for "European" and "Native" spectators, although one newspaper warned that "[...] the music sounds a bit strange to European ears".[391] Complaints were also being made about the fact that the Kapasan Theatre was not allowed to sell alcohol, "[f]or the European visitors of the Victoria Parsi Theatrical Company, it is certainly no less enjoyable to be able to get a brandy or whiskey soda".[392] The newspaper further reasoned that Kapasan Theatre was probably denied a permit because riots have been known to erupt there when too much alcohol was being consumed; however, since spirits were sold at circus tents, it was believed this decision should be reconsidered. With or without the aid of alcohol, occasional riots did break out between audience members, especially in the fourth class.[393] Despite these problems, increasingly more European spectators were attending the shows, showing appreciation of the fact that the Dutch national anthem was sung by the choir to the accompaniment of the orchestra at the end of every show.[394] One Saturday evening show was reportedly so busy that it brought in an income of more than 600 guilders.[395] Only the heavy rain falls were able to deter spectators from coming to the shows.[396]

On 8 December, in a show that was to be attended by Captain of the Chinese in Surabaya and his family, the Cinematograph was finally included on the programme again.[397] And while the Cinematograph reaped "great acclaim" during the last month of shows in Surabaya, the device was once again put up for sale along with a phonograph, both advertised as being "in good condition".[398] After giving a couple of special shows of theatrical acts and *tableaux* at

---

389 "Nederlandsch-Indië", *Soerabaiasch-Handelsblad* (14 November 1898); "Nederlandsch-Indië", *Soerabaiasch-Handelsblad* (22 November 1898); "Nederlandsch-Indië", *Soerabaiasch-Handelsblad* (5 December 1898).

390 See Cohen, *The Komedie Stamboel*, 280.

391 "Nederlandsch-Indië", *Soerabaiasch-Handelsblad* (15 November 1898).

392 "Nederlandsch-Indië", *Soerabaiasch-Handelsblad* (17 November 1898).

393 "Nederlandsch-Indië", *Soerabaiasch-Handelsblad* (28 November 1898).

394 "Nederlandsch-Indië", *Soerabaiasch-Handelsblad* (19 November 1898).

395 "Nederlandsch-Indië", *Soerabaiasch-Handelsblad* (5 December 1898).

396 "Nederlandsch-Indië", *Soerabaiasch-Handelsblad* (26 November 1898); "Nederlandsch-Indië", *Soerabaiasch-Handelsblad* (1 December 1898).

397 Advertisement, *Soerabaiasch-Handelsblad* (6 December 1898).

398 "Nederlandsch-Indië", *Soerabaiasch-Handelsblad* (10 December 1898); Advertisement, *Soerabaiasch-Handelsblad* (12 December 1898).

1 – Trials and Tribulations of Early Travelling Shows, 1896–1898

the Surabaya Theatre on the last week of December, simultaneously running stage shows and screenings of the Cinematograph at the Kapasan Theatre, the Victoria Parsi Theatre finally left for Singapore at the end of December.[399]

1.3.4 Magician Carl Hertz's Cinematographe

Before introducing moving pictures into his programme, beginning with his tour of South Africa in May 1896, American magician Carl Hertz had already travelled the globe extensively. Hertz began his career as a touring magician with a travelling circus in the US, moved to Britain and toured Europe with his stage acts, moved back to the US, and then went on tour again to Australia and New Zealand.[400] And although he advertised his device as a "Cinematographe", alluding to the Cinematographe Lumière, it was in fact a machine that he acquired from British film pioneer R. W. Paul when he was visiting in London before setting off for South Africa.[401] A few days later, Hertz already boarded a steamship headed to Johannesburg with his newly acquired attraction, which he was testing out on the other passengers in the middle of the sea voyage.[402]

However, with only five fifty-feet films in his possession and unable to order new films from London, his options of programme changes were limited and he quickly felt that he was losing his audience in Johannesburg.[403] He did apparently buy twenty films for ten pounds from the proprietor of a Kinetoscope parlour in Johannesburg, which he quickly discovered did not fit his device because the sprocket holes did not match. But Hertz thought of a solution, "[...] and accordingly set to work to cement all the spracket-holes [sic] with fresh strips of film and make fresh spracket-holes [sic] which would fit [his] machine".[404] The films still ran slower than they were intended to, which Hertz claimed was due to the fact that "[...] the films were worked on the Kinetoscope by electricity, whereas the first cinematograph machines were

399 "Nederlandsch-Indië", *Soerabaiasch-Handelsblad* (27 December 1898).

400 See Carl Hertz, *A Modern Mystery Merchant: The Trials, Tricks and Travels of Carl Hertz, the Famous American Illusionist* (London: Hutchinson & Co., 1924).

401 Ibid., 139. According to his memoirs, Hertz in fact saw a Cinematographe Lumière exhibited by Trewey at the Royal Polytechnic Institution in London and was interested in hiring a machine for his upcoming tour in South Africa, yet Trewey did not consent. He thus began negotiating with Paul, who was willing to sell him a device for 50 pounds, yet was only able to deliver it within two or three months. After some coaxing, Hertz finally managed to buy one of Paul's two devices, which were at that moment both used for his shows at London's Alhambra Theatre, paying 100 pounds in cash.

402 Ibid., 141.

403 Ibid., 142.

404 Ibid., 145. This was probably one of many exaggerated stories included in Hertz's memoir. Edison films were available from Paul, who built a camera to produce new films for the Kinetoscope and a projector (Theatrograph) with four perforations on both sides (see Deac Rossell, *Living Pictures. The Origins of the Movies* (New York: SUNY, 1998), 139). As Sabine Lenk suggested to me, changing the perforation by cementing the holes would have made the perforation thicker and irregular, making it difficult to pass through the gate and otherwise would have caused image trembling. It would have further made the films more vulnerable by putting the perforation and/or filmstrip at higher risk of breaking or catching fire more easily.

worked by hand".[405] The audience nevertheless found the slow movements of people and animals to be funny, and the shows were a success.

According to Tofighian, Hertz "[...] toured with the cinematograph in South Africa, Australia, New Zealand, India, and Ceylon in 1896 and 1897. After India, he went to Rangoon and Mandelay in Burma, to Singapore for a week, Manila for two weeks, back to Singapore for a week, to Java and Borneo, back again to Singapore, Saigon for a week, Hong Kong, Shanghai for two weeks, Japan, Hawaii, and San Francisco."[406] As this research has found, Hertz began his tour of Java in Batavia, moving on to Semarang and Surabaya, hiring the services of experienced manager Edwin Geach, who later toured with the successful acrobatic act The Flying Jordans.[407]

Hertz arrived in Batavia at the beginning of July 1898 on board the steamship *Both* from Singapore with his wife, Mademoiselle d'Alton, who was also an on stage assistant especially for the magic trick of the vanishing lady.[408] Advertisements and reports about the upcoming shows at the Batavia Theatre began appearing in Dutch and Malay newspapers a couple of weeks before, highlighting the wonderful magic tricks which are all the rage of London and Paris and emphasising the "beautiful and natural movements" of the films, thus hyping up the expectations for the opening show on 19 July.[409] "Do not forget to come see the coloured living pictures of the cinematograph – 20 known and entertaining topics", read the advertisements, offering tickets at three guilders for a box seat, two guilders for the parterre, and one guilder for a balcony seat. Advertising bills were posted around the city, presumably comprised of similar text to the newspaper advertisements. Soldiers below the rank of officers and children below ten years of age received a discount on all classes of tickets, and there was also an option to reserve a seat for 50 cents extra. With moving pictures no longer being a technical novelty by 1898, the expensive ticket pricing reflect the kind of audience Hertz was aiming at, namely – higher class spectators who could afford to pay a premium price for his magic, variety show.

However, on the day of the show, the opening suddenly had to be postponed due to what a newspaper advertisement described as "a slight indisposition".[410] Hertz's memoir helps to clear up the situation, as he wrote:

> On reaching Batavia, I fell ill with malaria and was laid up for a fortnight, in consequence of which we were, of course, unable to open at the advertised time.

405   Hertz, *A Modern Mystery Merchant*, 145. Since Hertz's Cinematographe device was hand cranked, reaching around sixteen to eighteen frames per second, it was probably difficult to turn it fast enough to meet the thirty frames per second of the electrically-run Edison Kinetoscope, which led to the slowing down effect. Thanks are due to Frank Kessler for this clarification.

406   Tofighian, *Blurring the Colonial Binary*, 111.

407   Advertisement, *Java-Bode* (5 July 1898). His advance agent in Singapore was advertised as Harry Lyons (Advertisement, *The Singapore Free Press* (14 March 1898)).

408   "Aangekomen passagiers", *Bataviaasch Nieuwsblad* (19 July 1898).

409   Advertisement, *Java-Bode* (5 July 1898); Advertisement, *Bataviaasch Nieuwsblad* (5 July 1898); Advertisement and "Chabar Betawi", *Pembrita-Betawi* (12 July 1898); "Nederlandsch-Indië", *Java-Bode* (6 July 1898).

410   Advertisement, *Java-Bode* (19 July 1898).

1 – Trials and Tribulations of Early Travelling Shows, 1896–1898

I was told that everyone gets malaria in Java, and, so soon as I was convalescent, I was taken to see the cemetery, which is one of the sights of Batavia and is known as "The Actors' Graveyard", being so named because nearly every theatrical company which goes there leaves someone behind. I felt thankful that I had managed to pull through, and, though during our stay in Java nearly every member of our company was taken ill with malaria, we were fortunate enough to lose no one.[411]

As we have seen in the case of Harley (see Section 1.1) and as Hertz's account further indicates, a debilitating disease, in the better case scenario, or a lethal illness, in the worst case, was a common threat that had to be taken into account when travelling in the region. In light of this account, it probably should not come as a surprise that Hertz stayed in Java for merely a month, giving shows in the main cities accessible via steamship, rather than travelling by railway into the hinterland as other exhibitors had done before him.[412] Moreover, it appears that Hertz's strategy was, in any case, to skim the surface and add more countries to his tour list, rather than thoroughly cover every possible town in each location. "It was", according to Tofighian, "a good marketing strategy for entertainment companies to go abroad in an increasingly inter-connected entertainment world".[413] They could use the checklist of sites they have visited as a promotional tool, at home and abroad.[414]

Hertz's opening show in Batavia finally took place on 21 July. The hall was reportedly well attended, and the public's high expectations were largely met.[415] According to *Pembrita-Betawi*, many of the spectators were Chinese.[416] The Cinematograph added to the programme's variety, but the films were apparently spun too fast.[417] According to *Java-Bode* the films exhibited included: a park with vehicles and cyclists, a race, a funny courtship between lovers, a serpentine dance in colour, and a trick scene of a magician and a creepy ghost.[418] The advertisement for the last shows on 30 and 31 also mentioned a film depicting Queen Victoria's Diamond Jubilee procession.[419] And while

411 Hertz, *A Modern Mystery Merchant*, 168–169.

412 According to the account in his memoir, Hertz may have had another unidentified town on his tour of Java. He writes: "At one of the towns in Java which I visited I was unable to obtain a suitable building to give my performance in, so my advance-agent had to have one put up. The total cost came to just 1 pound. It was made of palm leaves and bamboo, and the wood used was borrowed, and returned at the end of my engagement" (ibid., 163). Unfortunately, Hertz does not name the town and this research was unable to decipher where he might have gone. Since only a couple of days separated between his shows in Batavia and Semarang, it could be that he travelled to Buitenzorg (Bogor) for one show. Other options might be Solo (Surakarta) or Yogyakarta, in between his shows in Semarang and Surabaya. After the shows in Surabaya, Hertz was unexpectedly approached by an agent of a wealthy Raja from Borneo and set out to give private shows at the palace (ibid., 169).

413 Tofighian, *Blurring the Colonial Binary*, 48.

414 However, as we shall see in Chapter 3, by 1905 some commentators were questioning the function of foreign companies in the Indies and the benefits they were bringing to the local population in return for the money spent on these entertainments.

415 "Nederlandsch-Indië", *Bataviaasch Nieuwsblad* (22 July 1898).

416 "Chabar Betawi", *Pembrita-Betawi* (22 July 1898).

417 "Nederlandsch-Indië", *Bataviaasch Nieuwsblad* (22 July 1898).

418 "Nederlandsch-Indië", *Java-Bode* (22 July 1898).

Figure 1–11. Advertisement for Carl Hertz's magic show with Cinematograph, *Bataviaasch Nieuwsblad* (8 July 1898). Retrieved from Delpher on 5 October 2015, http://resolver.kb.nl/resolve?urn=ddd:011032138:mpeg21:a0030.

Hertz's magic tricks as well as Miss d'Alton's singing were very much appreciated by spectators, it was the Cinematograph that drew "[...] lively interest and reaped the admiration in the higher ranks of the theatre to deafening screams, whistles and pounding".[420] According to the shipping lists from 5 August, Carl Hertz, his wife and manager arrived in Semarang on board the steamship *Van Diemen* from Batavia.[421] His advance agent, H. P. Lyons, was reportedly in Semarang already two weeks earlier, presumably to make all the necessary arrangements for the show at the Semarang Theatre. Lyons also dropped by the office of *De Locomotief* to put in a good word for the upcoming show.[422] Nevertheless, with ticket prices at 2.40 guilders for box and stool seats and one guilder for parterre, again – with discount for children and soldiers, the shows on 7, 8, 9 and 10 August were apparently not particularly well-attended.[423] Reporters were less than impressed with Hertz's magic tricks, claiming they were not any better than those performed by magicians even thirty years ago.[424] No mention of the Cinematographe was found, even though it was definitely advertised on the programme.

Hertz may have been hoping for better luck in Surabaya. By the beginning of August, newspapers there also began reporting about Hertz's shows in Batavia, expressing concern that he would not be able to visit Surabaya as planned the following week since there was no appropriate venue available.[425] In fact, two other magic acts, which were deemed by the *Soerabaiasch-Handelsblad* to be inferior to Hertz's magical skills, were being shown in Surabaya at the time in venues that would have been attractive to Hertz as well: Calabresini was playing at the Kapasan Theatre, and the Sphinx at the Surabaya Theatre.[426] To the relief

419 Advertisement, *Java-Bode* (30 July 1898).
420 "Nederlandsch-Indië", *Java-Bode* (27 July 1898).
421 "Aangekomen Passagiers te Semarang", *De Locomotief* (5 August 1898).
422 "Voorloopige aankondiging", *De Locomotief* (23 July 1898).
423 Advertisement, *De Locomotief* (8 August 1898); "Nederlandsch-Indië", *De Locomotief* (9 August 1898).
424 "Nederlandsch-Indië", *De Locomotief* (8 August 1898).
425 "Nederlandsch-Indië", *Soerabaiasch-Handelsblad* (1 August 1898).
426 Advertisements, *Soerabaiasch-Handelsblad* (10 August 1898).

of the Surabaya newspapers, the Surabaya Theatre was made available after all as of Saturday, 13 August, the day that Hertz and his wife arrived in Surabaya on board the steamship *Coen*.[427] Ticket prices ranged from three guilders for a box seat, two guilders for a parterre seat, and one guilder in the balcony, with discount for children and soldiers, and an extra 50 cents for a seat reservation.[428] However, and perhaps due to the over-presence of magicians, with one following in the footsteps of the other, Hertz's first shows did not seem to draw the crowds after all: "Saturday night the theatre was fairly busy, but Sunday night was less frequented than the previous evening […] May his farewell shows yield better financial results for him."[429] The reports in Surabaya then were generally more appreciative of Hertz's show, compared to Semarang at least, but although the Cinematographe was apparently to the audience's liking, *Soerabaiasch-Handelsblad* noted that the flickering was quite severe, wondering if the device were not placed perhaps on a "vibrating floor".[430] By the time of his fourth and last show in Surabaya a week later, and after offering special children's programmes, the crowd warmed up to Hertz and his shows were better attended, and apparently surpassed those of the Sphinx séance shows.[431]

1.4 Conclusion

This chapter outlined the first years of moving picture shows in the Netherlands Indies by focusing on the journeys of several itinerant performers through the archipelago. The examples brought here are rather striking in terms of the different approaches they demonstrate to the exhibition of moving pictures and the rich variety of combinations with other entertainment forms.[432] Early moving picture shows in the Netherlands Indies were "intermedially embedded", and most spectators at the time, it is likely to assume, had their first encounter with moving images within the context of another mode of amusement, for instance: as a side show on the circus grounds, on stage as part of a variety act, as a bonus item at the Parsi theatre, or as a new trick at a

---

427 "Aangekomen", *Soerabaiasch-Handelsblad* (17 August 1898).

428 Advertisement, *Soerabaiasch-Handelsblad* (9 August 1898). By comparison, tickets for the Sphinx were priced at 2.50 guilders per box and parterre seat and one guilder for the balcony, with 25 cents extra for a seat reservation. No discounts were offered.

429 "Nederlandsch-Indië", *Soerabaiasch-Handelsblad* (15 August 1898).

430 Ibid.

431 "Nederlandsch-Indië", *Soerabaiasch-Handelsblad* (17 August 1898).

432 It should be noted that these examples are not the only instances of moving picture shows exhibited in this period, but rather they are the ones that have left the most prominent traces. Beyond the exhibitors mentioned in this chapter, another exhibitor of moving pictures, Mr. Holton and his Cinematographe, was found to be touring in 1897. I have not found any indication that he offered shows outside European Club houses, such as the *Sociëteit Harmonie* in Semarang and Solo (Surakarta), which were usually offered free of charge to members ("Sociëteit Harmonie", *De Locomotief* (15 November 1897); Advertisement, *De Nieuwe Vorstenlanden* (3 December 1897)). Surabayan photographer H. Salzwedel, who will be discussed in the following chapter in connection with the Java Biorama, began experimenting with a Kinematograph in 1897 ("Nederlandsch-Indië", *De Locomotief* (9 December 1897)).

magic show.[433] The incorporation of moving picture technology enabled all of the above entertainers to pique spectators' curiosity by claiming that they were propagating the latest achievements of modern science and, thus, by extension, that they themselves were modern and up-to-date.[434] Spectators, in turn, were expected to excuse any technical problems because what they were being shown was novel, experimental and ground-breaking.

The fact that Talbot's Scenimatograph shows were comprised solely of films, including films that he had shot himself locally, is equally remarkable, considering the number of titles which would have been required to fill up roughly an hour-long programme.[435] His shows were clearly the exception rather than the norm, compared to the intermedial examples above which used only imported films on their programmes. And while his shows may have been exclusive in terms of audience composition, compared to the circus or Parsi theatre, the Scenimatograph's effect on the early movie-going scene in the Indies in those years was palpable. As various competing exhibitors and technologies followed suit, the name of the Scenimatograph and, in some cases, the positive impressions left by Talbot's earlier shows, continued to be evoked in the newspapers whenever a new device was presented to the public. If initially the local Indies newspapers had to use Edison's name in order for their readers to recognize the new invention and draw the appropriate connections to other related devices, by the time Talbot was halfway through his tour of Java, it seems his Scenimatograph, in many respects, turned into a brand name in and of itself.[436] The Scenimatograph, in short, became a benchmark against which other devices for the projection of moving pictures were to be measured, only to soon go unheeded as even newer innovations in the field were to be introduced over the next few years. His local views were definitely forgotten and, about a decade later, another exhibitor claimed to be the first to be showing local views of Java.[437]

---

433 Shail, "Intermediality", 5. Tofighian's findings regarding early moving picture shows in the entire region further support this assertion, see Tofighian, *Blurring the Colonial Binary*, 46–52. Similarly, audiences in the West would have first seen moving pictures as part of variety entertainment at vaudeville halls in urban centres, or on fairground and festival tents in rural areas or smaller towns (Robert C. Allen, "From Exhibition to Reception: Reflections on the Audience in Film History", *Screen* 31, 4 (1990): 349). See also: Lee Grieveson, "Audiences: Surveys and Debates", in Abel (ed.), *Encyclopedia of Early Cinema*, 64–69.

434 As Gillian Arrighi claims, nineteenth century circuses played a crucial role in spreading modernity globally, thanks to their commitment to proving that they were in possession of the latest technologies (Arrighi, "The Circus and Modernity", 171).

435 Films at the time averaged 30 to 60 seconds in length, and reel changes would have also required some time. Therefore, it is likely to assume that at least part of Talbot's show was dedicated to lecturing about the new technology.

436 By the time Talbot left Sumatra, another so-called Scenimatograph (*Scenimatograaf*) device was being exhibited by L. Rosenberg at *Sociëteit Ons Genoegen* in Padang in early 1898. It was again promoted as "the only French device in the Netherlands Indies" and the advertisement further warned against confusing it with the "Kinematograph, Ripograph and other imitations". The name J. Schvartz appeared on the advertisement as manager (Advertisement, *Sumatra Courant* (25 March 1898)).

437 See further on Abdullly Esoofally's Royal Bioscope in Section 3.2.

2

The Dutch Come into the Picture

Wednesday night at the Manège in [Tanah] Abang was justifiably cheerful. The 2nd Reserve battalion was the guest of the American Biograph. They sat together in camaraderie. Natives and Europeans, full of anticipation of things to come. […] Suddenly it became dark and the show began. Boy oh boy, how enthusiastic was the singing. The Natives did not understand. They were overwhelmed. Does "toean satan" sit in this cabinet? After each number, they looked back with superstitious curiosity. The military scenes naturally attracted the most attention. […] Then during the jumping [of English cavalrymen], when one of the riders fell over with his horse, the illusion was so powerful that a European manifested his fright rather too candidly. […] We also saw a warship being launched, a high sea, "joies" in Scheveningen when the fish catch comes home, a… oh let's end it here, there was too much for us to mention. Finally, the men could see Her Majesty our dear Queen arriving in Amsterdam, the entrance to the church for attending the investiture and Her Majesty being cheered on the balcony of the Palace at the Dam. One can imagine how the soldiers, white and brown, were delighted. Though during the days of September 1898 they were striking in Pedir,[438] now they had the chance to see it at least as good as the Amsterdammers! The Javanese knew Her Majesty only from a still portrait, and now, thanks to this wonderful invention, it was as if she appeared in front of them in flesh and blood.
"De Biograaf en het Garnizoen van Batavia", Albrecht's Zondagsblad *(14 May 1899).*

Following the introduction of moving pictures in the Indies by local and foreign entrepreneurs of various nationalities, the Indies moving pictures scene suddenly underwent somewhat of a Dutch turn. Firstly, the Dutch subsidiary of the American Mutoscope and Biograph Company began trading in the Indies, albeit for a short period of a couple of years, and it appears that other companies were receiving at least some of their films from distributors in the Netherlands. Secondly, certain images and themes of relevance to the Dutch became subjects of films made and exhibited at the time. Thirdly, as moving picture shows became more common and a growing number of companies were travelling and establishing themselves in the Indies, the Dutch colonial authorities were increasingly required to address companies' incorporation procedures, in addition to control of moving picture shows, in terms of ticket sales, public safety, and the morality of its content. Finally, the seating and pricing tiers of moving picture shows increasingly came to reflect the colonial racial classification system, at times drawing on the census system's

---

438 A punitive expedition of the Aceh War (see footnote 261 in Section 1.2.2).

differentiation between "Natives", "Europeans" and "Foreign Orientals" (see further in the Introduction). In sum, the constitution of a local market for moving picture distribution, exhibition and consumption was well underway.

This chapter highlights the period 1899 to 1905, focusing on three different companies active at this time. The first is the *Nederlandsche Biograaf- en Mutoscope Maatschappij*, the Dutch subsidiary of the American Mutoscope and Biograph Company, which was the first to screen films of the investiture of Queen Wilhelmina in the Indies.[439] The second is Herman Salzwedel's Java Biorama, which advertised that its screenings were given with an American Biograph unit (and may have been an offshoot of the earlier American Biograph).[440] Finally, the third is the Java Cineograph Company, which appears to have been the first moving picture company to be incorporated in the Indies. Various aspects of exhibition practices will be considered in the discussion of each company, in addition to a particular focus on certain films or themes in their programmes which will serve as a basis for comparisons with other contemporary competitors. The subjects in focus include the investiture ceremony of Queen Wilhelmina in September 1898, the period of engagement to Hendrik van Mecklenburg-Schwerin in October 1900, and the royal wedding in February 1901. Two additional topics are the Second Boer War (or Second South African War) of 1899–1902 and the Russo-Japanese War of 1904–1905, two international conflicts alerting the Dutch of their precarious position on the global political stage.[441] Thus, the novelty of the new technology, still appreciated for its vivid effect of bringing still images to life as in the above description of a screening of Queen Wilhelmina's investiture, was nevertheless slowly declining. While companies were still trying to set their devices apart as superior to those used by their predecessors or competitors, the emphasis was gradually placed more on moving pictures as a living newspaper, or a modern learning tool for conveying information and reporting on current events, as well as a form of modern entertainment.

2.1 The Dutch Subsidiary of the American Biograph

2.1.1 First Steps in the Indies

The American Mutoscope Company with its Biograph projector became the leading motion picture company in the United States in 1897, when it also premiered in Europe and Australia. Two years later the company had eight sister companies in Britain, France, Germany, the Netherlands, Belgium,

---

439 In the Netherlands, the ceremony in which a new monarch becomes the reigning king or queen is known as an investiture (*inhuldiging*) rather than a coronation. I wish to thank Nico de Klerk for clarifying this point and the English term to be used.

440 Sections 2.1 on the American Biograph and 2.2 on the Java Biorama, in a slightly different version, also form part of a pending publication written with Nadi Tofighian on the transnational distribution of the American Biograph in the region (see Dafna Ruppin and Nadi Tofighian, "Moving Pictures across Colonial Boundaries: The Multiple Nationalities of the American Biograph in Southeast Asia", *Early Popular Visual Culture* 14, No. 2 (2016): 188–207).

441 See Dijk, *The Netherlands Indies and the Great War, 1914–1918*, 10–16.

2 – The Dutch Come into the Picture

South Africa, Italy and India.[442] The *Nederlandsche Biograaf- en Mutoscope Maatschappij* was established as a subsidiary of the American Mutoscope and Biograph Company in Amsterdam in December 1898. Apart from its dealings in Mutoscope devices and Biograph projectors in the Netherlands, from its very establishment one of the company's stated goals was to trade in the Dutch colonies and overseas possessions, under the name "The International Mutoscope and Biograph Syndicate".[443] For the purpose of trading in the Netherlands Indies, the company partnered up with a local firm, the Anglo-Java Trading Company (*Engelsch-Javasche Handelsmaatschappij*), formerly known as *Myer en Compagnie*, under the direction of Jan Dirk Myer.[444] Upon its establishment, the Anglo-Java Trading Company had offices in Rijswijk (Batavia) and in Bandung, and further operated sub-contractors in Semarang and Solo (Surakarta).[445] Over the years it was involved in import of bicycles, tracks and parts for electric and steam trams, highly durable flooring material for factories and machines for the sugar, coffee, tea and rice industries, as well as dynamite and petroleum residue fuel.[446] As a company that had experience trading with explosives, it was probably placed in an advantageous position for shipping celluloid films.

In March 1899, *De Locomotief* reported that the *Nederlandsche Biograaf en Mutoscope- Maatschappij* has sent a technician to the Indies, along with the latest model of the Biograph projection unit, in order to hold performances in a specially rented and furnished building. The films on the programme were to include scenes of recent political significance and of high artistic quality.[447] The company reportedly also sent no less than twenty-five Mutoscopes, coin-operated devices for individual viewing, to be stationed in crowded locations. Each mail boat from Europe brought new scenes capturing the latest events, enabling the film programmes to be changed weekly.[448]

442 Charles Musser, *The Emergence of Cinema: The American Screen to 1907* (New York: Scribner, 1990), 145, 172, 176, 264.

443 *Koloniaal Verslag van 1900. Nederlandsch (Oost-) Indië, Bijlage D.*, [3.6.], 15.

444 "Naamlooze Vennootschap", *De Locomotief* (30 January 1899).

445 "Verspreide Nieuwtjes", *Sumatra Post* (7 February 1899); Advertisement, *De Locomotief* (23 June 1899).

446 Advertisement, *De Locomotief* (2 January 1896); "Stoom- of electrische trams", *De Locomotief* (3 February 1899); "Verspreide Indische Berichten", *De Locomotief* (24 March 1899); Advertisement, *De Locomotief* (23 June 1899).

447 "Iets nieuws", *De Locomotief* (10 March 1899).

448 "De Mutoscopen", *Bataviaasch Nieuwsblad* (18 April 1899). Interestingly, Dutch newspapers in the Indies often advertised the show as American Biograph, while Malay newspapers tended to mention the *Nederlandsche Biograaf en Mutoscope-Maatschappij*. A report in *Bataviaasch Nieuwsblad* suggested that foreign names were more attractive than the local variety, so the naming might have been a strategy for audience appeal, depending on each segment of the population and respective newspaper readership ("Nederlandsch-Indië", *Bataviaasch Nieuwsblad* (18 May 1899)). Similarly, the Royal Bioscope later was often advertised and/or referred to as Royal Bioscope in the Dutch press and as *Koninklijke Bioscoop* in the Malay newspapers (see Section 3.2). In Singapore, the American Biograph immediately tried to distinguish itself from its competitors. A lengthy advertisement, which claimed to present "the latest and best invention for the representation of animated photographs" read: "The public of Singapore are kindly requested to note that in no respect is the American Biograph to be connected with the Cinematograph, Kinematograph, Vicograph, or other machines which have shown animated pictures" (Advertisement, *The Straits Times* (11 November 1899)).

The Biograph screenings, under the management of Mr. Ten Broeke, were initially given in a structure rented by the Anglo-Java Trading Company, which previously served as the Fuchs stables (Manège Fuchs) at Tanah Abang, a fashionable European quarter in Batavia's upper town (*bovenstad*, also known as Weltevreden).[449] The space was specially decorated for the performances which were expected to begin in April, as soon as the next French mail boat arrived with the said devices, film reels, and a technician.[450] Interestingly, while other entertainment troupes and moving picture companies often offered cheaper tickets and seating only to "Native" spectators, the American Biograph went one step further by differentiating between third class tickets at 50 cents for "Foreign Orientals" and fourth class tickets at 25 cents for "Natives".[451] Significantly, tickets for box seats at f 1.50, first class at f 1 and second class at f 0.75, presumably for "European" spectators, remained unmarked in the advertisements.

Tickets for the Biograph shows could be reserved at bicycle shop Mijer & Co. in Rijswijk, which was also home to at least one, yet presumably more, of the Mutoscope devices which were already operating for a few days before the Biograph's opening show.[452] Another two locations for Mutoscopes were also in the city's primarily European suburbs: at the G. W. Versteeg restaurant in Noordwijk, and in the recreation room of the Batavia zoo. The Mutoscopes at the zoo were available for viewing at night, between 9 and 12 pm, while the other venues did not specify opening times but pointed out that viewings were possible on Sundays as well. Reports on the new attraction immediately spread to Semarang, as the Batavia correspondent for *De Locomotief* commended admiringly:

> It is remarkable how well one can amuse oneself in Batavia. Balzofiore's company performs two or three operas every week and tonight will be the debut of the "Flying Jordans", a troupe of acrobats. Moreover, mutoscopes are stationed in three locations, where one for 10 cents can obtain a coin to slide into the slot and turn around a handle, summoning in front of their eyes images from a kinematograph.[453]

In June more Mutoscopes, or perhaps the same ones, were stationed at the Chinese *kampung* of Glodok and may have moved later to the nearby Pasar Senen. These were advertised only in the Malay newspapers and the charge was significantly cheaper than the earlier shows for 10 cents, at only f 0.025 per person.[454] By late July, Mutoscopes were placed at Pasar Tanah Abang and

449   The Manège Fuchs at Tanag Abang became home to plenty of other moving picture companies over the following years, many of them refurbishing the space according to their specific needs. See further in Section 5.1.
450   "De Mutoscopen", *Bataviaasch Nieuwsblad* (18 April 1899).
451   Advertisement, *Java-Bode* (22 April 1899).
452   "De Mutoscopen", *Bataviaasch Nieuwsblad* (18 April 1899).
453   "Uit Batavia", *De Locomotief* (20 April 1899).
454   "Chabar Betawi", *Pembrita Betawi* (7 June 1899); Advertisement, *Bintang Barat* (10 July 1899).

Pasar Meester Cornelis while the American Biograph moved its projected exhibition to a tent at Tanah Lapang Glodok (Glodok field), in the Chinese commercial district of Batavia.[455]

Upon opening in Batavia, the company's international flair was highlighted, pointing out that the American Biograph, invented by Herman Casler of New York, was showing "Scenes from France. Scenes from England. Scenes from Holland. Scenes from America [etc... and has been performing for] 2 years at London's Palace Theatre. 1¼ years at Paris's Casino Theatre. 14 months at Berlin's Wintergarten. 2½ years at New York's Keith Theatre. 7 months at Amsterdam's Circus Carré. The first show in the East Indies [on] Monday, 24 April" (see Figure 2–1).[456] Batavia, it implied, was now on the map too. However, although the American Biograph took great pains "not to be confused with the Kinematograph" and other devices, spectators, for the most part, probably did not pay heed to the technical differences between the various devices but cared more about the final result.[457] As the *Java-Bode* wrote: "In what way does a biograph differ exactly from a kinematograph is a question that only the expert may answer; all we can say is that the canvas on which the images are projected is of much larger dimensions and the performances are therefore clearer and more interesting".[458]

Figure 2–1. Advertisement for American Biograph's opening show next to a Mutoscope advertisement, *Bataviaasch Nieuwsblad* (22 April 1899). Retrieved from Delpher on 5 October 2015, http://resolver.kb.nl/resolve?urn=ddd:011032709:mpeg21:a0020.

---

455 Advertisement, *Bintang Barat* (19 July 1899); Advertisement, *Bintang Barat* (3 August 1899); Advertisement, *Bintang Barat* (8 August 1899).
456 Advertisement, *Java-Bode* (22 April 1899).
457 "Biograaf", *Soerabaiasch-Handelsblad* (18 August 1899).

The American Biograph's tent, which later that year travelled to places such as Yogyakarta, Bandung, Surabaya and Singapore, was promoted as the largest ever constructed in Java, at twelve and a half meters in height, allowing to show pictures on a screen twenty square meters bigger than in the Manège Fuchs at Tanah Abang.[459] It could supposedly do with better ventilation, but the electric lighting was deemed good and the seats comfortable, particularly the box seats.[460] The move to Glodok nevertheless meant that the tent was patronised by less European spectators, supposedly due to the distance from the European neighbourhoods.[461] It also involved more direct competition with other entertainers which were performing at the time in the Chinese parts of town, namely: a *bangsawan* troupe at Mangga Besar and Harmston's Circus, which similarly set up its tent at Glodok.[462] By the time the American Biograph returned to Batavia in April 1900 after touring the rest of Java, it chose to go back to the Manège in Tanah Abang, and advertisements stressed that the hall was now illuminated with electric lighting and cooled by electric fans.[463]

2.1.2 Moving Images of Queen Wilhelmina

One of the items on the programme which were found to be most pleasing by journalists and spectators were scenes from the investiture of Queen Wilhelmina which took place in September 1898. These were screened in Batavia for the first time by the American Biograph during its opening show in late April 1899.[464] While they were traded by the *Nederlandsche Biograaf- en Mutoscope Maatschappij*, these scenes were not filmed by the Dutch branch of the company but rather by William Kennedy-Laurie Dickson for the British Mutoscope and Biograph (THE CORONATION OF QUEEN WILHELMINA OF HOLLAND AT AMSTERDAM, British Mutoscope and Biograph Syndicate, 1898).[465] These scenes, showing Queen Wilhelmina and her entourage enter and exit the *Nieuwe Kerk* (New Church) in Amsterdam, to the enthusiastic waving and cheering of the crowds on the street, were purportedly the high point of every American Biograph screening across the Indonesian archipelago over the following months.

458 "Nederlandsch-Indië", *Java-Bode* (25 April 1899). This article also mentions that there was a lecturer who introduced each picture.
459 Advertisements, *Bintang Barat* and *Java-Bode* (19 July 1899).
460 "Uit Soerabaja", *De Locomotief* (11 September 1899). The tent for the second show in Surabaya was full, to the extent that spectators in the box and first class seats had to be turned away ("Nederlandsch-Indië", *Soerabaija-Courant* (9 September 1899)).
461 "Nederlandsch-Indië", *Bataviaasch Nieuwsblad* (27 June 1899).
462 "Nederlandsch-Indië", *Java-Bode* (6 July 1899).
463 Advertisement, *Bataviaasch Nieuwsblad* (2 April 1900).
464 "Nederlandsch-Indië", *Java-Bode* (25 April 1899).
465 The copy held in the collection of Eye Film Institute Netherlands in Amsterdam includes the following scenes: "Solemn entry of HM Queen Wilhelmina in Amsterdam", "HM Queen Wilhelmina on her way to the church", "HM Queen Wilhelmina crowned Queen of the Netherlands", "HM Queen Wilhelmina and her people", "The 'Prins Maurits' company at the entry" ("The Coronation of Queen Wilhelmina of Holland at Amsterdam", Eye Film Institute Netherlands, accessed on 2 February 2016, https://www.eyefilm.nl/en/collection/film-history/film/the-coronation-of-queen-wilhelmina-of-holland-at-amsterdam).

2 – The Dutch Come into the Picture

Spectators were invited to "go on leave to Holland for a few minutes" with a programme that also included beach scenes from Scheveningen (DE BOULEVARD VAN SCHEVENINGEN, British Mutoscope and Biograph Syndicate, 1898) in addition to other pictures, including: scenes showing Dreyfus and Mrs. Dreyfus in the Rennes Military Prison (likely filmed by the French subsidiary, Société Française de Mutoscope et Biographe),[466] *The launch of H.M.S. "Formidable"* (LAUNCH OF H.M. BATTLESHIP "FORMIDABLE" AT PORTSMOUTH, British Mutoscope and Biograph Syndicate, 1898),[467] *Cavalry of 1,500 French Cuirassiers* (DE CUIRASSIERS, British Mutoscope and Biograph Syndicate, 1897),[468] *Panorama of Conway Castle N. Wales* (CONWAY CASTLE: PANORAMIC VIEW OF CONWAY ON THE L. & N.W. RAILWAY, British Mutoscope and Biograph Syndicate, 1898),[469] *A Duel to the Death* (DUEL TO THE DEATH, British Mutoscope and Biograph Syndicate, 1898)[470] and *A Railway Scene* (could be one of various railway phantom ride scenes filmed by various Biograph subsidiaries).[471] Advertisements in Dutch and Malay newspapers read: "A show filled with emotions. A show filled with pleasure. […] A show filled with patriotism."[472] These American Biograph screenings, often accompanied by the sounds of the Dutch national anthem, were thus presented in a way that tried to foster a sense of a shared national identity around the figure of the Queen among the entire spectrum of spectators.[473]

The impact of these scenes naturally went beyond Batavia and ordinary, paying spectators. Screenings were attended by dignitaries, such as the Residents of Surabaya and Madura and the Sultan of Deli.[474] Free shows were offered to orphans of all (Christian) denominations, who were cheering excitedly when they saw the Queen waving at them on screen.[475] Soldiers of the lower ranks of the Dutch Royal Army stationed in Batavia were invited for a free screening, and since three or four evenings were required in order to host all soldiers from

---

466 See "Lives in Film no. I: Alfred Dreyfus – Part 2", The Bioscope, Luke McKernan, accessed on 2 February 2016, http://thebioscope.net/2010/03/11/lives-in-film-no-1-alfred-dreyfus-part-2/. See Stephen Bottomore, "'Zischen und Murren': Die Dreyfus-Affäre und das frühe Kino", *KINtop* 2 (1993): 69–82.

467 See "The Wonders of the Biograph", La Cineteca del Friuli, accessed on 2 February 2016, http://www.cinetecadelfriuli.org/gcm/ed_precedenti/edizione2000/biograph2000.html.

468 Ibid.

469 See Giovanna Fossati, "Multiple Originals: The (Digital) Restoration and Exhibition of Early Films", in Gaudreault et al. (eds.), *A Companion to Early Cinema*, 555.

470 See Elizabeth Carolyn Miller, *Framed: The New Woman Criminal in British Culture at the Fin de Siècle* (Ann Arbor: University of Michigan Press, 2008), 107.

471 "Uit Soerabaja", *De Locomotief* (11 September 1899); Advertisement, *Bintang Barat* (27 April 1899); Advertisement, *Java-Bode* (27 April 1899).

472 Advertisement, *Java-Bode* (29 April 1899); Advertisement, *Bintang Barat* (1 May 1899).

473 "Uit Soerabaja", *De Locomotief* (11 September 1899).

474 "Nederlandsch-Indië", *Soerabaiasch-Handelsblad* (13 September 1899); Advertisement, *Sumatra Post* (10 March 1900).

475 "Nederlandsch-Indië", *Java-Bode* (3 May 1899); "Nederlandsch-Indië", *Bataviaasch Nieuwsblad* (8 May 1899).

the garrison in Surabaya, the *Cantinefonds* was asked to cover the cost of coal used for electric lighting and other operational costs.[476]

The reception of the inauguration scenes also preoccupied journalists reporting about the shows. "One can imagine how the soldiers, white and brown, were elated", *Albrecht's Zondagsblad* reported from a screening for a mixed audience of "Native" and "European" soldiers in Batavia.[477] "The Javanese knew Her Majesty only from her still portrait and now, thanks to this wonderful invention, she appeared in front of them as if in flesh and blood."[478] The *Sumatra Post* in Medan later wrote in regards to repeated screenings of the scenes of Queen Wilhelmina's investiture that "[...] nobody will complain about seeing the graceful apparition of our Queen once more".[479] However, not all spectators were awed into submission by the images of Her Majesty. During a show in Surabaya that hosted students from the Dutch-run secondary school (*Hogereburgerschool*, or HBS), the manager had to request spectators in the front – the location of the cheaper seats for "Natives" – to remain seated while the show was in progress as they were blocking the view of spectators in the back – the higher-paying seats.[480] Several youngsters apparently accompanied the images with whistling and screaming. "Only rascals make such noise", complained *Soerabaiasch-Handelsblad*.[481]

Yet, the American Biograph was not the only company showing scenes from Wilhelmina's investiture at the time. In fact, by the time the American Biograph reached Surabaya with these images in August 1899, similar pictures identified as "the coronation procession in Amsterdam" were already shown in the city by Meranda's Kinematograph and Xylophone in June of that year (for more on Miss Meranda and her Kinematograph shows, see Section 1.3.2).[482] These may have been scenes, commissioned by Franz Anton Nöggerath Sr. of the Variété Flora theatre in Amsterdam, which were filmed by two cameramen invited over especially from London, among them Charles Urban who was then managing director of the Warwick Trading Company (INHULDIGING KONINGIN WILHELMINA TE AMSTERDAM, Filmfabriek F.A. Nöggerath, 1898).[483] Nevertheless, Miss Meranda's screenings were a far less

---

476 "Nederlandsch-Indië", *Java-Bode* (8 May 1899); "Uit Soerabaja", *De Locomotief* (18 September 1899). Before an agreement on the deal was reached, on the first night of shows for soldiers in Surabaya, 2,000 spectators attended and the *Cantinefonds* paid 165 guilders.

477 "De Biograaf en het garnizoen van Batavia", *Albrecht's Zondagsblad* (14 May 1899).

478 Ibid.

479 "De Biograph", *Sumatra Post* (26 February 1900). The newspaper set out to defend the American Biograph against the common misconception that it was changing its programmes every night, explaining that changes were less frequent and that only the inauguration scenes were to be repeated again.

480 "Biograaf", *Soerabaiasch-Handelsblad* (18 September 1899).

481 Ibid.

482 "Uit Soerabaja", *De Locomotief* (6 June 1899). Miss Meranda further screened these scenes in Semarang in August, and most likely in other parts of Java ("Nederlandsch-Indië", *De Locomotief* (28 August 1899)).

483 See Charles Urban, *A Yank in Britain: The Lost Memoirs of Charles Urban, Film Pioneer*, edited by Luke McKernan, Hastings East Sussex: The Projection Box, 1999), 62; "Inhuldiging Koningin Wilhelmina te Amsterdam", Eye Film Institute Netherlands, accessed on 2 February 2016, https://www.eyefilm.nl/en/collection/film-history/film/inhuldiging-koningin-wilhelmina-te-amsterdam.

2 – The Dutch Come into the Picture

inclusive affair than the one orchestrated by the American Biograph. The Kinematograph shows were given at the Surabaya Theatre and tickets were offered at one guilder per person for early evening shows (and children under the age of ten years at half price), and later evening shows at two guilders for a man and one guilder for a woman, doubtless in an attempt to encourage couples to go to the show together rather than an appeal to single women to attend the theatre.[484] No advertisements for these shows were found in the Malay newspapers.

Moving images of Queen Wilhelmina continued to feature over the next couple of years on film programmes of various companies. H. Salzwedel's American Biograph or Java Biorama, which may have taken over Ten Broeke's outfit, screened throughout 1900 and 1902 at various locations the scenes taken on the occasion of the investiture and billed as "Arrival of H.M. the Queen in Amsterdam" (possibly PLECHTIGE INTOCHT VAN H.M. KONINGIN WIL-HELMINA IN AMSTERDAM, British Mutoscope and Biograph Syndicate, 1898).[485] In addition, Salzwedel screened pictures from Wilhelmina's wedding to Duke Hendrik van Mecklenburg-Schwerin, which took place in February 1901 (HUWELIJKSSTOET TER GELEGENHEID VAN HET HUWELIJK VAN WIL-HELMINA EN HENDRIK, Nederlandsch Biograaf- en Mutoscoop Maatschappij, 1901 and/or DE HUWELIJKSPLECHTIGHEDEN TE 'S-GRAVENHAGE, Nederlandsch Biograaf- en Mutoscoop Maatschappij, 1901. See more on Salzwedel in Section 2.2 below).[486]

The Netherlands Bioscope Company (*Nederlandsche Bioscope Maatschappij*) screened images of Wilhelmina and her husband-to-be at the Manège Fuchs in Batavia in December 1900.[487] Nast's Kinematograph and Xylophone screened scenes described as "the arrival of H. M. the Queen in Amsterdam" and "the royal wedding celebrations" in Surabaya in August 1902, in direct competition with the Java Cineograph Company which was showing at the same time Nöggerath's FEESTELIJKE ONTVANGST VAN H.M. KONINGIN WIL-HELMINA EN DEN PRINS-GEMAAL TE SCHWERIN (Filmfabriek F.A. Nöggerath,

---

484 Advertisement, *Soerabaiasch-Handelsblad* (21 May 1899).

485 See "Plechtige Intocht van H. M. Koningin Wilhelmina in Amsterdam", Eye Film Institute Netherlands, accessed on 2 February 2016, https://www.eyefilm.nl/en/collection/film-history/film/plechtige-intocht-van-hm-koningin-wilhelmina-in-amsterdam.

486 Advertisement, *De Locomotief* (24 December 1900); Advertisement, *Bintang Soerabaia* (11 February 1901); "Uit Bandoeng", *Het Nieuws van den Dag voor Nederlandsch-Indië* (29 June 1901); Advertisement, *Bataviaasch Nieuwsblad* (16 September 1901); "Kindervoorstelling", *Sumatra Post* (21 July 1902). See "De Huwelijksplechtigheden te 's-Gravenhave", Eye Film Institute Netherlands, accessed on 2 February 2016, https://www.eyefilm.nl/en/collection/film-history/film/de-huwelijksplechtigheden-te-s-gravenhage; "Huwelijksstoet ter gelegenheid van het huwelijk van Wilhelmina en Hendrik", Eye Film Institute Netherlands, accessed on 2 February 2016, https://www.eyefilm.nl/en/collection/film-history/film/huwelijksstoet-ter-gelegenheid-van-het-huwelijk-van-wilhelmina-en.

487 Advertisement, *Bintang Betawi* (5 December 1900). According to descriptions, these scenes may have been INTOCHT VAN H.M. DE KONINGIN EN HERTOG HENDRIK TE DEN HAAG (1900) and Nöggerath's INTOCHT VAN HERTOG HENDRIK VAN MECKLENBURG EN H.M. DE KONINGIN AAN HET STAATSSPOOR TE 'S-GRAVENHAGE (1900).

1901).[488] Finally, Abdulally Esoofally first screened the investiture scenes in Medan in October 1901 as the New Bioscope ("The Coronation and arrival of H. M. the Queen"), and continued screening them later as the Royal Bioscope in Batavia in April 1903 until as late as January 1905 ("The Coronation of H. M. the Queen of Holland", possibly again INHULDIGING KONINGIN WILHELMINA TE AMSTERDAM, Filmfabriek F.A. Nöggerath, 1898. For more on Esoofally, see Section 3.2).[489]

2.1.3 Slow Decline

After completing his tour of Java, on 13 October 1899, the *Soerabaija-Courant* reported that Mr. Ten Broeke, director of the American Biograph, was to leave the next day for Singapore on board the steamship *Japara*, to be followed by the Biograph on 25 October.[490] It had a successful run of nearly two months in a tent located in front of the Beach Hotel in Singapore, showing many of the titles that were earlier included on its tour of Java. Before heading from Singapore to Sumatra, the American Biograph offered up for sale in auction its portable engine and a dynamo: "1. A to H. P. Portable Engine, nearly new, by Marshall and Co. In perfect working order. 2. A Schukert Dynamo, 72 amperes, 110 volts, (direct) mounted on a 2 wheel tumbril. In good working order, with windlass for cable."[491] The *Sumatra Post* later explained that these machines were left behind in Singapore since the local electricity company in Medan (*Electriciteit-Maatschappij Medan*) could provide the operator with the necessary electric power for the shows.[492] The only issue remaining was that the company provided alternating current, so a converter was required in order to get direct current to operate the device. The newspaper further speculated, after consulting with a local "specialist", that the cost of the Biograph device was in the region of thirty to forty thousand Mexican dollars, thus between 43,000 and 57,000 guilders (at an exchange rate of 0.7 per guilder), and that each film of twenty pictures could cost between 1,000 and 1,500 guilders.[493]

488 See "Uit Soerabaja", *De Locomotief* (12 August 1902); Advertisement, *Soerabaiasch-Handelsblad* (15 August 1902). "Feestelijke ontvangst van H.M. Koningin Wilhelmina en den Prins-Gemaal te Schwerin", Eye Film Institute Netherlands, accessed on 2 February 2016, https://www.eyefilm.nl/en/collection/film-history/film/feestelijke-ontvangst-van-hm-koningin-wilhelmina-en-den-prins-gemaal-te. On the possible connection between Nast and Miss Meranda, see section 1.3.2.

489 "De Bioscope-voorstelling", *Deli Courant* (7 October 1901); "De Bioscoop", *Het Nieuws van den Dag voor Nederlandsch-Indië* (2 April 1903); Advertisement, *Het Nieuws van den Dag voor Nederlandsch-Indië* (11 January 1905).

490 "Nederlandsch-Indië", *Soerabaija-Courant* (13 October 1899). According to the shipping lists, Ten Broeke in fact left for Singapore on 17 October ("Vertrokken passagiers", *De Locomotief* (19 October 1899)).

491 Advertisements, *The Straits Times* and *The Singapore Free Press* (22 January 1899). It is not clear why an exhibitor would have opted to sell equipment that could have come handy again later, but it appears that many exhibitors often unloaded themselves of all sorts of equipment, as we also saw in Chapter 1. As Suryadi found in his research on gramophone and phonograph operators in the Indies, and as he related to me in a private exchange, many of these exhibitors also used to put their equipment up for sale when leaving one island or another. Further research of this behaviour is required.

492 "Plaatselijk Nieuws", *Sumatra Post* (21 February 1900).

493 This is likely to be an exaggerated price based on the fact that, just a few years earlier, the Ripograph or Giant Cinematograph advertised in the Singaporean and Indies newspapers that it was imported from Paris at a cost of 10,000 (presumably, Mexican) dollars (Advertisement, *The Straits Times* (12 May 1897); Advertisement, *Java-Bode* (29 May 1897)).

2 – The Dutch Come into the Picture

Ten Broeke paid a personal visit to the offices of *Sumatra Post* to relay that the American Biograph "[...] 'is completely different from the kinematograph which was shown here recently', [...]. But what it was exactly, he would not say."⁴⁹⁴ Shows in Medan were given in the building of the Gymnastics Union relatively early in the evening, at quarter past six. The tickets advertised in the Dutch newspapers were rather expensive for this sort of entertainment: stalls for $1.50 and first class for $1. There were presumably cheaper tickets for unadvertised lower classes available, as suggested by the designation of "first class" seats, but probably only for "Native" spectators.⁴⁹⁵ Possibly due to this, and despite all the attention and promotion efforts of Ten Broeke, the one-month run in Medan was not very successful. The opening show hardly drew in any spectators, and returning spectators constantly complained that not enough new pictures were being offered from one programme to the next.⁴⁹⁶ "The Biograph attracts many visitors and remains a remarkable invention", wrote the *Sumatra Post* a few days later, possibly endorsed by Ten Broeke. "It is only a pity that it is not available always and everywhere."⁴⁹⁷ After offering a free show to soldiers of the garrison, the American Biograph suddenly changed its name on the advertisements to the Netherlands Mutoscope and Biograph Company (*De Nederlandsche Mutoscoop en Biograph Maatschappij*).⁴⁹⁸ For its last few nights it also moved to the structure of the *bangsawan* troupe, and cheaper tickets were now advertised: first class seats at $1.50, second class at $1, and third class at $0.50.⁴⁹⁹

Ten Broeke and his wife travelled from Medan to Batavia on board the steamship *Reyniersz* on 20 March 1900, and the opening show of the second run in Batavia began on 4 April at the Manège in Tanah Abang.⁵⁰⁰ The highlights of the programme were scenes from the streets of Amsterdam, as well as pictures depicting the Boer War (see further in Section 2.2.2).⁵⁰¹ At this point, the manager decided to sell whatever Mutoscopes were still in his possession, asking to be contacted directly at the Manège for further details and prices. The advertisement here too was signed by *De Nederlandsche Indische Mutoscopen en Biograph Maatschappij*.⁵⁰² Some Mutoscopes were still being

494 "American Biograph", *Sumatra Post* (20 February 1900). Ten Broeke was possibly referring to the fact that the Biograph device was designed to project 68mm film strips, as opposed to other projection units intended for 35mm format.
495 Advertisement, *Sumatra Post* (18 February 1900). This research unfortunately did not find advertisements for these shows in Malay newspapers.
496 "American Biograph", *Sumatra Post* (24 February 1900); "De Biograph", *Sumatra Post* (26 February 1900); "American Biograph", *Sumatra Post* (28 February 1900).
497 "Zaterdagsche Causerie", *Sumatra Post* (3 March 1900).
498 Advertisement, *Sumatra Post* (5 March 1900); Advertisement, *Sumatra Post* (6 March 1900).
499 Advertisement, *Sumatra Post* (8 March 1900).
500 "Vertrokken passagiers", *Sumatra Post* (21 March 1900); Advertisement, *Bataviaasch Nieuwsblad* (2 April 1900).
501 Advertisement, *Bataviaasch Nieuwsblad* (2 April 1900); Advertisement, *Bataviaasch Nieuwsblad* (4 May 1900).
502 Advertisement, *Bataviaasch Nieuwsblad* (14 April 1900).

operated a month later by Ten Broeke in Surabaya, where he obtained a license to place Mutoscopes at Grimm & Co. restaurant, located on one of the city's main interchanges at Pasar Besar (see further on this location for moving picture shows in Section 4.1).[503] These Mutoscopes were finally offered up for sale in Surabaya in June 1900.[504] Mr. Obdam, a member of the *Indische Bond* (the union of Indo-Europeans) in Surabaya, was trying to convince fellow members to take over the operation of the "mutoscope company" with an investment of 8,500 guilders, specifically: 100 guilders per share – accounting for 8,000 guilders, in addition to 500 guilders for the cost of operation and exchange of new film reels. This enterprise was expected to prove profitable and to provide employment for union members.[505]

It is unclear to what extent the *Nederlandsche Biograaf- en Mutoscope Maatschappij* was involved in the Indies enterprise by this point, if at all. By July 1900, the manager of the Dutch subsidiary in Amsterdam, Daniel Louis Uyttenboogaart, was fired by the company's board, in part, at least, due to poor management and reporting on business in the Indies.[506] *The Nederlandsche Biograaf- en Mutoscope Maatschappij* was declared bankrupt on 27 June 1902.[507]

2.2 The American Biograph as Java Biorama

The operator of the Java Biorama was Mr. Herman Salzwedel, a German photographer who first arrived in the Indies from Shanghai in May 1877. He initially opened a photography studio in Batavia in March 1878, and in May 1879 opened a studio in Surabaya, where he moved to a year later. In the mid-1880s Salzwedel sold his studio and left the Indies for Shanghai and later the Netherlands. Other branches of Salzwedel's studio were opened in Medan in 1886 and in Makassar in 1887. The studio was registered as a public limited company in 1900, yet Versnel, the leading shareholder, went bankrupt in July 1901.[508] Salzwedel returned to the Indies in the early 1890s and began dabbling with moving pictures in the form of dissolving views (magic lantern) and Kinematograph shows in 1897 and 1898, holding screenings at European Club houses, as well as shows targeting "Native" audiences, for instance, when performing at the *Sekaten* festival in Solo (Surakarta), a Javanese traditional week-long celebration marking the birth of the Islamic prophet Muhammad.[509]

503 "Onze Nieuwtjes", *Soerabaija-Courant* (22 May 1900).
504 "Uit Soerabaja", *De Locomotief* (5 June 1900).
505 Ibid.
506 "Biograaf en Mutoscope", *De Tijd* (27 July 1900).
507 See "Nederlandsche Biograaf- en Mutoscope Maatschappij", Eye Film Institute Netherlands, accessed on 2 February 2016, https://www.eyefilm.nl/en/collection/film-history/company/nederlandsche-biograaf-en-mutoscope-maatschappij.
508 For more on Salzwedel and the history of his namesake photography studio, see Steven Wachlin, "Salzwedel", in Karin Peterson and Steven Wachlin (eds.), *In het Voetspoor van Louis Couperus* (Amsterdam: KIT Publishers, 2009), 112–118.
509 "Nederlandsch-Indië", *De Locomotief* (9 December 1897); "Uit Loemadjang", *Soerabaiasch-Handelsblad* (10 January 1898); "Uit Solo", *De Locomotief* (3 August 1898).

2 – The Dutch Come into the Picture

From October 1900 to August 1902 Salzwedel was touring in the region with shows advertised as the American Biograph or Java Biorama. Since it appears that he performed some of the films on the American Biograph's earlier programmes, such as the investiture of Queen Wilhelmina or scenes from the Boer War, it is possible that Salzwedel took on the Biograph outfit from Ten Broeke or that they partnered up. In December 1900 the public in Surabaya was told to expect a visit by the American Biograph, a company described as having toured some of the main locations in the Indies over the past couple of years and owned by "two of our townspeople".[510] In February 1901, when the shows in Surabaya approached, *Soerabaija-Courant* pointed out that the "biograph is the same such as the one shown at the time by Mr. van den [sic] Broeke".[511] Moreover, while Salzwedel's name appeared at the bottom of the Surabaya advertisements throughout the entire stint, in March Ten Broeke was suddenly mentioned in newspapers as a returning performer in connection with the Java Biorama.[512]

The Java Biorama had a successful run for almost two years, visiting locations such as Malang, Semarang, Pekalongan, Tegal, Cirebon, Surabaya, Bandung and Batavia on Java, Kuala Lumpur and Singapore in British Malaya, and Medan and Binjai on Sumatra.[513] In its advertisements the public, once again, was "[...] kindly requested not to confuse the Biograph with the Cinematograph, as the Biograph is an entirely new invention which has never been shown here before".[514] Paradoxically, the promotion material simultaneously stressed that the company had been giving shows in the Indies before. The Biorama was billed as "an improved cinematograph, keeping flickering down to a minimum" or simply as the "King of Cinematographs", reportedly earning 700–800 guilders per night in Surabaya.[515] In Medan, the Java Biorama was even found to be "better than the American Biograph", which is ironic considering that the Java Biorama repeatedly advertised that its shows were given by an American Biograph unit.[516] Nevertheless, many of the new scenes offered by Salzwedel appear to have been 35mm films, which would not have

510 "Uit Soerabaja", *De Locomotief* (11 December 1900).
511 "Onze Nieuwtjes", *Soerabaija-Courant* (1 February 1901).
512 "Onze Nieuwtjes", *Soerabaija-Courant* (16 March 1901).
513 "Ditjes en Datjes uit Malang", *Sumatra Post* (17 October 1900); "Nederlandsch-Indië", *De Locomotief* (17 December 1900); "Nederlandsch-Indië", *De Locomotief* (19 January 1901); Advertisement, *Soerabaiasch-Handelsblad* (8 February 1901); "Uit Bandoeng", *Het Nieuws van den Dag voor Nederlandsch-Indië* (29 June 1901); Advertisement, *Bataviaasch Nieuwsblad* (16 September 1901); Advertisement, *Malay Mail* (15 February 1902); Advertisement, *Malay Mail* (12 March 1902); Advertisement, *Sumatra Post* (18 June 1902); Advertisement, *Sumatra Post* (22 August 1902). I thank Nadi Tofighian for the references to the Java Biorama shows in Singapore and Kuala Lumpur.
514 Advertisement, *De Locomotief* (24 December 1900).
515 "Nederlandsch-Indië", *De Locomotief* (24 December 1900); Advertisement, *Soerabaiasch-Handelsblad* (13 March 1901); "Uit Soerabaja", *De Locomotief* (23 August 1902). The 700 to 800 guilder profit per night seems to be an exaggeration. According to an advertisement that appeared in Surabaya and Semarang newspapers in late December 1900, a "Cinematograph (Biograph)" available for immediate operation was up for sale, and promoted as able to generate an income of 50 to 200 guilders per day (Advertisements, *De Locomotief* and *Soerabaiasch-Handelsblad* (21 December 1900)).
516 "Java Biorama", *Sumatra Post* (12 July 1902).

been possible to screen with a Biograph projector of 68mm (see further in Section 2.2.3). Showmen in this period would have often used names of projection devices other than the ones they were using, simply to benefit from a recognisable and recognised brand name. It is therefore possible that Salzwedel might have travelled with more than one device, such as the Kinematograph he already performed with since 1897 in addition to a Biograph device acquired later, but that he chose to highlight the Biograph due to the positive reputation it had already. Alternatively, he could have simply been using the "Biograph" as a marketing strategy, considering Ten Broeke's earlier success.

2.2.1 Touring Pains on Java, 1900–1901

The first records found in this research of Salzwedel's shows as Java Biorama are from Malang, in East Java. These were reported about in several Indies newspapers – from Java and Sumatra – in October 1900.[517] "The big tent of Mr. Salzwedel from Surabaya is stationed at the moment on the *Alun Alun*, where for the first time here the Biograph, or the Java Biorama, as he named it, can be admired by anyone who wants to keep up with the new inventions, which in this field rapidly follow each other these days."[518] The tent, located next to a carousel and surrounded by "Native and Chinese *warungs*", was reportedly pretty much packed on the opening night, and the good reviews passed by word-of-mouth meant that soon the tent was so full that spectators were refused entry and forced to try their luck again another night.[519] Even after a month of shows, reports claimed that the Java Biorama's tent was still well occupied since the prices were reduced and the tickets for "Natives" cost only 10 cents.[520] According to one reporter, other seating ranks of the Java Biorama were also fairly well attended thanks to the many foreigners who were staying in Malang at the time, fully occupying the hotels.[521] It was outdoing the carousel which, at the same cost of ten cents per ride, was found to be too expensive.

Shows the following month in Semarang were initially less enthusiastically received, despite the advertisements claiming that "the tent is packed every night".[522]

> Unknown, unloved; this is what the owner of the Biorama experienced at his first show yesterday evening, as many places in the neat tent remained unoccupied. It seems that the public [confused] his device with the kinematograph [*kinematograaf*], which is linked with so many unpleasant memories for our eyes.

517 "Ditjes en Datjes uit Malang", *Het Nieuws van den Dag voor Nederlandsch-Indië* (17 October 1900); "Ditjes en Datjes uit Malang", *Sumatra Post* (17 October 1900); "Uit Malang", *De Locomotief* (19 October 1900).

518 "Uit Malang", *De Locomotief* (19 October 1900), emphasis added.

519 "Uit Malang", *Het Nieuws van den Dag voor Nederlandsch-Indië* (27 October 1900), emphasis added; "Uit Malang", *De Locomotief* (19 October 1900).

520 "Uit Malang", *Het Nieuws van den Dag voor Nederlandsch-Indië* (8 November 1900).

521 "Uit Malang", *De Locomotief* (10 November 1900).

522 Advertisement, *De Locomotief* (24 December 1900).

2 – The Dutch Come into the Picture

The Biorama is an improved kinematograph, the troublesome flicker of the transmitted images is brought down to a minimum, and [...] it is almost entirely successful, the annoying vibrations are gone, the images are clear and so big that one can easily recognise the people as if they were among one's acquaintances. Indeed we have seen a known sight and naturally also recognised: Uncle Paul [Kruger] riding from his home to the *Volksraad* in his carriage. In one word, it was beautiful![523]

To counter this trend, Salzwedel immediately decided to add more shows at cheaper prices, with special emphasis on enabling children to attend screenings as well: shows from 7 to 8 pm at f 1 for first class, f 0.75 for second class, f 0.25 for third class and f 0.15 for fourth class; and more expensive shows from 9 to 10.30 pm, with the same pricing of the opening show, at f 1.50 for first class, f 1 for second class, f 0.50 for third class, and f 0.25 for fourth class "for Javanese only".[524] This seemed to improve the situation, as both early and late evening shows became increasingly busier, and Chinese spectators were singled out as the keenest visitors attending performances in both time slots.[525] The Resident with his family and the Regent with his wife also attended a screening.[526] "Everyone who has seen [the Biorama...] declares that a visit to the tent would absolutely be worth your while", *De Locomotief* commented. "It is also remarkable [to witness] the technical progress in this sort of amusement."[527] A couple of weeks later, as the monsoon rains became heavier, Salzwedel informed via the newspapers that it was becoming too difficult to continue holding shows in the early evenings. "Parents wanting to give their children a few pleasant hours should not delay going to the tent for too long, as they only have a couple of more days left [of early evening shows]. The later evening shows will continue as usual."[528]

By the end of his stay in Semarang in mid-January 1901, Salzwedel's departure was lamented: "The Biograph cannot constantly remain in Surabaya, other inhabitants of Java also want to benefit from this truly enjoyable entertainment."[529] Among the locations on Salzwedel's planned route were reportedly Pekalongan, Tegal and Cirebon in Central Java, west of Semarang.[530] However, the most immediate destination was Surabaya. The large tent was set up on the grounds next to the Courthouse, which was previously occupied by a steam carousel. The same trick of early evening shows at cheaper entrance prices and later evening shows for more expensive tickets was repeated.

---

523 "Nederlandsch-Indië", *De Locomotief* (24 December 1900), emphasis added.
524 Advertisement, *De Locomotief* (24 December 1900); Advertisement, *Selompret Melajoe* (22 December 1900).
525 "Promotie", *Bataviaasch Nieuwsblad* (12 January 1901).
526 "Nederlandsch-Indië", *De Locomotief* (2 January 1901).
527 "De voorstellingen", *De Locomotief* (27 December 1900).
528 "De Biograaf", *De Locomotief* (11 January 1901).
529 "De laatste voorstelling", *De Locomotief* (19 January 1901).
530 Ibid.

Nevertheless, the monsoon rains continued to plague the Java Biorama's allegedly "completely waterproof tent".[531] Just a few nights after the successful opening show which was attended by "many people", only twenty spectators braved the elements and ventured to the tent, leading to the show's cancellation.[532] "Good business will probably not be made", *De Locomotief*'s Surabaya correspondent speculated, "because we are, so to speak, in the midst of the West Monsoon."[533] Nevertheless, Salzwedel stuck it out in Surabaya until the end of May, as attendance figures gradually improved and newspaper reports lent more support.[534]

It appears that outright box office success continued to elude Salzwedel. By late June the Java Biorama's tent was stationed in Bandung and was often under-performing in comparison with other popular entertainment forms on site. Thus, the musical evening at the *Sociëteit* supposedly robbed the Biorama's opening show of potential spectators.[535] And as soon as the Java Biorama was joined at the *Alun Alun* by a steam carousel and the tent of Harmston's Circus in early August, the competition only got tougher. "The local residents of Kerkplein can say our 'rest is gone' [*Ruhe ist hin*], because aside for the circus with its own music corps, [there is] also a carousel that goes round to its own organ sounds. And between the circus and carousel stands the tent of Mr. Salzwedel's Biograph, which entertains the public in a calmer manner. The square now provides the spectacle of a true Dutch fairground [*kermis*]."[536] Salzwedel's determination to stay in Bandung under these conditions, a reporter for the *Bataviaasch Nieuwsblad* opined, was not so much a reflection of the good business he was making there as much as an attempt to uphold his favourable reputation.[537]

By the time Salzwedel reached Batavia in September, the *Java-Bode* recommended a visit to the Java Biorama's tent at Koningsplein based on positive reviews from other newspapers on Java, noting that the admission prices were moderate: first class for ƒ 1.50, second class for ƒ 1, third class for ƒ 0.50, and fourth class for ƒ 0.25 ("for Natives only").[538] However, the enthusiasm somewhat abated after the opening show, once it was realised that the pictures

---

531 Advertisement, *Bintang Soerabaia* (11 February 1901); "Onze Nieuwtjes", *Soerabaija-Courant* (1 February 1901).
532 "India Ollanda", *Bintang Soerabaia* (12 February 1901). A few months later, in Bandung, spectators did not find the boggy terrain on which the tent was set up particularly appealing for an evening's outing. "Uit Bandoeng", *Het Nieuws van den Dag voor Nederlandsch-Indië* (3 July 1901).
533 "Uit Soerabaja", *De Locomotief* (14 February 1901).
534 "Nederlandsch-Indië", *Soerabaiasch-Handelsblad* (20 April 1901); Advertisement, *Soerabaiasch-Handelsblad* (29 May 1901).
535 "Uit Bandoeng", *Bataviaasch Nieuwsblad* (29 June 1901).
536 "Uit Bandoeng", *De Locomotief* (8 August 1901).
537 "Uit Bandoeng", *Bataviaasch Nieuwsblad* (5 August 1901).
538 "Java-Biorama", *Java-Bode* (16 September 1901); Advertisement, *Bataviaasch Nieuwsblad* (16 September 1901).

had clearly been in use for a considerable time and some left much to be desired in terms of clarity.[539] To add to Salzwedel's strife, a few days later, the Batavia police had to remove a "Native" employee of the Java Biorama who was diagnosed with cholera and shut down the tent for three days, by order of the Assistant Resident, while the area was disinfected.[540] Several touring entertainment companies, particularly those that had to enter by steamship from locations outside the Indies, were struggling to obtain permits for their shows at the time.[541] Even companies already on site were facing problems related to hygiene and healthcare (see also the case of the Java Cineograph in Section 2.3).

The Java Biorama stayed in Java until the beginning of 1902, when Salzwedel, with his wife and children, travelled from Batavia to Singapore on board the steamship *Mossel* on 17 January.[542]

2.2.2 Touring Successes on Java: The Boer War on Screen

Although the objective success of Salzwedel's Java Biorama tour on Java seems questionable in the light of the findings presented here, he did reap some successes. The scenes on the programme were generally found to provide great variety, with each number clearly announced "in advance with clear letters on screen by the Biograph itself".[543] Another report mentioned that Salzwedel had a repertoire of about 120 pictures in his possession, with 24 screened in a single programme.[544] The scenes highlighted in several reports were "old memories", in which a few older men revive the fire of their youth when browsing through illustrations of beautiful female figures, "the astronomer's dream", "a cockfight", a scene showing a stormy sea, and the arrival of H.M. Queen Wilhelmina. "The two-hour [show...] flies by."[545]

The images that attracted most Dutch spectators' attention were scenes from the Boer War (also known as the Second Anglo-Boer War, or the South African War), which broke out on 11 October 1899, with Boer strikes in Natal and the Cape Colony, and ended up as a drawn out guerrilla war, finally stamped out by the British who annexed the Boer territories to the British Empire in May 1902. The Dutch government in the Netherlands tried to maintain a form of "aloofness" around the conflict between the British and the Boer states of the

---

539 "Java Biorama", *Bataviaasch Nieuwsblad* (18 September 1901).
540 "Verspreide Indische Berichten", *De Locomotief* (23 September 1901).
541 Harmston's Circus, for instance, was turned away by the local authorities in Surabaya due to the cholera situation ("Een kopje voor Harmston", *De Locomotief* (24 September 1901)). Other preventative measures employed were banning mobile street food stalls (*warungs*) and forbidding minor class sailors from disembarking arriving vessels ("Uit Atjeh", *Sumatra Post* (1 August 1901); "Correspondentie", *Het Nieuws van den Dag voor Nederlandsch Indië* (3 July 1901)).
542 "Vertokken Passagiers", *De Locomotief* (20 January 1902).
543 "Uit Malang", *De Locomotief* (19 October 1900).
544 "Uit Malang", *Het Nieuws van den Dag voor Nederlandsch-Indië* (22 October 1900).
545 "Uit Malang", *De Locomotief* (19 October 1900). The astronomer scene was possibly LA LUNE À UN MÈTRE (Méliès, 1898). The cockfight might have been COMBATS DE COQS (Pathé Frères, ca. 1897) or GROS TEMPS EN MER (Pathé Frères, 1900) or TEMPÊTE EN MER (Pathé Frères, 1900).

South African Republic (Transvaal Republic) and the Orange Free State, very much in order to protect its colonial interests in the Indies.[546] Any breach of neutrality, officials in The Hague feared, might be used as an excuse by the British to encroach on Java.[547] However, public opinion among the Dutch in the Netherlands and Netherlands Indies generally tended to lean in favour of the Boers and was, at times, openly disappointed with the Dutch government's inaction.[548]

Indies newspapers reported about the ongoing war on a daily basis, "Boer songs were sung and played everywhere and local *Transvaalfonds* were established in all cities and large towns of the Indies".[549] Auguste Mahieu's Sinar Stamboel company held a performance in Semarang in November 1899 for the benefit of the Transvaal cause, which even concluded with a Boer anthem translated into Malay.[550] Other *stambul* companies and cultural organisations, including Mr. Silbermann's wax museum and stereoscope pavilion, were also putting together war benefits across the Indies.[551] In addition, other popular entertainment forms, such as moving picture shows and panoramas, were displaying images depicting the battle scenes.[552] Many of the Boer War films were in fact staged scenes made by various companies in different countries in order to meet demand for such depictions and, according to Stephen Bottomore, "most showmen and spectators would have realised that these were merely representations, illustrations of war, and not reproductions of actual incidents – though there were many spectators who did not know".[553] There were also some eight cameramen filming in South Africa during the war (including Dickson, mentioned above, and Joseph Rosenthal who will be mentioned below in connection with the Russo-Japanese War) representing the British Mutoscope and Biograph Company, the Warwick Trading Company, and Robert Paul, among others.[554]

---

546 See Maarten Kuitenbrouwer, *The Netherlands and the Rise of Modern Imperialism: Colonies and Foreign Policy, 1870–1902*, trans. Hugh Beyer (New York: Berg, 1991), 294–320.

547 Dijk, *The Netherlands Indies and the Great War*, 12. The Dutch were also reliant on Britain for lines of communication between the Netherlands and Netherlands Indies, as most of the submarine telegraph lines were under British control, and this raised great concern and even calls for initiating telegraphic lines between the colony and the mother country which were independent of Britain (ibid., 13).

548 See further on Dutch reactions to the Boer War in Kuitenbrouwer, *The Netherlands and the Rise of Modern Imperialism*, 282–230.

549 Cohen, *The Komedie Stamboel*, 290, emphasis added.

550 Ibid., 291. "Gross income was 369.55 guilders from ticket sales, with an additional 83.60 guilders from donations solicited from spectators. When 139.49 guilders were deducted for expenses this yielded a net income for charity of 313.66 guilders – 'a splendid result indeed!' The sum raised was directly comparable to the gross income of 468 guilders raised for the Transvaalfonds from a soirée variée held at Semarang's schouwburg on 30 October" (Cohen, *The Komedie Stamboel*, 430, endnote 50, quoted from *De Locomotief* (17 November 1899).

551 "Nederlandsch-Indië", *Java-Bode* (26 October 1899).

552 For instance, J. Paul's Grand Panorama and Panopticum Company travelled from Singapore to Surabaya in March 1900 ("Nederlandsch-Indië", *Soerabaiasch-Handelsblad* (10 March 1900)).

553 Bottomore, *Filming, Faking and Propaganda*, Chapter 10, 1.

554 Ibid., Chapter 9, 2.

2 – The Dutch Come into the Picture

The Java Biorama's programme headlined scenes of "[...] the Boers marching to the border, upon which the Transvaal anthem was heard".[555] "The applause did not stop", the *Soerabaija-Courant* reported.[556] But while the authenticity of these scenes was not questioned, the precision of their presentation was. As the *Bataviaasch Nieuwsblad* later noted, "Boers marching to the border" was actually a mistitling since the scenes were in fact of English volunteers, identified by the slouch hats they were sporting.[557] "The titling of the photoplays [*lichtbeelden*] can do with a bit more accuracy."[558] Advertised as "Battle of the Boers at Spion Kop", it was likely used to achieve the exact opposite effect at locations with pro-Anglo sentiments.[559] As *Het Nieuws van den Dag voor Nederlandsch-Indië* wrote:

> "The Departure [*vertrek*] of Boers to the Border" drew a spontaneous outburst of enthusiasm from the Dutch section of the audience. Unfortunately, it was skullduggery [*Boerenbedriegerij*] and a tableau of double usage. Because as soon as the Biorama is displayed in an English site, the Bioramist will immediately change the Boers into Englishmen and call the tableau: "Cape Volunteers, advancing to the border". The destination remains but the name of the trekkers changes.[560]

Other Boer War scenes found during the Java Biorama's tour of Java were: "Ambulance in South Africa"[561] and "President Kruger getting into the ceremonial carriage".[562] These pictures similarly attracted the attention of the Malay press, which highlighted the comic aspect of the scenes showing "big and fat" President Kruger carried by a large horse-drawn carriage.[563]

---

555 "Onze Nieuwtjes", *Soerabaija-Courant* (20 April 1901).

556 Ibid.

557 "Java Biorama", *Bataviaasch Nieuwsblad* (18 September 1901).

558 Ibid.

559 It was possibly one of Dickson's (Biograph films (BATTLE OF SPION KOP: AMBULANCE CORPS CROSSING THE TUGELA RIVER, British Mutoscope and Biograph Syndicate, 1900) or a scene from Pathé (ÉPISODE DE LA BATAILLE DE SPION-KOP, Pathé Frères, 1900). See "Battle of Spion Kop: Ambulance Corps Crossing the Tugela River", Colonial Film: Moving Images of the British Empire, accessed on 2 February 2016, http://www.colonialfilm.org.uk/node/1943; Henri Bousquet (ed.), *Catalogue Pathé des années 1896 à 1914* (s. l. [Bures-sur-Yvette]: Henri Bousquet, 1993–1996), 858. According to the Cinema Context database, the corresponding film title in the Netherlands might have been *Het Gevecht bij Spionkop en de Toegoela* ("Boer War Films", Cinema Context, accessed on 2 February 2016, http://www.cinemacontext.nl/id/F032064). See also: Luke, McKernan, *The Boer War (1899–1902): Films in BFI Collections, National Film and Television Archive*, Second Edition (London: National Film and Television Archive, 1999 [1997]).

560 "Het Java-Biorama", *Het Nieuws van den Dag voor Nederlandsch-Indië* (18 September 1901).

561 Possibly one scene out of the three-part Dickson film, or FIELD AMBULANCE CROSSING THE VAAL RIVER (Warwick Trading Company, 1900); or AMBULANCE CROSSING THE MODDER [AKA MODDER RIVER DRIFT] (R.W. Paul, 1899); or AMBULANCE TRAIN (R. W. Paul, 1899); or AMBULANCE CORPS AT WORK (John Montagu Benett-Stanford, 1899). See "Field Ambulances Crossing the Vaal River", Colonial Film: Moving Images of the British Empire, accessed on 2 February 2016, http://www.colonialfilm.org.uk/node/1950; Bottomore, *Filming, Faking and Propaganda*, Chapter 9, 11.

562 "Onbekend maakt onbemind", *De Locomotief* (24 December 1900); "Nederlandsch Indië", *De Locomotief* (2 January 1901). The film was probably EX-PRESIDENT KRUGER LEAVING HOTEL DE VILLE (Société Française de Mutoscope et Biographe, 1900), or PRESIDENT KRUGER (Warwick Trading Company, 1898). See McKernan, *The Boer War*, 30, 5–6.

563 "Hindia Ollanda", *Primbon Soerabaia* (15 February 1901).

Again, the Java Biorama was not the only company to have shown Boer War pictures. As mentioned above, Ten Broeke's American Biograph screened scenes advertised as "several pictures from the Transvaal" towards the end of his stay in Batavia in May 1900, but no further description has been found.[564] In Surabaya in June, Mr. Coops's Cosmograph (*Cosmograaf*) was offering shows at the *Eendracht Sociëteit*, attended by club members as well as non-members, which included "Scenes from the Transvaal War", received to a loud cheer of "Long live the Boers".[565] J. Calabresini & Co., a touring magician, similarly advertised "pictures from the Transvaal War" as part of his Animatograph (*Animatograaf*) shows in Batavia in January and February 1901.[566] The Java Cineograph, to be discussed further below, also showed scenes of the Transvaal War: "It goes without saying that the topic of the day, the South African War, plays a big part here. The battle at Spion Kop must be great", *De Locomotief* pre-empted the opening show.[567] Abdullaly Esoofally was touring in Sumatra at the time with the New Bioscope (*Nieuwe Bioscope*) showing "pictures from the South African War" (see further on Esoofally in Section 3.2).[568] Esoofally later reflected on his earlier career as a travelling showman in Southeast Asia, referring directly to these Boer War films:

> When I started my bioscope shows in Singapore in 1901, little documentary films I got from London helped me a lot in attracting people. A short documentary about Queen Victoria's funeral and another about the Boer War showing the British Commander-in-Chief Lord Roberts' triumphant entry into Pretoria against the forces of Paul Kruger, the President of the Transvaal Republic, proved wonderful draws. People who had merely heard or read some vague reports about the war were thrilled beyond description when they saw the famous figures of the Boer War in action.[569]

The films were possibly obtained from Warwick Trading Company, which had 15 scenes relating to the funeral procession through London, the longest among them: THE FUNERAL AT HYDE PARK CORNER and THE FUNERAL AT STANHOPE GATE (Warwick Trading Company, 1901). According to the description in the quote, the Boer War scene was probably LORD ROBERTS HOISTING THE UNION JACK AT PRETORIA (Warwick Trading Company, 1900) or THE ENTRY OF LORD ROBERTS INTO PRETORIA (Warwick Trading Company, 1900).

564 Advertisement, *Bataviaasch Nieuwsblad* (4 May 1900).

565 Advertisement, *Soerabaiasch-Handelsblad* (6 June 1900); "Nederlandsch-Indië", *Soerabaiasch-Handelsblad* (8 June 1900). Coops was also exhibiting life-size photographs at Grimm café at the time, and was planning to move on to the hinterland, with Solo (Surakarta) up next on his tour plan ("Onze Nieuwtjes", *Soerabaija-Courant* (7 June 1900)).

566 Advertisement, *Bintang Betawi* (10 January 1901). Advertisements for these shows were found only in the Malay newspaper, and the shows at Tanah Lapang Glodok, in the Chinese part of town, offered separate seating for women.

567 "Cineograaf", *De Locomotief* (7 May 1901).

568 "Bioskoop", *Sumatra Post* (18 September 1901).

569 *Indian Talkie, 1931–56: Silver Jubilee Souvenir* (Bombay: Film Federation of India, 1956), 121–122, quoted in Erik Barnouw and S. Krishnaswamy, *Indian Film* (New York/London: Columbia University Press, 1963), 8–9.

Even after the conclusion of the war, such scenes that initially had newsworthy appeal continued to feature on various companies' programmes over the next few years. In August 1902, Nast's Kinematograph chose to screen "episodes from the war in the Transvaal" alongside pictures of the Boxer Uprising in China.[570] Another device simply advertised in Semarang as "The Biograph" was showing "Captain Wilson and his men's last stand against the Zulus in Africa" in 1905.[571] Finally, the latest performance of Boer War films in May 1906 in Surabaya was probably the most intriguing: the Edison Bioscoop owned by Mr. M. Strauss claimed that Strauss himself was part of the Boer Campaign and therefore had the opportunity to shoot the most sensational events.[572] A year earlier, Strauss was performing in Batavia with a device advertised as the Cineograph or Chineograph, and the programmes included scenes from the Boer War, Spanish-American War, Russo-Japanese War, and the Dreyfus affair.[573] Among the films promoted in the advertisement in 1906 were: "President's Kruger's departure to the battlefield", "Fighting in Ladysmith, Mafeking, Modder River, and Spion Kop: Imprisonment and condemnation of a Boer Spy".[574] We can obviously question these scenes and whether Strauss indeed shot them, or, at the very least, their titling. Kruger, by then President of the Transvaal Republic, did not set out to the battlefield, but perhaps this was again the scene of his departure in a carriage to the *Volksraad*. The British Mutoscope and Biograph Company had a film about the fighting at Ladysmith (GORDON HIGHLANDERS IN LADYSMITH, 1900). Several pictures of the Modder River are known: AMBULANCE CROSSING THE MODDER (Paul's Animatograph Works, 1899), LANCERS CROSSING THE MODDER RIVER (Warwick Trading Company, 1899), and TROOPS PASSING OVER MODDER RIVER BY TRAIN (Warwick Trading Company, 1899).[575] The last scene about a Boer spy might have been an R. W. Paul staged scene SHOOTING THE SPY dated November 1899, or Pathé's ARRESTATION D'UN ESPION BOËR OR SON EXÉCUTION.[576]

2.2.3 *The Java Biorama Outside of Java, 1902*

In February 1902, Salzwedel advertised the American Biograph in Kuala Lumpur where he performed for a month on High Street.[577] Among the twenty-five films on the programme, mentioned in a review from Singapore a few months later, were: PICCANINNIES AT LION CUBS (Warwick Trading Co, 1899), PHOTOGRAPHING A GHOST (George Albert Smith, 1898), THE IMMATURE PUNTER (Cecil M. Hepworth, 1898), LES ILLUSIONS FANTASMAGORI-

---

570 "Onze Nieuwtjes", *Soerabaija-Courant* (7 August 1902).
571 Advertisement, *De Locomotief* (17 June 1905).
572 Advertisement, *Soerabaiasch-Handelsblad* (15 May 1906).
573 Advertisement, *Het Nieuws van den Dag voor Nederlandsch-Indië* (17 March 1905); Advertisement, *Het Nieuws van den Dag voor Nederlandsch-Indië* (31 March 1905).
574 Advertisement, *Soerabaiasch-Handelsblad* (15 May 1906).
575 See McKernan, *The Boer War*, 14–15.
576 See Bottomore, *Filming, Faking and Propaganda*, Chapter 10, 7, 25.
577 See also Ruppin et al., "Moving Pictures across Colonial Boundaries".

Figure 2–2. Advertisement in Dutch for Java Biorama with English illustration, *Sumatra Post* (12 July 1902). Retrieved from Delpher on 5 October 2015, http://resolver.kb.nl/resolve?urn=ddd:010321642:mpeg21:a0006.

Figure 2–3. Advertisement in Malay for Java Biorama with English illustration, *Sumatra Post* (29 August 1902). Retrieved from Delpher on 5 October 2015, http://resolver.kb.nl/resolve?urn=ddd:010321682:mpeg21:a0067.

QUES (Georges Méliès, 1898), LES RAYONS RÖNTGEN (Georges Méliès, 1898), LUTTES EXTRAVAGANTES (Georges Méliès, 1899), LA LUNE À UN MÈTRE (Georges Méliès, 1898), MAN OVERBOARD (Warwick Trading Co, 1899), and THE RAILWAY CYCLE RACE (Warwick Trading Co, 1899). There were also military scenes in the form of MAJOR WILSON'S LAST STAND (Warwick Trading Co, 1899), "Infantry Parade" (possibly DISPERSING THE TROOPS AT WINDSOR AFTER PARADE, Warwick Trading Company, 1899), "Highlander's Drill" (possibly SEAFORTH HIGHLANDERS: PHYSICAL DRILL, Warwick Trading Company, appearing in 1902 catalogue but likely filmed earlier) and "African Troops". The highlights of the programme were, reportedly, two other films by Georges Méliès, LE MIROIR DE CAGLIOSTRO (1899) and NEPTUNE ET AMPHITRITE (1899), which "[...] would more than compensate any inconvenience endured by passing the tent a visit".[578] Some of these 35mm films, like LA LUNE À UN MÈTRE, had been screened before on Java, suggesting that Salzwedel might have travelled with more than one device: one for the 68mm Biograph films, and another for the 35mm films.[579] It is surprising that none of what appear to be Biograph films of the Boer War, which were exhibited earlier on Java, seem to have been shown by the Java Biorama in Singapore, in light of the obvious interest these would have aroused among spectators of this British colony. These may have been discarded by that point because they were rundown due to overuse. It is also possible that the Biograph device was castoff and that Salzwedel simply chose to continue advertising under the Biograph brand name.

The American Biograph as Java Biorama travelled to Sumatra for almost two months in July and August 1902, after performing in British Malaya for a

578 "The American Biograph", *The Straits Times* (6 May 1902).

579 "Uit Malang", *De Locomotief* (19 October 1900).

2 – The Dutch Come into the Picture

couple of months. Its shows in Medan, "with the improved American Biograph", reportedly included "historical scenes from wars", stories from "1001 Nights, nice fantasy pieces, ballets, African dances, and what not" (see Figure 2–2).[580] At first the tent was not entirely full, but as the shows continued and newspaper reviews persistently praised Salzwedel's programme and the quality of his tent, the shows filled up, particularly – and importantly – the high-paying European section.[581] The *Sumatra Post* claimed that, since the shows were well-attended, Salzwedel decided to extend his stay in Medan by another week.[582] The last Java Biorama shows this research found in the Indies was given in Binjai in August 1902 (see Figure 2–3), after which Mr. Salzwedel, with his wife and two children, left on board the steamship *Sumatra* for Penang on 4 September 1902.[583]

2.3 The Java Cineograph Company

The Java Cineograph Company, which also had its offices in Surabaya, was established in mid-1901 for a period of ten years – with extension of the deed to be considered again one year prior to its expiry.[584] It declared a capital upon establishment in the sum of 20,000 guilders, divided into twenty shares worth a thousand guilders each: 15 shares owned by Mr. Henricus Julius Edgarus Naus of Pekalongan, and the remaining five shares by Mr. Emile Victor van der Schalk of Pasuruan. Representing the two in front of the notary was Company Chairman Mr. Thomas Charles Etty of Blitar, who was also charged with acquiring the Cineograph devices required for the shows. It appears that all three were also involved in the sugar industry on Java.[585] Board members were identified as Mr. Albert Jan Hendrik Kluyt, a broker from Surabaya, and Dirk Kluyt, a mechanic from Surabaya. As of July 1902, another manager by the name V. Knepper was mentioned in various reports and up to the company's last shows in October 1905.[586] It is possible that the Java Cineograph operated more than one device simultaneously, as this research found shows

580   Advertisement, *Sumatra Post* (12 July 1902); "Java Biorama", *Sumatra Post* (14 July 1902).
581   "Het Java Biorama", *Sumatra Post* (17 July 1902).
582   "Java-Biorama", *Sumatra Post* (4 August 1902). Admission prices were: $2, $1, $0.50 and $0.25, with the cheapest tickets reserved for "Natives", which was in line with prices other cinematographic exhibitors charged on Sumatra (Advertisement, *Deli Courant* (21 July 1902)).
583   "Het Java-Biorama", *Sumatra Post* (5 September 1902).
584   *Extra-Bijvoegsel der Javasche Courant* 1901, no. 58. No date appears on the *Extra-Bijvoegsel*, but a report in *De Locomotief* from early July announced that the company's establishment was approved ("Uit Buitenzorg", *De Locomotief* (2 July 1901)).
585   Naus was manager of the sugar factory Gending in Kraksaan ("Gouvernementsdienst", *De Locomotief* (1 December 1900)). Etty, who was of English descent, came from a family of entrepreneurs in the sugar industry which spanned factories from India to Java, and was superintendent of the Etty factories on Java from 1892 to 1893 (H.Ch.G.J. van der Mandere, "De Cultuurmaatschappij Wonolangan (1895–1925)", *Indië: Geïllustreerd Tijdschrift voor Nederland en Koloniën* 9, no. 19 (9 December 1925): 309). Van der Schalk was married to a member of the Etty family, Janette A. Etty (Advertisement, *Soerabaiasch-Handelsblad* (27 March 1899)).
586   "Nederlandsch-Indië", *Soerabaiasch-Handelsblad* (30 July 1902); "The Java Cineograph Coy", *Bataviaasch Nieuwsblad* (23 September 1905). Etty was still mentioned as owner in July 1902 ("Nederlandsch-Indië", *Soerabaiasch-Handelsblad* (11 July 1902)),

in Surabaya in July and August 1903 while Tofighian mentions shows at the same time in Makassar.[587]

2.3.1 Cholera, Controversy and Control of Moving Picture Shows, 1901–1903

"We have had the kinematograph, the biograph and a few other graphs, but we have not gotten to know the Cineograph yet", *De Locomotief* wrote upon the first Java Cineograph shows found in this research, which took place at the *Alun Alun* in Semarang in May 1901.[588] The Cineograph was promoted as an American invention for the display of living images bigger than life-size, projected with hardly any shaking. The operation by electric lighting was described as "quite American", and the programme was found to provide ample variety, as the device came with 300 pictures, including of the Boer War.[589] During the Java Cineograph's one-month stay in Semarang, several charity shows were offered to orphans, in order to be able to accommodate all children from the Protestant and Roman Catholic orphanages.[590] Ticket prices for regular shows varied greatly: from box seats for ƒ 2, first class for ƒ 1, second class for ƒ 0.50, and third class, for "Natives" only, for ƒ 0.15.[591] No designated category was allocated to Chinese spectators, as the American Biographs did earlier. Nevertheless, the latter were presumably avid patronisers of the Java Cineograph's tent, if to judge by a report in *Selompret Melajoe* claiming that, during a visit of a Chinese *wayang* show to Semarang, low attendance figures were recorded by the Java Cineograph and another visiting *komedi stambul*, since the Chinese were attending the *wayang* instead of the latter venues.[592]

In mid-June the tent of the Java Cineograph was dismantled and moved to Solo (Surakarta) and presumably continued from there to other locations on Java.[593] However, the company's tour of Java in 1901 was hampered by the outbreak of cholera which, as may be recalled, also disrupted Salzwedel's Java Biorama shows at the same time (see Section 2.2.1). Stranded in Yogyakarta for a while without much business, the Java Cineograph applied for permits to perform in Semarang, Magelang, and Purworejo, among other places, yet its requests were refused in every single one of these locations due to the raging cholera crisis (see further examples of outbreak of diseases and their effect on moving picture shows in Sections 3.3.7 and 4.3).[594]

---

587 Advertisement, *Makasaarsche Courant* (30 July 1903); Advertisement, *Makasaarsche Courant* (11 August 1903), references from Tofighian, *Blurring the Colonial Binary*, 232, footnote 167.

588 "Cineograaf", *De Locomotief* (7 May 1901).

589 Ibid. The word "quite" was used in English in the original. The association with "American" was so strong, that the company was later identified in the newspaper as the "American Cineograph Company" ("De cineograaf", *De Locomotief* (1 June 1901)).

590 "De Cineograaf", *De Locomotief* (31 May 1901).

591 Advertisement, *De Locomotief* (10 June 1901).

592 "Kirimian", *Selompret Melajoe* (13 June 1901).

593 "Cineograaf", *De Locomotief* (16 June 1901).

594 "Uit Djocja, *De Locomotief* (12 December 1901).

2 – The Dutch Come into the Picture

A report in *De Locomotief* about the Java Cineograph's shows in Yogyakarta demonstrates that, while the business situation was grim, there was no shortage of excitement and controversy around the Java Cineograph's tent, particularly when a special gentlemen's programme was advertised in Yogyakarta for a hefty 2.50 guilders entrance fee:

> On Friday evening at half past nine the Java Cineograph gave a special gentlemen's show. That is not so bad in itself, but we felt it highly inappropriate that in the morning handbills were distributed profusely throughout the city depicting the main numbers on the programme that would be shown vividly and in life-size on the canvas, including: caught in the act of illicit adultery, a painter's nude model, scenes from the Moulin Rouge, etc. Schoolchildren found these coloured programmes on the street and made themselves merry over the scenes that daddy would get to see in the evening.[595]

The Java Cineograph's gentlemen's programme in Semarang a few months later is the first instance found in this research in which the screen was used to separate spectators. Box seat tickets were sold for f 2.50, first class for f 2, second class for f 1.50, and, finally, third class for f 1 were identified in the advertisement as located "behind the screen", although without mentioning "Natives" specifically (see further on this practice in the Introduction and in Section 3.3.2).[596] No persons under the age of 18 years were allowed to enter.

While there was no official censorship in force at the time, such shows drew the attention of local police forces, charged with keeping the public order. Prior to the reorganisation of the police in the 1910s, around 1900 the government or general police on Java and Madura consisted of about five thousand ordinary policemen (*oppassers*) and 45,000 constables assigned to particular jobs: "[...] watchmen, guardians of district prisons, supervisors of prisoners, and the special coffee, salt, forest and opium police".[597] The superior and intermediate ranks consisted of Europeans, while the subordinate personnel were Indonesians. Patrols in the major cities were delineated along segregated racial lines: European neighbourhoods, Chinese and Arab neighbourhoods, and the "Native" *kampung*. While night patrols, similarly to their role at other venues for popular entertainments, were often present in and around moving picture tents in order to guard public safety and sometimes intervene in case of violent arguments erupting between spectators, it is not entirely clear who was directly in charge or even expected to control film content itself.

One case in 1902 went as far as being discussed in court in Surabaya, with a

---

[595] Ibid. The first two scenes could have been FLAGRANT DÉLIT D'ADULTÈRE (Pathé Frères, 1897) and PEINTRE ET MODÈLE (DÉSHABILLÉ) (Pathé Frères, 1897).

[596] Advertisement, *De Locomotief* (30 May 1902). These were pricey tickets, compared to tickets for regular shows which, while not mentioning anything about seating behind the screen, did offer cheaper tickets for "Natives" at f 0.10, and all other categories were significantly cheaper and in line with the customary pricing for moving picture shows at the time. The Java Cineograph was so popular that, by the time it continued on to Solo (Surakarta) for the *Sekatenfeesten*, a very large bamboo tent had to be reserved for it since the regular tent, stationed in Semarang then, last time proved to be too small for the rush of visitors ("Uit Solo", *De Locomotief* (3 June 1902)).

[597] Marieke Bloembergen, *De geschiedenis van de politie in Nederlands-Indië. Uit zorg en angst* (Amsterdam: Boom, Leiden: KITLV Uitgeverij, 2009), 86.

warrant issued in June against Nast's Kinematograph, under the "good morality article 4 no. 18 of the police act", requiring local authorities to report the exhibitor, suspected to be headed for shows further eastward on Java, and to seize his films.[598] It seems that the offence was deemed even more serious due to the fact that the exhibitor failed to announce that such scenes would be included in the programme, alternating these with more naïve scenes, to the "amusement of the natives" and to the shock and terror of parents who had brought their children along.[599] While this kind of criticism was earlier voiced about Miss Meranda's mixing of similarly inappropriate content in a show for the whole family in Solo (Surakarta) in 1897, the authorities did not seek any action against her.[600] And although more official censorship would not be introduced before the 1910s, as will be further discussesd in relation to each city in Part II and in the Indies as a whole in the Concluding Remarks, the uproar created by Nast's films suggests that in 1902 the authorities were beginning to pay closer attention to the contents on screen, and even evoking articles of existing laws to yield more control over it. The said films shown by Nast were finally spotted in Yogyakarta three months later and promptly transferred to Surabaya, where they were privately screened to four prosecutors. "The outcome is 'secret'" because the police kept curious passers-by away from the door while the "gentlemen of the law enjoyed the dreadful show", *Het Nieuws van den Dag voor Nederlandsch-Indië* reported.[601] However, the report continued, this was probably the least of the Kinematograph owner's worries, since he was in hospital after being diagnosed with cholera and was putting up his device for sale for 5,000 guilders.[602]

Other controversies surrounding the Java Cineograph's shows related to its screenings of Passion Plays, specifically to its arguably poor choice of musical accompaniment for the scenes. Thus, a report from Solo (Surakarta), under the heading "Shocking", related a spectator's complaint according to which, during the crucifixion scene, "[...] the organ played [the popular vaudeville song] 'Ta-ra-ra Boom-de-ay'".[603] "It would already be shocking if a funeral procession passing through or the execution of a convicted person were to be accompanied by the sounds of a jolly tune, but in this case it was [...] particularly offensive", the spectator reportedly claimed.[604] The newspaper disagreed with these statements, arguing that the exhibitor had no intention of

598 "Nederlandsch-Indië", *De Nieuwe Vorstenlanden* (20 June 1902).
599 Ibid.
600 "Nederlandsch-Indië", *De Nieuwe Vorstenlanden* (2 August 1897). See further on the earlier *risqué* shows of Miss Meranda's Kinematograph in Section 1.3.2.
601 "Zedekwestend", *Het Nieuws van den Dag voor Nederlandsch-Indië* (8 September 1902).
602 Even Esoofally's Royal Bioscope, discussed further in Chapter 3, sometimes offered "gentlemen's shows", but ceased them upon request, assuring the audience in Surabaya in June 1905 that there will be no more reason for anyone to find its shows objectionable (Advertisement, *Nieuwe Soerabaja Courant* (8 June 1905)).
603 "Stuitend", *Het Nieuws van den Dag voor Nederlandsch-Indië* (8 July 1901).
604 Ibid.

offending anyone and was simply tapping into "the ordinary Indies resident's lukewarm attitude towards religion. Yet the manager should take into account spectators who come especially for the Passion Plays", the journalist reasoned.[605] The music indeed did not seem to bother many other spectators, and when the Java Cineograph returned to Solo (Surakarta) the following year, a large bamboo tent was reserved for the shows since the ordinary tent used before proved to be too small for the swarm of visitors.[606]

The earlier report from Solo (Surakarta) also found it relevant to mention that the "[...] native audience does not understand the Passion Plays; it believes that seeing one picture is just the same as another picture".[607] However, descriptions in the Malay press about the reception of screenings of the Oberammergau Passion Plays by the Royal Bioscope signalled that these scenes of "the great prophet Jesus" were not only understood, but also proved to be problematic for a Muslim audience.[608] Making a spectacle of the Christian prophet, *Bintang Betawi* reasoned, based on the proscription against producing images of God in Islam, "[...] must be condemned, the same as if a spectacle were made about the prophet of Islam".[609]

In 1902 the authorities in Surabaya decided to intervene in ticket sales for moving picture shows, in light of the rising number of visitors to the tents of the Java Cineograph and the number of spectators having to stand up or refused entry, even against the presentation of a valid ticket.[610] The Java Cineograph and its far less successful competitor at the time, Nast's Kinematograph, were thus instructed by the local government to stop selling more tickets than their tents could actually seat.[611] Shows of the Java Cineograph in Surabaya were priced at box seats for f 1, first class for f 0.50, and second class for f 0.25, noting that "second class is NOT accessible to Europeans".[612] Yet it seems the separation was not necessarily closely observed, as just a few days later a report

605 Ibid.
606 "Uit Solo", *De Locomotief* (3 June 1902).
607 "Stuitend", *Het Nieuws van den Dag voor Nederlandsch-Indië* (8 July 1901).
608 Reports in 1902 also identified the Java Cineograph's scenes as "Obbermergau [sic] Passion Plays" (Advertisement, *Soerabaiasch-Handelsblad* (25 July 1902)). The Passion Plays continued to star on the Java Cineograph's programme, and the company continually received to receive new versions, including the "Passion Plays, recorded in Horitz (Bohemia)", which were possibly THE HORITZ PASSION PLAY (Warwick Trading Company, 1902) (Advertisement, *Soerabaiasch-Handelsblad* (17 July 1903)). These were found to be satisfyingly more comprehensive than the scenes showed in previous years, since it began with scenes of Adam and Eve in heaven and concluded with the Resurrection of Jesus ("Onze Nieuwtjes", *Soerabaija-Courant* (20 July 1903)).
609 "Kabar sehari-hari dari Betawi dan laen-laen negri", *Bintang Betawi* (11 May 1903). The issue of an actor incarnating Christ was the subject of much debate in the US (see Charles Musser, "Passions and the Passion Play: Theatre, Film and Religion in America 1880–1900", *Film History* 5, no. 4 (1993): 419–456).
610 Upon arrival in Surabaya in July 1902 and while still preoccupied with setting up its tent next to the Courthouse, the Java Cineograph immediately advertised that it was looking to hire a good pianist for a period of one month, who was expected to play every evening (Advertisement, *Soerabaiasch-Handelsblad* (6 July 1902)).
611 "Onze Nieuwtjes", *Soerabaija-Courant* (13 August 1902).
612 Advertisement, *Soerabaiasch-Handelsblad* (31 July 1902), emphasis in original.

in *Soerabaija-Courant* mentioned that it was so crowded in the big tent that "[...] several Europeans had to be content with a place among the natives, while many others were not admitted".[613] Such a blatant breaking down of the racial divide was probably not quite what the local administration expected when proposing the scheme.

Finally, when the Java Cineograph was getting ready to depart for Probolinggo in early October 1902, after three months of shows in Surabaya, a court order was suddenly presented to Etty due to a claim made by an individual, identified as the Chinese Tan Sioe Thwan, demanding to be paid 110 guilders in respect of merchandise used.[614] Two officials showed up at the tent, demanding the payment in order to allow the continuation of shows in Surabaya and the move to Probolinggo. The seizure of the Java Cineograph was lifted the next day, after the money owed was paid, with Etty explaining that the failure to pay was simply due to a misunderstanding.[615]

2.3.2 Competition Intensifies: The Case of the Russo-Japanese War on Screen, 1904–1905

The Java Cineograph continued touring in the Indies against the backdrop of ever-growing rivalry from other itinerant moving picture companies, whether arriving from outside or established locally in the Indies. In order to examine the scale of competition that the Java Cineograph was faced with in its final years of operation, scenes of the Russo-Japanese War on screen provide a good case study. The Russo-Japanese War of 1904–1905 which saw the Japanese succeed in vanquishing the Russian Imperial Army in the Far East, an Asian power thus defeating a European one in a conflict conducted with modern arms, had a global impact that reached far beyond the theatre of war and drew worldwide attention to the ongoing conflict.[616] The Dutch, who were once more struggling with finely balancing their neutral position in the conflict, were openly nervous about the possible outcomes of a Japanese victory, whether in the form of a Japanese move towards Southeast Asia and the Netherlands Indies in particular, or in the form of inspiration for other peoples in Asia (and various oppressed parts of the world) who might rise against dominant European powers.[617] Once again, reports from the battlefield appeared in every newspaper, and books and maps about the conflict were put up for sale during and following the war. It was also a popular topic on film programmes in the Indies from merely a few months after the outbreak of war in 1904 until as late as 1912, as filmmakers quickly responded to the desire of

---

613 "Onze Nieuwtjes", *Soerabaija-Courant* (11 August 1902).

614 "Onze Nieuwtjes", *Soerabaija-Courant* (1 October 1902). The report unfortunately does not specify what kind of merchandise was at the heart of the dispute.

615 "Onze Nieuwtjes", *Soerabaija-Courant* (2 October 1902).

616 For more on the Russo-Japanese War and its global impact, see Rotem Kowner (ed.), *The Impact of the Russo-Japanese War* (London: Routledge, 2007).

617 See Dijk, *The Netherlands Indies and the Great War*, 14–16, 73–74.

2 – The Dutch Come into the Picture

film audiences worldwide for moving images of the war, resulting in war re-enactments as well as limited footage provided from the scene.[618] Russo-Japanese War scenes were screened by various competing companies, among them: the Java Cineograph,[619] the Netherlands Indies Biograph Company,[620] the American Animatograph,[621] Aldow's Funny Frenchmen with a device referred to as Biorama or Cinematographe,[622] S. M. Aidid's Edison Bioscope Company and later Urban Bioscope,[623] M. Strauss's Cineograph,[624] and E. Bartelle's Imperial Bioscope.[625] The most intriguing screenings of Russo-Japanese War films were arguably the ones given by companies coming from Asia, although the films were most likely of Western origin.[626] For instance, the New Biograph Company from Bombay (*Biograph Compagnij Baroe dateng dari Bombaij*), which visited Batavia for a month in June 1904, claimed to be screening images of the Russo-Japanese War that were just received,

---

618 Advertisement, *Soerabaiasch-Handelsblad* (25 June 1904); Advertisement, *De Locomotief* (23 July 1912). The Charles Urban Trading Company in Britain, for instance, filmed war re-enactments, yet also dispatched its cameraman Joseph Rosenthal behind the lines of the Japanese, and another cameraman, George Rogers, behind the Russian side in order to produce actualities from the scene (see Urban, *A Yank in Britain*, 75). Meanwhile, the Edison Company and the Biograph Company in the US, wanting to satisfy the craving for images of the war while keeping production costs low, resorted to filming war re-enactments in New York and New Jersey based on news from the front (see Musser, *Before the Nickelodeon*, 273–274). In France, Pathé Frères similarly invested in a series of war re-enactments generally known as *Évènements russo-japonais* which, according to its set designer, were also filmed in accordance with reports on the war in major French newspapers of the day (see Bousquet, *Catalogue Pathé*, 889). Remarkably business-minded, Pathé offered exhibitors two options for the films' final intertitle – "Vive le Japon!" or "Vive la Russie!" – in six different languages, opening up the possibility for these films to be used in film programmes expressing directly opposite sentiments (Georges Sadoul, *Histoire générale du cinéma. Tome 2: Les Pionniers du cinéma, 1897–1909* (Paris: Denoël, 1973), 302). Selig Polyscope also made Russo-Japanese War "reproductions", such as TORPEDO ATTACK ON PORT ARTHUR, THE ATTACK ON PORT ARTHUR, and THE BATTLE OF CHEMULPO, advertised in their catalogue from 1903–1904 (see "Films of the Passion Play", Rutgers University Community Repository, accessed on 2 February 2016, http://dx.doi.org/doi:10.7282/T3X92BMJ). For more on exhibition and reception of Russo-Japanese War scenes in the Netherlands and the Netherlands Indies, see Dafna Ruppin, "Views from the Japanese-Russian War': Re-titling Russo-Japanese War Film Programmes in the Netherlands and Netherlands Indies", in Angel Quintana and Jordi Pons (eds.), *The Construction of News in Early Cinema*, (Girona: Fundació Museu del Cinema & Ajuntament de Girona, 2011), 191–202. For more on the exhibition of Russo-Japanese War films in Southeast Asia, see Tofighian, *Blurring the Colonial Binary*, 235–246.

619 Programme included unidentified scene from the Russo-Japanese War (Advertisement, *Soerabaiasch-Handelsblad* (25 June 1904). See further discussion of the films shown by the Java Cineograph below.

620 Programme included unidentified scenes from the Russo-Japanese War, screened alongside scenes from the Boxer Uprising (Advertisement, *Soerabaiasch-Handelsblad* (22 July 1904)).

621 "Attack on a Russian Outpost" (Advertisement, *Java-Bode* (2 September 1904)).

622 "Military battle in Japan" (Advertisement, *Taman Sari* (4 January 1905)).

623 "Two Torpedo Boats in Port Arthur", "Japanese and Russian Battle at Yalu", "Japanese and Russian Battle at Liaoyang" (Advertisement, *Kabar Perniagaan* (24 February 1905)). Urban Bioscope later advertised unidentified scenes from the Russo-Japanese War (Advertisement, *Kabar Perniagaan* (17 June 1905)).

624 Programme included unidentified scenes from the Russo-Japanese War (Advertisement, *Het Nieuws van den Dag voor Nederlandsch-Indië* (17 March 1905)). Further discussion of the films shown by M. Strauss in 1906 below.

625 Programme included unidentified scene from the Russo-Japanese War (Advertisement, *Taman Sari* (2 November 1905)).

626 See also Tofighian, *Blurring the Colonial Binary*, 152–153.

alongside related scenes described in the Malay press as the "assassination of the Soviet Raja and Empress".[627]

Matsuno's Japanese Cinematograph (*Japansche Kinematograaf*) was exhibiting Russo-Japanese War films in Medan in late August and early September 1905 (see Figure 2–4).[628] The films on the programme, depicting Japanese soldiers striking bearded Russian soldiers and Russian battleships attacked by Japanese torpedoes, were initially praised for their artfulness: "[...] such wonderfully harmonious colours, how true to nature [are] the human figures. One might say: they stepped out of the battlefield. All that red, blue, green, yellow is greatly attractive."[629] These films appealed to newspaper reporters so much that they continually described these scenes, their exhibition setting, and spectators' responses to them. The Japanese Cinematograph apparently managed to gather together in front of the screen "[...] [i]n no time a throng of Natives, Chinese, Klings [Tamil immigrants], and whatever other peoples there are here [...]. Eyes wide open, wrinkles at the corners of their mouths, some even with mouths wide open, as they stood there. [...] Not a word was spoken; who better enjoys the art of silent pleasures than the Oriental [*Oosterling*]?"[630] The only disruptions of the silence came in the form of a drunken gentleman wearing khaki, who took it upon himself to explain the images on screen, as well as a police sergeant who stood in the very front, asserting his position of power and lecturing to the "Native" spectators: "[...] a general who has missed his calling".[631]

Another description of a screening of Abdulally Esoofally's Royal Bioscope in Sukabumi from December 1904 gives a good sense of the atmosphere:

> The Royal Bioscope with its shows always draws large crowds. Chinese and natives especially love such amusements and of course the favourite topic of such spectacles: the Russo-Japanese War. On war evenings, as we shall call them, it was packed and with every new Japanese victory came a loud applause.[632]

627 Advertisement, *Bintang Betawi* (25 June 1904).

628 Advertisement, *Sumatra Post* (19 August 1905). Tofighian has found several mentions of "Japanese Cinematograph" in the region since January 1905 (Tofighian, *Blurring the Colonial Binary*, 149). However, the ownership structure remains unclear and most likely there was more than one company by that name (ibid., 150–151). Matsuno's Japanese Cinematograph was advertised as "Matsuo's Japanese Cinematograph" as his tour of Southeast Asia continued in 1906–1907 (ibid., 152–154).

629 "Langs den Weg", *Sumatra Post* (24 August 1905). During the next day's show, however, the projection unfortunately failed to produce a clear image, despite attempts by the exhibitor to correct the situation, and spectators finally were given their money back ("De Kinematograaf", *Sumatra Post* (26 August 1905)). According to Tofighian, advertisements in Singapore in January 1905 mentioned "Fighting at Mukden, Liaoyang, Port Arthur, Yantai. Views taken at the seat of war" (Advertisement, *The Straits Times* (9 January 1905), referenced in Tofighian, *Blurring the Colonial Binary*, 240, footnote 205). As victory drew nearer, Tofighian notes that the Japanese Cinematograph in Singapore began referring to these as "Japanese-Russian War" films, which was also the case in the later shows in Medan (see Figure 2–4), and these included: "Many land battles at Kiu-Len-Chan, Kinchow, Teriji, Taiseko, Liaoyang, and a Naval Battle of Port Arthur" (Advertisement, *The Straits Times* (17 January 1905)); Advertisement, *The Straits Times* (19 January 1905), referenced in Tofighian, *Blurring the Colonial Binary*, 240, footnote 207).

630 "Langs den Weg", *Sumatra Post* (24 August 1905).

631 Ibid.

632 "Het Land der Gepensionneerden [sic]", *Het Nieuws van den Dag voor Nederlandsch-Indië* (14 December 1904). For more on Abdulally Esoofally and the Royal Bioscope, see Section 3.2.

2 – The Dutch Come into the Picture

The films of the Japanese Cinematograph were met with equal excitement, according to a journalist who noted the audience's "ecstasy", "rejoicing" and "spontaneous joy".[633] Spectators seemed to be content with (nearly) any footage they could get from the current conflict, but especially the footage filmed by Joseph Rosenthal, the Urban Trading Company's cameraman sent to film on the Japanese side, received extra attention when screened by the Royal Bioscope (see Figure 2-5). For instance, when these scenes were screened in Batavia in 1905, *Het Nieuws van den Dag voor Nederlandsch-Indië* wrote:

Figure 2-4. Advertisement for the Japanese Cinematograph, *Sumatra Post* (22 August 1905). Retrieved from Delpher on 5 October 2015, http://resolver.kb.nl/resolve?urn=ddd:010321976:mpeg21:a0019.

[…] these images are real, not a game of smoke and mirrors of extras dressed as Japanese, but rather the actual exodus of the Russian prisoners from the captured Port Arthur, the actual arrival of the victorious Japanese army […]. Of course, these recordings had to be approved by the Japanese military's administration, which ensured that neither the best looking Russian troops, nor the least among the Japanese soldiers appear strong, sturdy, and energetic.[634]

Spectators may have been receptive of "faked" representations, but it appears that images that could claim a certain degree of authenticity were appreciated, even while acknowledging that there was a certain degree of staging in the choice of what to film in order to obtain Japanese military consent. The interest in the Russo-Japanese War further spawned a local Indies trade in maps and postcards, as well as a variety of stage acts, public lectures, and *tableaux vivants*, depicting a glorious Imperial Japan.[635] The news stories of the Russo-Japanese War thus got their own run on the local entertainment scene, on stage and on screen.

The Java Cineograph appears to have been one of the first companies to have shown scenes of the Russo-Japanese War as early as in June 1904 in Surabaya, at a tent next to the Courthouse.[636] After the first show, exhibiting "beautiful

---

633 "Langs den Weg", *Sumatra Post* (24 August 1905).

634 "Royal Bioscope", *Het Nieuws van den Dag voor Nederlandsch-Indië* (11 September 1905). According to advertisements, the films on the programme included: DOROTHY'S DREAM aka A DREAM OF FAIRYLAND (G.A. Smith, 1903), LES AVENTURES DE ROBINSON CRUSOË (Star Film Company, 1902), and SIEGE AND SURRENDER OF PORT ARTHUR (Rosenthal for Warwick Trading Company, 1904).

635 Advertisement, *Kabar Perniagaan* (18 September 1905); Advertisement, *Taman Sari* (20 October 1905); "Perang Japan dan Roes", *Taman Sari* (10 January 1907); Advertisement, *Het Nieuws van den Dag voor Nederlandsch-Indië* (11 October 1905); Advertisement, *Het Nieuws van den Dag voor Nederlandsch-Indië* (28 October 1905).

636 Advertisement, *Soerabaiasch-Handelsblad* (25 June 1904).

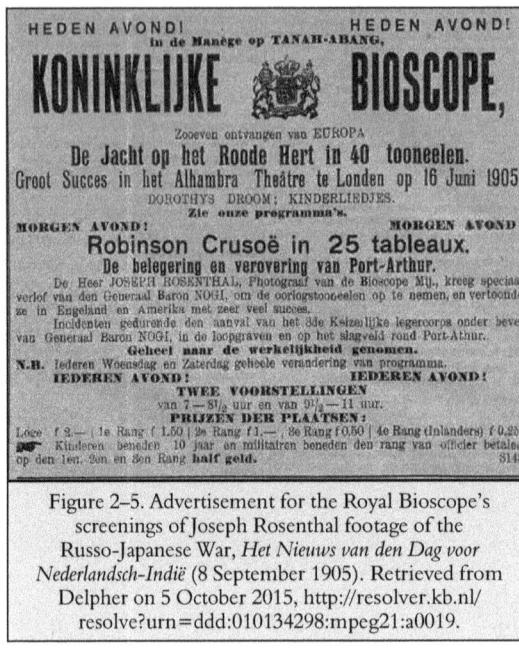

Figure 2–5. Advertisement for the Royal Bioscope's screenings of Joseph Rosenthal footage of the Russo-Japanese War, *Het Nieuws van den Dag voor Nederlandsch-Indië* (8 September 1905). Retrieved from Delpher on 5 October 2015, http://resolver.kb.nl/resolve?urn=ddd:010134298:mpeg21:a0019.

scenes from the Russo-Japanese War (Living Images)" which "achieved great success in Europe", new pictures were delivered by the *Internationale Crediet- En Handelsvereeniging* "*Rotterdam*" at Gubeng station, and from there went directly on screen the same day.[637] The films attracted so many spectators that the manager reportedly had to refuse entry to five hundred people. "One can spend a few hours and behold many different war scenes, as well as charming Japanese geishas, etc.", another report further promoted the shows.[638]

The Java Cineograph continued to receive new films, specifically pointing out that they were shipped from the Netherlands, reportedly at a cost of 4,000 guilders every month.[639] Apart from land and sea battle scenes from the Russo-Japanese War, programmes included coloured films, such as "Cinderella", possibly Méliès's CENDRILLON (Star Film Company, 1899), and sensation films, including "The Great Fire in Hamburg and Bullfight", in addition to "The Pope at the Vatican", "Death of Leo XIII", and the "original *Cake Walk*", on top of which spectators were advised to further consult the handbills distributed.[640] One month into its shows in Surabaya, a new device was received from Europe, with the goal of bringing flickering down to a minimum. In addition, ticket prices were made even more attractive: from box seats for ƒ 1.50, first class for ƒ 1, second class for ƒ 0.50, third class ("Chinese and Arabs") for ƒ 0.25, and fourth class ("Javanese") for ƒ 0.10 at the beginning of

637 Ibid.; "Onze Nieuwtjes", *Soerabaija-Courant* (27 June 1904). The *Internationale Crediet- En Handelsvereeniging "Rotterdam"* (shorthand: Internatio), was the largest trader in pepper from the Netherlands Indies, but its activities further included sugar, tobacco, coffee, tea, and rubber. As of 1878, it also ran the *Rotterdamsche Lloyd* shipping company's operations (see Michael B. Miller, *Europe and the Maritime World: A Twentieth-Century History* (New York: Cambridge University Press, 2012), 104–107). Among its dozens of branches was one in Surabaya.

638 "De Cineograaf", *Soerabaiasch-Handelsblad* (30 June 1904).

639 "Cineograaf", *Soerabaiasch-Handelsblad* (13 July 1904); "De Java Cineograph Coy", *Soerabaiasch-Handelsblad* (18 April 1905).

640 Advertisement, *Soerabaiasch-Handelsblad* (22 July 1904); Advertisement, *De Locomotief* (28 October 1904); "Cineograaf", *Soerabaija-Courant* (27 July 1904). "The Great Fire in Hamburg" was possibly COURSE DE TAUREAUX À BEZIERS – FRANCE (Pathé Frères, 1904). The Pope scenes could have been LE PAPE LÉON XIII AU VATICAN (Pathé Frères, 1903), MORT DU PAPE LÉON XIII (Pathé Frères, 1903). Pathé also had a cake-walk scene: DANSE DU CAKE-WALK (Pathé Frères, 1903).

its run, prices towards the end of its stay were cut to box seats for ƒ 1, first class for ƒ 0.50, second class for ƒ 0.25, third class ("Chinese and Arabs") for ƒ 0.15, and fourth class ("Javanese") for ƒ 0.05.[641] According to a report from Semarang a couple of months later, the seats "for the brown brother [were] hidden from view of the other visitors" to the tent, so presumably the seating of "Native" spectators behind the screen continued.[642] Nevertheless, the boundless "'wahs' of the little brown men" during screenings of Méliès's LE ROYAUME DES FÉES (1903) could not be obscured from anyone.[643]

Back in Surabaya again in March 1905, in a tent set up in front of the military garrison, the fanfare music, which drew complaints earlier, was replaced by piano accompaniment and later by a string orchestra.[644] Spectators "are not constantly treated to the melody of tsjek-tsjek-tsjek for all pictures", a Batavia newspaper later commended the new musical choice.[645] The influx of visitors at times required the police to interfere. This was probably due to the fact that, as opposed to the earlier order given by the authorities, the Java Cineograph again failed to (or chose not to) properly match the number of tickets sold against seats available. Thus, for a show beginning at 7 pm, the tent was "packed full of Europeans and Natives" by 6.30 pm, and many spectators "who had bought a ticket had to wait until the [later] evening performance".[646] Since the tent continued to be full and the seventh Sugar Congress was coming up, expected to draw in more visitors for popular entertainment shows, the Java Cineograph took a few measures in preparation: "The tent is nearly twice as big and by an arrangement of the side walls the necessary ventilation is provided. The décor is worth a visit."[647]

The last shows of the Java Cineograph found in this research were given in Batavia in September and October 1905, in a tent set up next to the Manège at Tanag Abang.[648]

2.4 Conclusion

After the first wave of moving picture companies, such as Talbot's Scenimatograph, which presented the novelty of the new technology, the American Biograph, Java Biorama, and Java Cineograph were among the prominent follow-ups signalling that moving pictures were there to stay, even if the

---

641 Advertisement, *Soerabaiasch-Handelsblad* (24 June 1904); Advertisement, *Soerabaiasch-Handelsblad* (22 July 1904).

642 "De Cineograph", *De Locomotief* (26 September 1904).

643 "De Java Cinematograph Cie", *Soerabaiasch-Handelsblad* (6 March 1905).

644 In 1902, the Java Cineograph advertised that it was seeking a pianist for performances in Surabaya every evening over the course of one month (Advertisement, *Soerabaiasch-Handelsblad* (6 July 1902)). Advertisements in 1905 mentioned that the shows were accompanied by the sounds of an Italian Quintet (Advertisement, *Soerabaiasch-Handelsblad* (16 March 1905)).

645 "Nieuwe cineografen op komst", *Het Nieuws van den Dag voor Nederlandsch-Indië* (23 September 1905).

646 "De Biograaf", *Nieuwe Soerabaja Courant* (6 March 1905).

647 "De Suikerfeest", *Soerabaiasch-Handelsblad* (4 April 1905).

648 "Nieuwe cineografen op komst", *Het Nieuws van den Dag voor Nederlandsch-Indië* (23 September 1905).

companies themselves were short-lived. Unlike the earlier companies which tended to move around from one location to another after a few days of shows in smaller towns and up to a month's stay in major cities, many of the companies discussed in this chapter often stayed on in one place, whether in a tent or in an existing structure converted into an exhibition space, for several months. Some were recycling old stock while others received regular shipments of new films from Europe and the United States, to sustain the variety of their programmes in order to attract repeat visitors and to keep abreast of current affairs reported in the newspapers. The modernity of moving pictures lay in their up-to-dateness and ability to represent current events, whether in actualities or staged films, making wars into spectacles to be consumed on screen.

Moving pictures of Queen Wilhelmina presented her colonial subjects with a living image of their monarch, who in fact never set foot in the Indies. At times, the reception of such images supported an idyllic notion of a unified colonial society, with spectators of all ethnicities applauding and cheering the Queen together. Similarly to Benedict Anderson's understanding of the advent of print-capitalism as helping to form an "imagined community" among people who have never encountered each other in person, the multi-ethnic residents of the Indies were perceived as patriotically banding together at the sight of mechanically reproduced moving images of Queen Wilhelmina.[649] Other instances, such as when the HBS schoolchildren in Surabaya, the colony's future "cultural citizens", insolently stood up in the front seats, or when Chinese and "Native" spectators cheered at the Japanese victories over the Russians, revealed the cracks forming in Dutch colonial sovereignty, even if contemporary commentators seemed to be blissfully unaware of these.[650]

Finally, between the films of current events, sensational pictures and comic scenes discussed in this chapter, Indies audiences were apparently still lacking another element that would transform moving pictures fully into a local form. As a 1904 review in *De Locomotief* of the Java Cineograph put it:

> The living pictures screened were almost all new to us, the audience was one-and-all at attention, especially for the lady floating in the sky and the small "pocket boxers". These were "very nice". After each successful living picture were shown good recordings of landscapes, cities and ruins from Turkey or Asia Minor. This variety is very good: it gives the eye a rest. When sights from Java would be shown instead, the audience would definitely find it more interesting.[651]

In the following chapter, we shall see that calls for more local scenes were growing and encountered companies that began to include local views of the Indies in their film programmes on a regular basis, alongside imported scenes.

---

649 See Benedict Anderson, *Imagined Communities: Reflections on the Origin and Spread of Nationalism*, Revised Edition (London/New York: Verso, 2006 [1983]).

650 By the 1940s, according to Mrázek, Indonesian spectators were recorded by colonial officials as raising a ruckus while images of Queen Wilhelmina were projected on screen, even as the Dutch anthem was played (Mrázek, *Engineers of Happy Land*, 111).

651 "De Cineograph", *De Locomotief* (26 September 1904).

3

Komedi Bioscoop, Indische Films and the Localisation of Film Exhibition

> *The* Royal Bioscope *attracts many people and, I must say, the shows are always entertaining and varied. But why are there not more I n d i s c h e scenes being shown? What does a fire in Toronto or a visit to Allahabad have to do with us, as interesting as these things may be. I'm planning to associate myself with the excellent Mr. Yousoof, and we will soon be showing a series of films that are current and also specifically Indisch.*
> "Zaterdagsche Causerie", Het Nieuws van den Dag voor Nederlandsch-Indië *(28 January 1905), emphases in the original.*

The above quote is an excerpt from an editorial by Diederiek Baltezardt, the pseudonym of *Het Nieuws van den Dag voor Nederlandsch-Indië*'s editor, Karel Wybrands. After laying out his arguments in favour of more locally relevant filmmaking and exhibition, it further details a film to be made in 31 tableaux titled "Wonders of the Deep", borrowing its name from a highly popular *féerie* of the day, Méliès's LE ROYAUME DES FÉES (advertised in Dutch as *"De wonderen der diepten"*).[652] Intended to touch on issues of municipal corruption under the recently introduced decentralisation scheme, among the scenes to be included were: "The inspector of finances", "'I have heard nothing, I have seen nothing'", "Who should pay the deficit? (Comic scene.)", and "Reports and Business trips (Moving panorama, beautifully coloured.)".[653] The programme was envisioned to be complemented by another short reel, "'The lost letter', recording from nature", and a note in the end remarked: "The management reserves the right to modify the programme according to circumstances".[654] While this is a rather cynical piece of writing, it nevertheless hints at several developments occurring at the time regarding the way in which moving pictures were being understood and consumed by local audiences in the Netherlands Indies. In order for the satire to be effective, the editor had to assume that readers (and spectators) could identify the construction and conventions of a film programme which he was evoking. It also indicates that, while audiences were being flooded with a plethora of imported productions of various sources, there was a growing appetite in the Indies for more locally informed films, or, as the article labels them, "*Indische* scenes".

652 Advertisement, *Java-Bode* (2 January 1905).
653 "De Royal Bioscope", *Het Nieuws van den Dag voor Nederlandsch-Indië* (28 January 1905).
654 Ibid.

This chapter proposes to explore this period in the development of movie-going in colonial Indonesia by evoking the term *Indische*, meaning "Indies-like". In historical and social research *Indische* has often been used to refer to the Indies as a colonial or racially mixed society, marked by intermarriage and Mestizo offspring.[655] Others yet have employed it to describe "all cultural phenomena which were composed of mixed European and Indonesian elements", for example: building and architecture, Europeans adopting *sarong* and *kabaja* dress, or serving *rijsttafel* for dinner.[656] "Indische" as it is used here comes from a tradition of engaging with the term in order to describe hybrid text- and performance-based cultural phenomena, springing up in the Indies in the late nineteenth and early twentieth centuries. This chapter therefore first provides background on the traditions of *Indische roman* and *Indische* theatre as local cultural practices, blending local forms with outside influences from the region and beyond, as consumed by modern readers and *stambul* spectators in the Indies. It then proposes to apply the term *Indische* to the Indies early cinema scene, by focusing on two of the leading local exhibition and production companies of the time which serve as examples of hybrid cultural mediators, experimenting with localised practices.

The role of the cinema exhibitor as an intermediary figure who could blend the global into cultural practices that appealed and made sense to local audiences has been previously outlined by Thunnis van Oort in the context of cinema exhibition in the Catholic south of the Netherlands. He writes: "The cinema exhibitor acted as an intermediary, not only between the local, the national and international contexts, but also in drawing the novelty of cinema into the cultural and social life of the region".[657] As we shall see, the local exhibitors discussed in this chapter, who were essentially responsible for early cinema's hybridisation and embedding in the Indies, were often "hybrid individuals" themselves.[658] They contributed to shaping the highly dynamic and evolving local cinema-going scene within the existing popular entertainment landscape which included, among others, travelling *komedi stambul* companies, *bangsawan* troupes, *wayang* shows, circus outfits, and acrobats and magicians (see further details in Introduction). In fact, movie-going became

---

655 For an overview of historical research and the problems with the term, see Ulbe Bosma and Remco Raben, *Being "Dutch" in the Indies: A History of Creolisation and Empire, 1500–1920*, trans. Wendie Shaffer (Singapore: NUS Press, 2008).

656 W. F. Wertheim, *Indonesian Society in Transition: A Study of Social Change*, Second Revised Edition (The Hague: W. van Hoeve Ltd, 1959 [1956]), 173. See also: Jean Gelman Taylor, *The Social World of Batavia: Europeans and Eurasians in Colonial Indonesia*, Second Edition (Madison: The University of Wisconsin Press, 2009 [1983]); Pauline Dublin Milone, "Indische Culture and Its Relationship to Urban Life", *Comparative Studies in Society and History* 9 (1967): 407–26.

657 Thunnis van Oort, "'That pleasant feeling of peaceful coziness': Cinema Exhibition in a Dutch Mining District during the Inter-war Period", *Film History* 17, no. 1 (2005): 148.

658 Peter Burke writes that "hybrid individuals, whether they were born into this situation because their mothers and fathers came from different cultures, or entered it later, willingly or unwillingly", can serve as cultural mediators. "A life in between cultures often results in a 'double consciousness', to use the famous phrase of W. E. B. Du Bois (1868–1963) about North American blacks" (Peter Burke, *Cultural Hybridity* (Cambridge: Polity Press, 2009), 31).

3 – *Komedi Bioscoop, Indische* Films and the Localisation of Film Exhibition

so prevalent in the Indies commercial entertainment scene, known in Malay as *komedi*, that the terms used for describing moving picture shows were vernacularized as *komedi bioscoop* or, more commonly, *komedi gambar hidup* (literally, living picture, which parallels the Dutch term *levende beelden*).[659]

The time-period highlighted in this chapter is 1905 to 1909, with a few years' leeway in either direction, since the companies under discussion were often active before or after this period. The two examples highlighted here will serve to show the way in which exhibition companies were attempting to embed themselves within the local popular entertainment environment. It views the fact that *Indische* films were produced with local audiences in mind as part of exhibitors' localisation strategies, making their companies an integral part of the *komedi* circuit. In this vein, it further considers the physical conditions of moving picture exhibition which were adjusted to best-suit Indies society: whether through the separated seating arrangements, the materials used for the construction of cinema spaces, such as bamboo tents (further elaborated on in Part II), or the incorporation of moving pictures as part of the entertainment forms on offer at the *Pasar Malam* (night market) and *Pasar Gambir* (the annual great market in Batavia). Each example is set into context against other contemporary companies exhibiting moving pictures, in order to provide a wider overview of the ever-growing cinema-going scene, local film exhibition practices, and the authorities' attempts to bring these under control. With movie-going constantly gaining in popularity and local issues such as the 1904 peasant uprising in Gedangan supposedly to be represented on screen, the colonial authorities, which previously appeared to be oblivious of the potential disruptiveness of scenes of the Russo-Japanese War to the colonial order, were about to be roused from their slumber.

The first case is British-Indian exhibitor Abdullaly Esoofally and his Royal Bioscope, who toured extensively in the region from 1901 to 1906.[660] Throughout, we shall see various strategies employed by Esoofally in order to gain repeat visitors to his shows. These strategies include carefully cultivated relationships with various newspaper desks, as well as a habit of offering charity shows to benefit various causes, all seemingly executed with a keen sense of self-promotion. In the process of mapping out Esoofally's activities in the Indies, the films on the Royal Bioscope's programmes, as well as those of its

---

659 When Talbot performed his animated pictures, the Malay term used to describe the show was "pertunjukan gambaran ajaib", meaning magic picture show, while the advertisement read "pertunjukan gambaran hidup", meaning living pictures show ("Betawie, 8 Maart 1897", *Bintang-Barat* (8 March 1897); Advertisement, *Bintang-Barat* (8 March 1897)). The earliest use of "komedi gambar" I came across was made in reference to the Kenotograph show in Surabaya's Kapasan district, the home of *komedi*, and since then it appears that it was not in use until 1903, when referring to Esoofally's shows ("India Ollanda", *Bintang Soerabaia* (28 April 1897); "Kabar sehari-hari dari Betawi dan laen-laen negri", *Bintang Betawi* (27 April 1903)).

660 According to Suresh Chabria, another company by the name Royal Bioscope was founded by Hiralal Sen and his brother Motilal in 1899 (see Suresh Chabria, "Royal Bioscope", in Abel (ed.), *Encyclopedia of Early Cinema*, 555). Among their films was a stage performance of ALIBABA AND THE FORTY THIEVES (1904). Nevertheless, this research was not able to find convincing proof of any link between their company and Esoofally's Royal Bioscope.

competitors, are considered in relation to the stories consumed by local audiences in print and on the *komedi stambul* stage at the time. The analysis pays special attention to the Royal Bioscope's reported recording in 1906 of a performance of the popular Javanese folklore story *Nyai Dasima*, the tragic tale of an Indonesian woman named Dasima who becomes an Englishman's *nyai* (concubine or informal native wife). These programming choices are viewed as commercial strategies for winning over consumers of other popular entertainments of the day.

The second case is of local Armenian exhibitors Amirkan Johannes and Mackertich Johannes of Kediri and Mackertich Abraham Nahapiet of Surabaya and their Netherlands Indies Biograph Company. Beginning to operate in 1904 as a touring enterprise, this company continued to run under one guise or another up until 1913, bridging over to a period in which cinema was becoming a more permanent fixture of urban life, as will be further elaborated on in the final four chapters of this book. In the present chapter, emphasis will be placed on the strategies used by the Netherlands Indies Biograph Company and its daughter companies (Johannes Biograph and Vardon Biograph) to industrialise cinema exploitation in the Indies. Their involvement in the local industry covers, on the one hand, local exhibition practices, namely, the institutionalisation of separating "Native" from "European" audiences by using the screen as a separator, and, on the other hand, film production and distribution as manifested in their endeavours of producing, exhibiting and distributing films of local interest: from an alleged recording of a peasant uprising in Gedangan to street scenes in Surabaya.

3.1 Manifestations of the *Indische* in Local Popular Culture
3.1.1 The *Indische* Roman *and Modern Readership*

The advent of the vernacular Malay press in the mid-nineteenth century, as discussed in the introduction, is often seen as having directly contributed to the formation of Malay popular literature. On the one hand, it developed a broad-based, mass market of readers in Low or Market Malay – the *lingua franca*, as opposed to High Malay of traditional court literature or regional languages, such as Javanese or Madurese. On the other hand, it produced a skilled workforce of publishers, editors, writers and translators.[661] Malay newspapers printed traditional prose literature, *The Thousand and One Nights* stories, various animal fables (including *Aesop's Tales*), *jinn* and *raja* mythical stories, and occasionally Chinese stories as well as original material, often in serialised form (*feuilleton*).[662] In the closing decades of the nineteenth century, printed schoolbooks, storybooks and poetry books in Malay began to appear more promi-

---

661 See Kenji Tsuchiya, "Popular Literature and Colonial Society in Late-Nineteenth-Century Java – *Cerita Nyai Dasima*, the Macabre Story of an Englishman's Concubine", *Southeast Asian Studies* 28, no. 4 (1991): 461.

662 See C. Watson, "Some preliminary remarks on the antecedents of modern Indonesian literature", *Bijdragen tot de Taal-, Land- en Volkenkunde (BKI)* 127, no. 4 (1971): 423–424.

nently.[663] As opposed to the vernacular press, it was also hardly subject to censorship by the colonial authorities at this stage.[664] Books could be acquired by mail order or at shops, alongside notepads, cigars, and medications, umbrellas and shoes.[665] Lending libraries were also available, sometimes with titles of a more "erotic nature".[666]

Popular literature in Malay, according to Jedamski's study of Sherlock Holmes in the Indies, "entered the indigenous literary world almost unaltered and without any literary label attached to it that might stigmatize it as inferior", as was the case in the West.[667] Among the popular literature available in Malay at the time were publications coming in from Singapore and Penang in the Arabic script (*Jawi*), including print versions of earlier stories available as manuscripts, reproductions of Middle Eastern and Indian tales and serially published Malay versions of Chinese tales. There was also a local book market under development in Batavia, Semarang, Yogyakarta and Surabaya which presented readers with texts in Romanised script, many of them adaptations of Chinese stories, historical narratives transmuted into works that were journalistic in style.[668] Translations into Malay of best sellers from both East and West included *Robinson Crusoe* in 1875, *The Adventures of Sinbad* in 1896, *Around the World in Eighty Days* in 1890, a Chinese historical work known as the *Records of the Three Kingdoms* (or by its Chinese title, *Sanguozhi*) in 1893, and *Count of Monte Cristo* between 1894 and 1899.[669] There was even a *syair* (traditional Malay poetry) version of *Cinderella* published in 1890, using the Dutch name "Asschepoester" in the Malay title: *Boekoe Pantoen Dari Tjeritnja Nonah Asschepoester. (Anak jang dihinaken oleh Mamatirinja).*[670]

---

663 See Maier, "Explosions in Semarang", 4.

664 Interestingly, popular literature continued to go under the radar of the Dutch censorship system for quite some time, even into the late 1920s, although the authorities were growing more vigilant (see Doris Jedamski, "The Vanishing-Act of Sherlock Holmes in Indonesia's National Awakening", in Doris Jedamski (ed.), *Chewing Over the West: Occidental Narratives in Non-Western Readings* (Amsterdam/New York: Rodopi, 2009), 383–413). Original crime fiction and translations continued to appear in the 1930s and 1940s, with the villains often presented as Chinese or Arab. Europeans were not portrayed as villains, but it is not known whether this was due to any outside pressure or direct censorship (see ibid., 405–406).

665 Maier, "Explosions in Semarang", 7.

666 Watson, "Some preliminary remarks", 421. Books were by no means a cheap commodity: "Books of verse were in the lower price range, usually around f 1.00; books of laws were the most expensive, often more than f 3.00; and storybooks in prose were in between" (Maier, "Explosions in Semarang", 7).

667 Jedamski, "The Vanishing-Act of Sherlock Holmes", 385. Jedamski pays particular attention to the publication activities of the Chinese-Malay, who were the first to translate Sherlock Holmes stories. Although Balai Pustaka, the official government publishing house, began publishing novels in Malay in an attempt to offset the success of the Chinese-Malay publishers and set up a distinction between "high" and "low" culture, the former eventually relented and also published Malay translations of Sherlock Holmes tales (ibid., 388–389). For more on Chinese-Malay literature, see Claudine Salmon, *Literature in Malay by the Chinese of Indonesia; a Provisional Annotated Bibliography* (Paris: Éditions de la Maison des Sciences de l'Homme, 1981).

668 Ibid., 5.

669 See Tsuchiya, "Popular Literature and Colonial Society", 472.

670 See Watson, "Some preliminary remarks", 422.

Original Malay popular novels, or *Indische roman*, then started appearing on the scene, continually growing in quantity.[671] Reports on sensational stories in the newspapers involving crimes, such as murder, rape, infidelity and theft, influenced this body of work, serving as source material for authors of popular novels.[672] It was a literary genre, written in Dutch and Malay, telling stories set in the Indies and targeting local readers.[673] Veering between the realist and supernatural, fiction and the retelling of true past and present crime stories, the *Indische roman* was peppered with "[v]irgin abductions, opium smugglers, last-minute rescues, treacherous concubines, desolate hideouts, stalwart heroes, inscrutable mandarins, robber barons, pirate chiefs, lascivious landlords, unscrupulous spies, and dark and stormy nights [...]".[674]

The readers consuming such popular literary works, according to Tsuchiya,

> [...] constituted the first wave of a racially mixed group of "modern readers" that populated the colonial city. By "modern readers" I mean that they were a group able to communicate personally with the novels' authors through the print media, which they read quietly in their living rooms and bedrooms. They were the first generation of the new "urban bourgeoisie", who from the latter half of the nineteenth-century experienced a change in the form of their literary enjoyment from stories that were read aloud (the world of the storyteller) to stories that were read in silence.[675]

Throughout the following decades, as the number of institutions for education under the Ethical Policy expanded, literacy figures improved and the number of such "modern readers" increasingly grew. "Books were produced to be sold", Maier underlines, "and if they failed to create an audience, their producer could be forced to roll up his mats".[676] It was thus a modern book market, adhering to the laws of supply and demand.

3.1.2 The Komedie Stamboel as Indische Theatre

Similarly to the literature printed in Dutch and Malay newspapers and books, the popular Malay opera form of *komedi stambul* also drew inspiration and borrowed stage techniques from a wide range of sources. Plays based on *The Thousand and One Nights* were often staged by *komedi stambul* companies, alongside the *Faust* tale, adapted for the first time in 1891 as *Fathul Achmat, or The Faust of Arabia*, and *Bluebeard* which was one of the most popular titles of the *stambul* repertoire.[677] *Komedi stambul* troupes also drew on European theatrical technology, introduced in the shows of travelling European opera and theatre groups performing in the Indies during the second half of the nineteenth century, including: "The proscenium stage, wing-and-drop set, focused

---

671 See Tsuchiya, "Popular Literature and Colonial Society", 472.
672 See Watson, "Some preliminary remarks", 424.
673 See Cohen, *The Komedie Stamboel*, 277.
674 Ibid., 278.
675 Tsuchiya, "Popular Literature and Colonial Society", 476.
676 Maier, "Explosions in Semarang", 6.
677 See Cohen, "The Komedie Stamboel", 72.

stage lighting, emotive character-based acting, musical orchestra accompaniment, division of plays into scenes and acts, makeup and costumes [...]".[678] Another source of influence was the Parsi theatre, delivering a repertoire of songs and stories from Persia and India to Southeast Asia in the same period (see Section 1.3.3 on Parsi Theatre and the Cinematograph).[679] Therefore, the *komedi stambul*, whose cast would have been made up of a mix of Indonesian, Chinese and Eurasian performers, may have used European dramaturgy and theatrical technology, but by doing so in their own language and idioms they were in fact appropriating and localising it, presenting "an indigenized form" of European theatre.[680] "*Stambul* staged a modern model for representation, both in theatre and in real life. As commercial entertainment performed in readily accessible Malay language in public theaters, depicting characters mechanically reproduced or re-presented from social life, it was not contingent on expert spectators, local religious practices, or place spirits. [...] It was a place for exploration of possibilities, including ones overtly forbidden by the colonial regime" (see further in Introduction).[681]

For Cohen, the period in which the troupe known as Komedie Stamboel can be identified as "An Indische Theater" is clearly demarcated in the fifth chapter of his book bearing that title as the years between 1898 and 1903.[682] It begins with Komedie Stamboel Boenga Mawar's performance in Semarang in late 1898 of "a new sort of play [...], a social drama with a contemporary Indies setting entitled *Secrets of Semarang by Day and Night*", which Cohen designates as "the theatrical equivalent of an *Indische roman*".[683] Unlike the adaptations of Western plays or of stories from *The Thousand and One Nights*, *Indische roman* plays performed by this and other *stambul* companies which came to be known in the trade as "*rusia* (secret) plays, likely after the Malay title of *Secrets of Semarang*", offered something different to spectators.[684]

> Stories of this sort played on motifs that are familiar to Javanese more from Indic tales enacted as wayang and topeng than from the *Arabian Nights*. Magic arrows, men posing as women and women as men, hand-to-hand combat with raksasa, deposed kings posing as beggars, bodies cast adrift at sea. All these are devices found in tales that have existed in Java for at least a thousand years. With a bit of tweaking, the same plot could be transposed to the mythical universes of the Mahabharata or Panji.[685]

Among the *Indische romans* adapted by the company under the direction of Mahieu were: *Secrets of Batavia; Nyai Dasima; Rosina; Si Conat, the Bandit Chief*

---

678 Ibid., 41.
679 Ibid.
680 Ibid., 185.
681 Ibid., 345, emphasis added.
682 Ibid., 275–339.
683 Ibid., 277, italics in original. The death of the company's legendary director, Auguste Mahieu, marks the end of this period of "Indische theatre".
684 Ibid., 278, italics in original.
685 Ibid., 286, italics in original.

of Tangerang; Siti Rohaya: A Tale from Batavia; and *Revenge, or Oeij Kim Nio* and *Lie Koen Njan.* These became part of a growing effort "to indigenize the *stambul* form" and appeal to rural audiences on Java.[686] On top of the *Indische roman* plays, the company's repertoire continued to represent highly diverse source materials, including plays from Parsi theatre and *bangsawan*, and adaptations of European operas, such as *Faust* and *Aïda.* "There was a play based on a Siamese chronicle, *The Battle of Achmad Mohamad: The Origin of the Genie King,* also known as *The Monk King, or a War Tale Concerning the King of Siam.*"[687]

European spectators were often curious to see how the Komedie Stamboel adapted operas like Gounod's *Faust*, Bellini's *Norma* and *La sonnambula*, and Verdi's *Aïda*. However, *stambul* treatments of these texts were often not accepted by Europeans as "the genuine articles".[688] By comparison, non-European spectators had different expectations when coming to watch the company's appropriations of Western operatic classics. Komedie Stamboel might have performed its operas on improvised makeshift stages, rather than at colonial theatre buildings used by visiting European opera companies. However, Cohen writes, "[...] the masses accepted the Komedie Stamboel uncritically and without reserve as *De Oost Indische Opera* – the opera of the East Indies".[689]

3.2 Abdulally Esoofally

The Royal Bioscope, owned by a British-Indian entrepreneur by the name Abdulally Esoofally, travelled throughout Southeast Asia from 1901 to 1907, holding shows in Singapore, Sumatra, Java, Burma (Myanmar) and Ceylon (Sri Lanka).[690] According to Erik Barnouw and S. Krishnaswamy's work on the history of Indian cinema, "[...] from 1908 to 1914 [Esoofally] continued his cinema travels in India. His tent was 100 feet long and 50 feet wide, propped by four posts, and could hold a thousand people. The short items shown were purchased outright by Esoofally, according to the practice of the time, and were used till the prints wore out."[691] According to Esoofally's own account, he would "[...] buy these bits at the rate of 6d. per foot and 40 or 50 pictures composed [his] full programme. The films, however small, provided a varied fare. They included comedy gags, operas, travel films, sports events, etc. The maximum length of those films ranged between 100 and 200 feet and only in 1908 I remember to have shown my biggest films – 1,000 feet in length – in my traveling cinema."[692]

686 Ibid., emphasis added.
687 Ibid., 302, italics in original. For a list of plays and tableaux performed by the Komedie Stamboel between 1891 and 1901, see Appendix to Cohen's book (ibid., 381–390).
688 Ibid., 175.
689 Ibid., 176, italics in original.
690 See Barnouw et al., *Indian Film*, 8. I would like to thank Rianne Siebenga for helping me in identifying Esoofally.
691 Ibid.
692 Ibid.

3.2.1 First Run in Sumatra: The New Bioscope, 1901

Apart from the fact that his name was often spelled differently in advertisements and reports – either A. A. Josep, Jousoof, Jusuf, Yusuf or Yousoof, the spelling very much depending on whether the newspaper was in Dutch or Malay – Esoofally travelled by various stage names in Java and Sumatra. Instead of the later Islamic-sounding name, it appears that at first he went by the Anglicised name John Joseph, with a tent show set up in Medan's Esplanade and advertised in October 1901 as the New Bioscope (*De Nieuwe Bioscoop*).[693] It was only during the last week of the New Bioscope's tour that the shows were advertised under the management of A. A. Esoofally.[694] The most expensive films on the opening night, scheduled for Saturday, 5 October at 500 Mexican Dollars apiece and 750 feet in length, were identified in one newspaper report as: "[...] the funeral of Queen Victoria [...], coronation celebrations [of Wilhelmina] in Amsterdam, cavalry in full battle, and Aladdin and the wonder lamp (performed by the Lyric Theatre in London)".[695] Another report following the screening identified the battle scenes as "snapshots from the war in China [Boxer Uprising] and the battle of Glencoe" (see also advertisement in Figure 3–1).[696]

The hype in the newspapers built up as the opening show approached: "A bioscope is, as it were, a giant cinematograph [*cinematograaf*] as is known. It is also known that there are two kinds, one that is unpalatable due to the jittering and flickering, and another that projects stable pictures. According to the manager of 'this' bioscope [it] is of the latter sort."[697] Nevertheless, despite many promises by the manager that the technical qualities of his device were superior to those of another recently visiting company, problems emerged immediately. On the first night, although many spectators had already lined up outside the tent, "[...] Mr. Joseph sent them all away because he tested the electric light, provided to him by the electricity company, and found it lacking".[698] The next night he apparently felt he could wait no longer and decided to go on with the show, even though the light was still not quite right. The earlier part of the show, which included the scenes showing Queen

---

693   The first advertisement appeared already a couple of weeks ahead of the opening show in *Sumatra Post* (18 September 1901).

694   Advertisement, *Deli Courant* (23 October 1901). I would like to thank Nadi Tofighian for pointing out the advertisement in *Deli Courant* to me. The change of names was likely for commercial resaons, presumably starting out as John Joseph in Singapore which would have made sense in a British colonial context. The later choice of the name Yusuf and its variants was probably intended to appeal to a more Muslim audience.

695   "De nieuwe bioscoop", *Deli Courant* (21 September 1901).

696   "De Bioscope-voorstelling", *Deli Courant* (7 October 1901). The films could be from Pathé Frères: FUNERAILLES DE LA REINE VICTORIA (Pathé Frères, 1901), ÉVÉNEMENTS DE CHINE: BATAILLE AU PIED DE LA MUREILLE DE PEKIN (Pathé Frères, 1901), UNE ESCARMOUCHE PRÈS DE GLENCOË or ASSAUT D'UNE COLLINE PRÈS DE GLENCOË (Pathé Frères, year not given), ALADIN ET LA LAMPE MERVEILLEUSE (Pathé Frères, 1901).

697   "De nieuwe bioscoop", *Deli Courant* (21 September 1901).

698   "De bioskoop", *Sumatra Post* (7 October 1901).

> **Komt, ziet en overtuigt U!!**
> Een buitengewoon mooie
> **VOORSTELLING,**
> van de Nieuwe Bioscope,
> **In de Tent tegenover het Station.**
> Men zal er de meest wondervolle en interessante
> **"Levende" Photos**
> te zien krijgen, als nooit te voren vertoond.
> o. a. ALADIN en de WONDERLAMP,
> Scènes van de TRANSVAAL- en CHINA-
> OORLOGEN, enz., enz, enz.
> **Prijzen der plaatsen als gewoonlijk.**
> **Deuren geopend 8 uur. Aanvang
> 9 uur n. m. precies.**
> 1004 JOHN JOSEPH, Manager.

Figure 3-1. Advertisement for the New Bioscope with John Joseph as manager, *Sumatra Post* (8 October 1901). Retrieved from Delpher on 5 October 2015, http://resolver.kb.nl/resolve?urn=ddd:010320670:mpeg21:a0014.

Wilhelmina, suffered due to the lack of light, but it was generally agreed upon that the later part of the evening was much better because, as the *Sumatra Post* explained it, "[...] less houses were using light as the evening went on and so more electricity went to the cinema".[699] The show was nevertheless recommended, "[...] especially if, as Mr. Joseph hopes, the electricity company fixes the light so that it's more powerful also at the beginning of the evening".[700]

It was the final statement that got "Mr. Joseph" into an argument with the electricity company running over the pages of the newspapers for the next few days. It was not the case that the electricity company could not provide sufficient light, the *Sumatra Post* was required to correct the earlier claim, but in fact the plant could provide more than the cinema was able to use, and so the fault for the poor light quality lay with the less than perfect design of the "Biographman".[701] The company further went on to clarify that it provided

---

699 Ibid.

700 Ibid.

701 "Het licht in de bioskoop", *Sumatra Post* (9 October 1901).

3 – Komedi Bioscoop, Indische Films and the Localisation of Film Exhibition

alternating current (AC) while the device worked on direct current (DC), and, since the exhibitor did not have the right transformer, the voltage going into the machine was wrong. Moreover, the electricity company claimed, the actual voltage was too high leading to flickering and overheating which made the light blue. They prepared a quick fix for him, so that the correct voltage and current could go into the device. While the result was still less than perfect, the machine was heating up a lot, gradually increasing the electrical resistance. Therefore, more power was dissipated as heat and the actual light itself improved, concluded the report.[702]

According to other reports later on his tour, Esoofally was also showing scenes from the Boxer Uprising, Greco-Turkish War and Boer War.[703] The images, including several coloured ones, were to the liking of the numerous spectators across all seating classes.[704] At times, watching other film-goers proved to be "just as fascinating as the show itself":

> The grilling of the 'toean pandita' [missionary pastor] was an uplifting moment especially for the Chinese [...]. During the storming of the walls of Peking, however, they were all silent. [...]
> Of course, the Turkish army has its share in the success of the evening, as the little friends deplete a Greek house in about 60 seconds, stabbing the residents with knives, avoiding the women and plundering the safe [... received by those] in the first class, i.e. [the "Native" spectators] seated in the front, in ecstasy!
> One of them, apparently a craftsman, applauded fervently when these chests with "goodies" were struck open and cried with tears of emotion in his eyes [...] full of admiration for his brethren, also by the release of the prisoner a buzz of admiration arose from the avant scène. The show now works to educate the masses!
> The artillery of the Turkish Sultan was also much admired, but the Turkish warship swaying back and forth at sea, was probably an oversight, because that fleet at the time had no floating warships.[705]

After a month of shows in Medan, Esoofally presumably stayed on Sumatra, as this research found a couple of shows given in Binjai in November 1901.[706]

---

702 Ibid.
703 "De Bioscoop", *Deli Courant* (31 October 1901). See further on the Boer War in Section 2.2.2.
704 "De bioskoop", *Sumatra Post* (7 October 1901).
705 "De afgeloopen week", *Deli Courant* (12 October 1901), italics in original. The reference to the reactions to the Boxer Uprising film was likely the scene mentioned above in footnote 696 along with MARTYRE D'UN MISSIONNAIRE À PAO-TING-FOU – INTERVENTION DES TROUPES ALLIÉES (Pathé Frères, 1901, part of ÉVÉNEMENTS DE CHINE). Greco-Turkish War scenes could have been MASSACRE EN CRÈTE and BOMBARDEMENT D'UNE MAISON (Méliès, 1897). The Turkish warship scene was probably one of Méliès' Greco-Turkish War films, surviving in the National Film and Television Archive in the UK with the attributed title 'Action on Deck of Warship' (Bottomore, *Filming, Faking and Propaganda*, Chapter 3, p. 13). As Sabine Lenk has proposed to me, if Esoofally got his films from London, he might have obtained Pathé's films through their London representative (Sourcy & Cie) and Méliès films via Warwick.
706 "Onze Nieuwtjes", *Deli Courant* (5 November 1901).

By mid-November, Esoofally boarded the steamship *Sumatra* and headed for Penang.[707]

3.2.2 On the Komedi Circuit in Java: The Royal Bioscope, 1903–1906

Esoofally apparently returned again to the Indies only in March of 1903, giving shows at the Manège in Tanah Abang under a new company name: the Royal Bioscope.[708] Tickets were advertised at f 2 for box seats, f 1 for first class, f 0.50 for second class, and the third class, mentioned only in the Malay advertisements, at f 0.25 to Muslims and Javanese.[709] Having most likely been exposed to the raving reviews coming from Singapore, the Batavia newspapers were drumming up the expectations for the upcoming shows whose attractions were to include "Princes of Europe, wars, parades, courts, churches, prisons, waterfalls, etc. etc.".[710] Unfortunately, the opening show scheduled for Saturday, 28 March had to be postponed, once again, until further notice. The excuse this time was that the technician had yet to arrive.[711]

The opening finally took place on 1 April 1903 to a well-attended hall, with the programme including the previously shown scenes of the coronation of Queen Wilhelmina, as well as a recording of a football match in England and the Oberammergau Passion Play (see discussion of the controversy and response to the Passion Play films in Section 2.3.1).[712] On the whole, the Malay reviews usually showed more enthusiasm about the Royal Bioscope's shows than the Dutch ones, describing many of the scenes in detail. According to *Bintang Betawi*, the exhibition space was often crowded, especially on Friday nights. Many of the spectators were identified as young Chinese men and women, and the newspaper was actively encouraging (male) readers to come with their wives and children to watch the wonderful presentations and to enjoy a good laugh and some excitement.[713] The kind of marketing language used by this and other newspapers suggests these were self-promotional pieces written by Esoofally himself.

By the end of April, supposedly by request of many Chinese, the Royal Bioscope moved from the south-western district of Tanah Abang, with its high

---

707 "Vertrokken", *Sumatra Post* (18 November 1901).

708 Advertisement, *Bintang Betawi* (24 March 1903). In between these two instances in which he appeared in the Indies, this research has found shows of the Royal Bioscope in Singapore from October 1902 until the end of January 1903 (Advertisement, *The Singapore Free Press* (29 September 1902)). Although the Singapore tour does not identify Esoofally by name at any point, the films on the programme of the Royal Bioscope there match the titles later shown in the Indies, as well as in the quote from the interview with Esoofally. The final report in Singapore stated that the company was leaving for Java the following week (Untitled, *The Straits Times* (31 January 1903)).

709 Advertisement, *Bintang Betawi* (24 March 1903).

710 "De Bioscoop", *Het Nieuws van den Dag voor Nederlandsch-Indië* (27 March 1903).

711 Advertisement, *Het Nieuws van den Dag voor Nederlandsch-Indië* (28 March 1903).

712 "De Bioscoop", *Het Nieuws van den Dag voor Nederlandsch-Indië* (2 April 1903).

713 "Kabar sehari-hari dari Betawi dan laen-laen negri", *Bintang Betawi* (8 April 1903).

proportion of European population, to a more central location in Mangga Besar, part of Batavia's Chinatown district. The *"komedi bioscoop"* or *"komedi gambar hidup"*, as it was now referred to in Malay, was to occupy the hall of *komedi Tjindra Bangsawan*.[714] The advertisements promised an entirely new programme and newspaper reports mentioned that a new device had arrived along with the films, which obviously led to new technical problems when first trying to operate it.[715] The reports do not indicate where the films and device were shipped from, but if to judge by an earlier mention during the run in Singapore, as well as by Esoofally's own statements brought here earlier, they arrived from London.[716] Shows were offered every night at 9 pm, with doors opening already at 8 pm. On Wednesday and Friday afternoons there were special programmes for children at half price.

The advertisements also provided information on the professional team operating the Royal Bioscope: Manager H. van Hausen – in Malay, or H. van Housen – in Dutch, Owner A. A. Josep – in Malay, or A. A. Yusuf – in Dutch, and Mechanic-Electrician A. Louis – in Malay, or A. Lewis – in Dutch.[717] Van Housen was praised in a letter from Captain of the Chinese Tio Tek Ho published in the Malay daily *Bintang Betawi*, stressing the impact the show made on the Captain and his family after their visit to the Royal Bioscope.[718] Over the years, the Royal Bioscope continued to reap, and publicly share, diplomas and medals from the King of Siam and the Sultan of Johore, as well as praises from places such as "Batavia, Buitenzorg [Bogor], Semarang, Surabaya, Malang, Banjarmasin [in South Kalimantan, or Indonesian Borneo], etc.".[719]

Van Housen was clearly an important and trusted employee, in mid-Maay Esoofally announced that the former was leaving Java for ten days to Singapore in the interest of the company.[720] Before his departure, van Housen reportedly dropped by the offices of *Bintang Betawi*, explaining that he was going away in search of a proper venue for shows in Singapore and wanted to thank all the people who have been attending the shows in Batavia.[721] Nevertheless, Esoofally was not as lucky with all members of his staff. Around the same time a special notice appeared next to the regular advertisements for the shows, announcing that, as of 7 May 1903, Mr. T. Edward had ceased to be employed as agent for the Royal Bioscope, and that Esoofally could not be held liable for

714 "Kabar sehari-hari dari Betawi dan laen-laen negri", *Bintang Betawi* (27 April 1903), italics in original.
715 "Kabar sehari-hari dari Betawi dan laen-laen negri", *Bintang Betawi* (30 April 1903).
716 According to advertisements, a new stock of films arrived on board the steamship *Malacca* (Advertisement, *The Straits Times* (8 November 1902)). The shipping lists of the previous day indicate that the vessel, which left London on 4 October, arrived in Singapore on 6 November ("Arrivals", *The Straits Times* (7 November 1902)).
717 Advertisements, *Bintang Betawi* and *Het Nieuws van den Dag voor Nederlandsch-Indië* (9 May 1903).
718 "Soerat Kiriman", *Bintang Betawi* (12 May 1903).
719 Advertisement, *Preanger-Bode* (17 May 1906).
720 Advertisement, *Het Nieuws van den Dag voor Nederlandsch-Indië* (14 May 1903).
721 "Kabar sehari-hari dari Betawi dan laen-laen negri", *Bintang Betawi* (15 May 1903).

any engagements entered into with Edward from that date onward.[722] Following Van Housen's departure, the Royal Bioscope stayed for a few more shows in Batavia before reportedly continuing for shows in Buitenzorg (Bogor).[723] "The public in Bogor should consider themselves lucky to be getting a visit from this renowned bioscope", noted *Bintang Betawi*.[724]

By the time the Royal Bioscope arrived for shows in Semarang in January 1904, Esoofally was able to find a trusted manager. A new agent and accounts manager by the name L. Wenzel was signed at the bottom of the advertisements and he remained with the company until August 1905.[725] Wenzel reportedly obtained a permit from the local authorities to offer shows at Semarang's *Alun Alun* during the course of one month, and the next day immediately began to set up the bioscope tent.[726] With ever growing competition from other devices, the Royal Bioscope tried to differentiate itself from the rest as "[...] showing vivid scenes of current events, it gives you a whole world tour [...] our bioscope is operated by a special motor free of any faults of other Kinematographs. Allow us to point out that, out of all the other Kinematographs which have visited this colony, none can be compared to our machinery and our pictures. They are so pure, bright, exciting and of course [...] interesting, entertaining and surprising."[727] Tickets for the opening show on 2 January were offered at four different price categories (box for f 2, first class for f 1.50, second for f 1, third for f 0.50, fourth for f 0.25), with discount to military below the rank of officer.[728] The show was to be accompanied by the Royal Bioscope's very own string orchestra.[729]

However, despite the efforts of the new manager, the Royal Bioscope was not very successful in Semarang and failed to draw big crowds. The roof of the tent often failed to withstand the torrential rainfall and, other than a few people finding dry spots in the back, most spectators apparently felt like they were sitting in the open air, "[...] letting themselves be sprinkled by the [Roman]

---

722 Advertisements, *Bintang Betawi* and *Het Nieuws van den Dag voor Nederlandsch-Indië* (14 May 1903). T. Edward may have been Thomas Edward who, a few months earlier, served as the agent for the Komedie Indra Zanzibar, owned by S. Kassim and managed by Hamid (Advertisement, *Soerabaiasch-Handelsblad* (13 November 1902)). Esoofally encountered a similar problem a couple of years later, in July 1905, when a new manager by the name H. C. Mason was hired for shows in Batavia only to be dismissed a few days later, posting a notice next to the regular advertisements according to which "Mason is no longer connected to the Royal Bioscope. Tickets acquired from this gentleman are not accepted" (Advertisement, *Het Nieuws van den Dag voor Nederlandsch-Indië* (26 July 1905); Advertisement, *Het Nieuws van den Dag voor Nederlandsch-Indië* (31 July 1905)).

723 Advertisement, *Het Nieuws van den Dag voor Nederlandsch-Indië* (19 May 1903).

724 "Kabar sehari-hari dari Betawi dan laen-laen negri", *Bintang Betawi* (20 May 1903).

725 Advertisement, *De Locomotief* (30 December 1903). By the end of 1905, when the Royal Bioscope returned to Java again for shows in Semarang, a new manager appeared in the ads by the name C. I./L. Schaaff, later manager and partner of The Chrono (Advertisement, *Selompret Melajoe* (7 December 1905); Advertisement, *Taman Sari* (9 April 1906)).

726 "De Royal Bioscope", *De Locomotief* (29 December 1903).

727 Advertisement, *De Locomotief* (30 December 1903).

728 Advertisement, *De Locomotief* (2 January 1904).

729 Advertisement, *De Locomotief* (6 January 1904).

god Pluvius".[730] One report claimed the disappointment was not only due to the West Monsoon rains, but also to the fact that the previous cinematograph tent to visit Semarang lingered for so long that it "[...] sucked up all of the public's curiosity [*kijklust*]".[731] If at the conclusion of the month no permit extension will be requested", another newspaper claimed, "no Semaranger will be sorry about that".[732] What is more, new competition was on its way in the form of the N. V. Biograph, in a waterproof tent at Karang Tengah in the Chinese *kampung*, and for cheaper entrance prices (box *f* 1.50, first class *f* 1, second *f* 0.50, third for "Foreign Orientals" *f* 0.25, fourth for "Natives" *f* 0.10, and half price for children below the age of ten years and for military below the rank of officers).[733] And while the quality of the latter's device "left something to be desired", the tent itself was found to be "[...] spacious, airy and very clean, the three factors that count, while the installation [of electric lighting] is a triumph for the company De Vlijt".[734] "The genre of the films is by no means inferior to that of the Royal Bioscope", the report in *De Locomotief* continued, "but tastes differ [... so] the critical public should go judge for itself."[735]

The Royal Bioscope tried to compete by lowering its own ticket prices: box *f* 1.50, first class *f* 1, second *f* 0.75, third *f* 0.30, fourth *f* 0.15.[736] And while this appeared to improve the attendance figures, the one-month permit was nearly up by that point.[737] The Royal Bioscope apparently was interested in staying on for additional shows, yet the local government refused to extend its permit as it was eager to make progress on its plans for the city garden on the premises previously occupied by the tent.[738] On 1 February 1904 the Royal Bioscope gave its last show in Semarang before heading out to Kudus.[739]

It is not clear where the Royal Bioscope went to from there. It was back in Java for shows in Sukabumi only in December 1904.[740] In January 1905, the Royal Bioscope finally returned for shows in Batavia, to a warm welcome by newspapers and audiences. In advertisements promoting the upcoming shows a couple of weeks before the opening, the Royal Bioscope, still under the management of L. Wenzel, was literally trying to make a name for itself, during a time in which a variety of titles were used for moving picture shows:

730 "Royal Bioscope", *De Locomotief* (19 January 1904). For more on the strife of exhibitors with weather conditions in Semarang, see Section 6.2.
731 "Royal Bioscope", *De Locomotief* (7 January 1904).
732 "Brieven uit Semarang", *Het Nieuws van den Dag voor Nederlandsch-Indië* (12 January 1904).
733 "Concurrentie", *De Locomotief* (21 January 1904).
734 "Biograaf", *De Locomotief* (22 January 1904).
735 Ibid.
736 Advertisement, *De Locomotief* (19 January 1904).
737 "Royal Bioscope", *De Locomotief* (27 January 1904).
738 "De Royal Bioscope en stadstuin", *De Locomotief* (2 February 1904).
739 Ibid.
740 "Het Land der Gepensioneerden [sic]", *Het Nieuws van den Dag voor Nederlandsch-Indië* (14 December 1904).

The Royal Bioscope, The King of Cinematographs, Biographs, Cinematoscopes, Animatoscopes, etc. etc. etc. is expected here. No flickering. Vast and bright light. Following a trip around the world and a journey across Java, where the owners of this Bioscope have gained much success, they return again to this city next week for shows at the Manège in Tanah Abang, of the same genre as those that are attracting so much attention now at the Alhambra Theatre in LONDON. The most interesting scenes will be displayed on screen, without flickering, bright and sharp. So perfect, never before seen here. The big opening show will be announced.[741]

A few days later, another advertisement explained that the Royal Bioscope was the best and most unique of its kind because "[...] this is the only Bioscope that has had the honour of performing to almost all Crowned Heads of the world. That is why it has the right to be called the King of Bioscopes."[742] Interestingly, the advertisements in Dutch generally used the name "Royal Bioscope" in English, presumably to retain the connection to the London metropole, while the Malay advertisements opted for the Dutch "Koninklijke Bioscope", perhaps assuming the royal designation in Dutch would be more readily recognisable and royal-sounding to its readers.[743] In any case, the two names were used interchangeably in Dutch and Malay newspaper reports over the following weeks. *Kabar Perniagaan* even went so far as dubbing it the "*Raja Bioscope*".[744] By now the Malay newspapers not only borrowed from the jargon of *komedi* to refer to the Royal Bioscope, but also from that of the *wayang kulit*, referring to the exhibitor as a *dalang*, the term used for the puppeteer in the Javanese shadow play.[745] Dutch and Malay newspapers also differed in the ways they presented the schedule. While Dutch newspapers noted that programme changes took place every Wednesday and Saturday, the Malay newspapers went by the Islamic calendar system in which a new day begins at sundown of the previous day, therefore mentioning the programme change taking place on the eves of Thursday and Sunday.[746]

When it was finally time for the opening, Esoofally dropped by the desk of *Bintang Betawi* in person, to announce that the opening show would take place on 1 January 1905, "at the usual place" in Tanah Abang.[747] He presumably also paid a visit to the offices of *Pembrita Betawi*, which ran a promotional piece similar in tone on the same day, highlighting the Royal Bioscope's success and the praise it has received everywhere it had played.[748] It further drew attention to the tickets available to Muslim spectators, which were deemed to be "not

---

741 Advertisement, *Bataviaasch Nieuwsblad* and *Het Nieuws van den Dag voor Nederlandsch-Indië* (20 December 1904); emphasis in original. Practically identical advertisements appeared a week later in the Malay newspapers: Advertisement, *Bintang Betawi* and *Pembrita Betawi* (28 December 1904).

742 Advertisement, *Java-Bode* (29 December 1904).

743 Only the *Java-Bode* used "Koninklijke Bioscope" in some of the advertisements.

744 "Radja Bioscope", *Kabar Perniagaan* (4 January 1905), emphasis added.

745 "Kabar sehari-hari dari Betawi dan laen-laen negri", *Bintang Betawi* (24 January 1905).

746 Advertisement, *Pembrita Betawi* (3 January 1905).

747 "Kabar sehari-hari dari Betawi dan laen-laen negri", *Bintang Betawi* (28 December 1904).

748 "Gambar Hidoep", *Pembrita Betawi* (28 December 1904).

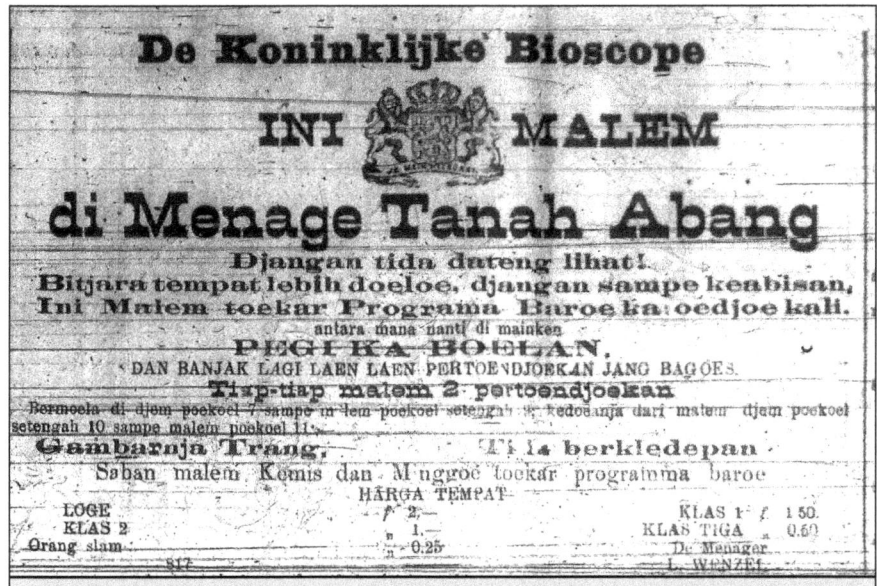

Figure 3–2. Advertisement for the Royal Bioscope's screening of LE VOYAGE DANS LA LUNE ("Pegi ka boelan"), *Pembrita Betawi* (21 January 1905). Scan courtesy of PNRI, Jakarta.

too expensive [at] only 25 cents".[749] The newspapers appear to have agreed with the statements in the advertisements. For instance, *Bintang Betawi* noted that while other shows may claim that they should be called "bioscope", none of them were nearly as good as the shows offered by the Royal Bioscope.[750] *Pembrita Betawi* animatedly reported: "We asked a couple of people, why not come to watch, and they answered: 'why should I go again, I have seen these pictures before and this *komedi* is not so different from other *komedi* we have seen before.' But the newspaper assures that this is unlike any other previous *komedi*, big difference: good pictures, good lighting, seats, all neat and entertaining for the spectators. Come and see for yourself."[751]

It is difficult to discern to what extent all of these were objective reports. The Dutch newspapers similarly commended the steady electric light of the Royal Bioscope's projection device, which brought flickering down to a minimum, the superior conditions achieved in the conversion of the Manège into a screening room, as well as the frequent change of programme with longer reel films, such as Edwin S. Porter's THE GREAT TRAIN ROBBERY (1903), Georges Méliès's LE VOYAGE DANS LA LUNE (1902, see Figure 3–3), LE VOYAGE À TRAVERS L'IMPOSSIBLE (1904, which reportedly cost 800 guilders or 18 pound sterling[752]) and LE ROYAUME DES FÉES (1903), referred to in one of the Malay newspapers

749 Ibid.
750 "Kabar sehari-hari dari Betawi dan laen-laen negri", *Bintang Betawi* (23 January 1905).
751 "Gambar Hidoep", *Pembrita Betawi* (13 January 1905), emphasis added.
752 Advertisement, *Het Nieuws van den Dag voor Nederlandsch-Indië* (23 January 1905); Advertisement, *Bintang Betawi* (24 January 1905).

as "Miracle of the Sea or the Kingdom of the *Jin* and Elves".[753] The Malay-language newspapers in Batavia were absolutely taken with the Royal Bioscope, with rave reviews of the shows appearing in *Bintang Betawi*, *Pembrita Betawi* and *Kabar Perniagaan* nearly every single day of that month, including its earnings which reportedly exceeded 1,200 guilders for the first two nights alone.[754] Likewise, upon returning to Semarang for shows in April and May 1905, *Selompret Melajoe* was referring to the Royal Bioscope every other day reporting that, while in the past it seemed as if people were bored with the shows, now they were willing to come back two or three times making the tent nearly full every night.[755] By the end of its stint in Semarang, one reporter finally remarked: "[...] the author is tired of saying this, but this *komedi* is great".[756]

Even during the continuation of the tour in Surabaya, when just days earlier the Malay newspaper *Bintang Soerabaia* was still complaining about commercial entertainments, such as the Biograph, Bioscope, Cinematograph, and European circus acts which, the newspaper claimed, were just out to grab the money of the people of Java, taking all of it back to Europe and being of absolutely no benefit to the local economy or people,[757] the following opinion appeared in the same newspaper:

> Don't miss the Royal Bioscope because it is better than any other show that has visited here before. We have always denounced the picture entertainment because the price is very expensive, if this entertainment is compared with other kinds of shows. But the case of the Royal Bioscope has changed our minds because that novelty is worth watching.[758]

In 1906, while the Royal Bioscope was in Buitenzorg (Bogor) and planning to return to Batavia again, *Pembrita Betawi* went as far as urging its readers not to be "[...] too wasteful and save [their] money for watching this *komedi* when it comes here".[759] It is highly likely that there were all sorts of dealings behind the scenes, and the fact that Esoofally and his staff members were visiting newspaper desks directly might serve as a clue to this. Another more open instance of this is a reply in 1906 from the editor of *Het Nieuws van den Dag voor Nederlandsch-Indië* in response to a query received from the Bioscope showing at the time in Buitenzorg (Bogor), which was in fact the Royal Bioscope, confirming that: "Your piece can be placed under the Advertorial Section [*Ingezonden Mededeelingen*] for 30 cents per line".[760] There was also a

---

753 "Gambar Hidoep", *Pembrita Betawi* (23 January 1905), emphasis added. See Section 3.2.3 for more information on the Royal Bioscope's film programmes.

754 "Gambar-idoep", *Pembrita Betawi* (3 January 1905).

755 "Cinematograaf (Gambar Hidoep)", *Selompret Melajoe* (25 March 1905).

756 "Bioscope", *Selompret Melajoe* (11 May 1905), emphasis added.

757 "India Ollanda", *Bintang Soerabaia* (2 June 1905).

758 "India Ollanda", *Bintang Soerabaia* (8 June 1905). During the earlier part of the Royal Bioscope's stay in Surabaya, newspapers warmly recommended a visit, but at the same time noted that the tickets were too expensive ("De Royal Bioscope", *Soerabaiasch-Handelsblad* (26 May 1905)).

759 "Royal Bioscoop", *Pembrita Betawi* (18 June 1906), emphasis added.

760 "Correspondentie", *Het Nieuws van den Dag voor Nederlandsch-Indië* (22 June 1906).

practice of providing free tickets to the press which must have contributed, at the very least, to the scale of coverage if not its tone. We should therefore assume that some of the positive reviews and reports were sponsored in one way or another and probably self-written.

Moreover, Esoofally often donated money to charity as was common practice by other entertainment companies, which is yet another act that can be construed as a tool of self-promotion. For example, during his run in Surabaya from the end of May until the beginning of August 1905, he gave a portion of one night's income to the Protestant and Catholic orphanages, on top of which the children of these institutions were invited for special free screenings on two nights, one intended for the boys, and the other – for the girls.[761] Half of the revenues from the shows a few nights later were donated to the Chinese school Hoo Tjiong Hak Tong, with a programme "especially selected to suit the tastes of Chinese spectators".[762] The last show in Surabaya raffled golden watches among ticket buyers.[763]

Back in Batavia in July 1905 en route to Singapore, the Royal Bioscope was, once again, eagerly anticipated, with *Bintang Batavia* highlighting the new coloured pictures on the programme.[764] At this point there were in fact two Royal Bioscope outfits running at the same time: one in Surabaya until the beginning of August, and the other opening in Batavia in mid-July.[765] Upon its opening show at Tanah Abang, *Het Nieuws van den Dag voor Nederlandsch-Indië* especially commended the improved electric lighting, which apparently was now provided by its very own electrical installation producing approximately four horsepower.[766] Although the new installation was not particularly quiet, it provided powerful and constant lighting. The conversion of the Manège into an auditorium, in terms of the hospitality and comfort, was found to be in excellent order, suggesting that other companies "should use the 'Royal' as an example".[767]

At this point, the Royal Bioscope and some of its competitors were beginning to be introduced under new exhibition contexts, as part of local European and Javanese celebrations. For instance, during the first *Pasar Gambir* (great market) in Batavia at the end of August 1905, celebrating the birthday of Queen Wilhelmina, the Royal Bioscope moved to the festival venue at

---

761 "De Koninklijke Bioscope", *Soerabaiasch-Handelsblad* (20 June 1905).
762 Advertisement, *Bintang Soerabaia* (21 June 1905).
763 Advertisement, *Soerabaiasch-Handelsblad* (4 August 1905).
764 Advertisements, *Java-Bode* and *Bintang Batavia* (18 July 1905). *Bintang Betawi* changed its name to *Bintang Batavia* in July 1905.
765 There appears to be an overlap of a couple of weeks with shows in Surabaya and Batavia. Since Esoofally was continually having films shipped during his stay in Surabaya, it is also possible that another device was received at this point.
766 "Koninklijke Bioscope", *Het Nieuws van den Dag voor Nederlandsch-Indië* (24 July 1905).
767 Ibid.

Koningsplein.[768] Even within close proximity to other entertainments, the Royal Bioscope played to full houses, with some spectators having to remain standing during the entire show.[769] In 1906, the Royal Bioscope was also featured as part of the entertainment on offer at the *Sekaten* celebrations in Solo (Surakarta), to commemorate the birth of the prophet Muhammad, achieving "enormous success" even when in competition against five other bioscopes.[770] The advertisement in the *Preanger-Bode* and later reappearing in *Bintang Batavia* further related: "During the festival which lasts seven nights, the Royal Bioscope was visited by more than 60,000 Javanese and 15,000 Europeans and Foreign Orientals".[771]

Newspapers were torn between different companies. For example, when the Royal Bioscope and the Royal Vio were deeply involved in a war of attrition over the advertisement section of the Batavia newspapers, each trying to outdo and tarnish the other, *Kabar Perniagaan* claimed people have been asking to get its professional opinion on which one is truly the best.[772] The newspaper obliged diplomatically, claiming that both are just as good, yet pointing out that the Royal Bioscope had many pictures, thanks to the fact that it had agreements with several manufacturers and therefore were always able to obtain new and good pictures.[773]

3.2.3 "Komedi *within* Komedi": *Film Programmes and Points of Convergence with Texts in Circulation in the Indies*

Many of the films screened by the Royal Bioscope, as well as several of its competitors, would have been previously known to spectators thanks to their earlier translations into Malay or their stage adaptations (see Section 3.1).

Versions of *Faust*, the first Western text adapted by the Komedie Stamboel in 1891, were screened by the Royal Bioscope (in 30 tableaux) and the Netherlands Indies Biograph Company during their runs in 1905, and by the Chrono and the General Bioscope Company (owned by the Shahab brothers) in 1906.[774] Newspapers immediately drew the connections between stage and screen, for example: when *Faust* was shown in Semarang by the Royal Bioscope in May 1905, *Selompret Melajoe* noted that this is a case of "*komedi* within

768 Advertisement, *Het Nieuws van den Dag voor Nederlandsch-Indië* (29 July 1905).

769 "Komedie Gambar Roijal Bioscope", *Pembrita Betawi* (1 September 1905).

770 Advertisement, *Preanger-Bode* (17 May 1906).

771 Ibid.; Advertisement, *Bintang Batavia* (18 July 1906). In 1905, the population of Solo (Surakarta) totalled 118,378: 109,524 Javanese, 6,532 Chinese, 1,572 Europeans, 413 other Foreign Orientals, and 337 Arabs (see Kuntowijoyo, "Making an Old City a Pleasant Place to Stay for *Meneer* and *Mevrouw*: Solo, 1900–1915", *Humaniora* XII, no. 2 (2000): 139).

772 "Royal Bioscope Company", *Kabar Perniagaan* (2 July 1906).

773 Ibid.

774 "Betawi 22 Juli 1905", *Taman Sari* (22 July 1905); Advertisement, *Soerabaiasch-Handelsblad* (4 August 1905); Advertisement, *Het Nieuws van den Dag voor Nederlandsch-Indië* (31 March 1906); Advertisement, *Sumatra Post* (20 October 1906). From the available information in the newspapers, I was unable to identify which version of *Faust* was screened.

komedi".⁷⁷⁵ In Batavia, where it was referred to by the name used for the stage adaptation "Fatoel Achmad", it was admired for its entertainment and educational value.⁷⁷⁶ And, while it was advertised as "Goethe's Faust",⁷⁷⁷ by the time the Royal Bioscope showed it in Surabaya a few weeks later, *Soerabaiasch-Handelsblad* found it important to note that the manner in which the story of Faust is presented in the film is "very American".⁷⁷⁸ Another more lengthy report from Semarang gives more information about the film and its reception:

> The Royal Bioscope's tent was packed full with curious spectators yesterday evening; we must assume that the main reason to do so was to wait a minimum time to see the performance of the famous opera Faust as the public [normally] gets on the big stages. This film, which should be of a respectable length, evidently had the large auditorium greatly satisfied. There was good reason [for rushing to see it]. The beautiful décor, the large number of people who came to the theatre, the beautiful costumes and beautiful ballet performed by ballet dancers to be seen, all made the audience charged with energy. Mephisto's palace and Hell were no less attractive, [...] one might pass the boredom of eternal roasting there by admiring the numerous female godly spirits.⁷⁷⁹

Some reports claimed that the Royal Bioscope was even better than the *komedi stambul*. For instance, *Pembrita Betawi* found the Royal Bioscope's version of "Aladdin and his magic lamp in 45 tableaux" to be better than its *stambul* stage performances.⁷⁸⁰ "Readers [and, thus, spectators] are already familiar with the story of Aladdin and the Wonder Lamp, which is often staged by the *komedi stambul* and many other Malay *komedi* troupes", noted *Bintang Betawi*.⁷⁸¹ Described in the Singaporean press as a "representation of a burlesque of 'Aladdin'", it was singled out already in Esoofally's earlier run as the New Bioscope in Medan as "[t]he most beautiful series [...], the captivating magic fairy tale [*tooversprookje*], which especially captured the attention of the Orientals [*Oosterlingen*]".⁷⁸² Presumably, "Orientals" in this case was referring to Chinese and Malay spectators, while another report a few days later in the same newspaper honed in on the latter group: "The more fantastic, the better for the Malays,

---

775 "Royal Bioscope", *Selompret Melajoe* (6 May 1905), emphasis added.
776 "Betawi 24 Juli 1905", *Taman Sari* (24 July 1905); "Pertoendjoekan Gambar Idoep", *Taman Sari* (25 July 1905).
777 Advertisement, *De Locomotief* (5 May 1905).
778 "De Royal Bioscope", *Soerabaiasch-Handelsblad* (26 May 1905).
779 "De Royal Bioscope", *De Locomotief* (8 May 1905).
780 "Gambar Hidoep", *Pembrita Betawi* (28 January 1905).
781 "Kabar sehari-hari dari Betawi dan laen-laen negri", *Bintang Betawi* (13 May 1903). As Sabine Lenk has pointed out to me, the Pathé-version (ALADIN ET LA LAMPE MERVEILLEUSE, Pathé Frères, 1900) was announced in the catalogue of March 1902 with 45 scenes (230m for 460 French francs, see Bousquet, *Catalogue Pathé*, 856). The catalogue gives a screening time of 15 minutes. The term "scene" here is ambivalent, as the scenes listed in the catalogues at that time could represent just a part of an action, whereas on the stage a scene is an autonomous unit of a play. The high numbers of scenes announced by producers and exhibitors (as is the case also for the 30 "scenes" of *Faust* above) may have been a trick to lure theatre lovers into the cinema tent.
782 "The Royal Bioscope", *The Straits Times* (30 December 1902); "De Bioscope-voorstelling", *Deli Courant* (7 October 1901). Since the film was first shown already in 1901, it might have been Pathé's ALADIN ET LA LAMPE MERVEILLEUS (Pathé Frères, 1900).

and the dream of the *raja*, as well as Aladdin and the magic lamp won their full attention. Then they sit quietly huddled, dreaming with big open eyes and enjoying."[783] The above quotations, published between 1901 and 1905, reveal that spectators were fascinated with the content of these fairy tales, which were repeatedly performed and screened over the years.

Other films in this vein, screened by the Royal Bioscope as well as by several of its contemporaries, were "Ali Baba and the Forty Thieves", "Bluebeard", and "Robinson Crusoe".[784] Nevertheless, most of the films from this period were actualities rather than fiction, which to an extent mirrored the pages of Dutch and Malay newspapers that presented current news stories alongside serialised novels. The Russo-Japanese War of 1904–1905, as discussed in Chapter 2, was a popular topic on film programmes in the Indies at the time. A screening of the Royal Bioscope in Batavia in September 1905 thus lined up "Robinson Crusoe in 25 tableaux" alongside scenes from the battlefield at Port Arthur, pointing out that the Charles Urban cameraman Joseph Rosenthal received "special permission from the General Baron Nogi to capture [Russo-Japanese] war scenes, and has shown these in England and America to great success" (see Figure 2–5).[785] A review of the show a couple of days later further drew a comparison between the scenes of shelling at Port Arthur and the use of firearms in LES AVENTURES DE ROBINSON CRUSOË, with each shot from the more primitive armoury nevertheless managing to blow off "[...] a whole troop of cannibals [...]. Thus one sees: history repeats itself."[786]

3.2.4   An Indische *Film: The Case of* Nyai Dasima

As suggested earlier, film programmes at the time often also shared other stories and themes in common with popular literature in Dutch and Malay, which were further adapted to the *komedi stambul* stage. The case of *Nyai Dasima* stands out among these. While adaptations of titles such as *Faust, Bluebeard*,

---

783 "De afgeloopen week", *Deli Courant* (12 October 1901), emphasis added. The *raja* film could have been LE RÊVE DU RADJAH (Méliès, 1900). Versions of Aladdin were also screened at the time by the Java Cineograph Company and by M. Strauss's Cineograph or Chineograph (Advertisement, *Soerabaiasch-Handelsblad* (25 July 1902); Advertisement, *Het Nieuws van den Dag voor Nederlandsch-Indië* (31 March 1905)).

784 Méliès made BARBE-BLEUE (Star Film Company, 1902) and LES AVENTURES DE ROBINSON CRUSOË (Star Film Company, 1902). Ferdinand Zecca made ALI BABA ET LES 40 VOLEURS in 1902 for Pathé Frères, and later screenings might be referring to Segundo de Chomón's 1905 ALI BABA ET LES QUARANTE VOLEURS, also for Pathé Frères. Versions of "Ali Baba" were screened by N. V. Biograph, the Netherlands Indies Biograph, the Royal Bioscope, Phono Animatograph, S. M. Aidid's Royal Optigraph and Cine Lumen (Advertisement, *De Locomotief* (21 January 1904); Advertisement, *Bintang Soerabaia* (1 October 1904); Advertisement, *Het Nieuws van den Dag voor Nederlandsch-Indië* (7 January 1905); Advertisement, *De Locomotief* (2 April 1906); Advertisement, *Kabar Perniagaan* (10 December 1906); Advertisement, *Bataviaasch Nieuwsblad* (20 March 1908)). *Bluebeard* was on the programmes of the Netherlands Indies Biograph Company and Eastern Bioscope Company (Advertisement, *Bintang-Soerabaia* (1 October 1904); Advertisement, *Het Nieuws van den Dag voor Nederlandsch-Indië* (27 April 1905)). Film versions of "Robinson Crusoe" were shown by the Netherlands Indies Biograph Company, the Royal Bioscope, the Royal Optigraph and Cinema Orion (Advertisement, *Soerabaiasch-Handelsblad* (22 July 1905); Advertisement, *Het Nieuws van den Dag voor Nederlandsch-Indië* (8 September 1905); Advertisement, *Kabar Perniagaan* (4 December 1906); "Cinema Orion", *Sin Po* (27 August 1915)).

785 Advertisement, *Het Nieuws van den Dag voor Nederlandsch-Indië* (8 September 1905).

786 "Royal Bioscope", *Het Nieuws van den Dag van Nederlandsch-Indië* (11 September 1905).

3 – *Komedi Bioscoop*, *Indische* Films and the Localisation of Film Exhibition

Aladdin, Ali Baba and the Forty Thieves and *Robinson Crusoe* shown on screen by the Royal Bioscope and its contemporaries were Western productions (as discussed in the previous section), *Nyai Dasima* was a local production of a quintessentially *Indische* folklore tale. *Nyai* stories in general, which feature a colonial man and his *nyai* (informal "Native" wife) were some of the most popular tales of the *Indische roman* genre.[787] Among these *Nyai* stories, Watson rates Gijsbert Francis' *Nyai Dasima* as "far superior in style" thanks to the "smooth progression of the narrative, and lively dialogue" compared to other stories fitting this formula.[788]

The story of *Nyai Dasima* was in fact in circulation in the Indonesian archipelago for at least 250 years, but was first committed to paper in 1896 by Eurasian journalist and illustrator Gijsbert Francis and published by the Kho Tjeng Bie & Co. publishing house. It was, according to Tsuchiya, "a literary work born from definite 'hybrid' conditions": written in Malay by a man of mixed European and Asian descent, distributed through a Chinese publishing house, and circulating in an ethnically mixed late nineteenth century Dutch colonial society.[789] On top of that, since its first publication, *Nyai Dasima* has been re-written several times by Indonesian, Dutch and Chinese authors and poets, featured on the regular repertoires of every *komedi stambul* theatre company, and later adapted to contemporary theatre, ballet, opera, television programmes and cinema. It is still present and referenced in Indonesian popular culture to this day.

While the earliest film version known until now has been the highly successful 1929 production of NJAI DASIMA by the Chinese Indonesian Tan Koen Yauw film company, this research has discovered records of an earlier screen adaptation from 1906.[790] Mentioned in an advertisement for Esoofally's Royal Bioscope as "Njai Dasima. Specially recorded by the Royal Bioscope Company" (see Figure 3–3), it was included in the line-up for the company's upcoming tour of Batavia, alongside other non-fiction local views of Yogyakarta and Surabaya and many fiction and non-fiction scenes of Western origin, such as stories from *A Thousand and One Nights*, the San Francisco earthquake, the wedding of King of Spain Alfonso, British Navy manoeuvres, Esmeralda – "the latest drama by Victor Hugo", a boxing championship which took place two months earlier, and others.[791] The discussion here will provide

---

787 See Watson, "Some preliminary remarks", 428. The man in these stories could be English, Dutch, or, in some versions, Chinese.

788 Ibid., 421.

789 Tsuchiya, "Popular Literature and Colonial Society", 467.

790 As to my knowledge, no copy of the 1929 version has been retrieved either.

791 Advertisement, *Bataviaasch Nieuwsblad* (26 June 1906). Possible films on the programme: SAN FRANCISCO APRÈS LA CATASTROPHE (Pathé Frères, 1906), THE ERUPTION OF VESUVIUS (Director: A.C. Bromhead, Gaumont, 1906), DICK TURPIN'S LAST RIDE TO YORK (Director: Charles Raymond, Warwick, 1906) or DICK TURPIN'S RIDE TO YORK (Director: Lewin Fitzhamon, Hepworth, 1906), MARIAGE DU ROI D'ESPAGNE (Pathé Frères, 1906) or GRANDE PARADE À MADRID À L'OCCASION DU MARIAGE DU ROI ALPHONSE XIII (Director: Segundo de Chomón, Pathé Frères, 1906), THE GREAT HACKENSCHMIDT V. MADRALI MATCH (Urban, 1906), LA ESMERALDA (Gaumont, 1905).

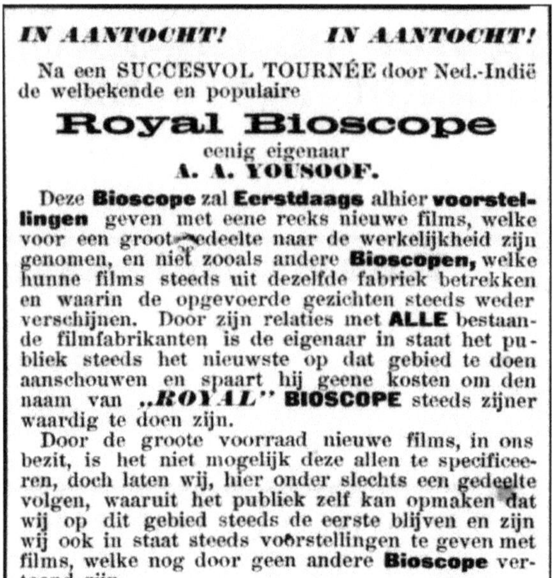

IN AANTOCHT! *IN AANTOCHT!*

Na een SUCCESVOL TOURNÉE door Ned.-Indië de welbekende en populaire

Royal Bioscope

eenig eigenaar

A. A. YOUSOOF.

Deze **Bioscope** zal **Eerstdaags** alhier **voorstellingen** geven met eene reeks nieuwe films, welke voor een groot gedeelte naar de werkelijkheid zijn genomen, en niet zooals andere **Bioscopen,** welke hunne films steeds uit dezelfde fabriek betrekken en waarin de opgevoerde gezichten steeds weder verschijnen. Door zijn relaties met **ALLE** bestaande filmfabrikanten is de eigenaar in staat het publiek steeds het nieuwste op dat gebied te doen aanschouwen en spaart hij geene kosten om den naam van *„ROYAL"* **BIOSCOPE** steeds zijner waardig te doen zijn.

Door de groote voorraad nieuwe films, in ons bezit, is het niet mogelijk deze allen te specificeeren, doch laten wij, hier onder slechts een gedeelte volgen, waaruit het publiek zelf kan opmaken dat wij op dit gebied steeds de eerste blijven en zijn wij ook in staat steeds voorstellingen te geven met films, welke nog door geen andere **Bioscope** vertoond zijn.

1. Een Arabische nachtelijke vermakelijkheid (Duizend en één nacht).
2. San Francisco ramp.
3. De laatste uitbarsting van de Vesuvius.
4. Dick Turpin laatste rit naar York.
5. Koning Alphonso's huwelijk en de Anarchist.
6. Engelands laatste Marine Manoeuvres.
7. Het worstel Wereld-Kampioenschap te Olympia, 28 April 1906, tusschen Hachenschmidt, de Russische Leeuw en Madrali, de verschikkelijke Turk.
8. Esmeralda, laatste Drama van Victor Hugo.
9. Njai Dasima, met speciale toestemming gefotograveerd door de **Royal Bioscope Company.**
10. Djokdjasche skaten feesten, gefotograveerd door de **Royal Bioscope Company.**
11. Landschaps Panorama's door geheel Java. Gefotograveerd door de **Royal Bioscope Company.**
12. Soerabaia — Passar Besaar tot Wonokromo, gefotograveerd door de **Royal Bioscope Company.**

5016

Figure 3–3. Advertisement for the Royal Bioscope's upcoming visit to Java, including recording of "Nyai Dasima" and other local views, *Bataviaasch Nieuwsblad* (26 June 1906). Retrieved from Delpher on 5 October 2015, http://resolver.kb.nl/resolve?urn=ddd:010134459:

some background on the institution of the *nyai*, as well as its reincarnations in the *Indische roman* and *Indische* theatre. Nevertheless, it will not focus on analysing either the story, which has been the subject of numerous studies, or the film itself, of which no known copy survives. Rather, it wishes to reflect on the way that incorporating this classic story into the Royal Bioscope's repertoire was a further move by Esoofally towards localising moving pictures for Indies audiences.

The institution of the *nyai*, the colonised woman living as a concubine to a European man, has been a topic of interest drawing much literary, theatrical, cinematic and scholarly attention. Since for hundreds of years the Dutch restricted the migration of European women to the colonies, colonial men – employees of the Dutch East India Company (VOC), recruits to the Royal Army, imperial government workers and plantation owners – were expected to rely on the company of local women as housekeepers and sexual partners.[792] One outcome of this widespread practice was the proliferation of Eurasian children, which led to anxieties about the future of European society and the Dutch race in the colonies. As Dutch families began arriving from the 1870s, European women were "charged with regenerating [...] the metropolitan affinities and the

792 See Stoler, "Making Empire Respectable", 637.

imperial purpose of their men".⁷⁹³ Keeping a *nyai*, who would often be a figure holding some power in the domestic space, was becoming less prevalent.

Francis's novella of 39 pages titled *Cerita Njai Dasima* (The Story of Nyai Dasima: A Victim of Seduction) from 1896, supposedly based on a true story that occurred around 1813, was therefore written at a time of rapid modernisation, when the keeping of a *nyai* in the domestic space was being perceived as ever more scandalous in the public sphere.⁷⁹⁴ Nevertheless, and possibly due to this, news stories about the lives of these women were often reported in the vernacular press, finding their way into so-called *"nyai* tales" in book form, which were consumed voraciously by the newly rising modern reading public in the Malay language.⁷⁹⁵

The plot summary of *Cerita Njai Dasima* is as follows. Edward W, an English administrator in West Java, moves to Batavia with a Muslim woman by the name Dasima as his *nyai*. "She was very beautiful. Her skin was fair and her hair was long. Willingly she had studied all the things a woman should know – cooking, sewing and dressmaking […] Dasima was a diligent and intelligent person. Mr. W loved her as though she were his legal wife. He entrusted the care of all his property to her. Dasima had even given him a pretty girl, named Nancy."⁷⁹⁶ Mr. W would buy Dasima all sorts of luxury items, on top of giving her generous amounts of money to spend, which she would set aside and save. After selling his land, they move together to Batavia, where the wealth and beauty of Dasima becomes the talk of the Muslim community. One Muslim man named Samiun decides to seduce her and manages to infiltrate the household by sending in an old lady named Ma Buyung as his spy. After becoming Dasima's housekeeper and gaining her trust, Ma Buyung uses a magic potion produced by a witch doctor to convince Dasima to leave Mr. W and their daughter, marry Samiun, and fully embrace Islamic life. Mr. W is hurt and bewildered, but allows Dasima to leave with her money. Once Dasima realises that Samiun is not going to leave his first wife, she begs him to let her go and return her possessions. Samiun then contracts a man to murder Dasima. Her body is thrown into the river and washes up on the river banks of Mr. W's house. The story ends with all parties involved in the murder arrested and imprisoned.

According to Tsuchiya, the re-incarnation of the Nyai Dasima story over decades, in various forms and beyond print media, is "[…] a rare occurrence in the literary history of Indonesia, and shows well how deeply the story of Dasima, the fated concubine, permeated popular culture during that period".⁷⁹⁷ While later versions often played down the anti-Muslim commen-

793   Ibid., 649.
794   G. Francis, *Tjerita Njai Dasima* (Batavia, 1896).
795   Tsuchiya, "Popular Literature and Colonial Society", 474.
796   Ibid., 468, quoted from G. Francis, *Nyai Dasima*, Working Paper no. 46, trans. Harry Aveling (Clayton, Australia: Monash University, 1988), 2.
797   Tsuchiya, "Popular Literature and Colonial Society", 477.

tary, and Mr. W's ethnicity was subject to change – sometimes presented as Dutch and at other times as a member of the native elite class or a Chinese – the figure of Dasima as victim would remain constant.[798] These include a verse poem in Chinese published by Tjiang in 1897, a novel written in 1926 in Dutch by possibly another Eurasian by the name of Manusama (who also contributed scripts to the *komedi stambul*), the 1929 film produced by Tan Koen Yauw film company, and a post-independence script written by S. M. Ardan in 1965.[799]

As mentioned above, *komedi stambul* troupes embraced *Nyai Dasima*, as did their mixed audiences. Matthew Cohen quotes at length from a review in a Malay-language newspaper of a *komedi stambul* adaptation of *Nyai Dasima* which was performed in Batavia in 1900, stressing the visceral response of spectators:

> People work in the city of Batavia for the sake of their physical sustenance – that is, to pay for food, clothes, and accoutrements. Is it not surprising, then, that the Sinar Hindia company, and its accomplished director, have been accepted with open arms and hearts?
>
> Every night that Sinar Hindia performs at Meester Cornelis, the people of Batavia and surroundings indicate that they understand how great the benefits are that accrue in receiving food for the soul. I have always looked after myself and insured that the food supplied to my body and soul are in balance, but I feel that Mahieu's performances are a sort of new sustenance serving to reinvigorate the nerves and elevate thoughts from the commonplace.
>
> Starting from the performance of *Nyai Dasima*, a story that causes tears to flow from the eyes of girls and women, Sinar Hindia has continually healed the ailing souls of the people who live here. ... Over the last nights, I have seen spectators from all parts come to the theater, where this community [*kaum*] is treated by the performing ensemble onstage, which is so lively and attractive in all aspects, including the smallest details, so that in the melancholic sections all the spectators look for a handkerchief to dry their eyes, and when it is animated [onstage] everyone feels that they live in fellowship.[800]

As Tsuchiya suggests, modern readership of newspapers and books, torn between tradition and modernity within the cultural plurality of the colonial city, "[...] was drawn emotionally into a literary world of things which could be understood by neither the modern intellect nor modern rationalism".[801] A similar emotional attachment seems to have been at work for the *komedi stambul* audience, which was even larger and farther-reaching due to the fact that enjoying the stage performance was not limited to a literate audience and could

---

798 See Jean Gelman Taylor, "Nyai Dasima: Portrait of a Mistress in Literature and Film", in Laurie J. Sears (ed.), *Fantasizing the Feminine in Indonesia* (Durham/London: Duke University Press, 1996), 225–248.

799 O. S. Tjiang, *Sair Tjerita di tempo tahoen 1813 Jang Belom Brapa Lama Soeda kadjadian di Betawi Terpoengoet Dari Boekoe: Njaie Dasima* (Batavia: Ijap Goan Ho, 1897); A. Th. Manusama, *Njai Dasima, Het Slachtoffer van bedrog en misleiding, een historische zedenroman van Batavia* (Batavia, 1926); "Njai Dasima", Film Indonesia, accessed on 2 February 2016, http://catalogue.filmindonesia.or.id/movie/title/lf-n011-29-352520_njai-dasima-i; S. M. Ardan, *Njai Dasima* (Jakarta: Pustaka Jaya, 1965). It was also referenced in the *Buru Quartet* by acclaimed Indonesian author Pramoedya Ananta Toer, see Pramoedya Ananta Toer, *This Earth of Mankind* [*Bumi Manusia*], trans. Max Lane (New York: Penguin, 1990 [1975]).

800 *Primbon Soerabaia* (19 October 1900), quoted in Cohen, *The Komedie Stamboel*, 303, italics in original.

801 Tsuchiya, "Popular Literature and Colonial Society", 474.

3 – *Komedi Bioscoop, Indische* Films and the Localisation of Film Exhibition

be consumed collectively, as suggested in the review above, rather than in the private confines of one's home.

Unfortunately, we can only imagine the response of Indies spectators to seeing the Royal Bioscope's *Nyai Dasima* on screen. Apart from several advertisements in the Batavia newspapers leading up to Esoofally's upcoming visit, this research has not been able to find any mention of an actual screening of the film, either in Batavia or elsewhere in Java, in the Dutch- or Malay-language press. Since the only clue to the existence of the film is found in the advertisements, it has in fact proven to be as ephemeral as its stage adaptations. While it is highly likely that the filmed version featured a performance by local *komedi stambul* actors, we cannot say for certain which troupe might have been filmed. In fact, it is entirely possible that the recording by the Royal Bioscope did not produce a projectable copy, as occurred to various contemporary entrepreneurs in the Indies.

At the same time, whether or not the Royal Bioscope's filmed version of *Nyai Dasima* was ever shown to the public seems almost beside the point. What is interesting is the way in which Esoofally was attempting to integrate the content of his Royal Bioscope shows into the canon of stories offered by popular commercial entertainment in the Indies.[802] His answer to Wybrands's challenging call for more *"Indische* scenes" combined localisation of content and technology or, in Peter Burke's terms, "hybrid texts" and "hybrid practices".[803] As an outsider to both Dutch an Indonesian culture, Esoofally appears to have served as an ideal cultural mediator, adapting a foreign entertainment form to blend in with the local culture, making it ever more relevant for local audiences.

3.2.5 *"Cinemania": Esoofally's Impact on the Local Movie-going Scene*

The time period in which Abdulay Esoofally was active in the Netherlands Indies as a moving picture exhibitor (1901–1906) was at the height of itinerant shows. Several touring companies were running along similar travel routes in the region, competing over audience sympathies, at times even in direct competition with one another in the same town. The case of Esoofally reveals several strategies employed by a seasoned professional with vast touring experience reaching beyond the local scene. His stage name and company moniker underwent several alterations, in order to best suit the cultural environment in which he was operating. Esoofally or a manager on his behalf paid regular visits to local newspaper desks, and most likely composed themselves some of the raving reviews lavished on the Royal Bioscope. Charity shows for the

---

802 "Nederlandsch-Indië", *Java-Bode* (9 July 1906).

803 According to Burke, translations are the clearest examples of "hybrid texts, since the search for what is often called 'equivalent effect' involves the introduction of words and ideas that are familiar to the new readers but might not be intelligent in the culture in which the book was originally written" (Burke, *Cultural Hybridity*, 17). "Hybrid practices may be identified in religion, music, language, sport and other cultural domains", wherein one culture adopts and adapts the cultural forms of another culture (ibid., 21–25).

benefit of orphans or victims of natural disasters were held, as was customary at the time, while also serving the Royal Bioscope's own commercial interests.

Esoofally's programming choices, initially highlighting current affairs, were gradually based on more fiction films, possibly reflecting the development in his audiences' preferences. And although most films were presumably made with a Western audience in mind, it is striking that many of these film titles mirrored stories which would have been familiar to local Indies spectators from their previous translations into Malay or from their earlier adaptations to the *stambul* stage. Finally, the recording of a local folk tale such as *Nyai Dasima* is further proof of Esoofally's efforts to tailor his programmes to the tastes of his local audiences. The emphasis in the Royal Bioscope's advertisements, which in earlier phases of moving picture exhibition in the Indies highlighted the novelty of the new technology, was now placed on these recognisable film titles, reflecting frequent programme changes that were to attract repeat visitors over the course of however many days or weeks the Royal Bioscope's tent was stationed in each town.[804]

There is no question that the Royal Bioscope succeeded in drawing in the local crowds. As a 1905 report from Buitenzorg (Bogor) under the heading "Cinemania" (*Bioscoop-mani*) grumbled during one of Esoofally's visits to the city:

> Everything here revolves around the bioscope [*bioscoop*]. They get together at the bar of the Royal. Young girls are constantly flirting in the evening dusk of the bioscope. Natives steal, and if they are caught they excuse themselves by saying that they had no money to go to the bioscope. A father [...] complained that his daughter had disappeared; last night she went to the cinema and since then she has been missing. [...] Employees ask for advance payment no longer because their father or mother passed away, – I had a stable boy who lost seven mothers, – but because they want to go to the bioscope. We are smothered by the heat of the day and look forward filled with hope to the clouds, [... but] then there is always someone who says: "I still hope that the evening remains dry, otherwise we can't go to the bioscope". Even the washer man [...] lends white pants and jackets to unfortunate native dandies who also want to go to the bioscope in style [*chic*]. [...] The owners [...] make a fortune with their bioscope. And if in the beginning of the month a lady moans because hubby is so tight with his household budget, the man says: "Yes, we have to set aside some of the money for the bioscope".[805]

Esoofally's Royal Bioscope was thus identified as a central player in the "Cinemania" that has struck "Native" spectators in the Indies. Moving pictures

---

804 Interestingly, Méliès's name was not used to promote his films. Pathé Frères were similarly left out of the advertisements of the Royal Bioscope and its contemporaries, although spectators most likely recognised the company's rooster trademark, which would have also been familiar to them from the company's earlier trade in phonograph devices and plates in the region.

805 "Bioscoop-mani", *Het Nieuws van den Dag voor Nederlandsch-Indië* (12 October 1905).

became a genuine need in their life, and it appears that nothing could stop them from going to the bioscope except, perhaps, the rain.

3.3   The Netherlands Indies Biograph Company

3.3.1   *Background: Armenians in Southeast Asia and in the Local Photography and Moving Picture Trades*

The Netherlands Indies Biograph Company was registered as a public limited company (*Naamloze Vennootschap*, or N.V.) on 12 December 1904.[806] Amirkan Johannes, a private individual who was resident of Kediri, was announced as the company's director, while Mackertich Johannes, also identified as a private individual from Kediri, and Mackertich Abraham Nahapiet, a tradesman from Surabaya, were appointed as the company's commissioners, with all three together making up the company's board. Nahapiet was earlier the importer and sole distributor of cigars in the Indies for *De Jonge Amerikaan Sigaren* and *Koninklijke Sigarenfabriek Dresselhuys & Nieuwenhuysen*, as well as of premium Dutch butter.[807] Based on several newspaper reports from later years, all three were of Armenian descent. Another Armenian by the name A. C. Vardon, sometimes spelled Warden or Varden, was first mentioned in connection with the company as its manager during its shows in Batavia in October 1905.[808] As we shall see, the Netherlands Indies Biograph continued operating under various company names, including Johannes Biograph, Royal Vardon Biograph, and Royal Standard Biograph, up to 1913. The nature of the connection between the different companies and these individuals is difficult to ascertain and it is likely that, at a certain point, they became competitors rather than remaining as partners. Nevertheless, for the majority of the period, they appear to have shared films and exhibition venues.

In an overview of Armenian traders and communities in Southeast Asia, Margaret Sarkissian notes that "Armenians have always been associated with trade, particularly in the minds of non-Armenians".[809]

> Two major elements, besides a natural aptitude, have probably contributed to this penchant for trade. Firstly, the geographical situation of Armenia has always ensured contact with the overland east-west trade routes. Almost all the trade routes from the Mediterranean or the Black Sea were forced through or near Armenia in order to pass south of the Caspian Sea. From Armenia the traders could either follow the Silk Route to China or take a more southerly path to the Indo-Ganges plains of northern India [...]. Secondly, the turbulent history of Armenia [which in the seventeenth century was the subject of tension between the Ottoman and Persian Empires, and finally invaded by the latter] has meant

---

806 "Naamlooze-Vennootschap Nederlandsch-Indische Biograph Compagnie. No. 26", *Extra-Bijvoegsel der Javasche Courant van 28/4–1905*, no. 54 (28 April 1905).

807 Advertisement, *Soerabaiasch-Handelsblad* (20 November 1901); Advertisement, *Soerabaiasch-Handelsblad* (21 January 1903); Advertisement, *Soerabaiasch-Handelsblad* (24 September 1902).

808 Advertisement, *Het Nieuws van den Dag voor Nederlandsch-Indië* (25 October 1905).

809 Margaret Sarkissian, "Armenians in South-East Asia", *Crossroads: An Interdisciplinary Journal of Southeast Asian Studies* 3, no. 2/3 (1987): 1.

that there have probably always been migrations, forced or otherwise, of Armenians from their homeland [and thus a widespread network of potential contacts].[810]

Armenian traders from India first arrived in Southeast Asia in the sixteenth century, with the first Armenians appearing in Aceh and Batavia in the seventeenth century, and a proper Armenian community established in Batavia in the eighteenth century, signalled by the construction of a church and a school.[811] The Armenian minority in Surabaya, representing 1.0% of the population of Surabaya according to the 1930 census, began to arrive in this major port city of East Java during the second half of the nineteenth century.[812] At this time, there was further movement of Armenian communities to Semarang, Makassar (on Sulawesi), and Buleleng (on Bali).[813] Armenians were reputed for speaking many languages, often serving as interpreters for other Europeans in Southeast Asia and, at times, as go-betweens for the Dutch and British governments.[814]

Armenians in the Netherlands Indies, and in Surabaya specifically, already had a reputation in the field of still photography thanks to photographer Ohannes Kurkdjian (1851–1903), who "opened a photographic studio in Surabaya in 1888, which continued operating until 1936. After his death the Englishman G.P. Lewis ran the studio. The Kurkdjian & Co photographic studio created carefully staged photographs in which the choice of subject, the composition, the framing, the use of light and the scene atmosphere were striking. Such images had a great influence on the ways the colony was perceived", also back in the Netherlands.[815]

Established for a period of at least thirty years, the Netherlands Indies Biograph Company declared a capital in cash upon establishment in the sum of 30,000 guilders, divided into 300 shares worth 100 guilders each.[816] The shareholders were not specified by name. Compare this to the information available on the Java Cineograph Company which was established in 1901 for a period of ten years – with extension of the deed to be considered again one year prior to its expiry – and a capital of 20,000 guilders, divided into twenty shares worth a thousand guilders each, divided between one majority shareholder and one minority shareholder (see Section 2.3).[817] So it appears that, whereas the Java

810 Ibid.
811 Ibid., 3, 9–10.
812 See H. W. Dick, *Surabaya: City of Work: A Socioeconomic History* (Athens: Ohio University Press, 2002), 125; Sarkissian, "Armenians in South-East Asia", 11.
813 Ibid., 11–13.
814 Ibid., 1, 13.
815 Rob Jongmans and Janneke van Dijk, "From colonial topicality to cultural heritage: the history of the photograph collection", in Janneke van Dijk, Rob Jongmans, Anouk Mansfeld, Steven Vink and Pim Westerkamp (eds.), *Photographs of the Netherlands East Indies* (Amsterdam: KIT Publishers, 2012), 15–37, here 27.
816 "Naamlooze-Vennootschap. Nederlandsch-Indische Biograph Compagnie. No. 26", *Extra-Bijvoegsel der Javasche Courant van 28/4–1905*, no. 54 (28 April 1905).

Cineograph was run practically as a privately-owned company, the Netherlands Indies Biograph was reaching out to a wider base of middle-class investors. The documents of the latter were certainly clearer about what was expected of the company in terms of its books of accounts presenting the company's profit and loss statements, which were to be submitted in December of every year, as well as in regards to shareholder meetings and voting on dividend distribution to take place every year during the month of May.

Based in Surabaya, the "purpose of the Company [was]: to sell biographs or similar devices to produce photoplays [*lichtbeelden*]".[818] While the Netherlands Indies Biograph certainly produced its fair share of local views of the Indies, it seems that the use of the verb "to produce" (*produceren*) was not limited to what we would now associate with film production, but rather can be interpreted in the sense of film projection, or producing images on screen.[819] At times the company's local views were commissioned by commercial companies as a form of promotional material, such as the engineering workshop Der Vorstenlanden in Yogyakarta (*N.V. Constructie Atelier der Vorstenlanden*), which reportedly paid 600 guilders to the Johannes Biograph for filming its atelier.[820] Such films were presumably made to be shown at the various arts and crafts festivals across the Indies (i.e. *Pasar Malam* and *Pasar Gambir*), which were increasingly hosting cinema companies on the premises, *in lieu* or in addition to a physical exhibit by these commercial firms.

The Netherlands Indies Biograph later went into film sales as well: in 1907 it offered no less than 200,000 feet of films, while in 1909 the Johannes Biograph put up for sale around 80,000 feet of films by "various producers", although it remains unclear whether it was also selling its own pictures or only foreign prints that had finished their run with the various Biograph subsidiaries.[821] Furthermore, the different subsidiaries were advertising their services as exhibitors available for hire directly by local industrial companies, such as sugar factories, especially on the occasion of local festivities. For example, during the *maalfeest* (the sugar factory milling festival) in 1909, the Johannes Biograph, stationed in Surabaya at the time, advertised that it would require any interested company to provide electric current of minimum 25 and maximum 30 amperes for shows to take place, though it did not specify its fee.[822] Meanwhile, the Vardon Biograph in Solo (Surakarta) was asking for 250 guilders per night,

---

817 *Extra-Bijvoegsel der Javasche Courant* 1901, no. 58.

818 "Naamlooze-Vennootschap. Nederlandsch-Indische Biograph Compagnie. No. 26". *Extra-Bijvoegsel der Javasche Courant van 28/4–1905*, no. 54 (28 April 1905).

819 A similar sentence construction appeared in the announcement of the Java Cineograph Company's establishment from 1901 (*Extra-Bijvoegsel der Javasche Courant* 1901, no. 38).

820 "Uit Djokja", *Nieuwe Soerabaja Courant* (21 August 1908). The reporter in Yogyakarta expressed his disappointment that the film was not completed in time to be first screened in Yogyakarta, but rather had its premiere in Surabaya.

821 Advertisement, *Soerabaiasch-Handelsblad* (19 August 1907); Advertisement, *Soerabaiasch-Handelsblad* (17 July 1909). M. A. Nahapiet appeared as the contact person in the advertisement. It was repeated several times in various newspapers.

822 Advertisement, *Soerabaiasch-Handelsblad* (1 April 1909).

referring interested managers to seek recommendations from the directors of other sugar factories in Mojokerto and Pasuruan.[823] In later years Nahapiet and Vardon, though probably by that point not associated with each other, were also looking into constructing semi-permanent and permanent cinema houses in Surabaya.[824] The company's functions thus arguably developed in accordance with the needs of the local moving pictures scene, and at the same time instigating – at the very least, some – of these changes. As we shall see, their efforts to industrialise the exhibition of moving pictures similarly met with and simultaneously prompted increasing legislation by the colonial authorities.

3.3.2 Starting Out: Seating Practices and Struggles with Censorship, 1904–1905

The Netherlands Indies Biograph appears to have been the longest-running film company in the Indies at that point, performing, in one form or another, for about a decade.[825] The earliest shows as "Netherlands Indies Biograph Company" found in this research were given in Surabaya from July to December 1904, in a spacious tent in front of the artillery barracks, next to the chemist Moll & Co. at Pasar Besar in Surabaya. The Netherlands Indies Biograph offered attractive shows, including "bloody scenes from the Boxer Rebellion" and images of the Russo-Japanese War, screened alongside *Sleeping Beauty* and *Ali Baba*, in order to "restore the balance of the shocked public".[826]

Ticket prices for the shows varied by class and ethnicity: box seats for *f* 1.50, first class *f* 1, second class *f* 0.50, third class offered to "Chinese and Arab" spectators *f* 0.35, and fourth class for "Javanese", with seats located behind the

823 Advertisement, *Soerabaiasch-Handelsblad* (27 April 1909).

824 "Nederlandsch-Indië", *Soerabaiasch-Handelsblad* (28 September 1908); "Gemeenteraad van Soerabaja. Zitting van 24 Januari 1912", *Soerabaiasch-Handelsblad* (26 January 1912).

825 An advertisement from 1906 in fact claimed that the Netherlands Indies Biograph apparently already operated since 1902 (Advertisement, *Soerabaiasch-Handelsblad* (4 October 1906)). However, advertisements from 1910 along a similar line claimed the company started out in 1904 (Advertisement, *Soerabaiasch-Handelsblad* (11 October 1910)). There may have been a typo in the 1906 advertisements, or it was simply operating as a private company under a different name before. M. Johannes and M. A. Nahapiet were mentioned as passengers on board steamship *G. G. 's Jacob* from Surabaya to Singapore on 3 February 1902 ("Vertrokken", *De Locomotief* (6 February 1902)). They returned to Surabaya from Singapore at the end of February on board the steamer *Speelman* ("Aangekomen", *De Locomotief* (27 February 1902)). This research, however, has not been able to link them or this trip to Singapore to any cinema company active in the Indies at the time. There were several companies trading devices and films in this period, so this might have been a fact-finding mission ahead of entering the moving pictures business. Another passenger mentioned, on both legs of their trip, was L. M. Sarkies. In July 1901, Sarkies Johannes & Co., a Surabaya-based company that had been active on Java for 18 years, began operating in Singapore as well "as General Merchants, Auctioneers, Estate Agents, Commission Agents, Teak Timber Merchants and Teak Wood Furniture Manufacturers" (Advertisement, *The Straits Times* (10 July 1901)). The partners in the company were Eleazar Johannes and Arathoon Martin Sarkies in Singapore, and Lucas Martin Sarkies in Surabaya (ibid.). There was most likely some sort of connection to the Sarkies brothers (Martin, Arshak, Aviet and Tigran), who were famous hoteliers in Southeast Asia from the mid-nineteenth century, especially in Singapore where they founded the Raffles Hotel in 1887 (see Nadia H. Wright, *Respected Citizens: The History of Armenians in Singapore and Malaysia* (Melbourne: Amassia Publishing, 2003)).

826 "Nederlandsch-Indië", *Soerabaiasch-Handelsblad* (20 July 1904). Possible films on the programme: LA BELLE AU BOIS DORMANT (Pathé Frères, 1903), ÉVÉNEMENTS DE CHINE: MARTYRE D'UN MISSIONNAIRE aka UNE EXÉCUTION À PEKIN (Pathé Frères, 1900), ÉVÉNEMENTS RUSSO-JAPONAIS (Pathé Frères, 1904), ALI BABA ET LES QUARANTE VOLEURS (Pathé Frères, 1902).

screen, at ƒ 0.10.[827] Tickets for soldiers below the rank of sergeant and for children in box, first and second class seats were sold at half price. Advertisements in Semarang, where the Netherlands Indies Biograph set up its tent in September–October 1905, further specified that "foreign Orientals" were seated on chairs (ƒ 0.25), while "Natives" (ƒ 0.10) were presumably allocated a mat on the ground, behind the screen.[828]

An exceptional portrayal of this screening situation, which also provides a rare example of the description of an audience reacting to Méliès's LE VOYAGE DANS LA LUNE, was provided towards the end of the Netherlands Indies Biograph's stay in Surabaya in late December 1904. Following a visit to the tent, a reporter provided his account of "An Evening at the Biograph":

> Boom, boom, boom... Djing, djing... A high-pitched flute combined with the sound of clashing cymbals, the bang of a big drum and wirrr, wirrr of the machine. The tent is naturally chock-full.
>
> The natives sit open-mouthed gawking at the white screen in the middle. A shrill whistle announces that [the show] is about to begin. The electric arc lamps are turned off, the manager ascends to his booth. [...] then a bright circle appears which is immediately filled with a picture: the Kalimas at Goebeng [in Surabaya].
>
> "Waa...h!" sounds rise from behind the screen, the section for the natives. When there are compelling scenes, these children of nature cannot control their emotions. When a sleepwalker [...] is about to fall down, a good soul, mortally terrified, calls out: "*Allah, tobat!*" [Allah, have mercy] Or when the little moon people come into battle with the earthlings who, à la Jules Verne, land on the moon, and evaporate into gas, they do not understand much, but that does not bother them: there is so much action in the most charming pictures, that the attention remains stimulated. [...]
>
> The natives laugh themselves into seizures at the scenes with the enchanted clothes, the white people shudder at the poignant depiction of the life of an actor, finally hung for committing murder [...].
>
> During the scene of a fire that also impresses the natives, a nervous lady is startled and says excitedly to her husband: "Good man, if there were a fire here now... at our home... our baby... I'm going home... I'm leaving, leaving!" The man tries to calm her down, "Come on wifey, don't get wound up, nothing is happening", but the anxious mother already has one foot out the tent.[829]

This description, closely capturing the exhibition setting of the Netherlands Indies Biograph in such minute detail, is a rare one. At the same time, it does not mean that this particular arrangement of the cinema space was an anomaly, since I have come across plenty of evidence that this layout was widely employed throughout the entire period and in many venues across the archipelago. Even the luxurious cinema palace of Umbgrove's East Java Bioscope,

---

827 Advertisement, *Bintang Soerabaia* (18 July 1904).

828 Advertisement, *De Locomotief* (7 October 1905). Ticket prices for box and first class seats were the same as in Surabaya.

829 "Een avondje bij de Biograaf", *Soerabaiasch-Handelsblad* (25 November 1904), emphasis added. Possible films on the programme: VOYAGE DANS LA LUNE (Méliès, 1902), LE DÉSHABILLAGE IMPOSSIBLE by Méliès (1900) or Pathé Frères (1901), and AU FEU! (Pathé Frères, 1903) or RESCUE FROM THE FIRE (Sigmund Lubin, 1903).

which was built in 1913 to accommodate 750 "Europeans" and 400 "Natives", offered cheaper seats for "Native" spectators behind the screen (see further in Section 4.5).[830] Furthermore, it appears that seating restrictions were either not strictly enforced or not properly adhered to. For instance, a journalist who attended a Netherlands Indies Biograph show in Blitar in April 1905 reported that he was sitting in first class "on hard stools" next to a Javanese woman (see further discussion of spectatorial positions in the Introduction).[831]

The first local view advertised by the Netherlands Indies Biograph also happened to be the most controversial one. In October 1904, their programme in Surabaya included the title *Uprising in Gedangan* ("*Oproer in Gedangan*" in Dutch and "*Resoesoehan di Gedangan*" in Malay, see Figure 3–5).[832] It is not clear whether this was an actuality or re-enactment of events, or even if this was authentic footage or a re-titling of another riot scene filmed in an entirely different context, but it was presumably referring to the uprising of May 1904 in the village of Kebonpasar in Gedangan district of Sidoradjo regency, eastern Java. Led "by a certain Kasan Mukmin, a *kyai* or rural religious teacher", a small band of just over a hundred "[...] followers were allegedly going to kill Europeans in the area and overthrow the foreign yoke for a new order under Mukmin, who claimed to be an incarnation of Imam Mahdi, a messianic figure in Islamic eschatology. He would abolish all burdensome levies imposed by the colonial state, it was said, and allow people to live in peace and prosperity. The local government was caught by surprise, but quickly suppressed the uprising in a bloody confrontation, killing a number of rebels including Mukmin himself."[833] Social protests were henceforth denounced "as a threat to 'peace and order'" and any challenge to colonial rule was to be dealt with decisively.[834]

The fact that the unrest took place merely an hour's train ride away from Surabaya, according to Bloembergen, was one of the main causes of alarm among the European population of the city at the time, which subsequently led to reorganization of the municipal police in the three major Javanese cities (Batavia, Surabaya and Semarang) from 1911 to 1918.[835] In light of the colonial authorities' interpretation of the uprising, it comes as no surprise that the much anticipated screening of *Uprising in Gedangan* ended up being banned by the police, to the disappointment of many in the audience. If the film's screening was indeed forbidden by the police, the *Soerabaija-Courant* further commented, "[...] then it seems to us that this was wisely done. The less these scenes are recalled in the memory, the better."[836]

830 "Oost Java Handels Mij en Oost Java Bioscope", *Soerabaiasch Nieuwsblad* (10 November 1913).
831 "Wel gevoel", *Het Nieuws van den Dag voor Nederlandsch-Indië* (14 April 1905).
832 Advertisement, *Soerabaiasch-Handelsblad* (1 October 1904).
833 M. R. Fernando, "The Trumpet Shall Sound for Rich Peasants: Kasam Mukmin's Uprising in Gedangan, East Java, 1904", *Journal of Southeast Asian Studies* 26, no. 2 (September 1995): 242, italics in original.
834 Ibid. For a detailed socio-economic analysis of the breakout of the Uprising, see Fernando's article.
835 See Bloembergen, *De geschiedenis van de politie in Nederlandsch-Indië*, 77–78.

By that point, the Netherlands Indies Biograph's tent was stationed in Surabaya for nearly three months, and it appears that this minor mishap was forgiven, by authorities and spectators alike.[837] The fact that it was heavily involved in charity shows for orphans, especially immediately after the latest incident, when it offered all proceeds over the course of the following week to the *Van Heutsz-Fonds* for the benefit of "children of casualties among the lower ranks", most likely served their own cause at the same time.[838] The company managed to obtain an extension of its permit and advertisements pointed out that shows would now be given using a new device, recently "awarded the first prize at the exhibition [World's Fair] in St. Louis".[839] Programmes were to be boosted with around 30,000 feet of new films, some of them had already been brought by the steamship *Sindoro* and the rest expected to arrive shortly by the steamships *Salak* and *Lawoe*.[840] Among the new films highlighted were *Bluebeard*, *Ali Baba*, *Rip van Winkel*, as well as new scenes from the Russo-Japanese War and the Greco-Turkish War (see further on the Russo-Japanese War in Section 2.3.2).[841] The Netherlands

Figure 3–4. Advertisement for new films to be screened by the Netherlands Indies Biograph, including Uprising in Gedangan, *Soerabaiasch-Handelsblad* (1 October 1904). Retrieved from Delpher on 5 October 2015, http://resolver.kb.nl/resolve?urn=ddd:011087948:mpeg21:a0078.

---

[836] "Nederlandsch-Indië", *Soerabaija-Courant* (4 October 1904). The earliest example of censorship imposed on moving pictures found in this research was of a film screened by Nast's Kinematograph across Java, which was seized in Yogyakarta on account of its questionable morality and was brought to Surabaya for review (see Section 2.3.1). This research has not come across any previous bans of battle or fighting scenes, such as the atrocities in Greece or the Boxer Uprising.

[837] Initially, during July and August, it was in competition with the Java Cineograph, whose tent was first set up by the Courthouse and later moved to the nearby *Stadstuin* (Advertisement, *Soerabaiasch-Handelsblad* (24 June 1904); Advertisement, *Soerabaiasch-Handelsblad* (19 July 1904)).

[838] "Royaal", *Soerabaiasch-Handelsblad* (7 October 1904). The specially selected programme for the charity show was to be accompanied by the orchestra of the 13th Battalion (Advertisement, *Soerabaiasch-Handelsblad* (7 October 1904)).

[839] Advertisements, *Bintang Soerabaia* and *Soerabaiasch-Handelsblad* (1 October 1904).

[840] Ibid.

Indies Biograph's permit was extended three more times: in mid-November, at the end of November in order to hold shows in the run-up to Saint Nicholas Eve, and finally in mid-December to give a chance to the public to attend shows during Christmas and New Year's Eve.[842]

The Netherlands Indies Biograph Company likely visited several other locations in eastern Java before returning for shows in Surabaya in May 1905, setting up its tent once again next to the military barracks. The advertisement for its forthcoming shows drummed up anticipation:

> The Well-known Netherlands Indies Biograph Company which had such wonderful success here last year, is coming back to Surabaya within a few days, with its Huge waterproof tent that will be set up at the same site as before in front of the Barracks of the Mountain Artillery. This tent, specially made in America for the Tropics can easily hold 2,500 people. A large and entirely new stock of pictures from the best French companies. Very long pieces! Magic spells, Ballets and Opera, Historical and Political events, Funny scenes, Plights and Atrocities in Russia and Macedonia, Murders among Russian Lords and last but not least, terrible scenes of the Russo-Japanese War on land and at sea, etc. etc. These pictures have been wonderfully successful all over Europe. They will soon be seen in Surabaya!! The opening will be announced through an advertisement.[843]

The *Nieuwe Soerabaja Courant* noted: "We have here two biographs. Mr. Johannes is busy setting up his tents at Pasar Besar, on the site in front of the third mountain artillery. He believes he will be able to begin his shows here in the coming days. Being a biograph-owner seems to be the best job these days."[844]

There were in fact three companies in Surabaya at the time (and henceforth there were usually at least three moving picture shows offered simultaneously in the city), all with different variations of "Biograph" and/or "Royal" in their names: on top of the Netherlands Indies Biograph, Esoofally's Royal Bioscope was giving shows at Pasar Turi next to the Courthouse, while E. H. Stevenson's company advertised as Royal Biograph Burlesque (*Koninklijke Biograph Kluchtspel*) was performing at Kapasan Theatre, though for a limited duration – coinciding with the *Pasar Malam* celebrations in Surabaya.[845] This caused plenty of confusion in the local newspapers, for instance: Esoofally's Royal Bioscope was dubbed "Royal Biograph" while the Netherlands Indies Bio-

---

841 Film titles were possibly BARBE-BLEU (Méliès, 1901), ALI BABA ET LES QUARANTE VOLEURS (Pathé Frères, 1902) and Sigmund Lubin's RIP VAN WINCKLE (1903). As Sabine Lenk has pointed out, this could suggest that the Netherlands Indies Biograph got some of its films from Lubin, meaning that films were shipped from Europe as well as the US.

842 Advertisement, *Soerabaiasch-Handelsblad* (18 November 1904); Advertisement, *Soerabaiasch-Handelsblad* (30 November 1904); Advertisement, *Soerabaiasch-Handelsblad* (16 December 1904).

843 Advertisement, *Soerabaiasch-Handelsblad* (20 May 1904). The same advertisement appeared in *Bintang Soerabaia* over the next few days, although the location there simply mentioned Pasar Besar. Possible film titles on the programme: ATROCITÉS TURQUES (Pathé Frères, 1903) concerning Macedonia, and Russo-Japanese War scenes such as ÉVÉNEMENTS RUSSO-JAPONAIS (Pathé Frères, 1904) and ASSASSINAT DU MINISTRE PLEHVE (Pathé Frères 1904).

844 "Nog een biograaf", *Nieuwe Soerabaja Courant* (26 May 1905).

845 Advertisement, *Soerabaiasch-Handelsblad* (20 May 1904); Advertisement, *Bintang Soerabaia* (22 May 1905).

3 – *Komedi Bioscoop, Indische* Films and the Localisation of Film Exhibition

graph was labelled "Netherlands Indies Cinematograph".[846] The mix-up was only magnified by the fact that the two companies often had practically the same programmes running in parallel. Thus, on 2 June 1905 the Royal Bioscope's advertisements highlighted the films "Christophorus Columbus. Historical Scenes in 8 pictures and one tableau" and "The great Fire in Toronto. The great fire on the eve of 19 April 1904. In eight hours' time damage of 1,300,000 pound str., 144 buildings burned down, 250 firms could not continue their business and 7,000 people were out of work."[847] The Netherlands Indies Biograph Company meanwhile was promoting "Christophorus Columbus (In 9 Tableaux). The great Fire in America. Many buildings burned down."[848] Nevertheless, both companies reportedly enjoyed "[...] great success. The tickets for the [high-paying] first and second classes were sold out."[849] Those who still wanted to attend a show apparently had to make do with standing room only.

By July, as competition between the Netherlands Indies Biograph and the Royal Bioscope was still raging in Surabaya, the former decided to introduce a new device, announcing in its advertisements: the "Gaumont Chronophone (Talking Cinematograph) the greatest miracle of this century, has arrived here, and will be shown for the first time in the Netherlands Indies. This device has enjoyed great success at the Hippodrome in London and in Paris."[850] Programmes from now on were to include a couple of films screened with the Biograph, such as *Robinson Crusoe*, *A Trip to the Moon*, *Marie Antoinette*, and scenes from the Russo-Japanese War, and – after a break – a few Chronophone representations, mostly opera, dance and musical numbers.[851] The trumpet for playing the sound was placed in the middle of the tent, on the side of the screen onto which the images were projected, thus facing the more expensive seats in the tent.[852] A promotional piece further explained the concept: "[...] one will be able to enjoy simultaneously with eyes and ears beautiful and nice graphics and mono[logues] and dialogues. The effect must be surprising and we recommend to everyone [...] to go see it."[853] However, the first show did not go quite as planned "due to a defect in the talking machine", and Johannes apologized over the pages of the newspaper to the numerous disappointed spectators.[854] "Yesterday evening, however, according to our reporter the show

---

846 "De Royal Biograph", *Soerabaiasch-Handelsblad* (29 May 1905); "N. I. Cinematograaf", *Soerabaiasch-Handelsblad* (29 May 1905).

847 Advertisement, *Soerabaiasch-Handelsblad* (2 June 1905). Columbus could be CHRISTOPHE COLOMB (Pathé Frères, 1904).

848 Advertisement, *Soerabaiasch-Handelsblad* (2 June 1905).

849 "Veel success gehad", *Nieuwe Soerabaja Courant* (5 June 1905).

850 Advertisement, *Soerabaiasch-Handelsblad* (7 July 1905).

851 As mentioned earlier, there was a 1902 Méliès production of LES AVENTURES DE ROBINSON CRUSOË (Star Film Company, 1902). *Marie Antoinette* was possibly MARIE-ANTOINETTE (Pathé Frères, 1904).

852 "De Chronofoon", *Soerabaiasch-Handelsblad* (20 July 1905).

853 "Biograaf-Chronofoon", *Soerabaiasch-Handelsblad* (7 July 1905).

854 "Biograaf-Chronofoon", *Soerabaiasch-Handelsblad* (10 July 1905).

was an utter success", the report added.[855] The performances improved from then on, with one report noting that the sound produced by the machine was so clear during a scene at the dentist, that one could recognise the authentic German Berliner accent spoken in the scene.[856] Interestingly, Johannes then repeated the text to his audience in English. The Netherlands Indies Biograph reportedly spared no expense when it came to making the shows ever more enjoyable for spectators and, as of mid-August, an Italian quintet could be heard between the different numbers.[857]

At the beginning of September 1905, Johannes moved his tents to the *Alun Alun* in Semarang, where he received a permit to perform for one month.[858] In advertisements the Netherlands Indies Biograph tried to build on its earlier reputation, mentioning that it had given praiseworthy shows in Surabaya over the course of six months.[859] *De Locomotief* provided impressions from the second evening of the Biograph, noting that the show was so full and that many people had to stand since the ticket booth failed to keep count of the available seats. The music of the phonograph accompanying the show was deemed beautiful and the programme was found to be varied, showing "[...] the 'incident' at Hull, Jeanne d'Arc and [...] the wonders under the sea [which] was very successful. Too bad that the tent has as good as no ventilation, one sits as if in a steam bath." [860] But, the manager promised the reporter, a ventilation system was going to be installed, and the newspaper thus had no doubts about recommending a visit to the tent. And the public apparently came: "The cinematograph currently on the *Alun Alun* has no reason to complain about the public's interest, the tent is always full in both the early and late evening [shows]. The films accompanied by the phonograph are especially to [the public's] liking; it is then also something new for Semarang."[861] Johannes apparently continued to receive new films as he was stationed in Semarang.[862] Nevertheless, Johannes's stay in Semarang was short-lived and by the end of October he was moving on to Batavia. To finish off his visit on a positive note, Johannes offered free shows to children from the Protestant orphanage.[863] During the last week of shows, spectators could win prizes in a raffle held every night.[864]

---

855 Ibid.
856 "De Chronofoon", *Soerabaiasch-Handelsblad* (20 July 1905). The film was possibly AT THE DENTIST'S, a comical scene by M. Schwartz, in German (Gaumont). Title found in the British Gaumont catalogue of 1906, but the film was certainly made before.
857 "Nederlandsch-Indië", *Soerabaiasch-Handelsblad* (14 August 1905).
858 "Alweer een cinematograaf", *De Locomotief* (4 September 1905).
859 Advertisement, *Selompret Melajoe* (9 September 1905).
860 "Nederlandsch-Indië", *De Locomotief* (12 September 1905). Films on the programme were possibly: JEANNE D'ARC (Méliès, 1900), and LE ROYAUME DES FÉES (Méliès, 1903).
861 "De cinematograaf", *De Locomotief* (19 September 1905), emphasis added.
862 For example, new films reportedly arrived from Europe aboard the steamship *Willem I* ("De cinematograaf", *De Locomotief* (23 October 1905)).
863 "De cinematograaf", *De Locomotief* (24 October 1905).

3 – *Komedi Bioscoop, Indische* Films and the Localisation of Film Exhibition

In Batavia at the end of October 1905, the Netherlands Indies Biograph was, once again, drawing on its earlier success elsewhere to build up the hype for its upcoming shows: "The Netherlands Indies Biograph Company, the largest Company in the Netherlands Indies, Living, talking Paintings. The latest invention in the field. The greatest miracle of the 20th century. The flickering image is completely eliminated by a new invention. Everything is operated by its own electric machines. Shown in Semarang and Surabaya with tremendous success. The grand opening show will be further announced. A. C. Warden, Manager."[865] The shows in Batavia were not given in a tent, but rather in the Manège at Tanah Abang, and tickets could be reserved directly with Warden at Hôtel Ort. It was presumably planning on arriving in Batavia even earlier, in which case it would have been in direct competition with the Java Cineograph which was performing in September and October at Tanah Abang, in a tent set up next to Manège Fuchs.[866] Nevertheless, the Netherlands Indies Biograph experienced delays in obtaining a permit in time from the police.[867] Even so, it still had to compete against E. Bartelle's Imperial Bioscope at Pasar Pisang Senen and the Shahab Brothers' General Bioscope Company at Tanah Lapang Mangga Besar, both stationed in the Chinatown district of Batavia.[868]

The new manager appears to have reversed the order of the show, compared to Johannes. At least initially, the Chronophone was displayed first and after a ten-minute break the "silent films" were played.[869] People love the talking pictures, *Bintang Batavia* reported, and once they were exposed to it they made repeat visits.[870] *Het Nieuws van den Dag voor Nederlandsch-Indië* was somewhat less enthusiastic about the Chronophone's talking pictures, which it found to be less successful than the ordinary non-sound Biograph films. Overall, the review was extremely positive: "A large number of new and good films, good lighting, a good projection device, so by the majority of images screened no vibration was observed [...] The locale of the manège is excellent for this kind of event and was, moreover, refurbished once again. On Saturday the manager had a packed hall and will undoubtedly make good business with these appealing shows."[871]

The Netherlands Indies Biograph stayed in Batavia until the beginning of 1906, and while it was commended at one point in the Malay press as "better than Esoofally's Royal Bioscope" and was even attended by Governor General Van Heutsz with his wife and kids in December of 1905, it generally did not draw

864 Advertisement, *Selompret Melajoe* (12 October 1905).
865 Advertisement, *Het Nieuws van den Dag voor Nederlandsch-Indië* (25 October 1905). The same ads appear also in *Bintang Batavia* and *Taman Sari*.
866 Advertisement, *Het Nieuws van den Dag voor Nederlandsch-Indië* (23 September 1905).
867 "Nieuwe cineografen op komst", *Het Nieuws van den Dag voor Nederlandsch-Indië* (23 September 1905).
868 Advertisement, *Taman Sari* (2 November 1905); Advertisement, *Taman Sari* (28 November 1905).
869 "Kabar sehari-hari dari Betawi dan laen-laen negri", *Bintang Batavia* (6 November 1905).
870 Ibid.
871 "Ned. Ind. Biograph Coy.", *Het Nieuws van den Dag voor Nederlandsch-Indië* (6 November 1905).

too much attention in the press.[872] Other, more expensive, stage entertainments arriving from the Netherlands received more coverage in the Dutch newspapers at the time, such as the Brondgeest ensemble or reports in anticipation of the arrival of the Louis Bouwmeester company.[873] However, how successful such acts were in the box office is doubtful, as a report from the *Haarlem Courant* quoted in *Bataviaasch Nieuwsblad* claimed:

> There seems to be a rage among performers [in the Netherlands] to go to the Netherlands Indies. One hears murmurs about fabulous sums which have been earned by agents. The craze goes so far that artists are already willing to forgo good contracts for next season in order to try to pick up a fortune there. These days we received a letter from the Indies from one of the performers in Brondgeest's ensemble, which shows that the Indies are not all rosy. It refers to the 'high fevers,' which all members of the ensemble suffered. "It is", so is written, "a boring, dull and unhealthy land. Artistic success here is so so. Financial also so so. But we hope to stay healthy and to return to Holland as soon as possible." The above said is like a warning for those who have plans to sacrifice their position for the sake of ... a chimera.[874]

By comparison, several circus outfits and *stambul* troupes visiting Batavia around the same time were making handsome profits, according to a report appearing in *Taman Sari*: the European Circus made around 8,500 guilders, Warren's Circus – more than 20,000 guilders, Professor Bose's Circus – 11,000 guilders, and the *stambul* troupe of Mr. Hunter – 15,000 guilders.[875] All these foreign companies, the newspaper lamented, were coming to Batavia and taking away the money of the city's poor residents, making them neglect their families and leaving children "[...] desperate for a mouthful of rice. That is what is called progress [*kemadjoean*] in Batavia".[876] The report unfortunately does not state how long each of these companies performed in Batavia; therefore, it is difficult to determine whether the differences between their incomes were due to popularity or length of time they spent in the city. Based on advertisements observed in the newspapers at the time, circuses usually had runs of one month in Batavia performing in their own tents for thousands of spectators. Moving picture companies can be grouped into three different categories. First, the bigger moving picture companies with their luxurious tents stationed in central locations, like the Royal Bioscope or the Netherlands Indies Biograph, would stay in town for between one to five months in one go, bringing in new films from Europe or the US to revitalise their stock and to keep up with programme changes twice per week. Second, smaller moving

---

872 "Kabar sehari-hari dari Betawi dan laen-laen negri", *Bintang Batavia* (8 November 1905).

873 "Brondgeest-ensemble", *Het Nieuws van den Dag voor Nederlandsch-Indië* (6 November 1905); "Het vertrek van Bouwmeester", *Het Nieuws van den Dag voor Nederlandsch-Indië* (7 November 1905).

874 "Tooneelspelers in Indië", *Bataviaasch Nieuwsblad* (10 January 1905). The Brondgeest ensemble was even more plagued by the time it was in Batavia again in late 1905, simultaneously with the Netherlands Indies Biograph, with shows postponed due to the illness of cast members ("Brondgeest-ensemble", *Het Nieuws van den Dag voor Nederlandsch-Indië* (6 November 1905)).

875 "Betawi 22 Juni 1905", *Taman Sari* (22 June 1905).

876 Ibid.

picture companies stationed in the *kampung* for a couple of months at a time offered cheaper tickets and relied mostly on re-used films with little change in the programme. Finally, one-off exhibitors of moving pictures, often performing as part of variety shows or amusement companies, would have come in for a handful of shows over the course of a couple of weeks. And while it seems many of them were using old films, their venues were often the higher-end European theatre buildings.

Meanwhile, reports from all around the archipelago were calling for more control and monitoring of moving picture shows. For instance, a film advertised on the Netherlands Indies Biograph programme as "One Man and 10 Women" was singled out in *Taman Sari* as a picture that won plenty of laughs, but which did not necessarily convey the right message to spectators.[877] A film showing the slaughter of a pig in minute details further drew complaints from spectators of the Netherlands Indies Electro Bioscope in Surabaya at the same time. One anonymous spectator signed "Homo" even sent a letter to the editor of *Soerabaiasch-Handelsblad*, to voice his discontent at the police's incapability and absence from the scene of the screening.[878] The newspaper itself wrote: "The monitoring of Kinematographs [*Kinematografen*] and similar devices has recently proven to be inadequate. […] it is time that systematic [control] against giving immoral […] shows is put in place. The most effective way for this is that no kinematograph or biograph performs here before the police are satisfied that the films do not exhibit anything immoral or offensive."[879] As we have already seen and shall see further in the following chapters, such suggestions were made repeatedly but continued to be very difficult to implement in practice.

3.3.3 Imported Scenes and Local Production: From Netherlands Indies Biograph to Johannes Biograph, 1906–1907

When the Netherlands Indies Biograph arrived for the third time in Surabaya in July 1906, for shows in a tent in front of the military barracks, "[…] the marvellous Chronophone (talking machine) [was] graced with a Spanish Orchestra conducted by Mme. Geicha".[880] Advertisements boasted that it was the only Biograph that was visited by the Governor General and his wife.[881] Ticket prices were now slightly more expensive: box seat for f 2, first class f 1.50, second class f 1, third class f 0.50 fourth class f 0.15 (only for "Natives"). A new category of fourth class for "Native" children was introduced at f 0.10. From now on, the Netherlands Indies Biograph shows were also mentioned on the

---

877 "Gambar Hidup", *Taman Sari* (7 November 1905). Films on the programme were possibly: DIX FEMMES POUR UN MARI (Pathé Frères, 1905) and EGORGEMENT D'UN PORC (Pathé Frères, 1905).
878 "Een ergelijke vertooning", *De Locomotief* (9 November 1905).
879 "Nederlandsch-Indië", *Soerabaiasch-Handelsblad* (9 November 1905).
880 Advertisement, *Soerabaiasch-Handelsblad* (27 July 1906).
881 The same tag line was used also for its shows in Solo (Surakarta) and Semarang (Advertisement, *De Nieuwe Vorstenlanden* (6 April 1906); Advertisement, *De Locomotief* (17 May 1907)).

daily agenda of the newspaper – "Every evening. Shows of the Netherlands Indies Biograph Comp." – alongside announcements of other events at the *Stadstuin*, or public auctions.[882]

Stationed in Surabaya until the beginning of January, it received several shipments of about 30,000 feet of new films, arriving on board the steamships *Prinses Sophie*, *Koning Willem II* and *Koningin Wilhelmina*.[883] Programmes were now officially being changed twice a week: on Wednesdays and Saturdays. Other contemporary companies were apparently re-screening films many times over, sometimes simply changing the title of a film. The Royal Vio, in Batavia at the time, even felt compelled to explain in its advertisement: "The Royal Vio doesn't have thousands of dancing movies, which have been travelling in Java, but the latest perfected novelties. The Royal Vio sometimes shows the same picture twice, but always the most sought after, that our numerous visitors would like to see twice. These pictures are always announced under the same title, so that the public is not deceived."[884]

Alongside old favourites, such as *Ali Baba* and *Sleeping Beauty*, new scenes of the Russo-Japanese War were still attracting audiences to the Netherlands Indies Biograph. These scenes were supplemented by a growing collection of local views, as the *Soerabaiasch-Handelsblad* promoted the upcoming shows: "One will be able to see Javanese folk games [*volksspelen*], *sedekah* [giving alms], *topeng* [masquerade], *tandak* [Javanese dancers] in Bandung, [and] native weddings".[885] Nevertheless, the source of these films is not clear. They were most likely not made by the Netherlands Indies Biograph since in later instances, when their own productions were exhibited, this point was clearly mentioned. More curious still is the fact that the Royal Vio, which was performing at the Manège Fuchs in Batavia at the time and often advertised that its programmes consisted of Pathé titles, was showing films whose descriptions closely resembled the ones on the Netherlands Indies Biograph's programme. These were advertised as "a great collection of new images, including scenes of Batavia and Java, arrived with the latest mail boat".[886] A review the next day further described the scenes: "The photoplays [*lichtbeelden*] which showed our manners and customs on Java will certainly arouse great

---

882 "Dag-Agenda", *Soerabaiasch-Handelsblad* (1 September 1906).

883 Advertisement, *Soerabaiasch-Handelsblad* (17 September 1906).

884 Advertisement, *Java-Bode* (10 October 1906).

885 "Nederlandsch-Indië", *Soerabaiasch-Handelsblad* (4 October 1906), emphasis added. *Tandak* "is a dance by one or more young women, accompanied by song and gamelan, on the occasion of marriages, circumcisions, changes of name and other celebrations, for a small payment. These women were usually of the poorest classes or reduced to this profession because of bad character" (Ann Kumar, *Java and Modern Europe* (Surrey: Curzon Press, 1997), 136). "The *topeng*, or masquerades, was played by masked men, and the stories were the same as those of *wayang gêdog* [puppets of buffalo leather]" (ibid.).

886 Advertisement, *Java-Bode* (13 September 1906). The Royal Vio pointed out in advertisements that its films included the "cock [*hannetje*] in the title" (Advertisement, *Java-Bode* (10 October 1906)).

interest in Europe. The film showed one impeccable recording of a Javanese celebration, which included, of course, the obligatory *tandak*."[887] The next day's programme included a scene titled *"Tandak* and *Topeng* in Batavia".[888] The earliest scenes filmed in Java appearing in the Pathé catalogue are titled JAVA PITTORESQUE, as announced in the supplement to the catalogue for February–March 1907, which included: views of sunny, mountainous Java, "the features of its little people laughing and shaken, ancient Buddahs perched on lotus chalices", as well as dance scenes typical of Java, street vendors, opium dens, and the capture of a crocodile.[889] The scenes shown by the Netherlands Indies Biograph and the Royal Vio may have well been scenes filmed in the Indies by or for a foreign company (possibly indeed for Pathé), developed in Europe, and shipped back to the Indies for distribution.[890]

Less than a year later, the Netherlands Indies Biograph was already showing scenes captured by its own cameramen. Back in Surabaya in August 1907, its brand new tent was placed nearby the previous location, at the *Alun Alun* next to the Courthouse, and musical accompaniment was provided by a Spanish Quartet. "An old friend with a new outfit", read the advertisements, and the *Soerabaiasch-Handelsblad* further elaborated: "This biograph has earlier made here an eminent impression; they always had the latest and greatest in the field of these attractive photoplays [*lichtbeelden*]. The manager assures us that what is currently offered is even better than what has previously been shown."[891]

---

887 "Royal Vio", *Java-Bode* (14 September 1906), emphasis added. Other films on Javanese traditions were made before but not in Java, which indicates there was a certain interest in such scenes in Europe before. For instance, DANCE DES JAVANAIS (Pathé Frères, 1899/1900).

888 Advertisement, *Java-Bode* (15 September 1906), emphasis added.

889 "Java pittoresque", Fondation Jérôme Seydoux-Pathé, accessed on 6 June 2011, http://filmographie.fondation-jeromeseydoux-pathe.com/453-java-pittoresque accessed on 2 February 2016. I would like to thank Rianne Siebenga for pointing out this film to me. These scenes may have been shown by the Flying Bioscope in Batavia in December 1907, under the title "Idyll in the Indies (A very beautiful film)" (Advertisement, *Het Nieuws van den Dag voor Nederlandsch-Indië* (21 December 1907)). A 1907 reviewer of the film in the trade press noted that "'several hundred' Javanese children were 'conscious [...] before the camera, dancing and cutting capers before the lens'". (Alison Griffiths, *Wondrous Difference: Cinema, Anthropology, and Turn-of-the-Century Visual Culture* (New York: Columbia University Press, 2003), 203, quoting from "Picturesque Java" (Pathé Frères, 1907), *Film and View Index*, vol 2).

890 Earlier views of Java appear in the Gaumont-Pathé online catalogue as part of the Gaumont (Boites Vertes) collection of actualities from 1900 to the 1950s with the following description: "Reel 1: Various views of Java in Indonesia. Train, Dwelling, Inhabitants, men, women and Javanese children in the streets carrying out their activities. Large water lilies. Wooden bridge, Basin with water jet [...] Reel 2: Various views in Java in Indonesia. Row of almost identical houses with small gardens. Cars of the 1950s. Passers-by in a street, shops. Panorama of a Javanese town [...]." Despite the fact that the release date appears as 1 January 1900, probably the date marker was used for any scenes that are estimated as pre-1905. Therefore, it is not clear when these views were captured exactly and by whom, and none fit the description of the films here ("Gaumont (Boites Vertes) Actualité", Gaumont-Pathé Archives, accessed on 2 February 2014, http://www.gaumontpathearchives.com/indexPopup.php?urlaction=doc&id_doc=158645&rang=4).

891 Advertisement, *Soerabaiasch-Handelsblad* (16 August 1907); "Nederlandsch-Indië", *Soerabaiasch-Handelsblad* (16 August 1907).

The programme of the opening show included: "The Disaster of 'Berlin' at Hook of Holland and the Rescue mission of the Shipwreck".[892] It was at this time that the Netherlands Indies Biograph further decided to sell no less than 200,000 feet of films, offered for sale via an advertisement in the Surabaya newspapers, thus revealing that used films were traded on a local level (see also Section 3.3.4).[893]

"The Netherlands Indies Biograph Company, known by the Native as the Johannes-biograph", had successful shows on its first two nights which lived up to the reputation left in the memories of local spectators.[894] The new tent, "[...] which is more than one and a half times the size of the previous one [i.e. accommodating around 4,000 spectators], was over-crowded and many native spectators could not be admitted. This bioscope has excellent projection devices and nearly all new films, which have not been shown here before."[895] The praise continued a few days later:

> The Johannes-Bioscope. When writing about the recent bioscopes which gave performances here, we could keep [our reports] short and simply mention that the images were crisp and clear. The new bioscope, however, the Johannes-bioscope, certainly deserves a few more words.
>
> Johannes seems to be a man who has been to Europe and who has seen that, in order to attract audiences, one should not hesitate to spend loads of money. His tent looks neat, the greenish tent is pleasing on the eye and it is a pleasure to sit inside [...]. The bioscope is excellent, all new pictures, with only a single rupture here or there, and the programme last night had the crowded tent roaring with laughter. And then what is for the Indies entirely new is the phono-bioscope [*phonobioscoop*]. In Europe, the attempts to put together a good phono-bioscope have failed and the one which is to be heard and seen here is not perfect, but definitely worth a visit. Besides, it worked pretty well yesterday evening. If one looks steadily at the mouths of the moving images on the screen, one gets a moment of illusion that they are actually imbued with life. [...]
>
> And another attraction of this bioscope is the so-called Spanish quartet.
>
> No annoying Native-music but gentle, compelling up-to-date waltzes performed by a pretty good quartet.
>
> We can recommend a visit to the new bioscope.[896]

---

892 Advertisement, *Soerabaiasch-Handelsblad* (19 August 1907). The Imperial Bioscope was actually advertising the same film, to coincide with the Netherlands Indies Biograph's opening night (Advertisement, *Soerabaiasch-Handelsblad* (17 August 1907)). The incident occurred in February 1907 and was the subject of the actuality by Filmfabriek F. A. Nöggerath HOEK VAN HOLLAND NACH DER KATASTROPHE. DER SCHIFFBRUCH DES DAMPFERS BERLIN ("Hoek van Holland nach der Katastrophe. Der Schiffbruch des Dampfers Berlin", Eye Film Institute Netherlands, accessed on 2 February 2016, https://www.eyefilm.nl/en/collection/film-history/film/hoek-van-holland-nach-der-katastrophe-der-schiffbruch-des-dampfers). The film shown could have also been WRECK OF THE S.S. BERLIN, HOOK OF HOLLAND DISASTER (Warwick, 1907).

893 Advertisement, *Soerabaiasch-Handelsblad* (19 August 1907). The 200,000 feet (about 65,000 meters) of nitrate films were presumably collected by the Netherlands Indies Biograph over the course of several years of activities. This research was not able to find source material on how moving picture companies were able to travel with films and maintain them in good condition in the humid climate of the Indies. Further research is required on this essential issue.

894 "Nederlandsch-Indië", *Soerabaiasch-Handelsblad* (19 August 1907).

895 Ibid.

About a month later when the electric fans arrived, providing relief to spectators inside the tent, the *Soerabaiasch-Handelsblad* wholeheartedly recommended a visit to the Netherlands Indies Biograph: "what more could one want?" the report asked rhetorically.[897]

In late August, Johannes reportedly travelled to Yogyakarta himself in order to film the wedding ceremony of the Javanese Crown Prince.[898] "Tomorrow evening, the manager assures us, one will be able to admire the very successful recording of the marriage celebrations of the crown prince of Djokja. The operator of the bioscope has been to Djokja himself and was successful [in capturing] a faithful representation of the celebrations [...]."[899] The films were purportedly "a source of admiration especially for the Natives".[900] Only one other film in 1907 was credited to Johannes: "The latest [horse] races in Djokja".[901] This was clearly not enough to fill up the programmes of the Netherlands Indies Biograph, which had a reputation for bringing in new films all the time and offering frequent changes of programme.[902] The company therefore continued to receive more films from Europe every month: 60,000 feet by the steamship *Koningin Wilhelmina* in September, further "neat and fascinating films" arrived by the steamer *Oranje* in October, another 40,000 feet were brought by steamship *Koning Willem I* in November, and yet another unspecified load of films came in on board the steamer *Wilis* in December.[903]

By the beginning of 1908, the Netherlands Indies Biograph formally adopted its popular nickname and began advertising itself as "The Netherlands Indies Biograph Company. Johannes Biograph" in the Dutch press and as "Living Pictures *Tuan* Johannes" ("*Gambar Idoep Toewan Johannes*") in the Malay newspapers.[904] This sometimes caused even further mangling of the name, such as a report in *Bintang Soerabaia* that referred to the company as "*Komedi* [living] pictures Johannes Netherlands Bioscope" ("*Komedi gambar Johannes Nederlandisch Bioscoop*").[905]

In preparation for the approaching west monsoon season in Surabaya, Johannes was interested in constructing "a sturdy tent of temporary materials, such as bamboo, *pinang* [areca palm] tree trunks, etc.".[906] He was allocated the land

---

896 "De Johannes-Bioscoop", *Soerabaiasch-Handelsblad* (22 August 1907).
897 "Nederlandsch-Indië", *Soerabaiasch-Handelsblad* (15 September 1907).
898 "De Johannis[sic]-Bioscoop", *Soerabaiasch-Handelsblad* (30 August 1907).
899 Ibid.
900 "De Johannes-Bioscoop", *Soerabaiasch-Handelsblad* (2 September 1907).
901 Advertisement, *Soerabaiasch-Handelsblad* (9 December 1907).
902 "Johannes-Bioscoop", *Soerabaiasch-Handelsblad* (25 November 1907).
903 Advertisement, *Soerabaiasch-Handelsblad* (11 September 1907); Advertisement, *Soerabaiasch-Handelsblad* (25 October 1907); Advertisement, *Soerabaiasch-Handelsblad* (23 November 1907); Advertisement, *Soerabaiasch-Handelsblad* (9 December 1907).
904 Advertisement, *Soerabaiasch-Handelsblad* (20 December 1907); Advertisement, *Bintang Soerabaia* (7 January 1908).
905 "Hindia Ollanda", *Bintang Soerabaia* (13 January 1908).
906 "Nederlandsch-Indië", *Soerabaiasch-Handelsblad* (7 January 1908), emphasis added.

opposite the military garrison free of charge and, in return, was expected to offer free tickets to lower ranked soldiers or to contribute to the canteen trust. "Obviously we have nothing against the generosity of the military authorities", the *Soerabaiasch-Handelsblad* ruminated:

> The Johannes bioscope is one of the best, if not the best, that we have in the Indies, and Surabaya should not lack such a spectacle that provides a jovial evening to so many. And its appropriate place is in the city centre.
>
> But in addition we think that it requires that the police and military authorities should put an end to the disgusting scenes of immorality, which are given regularly after every bioscope which has stood on *this* site.[907]

The central location of the bamboo tent, right at the heart of Surabaya, aroused particular concern: "If there is a bioscope, no lady will be able to go for a walk from Pasar Besar to Polacstraat, along the road to the church, after seven o'clock in the evening", the report continued, finally calling on the police to take decisive action against this scandalous situation.[908]

3.3.4 "[...] that is more than many sugar companies distribute to their shareholders!": Economic Success Rouses Regulators

An annual shareholders' meeting of the Netherlands Indies Biograph Company was held on 24 January 1908, at the offices of the Executive Board. Points to be discussed included profit and loss statements, deciding on the dividend for 1907, and electing a new Board or re-electing the existing one.[909] A few days later, the Netherlands Indies Biograph announced over the pages of the newspaper that the profit and loss statements were approved, and that the dividend for 1907 was f 40 per share, payable upon presentation of a coupon at the office. The old Board was unanimously re-elected.[910]

Bataviaasch-Handelsblad further tried to analyse the finances behind the moving picture business. In response to repeated complaints about expensive patent tax paid by agricultural firms in eastern Java, cinemas, the report pointed out, were the exception to this norm. It estimated that a bioscope was making about 300 guilders in cash per day from ticket sales for early and late evening shows, making a total of approximately 9,000 guilders per month.[911] Even on seldom occasions when there were continuous torrential rains, the report assessed that the bioscope was still making at least 140 guilders per day. "And what were the expenses of this spectacle [*kijkspul*]. Not even f 900 a month! In those expenses are included the salaries of the manager, attendants, cashiers, electricians, rental of chairs, regular expenses of the electric lighting, musicians, film purchasing. Suppose that the interest that must be paid on recorded capital was f 100 per

---

907 Ibid., italics in original.
908 Ibid.
909 Advertisement, *Soerabaiasch-Handelsblad* (18 January 1908).
910 Advertisement, *Soerabaiasch-Handelsblad* (25 January 1908).
911 "Bioscopen en Fiscus", *Bataviaasch-Handelsblad* (5 February 1908).

month, then the total expenses are never higher than ƒ 1,000 per month and the net profit thus ƒ 8,000, in words eight thousand guilders per month! And what does the bioscope pay on patent tax [*patentbelasting*] per month? Exactly twenty whole guilders!"[912] No wonder then that the Netherlands Indies Biograph, "[...] operator of one or more bioscopes, was able to distribute a forty per cent dividend in respect of the past year; the amount of profit going to the reserve fund[913] was wisely not made public by the management. Forty per cent, that is more than many sugar companies distribute to their shareholders!"[914]

All this was about to change very soon after. Some local authorities, such as in the Preanger, Malang and Buitenzorg (Bogor), were exasperated by the fact that "Native" spectators were allegedly spending their money on moving picture shows rather than paying their taxes to the authorities, and therefore halted handing out permits to exhibitors, at least temporarily. "*Ça coute si peu et ça fait tant de plaisir*" (it costs so little and it gives so much pleasure), explained a newspaper report.[915] Other, more entertainment-friendly authorities, like Surabaya, decided to try capitalising on moving picture shows' success (see further information on Surabaya's taxation of public amusements in Section 4.2). Thus, the tax on public amusements was in the process of shifting from being based on net profits to revenues in total, and any deductions were to be carefully scrutinized from now on.[916]

Although the profit margins presumably became smaller under the new conditions, some companies, at least, continued to make handsome profits. The Stella Ripograph, a contemporary competitor of the Netherlands Indies Biograph which was itself part of a syndicate of moving picture companies, was criticized after holding a charity show in Solo (Surakarta) in 1909 and subsequently donating only 60 guilders to the unfortunates of Kaliwungu, revealing that its receipts usually averaged 80 guilders per show.[917] Furthermore, its free show the next day apparently offered the exact same programme as the night before, and was obviously fully packed. Asked about the poor box office

---

912 Ibid.
913 A profitable public limited company usually does not distribute all of its profits as dividend to shareholders, but transfers a certain proportion to a reserve fund. This is regarded as reinvestment in the company, strengthening its ownership capital and credit worthiness.
914 "Bioscopen en Fiscus", *Bataviaasch-Handelsblad* (5 February 1908).
915 "Bioscoop-vergunningen", *Het Nieuws van den Dag voor Nederlandsch-Indië* (31 March 1908), emphasis added.
916 "Belasting op publieke vermakelijkheden", *Het Nieuws van den Dag voor Nederlandsch-Indië* (7 October 1907).
917 According to reports in 1910, the Stella Ripograph was owned by a Mr. Hartman (1909–1910) ("Nederlandsch-Indië", *Soerabaiasch-Handelsblad* (21 June 1910)). Hartman was also associated with the Java Cinematograph in 1905 ("Alweer een cinematograaf", *De Locomotief* (31 October 1905)). The Hartman Brothers were the owners of the Wilhelmina Bioscope (1906–1909) ("Wilhelmina Bioscoop", *De Locomotief* (25 August 1906)). Hartman Jr. owned the Emma Ripograph (1908–1912) ("De 'Electrische ceintuur'", *Soerabaiasch-Handelsblad* (23 July 1908)). W. F. Hartman Jr. (probably the same as the above) was linked to the Ideal Ripograph in 1910–1911, and his name was later mentioned in regards to film shipping ("Nederlandsch-Indië", *Soerabaiasch-Handelsblad* (21 January 1911); Advertisement, *Soerabaiasch-Handelsblad* (25 October 1912)). A. Hartman was the proprietor of the Cinerama Theatre de Paris in Surabaya in 1912 ("Nieuwe bioscoop", *Nieuwe Soerabaja Courant* (16 April 1912)).

performance, the manager went on the defence by complaining. This left the journalist unimpressed:

> Complaints are uncalled for, I thought to myself, because when one hears that such a man rakes in f 2,400 per month, then this seems to us not to be such a bad job after all. The "standing" fees here are not so high, one and a half cents per square meter, so [with a] tent of 320 square meter floor area each evening [is] f 4.80. He calculated for us that per month he had expenses of f 1,300 on staffing and lighting, so the other f 1,100 are left for purchase [of films], travel and transportation costs. The journey between here and Madiun[918] cost him f 500, so there would be about 600 remaining for new films. One meter of (uncoloured) film costs 60 cents. Each film is at least 100 meters long, ergo one film represents a value of f 60. Every evening 1,300 meters of film are spun, thus the first night for f 780 ($=13$ x f 60). One sees that the guy is really running short. I looked at him and smiled and said that, firstly, one can use the same film for at least one and a half years, secondly, that it was customary [among exhibitors] to agree to exchange among themselves, [thirdly], that he has already been in Solo [Surakarta] for more than a month and had saved f 500 on travel. "Cut it out, sir, or you'll convince me that I'm wealthy" [the manager said and] walked away. He looked back for a moment and smiled, which to me was a sign: you got me.[919]

This research has not found any evidence to corroborate or refute these estimates by the journalist. Nevertheless, taken together with the earlier figures in regards to the Netherlands Indies Biograph's profits, this seems to have been a golden age for touring moving picture companies. (See further information on profitability and taxation below, in Section 3.3.7).

3.3.5 Local Production Fever: The Johannes-Nahapiet-Vardon Connection, 1908

As the above report from *Bataviaasch-Handelsblad* noted, the Netherlands Indies Biograph Company operated more than one exhibition company. Another company found to be associated with the Johanneses and Nahapiet was A. C. Vardon's Royal Biograph, which was also known as Vardon Biograph, sometimes Royal Biograph or Vardon Bioscope. Earlier, in 1905, A. C. Warden was mentioned as manager of the Netherlands Indies Biograph Company in Batavia.[920] The spelling of his name shifted several times, from Warden to Varden until finally Vardon was in regular use.

The Vardon Biograph's opening show at the Pasar Besar in Surabaya, in a structure next to chemist Moll & Co., took place just a few days after the departure of Johannes Biograph from the scene. In fact, one report explained, it was widely known that the "Royal Biograph, also known as Vardon Bioscope", was "owned by the same company which [previously] had great success with the Johannes Biograph" in Surabaya.[921] Made of sturdy materials,

---

918 Madiun is a city on the western edge of East Java, and is located approximately 80 kilometres east of Solo (Surakarta).

919 "Solo", *De Locomotief* (14 August 1909).

920 Advertisement, *Het Nieuws van den Dag voor Nederlandsch-Indië* (25 October 1905).

921 "Nederlandsch-Indië", *Soerabaiasch-Handelsblad* (7 February 1908).

such as *pinang* and bamboo trunks and covered with zinc, the interior was decorated with antique muslin so the raw materials remained hidden from view. The box seats and lower seating ranks had solid wooden floors. The former, which was very spacious, was also provided with a separate exit, to avoid any potential risk upon exiting the tent. Good, spacious seats were provided across the board in all ranks, and the tent remained dry even under the heaviest downpour.[922] At the back of the tent was hung a plate with the inscription "Long Live Queen Wilhelmina" made out of English post stamps.[923] Lighting in this bamboo tent was provided by mercury-vapour lamps, which were more energy- and heat-efficient than the arc lamps used in other bioscopes, although the "obnoxious bleak colour" effect on people's faces was not found to be very attractive.[924] (For further discussion of semi-permanent bamboo tents and the municipal legislation concerning them in Surabaya, see Sections 4.1 and 4.2).

Yet, even before the tent ever opened its doors to spectators, the Vardon Biograph placed an advertisement in the newspapers calling on people to show up outside the Grimm Café and Hellendoorn Restaurant at Pasar Besar on a Sunday morning with their bicycles, cars and carriages, "preferably with open tops", in order to appear in a film (see Figure 3–6).[925] Vardon may have placed this advertisement in the knowledge that the corner in question was otherwise likely to be empty on a Sunday morning due to the busy urban nightlife culture in Surabaya (see further in Section 4.2). The *Nieuwe Soerabaja Courant* was further attempting to get Surabayans to take part in the filming: "The more people, the more fun! And the more vehicles, the brighter the impression that others will get of the busiest intersection in Surabaya. Especially if they are occupied by Chinese!"[926] The local cameramen on behalf of the Vardon Biograph were identified as Mr. V. Verder and Mr. Van der Kloet. The latter would later assist the Colonial Institute's cameraman J. C. Lamster for a short time as of August 1912.[927] Following the initial screenings in Surabaya, this film was to be presented as a gift to Queen Wilhelmina, to give her an impression of the busiest city in the Netherlands East Indies.[928]

Whether the film was ever presented to Queen Wilhelmina is doubtful. Nevertheless, suggestions of films to be made and shipped to the Netherlands began to pop up in several Dutch-language newspapers across the archipelago

922 Ibid.
923 "Onze Nieuwtjes", *Nieuwe Soerabaja Courant* (7 February 1908).
924 "Onze Nieuwtjes", *Nieuwe Soerabaja Courant* (4 March 1908). The report was also picked up by *Het Nieuws van den Dag voor Nederlandsch-Indië* a few days later. "Kwikdamp-lampen", *Het Nieuws van den Dag voor Nederlandsch-Indië* (7 March 1908).
925 Advertisement, *Soerabaiasch-Handelsblad* (31 January 1908).
926 "Onze Nieuwtjes", *Nieuwe Soerabaja Courant* (1 February 1908).
927 See Nico de Klerk, "Een onmogelijke opdracht: J. C. Lamster filmopnamen voor het Koloniaal Instituut", in Janneke van Dijk, Jaap de Jong and Nico de Klerk (eds.), *J. C. Lamster, een vroege filmer in Nederlands-Indië* (Amsterdam: KIT Publishers, 2010), 79–114, here 86.
928 Advertisement, *Soerabaiasch-Handelsblad* (31 January 1908).

Figure 3–5. Advertisement for Vardon Biograph's upcoming shoot at Pasar Besar, *Soerabaiasch-Handelsblad* (31 January 1908). Retrieved from Delpher on 5 October 2015, http://resolver.kb.nl/resolve?urn= ddd:011088845:mpeg21:a0068.

around this time.[929] As opposed to the entertainment value emphasised in the Vardon Biograph's advertisement, other initiatives were focused on the pedagogical potential of such an undertaking. The editor of the *Java-Bode* envisioned a project wherein Dutch schoolchildren would get to watch moving images of the colonies, while Indies schoolchildren would be exposed to scenes from the Netherlands, estimating that such a project would require 25,000 guilders in the first year, for the purchase of devices and hiring (and possibly, training) of individuals, "preferably teachers", to operate these in the motherland and in the colonies.[930] Among the Dutch scenes proposed for the Indies youth were: a farm during milking time, a snowy winter, how cotton is made, how a railway bridge is built, children in working class neighbourhoods, a middle-class home from the inside, and a busy railway station. The Dutch youth were to watch scenes of *kampung* life, a volcano, an Indies city, a tea plan-

---

[929] The earliest suggestion of this sort found in this research was raised in 1904 in *Het Nieuws van den Dag voor Nederlandsch-Indië* quoting *Het Nieuws van den Dag* from Amsterdam, in response to a screening in Amsterdam of moving images of British North Borneo, captured by Urban Bioscope's cameraman Lomas, which failed to show the Dutch-held part of the island. "Would nobody in our country want to produce in this way images of the Indies and its inhabitants for Dutch [audiences]? It might be a lucrative venture" ("Britsch Noord-Borneo", *Het Nieuws van den Dag voor Nederlandsch-Indië* (15 January 1904)). I would like to thank Sarah Dellmann for sharing this article with me.

[930] "Cinematograaf en Onderwijs", *Java-Bode* (28 September 1908). The same report further acknowledged that it would not be possible to equip all schools immediately with the equipment for film screenings, and therefore the films were to move every once in a while from one town to another while more equipment would be bought every year.

3 – *Komedi Bioscoop, Indische* Films and the Localisation of Film Exhibition

tation, how the "Natives" weave and cultivate the land, how to fish, how local festivals are celebrated, and even a railway trip through Java. Teachers were to receive a printed text that they could use in order to explain the images to the children.

The report made waves across Java and suggestions for other scenes that should be filmed immediately sprang up in response in *De Locomotief*: the paddy field, the rice crop, a sugar factory, a coffee, tea and cinchona enterprise, some impressive scenery and waterfalls, the ascent of a mountain, an active volcano, a cliff on Sumatra, a railway journey through the Preanger, Hindu monuments, the cities of Batavia, Semarang, Surabaya, Padang, Palembang, Ambon, Makassar, etc., hunting tableau, the buffalo (in the field and entering a pool of water), a forest, weaving and batik-making, *ronggengs*, *wayang wong* and *wayang golek*, an opium den, a Chinese parade, mobile Chinese vendors selling *kelontong* (small wares) or noodles, etc., a horse race, an Indies home with different interiors, military barracks, a group of soldiers, a *warung*, etc.[931] *De Locomotief*, *Nieuwe Soerabaja Courant* and *Java-Bode* further reported that the Resident of Demak had in fact already ordered films to be made of characteristic Javanese scenes, and was indeed planning on shipping them to the Netherlands at some point for educational purposes.[932] Again, it is doubtful whether any of these plans ever came to fruition.

The Vardon Biograph, meanwhile, continued to show scenes that were filmed locally, in addition to "[...] weekly shipments of films from Europe and the United States [showing] the latest events".[933] Verder and Van der Kloet were once again credited with recording a football match between local teams E.C.A. and T.H.O.R. which was attended by an estimate of 10,000 spectators, with the debut screening of the film taking place just a few days after the match was played in Surabaya at the beginning of April.[934] About a month later, the film was shown by the Johannes Biograph, which was giving performances in its famous green tent, stationed at the *Alun Alun* in Semarang.[935] However, the recording apparently left much to be desired, according to *Soerabaiasch-Handelsblad*: "The Bioscope recording from Sunday, 29 March of the football match between T.H.O.R. and E.C.A. was very disappointing to us and to others. [...] the cameraman did not manage to record any compelling moment from the match and confined himself to aimlessly reeling his device, mainly along the quietly on-looking crowd. That is not the way to do it. A good example was

931 "Cinematograaf en Onderwijs", *De Locomotief* (2 October 1908).
932 "De cinematograaf in dienst van het onderwijs", *De Locomotief* (6 October 1908), *Nieuwe Soerabaja Courant* (8 October 1908), *Java-Bode* (9 October 1908).
933 Advertisement, *Soerabaiasch-Handelsblad* (4 February 1908). Films were received "from Paris" towards the end of February (Advertisement, *Soerabaiasch-Handelsblad* (22 February 1908)). Another load arrived on board the Rotterdamsche Llyods steamship Kawi at the beginning of March and again at the end of June (Advertisement, *Soerabaiasch-Handelsblad* (5 March 1908); Advertisement, *Soerabaiasch-Handelsblad* (23 June 1908)).
934 Advertisement, *Soerabaiasch-Handelsblad* (9 April 1908).
935 Advertisement, *De Locomotief* (15 May 1908).

recently screened at the same bioscope, a recording of a rugby match, which was magnificently successful. The unit was stationed on the side-lines of the field; here [in Surabaya] – next to the goal, which is of course absolutely wrong. Better luck next time."[936]

Verder and Van der Kloet's next opportunity came a few weeks later during the *Sekaten* festival in Solo (Surakarta), the annual week-long Javanese celebration commemorating the birth of the prophet Muhammad, celebrated with a daytime fair and night market (*pasar malam*).[937] In order to make these recordings, the Vardon Biograph's advertisement assured, "no trouble nor expense had been spared".[938] According to a review from Semarang, where the film was shown by the Johannes Biograph a month later, the scenes of the *Sekaten* festival from 16 April, identified as its "own recording", were especially beautiful.[939] "This film gave a good picture of this Oriental fair [*kermis*], full of life and amusement."[940]

In June the Vardon Biograph screened its own recordings in 35 tableaux of the annual *Pasar Malam* in Surabaya, also known as the craft-fair (*Jaarmarkt*) exhibition, although no cameraman was mentioned by name in this case.[941] A special screening to journalists one day before the official debut enabled to assure the public that the recordings were excellent: "The series begins with a beautifully lit image of the influx of the public to the main gate, seen from the 'Tobacco Plant'. Then follows a series of images, particularly clear, from the opening of the exhibition, seen from inside [the exhibition grounds]. We see them streaming in, curious spectators of all nationalities, but especially women in neat outfits […]. Then the bioscope takes you through everything one could see at the exhibition, along the vast rows of sheds, along the restaurants, along the dancers and swordsmen, along the *gamelan* and through the *kampong toekang* [Javanese craftsmen]!"[942] The debut was attended by the recently appointed Resident of Surabaya and more screenings were added due to popular demand.[943]

Vardon Biograph remained in Surabaya until the end of June 1908, occasionally offering variety acts alongside the film screenings, such as a *Variété* troupe comprised of tightrope walkers, acrobats, a famous pianist and singer, dancers, gymnasts, trapeze artists, snake performers, sword swallowers, and a woman

---

936 "Nederlandsch-Indië", *Soerabaiasch-Handelsblad* (13 April 1908).
937 Advertisement, *Soerabaiasch-Handelsblad* (23 April 1908).
938 Ibid.
939 "Johannes-Biograph", *De Locomotief* (14 May 1908).
940 Ibid.
941 Advertisement, *Soerabaiasch-Handelsblad* (19 June 1908).
942 "De Jaarmarkt-tentoonstelling in de Bioscoop", *Soerabaiasch-Handelsblad* (20 June 1908), emphasis added.
943 Advertisement, *Soerabaiasch-Handelsblad* (23 June 1908). The Chiefs of Aceh and Boni also attended Vardon Biograph shows upon visiting Surabaya ("Nederlandsch-Indië", *Soerabaiasch-Handelsblad* (5 June 1908)).

of 891 pounds.[944] Vardon then travelled to Semarang, where he replaced the Johannes Biograph which had just left the *Alun Alun* a couple of weeks earlier.[945] It was the Vardon Biograph then which showed the scenes from the *Pasar Malam* in Surabaya to audiences in Semarang in mid-July.[946]

With the city of Semarang in the midst of preparations for its own *Pasar Malam* and "exhibition of Native industry and agriculture", certain people were eyeing the Vardon Biograph's tent, presumably some sort of bamboo structure as the one it had erected in Surabaya, as a potential site for the exhibition since it was "spacious, sealed, and sturdy".[947] It was therefore proposed to the organizing committee to take over the tent and use it as a "[...] Native theatre, or as a workshop for *toekangs*. Besides, should the organizing committee choose to have bioscope screenings, the tent is naturally built for this purpose."[948] The Vardon Biograph was also the obvious candidate for the job. Finally, it was agreed upon that Vardon's tent at the *Alun Alun* would be used for Javanese court performers from Yogyakarta, while the Vardon Biograph itself temporarily moved to another tent next to the post office and tram stop. After sunset, the site of the temporary Vardon tent was joined with the site of the exhibition by a tram connection, which allowed visitors to the exhibition grounds to attend Biograph shows as well, offered free of charge during the celebrations.[949] Among the films shown during the *Pasar Malam* in Semarang were the views of the *Pasar Malam* in Surabaya, along with Vardon's recordings of Mr. Watson's iron factory in Yogyakarta, in addition to images of Borobudur, a ninth-century Buddhist Temple in Central Java.[950]

Vardon also took advantage of this opportunity to film scenes of the *Pasar Malam* in Semarang, for which the organizing committee awarded him an honorary certificate. The *Nieuwe Soerabaja Courant* later noted in this respect: "[...] it is not an easy task to make a recording in Semarang which is well worth seeing, and Semarangers should be grateful to him that he has saved these rare moments from oblivion".[951] Semarangers themselves seem to have been aware of their poor standing, compared to the entertainment capital of the Indies in Surabaya, as can be inferred from their response to another local view of Semarang initiated by Vardon. "There [in Surabaya] one feels one is in a city, while here [in Semarang] one gets the feeling of being in a cramped small

---

944 Advertisement, *Soerabaiasch-Handelsblad* (26 March 1908). At the end of May, Vardon once again teamed up for a few nights with a French troupe of artistes, acrobats and clowns (Advertisement, *Soerabaiasch-Handelsblad* (26 May 1908)).

945 Advertisement, *De Locomotief* (4 July 1908); Advertisement, *De Locomotief* (13 June 1908).

946 Advertisement, *De Locomotief* (13 July 1908).

947 "Passer-malem", *De Locomotief* (9 July 1908).

948 Ibid., emphasis added.

949 Vardon Biograph was not the only moving picture show available during the Pasar Malam in Semarang. Open-air screenings were offered at the *Stadstuin*, as well as in the hall of the Regent of Yogyakarta ("Passer Malem", *De Locomotief* (2 September 1908)).

950 Advertisement, *De Locomotief* (25 August 1908).

951 "Bioscoop-opnamen", *Nieuwe Soerabaja Courant* (10 October 1908).

village. The Vardon Biograph, which made recordings of street crowds here and in Surabaya, can testify to the difference between the two cities. In Surabaya thousands responded to the request of the bioscope owner; there it became an opportunity to have a kind of a party, and here? A few hundred people at most turned up, so the film will not be very interesting. Semarang is truly asleep, and that is a shame for such a beautiful city."[952]

3.3.6 The Oranjefeesten: Competition Heats Up in Surabaya, 1909

Though the Vardon Biograph left Surabaya at the end of June and the Johannes Biograph returned only at the end of December 1908, the presence of the Netherlands Indies Biograph Company was felt in the intervening months. Nahapiet was apparently the owner of a new "permanent tent" set up next to the Courthouse in September 1908 and housed at the time by the Netherlands Indies Electro Bioscope.[953] Then, in November, while J. Hartmann Jr.'s Emma Ripograph, aka Hartmann Bioscoop or Hartman's Emma Ripograph, was performing in Surabaya, his tent structure at Pasar Besar, next to Moll & Co., experienced a series of sabotage attempts. Hartman did not hesitate to point accusing fingers at a "few Armenians, in one way or another connected to the soon expected competing Biograph".[954] The unnamed Armenians allegedly attempted to drive the "Native" audience away from the Emma Ripograph, by throwing hollowed out *pinang* nut shells filled with notes containing malevolent messages, or by piercing holes in the gutters of the tent in order to get it drenched under water. No official charges were ever made, and while it is unknown if anyone associated with the Netherlands Indies Biograph was indeed behind these acts, it is nevertheless a sign that competition between the ever-growing number of companies was heating up (for more on Surabaya's lively moving picture scene in this period, see Chapter 4).

Johannes Biograph's opening show took place in Nahapiet's bamboo tent on 23 December 1908 under a new manager by the name Erdtsieck.[955] The new manager was perceived in one newspaper report to have given a boost to the "dear old friend", by bringing everything up to date: "No carnival-like knick-knacks such as paper roses, light-coloured garlands, seat covers out of bed curtain. Everything is staid, sound, solid, entirely European. The walls are cheerful, light blue tinted. Separate boxes with velvet lining for four to six people. Innumerable electric bell-shaped and arc lamps. What beautiful paintings. For the ceiling, a garden with fresh plants and a fountain with coloured water jets."[956] Despite the claim that the exhibition space was now more "European", it was supposedly designed after the Mills Arcades in Chicago,

---

952 "Brieven uit Semarang", *Bataviaasche Nieuwsblad* (27 July 1908).
953 "Een nieuwe bioscop [sic]", *Nieuwe Soerabaja Courant* (11 September 1908).
954 "Speculatie op bijgeloof", *Soerabaiasch-Handelsblad* (20 November 1908).
955 Advertisement, *Soerabaiasch-Handelsblad* (23 December 1908).
956 "Johannes bioscoop", *Soerabaiasch-Handelsblad* (24 December 1908).

3 – *Komedi Bioscoop, Indische* Films and the Localisation of Film Exhibition

according to one advertisement.⁹⁵⁷ Every mail boat brought the very latest of films from six different companies, including Pathé "that of course occupies a place of honour", the advertisements guaranteed.⁹⁵⁸ By the beginning of March, the Johannes Biograph was hooked up to the telephone line and could be reached by phone for seat reservations.⁹⁵⁹

Nevertheless, the Board of Directors was apparently not satisfied with the performance of Mr. Erdtsieck, who was promptly discharged just a couple of weeks after the opening show.⁹⁶⁰ A wanted ad for a new manager for the Johannes Biograph was immediately posted, suggesting that the issue was alcohol-related: "Johannes Biograph is seeking an individual who is not addicted to strong drink and is suitable to act as Manager".⁹⁶¹ Those with previous working experience in the field would be given preference, and candidates were invited to present themselves to Mr. Johannes directly. An article running in the newspaper the same day stated that a few applications have already been submitted to the management, and further mentioned that a salary of 200 guilders per month was guaranteed, presumably with added bonuses to be given based on actual box office performance.⁹⁶² A new manager by the name Ch. F. Behrend was hired about a month later.⁹⁶³

Accusations of foul play continued to be raised, following the Johannes Biograph's decision to hold a charity show to aid victims of a recent natural disaster in Penjalu in Central Java, where a landslide took the lives of 200 to 300 people.⁹⁶⁴ Johannes Biograph quickly ordered via telegraph from Europe "some appropriate, current tragic scenes", and the two shows on Saturday and Sunday nights yielded 386.21 guilders for the cause.⁹⁶⁵ However, a few days

957   Advertisement, *Soerabaiasch-Handelsblad* (10 February 1909).
958   Ibid.
959   Advertisement, *Soerabaiasch-Handelsblad* (5 March 1909).
960   Advertisement, *Soerabaiasch-Handelsblad* (12 January 1909).
961   "Gevraagd", *Soerabaiasch-Handelsblad* (12 January 1909).
962   "Manager Johannes-Bioscoop", *Soerabaiasch-Handelsblad* (12 January 1909). For the sake of comparison, an office worker for an export company in Semarang would have earned between 300 and 350 guilders per month (Advertisement, *Bataviaasch Nieuwsblad* (4 October 1910)). A bookkeeper for the Batavia municipality had a starting salary of 250 guilders per month, with five two-yearly raises of up to 50 guilders each, in addition to a fixed pension plan (Advertisement, *Bataviaasch Nieuwsblad* (16 September 1910)). The starting salary of a European assistant on a plantation in Sumatra was 175 guilders per month ("Assistenten-Salarissen", *Sumatra Post* (4 May 1910)). A *toko* (shop) administrator or an office clerk in one of the main towns of Java would have earned between 100 and 150 guilders per month to start off (Advertisement, *Bataviaasch Nieuwsblad* (19 August 1910); Advertisement, *Het Nieuws van den Dag voor Nederlandsch-Indië* (9 June 1910); Advertisement, *Het Nieuws van den Dag voor Nederlandsch-Indië* (27 May 1910)). A Royal Packet Navigation Company (KPM) ship officer earned 150 guilders per month, and also got free room and board ("'De Draadlooze' en de Paketvaart", *Bataviaasch Nieuwsblad* (29 March 1910)). The starting salary of a *dokter djawa*, a Javanese healer with Western medical training, in 1910 was 150 guilders per month, "with four 3-yearly raises of ƒ25 to a maximum of ƒ250" (Liesbeth Hesselink, *Healers on the colonial market: Native doctors and midwives in the Dutch East Indies* (Leiden: KITLV Press, 2011), 172).
963   Advertisement, *Soerabaiasch-Handelsblad* (20 February 1909).
964   "De Vreeselijke Ramp in Pendjaloe", *Bataviaasch Nieuwsblad* (6 January 1909).
965   "De Liefdadigheidsvoorstellingen van de Johannes Bioscoop", *Soerabaiasch-Handelsblad* (15 January 1909); "Nederlandsch-Indië", *Soerabaiasch-Handelsblad* (19 January 1909).

later, a letter to the editor of *Soerabaiasch-Handelsblad* signed by a certain "Vio" related overhearing a conversation in which a gentleman said that it was "[...] a disgrace to the Dutch nation, that the native subjects must be helped in case of a disaster by a foreign Armenian fairground tent; [and, moreover] that this reflected positively on these Armenians, who commonly are considered such money-grubbers".[966] "Vio" actually disagreed with this statement, commending Johannes Biograph for its generosity while recognising the public relations ploy behind such an act of kindness. His problem was rather with the sum of money supposedly raised: "[...] how is it possible, just f 386.21 for two nights of packed tents, so full that the manager of the Johannes [B]ioscope himself publicised that the tent during those two evenings was so full that people had to be refused entry, i.e., that meant that there was between f 2,000 and f 2,500 to be collected, since free tickets were not valid on those evenings".[967]

Johannes Biograph replied immediately the next day, explaining that the original plan was to donate two-thirds of the gross proceeds from one night, but due to the expected poor weather conditions, it was decided to spread the risk and pledge one-third of the gross proceeds from two nights. On Saturday evening the receipts totalled f 509.90 and on Sunday f 650.55, thus a total of 1,160.45, one-third of which is f 386.21, which was indeed somewhat lower than for most other charity events. The Johannes Biograph attributed the result to the fact that higher ranked seats were not filled in the early evenings, while the lower paying sections were fully packed. "The piece by Vio in this newspaper does the owners of this bioscope and Armenians in general injustice in all respects", concluded the response letter.[968] Another anonymous "Armenian" sent in his own reply in defence of the defamed Johannes and Armenian community, enraged especially by the labelling "money-grubbers".[969]

The provenance of the accusations against Johannes Biograph is not clear, but there was certainly no shortage of disgruntled competitors around. By that point, Hartman Jr. and his Emma Ripograph had left the tent at Pasar Besar to be replaced by Hartman Sr.'s Royal Bioscope, aka Hartman Bioscope (not to be confused with Esoofally's Royal Bioscope).[970] Nevertheless, even when both tents offered similar film programmes, presumably mostly Pathé Frères films, the crowds seemed to prefer the Johannes Biograph.[971]

The exception to this was probably the excitement surrounding the birth of Dutch Princess Royal Juliana on 30 April. Following several months of anticipation and announcements of plans over the pages of the newspapers, news of the birth finally came in and the week-long celebrations, known as the "*Oran-*

---

966 "Ingezonden stukken. De weldadigheid van de Johannes bioscoop", *Soerabaiasch-Handelsblad* (26 January 1909).

967 Ibid.

968 "De Johannes Bioscoop en de Liefdadigheid", *Soerabaiasch-Handelsblad* (27 January 1909).

969 "Ingezonden stukken. Een open Brief aan het adres van Vio", *Soerabaiasch-Handelsblad* (27 January 1909).

970 "Weer een nieuwe bioscoop", *Nieuwe Soerabaja Courant* (15 January 1909).

971 "Mooie Films", *Soerabaiasch-Handelsblad* (5 March 1909).

3 – *Komedi Bioscoop, Indische* Films and the Localisation of Film Exhibition

jefeesten", could commence. This was an opportunity for local filming that was not to be missed, and several cameramen were in action. The first was Vardon, initially misidentified in the newspaper report as Nahapiet, who recorded scenes at the Pasar Besar for the Johannes Biograph. "Thus we will be able to re-live at the bioscope what we can now experience in the flesh once the festival week is up", *Soerabaiasch-Handelsblad* heralded the achievement.[972] As soon as the celebrations were over, the recordings were indeed screened at the Johannes Biograph. The scenes depicted, among others: "[...] the gun salute with the canons; the heavy traffic at Pasar Besar; the parade on *Alun Alun* Kemajoran; the arrival of 8,000 schoolchildren at the *Stadstuin*; children singing under the direction of Mr. Stoel; [...] Chinese schoolchildren; Javanese public amusements and prizes distributed at the *Alun Alun* Kemajoran; continuing with [...] the bottle game with eyes shut, the climbing of the mast, bicycle riding and running on smooth tree trunks. Finally, the parade of different nations, coloured."[973]

A report in *Soerabaiasch Nieuwsblad* noted that apparently it did not cost much to make such films, and practically anyone could handle such a device. Nevertheless, "[...] making a well-exposed film demands a lot of practice and sense of brightness and speed of movement. Mr. Vardon has already come a long way in this art. His achievements are constantly improving. It's worth going to watch them."[974] Another report in *Soerabaiasch-Handelsblad* singled out the views of the Pasar Besar, this time – taken from the terrace of the Grimm pastry shop, as the most successful scenes:

> [...] when one gets to look at the traffic along our main roads, one realises that the road is really not so badly laid out and that our city is not inferior in this respect to many European cities.
>
> For those who in the last few days celebrated there is an attractive opportunity in store to recognize themselves or other familiar faces. We therefore expect that, like last year with the recordings of the Pasar Malam, these films will also attract a large audience.[975]

On top of the screenings at the Johannes Biograph, the negatives of these scenes were apparently on their way to Europe, "[...] so that it will soon be possible to give a performance of *Indische* joviality there".[976] There is no evidence, however, that such scenes were ever shown in Europe. Yet they were shown in Semarang just a few weeks later, where Vardon travelled to – this time – as manager of the Johannes Biograph.[977]

972 "De Feesten en de Bioscoop", *Soerabaiasch-Handelsblad* (1 May 1909).
973 "Johannes Bioscoop", *Soerabaiasch Nieuwsblad* (8 May 1909), emphasis added.
974 "Nederlandsch Indisch Nieuws", *Soerabaiasch Nieuwsblad* (11 May 1909).
975 "De Johannes Biograph", *Soerabaiasch-Handelsblad* (11 May 1909).
976 "Johannesbioscoop", *Soerabaiasch-Handelsblad* (14 May 1909), emphasis added.
977 "Johannes-biograph", *De Locomotief* (1 June 1909). By mid-July, advertisements for Johannes Biograph with Vardon as manager were replaced by advertisements for Vardon Biograph (Advertisement, *De Locomotief* (12 July 1909)).

Nevertheless, as mentioned above, these were not the only scenes filmed of the *Oranjefeesten*.[978] J. C. Umbgrove, a Surabayan cameraman who was a member of "an old family from the Indies", was also filming for the Royal Bioscope of Mr. Hartman.[979] First screened for a small audience of invited guests, including journalists, the recordings were found to be very good, with one of the spectators commenting that they were

> [...] in no way inferior to those of Pathé. Indeed, [in terms of] sharpness and stability they left nothing to be desired and we suspect that this number on the Royal Biograph's programme will appeal to the public. In all the films the faces were clearly distinguishable, an attraction for our fellow citizens, who happily get to see themselves and their acquaintances immortalised, and no doubt will experience a pleasant sensation at the thought that their portraits will go all the way to Europe. Also for other reasons, it is an excellent idea of Mr. Umbgrove's to work for the European market. Thus, for example, it is by no means undesirable that in Holland they realise that our militia is a dashing outfit, as ready as the late Van der Werff to have one arm eaten up to fight with the other one, and marching in rank as if they had never done anything else. It really is worth the cost and effort to go see this film. Especially one that we saw later that was almost flawless in terms of technique. This film gives a representation of the company in the field of pottery near Surabaya. One sees the work on the well-known turntable, colours, and baking of pots and pans, all recorded with a sharpness that leaves no doubt as to what is done. We congratulate Mr. Umbgrove for this recording, which is truly unique.[980]

Again, while the idea of shipping these films to Europe was mentioned, it is unclear if this was ever done and Surabayans' ambition of becoming famous in Europe probably did not materialize. It would be another two years before Umbgrove were to establish the East Java Bioscope (*Oost-Java Bioscope*, or *N.V. Oost Java Handelscompagnie*) and begin to regularly make local views and deal with film distribution (for more on Umbgrove, see Section 4.5).

3.3.7 Hard Times for Travelling Exhibitors: Cholera Outbreaks and Tighter Regulation, 1910–1912

After the high-point of the *Oranjefeesten*, travelling moving picture exhibitors fell on hard times. Further new regulations and taxes on public amusements were being introduced – first in Surabaya and almost immediately adopted by other municipalities across the archipelago. Targeted regulation, it was

---

978 Local views of the *Oranjefeesten* were also made in Batavia by Mr. Demmeni and included various scenes, such as a parade, people at the square and riding in a *dos-a-dos*, the Native and Foreign Oriental celebrations at the zoo, *wayang wong*, military cyclists at the Waterlooplein ("Bioscoop-opnamen", *Java-Bode* (10 May 1909)). The plan was to screen these scenes the following week, probably at the Flying Bioscope which Demmeni was associated with. In 1908, his recording of the Batavia races was shown by the Flying Bioscope in Buitenzorg (Bogor) and was said to prove that in this field "we are not inferior to Europe" ("Uit Buitenzorg", *Soerabaiasch-Handelsblad* (11 November 1908)).

979 Bosma et al., *Being "Dutch" in the Indies*, 391. Charles Jacob Umbgrove was born on 15 February 1868 in Lumajang and died on 16 July 1936 in Surabaya. His parents were Jan Louis Umbgrove and Fatima Loemadjang ("Charles Jacob Umbgrove", Genealogie Online, accessed on 2 February 2016, http://www.genealogieonline.nl/genealogie-baert-cornelis-kalshoven/I10231.php).

980 "Nieuwe Films van de Oranje Feesten", *Soerabaiasch-Handelsblad* (13 May 1909).

3 – *Komedi Bioscoop*, *Indische* Films and the Localisation of Film Exhibition

believed, would make possible limitation of the nature and quantity of cinema tents and the duration of their emplacement, as well as the sale of alcohol on their premises.[981] Tighter inspection of ticket sales and an added tax on public amusements were among the means introduced (see further on tax and legislation in Surabaya in Section 4.2, in Batavia in Section 5.2, in Semarang in Section 6.3, and in Medan in Section 7.4).

Moreover, film distribution in the Indies was undergoing changes, from being based mostly on sale of films to a film rental system. One report argued that, while many believed that moving pictures were a lucrative business, this had been true only up until a few years before. Competition had grown to such an extent and the business required so much investment that a cinema company was now content if it made even a six per cent profit. Exhibitors had the option of either buying or renting films, and the more sophisticated "theatre films" were available for rental "[...] only under extremely severe conditions: no less than 50 per cent of the gross income must be paid to the film's rights holder".[982] Additionally, Pathé's agent in the Indies, L. Schwartz, also encroached on the territory of travelling exhibitors by advertising a projection device and dynamo for sale (at a total cost of 2,650 guilders), as well as films for rental available on a weekly basis, directly to planters and company owners for entertaining the coolies on their estates.[983]

Another grim problem exhibitors were faced with was a serious outbreak of cholera, especially on Java. The threat of cholera was a constant over the years, even claiming the life of at least one exhibitor in 1902, forcing the police to burn his canvas tent.[984] Yet, the 1910–1911 near-epidemic proved a difficult time for exhibitors, with most of them still operating travelling shows, as several local authorities opted for quarantine and simply refused to give out licenses for entertainment shows such as "bioscope and Native *komedie*".[985] Some companies thus could not travel further and were forced to extend their stay in the last town they had reached. In eastern Java, which was particularly hard hit, the flow of entertainments traditionally attended by more European spectators, such as violin concerts or *variété* companies, dried up. This reportedly made it more acceptable for Europeans to freely attend the only available amusement: the cinema.[986] Nevertheless, some exhibitors were luckier than others. For instance, the Emma Ripograph was stranded in Malang, where the authorities banned Javanese and Chinese spectators from going to the

---

981 "Tijdelijke afstand van wegen enz.", *Soerabaiasch-Handelsblad* (10 December 1908).
982 "Het Bioscoop-Bedrijf", *Soerabaiasch-Handelsblad* (23 December 1909). A similar report appeared again in 1910 ("Geldbelegging in Bioscopen", *Soerabaiasch-Handelsblad* (28 April 1910)).
983 Advertisement, *Het Nieuws van den Dag voor Nederlandsch-Indië* (11 January 1910). See further on Pathé's distribution in the Indies in Section 3.5.1.
984 "Onze Nieuwtjes", *Soerabaija-Courant* (22 October 1902).
985 "Telegrammen", *Sumatra Post* (29 July 1910), emphasis added.
986 "Nederlandsch-Indië", *Soerabaiasch-Handelsblad* (10 May 1910); "Uit Probolinggo", *Soerabaiasch-Handelsblad* (19 May 1910).

cinema.[987] This obviously led to unfortunate outcomes for the exhibitor, whose most loyal patronisers could not attend the shows.[988] By comparison, the Johannes Biograph, which was stuck in Probolinggo as the only form of entertainment in town, "[...] helped out the fun- and art loving residents to get through the quiet times and thus made excellent business".[989] But even this was short-lived, and the tent had to shut down soon due to growing numbers of cholera victims (for more on hygiene problems at cinema venues, see Sections 4.3 and 6.2).[990]

It might have been the difficult situation on Java that drove several companies at the time to travel for shows in Makassar, on Celebes. The Royal Standard Biograph under the management of Helant, who was one of the exhibitors receiving films from Dutch film entrepreneur Desmet, remained for shows there for the most part of 1910.[991] Vardon Biograph also spent a couple of months in Makassar in August–September 1910, where his local views of Chinese warships in Surabaya were enthusiastically received.[992] This was probably a film made in early 1908 capturing the ships "Haij Kie and Haij Yong and the celebrations in the *Stadstuin*".[993]

The last shows found in this research under the name Johannes Biograph were given in Surabaya at the beginning of January 1911.[994] Nevertheless, the name Johannes was once again mentioned as manager of the International Biograph a year later, when it performed in a structure next to the Courthouse in Surabaya from early May until early August 1912.[995] A semi-permanent structure was originally erected at this site by Nahapiet, but it was likely not the same one used for the International Biograph's shows. By this point, it appears that Johannes was no longer showing local views, and at least some of the films on his programme, including Asta Nielsen films, were provided via Umbgrove's East Java Bioscope Company.[996]

Vardon returned to Surabaya towards the end of 1911 and soon after sought to obtain a permit to set up a permanent cinema of brick and stone, on a piece of land just above the marsh of Prabanleiding, east of the Tunjungan-Gem-

987 The reports do not explain why Javanese and Chinese spectators were banned from attending the cinemas. Due to the poor sanitation conditions in the *kampung* areas, quarantine was practiced during times of epidemics.

988 "Nederlandsch-Indië", *Soerabaiasch-Handelsblad* (11 November 1910).

989 "Uit Probolinggo", *Soerabaiasch-Handelsblad* (19 May 1910).

990 "De cholera in den Oosthoek", *Het Nieuws van den Dag voor Nederlandsch-Indië* (26 May 1910).

991 Advertisement, *Makasaarsche Courant* (31 May 1910). According to Blom, from February to October 1914, Helant purchased second-hand prints for screening in his own cinema theatre, the Royal Standard Biograph in Yogyakarta, as well as for trading with other cinemas (Blom, Jean Desmet, 214).

992 "Stadsnieuws", *Makasaarsche Courant* (13 September 1910).

993 Advertisement, *Soerabaiasch-Handelsblad* (10 January 1908), emphasis added.

994 Advertisement, *Soerabaiasch-Handelsblad* (7 January 1911).

995 Advertisement, *Soerabaiasch-Handelsblad* (2 May 1912); Advertisement, *Soerabaiasch-Handelsblad* (3 August 1912).

996 "Asta Nielsen in de Bioscope", *Soerabaiasch-Handelsblad* (3 May 1912).

balongan bridge, parallel to Genteng. He was not the only bidder with similar plans for the same property, and one of his competitors was in fact Nahapiet.[997] Hughan, another bidder for the same property, proposed that the beautiful and monumental building that he was planning serve to conceal the "hideous view" of the *kampung* behind it.[998] However, none of these men received a permit, as the local authorities claimed that they had plans for widening the road.[999] Vardon, nevertheless, did obtain a permit to construct a "building of a temporary nature for giving moving picture shows" at Pasar Besar, north of Johorlaan, at a cost of 100 guilders rental per month.[1000] In 1913, Vardon Biograph exhibited another local view titled "Surabaya at every hour of the day", and the last shows found in this research were given on the New Year's Eve 1914.[1001]

3.4 Conclusion

The three cultural forms dealt with in this chapter, and especially their manifestations of *Indische* culture, have been literature, the *stambul* theatre, and moving pictures. Significantly, these forms as they developed into the 1920s and 1930s, according to Jedamski, have also "laid the foundation for modern Indonesian culture".[1002] She further argues:

> Not only did they introduce novel topics and discourses, but they also implemented Western forms of perception: a totally stage-centred and firmly guided theatre reception; individualized text reception introduced by the 'silent reading' of a book; and the camera-guided gaze at the film screen. In all three cases, the recipient, reader and spectator alike are supposed to experience a certain detachment from reality and to be entirely absorbed in the narrative for the duration of the reception process.[1003]

We may doubt whether such detachment was ever really achieved at turn-of-the-century moving picture shows, if we consider the screening conditions presented here, which were often disrupted by noises coming from inside and outside the venues, in addition to interruptions caused by electrical problems or weather conditions. Nevertheless, it certainly appears that modern readers of Malay novels[1004] and modern spectators of *stambul* in the Indies were

---

997 "Het Bioscooptheater te Soerabaja", *Soerabaiasch-Handelsblad* (16 January 1912).
998 "Een nieuwe bioscoop", *Nieuwe Soerabaja Courant* (20 January 1912).
999 "Zal niet gaan", *Nieuwe Soerabaja Courant* (25 January 1912).
1000 "Gemeenteraad te Soerabaja. Zitting van 27 Maart 1912", *Soerabaiasch-Handelsblad* (29 March 1912). For more on the construction of permanent cinema theatres in Surabaya, see Section 4.4.
1001 Advertisement, *Soerabaiasch-Handelsblad* (7 March 1913); Advertisement, *Soerabaiasch-Handelsblad* (30 December 1913).
1002 Jedamski, "... and then the lights went out", 484.
1003 Ibid.
1004 "Modern readers" refers to Chinese, Eurasian and Native elites who could read, consumed newspapers and literature, and were educated in the Dutch schools to become what Schulte Nordholt calls the colony's "cultural citizens" (see further discussion in Introduction).

identifying something that met their leisure expectations in moving picture shows.

The period highlighted in this chapter was marked by changes in the way early cinema was being exhibited, distributed and consumed. Moving picture exhibition, while still based mostly on itinerant show people on the move across the archipelago, and in Southeast Asia in general, was gaining ever more local features. The films on the programmes were echoing similar tales read in novels or watched on the *stambul* stages, on the one hand, and featured relevant actualities shot locally in the Indies, on the other hand. The contexts of moving picture consumption and the arrangement of exhibition spaces were further being localised and encountered on the various *pasar* fairgrounds in major cities and rural towns.

The two companies serving as the main focal points of this chapter, which were arguably the most successful of their day, reflect not only the localisation of film exhibition, but also the developments the industry was undergoing on a larger scale: from itinerant shows to a more permanent presence of moving pictures as a regular going-out option for urban dwellers. The Royal Bioscope's relative success in the local Indies entertainment scene can be gleaned, if not from the debateable swarm of positive reviews, then at least from Esoofally's repeated visits to the Indies over the course of five years. Nevertheless, ultimately, as the industry of moving picture exhibition was developing from tent shows into sedentary cinema houses, Esoofally settled back in India, taking over the Alexandra Theatre in Bombay (present-day Mumbai) with a partner in 1914.[1005] In 1918 they constructed the Majestic Theatre where, according to Barnouw and Krishnaswamy, the first Indian talking feature would be premiered.[1006]

The Netherlands Indies Biograph Company, as we have seen, underwent parallel processes on the local Indies scene. It was the longest running company of its day in the Indies, starting out in 1904, peaking around 1908–1909, and then slowly declining in the early 1910s, as itinerant exhibitors were becoming less visible in urban settings and replaced by fixed cinema houses.[1007] The enterprising spirit of Johannes, Nahapiet and Vardon in the field of moving pictures – spanning exhibition, distribution and production – helped shape the developing industry on the local level. Their attempts in the early 1910s of also going into ownership of fixed venues foreshadows the next stage in the development of moving picture exhibition, as will be discussed in the final four chapters. In turn, the growing presence of moving pictures and the increasing popularity of movie-going across colonial society set in motion regulation and

---

1005 See Barnouw et al., *Indian Film*, 9.

1006 Ibid.

1007 Moving picture shows were also making the rounds of entertainments for sugar company and plantation workers, as mentioned in this chapter (Sections 3.3.1 and 3.3.7) and will be further discussed in Section 7.3.

3 – Komedi Bioscoop, Indische Films and the Localisation of Film Exhibition

legislation procedures on the part of the colonial authorities, which previously did not pay much attention to this new entertainment form.

It is perhaps most fitting to conclude Part I of this book with statements attributed to C. J. Umbgrove, the local photographer-turned-lanternist-turned-cinema-entrepreneur whose endeavours will be highlighted in the following chapter on Surabaya, and whose impact as a film distributor reached far beyond this port city of eastern Java (see further in Section 4.5). Interestingly, it appears that Umbgrove first saw moving images when Esoofally came to Surabaya in 1905, according to his own account narrated to G. H. von Faber, the Dutch-German Surabaya-born author who was compiling memories and memorabilia for his volume *Nieuw Soerabaia: De Geschiedenis van Indië's voornaamste Koopstad in de Eerste Kwarteeuw Sedert hare Instelling 1906–1931*:

> Film was first introduced here [in Surabaya] by a British-Indian, a certain Joesoef, who in 1905 and 1906 travelled from one place to another in the Indies archipelago with a canvas tent, a simple projection device and a series of short "vibrating images" [*trilbeelden*]. Not much more can be said about this man. His "*gambar hidoep*" which was set up under the shade of a big jambul tree in an area along what is now "high road", north of the Courthouse, aroused great interest every evening among residents, especially the natives. The former Surabayan C. J. Umbgrove could tell us that the British Indian was the first, perhaps the only one, who showed recordings of the Russo-Japanese War.
>
> After him came Salzwedel [Java Biorama], who with Etty [Java Cineograph] screened film reels in a bamboo shed. This did not last very long. The company was dissolved. Salzwedel left for Semarang and was succeeded first by Johannes, and later by Vardon.[1008]

This summary of the early moving picture exhibition scene clearly reduces the actual scope of moving picture companies in the region, as outlined in this and the preceding chapters, which similarly have not been able to account for all exhibitors active in the Indies in the period. This was generally a time of explosion of film companies: from a handful of exhibitors around the turn of the century identified in this research, to seven or eight active companies on Java and Sumatra between 1902 and 1903, there were suddenly more than 20 companies touring the region between 1904 and 1905, most of them based locally. According to a report in *Nieuwe Soerabaja Courant*, by 1907 there were 35 exhibition companies active on Java.[1009] This research was able to identify by name 23 different companies showing moving pictures on Java in 1907, and several others which remain unidentified, which makes this figure plausible.[1010] And while the details provided in Faber's book are rather inaccurate

---

1008 G. H. von Faber, *Nieuw Soerabaia: De Geschiedenis van Indië's voornaamste Koopstad in de Eerste Kwarteeuw Sedert hare Instelling 1906–1931* (Bussum/Soerabaia: N.V. Boekhandel en Drukkerij H. van Ingen, 1936), 385–386, emphasis added.

1009 "Bioscoopconcurrentie", *Nieuwe Soerabaja Courant* (16 August 1907).

1010 Out of these 23 companies, only 18 of the owner names could be identified. Eleven of them have European-sounding names. As this does not exclude the possibility that some of them were in fact Eurasian, the trend in the ethnicity of moving picture entrepreneurs appears to shift towards more Chinese, Arab, and Indian owners in the mid-1900s.

and contain anachronisms, this description nevertheless attests to the lasting impressions that Salzwedel and Etty, and Esoofally, Johannes and Vardon, presented here, left on their spectators thirty odd years later and to the central role they played in embedding moving picture exhibition in the Indies archipelago.[1011] It does, nevertheless, obscure the ever increasing role played by Chinese and Arab entrepreneurs in the local movie-going scene, especially as more fixed exhibition venues began to pop up in the main cities from about 1907, as will be further elaborated on in the following chapters.

[1011] Salzwedel's Java Biorama and Etty's Java Cineograph, discussed in Chapter 2, came a couple of years before Esoofally. Moreover, Esoofally was neither the first nor the only one to have shown Russo-Japanese War films.

PART II

Local Cinema Cultures

4

Surabaya: Queen City of Moving Picture Venues

> *Cinemas here in the Indies continue to be housed in more or less primitive, sometimes already quite fashionably furnished tents or sheds. Now in Surabaya the finishing touches are underway on a real and permanent movie theatre* [bioscooptheater] *that has the ring of excellence about it [and] does not fall in any way behind the best European institutions of such a nature.*
>
> *"Soerabaja",* De Locomotief *(23 September 1913).*

Surabaya in East Java was a major coastal and military town and the principal mercantile centre of the Netherlands Indies. While Batavia was the "seat of government" and the city generally "perceived as [the] cosmopolitan metropole" of the colony, Surabaya served as the hub of the sugar, coffee, rubber and tobacco trades.[1012] With a recorded population of about 150,000 residents in 1906, this highly multicultural city was home to a Muslim majority of 124,473 Javanese and Madurese ("Natives" in Dutch colonial censi), 14,843 Chinese and 2,482 Arabs ("Foreign Orientals"), and 8,063 "Europeans" – mostly in fact Eurasians.[1013] Most importantly for the purposes of this research, popular entertainment had a prominent place on the landscape of Surabaya throughout the nineteenth and twentieth centuries. In the nineteenth century, the city was the breeding ground for the popular Malay opera form of *komedi stambul*, and frequently hosted French and Italian operetta companies, American magicians, British and Indian circus outfits and Australian and Japanese acrobats and performers.[1014]

Surabaya experienced the most irregular urban development of all the great cities of Java.[1015] "[I]n an alluvial delta", on land that rose just a few metres above sea level, the "fertility and accessibility of this rice-growing plain was the key to Surabaya's early prominence in the maritime trading world".[1016] It became a colonial trading post in the mid-eighteenth century, when a Dutch

---

1012 Cohen, *The Komedie Stamboel*, 29.

1013 Faber, *Nieuw Soerabaia*, 2. The population of Surabaya reached approximately 190,000 in 1920: 17,500 Europeans, 22,000 Chinese, and 150,000 Indonesians (ibid., 30).

1014 See Cohen *The Komedie Stamboel*, 9–12.

1015 See Faber, *Nieuw Soerabaia*, 17.

1016 Dick, *Surabaya: City of Work*, 326.

Figure 4–1. Map of Surabaya, Official Tourist Office, 1910.
Courtesy of Leiden University Library, Image code D E 53,7 i.

settlement was established alongside the original Javanese *kampung* to the west of the Kali Mas River.[1017] A parallel Chinese settlement on the east bank of the same river is also apparent in maps from the period.[1018] In 1835, when the city became a Dutch military installation, the old settlement was destroyed and the wooden buildings resting "among trees and streams" made way for "bridges, canals, paved streets, and buildings of brick and stone".[1019] By the end of the nineteenth century, as Surabaya gained in economic significance, "[...] it was the largest city in the Netherlands East Indies, an energetic, if unplanned, tangle of cultural styles and values, in which local tradition jostled for attention with modern technological power and a bustling international trade".[1020]

A guide book from 1897 probably gives the most vivid impression of Surabaya in the early days of moving pictures. After arriving at the harbour and travelling into the city by *kossong* (horse-drawn carriage) along streets filled with European and Chinese shops and offices, it quickly concluded:

> Surabaya compares unfavourably with other Dutch East Indian towns, on account of the greater part of the dwelling-houses not being detached, in the midst of beautifully shaded grounds, but built close together, and bordering on the streets. Besides this, the offices, warehouses, stores, shops, and dwelling-houses, European, Arabian, and native, are a great deal too much mingled together; and a separation between the lower or mercantile part and upper or European part of the town, is more difficult to define than in Batavia or Samarang.

> Now this may give to Surabaya a livelier and more European character, but it makes it at the same time dirtier, more oppressive, and less desirable to live in. Next to the finest private houses, we find little native tumble-down shops, or Chinese hovels, that are called *"Warungs"* [...] Once past the Concordia Club, the outward appearance of the town gets a little better. Here we come upon a cross-way, that to the left leads to the station, and to the right [...] to the Alun-Alun, on which there is a beautiful mosque. Before us, the road [Pasar Besar] has the appearance of an avenue [...] on the right side of which there is a small park called the *Stadstuin* (City Garden), where military concerts are given twice a week, and at the end, a small square, where a beautiful building is situated. This is the *Grimm Restaurant*, the finest café in the whole of the Dutch-Indies.[1021]

As a final point, and adding the disagreeable climate to its list of grievances, the guide book concludes by advising travellers "to stay no longer at Soerabaja than is necessary" (see Figure 4–2).[1022]

As the suburbs pushed steadily southwards and investment in infrastructure proceeded apace, various modes of transport, from *kossongs* and *sados* (aka *dos-*

1017 Ibid., 330.

1018 Ibid.

1019 William Hayward Frederick, *Visions and Heat: The Making of the Indonesian Revolution* (Athens: Ohio University Press, 1989), 2.

1020 Ibid.

1021 J. F. van Bemmelen and G. B. Hooyer, *Guide through Netherlands India, Compiled by order of the Koninklijke Paketvaart Maatschappij (Royal Packet Company)*, trans. B. J. Berrington, New Edition revised by Otto Knaap (London/Amsterdam: Thos. Cook & Son/J. H. de Bussy, 1903 [1897]), 81–82, italics in original.

1022 Ibid., 82.

4 – Surabaya: Queen City of Moving Picture Venues

Figure 4–2. Pasar Besar, with the Stadstuin on the right and Grimm Restaurant at the back (centred), behind steam tram, ca. 1900. Courtesy of Leiden University Library, Image code 6877.

à-dos, pony carts) through a horse omnibus service introduced in 1859 and the more advanced steam and later electric tram, eased movement through the growing city.[1023] Many Europeans owned their own horses and carriages to meet their daily travel needs, and a growing number of automobiles, first imported to Java in 1894, appeared on Surabaya's streets over the years: from 77 in 1906, to 3,761 in 1917, and up to 12,000 in 1930.[1024] Vehicle ownership for Indonesians meant bicycles and, according to available data, their number was approximately 9,000 in 1917, doubling to 18,000 in 1925, and doubling again to 36,000 in 1937.[1025] The 20-kilometre steam tram line, opened to the public in 1890 and connecting Surabaya's harbour to its outskirts, ran through the city once every half an hour from Wonokromo via Grudo, Keputran, Kaliasin, Tunjungan, and Pasar Besar to Ujung.[1026]

With goods and individuals transported at increasingly higher speeds through and around the city, Surabayan society was itself experiencing rapid changes. For one, it gained a stronger Dutch colonial flavour from the emergence of more exclusive ethnic hierarchies. "A key institution in this new pattern was the *soos* (colloquial for the *sociëteit* or club), a kind of clubhouse facility for

---

1023 See Dick, *Surabaya: City of Work*, 348.

1024 See Faber, *Nieuw Soerabaia*, 3, 202; Dick et al., *Cities, Transport and Communications*, 66; Bloembergen, *De geschiedenis van de politie in Nederlands-Indië*, 141.

1025 See Dick, *Surabaya: City of Work*, 349.

1026 See Faber, *Nieuw Soerabaia*, 3.

Europeans at which the binding ingredient was camaraderie in both drink and talk, serious and not."[1027] Hosting parties, musical *soirées*, amateur dramatic performances, and touring magicians, as well as some of the earliest moving picture shows, such institutions quickly developed a growing preoccupation with ethnic exclusivity among their members. The Ethical Policy of 1901, combined with laws on administrative decentralisation which led to the establishment of municipal governments, further strengthened the emphasis on ethnic divisions in colonial society. This effect was especially evident in the cities of the Netherlands Indies, "which were precisely the points at which European and indigenous forces threatened to meet and associate most closely".[1028] Thus, while the "population pressure, economic conditions and improved transportation [which] brought more, and more different, Indonesians to Surabaya" left urban *kampungs* increasingly diverse, these areas simultaneously became more "introverted".[1029] Neglected by the newly founded municipality of 1906, which focused its efforts on infrastructural development of European neighbourhoods, Surabaya's *kampungs* were literally "[h]emmed in by the city and separated in many ways from it [...]".[1030]

At the same time, Surabaya maintained and even increased its status as a centre for leisure and entertainment in this period, as can be gleaned from the following scene in December 1909, when three visitors to Surabaya from the interior of Java decided to go to a moving picture show.[1031] According to a report, appearing in the local Dutch-language daily newspaper *Soerabaiasch-Handelsblad*, an argument erupted among the trio over which venue they should patronise. One of the visitors had his heart set on the Aurora Biograph, which was giving shows in a "permanent tent" located just north of the Courthouse in the commercial and entertainment district of Pasar Besar, a structure constructed a little more than a year earlier and owned by a local Armenian cinema entrepreneur.[1032] Another member of the group favoured the next-door Royal Standard Bioscope, which had begun to offer shows a few days earlier in a Chinese-owned iron structure painted green and built just three months before on grounds belonging to Dutch military authorities. It had space for some 1,500 spectators: 700 "Europeans" and 800 "Natives".[1033] Finally, the party's driver claimed that it would be most worth their while to venture out to the Chinese *kampung*. He recommended the significantly cheaper Concurrent[1034] Biograph. "In the end we decided to go to the Aurora

---

1027 Frederick, *Indonesian Urban Society in Transition*, 17.

1028 Ibid., 32.

1029 Ibid., 45–46.

1030 Ibid., 46.

1031 "Aurora Biograph", *Soerabaiasch-Handelsblad* (23 December 1909).

1032 "Een nieuwe bioscop [sic]", *Nieuwe Soerabaja Courant* (11 September 1908). The owner was Nahapiet, of the Netherlands Indies Biograph Company (see Section 3.3).

1033 "De Irene-bioscoop [sic]", *Nieuwe Soerabaja Courant* (10 September 1909).

1034 Literally, "rival".

4 – Surabaya: Queen City of Moving Picture Venues

[…] which is well known in the hinterland for its exquisite films", one of the visitors reported to the Surabaya newspaper. "We were not disappointed and really enjoyed what we saw."[1035]

This anecdote from everyday life in colonial Surabaya, though in fact a thinly veiled promotional piece for the Aurora Biograph, gives us a sense of the scope of the exhibition of moving pictures in this urban centre of the Netherlands Indies at the beginning of the twentieth century. By the 1920s, another English-language travel guide noted: "As regards amusements Sourabaya enjoys the reputation of being the gayest city in the Dutch East Indies. There are two Night Clubs (Dance Clubs), two large Social Clubs, a Cabaret, an Ice Cream Palace and a number of Cinema Theatres."[1036] The range of entertainment options in modernising Surabaya led many commentators to dub the "Crocodile City" (*Krokodillenstad*), as it was commonly called, a *"ville lumière"* or city of light.[1037]

This environment of lively competition faced by entrepreneurs in Surabaya offering public amusements in general and moving pictures in particular, sets the starting point for this chapter, which explores the features that made Surabaya the leader in cinema amenities and comforts: from its canvas and bamboo tents, through iron monstrosities, to its very own modern cinema palace opened in 1913. As the first city in the Indies to have introduced a tax on public amusements in 1909, in an effort to cash in on the success of moving picture shows and fill the municipal coffers, this chapter unfolds how Surabaya came to set the tone for the rest of the cities and towns in the archipelago when it came to various aspects of film exhibition. Finally, this chapter explores new censorship schemes introduced and implemented in the city and principality of Surabaya during the 1910s, coinciding with the reorganisation and modernisation of the police force in Surabaya, in attempts to curb what was increasingly being perceived as cinema's threat to public order.

4.1 Canvas and Bamboo Tents at Pasar Besar

Since the very first moving picture shows given by Louis Talbot in Surabaya in mid to late April 1897, competition with other forms of entertainment as well as rival moving picture entrepreneurs was a prominent aspect of performing in this city.[1038] As moving picture shows began to move out of existing theatres (like the Surabaya Theatre and Kapasan Theatre) into larger circus tents or independently touring canvas tents, which often offered seats for "Native" spectators at lower prices, the increasing diversity of audiences and

---

1035 Aurora Biograph", *Soerabaiasch-Handelsblad* (23 December 1909).

1036 *See Java: Garden of the East. Issued by Michael's Java Motor Touring Co.* (Sourabaya: J. M. Chs. Nijland Ltd., ca. 1920), 4.

1037 Hein Buitenweg, *Krokodillenstad* (Katwijk aan Zee: Servire, 1980); "Uit de Krokodillenstad", *Het Nieuws van den Dag voor Nederlandsch Indië* (21 September 1911); K.M., "Reisherinneringen uit Indië. Soerabaja", *Indië: geïllustreerd weekblad voor Nederland en koloniën* 3, no. 44 (28 January 1920): 712, italics in original.

1038 See further on Talbot's Scenimatograph and the competition with the Kenotograph in Surabaya in Section 1.2.3.

the subsequent need to organize spaces accordingly were to become prominent features of the movie-going experience in Surabaya.[1039]

One of the main spots for popular entertainment and early movie-going in Surabaya was the street corner where the *Alun Alun* met Pasar Besar.[1040] The first shows in a canvas tent at Pasar Besar, set up in front of the military garrison, were offered by Ten Broeke's American Biograph from August to October 1899.[1041] His tent could seat approximately 2,000 spectators and was apparently almost entirely full every night, although undoubtedly at least some of the visitors were non-paying customers, such as soldiers or orphans who were often invited for free shows.[1042] After many complaints voiced in earlier years about the poor quality of the projection, the high quality of the Biograph's 68mm projector used by Ten Broeke set the bar high for the following showmen. From then on, and throughout the subsequent decade, showmen travelling with their own tents normally set up shop around the Pasar Besar: either at the *Alun Alun*, next to the military garrison or across from the Courthouse. When not in use by exhibitors of moving pictures, such public spaces were occupied by circus tents, steam carousels and other forms of public amusement.

Pasar Besar and its environs formed a central spot in the city which was recognisable and well-connected by public transport. Moreover, any erected tent there was assured to be surrounded by "Native" and Chinese *warungs*, enticing the visitors with food and drink.[1043] In addition, there were always plenty of other entertainment forms, if not other cinema tents, located in close vicinity. For instance, soon after Nast's Kinematograph arrived for shows in a tent next to the Courthouse, the number of public amusements in Surabaya multiplied, among them the next-door Java Cineograph Company and several concerts and stage performances at the Surabaya Theatre and in the various *soos* buildings.[1044] Occasionally, tents for moving picture shows were themselves used for variety shows which included moving picture screenings. For example, the tent of the Grand Eastern Phono-Cinematograph next to the Courthouse in August–September 1905 included a *café-chantant* performed by

---

[1039] Moving picture shows were screened at times also at European clubs. For example: Boer War screenings by Coops's Cosmograph at Vereeniging Eendracht (Advertisement, *Soerabaiasch-Handelsblad* (6 June 1900)).

[1040] Formerly Herenstraat, the street was originally a continuation of the Aloen-Aloen Straat going south. Pasar Besar itself, or the Great Market, moved to its new location at Pasar Turi in 1905.

[1041] Advertisement, *Soerabaiasch-Handelsblad* (21 August 1899). See further on Ten Broeke and the American Biograph in Section 2.1.

[1042] "Biograaf", *Soerabaiasch-Handelsblad* (18 September 1899).

[1043] Fixed and mobile street stalls are part of everyday life in many places across Southeast Asia to this day, providing food and nourishment. As we shall encounter here and in the following chapters, whenever a cinema tent was erected, such mobile kiosks would have set up shop outside the venue offering their goods to spectators.

[1044] "Nederlandsch-Indië", *Soerabaiasch-Handelsblad* (30 July 1902); Advertisement, *Soerabaiasch-Handelsblad* (24 July 1902); Advertisement, *Soerabaiasch-Handelsblad* (21 July 1902).

4 – Surabaya: Queen City of Moving Picture Venues

Figure 4–3. The bamboo tent of the East Java Bioscope, ca. 1912, "Het Nieuwe gebouw van de 'Oost-Java-bioscope' te Soerabaia", *Weekblad voor Indië* (30 November 1913), 772.

two Frenchwomen, gymnastics and juggling acts, in addition to H. de Beaucourt's Phono-Cinematograph.[1045]

Since audience turnout was inversely correlated to the extremity of weather conditions, especially the tropical rainstorms and humidity whose effects were only exacerbated by heat from the projector, exhibitors often made a point of including precise descriptions of their tents in advertisements and promotional pieces. Thus, in 1901 Salzwedel's Java Biorama advertised that it would present its shows in a tent that was "[...] extremely well ventilated and completely waterproof".[1046] In 1903, Abdulally Esoofally's Royal Bioscope toured with a tent "[...] 100 feet long and 50 feet wide, propped by four posts, [which] could hold a thousand people".[1047] By 1905, the Netherlands Indies Biograph Company was touring with "[...] a giant waterproof tent [...] made in America especially for the tropics, [which] can easily contain 2,500 people".[1048] Information on the cost of site rental for these tents remains rather sketchy. According to evidence for one case in 1905, the Royal Bioscope rented the space next to the military garrison for 250 guilders per month, and was required as part of this arrangement to offer free admission to soldiers once a month.

[1045] Advertisement, *Bintang Soerabaia* (12 August 1905). The Phono-Cinematograph was referred to in some newspapers as the "Biograph Pathé", and was touted as "the pinnacle of all biograph devices, without any vibration" ("Nederlandsch-Indië", *Java-Bode* (19 August 1905)). As Sabine Lenk has pointed out to me, Pathé Frères proposed its first "scènes ciné-phonographiques" in the supplement of May 1905, which means the Indies were up to date (see Bousquet, *Catalogue Pathé*, 904).

[1046] Advertisement, *Bintang Soerabaia* (11 February 1901). For more on the Java Biorama, see Section 2.2.

[1047] Barnouw et al., *Indian Film*, 9. For more on the Royal Bioscope, see Section 3.2.

[1048] Advertisement, *Soerabaiasch-Handelsblad* (20 May 1905). For more on the Netherlands Indies Biograph Company, see Section 3.3.

At the same time, its competitor, the Netherlands Indies Electro Bioscope, paid only 25 guilders per month for renting space on the grounds of the state railways.[1049]

Canvas tents soon gave way to gigantic, extravagant bamboo constructs which could seat thousands of people: the first class seats for Europeans were in elevated boxes at the rear, while the cheapest seats on the ground for the "Native" class of spectators were often located behind the screen (see Figure 4–3).[1050] Entrepreneurs already associated with the local cinema industry often erected these "bamboo tents" in place of the earlier canvas tents, built out of materials similar to those of the temporary pavilions constructed for the annual *Pasar Malam*, for the purpose of renting them out to exhibitors for several months at a time. Refreshment stalls provided by exhibitors on site as well as independent *warungs* surrounding it were available to patronisers of these venues. And, while the risk of fire in bamboo tents might seem real, in fact the more burning question in Surabaya concerned matters of hygiene (see Section 4.3).[1051] Acts of petty crime typical of an urban setting – pickpocketing, plundering the lemonade and tobacco stocks of stalls, theft of bicycles parked just outside tents – further plagued exhibition venues.[1052]

In January 1908 the Pasar Besar itself became a site for filmmaking when the Vardon Biograph placed an advertisement in the newspapers, announcing that filming of the heavy traffic of all kinds of vehicles and people outside Grimm and Hellendoorn restaurants will take place on a Sunday morning (see Figure 4–4, and see further on Vardon and his filming in Surabaya in Section 3.3.5).[1053] Vardon may have placed this advertisement in the knowledge that the corner in question was otherwise likely to be empty on a Sunday morning, as a description from 1910 of a typical Saturday night in Surabaya suggests:

> It's 8 o'clock. Party-going Surabaya is in full swing. Saturday night, the last night of the week, which is followed by a free day, a Sunday, a day of rest, a day of sleeping in. [...] The *Alun Alun* is the centre of Surabaya's big city buzz. The cinemas are bathing in a sea of electric light, which expands widely between the trees, with aspects of light hitting the surrounding buildings and the asphalt of the street. Cheerful music penetrates from the silent theatres to the outside, luring one to enter. Then suddenly the music ceases, but only for a few moments; the band resumes, the music becomes sadder, melancholic, the presently projected film is indeed a drama. It's not difficult to guess this.

1049 "Soerabaja", *De Locomotief* (8 November 1905).

1050 Coulter, "The Kinematograph in the East", 1039.

1051 The opposite was true of Batavia, which experienced several fires in bamboo cinemas and therefore introduced stricter regulations on the construction of exhibition venues ("Gemeenteraad van Batavia", *Het Nieuws van den Dag voor Nederlandsch-Indië* (15 October 1912)); see further in Chapter 5. It is likely that other municipalities, Surabaya among them, were aware of these developments, as were exhibitors and spectators. Stories about cinema fires in other cities, whether in the Indies or in Europe and the U.S., were regularly reported in local newspapers.

1052 "De Wederzijdsche te Soerabaia", *Het Nieuws van den Dag voor Nederlandsch-Indië* (9 March 1914); "Diefstal in het buffet van de Sirene", *Soerabaiasch Nieuwsblad* (27 November 1909); "Diefstallen", *Nieuwe Soerabaja Courant* (7 January 1908).

1053 Advertisement, *Soerabaiasch-Handelsblad* (31 January 1908).

4 – Surabaya: Queen City of Moving Picture Venues

Figure 4–4. Pasar Besar with Hellendoorn Restaurant (a cinema house, Rialto Bioscope, is visible to the right of the restaurant). Photo by G.C.T. van Dorp & Co., ca. 1920. Courtesy of Leiden University Library, Image code 181999.

The number of *kossongs*, which are rolling in from all directions [...] increases the hustle and bustle beyond measure; the hordes of coachmen with their whips; their shouts together, their sneering laughter and their irrational conduct as they run for the entrances of Hellendoorn or Grimm when they spot some people getting up to leave. All this gives an extraordinary impression of the busy city life. And were there not many natives to demonstrate the contrary, one would imagine one was in Europe, in the heart of the big cities.[1054]

While the sounds from the cinemas reached the surrounding streets, the noise and commotion from the road was equally likely to penetrate the cinemas, with an inevitable effect on spectators' viewing experience. The heavy, largely unregulated traffic, especially the presence of the steam tram in the midst of the crush of carriages, freight wagons and handcarts, served as a constant source of aggravation for shop owners and residents of this main quarter. Reports of accidents, some minor and others fatal and many involving pedestrians, appeared frequently in the newspapers of the day. At the same time, by locating their tents in strategic spots in the city, exhibitors ensured that potential customers had easy access to their venues. These venues, located among cafés and restaurants, also helped create in Surabaya a sense of a modern city centre, on par with the great cities of Europe. One recently arrived Dutchman, another newspaper reported, taking delight in the "[...] radiating light from the cinema and tart palace [on Pasar Besar...] even ventured to compare it to the Leidseplein in Amsterdam".[1055]

[1054] "Soerabaia op Zaterdagavond", *Soerabaiasch-Handelsblad* (4 July 1910), emphases added.

[1055] "Onze stadsklok", *Nieuwe Soerabaja Courant* (13 November 1914).

4.2 Tax and Legislation of Public Amusements in Surabaya

A persistent transience marked Surabaya's cinema spaces, even when canvas tents were replaced by bamboo or iron structures, due to the nature of legislation promoted by the Municipal Council of Surabaya, established in 1906 under the decentralisation scheme. Movie-goers who patronised these semi-permanent cinema houses were constantly reminded that the "[...] government may terminate the rental [of the land] any day. If now the tent looks as if built for eternity, one must remember that it can be fully dismantled."[1056] The legislation concerning public amusements – which governed kiosks, *warung*, tents, circuses, race tracks and cinemas – underscores the pertinence of this reminder.[1057] In accordance with the regulation on "the temporary use of public roads, streets, squares, parks and other grounds, with the exception of *pasars* in the Surabaya region", the local government (*Plaatselijk Bestuur*) could grant permits for a period of up to three months, while permits for longer periods required application to the regional council (*Raad*), a far more complicated and presumably more costly procedure.[1058] The municipality charged entrepreneurs a licence fee that took location, duration of use and size into account according to the following terms: for shorter durations (less than three months) and an area of a hundred square metres or less, ƒ 0.05 to ƒ 0.50 per square meter per day; for a space of 100 to 500 square metres, ƒ 0.50 to ƒ 2.00 per square meter per day; and for an area of 500 square metres or more, ƒ 2.10 to ƒ 10.0 per square meter per day. For durations longer than three months, it levied a charge of at least ƒ0.50 per square meter per month.[1059] Some exhibitors may have subverted the tight time limits by simply splitting up their company into two or three companies, with one company immediately following the other in renting the same space, once the three-month licence expired. For example, the Johannes Biograph and Vardon Biograph, as shown in Sectiom 3.3. Other cities beyond Surabaya later adopted similar legislation, and evidence of this sort of practice began to appear in newspaper reports from across the archipelago.[1060]

In any case, the abovementioned law very quickly proved inadequate. For one, it only covered use of public and not private spaces; use of the latter as venues for showing films became more and more common. Secondly, it was deemed that provisions should be put in place specifically for cinemas, in view of the "increasing indulgence of the [Native] population" in what have by now become "permanent fairgrounds" on practically every town square.[1061] Thus, in June 1909 the tax on public amusements came into effect in Surabaya.[1062] A

1056 "De Sirene-Bioscoop", *Soerabaiasch-Handelsblad* (9 September 1909).

1057 "Tijdelijke afstand van wegen enz.", *Soerabaiasch-Handelsblad* (10 December 1908).

1058 Ibid.

1059 Ibid.

1060 "Bioscoop-vreugde", *Bataviaasch Nieuwsblad* (17 March 1910).

1061 "Tijdelijke afstand van wegen enz.", *Soerabaiasch-Handelsblad* (10 December 1908).

1062 "De Belasting op Publieke Vermakelijkheden", *Soerabaiasch-Handelsblad* (3 June 1909).

4 – Surabaya: Queen City of Moving Picture Venues

municipal stamp would be added to every ticket, to be checked at the entrance by a European and a "Native" official. In addition, movie-goers were to hold on to the tickets because a policeman would check inside the cinema, to catch anyone who had snuck in. This system limited the number of free tickets that exhibitors could distribute, as they now had to pay tax in respect of all tickets issued. This change led exhibitors to stop offering free admission to residents living close to their venues, a practice that had presumably prevented them from complaining to the authorities about the noise (see also examples from Batavia in Section 5.2).

The new legislation did not make any concessions on the three-month duration of exhibition permits, even in the case of exhibitors who had invested substantial resources in constructing their venues. For example, the Chinese owner of the Sirene Bioscope, which opened in September 1909, rented land from military authorities and constructed an impressive building of iron on the site, housing a buffet and a *warung* for the pleasure of visitors.[1063] The interior was apparently just as striking as the sturdy-looking outside, with green-coloured wallpaper on the walls of the section intended to seat 700 "European" spectators, which was further equipped with electric lighting and excellent ventilation.[1064] The section for "Native" spectators, seating 800 people, was divided into two: one part intended for "*orang ketjil* [little people]", referring to the "Native" coolies, and another – for "*hooge inlanders* [high natives]", identified by the *Soerabaiasch-Handelsblad* as "wealthy Javanese who are not comfortable sitting beside the former".[1065] "Everything beams of novelty in the massive space, without any annoying pillar which hinders the view — the decoration is simple and tasteful, the furnishing of the interior is simply perfect for such a purpose."[1066] And yet, once his three-month exhibition permit expired, the owner could no longer show films himself. At least under the new legislation, he was not compelled to tear down his venue.[1067] He resorted to renting the space to other exhibitors for periods of up to three months, until he was again able to show films himself. Thus, when the Sirene's license expired in December 1909, Helant's Royal Standard Bioscope (*Royal Standard Bioscoop*) moved into the venue, boasting of his selection of the latest films arriving from Europe.[1068] Once Helant's license was up three months

---

1063 "De Sirene-Bioscoop", *Soerabaiasch-Handelsblad* (9 September 1909). The set up of a buffet and a *warung* seems to suggest there was a separation of their clientele according to the "European" and "Native" split of the audience. It remains unclear whether or not a "Native" spectator would have been able to approach the buffet, nor, conversely, if a "European" spectator would have purchased goods from the *warung*.

1064 "De Irene-bioscoop [sic]", *Nieuwe Soerabaja Courant* (10 September 1909).

1065 Ibid., emphases added; "De Sirene-Bioscoop", *Soerabaiasch-Handelsblad* (9 September 1909). No breakdown of the seating capacity in the two sections for "Native" spectators was provided. The "high natives" were reportedly to pay 20 cents per ticket. The prices of other seating ranks were not disclosed, but were supposedly in accordance with the rates charged at other cinemas.

1066 "Nederlandsch Indisch Nieuws", *Soerabaiasch Nieuwsblad* (13 September 1909).

1067 "Sirene-Bioscoop", *Soerabaiasch-Handelsblad* (8 December 1909).

1068 "De Sirenebioscoop", *Soerabaiasch-Handelsblad* (18 December 1909).

later, the same venue was quickly taken up by the Apollo Biograph in March 1910, as the *Nieuwe Soerabaja Courant* put it:

> The green shed beside the chemist shop Moll & Co. has been closed for merely a couple of evenings, and we already miss the magnificent arc lamps there. On Saturday evening the carbon arc lamps of the Apollo Biograph will have their brilliant beams of light pouring out over this part of town.[1069]

The situation continued for the next few years, leading to a state in which "[s]carcely has one bioscope left when another appears again with its signs at the ready".[1070]

4.3 The Plague and the Plight of Cinema Shows, 1910–1911

As of 1903, the Resident of Surabaya employed a Chinese healer or doctor, known as *sinse*, in order to "combat malaria, cholera, and especially the leprosy epidemic".[1071] Yet, neither this nor the introduction of iron, zinc and asbestos structures eliminated hygiene problems at cinema venues, as became clear during major epidemics. Although the Alhambra-Theatre Bioscope, playing in a shed next to the Hellendoorn restaurant from 8 July to 8 October 1910, claimed in its advertisements that a visit to the cinema could help the people of Surabaya to remain healthy better than "Pink pills" or "Abbey syrup" (*Abdijsiroop*), the truth of the matter was that the public could easily contract diseases in cinema spaces.[1072] Exposure to contaminated water and crowding were openings for potential contagion.

In 1911, the owner of the Sirene Bioscope faced inspection and closure of his cinema after dead rats were discovered buried just behind it during a major plague outbreak.[1073] As a military official informed the Surabaya newspapers, four live rats were captured and an equal number of dead rats were found in a state of decomposition, giving off a strong stench. However, what really got the Sirene's manager into trouble was the fact that he failed to report about the rats to the head of the local government, raising calls to launch an enquiry into the case.[1074] The police investigation found that the owner captured the rats

---

1069 "Bioscopen", *Nieuwe Soerabaja Courant* (24 March 1910).

1070 "De Transvalia Bioscope", *Soerabaiasch-Handelsblad* (13 January 1911).

1071 "Onze Nieuwtjes", *Soerabaija-Courant* (22 October 1902); Hesselink, *Healers on the colonial market*, 276.

1072 Advertisement, *Soerabaiasch-Handelsblad* (3 August 1910). The "Pink pills" presumably referred to the product "Pink Pills for pale people by Dr. Williams" which was also traded in the Netherlands, while "Abbey syrup" was a product of the Rotterdam pharmaceuticals company L. J. Akker ("Pink Pillen", Geheugen van Nederland, ReclameArsenaal, accessed on 2 February 2016, http://www.geheugenvannederland.nl/?/nl/items/RA01:30051001526331; Frank Huisman, "Struggling for the Market: Strategies of Dutch pharmaceutical companies, 1880–1940", in Viviane Quirke and Judy Slinn (eds.), *Perspectives on Twentieth-century Pharmaceuticals* (Bern: Peter Lang, 2010), 63–89, here 84). One of the films on the Alhambra's programme at the time was on microbes, and the cinema offered free admission to doctors and pharmacists (Advertisement, *Soerabaiasch-Handelsblad* (4 August 1910)).

1073 "Niet in den Haak", *Soerabaiasch-Handelsblad* (12 June 1911). The 1911 plague was well-documented in the newspaper articles and government reports of the day (see also Hesselink, *Healers on the colonial market*, 304).

1074 "Tiada baik", *Bintang Soerabaia* (13 June 1911).

himself and buried them, supporting earlier suspicions.[1075] By order of the local government, the cinema was shut down and underwent general cleaning. The bodies of the dead rats were dug up and burned.[1076] And although it was believed that the plague bacterium could remain alive in the ground for approximately 30 years, the Sirene Bioscope was reopened to the public within a matter of days.[1077] Interestingly, as soon as a municipal inspection committee approved the venue for running shows again, the exhibitor opted to capitalize on his tribulations by including a film about the cause, spread and control of the plague in his programme.[1078]

Periods of epidemics hit business hard for exhibitors in Surabaya and elsewhere in Java (as we have seen previously in Section 3.3.7). The precarious state of touring shows and temporary pavilions was likely one of the factors pushing entrepreneurs and legislators towards more permanent setups.

4.4 Building Plans in 1910s

In the 1910s, as Surabaya experienced rapid urban expansion and its division into a *benedenstad* (lower town) encompassing the port and business district and a *bovenstad* (upper town) of new residential neighbourhoods further to the south grew clearer, it gained a reputation in the Indies as the leader in cinema amenities and comforts.[1079] It was also believed to be a place where "[...] a cinema owner could become rich in the shortest time possible".[1080] By the beginning of 1912, cinema had come to be recognized as a genuine need in the life of Surabaya's residents, and the idea that competition would lead to cheaper ticket prices became current.[1081] In light of the trouble with the plague and cholera in previous years, the tendency was to construct cinemas out of iron or stone rather than bamboo and areca palm.[1082] The former were expected to provide better sanitary conditions compared to the bamboo tents, which were in more direct contact with the ground.

In 1912, as cinema companies were still battling it out over permits for shows at the permanent tents in Pasar Besar or for open-air screenings at the *Stadstuin*, several entrepreneurs, including Vardon and Nahapiet, began to eye property further down the road, on the cheaper-priced Prabanleiding marshland to the

---

1075 "Bioscope gesloten", *Het Nieuws van den Dag voor Nederlandsch-Indië* (13 June 1911); "Bioscoop gesloten", *Nieuwe Soerabaja Courant* (13 June 1911).

1076 "De Doode Ratten-Geschiedenis", *Soerabaiasch-Handelsblad* (13 June 1911).

1077 Ibid.

1078 "De Sirene-Bioscoop", *Soerabaiasch-Handelsblad* (16 June 1911).

1079 Dick, *Surabaya: City of Work*, 341; "Cine-Lumen", *Java-Bode* (6 October 1910).

1080 "Nieuwe bioscoop loods", *Nieuwe Soerabaja Courant* (10 April 1912).

1081 "Nieuwe permanente bioscoop", *Nieuwe Soerabaja Courant* (15 January 1912). Unfortunately, hardly any figures on ticket price are actually available from this period, with companies usually advertising that "ticket prices are as usual". Wherever prices are indicated, this will be mentioned below.

1082 The cinema of Helant was an exception to the norm, when in April 1912 it obtained a permit to convert a non-iron structure into a cinema venue ("Nieuwe bioscoop loods", *Nieuwe Soerabaja Courant* (10 April 1912)).

east of the Tunjungan-Gembalongan bridge.[1083] They even drew up competing building plans that they shared with city planners and journalists.[1084] Vardon, who sent a request to the Surabaya Municipal Council for renting or buying land for the purpose of constructing a cinema theatre, planned a building 50 meters long and 16 meters wide, with a "highly modern look".[1085] A terrace was sketched out at the front of the building for the use of visitors ahead of entering the show. From the terrace, one would enter a hallway where the ticket office was to be located, next to a women's restroom. According to the plans, the great hall was to be constructed in amphitheatre-style, and the entire building was to lie 35 meters away from the road, in order to provide a large square in front of the cinema theatre so as not to create congestion of traffic from arriving vehicles and queuing spectators.[1086] As previously mentioned, R. Hughan, another bidder for the same property, proposed that the beautiful and monumental building that he was planning "serve as a screen to conceal the hideous view of the *kampung* houses behind the ice factory on Gembalongan".[1087] The emphasis of both plans was clearly on constructing a "completely modern and beautifully finished stone cinema building".[1088] However, neither received a permit, as the local authorities claimed that they had plans for widening the road.[1089]

Other entrepreneurs, with deeper pockets to draw from, were still focusing on the more expensive locations off the main road connecting Simpang, Tunjungan, Gembalongan and Pasar Besar. Thus, Mr. Charles 't Sas received a permit from head of the local government for constructing a permanent cinema theatre at Pasar Besar, on land adjacent to the former bicycle shop G. E. Irving & Co. His plan was to empty out the shop and rent out the space, presumably to *warung* or restaurant operators, to serve as the entrance and front patio of his cinema.[1090] The opening of the "well-furnished extremely tidy shed" on the corner of Pasar Besar and Djoharlaan, scheduled for 7 September 1912, was nevertheless delayed.[1091] Just a couple of days before the first show, a municipal inspector did not approve of the roof which was built out of lighter materials than what was indicated in the building plans, since the owner was trying to

---

1083 See also discussion in Section 3.3.7. Due to the expensive costs of the more central locations, such as the cinema tent next to the Courthouse for which the rent stood at 5,000 guilders per month, Mr. Ch. Zecha gave up the license he had already obtained from the local government ("Geen tweede bioscoop", *Soerabaiasch-Handelsblad* (28 August 1913)).

1084 "Een nieuwe bioscoop", *Nieuwe Soerabaja Courant* (20 January 1912); "Bioscooptheaters te Soerabaja", *Soerabaiasch-Handelsblad* (24 January 1912).

1085 "Het Bioscooptheater te Soerabaja", *Soerabaiasch-Handelsblad* (16 January 1912).

1086 Ibid.

1087 "Een nieuwe bioscoop", *Nieuwe Soerabaja Courant* (20 January 1912), emphasis added.

1088 "Nieuwe permanente bioscoop", *Nieuwe Soerabaja Courant* (15 January 1912).

1089 "Zal niet gaan", *Nieuwe Soerabaja Courant* (25 January 1912).

1090 "Een nieuwe bioscoop", *Nieuwe Soerabaja Courant* (13 January 1912).

1091 "De Nieuwe Bioscoop", *Soerabaiasch-Handelsblad* (30 August 1912).

cut corners and save on construction costs.[1092] By 1913, it seems the "cinema tent" was occupied, at least temporarily, by Vardon, who applied for a permit from the inspector of public works in order to display advertisements on the outside wall, measuring 14 square meters on the western side and 150 square meters on the southern side.[1093]

Another entrepreneur by the name of Droste[1094] reportedly bought *kampung* land in Tunjungan from its Chinese owner, Han Kong Gie, for 11,000 guilders in early 1912.[1095] He planned to uproot the *kampung* dwellers from their homes and to build new residential housing, a *toko*, as well as a large cinema theatre intended for cinema shows and other *komedi* and variety entertainments, with an adjacent hotel for the use of travelling performers.[1096] "Both buildings [were] to be erected in modern style."[1097] The cinema theatre was, once again, planned to be constructed away from the road, leaving parking space for carriages and other vehicles.[1098] It is not clear what kind of compensation, if any, would have been offered to the "Native" population of the *kampung*, although by the 1910s the authorities were showing increasing concern for "Native" rights, even when private entrepreneurs were involved.[1099] Droste was further planning to construct a production company (*filmfabriek*) of his own, where he could make his own films. He was planning on travelling to Europe, where he would learn more about managing cinema theatres and create contacts with film companies there.[1100]

Meanwhile, Pathé Frères' representative in Batavia, Mr. Schwartz, also sought to buy land even further south, on the corner of the suburban Embong Malang and Simpang, from an Arab landlord. He awaited approval for the building plans while the municipality sought the neighbours' consent.[1101] He finally obtained his licence in September 1912, and construction was scheduled to start in November.[1102]

4.5 Constructing Cinema Palaces: C. J. Umbgrove's East-Java Bioscope, 1913

The most successful figure of this period by far was Charles Jacob Umbgrove, director of the East Java Bioscope earlier mentioned in Chapter 3 in connection

1092 "Het Nieuwe Bioscoopgebouw", *Soerabaiasch-Handelsblad* (5 September 1912).
1093 "Gemeenteraad van Soerabaja", *Soerabaiasch-Handelsblad* (11 April 1913).
1094 Sometimes spelled "Dreste".
1095 "Bioscooptheaters te Soerabaja", *Soerabaiasch-Handelsblad* (24 January 1912).
1096 "Een nieuwe woonwijk", *Nieuwe Soerabaja Courant* (5 March 1912).
1097 "Schouwburgplannen", *Nieuwe Soerabaja Courant* (24 January 1912).
1098 "Bouwplannen", *Nieuwe Soerabaja Courant* (23 January 1912).
1099 See Dick, *Surabaya: City of Work*, 355.
1100 "Schouwburgplannen", *Nieuwe Soerabaja Courant* (24 January 1912).
1101 "Bioscooptheaters te Soerabaja", *Soerabaiasch-Handelsblad* (24 January 1912).
1102 "Een bioscooptheater op Simpang", *Soerabaiasch-Handelsblad* (23 September 1912).

with films of the *Oranjefeesten* in Surabaya, who was most likely of mixed European and Indonesian descent (see Section 3.3.6). Although he had earlier experience with magic lantern shows, Umbgrove reportedly had to overcome a few difficulties – especially in the field of film development – before beginning to produce films himself. The main hindrance for this process in the Indies was, once again, the high temperature, which often rose above 30° Celsius.[1103] Many of the films were therefore failed attempts and hundreds of meters of film were destroyed in the process. "The outsider [...] is unfamiliar with the many difficulties that the entrepreneur had to overcome along the way to insure himself some chance of success; the uninitiated in *bioscopie* do not have the slightest view of the many disappointments that a filmmaker in the Indies experiences in the introduction of this new industry", as expounded in a special profile article about Umbgrove's East Java Bioscope.[1104] Nevertheless, the earlier experience Umbgrove obtained from producing lantern slides, having found suitable equipment for the local conditions, and having developed "an enviable knack" for printing photographic images on the glass plates, came in handy.[1105] Umbgrove managed to come up with a solution by which the development baths could be held at lower temperatures while fans were used to accelerate the drying of films. Mastering this process, *Weekblad voor Indië* claimed, Umbgrove could at last establish "[...] the first film company [*filmfabricatie*] in the tropics, which nobody had dared to do before. He was the founder of the first Indies production company [*Indische filmfabriek*] whose finished products also find a market in Europe and America."[1106]

The first records of films found in this research which can be attributed to Umbgrove were from the celebrations held in Surabaya to mark the birth of Dutch Princess Royal Juliana in April 1909, which were exhibited at Hartman's bioscope.[1107] Umbgrove's studio continued to produce films locally, utilising just about any opportunity that presented itself for capturing scenes on film: from the collapse of a department store building under construction at Pasar Besar in 1911, through the official visit of the Governor General to Surabaya that same year, the meeting of *Sarekat Islam* in the *Stadstuin*, the first equestrian competition, the establishment of the Boy Scouts, to the Colonial Exhibition in Semarang in 1914 (see Figure 4–5, and for more on the Colonial Exhibition, see Section 6.6).[1108] The local views shot in Surabaya and its surroundings and included on the film programmes were "projected as a surprise on the

---

1103 "Het Nieuwe gebouw van de 'Oost-Java-bioscope' te Soerabaia", *Weekblad voor Indië* 33 (30 November 1913), 771.

1104 Ibid., emphasis added.

1105 Ibid., 771. His dabbling in magic lantern slides was also reportedly what attracted him to film projection.

1106 Ibid.

1107 "Nieuwe Films van de Oranje Feesten", *Soerabaiasch-Handelsblad* (13 May 1909). See Section 3.3.6.

1108 "Nederlandsch-Indië", *Soerabaiasch-Handelsblad* (1 August 1911); "Oost-Java Bioscope", *Het Nieuws van den Dag voor Nederlandsch-Indië* (10 October 1911); "Het Nieuwe gebouw van de 'Oost-Java-bioscope' te Soerabaia", *Weekblad voor Indië* 33 (30 November 1913), 774; "Bioscopen", *Nieuwe Soerabaja Courant* (21 August 1914).

Figure 4–5. The East Java Bioscope filming at the Colonial Exhibition in Semarang, 1913. Courtesy of Leiden University Library, Image code 55987.

screen".[1109] In fact, in his cinema palace and adjacent film studio, Umbgrove had intended to "[...] compile a film archive, so that we will always be able to watch scenes from various Surabayan festivals on screen".[1110]

His first steps in film exhibition were taken in small towns, in order to gain confidence and experience, with the first show given on 7 January 1909 at the *Sociëteit* in Pamekasan, on the island of Madura. From there he continued to Sumenep where on 16 January he officially announced his "opening show".[1111] Despite the heavy rains on many nights, the dry spells, Umbgrove's good selection of films, and his improved lighting system meant that the East Java Bioscope was beginning to make a name for itself. With a permit finally obtained for shows in Surabaya, Umbgrove knew that the Surabaya public was not going to be easily impressed, so his programme needed to show the latest films in order to cope with competition in the city, which already had several cinemas in place. "Greater attention was then paid to the accompanying music."[1112] The acquisition of films required plenty of capital, and therefore

---

1109 "Het Nieuwe gebouw van de 'Oost-Java-bioscope' te Soerabaia", *Weekblad voor Indië* 33 (30 November 1913), 774.

1110 "Bioscopische opname van de passar malem", *Nieuwe Soerabaja Courant* (16 May 1914).

1111 "Het nieuwe gebouw van de 'Oost-Java-bioscope' te Soerabaia", *Weekblad voor Indië* 33 (30 November 1913), 773.

1112 Ibid.

in January 1911 Umbgrove established a Limited Company, the East Java Trading Company, with a registered capital of 100,000 guilders.[1113]

The East Java Bioscope's first shows in a "modern shed" in Surabaya, next to Hellendoorn Restaurant, were offered from July to October 1911 (possibly the same shed as in Figure 4–3).[1114] At that time, the company began to establish a reputation for itself by exhibiting good programmes on a regular basis. This was also when it started to become prominent in the field of film rentals, but the two sides of the business – the exhibition and distribution – were kept strictly separate in two different departments.[1115] There were also hardships along the way: its screenings in Malang had to come to a halt for an entire year due to the plague, and the tent had to be evacuated and burned. Despite this, the East Java Bioscope advanced to become the East Java Trading Company, owning no less than seven fixed cinemas – in Surabaya, Semarang, Malang, Pekalongan and Magelang – in addition to the operation of two travelling companies. On top of these activities, it operated a film rental office in Batavia. It was at that point that Umbgrove reportedly realised that the public was interested in more comfort, and the idea of a "new building, built, decorated, fully furnished and lit entirely in the manner of a modern European cinema theatre, while adapted to the Indies' climate", began to form in his mind.[1116]

When discussion of the proposed electric tram line was still in progress and while restaurants at Pasar Besar were fighting calls to shut them down before 1 am every night, the East Java Trading Company managed to secure land roughly a kilometre away, next to the gas works.[1117] And where others had failed, the company obtained all the necessary documents to enable it to construct a cinema out of brick along with a film development and rental depot, on land formerly occupied by the Oei Moo Liem First Indies Beer Hall at the crossroads of Baliwerti and Gembalongan. According to the report in *Soerabaiasch-Handelsblad*, the land, at more than 3,000 square meters, was originally bought by the local firm of Maurice Wolff, which intended to set up a large shop building, but the idea was dropped and the property went to a consortium

---

1113 Ibid.

1114 Ibid., 774; "De Oost-Java Bioscope", *Soerabaiasch-Handelsblad* (14 July 1911). Although the report in *Weekblad voor Indië* seems to suggest that the East Java Bioscope supposedly performed in Surabaya immediately after its shows in Madura, this research has not found any earlier screenings under the moniker "East Java Bioscope" in the city. Nevertheless, as mentioned above, Umbgrove's films of the celebrations of the birth of Princess Royal Juliana in April 1909 were screened at A.N. Hartman's Royal Bioscope in May 1909 ("Nederlandsch Indisch Nieuws", *Soerabaiasch Nieuwsblad* (26 May 1909)).

1115 The operation of the cinema under Umbgrove's management was apparently further separated from the management of the restaurant and bar at the East Java Bioscope which was managed by Mr. Meijers ("Oost Java Handels Mij en Oost Java Bioscope", *Soerabaiasch Nieuwsblad* (10 November 1913)). Running the distribution company was reportedly very time-consuming, and required close inspection of the cinemas traded with. For instance, in March 1914, Mr. Cartwright who was a cinema entrepreneur in Jember, rented the film THE LAST DAYS OF POMPEII but failed to return it, claiming that the print burned. The East Java Trading Company questioned the truth of this assertion and called for further investigation by the authorities ("Verdwenen film", *Nieuwe Soerabaja Courant* (25 March 1914)).

1116 "Het nieuwe gebouw van de 'Oost-Java-bioscope' te Soerabaia", *Weekblad voor Indië* 33 (30 November 1913), 774.

1117 "Soerabaja Vooruit", *Soerabaiasch-Handelsblad* (1 October 1912).

headed by Surabayan attorney Mr. Feenstra. The consortium subsequently reached agreements with the East Java Trading Company and Glaser Automobile Trading Company allowing them to set their businesses up on the property, receiving two-thirds and one-third of the land, respectively.[1118]

Building plans, as at 1 October 1912, included an office space for film rental, as well as a storage room for films along with a projection room, on the east side of the terrain facing Gembalongan. "The plan is to bring here an entirely modern theatre", *Soerabaiasch-Handelsblad* further reported after being shown the building plans:

> A large stage will be set up. Instead of the curtain now used when giving cinema shows, a white projection screen will be hung and the natives will arrive on the scene to be seated behind the screen. The natives will be let in through a separate entrance located on Baliwerti, the European audience observes nothing of them. [...]
>
> The hall for the European public is built amphitheatre-like and divided into four grades, providing also a balcony and box seats. The hall is thus tall and will be kept cool by fans. There will be space for around 800 European spectators.
>
> The main entrance will be located on the north side of the site [... with the plan] to build a very nice theatre front to the Buitzinglöwenplein. This front is divided into three sections. At the corners of Baliwerti and Gembalongan will be *tokos*, all glass [covered], while in the middle under the upstairs hall an indoor [*toko*] will be set up. The entrances to the theatre will go through this space, which will serve as a restaurant and where a splashing fountain will be placed in the middle. Nothing can be more original than this.
>
> One imagines this restaurant will be very attractively set up. It will be delightful to arrange it. It will be brilliant to have electric lighting and manage it with care.[1119]

The execution of the whole construction project was to be entrusted to the technical firm Knaud & Co., while the electrical installation was placed in the trusted hands of Siemens and Schuckert Werke. "Everyone will understand that the job is very costly, but this is no objection; the enthusiastic entrepreneurs have every confidence in its success."[1120]

Just over a year later, in November 1913, the East Java Bioscope had its grand opening and the two-part coverage of the occasion in the weekly magazine *Weekblad voor Indië* was a celebration not only of the East Java Bioscope's achievement, but also of the general progress in the exhibition of moving pictures in Surabaya over the last decade.[1121] In order to emphasise the headway that has been achieved with the new building, the report offered an overview of the recent history of moving picture venues in Surabaya: The first cinema sheds were of "primitive building style" and made of bamboo, with lime brush, wallpaper and red interlining to mask the splits in the bamboo, and Japanese

---

1118 Ibid.

1119 Ibid., emphasis added.

1120 Ibid.

1121 "Nieuw bioscoopgebouw", *Nieuwe Soerabaja Courant* (8 November 1913); "Het Nieuwe gebouw van de 'Oost-Java-bioscope' te Soerabaia", *Weekblad voor Indië* 33 (30 November 1913), 770-774; "Het Nieuwe gebouw van de 'Oost-Java-bioscope' te Soerabaia", *Weekblad voor Indië* 34 (7 December 1913), 786-789.

Figure 4–6. The new building of the East Java Bioscope in 1913, "Het Nieuwe gebouw van de 'Oost-Java-bioscope' te Soerabaia", *Weekblad voor Indië* 33 (30 November 1913), 773.

bamboo mats for the uneven floor. Even while these sheds appeared to be simple and primitive, the report continued, one should not think they were cheap to construct.[1122] First, the surface needed to be cultivated, and as soon as the "Native" contractor found out a cinema tent was to be built, the price of bamboo would shoot up.[1123] However, soon Surabaya could not be satisfied with these bamboo tents, introducing a transitional stage wherein suddenly "iron monsters, with zinc roofing and wooden panelling" were erected, while the projection room was built outside the hall in view of the risk of fire.[1124]

The many detailed descriptions of the new cinema theatre from various sources certainly give a sense that the building lived up to the expectations set by the earlier plans (see Figure 4–6). "Surabaya has been enriched with a modern building", *Weekblad voor Indië* continued its praise. "The Crocodile City currently has a 'movie palace' [*filmpaleis*] that would not make a bad figure even in one of the great European cities."[1125] "The new building at the Alun Alun Tjontjong, home to a restaurant and cinema spectacle [*tontonan bioscoop*], the most modern of all halls, is getting livelier every evening", *Bintang Soerabaia* commended.[1126] Built in accordance with the Dutch high architectural style of the day, it had separate entrances on either side of the building – one for the

1122 "Het Nieuwe gebouw van de 'Oost-Java-bioscope' te Soerabaia", *Weekblad voor Indië* 33 (30 November 1913), 773.

1123 Ibid.

1124 Ibid., 774.

1125 Ibid., 770.

1126 "Oost Java Bioscope", *Bintang Soerabaia* (13 November 1913).

Figure 4–7. The section for "European" spectators at the East Java Bioscope, "Het Nieuwe gebouw van de 'Oost-Java-bioscope' te Soerabaia", *Weekblad voor Indië* 34 (7 December 1913), 788.

Figure 4–8. The lobby of the East Java Bioscope, with bar to the left displaying bust of Queen Wilhelmina and stairs leading to the Balcon de luxe, "Het Nieuwe gebouw van de 'Oost-Java-bioscope' te Soerabaia", *Weekblad voor Indië* 34 (7 December 1913), 788.

higher-paying seats and the other for the section for "Natives". Positioned on a prominent Y junction, the cinema was a monumental building on one of Surabaya's main traffic arteries which could seat 750 "Europeans" and 400 "Natives" (see the section of the hall for "Europeans" in Figure 4–7).[1127]

The lofty two-storey façade was complemented by a neat and luxurious interior, "as good as a theatre in Europe", another daily publication proclaimed.[1128] Two spacious ticket booths, decorated with beautifully coloured stained-glass, were provided at the entrance. As soon as visitors passed through the entrance, they found themselves in a large hall (see Figure 4–8). Featuring busts of Queen Wilhelmina and her husband, the lobby opened by way of large mirror doors on to the bar to the left, where easy chairs enabled one to sit back comfortably and watch cars, carriages, trams and pedestrians moving busily all the way to Pasar Besar.[1129]

To the right of the lobby were buffets and a *toko* for buying beverages. Right in front of the entrance door was the monumental staircase leading up to the *Balcon de luxe*. With its swivel chairs and small tables, this expensive option at ƒ 2.50 (inclusive of municipal tax) provided a comfortable vantage point from which one had an unobstructed view of the screen and the audience in the hall.[1130] "Especially for visitors who like to sit somewhat up front, but would rather not sit in second or third class, this luxury box is a good solution. Multiple regular moviegoers have therefore already reserved their permanent seat."[1131] On the ground floor, to the right of the stairs, were the practically-equipped restrooms for ladies and gentlemen. To the left were the access ways to the regular box seats, as well as to the first, second and third class seats which were built amphitheatre-like, to enable a good view of the screen from every class. The regular box seats cost ƒ 2.20, and therefore it was arguably worthwhile for spectators who would normally go for box seats to invest another 30 cents "to enter the world of luxury".[1132] It was likely another way of differentiating between spectators, providing audience members of the higher end of European colonial society an opportunity to distinguish themselves from the Chinese or native elites, who would have also occupied box seats. Folding chairs were set out everywhere and nailed to the floor, "even in third class", and the size of the chair stood in direct correlation with the price paid for each seating class.[1133] Of course, there was no view of the "Native" spectators, whose

1127 "Oost Java Handels Mij en Oost Java Bioscope", *Soerabaiasch Nieuwsblad* (10 November 1913).

1128 "Het nieuwe gebouw van de Oost-Java bioscoop", *Soerabaija-Courant* (8 November 1913).

1129 "Het Nieuwe gebouw van de 'Oost-Java-bioscope' te Soerabaia", *Weekblad voor Indië* 34 (7 December 1913), 787.

1130 "Oost Java Handels Mij en Oost Java Bioscope", *Soerabaiasch Nieuwsblad* (10 November 1913); "Uit Soerabaja", *Bataviaasch Nieuwsblad* (13 November 1913).

1131 "Het nieuwe gebouw van de Oost-Java bioscoop", *Soerabaiasch-Handelsblad* (8 November 1913).

1132 "Uit Soerabaja", *Bataviaasch Nieuwsblad* (13 November 1913).

1133 "Het nieuwe gebouw van de Oost-Java bioscoop", *Soerabaiasch-Handelsblad* (8 November 1913); "Oost Java Handels Mij en Oost Java Bioscope", *Soerabaiasch Nieuwsblad* (10 November 1913); "Het Nieuwe bioscoop-restaurant", *Nieuwe Soerabaja Courant* (12 November 1913).

benches were behind the screen.[1134] These benches, occupying a space of 8 x 10 meters, could be covered when a variety troupe was to perform and a larger stage was necessary, thus essentially excluding them from attending such shows.[1135]

The staff of the East Java Bioscope dressed in neat uniforms, which they could put on in a changing room made available for them. Electric lighting was provided by Siemens, the grand piano was built on special commission, to accompany the orchestra, and the folding cinema chairs were specially imported from Vienna's finest furniture manufacturers, Jacob and Josef Kohn.[1136] The East Java Restaurant had a large hall on the ground floor in addition to an upstairs room behind the *Balcon de luxe* for banquets, meetings, or magic shows.[1137] The kitchen, located behind the smaller upstairs hall, was equipped with the latest inventions, including a gas stove as well as a new kind of refrigerator for storing meat.[1138] A lift connected the kitchen to the downstairs buffets.[1139]

The film studio was to be found above the engine room.[1140] It was a large space, with a dark room at the front and at the back, leaving a space of about ten meters long for making the prints and drying out the films. At least some of the films made by the East Java Bioscope were screened in other cities outside Surabaya, as the company supplied films to twenty cinema houses all over the Indies. Electricity was provided by a gasoline engine with a dynamo. An office was located on the Gembalongan side of the building, with a big safe for storing the films. Next to the office was a large dining room for the use of staff. The company invested in the most expensive technical equipment: "[...] the lantern of the projection device is entirely lined with asbestos. The latest ventilation devices are installed. The device is completely equipped with instruments to prevent fire when the film is standing still. This and the asbestos lining provide almost perfect protection against fire hazard. Just in case, a fire extinguisher is present at hand. Unlike [in other cinemas] where the machine is cranked by hand, the entire machine is set in motion by the electro-motor. There is also a [...] switchboard fitted here to turn the lights in the hall on and off."[1141]

1134 At the cost of eleven cents, the *Soerabaija-Courant* considered this to be a good bargain. "Het nieuwe gebouw van de Oost-Java bioscoop", *Soerabaija-Courant* (8 November 1913). *Bintang Soerabaia* mentioned tickets at the cost of 22 cents, although it did not specify their location ("Oost Java Bioscope", *Bintang Soerabaia* (13 November 1913)).

1135 "Het Nieuwe gebouw van de 'Oost-Java-bioscope' te Soerabaia", *Weekblad voor Indië* 34 (7 December 1913), 787.

1136 Ibid., 789. Electricity in Surabaya was not available before 1909.

1137 Ibid., 788. "Het Nieuwe gebouw van de 'Oost-Java-bioscope' te Soerabaia", *Weekblad voor Indië* (7 December 1913).

1138 "Het nieuwe gebouw van de Oost-Java bioscoop", *Soerabaija-Courant* (8 November 1913).

1139 "Oost Java Handels Mij en Oost Java Bioscope", *Soerabaiasch Nieuwsblad* (10 November 1913).

1140 Ibid.

1141 Ibid.

On opening night, Sunday night of 9 November 1913, Umbgrove gave a short speech in which he thanked the designers and builders, as well as the various suppliers, for the timely completion of the cinema theatre. Thereafter the sparkling wine was handed out, while the invited guests browsed around the theatre.[1142] The first two shows were rather well attended, while the restaurant continued to entertain visitors with the Stam and Weijns chamber music ensemble.[1143] The real draw was apparently the downstairs bar which was completely packed all evening.[1144] "The public in Surabaya loves occasions where people sit cosily, close together; the more crowded the better."[1145]

The East Java Bioscope's reputation preceded itself back in the Netherlands. As Dutch film importer and distributor Johan Gildemeijer, who was trading with Umbgrove's East Java Bioscope, pointed out in 1914:

> Elegant, bombastic theatres have risen not only in Montmartre and on the great boulevards of Paris, not only on the Friedrichstrasse or Nollendorf Platz in Berlin, the Rue Neuve in Brussels, or on our Kalverstraat, as appears in the above picture [same image as Figure 4–6] of the cinema theatre opened in Surabaya last year. The East Java Bioscope Company, directed by its energetic manager, C. J. Umbgrove, who from the beginning has taken an active role in improving cinematography [*kinematografie*] in the Dutch East Indies, should be proud of the outcome of his restless labour.[1146]

Yet, unfortunately, even cinema palaces were not destined to last. In 1918, and in spite of all the precautionary measures taken, the East Java Bioscope burned to the ground, and more than 100,000 metres of film were destroyed, presumably including many of Umbgrove studio's own productions.[1147] However, this loss apparently did to deter Umbgrove. The EYE Film Institute Netherlands in Amsterdam in fact holds three films from the late 1920s and early 1930s in its collection which are attributed to *Foto- en Kinoatelier Umbgrove*.[1148] These show Surabaya's new harbour and various street scenes in the city, including a panning shot of the Pasar Besar, with its heavy traffic of people and

---

1142 "Opening nieuw bioscoopgebouw", *Nieuwe Soerabaja Courant* (10 November 1913).

1143 The business partnership between the East Java Bioscope and Stam and Weijns unfortunately struck a sour note after a few months, when the latter claimed the former failed to pay the 8,000 guilders due ("Beslag gelegd", *Nieuwe Soerabaja Courant* (1 April 1914)). Legal action pursued by the performing troupe led to seizure of an inventory of drinks and other provisions ("Het Oost Java Restaurant", *Nieuwe Soerabaja Courant* (3 April 1914)). The East Java Restaurant nevertheless served that night as the location for a meeting of the fun-fair (Jaarmarkt) committee ("De a.s. Jaarmarkt", Nieuwe Soerabaja Courant (3 April 1914)).

1144 "De opening van de Oost-Javabioscoop", *Soerabaiasch-Handelsblad* (10 November 1913).

1145 "Uit Soerabaja", *Bataviaasch Nieuwsblad* (13 November 1913).

1146 Johan Gildemeijer, *Koningin Kino* (Amsterdam: De Nieuwe Tijd, ca. 1914), 38.

1147 See Faber, *Nieuw Soerabaia*, 386.

1148 The three films are even available for viewing online on the Indonesian Film Center website: "Soerabaia, het straatverkeer op pasar-besar 15 juli 1929", accessed on 2 February 2016, http://www.indonesianfilmcenter.com/pages/filmbox/filmbox.php?bid=6059; "Stadsgemeente Soerabaja mei 1930 haven en reede van Soerabaja", accessed on 2 February 2016, http://www.indonesianfilmcenter.com/pages/archive/watch.arcv?v=5620; "Rondvaart in het basin van het Marine Etablissement te Soerabaja 9 mei 1932", accessed on 2 February 2016, http://www.indonesianfilmcenter.com/pages/archive/watch.arcv. php?v =5650.

various kinds of vehicles, as well as a couple of cinema houses along the road and the building of the Grimm Restaurant at the top of the street.[1149]

4.6 Public Education or School for Crime: Local Censorship Initiatives, 1912

Contrasting claims regarding the positive or negative effects of cinema on Indonesian spectators, along with debates on the pedagogical potential of educational scenes versus the detrimental influence of detective or crime films, filled many pages of newspapers and official reports over the years. Thus, Esoofally's Royal Bioscope often promoted certain films as educational, for instance: scenes depicting the manufacturing processes of European factories or the printing of a newspaper. He then explicitly invited professionals or people working in similar areas in the Indies to watch these films in order "to get an idea of what goes on in European workshops".[1150] This approach received a significant boost from Cornelis Marinus Pleyte, who produced an official report about the *Pasar Gambir* in Batavia in 1906. In his report, Pleyte stated that the cinemas which, in his formulation, were brought brought forth by Europeans as forms of amusement, in fact proved to be "excellent means of public education".[1151] And while there were occasionally earlier calls for more police control, as we have seen in previous chapters, especially when it came to questions of the films' morality, the potential positive effects of cinema were generally the current view up to the 1910s.

As soon as the films on display could no longer be marketed as "educational", real-life acts of crime and theft were suddenly being linked to the scenes that "Native" spectators were watching on cinema screens, supposedly giving them inspiration and "modern" know-how.[1152] In July 1912 the Assistant-Resident of Police in Batavia decided to take action against cinema excesses, banning films that showed "murders, theft, adulteries, [or] robberies".[1153] Semarang, Surabaya and Medan immediately adopted these censorship measures, with a memorandum by the Procurer General in Surabaya circulated in the principality reading as follows: "Following letters received from various sources, the administration found that films screened at cinema shows which are contrary to good morals, or [which] display crimes or atrocities, are deemed to be injurious to the education of the population".[1154]

1149 See "Soerabaia, het straatverkeer op pasar-besar 15 juli 1929", accessed on 2 February 2016, http://www.indonesianfilmcenter.com/pages/filmbox/filmbox.php?bid=6059.

1150 "Royal Bioscoop", *Het Nieuws van den Dag voor Nederlandsch-Indië* (10 July 1906).

1151 Cornelis Marinus Pleyte, *Verslag Nopens de Pasar Gambir Gehouden op het Koningsplein te Weltevreden van 28 Augustus–2 September, 1906* (Batavia: Landsdrukkerij, 1907), 6.

1152 "De 'modern' manier", *Nieuwe Soerabaja Courant* (10 February 1910).

1153 "Bioscoop-censuur", *De Locomotief* (5 July 1912). This was reportedly inspired by earlier initiatives taken by the British in the Straits Settlements ("Soerabaja", *De Locomotief* (4 September 1912)).

1154 "De Bioscoop-Censuur", *Soerabaiasch-Handelsblad* (31 July 1912).

Although these measures could have been dismissed as "an assault on personal freedom" or "nanny state policies", as Surabaya correspondent for *De Locomotief* suggested, it was nevertheless useful and even necessary to have cinema censorship in a colony like the Netherlands Indies.[1155] It was not only the choice of subjects for film screenings that was problematic, but also the way they were displayed on "advertising and sandwich boards depicting the extreme nature of gore and sensuality (*'Petit Journal'* style)".[1156] A recent example of this was a "[...] garish coloured plate, depicting an episode from a San Francisco morality drama in which a Chinese is shown at work with the clearly dishonourable intentions of stabbing a fashionably dressed European lady. Anyone who acknowledges the suggestive power which emanates from such a representation", the journalist advocated, "will undoubtedly have to recognise that such advertising boards and such films should not be tolerated here".[1157]

The police in every city was charged with enforcing the ban, by order of article 4.18 of the General Police Regulations for Europeans in the Netherlands Indies, and was further expected to seize and destroy any films that were in breach of these regulations.[1158] By September 1912, a censorship commission in Semarang was reportedly watching films in the city twice per week.[1159] However, according to a report in the Dutch trade journal *De Kinematograaf* from July 1913, the police on Java soon decided, "on a trial basis", to leave the control of films to the managements of cinemas themselves, presumably because they could not keep up with that kind of workload.[1160] The municipal police in Surabaya was in fact in the process of reorganisation from 1911 to 1918, and under these circumstances might have not given cinema control much priority.[1161] The unavoidable result of this freedom, according to *De Kinematograaf*, was that "the most lurid content" was once again presented on screen.[1162] Whether films were controlled by police or by cinema entrepreneurs themselves, censorship was unevenly practiced in each city, leading to a situation in which cinemas in one place boasted that they were screening a film that was forbidden elsewhere.

1155 "Soerabaja", *De Locomotief* (4 September 1912).

1156 Ibid., emphasis added. The *Petit Journal* was a Parisian daily newspaper published from 1863 to 1944, often highlighting sensational stories. As of 1888, it included a weekly illustrated supplement, and in the 1890s reached a distribution of more than three million readers (see Michèle Martin, *Images at War: Illustrated Periodicals and Constructed Nations* (Toronto: University of Toronto Press, 2006), 15).

1157 "Soerabaja", *De Locomotief* (4 September 1912).

1158 "De Bioscoop-Censuur", *Soerabaiasch-Handelsblad* (31 July 1912). It seems the laws relating to censorship (also of the press) were given under the European law system. Although the "Native" and "Chinese" populations were generally subject to different legislative systems, I believe the regulations in this case were applied to all groups, as was the case in the printed press. The same regulations were previously evoked in relation to moving pictures already in 1902, when a film exhibited by Nast's Kinematograph was in the eye of the storm in Surabaya (see further in Section 2.3.1).

1159 "De keuring van de bioscoop-films", *De Locomotief* (4 September 1912).

1160 "Onoordeelkundige bioscoopvertooningen", *De Kinematograaf* 26 (18 July 1913): 166.

1161 See Bloembergen, *De geschiedenis van de politie in Nederlands-Indië*, 137–169.

1162 "Onoordeelkundige bioscoopvertooningen", *De Kinematograaf* 26 (18 July 1913): 166.

4 – Surabaya: Queen City of Moving Picture Venues

By 1914 it seems that these issues began to preoccupy legislators in the Indies more than ever before, especially in light of the seeming failure with the earlier censorship initiatives. So-called "lowbrow" detective and crime films of the Fantomas and Zigomar series were now replacing the "highbrow", "psychological" films starring Asta Nielsen and Valdemar Psilander, with sensational films making more money and apparently more attractive to male, and "Native", audiences.[1163] It was this tension around the veneration of violent films and specifically the gangster genre that drove the Resident of Surabaya, in the interest of public safety, to prohibit the screening of all detective films and any film in which a European person was seen "abused, injured or killed by Natives, Foreign Orientals or Indians", effectively banning most detective, cowboy and war films.[1164] These sanctions were soon after adopted by other districts across the archipelago.[1165]

"The cinema, almost the only regular leisure option for Surabaya's residents, is about to get a boost", opined the *Soerabaiasch-Handelsblad* in a lengthy piece under the heading "Morality and the cinema".[1166] Detective films were almost always the main item of programmes at that point, the report continued, with both

> [...] Europeans and Natives infinitely more attracted to sensational, emotion-filled films than the best dramas. Actors like Krauss and Psilander, Mlle Robins and Asta Nielsen (names which have managed to place the cinema business quickly in the foreground), are losing the battle against the 'Zigomars' and other detective films. It should be noted that indeed a strange charm is derived from these films. [...] The public, and especially the *Indische* and Native spectators, have now become fond of the sensational films. [...] And a cinema operator, being familiar with the taste of the public, cannot but give the public what they want.[1167]

Cinema operators in Surabaya arguably did occasionally try to sway public taste by bringing "outstanding dramatic works" to the screen, and sometimes even succeeded in making good business.[1168] But as soon as one of the competitors offered a detective film, spectators rushed to that cinema.

With the latest decree, the Resident of Surabaya at last decided to intervene, but this was "too little, too late", according to the *Soerabaiasch-Handelsblad*. "There is absolutely nothing more for the Natives to learn. They have already seen so much trickery on the screen that, should they imitate the examples

---

1163 "De zedelijkheid en de bioscoop", *Soerabaiasch-Handelsblad* (23 March 1914).

1164 Ibid. This development made the headlines also in Malay and Chinese-Malay newspapers in a wide range of towns, including Batavia, Makassar, Padang and Semarang ("De strijd tegen detective-films", *Het Nieuws van den Dag voor Nederlandsch-Indië* (24 March 1914); "Penllikan lebi doeloe boeat film bioscope", *Sin Po* (2 July 1914); "Film terlarang", *Pembrita Makassar* (1 April 1914); "Weg met Detective en Indianen Film", *Sinar Djawa* (24 March 1914)).

1165 Growing racial tensions in this period of budding Indonesian nationalism were likely the cause of such sweeping legislation. Chapter 7 on Medan, which was close to the conflict zone of the fighting in Aceh for decades, will further touch on these issues.

1166 "De zedelijkheid en de bioscoop", *Soerabaiasch-Handelsblad* (23 March 1914).

1167 Ibid., emphasis added.

1168 Ibid.

given to them, they do not need to learn anything else from the screen. Now they have grown accustomed to their '*Mas* Zigomar', their *toean* 'Niks Swinter', and they get no pleasure from staring at the modern dramas, which according to them lack action, lack movement, and which they do not understand the scope of because the intertitles are only in Dutch. Robbery stories they still understand, even without intertitles."[1169] The move by the Resident was expected to greatly hinder cinemas' ability to make a profit, "[f]or the Natives, who form the great majority of the 'clientele', will shun the cinema, and the European public rarely visits such facilities", the report concluded.[1170]

The Resident supposedly proposed that a committee of Surabaya citizens should be set up to watch and approve films. About twenty members were deemed necessary for the task at hand, and it was suggested that members of the Municipal Council should fill this role.[1171] Since films exhibited in other towns in the region mostly passed through Surabaya and would have presumably undergone the careful selection procedure in the capital of the district first, it was up to Assistant-Residents and inspectors in the Surabaya principality to monitor implementation of the new decree in their localities. Other reports still claimed enforcement of the decree in Surabaya would be entrusted in the hands of the police.[1172]

Police presence at exhibition venues and the expectation that they maintain public order was nothing new, as mentioned above, but policing of cinemas was becoming ever more intrusive. Thus, when a young man was making noise, "but not behaving in an annoying manner", during a screening at the East Java Bioscope, two policemen seized him and threw him down the stairs, to the sound of loud protests from the audience.[1173] It is not stated on which side of the screen the incident occurred. The police was also abusing the free tickets that public amusements were required to give out to police inspectors. Thus, about half a dozen policemen attended a circus show, taking up the most expensive seats in the tent. In another case, the police commissioner sought to receive free tickets for his wife for a cinema show. A newly issued order from September 1914 stated that police officers would not be allowed into the cinema, unless their presence was required there or if they had a valid ticket.[1174]

In the meantime, cinema operators were stuck with a whole inventory of detective films, and the next batch of orders from Europe, already dispatched, included further such titles. It was therefore agreed that the new decree would only go into effect as of 1 May 1914, so that exhibitors could make use of their

1169 Ibid., emphasis added. The disambiguation of "Nick Winter" appears in the original, indicating the nickname by which the film series was referred to in common parlance.

1170 Ibid.

1171 Ibid.

1172 "Weg met Detective en Indianen Film", *Sinar Djawa* (24 March 1914); "De strijd tegen detective-films", *Het Nieuws van den Dag voor Nederlandsch-Indië* (24 March 1914).

1173 "Zonderlinge politie", *Het Nieuws van den Dag voor Nederlandsch-Indië* (17 June 1914).

1174 "Vrijkaartjes", *Nieuwe Soerabaja Courant* (5 September 1914).

stocks and for "spectators to still have over a month to bask in debauchery".[1175] The *Soerabaiasch-Handelsblad* rather naively expected that Westerns would not be banned, at the end of the day: "After all, all [Westerns], without exception, end in favour of the whites, while the rebellious Indians are usually also punished at the final dramatic climax. There is nothing harmful or anything about these films, on the contrary, the Natives cheer loudly, expressing their joy when the whites prevail as always. In this cheering is [expressed] a certain skill to deduce what feels right, and certainly these cheers would not be heard if the Indians were the victorious party."[1176] It appears nothing was learned here from the earlier applause and displays of excitement among "Native" and Chinese spectators at the sight of earlier victory scenes of the Japanese over the Russians. The injurious potential of Westerns to the colonial order, nevertheless, did not escape the authorities' attention. Moving pictures were to come under even closer inspection with the legislation of the Bioscope Ordinance (to be discussed further in the Concluding Remarks).

4.7 Conclusion

This chapter examined the rise of moving picture venues in Surabaya, the liveliest city of the Netherlands Indies, in terms of commercial popular entertainment and nightlife options, catering to all levels of colonial society. It followed the development of moving picture venues, from canvas tents, through bamboo and iron structures, to modern cinema palaces of brick and stone. These advances were examined in relation to legislation and taxation in Surabaya, which were subsequently to be adopted by other cities across the archipelago. Umbgrove's endeavours with the East Java Bioscope, as filmmaker, exhibitor, film distributor, manager and even archivist, provided a particularly rich case study of the Surabayan movie-going scene. His cinema palace, deemed the most modern of all cinemas in Surabaya and therefore likely in the entire archipelago, was intended to attract discerning spectators. The entire set-up and film line-up were designed to give the popular practice of movie-going a more respectable, modern, "European" flair. It also set in stone the adaptation of the *wayang kulit* tradition of seating "Native" spectators behind the screen.

Thus, while the earlier cinema tents were attended by a majority of "Native" spectators, the cinema palaces that followed seemed to try to reverse this trend and even provided more seats to "Europeans" than to "Natives", in an attempt

---

1175 "De zedelijkheid en de bioscoop", *Soerabaiasch-Handelsblad* (23 March 1914).

1176 Ibid. This lengthy article on "Morality and the cinema" discusses, on the one hand, how the ban can help improve morality in the Indies, of "Europeans" and "Natives" alike, since they all are drawn to "sensational" films. On the other hand, it explains that if the ban is in place, then the profitability (for exhibitors and municipality) will drop because the "Natives", who are arguably the majority of cinema spectators, will no longer go. It would therefore also constitute a missed out opportunity for potential education of the "Natives" since the "Natives" supposedly cheer when the white man defeats the Indians and therefore seem to naturally know the "right" order of things.

to make movie-going a more respectable, "European" activity and avoid the stigma that was beginning to stick to the cinema as an entertainment for the "Natives". At the same time, since the proportion of "Europeans" out of the population was so small, exhibitors absolutely had to attract "Native" spectators as well in order to be profitable. It would have been professional suicide otherwise.

Movie houses were indeed among the most modern structures built over the following decades, including being the first buildings fitted with air conditioning.[1177] Nevertheless the attempts by Surabaya's cinema entrepreneurs, as well as local newspapers' coverage of these endeavours, of turning movie-going into a more "European", elitist, or middle-class leisure activity by linearly moving towards construction of increasingly modern amenities, were not uniformly representative of current trends in the early part of the twentieth century. As we have seen, at least some of the "permanent tents" on the Pasar Besar in fact outlasted Surabaya's movie palace of the East Java Bioscope, and other less luxurious options continued to operate in the Chinese parts of town.

1177 Mrázek, *Engineers of Happy Land*, 111.

5

Batavia: Capital of Chinese Cinema Venues

> *It is always somewhat unclear to me why it is that there are so many to be found in Batavia who complain about how little there is to do in the Indies and who are prompted to draw unfavourable comparisons between life in the Indies and in Holland. Yet the Batavian has truly no reason to complain. Recently, as I wrote in my last report, the amusements began to die down, but shortly after we got the races and the buck jumpers. This is how it always goes here: Hardly one entertainment has left us, and another already stands in the doorway, while there is usually no lack of variety. Then there are the permanent pleasures, like the concerts and parties at Concordia, Harmonie and the Zoo, the Indische performances at the Thalia Theatre, the cinemas, the football matches and the regularly recurring shows of the dilettantes.*
> "Batavia", De Locomotief *(8 October 1910)*, emphasis added.

Batavia (present-day Jakarta), capital of colonial Indonesia, was established by the Dutch East India Company (VOC) in 1619 on the east bank of the Ciliwung River in Jayakarta, West Java. Settlement in the area can be traced back to prehistoric times, and the city's origin as a port goes back to the twelfth century.[1178] The Dutch were previously stationed at the regional capital of Banten, but arguments between the Company, the Portuguese, the English and the Javanese led to the construction of a fort at the mouth of the river, in an environment identified as favourable for a harbour.[1179] In the seventeenth century, Batavia indeed became the hub for Dutch trade in Asia.[1180] However, the swampland and hostile climate proved to be less than hospitable, leading to a continuous chain of deadly plagues at the new VOC outpost.[1181]

The city's fortunes began to turn at the beginning of the nineteenth century, as the Company declined and Batavia turned into a colonial city under the rule of Governor General Herman Willem Daendels (1809–1811). Daendels decided to tear down the city walls, as well as some of the old buildings, and to widen the streets of the downtown area by the port.[1182] Furthermore, he began

---

1178 See Abeyasekere, *Jakarta*, 3–4.

1179 Ibid., 8–9.

1180 Ibid., 13.

1181 "Dutch records tell of 87,000 soldiers and sailors dying in the government hospital between 1714 and 1776, and of 1,119,375 dying at Batavia between 1730 and August, 1752" (Eliza Ruhamah Scidmore, *Java, The Garden of the East* (New York: The Century Co., 1897), 21). "Javanese were not permitted to live within the town, by Company decree" (Abeyasekere, *Jakarta*, 13).

1182 See Scidmore, *Java*, 22.

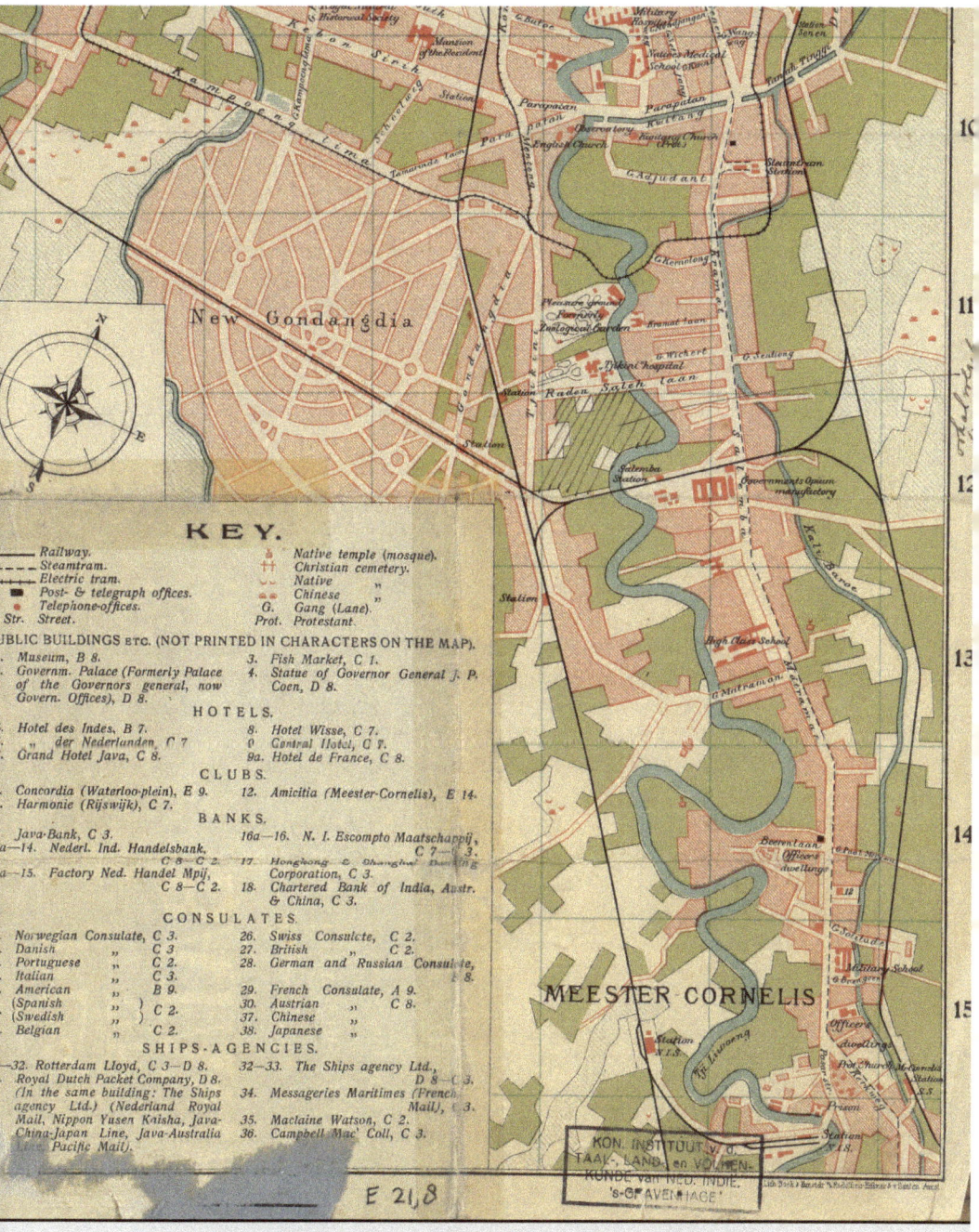

Figure 5–1. Plan of Batavia, Official Tourist Bureau, ca. 1910.
Courtesy of Leiden University Library, Image code D E 21,8.

building the new town, Weltevreden, in the higher suburbs to the south of the old city, which allowed more open construction and better airflow. The most important commercial businesses all had offices in the city. Tanjung Priok, the new harbour that could accommodate larger steamships, was opened some nine kilometres to the east in 1886. The sprawling city was connected to the harbour via road, canal and railway links. The most common vehicle used up to 1869 was a *sado* (or *dos-à-dos*), and that year horse-drawn trams were introduced.[1183] Steam trams, introduced in 1882, ran direct lines between the old town of Batavia and Meester Cornelis via Molenvliet, Rijswijk, Kramat and Salemba.[1184] Electric trams, which began running in April 1899 – three months before the first line in the Netherlands – followed a circuitous route from the old town by Menteng to Tanah Abang and Rijswijk, terminating at the *Harmonie* Club, thus avoiding Weltevreden and Kramat.[1185]

New visitors arriving were often unimpressed by the old town of Batavia (known in Dutch as the *benedenstad*), especially if they came in the evening when there was no commercial activity or any Europeans, Chinese, Indonesians, Indians and Arabs going about their business, and travellers were quickly whisked off to their hotels in Weltevreden (*bovenstad*).[1186] Crucially, as Milone notes in her in-depth study of the city from VOC times to 1870, "in spite of the difference in character between the cramped and deteriorated old town and the dispersed garden-town character of the new Weltevreden extension, Batavia did not develop the classic old town-new town dichotomy".[1187] The old town continued to serve as the busy commercial area, with banks and import-export companies all operating offices there, plenty of hustle and bustle of traffic coming from the port activity, and a lively Chinese quarter on the periphery. As Abeyasekere puts it: "One can almost hear the sigh of relief of the nineteenth-century traveller as his carriage bowled down the Molenvliet road".[1188] In contrast to the cramped terraces typical of the Chinese *kampung* with its crowded bazaars and streets, single-storey houses of Chinese officers lined the road along the paved canal, "where small natives splash and swim, women beat the family linen and men go to and from in tiny boats".[1189] These were followed by a sequence of European houses on wide avenues planted with tamarind and waringin trees, and finally, as the end of Molenvliet neared, the first of the large hotels serving travellers in the nineteenth century.

An English-language guide book from 1909 noted that the suburbs,

> [...] with their canals and pleasing open spaces [in addition to...] comfortable bungalows, in which European residents make their homes, seem for the most part to be enshrined in gardens of green foliage, and a stroll around the two great plains – Koningsplein and Waterlooplein, facing which many of the finest houses have been erected, enhances the suggestion, immediately formed, that the whole district is like one huge park. A few yards away from the quiet of the plains is to be found the principal business thoroughfare, which, during the early hours of the evening, presents a scene of gaiety and animation that can scarcely be equalled in any other Eastern city. Here are all the large and fashionable shops, of which

1183 See Abeyasekere, *Jakarta*, 51–52.

1184 Ibid., 445.

1185 See Dick et al., *Cities, Transport and Communications*, 7.

1186 See Abeyasekere, *Jakarta*, 52–53.

1187 Pauline Dublin Milone, *Queen City of the East: The Metamorphosis of a Colonial Capital*, PhD Dissertation (Berkeley: University of California, 1966), 322.

1188 Abeyasekere, *Jakarta*, 53–54.

1189 *Java, The Wonderland* (Weltevreden/Batavia: The Official Tourist Bureau, ca. 1900), 14.

5 – Batavia: Capital of Chinese Cinema Venues

Weltevreden can boast a considerable number, and several cafés, brilliantly illuminated with electric light, where bands play and the people sit in the foreground, in the Continental fashion, enjoying the cool evening air. The suburb has been well planned, it is kept scrupulously clean, and while the natives in their bright coloured clothes, quietly making their way hither and thither, give the required picturesque touch to the life in the streets, the absence of the crowded native dwelling houses prevents the occurrence of these objectionable features which so often destroy the charm of the towns in the Orient. It is the home of the Dutch residents in a far more real sense than any town east of the Suez can be said to be the home of the Englishman, and very naturally they have endeavoured to make it as attractive and cheerful a home as possible.[1190]

The fashionable areas of Batavia in the late nineteenth century and early twentieth century were Kramat, Salemba, Kebon Sirih, Parapatan and Pengangsaan, presenting rows of white houses with gardens along the main roads. The European settlement later extended to the south-east, while the extension of the tram and railway lines stimulated further development towards the military and market area of Meester Cornelis.[1191]

Many Europeans who spent substantial time in Batavia in the nineteenth century complained of the monotony of life in the city.[1192] Some of this may have changed by the early twentieth century. Similarly to the statements made in the opening quote of this chapter, an article published in *Het Nieuws van den Dag voor Nederlandsch-Indië* in 1905 under the heading "Batavia metropolis" argued as follows:

When the number of amusements determines whether a place should be included among the great cities, then Batavia these days is really heading in this direction. Complaints that "there is never anything to do here" are truly difficult to come by at present. At least certainly not these days. After the simple pleasures of beholding a brand new bioscope [*bioscoop*], which this evening begins its screenings at the Manège Fuchs in Tanah Abang, one can attend a musical matinee of the complete military band at the Zoo tomorrow. The theatre, recently abandoned by the untiringly Hamlet-interpreters, who yesterday for a fairly well-filled hall staged this opera for the 7th and last time, tomorrow evening will be taken up by the Stage Union Society, who will stir lovers of drama to tears with the performance of "Black Griet". Monday, however, there is a more serious [performance], worthy of the word muse, [by] the young violin artist Premislav [...]. What a divine art. What Tuesday adds to the agenda we do not know yet, but indeed one cannot complain these days in Batavia [...]. From the highest art to the most simple pleasures.[1193]

Batavia was not only the site of the earliest screenings of moving pictures found in this research, but also the first location for filming local views. In general, performing in Batavia was the highest aspiration of all entertainers in the Indies in that period. As Cohen articulates it in the case of the Komedie Stamboel,

---

1190 Wright, *Twentieth Century Impressions of Netherlands India*, 442.

1191 See Abeyasekere, *Jakarta*, 57.

1192 Most famously Bas Veth in his book *Het Leven in Nederlandsch-Indië* (Amsterdam: P.N. van Kampen & Zoon, 1900).

1193 "Batavia wereldstad", *Het Nieuws van den Dag voor Nederlandsch-Indië* (17 June 1905).

"[...] it was cosmopolitan, if-you-can-make-it-here Batavia that set the fashions emulated throughout the Netherlands Indies".[1194] However, when it came to cinema facilities, Batavians recognised that Surabaya was unsurpassed in terms of modern comforts and amenities, and entrepreneurs in Batavia (and elsewhere) aspired to emulate it.[1195]

In 1900 Europeans accounted for less than a tenth of the population of Batavia at only 1,363 (and it is unknown how many among them were Eurasian), the majority of Indonesians (Malays, Buginese, Balinese, Sumbawanese, Ambonese and others) numbered 78,000, and the Chinese made up almost a quarter at about 24,000.[1196] The large proportion of Chinese in Batavia, nearly doubling its population by the end of the nineteenth century, is also apparent in their strong representation as movie-goers and as entrepreneurs of moving pictures. Although the Chinese were clearly engaged in the business of moving pictures in other cities across the archipelago, the survival of extant material on Batavia from this period, including Chinese-Indonesian newspapers, enables to delve deeper into their contributions in the field in this chapter.

The Chinese population of the Netherlands Indies consisted of Indies-born Chinese known as *peranakan*, often the fruit of unions between Chinese male immigrants and local women, and newly arrived Chinese from the mainland known as *totok*. In many places the Chinese were confined to the Chinese districts of the cities and as of mid-nineteenth century their travel was restricted by the authorities which wanted to control their commercial activities. The 1863 pass system (*passenstelsel*) regulations were at times upheld so strictly that it the late nineteenth century a four-day stay away from home required a visa. Even a short trip from Batavia to Meester Cornelis, which took an hour by train, still required a pass in 1900, and anyone travelling without a pass or with a fake document risked fines and imprisonment.[1197] At the beginning of the twentieth century, the strict restrictions were somewhat relaxed, and as of 1904 travel passes were issued for a one-year period rather than for a single journey.[1198] In Batavia, the Chinese were mostly concentrated in the northern Chinese *kampung* of Glodok, but some also lived in the Chinese sections of Tanah Abang, Pasar Senen and Pasar Baru. Although many of them remained coolies or lower-rank tradesmen and hawkers, there were quite a number of successful Chinese businessmen in Batavia.[1199] They were generally repre-

1194 Cohen, *The Komedie Stamboel*, 119.

1195 "Cine-Lumen", *Java-Bode* (6 October 1910).

1196 See Abeyasekere, *Jakarta*, 57, 61, 65.

1197 See Williams, *Overseas Chinese Nationalism*, 30.

1198 See Claver, *Dutch Commerce and Chinese Merchants in Java*, 188. The shift in approach was due to the realisation that these restrictions were making it more difficult for the Chinese to trade in the countryside and collect their gains, and as a result of this the state coffers and European traders suffered because of the blow to profitability of their legitimate businesses (unlike opium trade, which these regulations were intended to curb). Finally, a compromise was reached between the authorities and the traders' lobby, which was made up of mostly European companies. The latter were largely acting out of their own self-interest, since restricting Chinese activity meant the Chinese could not honour their payments.

1199 See Cohen, *The Komedie Stamboel*, 121.

5 – Batavia: Capital of Chinese Cinema Venues

sented by Dutch-appointed heads of the community who made up the Chinese Council, who were also in charge of Chinese celebrations in the city, such as Chinese New Year.[1200]

Indonesian Chinese historically sponsored both indigenous and Chinese performances. Therefore, it is not surprising that they also played a major role in the moving picture industry. In 1901 Yap Goan Thay, the sponsor of Mahieu's successful Komedie Stamboel troupe, for instance, was even said to be experimenting with an improved Biograph device.[1201] Films and moving picture devices were offered for sale in Chinese shops from the beginning of the twentieth century (see Figure 5–2).[1202] Chinese entrepreneurs were also venue-owners, whether of structures made of bamboo or brick. They were thus involved in exhibition and distribution of moving pictures, as well as in their consumption. As spectators, the Chinese – men and women alike – were generally regarded to be enthusiastic movie-goers, attending shows throughout the night.[1203] Entrepreneurs thus depended on their attendance to a great extent in order to ensure their profit-making, and often offered a special class of tickets reserved for Chinese spectators, marked as either for "Chinese" or for "Foreign Orientals".[1204] At the same time, Chinese spectators were often the terror of foreign exhibitors. If members of the Chinese community ever felt that a Chinese was being mistreated – be it an inappropriate gesture towards a Chinese woman at the cinema or circus tent, or prejudicial treatment of a Chinese entrepreneur shown by the authorities – they would not hesitate to boycott a venue.

This chapter first examines some of the early venues for exhibiting moving pictures in Batavia, with an emphasis on the venues in the Chinese parts of town. It then moves on to review the new regulations and taxation schemes related to public amusements, introduced by the newly founded Municipal

---

1200 Ibid., 160.

1201 "Uit Soerabaja", *De Locomotief* (4 May 1901). For more on Yap Goan Thay and the Komedie Stamboel, see Cohen, *The Komedie Stamboel*, 40–41.

1202 In 1901, Tan Hoe Lo, the prime *peranakan*-Chinese *stambul* music maker and Batavia shop owner, advertised a complete cinematograph (*cinomotograaf*) for sale for as little as nine guilders, exclusive of shipping costs (Advertisement, *Bintang-Betawi* (4 December 1901). For more on Tan Hoe Lo, see Cohen, *The Komedie Stamboel*, 154–155 and Claudine Lombard-Salmon, "Le voyage du marchand Tan Hoe Lo à Paris (1889)", *Archipel* 54, No. 1 (1997), 177–188)). Based on the pricing of this device, it was probably an optical toy for home use or for children's entertainment, rather than for commercial use. By 1905, in the advertisement shown in Figure 5–2, a kinematograph (*kinemotograaf*) was offered at 50 guilders, in addition to six films for 12.50 guilders (Advertisement, *Kabar Perniagaan* (18 July 1905)). Compare these to the kinematograph device offered for sale by Nast in 1902 for 5,000 guilders, presumably along with some film stock, or the 1910 sale of a bioscope device with around 15,000 meters of film for 7,500 guilders ("Zedekwetsend", *Het Nieuws van den Dag voor Nederlandsch-Indië* (8 September 1902); Advertisement, *Pantjaran Warta* (2 April 1910)).

1203 "Kabar sehari-hari dari Betawi dan laen-laen negri", *Bintang Betawi* (8 April 1903); "Promotie", *Bataviaasch Nieuwsblad* (12 January 1901). One enthusiast, who could not afford a ticket and chose to peek inside a cinema tent at Kongsi Besar through a hole at the rear, was even caught in the act and picked up by police ("Een liefhebber van de bioscoop", *Het Nieuws van den Dag voor Nederlandsch-Indië* (4 August 1906)).

1204 It was sometimes noted that when Chinese spectators had other entertainment options on hand, such as a Chinese puppet theatre show, the cinema tent proved to be emptier ("Kirimian", *Selompret Melajoe* (13 June 1901)).

Figure 5–2. Advertisement for sale of a projector for children and films by Tan Hoe Lo & Co., *Kabar Perniagaan* (18 July 1905). Scan courtesy of PNRI, Jakarta.

Council as of 1907. Finally, it provides an overview of the major permanent cinema and variety theatres, some of them continuing their activities long beyond the period covered in this research. Identified in many of the municipal discussions and reports as the biggest enterprises, in terms of their share of the public amusements tax, these were: Cine Lumen at the Manège Fuchs in Tanah Abang, the Oriental Bioscope at Thalia Theatre in Mangga Besar, the Globe Bioscope in Pasar Baru, the West-Java Bioscope at Flora Theatre in Pasar Senen, and the Elite Bioscope in the area of the Sluisbrug. This chapter thus shows how, despite the Municipal Council's attempts to control the growth of the movie-going scene in Batavia, modern venues for the exhibition of moving pictures popped up essentially in every part of the city.

5.1 Venues for Early Shows

Upon the arrival of moving pictures in the Netherlands Indies and roughly during the decade that followed, Batavia had several venues that could host moving picture shows and generally served as locations for popular entertainment. Most of these were located in or around the new upper town area of Weltevreden. In fact, many companies, which initially scheduled just a certain number of shows and then decided to stay on for longer, often moved from one place to another in the city. This was either due to overbooking of the same site for other amusements, or it could have been a strategy of appealing to different audiences. Louis Talbot, for instance, exhibited moving pictures with his Scenimatograph at the Batavia Theatre, at the Botanical and Zoological Gardens – either as open-air screenings or inside the theatre on the premises – as part of a larger fairground event (alongside a carousel, *café chantant*, dances, military band music, and other amusements), and at the Concordia Military

5 – Batavia: Capital of Chinese Cinema Venues

Figure 5–3. Pasar Baru during the celebrations of Queen Wilhelmina's marriage, 1901. The Batavia Theatre (see Figures 1-4 and 1-5) is located across from the gate (left, off camera). Courtesy of Leiden University Library, Image code 31155.

Club.[1205] The Ripograph or Giant Cinematograph similarly started out at the Batavia Theatre, later moving to a roomy space on the premises of the Hotel and *toko* Cavadino when the Opera Club occupied the theatre, offered some children's programmes at the Botanical and Zoological Gardens over the weekend, and was even hosted by the Komedie Indra Bangsawan in Mangga Besar.[1206]

One could claim that the first screenings of moving pictures by Talbot were already given at a venue associated with the Chinese. Although the Batavia Theatre was a European-style building, its location just across the bridge from the Chinese neighbourhood of Pasar Baru (see Figure 5–3) meant that the theatre was surrounded by Chinese people, shops and eateries. In its report about Talbot's shows in 1897, *Bintang Barat* even referred to the theatre as "*Roemah Komedie Passar Baroe*".[1207] A review of Carl Hertz's magic show, also at the theatre in 1898, observed that the show was attended by many spectators, "especially Chinese".[1208] Nevertheless, more strictly speaking, it was the Ripograph or Giant Cinematograph which truly premiered moving pictures in the Chinese part of town, when it performed on the stage of the Komedie Indra

---

1205 Advertisement, *Java-Bode* (9 October 1896); "Nederlandsch-Indië", *Java-Bode* (14 July 1897); Advertisement, *Java-Bode* (16 July 1897). See further on Talbot's Scenimatograph in Section 1.2.

1206 Advertisement, *Java-Bode* (29 May 1897); Advertisement, *Java-Bode* (8 June 1897); Advertisement, *Java-Bode* (10 June 1897); Advertisement, *Pembrita Betawi* (14 June 1897). See further on the Ripograph or Giant Cinematograph in Section 1.3.1.

1207 "Betawie. 8 Maart 1897", *Bintang Barat* (8 March 1897), emphasis added. The advertisement appearing in the same newspaper that day did refer to the Batavia Theatre.

1208 "Chabar Betawi", *Pembrita Betawi* (22 July 1898).

Bangsawan in Mangga Besar (at Glodok, in the *benedenstad* of Batavia) in June 1897.[1209] The Victoria Parsi Theatre Company from Singapore with its own Cinematograph followed suit at Mangga Besar a year later.[1210]

In 1899, Ten Broeke's American Biograph chose to station Mutoscope devices in Glodok and in Pasar Senen.[1211] And while most of the screenings with the American Biograph were offered at the converted *Manège* in Tanah Abang, a couple of shows took place also in a tent at Tanah Lapang Glodok (Glodok field), "[...] larger than had ever been built in Java, height of 12 ½ meters. The images are 20 square meters larger than in the Manège Fuchs at Tanah Abang."[1212] Despite the more advantageous screening conditions at Glodok, it was projected that not many Europeans would attend the shows there because of the distance from Weltevreden.[1213] Another show of the Animatograph in 1901, also at Tanah Lapang Glodok, presumably in a tent, offered separate seats for female spectators.[1214] It is possible that this was done in order to provide gender-separation for a Muslim audience, which presumably attended this venue as well, similarly to the separation provided at S. M. Aidid's Urban Bioscope at Pasar Senen, which reserved its cheapest class of tickets for "Muslims".[1215] The American Animatograph, performing in 1905 at the building of Captain Tan Boen Koei in Kongsi Besar, also offered separate seats for women.[1216] It remains unclear whether any of these venues exercised gender-based separation in all seating ranks, i.e. also in the section for "European" spectators (if there even was one) and in the section for "Chinese" spectators, or only in the section reserved for "Muslim" spectators.

It is also quite likely that the separate seats in Glodok were intended to make women feel more comfortable to attend these venues for moving picture shows. There was no shortage of complaints about sexual harassment at cinema venues over the years, advances coming from other audience members or operating staff.[1217] Such misconduct by an "Indo" employee who was checking the tickets while inappropriately groping Chinese female visitors to a cinema tent set up by the company Het Centrum at Kongsi Besar, gave rise to a situation whereby at least a thousand spectators walked out of the screening. The Chinese vowed to boycott the venue henceforth, and the police was

---

1209 Advertisement, *Pembrita Betawi* (14 June 1897).

1210 Advertisement, *Java-Bode* (20 September 1898). For more on the Victoria Parsi Theatre, see Section 1.3.3.

1211 Advertisement, *Bintang Barat* (28 June 1899).

1212 Advertisement, *Bintang Barat* (29 July 1899).

1213 "Nederlandsch-Indië", *Bataviaasch Nieuwsblad* (27 June 1899). Such concerns would later arise again, in connection with the Thalia Theatre in Mangga Besar (see further in Section 5.3.2). For more on Ten Broeke's American Biograph, see Section 2.1.

1214 Advertisement, *Bintang Betawi* (19 January 1901).

1215 Advertisement, *Kabar Perniagaan* (29 March 1905).

1216 Advertisement, *Bintang Batavia* (21 September 1905). Tickets were priced at f 0.25 for "Chinese" and f 0.10 for "Muslims", and these were the only classes of tickets offered, advertised in this newspaper.

1217 For example: "Zaterdagsche Causerie", *Het Nieuws van den Dag voor Nederlandsch-Indië* (19 October 1912).

reportedly concerned that someone might set the cinema on fire.[1218] There were repeated cases of Chinese spectators boycotting amusements across the Indies, from circus tents to cinema companies, whether due to harassment of Chinese spectators, as above, or any other perceived discrimination (see further in Section 5.3.4).[1219]

5.2 Municipal Power and Taxation
5.2.1 Establishment of the Municipal Council

The switch from moving picture shows as a form of itinerant entertainment to a more institutionalised, fixed going-out option, seems to have coincided with the decentralisation of colonial rule, introduced by the colonial government in order to ease the administrative and financial pressure of urban responsibilities. The Batavia Municipal Council (*Gemeenteraad*) was formed in 1905 and was quickly gaining its own track record in attempts to control public amusements. According to Abeyasekere, upon its establishment the powers and finances of the Municipal Council were severely limited, and only in 1908 limited elections were held for some European Council members.[1220] The jurisdiction of Batavia's Municipality extended from Tanjung Priok to Matarman, including the *benedenstad*, Weltevreden, Kramat, Salemba, and Pagansaan.[1221] It was at this point that Meester Cornelis, further to the south, was clearly defined as independent from Batavia since it now had its own Municipal Council.

The Council was given an annual grant of 380,000 guilders from the colonial government, and its budget was supplemented with small amounts obtained from sale of water and rents for occupying municipal grounds. With this limited budget it was expected to repair roads and address sanitation issues in the entire district.[1222] Most of the budget items, "[...] such as road-building and maintenance, street-lighting, drinking-water provision, and payment of municipal personnel were items of expenditure largely on behalf of Europeans, since they were the ones who lived along and used roads most; street-lighting and drinking-water were largely restricted to their areas; and expenses on Europeans' salaries, overseas leave and pension provisions were a heavy burden on the budget."[1223] Where the investments went to was, thus, mostly to the European quarters. However, over the years Indonesian members of the

---

1218 "Boycot", *Het Nieuws van den Dag voor Nederlandsch-Indië* (1 July 1905); "Boycot", *Bintang Batavia* (3 July 1905); "Dari hal boycot", *Bintang Batavia* (4 July 1905).

1219 For instance: "Bioscoop di boijcot", *Pembrita Betawi* (5 March 1909); "Bioscoop di boijcot", *Pantjaran Warta* (30 January 1913); "Geboycot", *Het Nieuws van den Dag voor Nederlandsch-Indië* (13 January 1913).

1220 See Abeyasekere, *Jakarta*, 118. "In 1917, all twenty-seven seats were opened up for election but the conditions for election were still such as to protect European dominance, since fifteen seats were reserved for Europeans, leaving four for 'Foreign Orientals' (almost always Chinese) and eight for Indonesians. Voting was limited to males over twenty-three; Europeans who paid a yearly income tax of fl. 600 and could speak and read Dutch" (ibid.).

1221 See Wright, *Twentieth Century Impressions of Netherlands India*, 448.

1222 Ibid.

1223 Abeyasekere, *Jakarta*, 119.

Municipal Council managed to draw attention to the need for *kampung* improvement since, as they pointed out, Chinese, Arabs and poor Eurasians were also residents of these areas. Moreover, *kampung* settlements were scattered around Batavia and were located next to European workplaces and homes. Therefore health and hygiene, as well as fires in the tightly settled *kampung*, were of concern to Europeans too.[1224]

The Municipal Council often discussed rules and regulations relating to public amusements. The use of public roads, streets and squares, taxation and control, and later the construction of more permanent venues, were all issues relevant to entrepreneurs of moving picture shows. As Batavia often followed in the footsteps of Surabaya when it came to the field of legislation on entertainment, it was after the latter began to introduce new taxation on public amusements that the former jumped on the bandwagon. The first significant ruling was instated in late 1907, when operators of public amusements, who up until that point paid municipal taxes based on their net income, were thereof charged by their revenues in total.[1225]

The following year, another momentous decision, to go into effect as of 1 January 1909, was passed: moving picture shows were to be given only in the "Manège Fuchs, Pasar Tanah Abang, Jati Baru, Pasar Pisang, Senen, Tanah Abang, Salemba square and Kwitang".[1226] Moreover, while in 1908 there were at least 22 different moving picture shows in Batavia, some of which more or less fixed and others short-lived, from January 1909 onwards permits were to be issued for a one-month period only and tents were subject to a commission charged with assessing their safety. At the same time, doubts regarding the feasibility of upholding this regulation were expressed from the outset. It is possible that the legislation was never applied, since a company such as Cine Lumen, for instance, remained continuously operational from long before and well after this scheme (see Section 5.3.1). Moreover, the list peculiarly left out the Chinese areas of Glodok and Pasar Baru, which were districts with a significant going out scene for moving pictures and other entertainments. They were in fact increasingly becoming even more so, as we shall see below. The one-month limitation was extended to three months, which was still perceived as too restrictive since it did not encourage entrepreneurs to invest in the comfort and furnishing of their tents.[1227]

1224 Ibid., 121.

1225 "Belasting of publieke vermakelijkheden", *Het Nieuws van den Dag voor Nederlandsch-Indië* (7 October 1907). This was already the case in municipal tax collection from shops and other companies, and therefore public amusements were brought in line with this new measure.

1226 "Bioscoop-woede", *Java-Bode* (6 October 1908). It is not clear why Tanah Abang was repeated twice, but it appears there were a few potential sites in the same area.

1227 "Bioscopen", *Het Nieuws van den Dag voor Nederlandsch-Indië* (25 March 1909). This, the article pointed out, differed from the case of Surabaya, but that was true only to a certain extent. Exhibitors themselves were still tied down to limiting three-month permits in Surabaya, but owners of semi- and permanent venues were at least entitled to set up a cinema tent, maintain it and rent it out to other exhibitors ("Sirene-Bioscoop", *Soerabaiasch-Handelsblad* (8 December 1909)).

5.2.2 Discussions on Public Amusements Tax, 1911

In early 1911, inspired by similar legislation in Surabaya, the Municipal Council in Batavia sat down to discuss the planned new tax on public amusements. This kind of taxation was introduced in many cities and towns, but in Batavia a long time passed between the initial discussions and drafting of the taxation scheme, and its effectuation.[1228] It became the topic of endless Municipal Council meetings and newspaper reports, at times leading to accusations of the authorities using certain newspapers as their proxy.[1229] The new tax was intended to fill up the municipal coffers and to be put towards making "living in the city of 'Batavia more pleasant'".[1230] It was estimated that the proceeds from the new tax would be approximately 13,000 guilders: 3,000 guilders as a flat fee paid directly by entrepreneurs of public amusements, so about 250 guilders from each individual company, and another 10,000 paid proportionally, in the form of a ten per cent fee added to the entrance ticket, to be paid by spectators. The ten per cent tax, the memorandum of understanding stated, "seems to be not too high" and was based on a similar regulation which has been levied in Surabaya for a few years, where supposedly no complaints were made.[1231]

The Dutch newspapers in Batavia were dubious about the new tax regulation and the uses the income from it would be put towards. "In Amsterdam five per cent is imposed; why here in the Indies is asked double what is considered to be sufficient elsewhere is unclear to us. Are public amusements here so much better?" quipped one reporter.[1232] "Imposing 'tax' on public amusements makes sense in Paris, even in Amsterdam...., in an eerily boring place like Batavia it reeks of absurdity, not to use a stronger word", another article retorted. "That is yet another perk of Decentralisation; the Government would not come up with such a miserable idea, which was reserved for the Municipal Council."[1233] In the spirit of promising improvement of the city streets, a third report suggested the following:

[1228] Neighbouring Meester Cornelis issued a similar tax regulation around the same time. According to a report from that period, there was one active cinema at Meester Cornelis, in addition to "exhibitions, annual fairs, fancy fairs, sporting events, dances, operas, stage performances, lectures, singing and musical performances which certainly cannot be called numerous" ("Belasting op openbare vermakelijkheden", *Java-Bode* (20 September 1910)). Therefore, the 19 clauses of the draft regulation mostly related to the cinema. It was up to the municipality to decide which public amusements were provided in the interest of the public or for charitable purposes, and therefore would remain tax-free. One pessimistic estimate claimed the new tax on public amusements would only bring in about 50 guilders a year for the municipality at Meester Cornelis, but another estimated it should be between 2,500 to 3,000 guilders per year ("Belasting op openbare vermakelijkheden te Meester Cornelis", *Java-Bode* (27 September 1910)).

[1229] "Belasting op de Publieke Vermakelijkheden", *Het Nieuws van den Dag voor Nederlandsch-Indië* (23 September 1911).

[1230] "Belasting op openbare vermakelijkheden", *Het Nieuws van den Dag voor Nederlandsch-Indië* (10 January 1911).

[1231] Ibid.

[1232] Ibid. However, in late 1913, it was reported that the tax on public amusements in Amsterdam had been raised to fifteen per cent ("Brieven uit Amsterdam", *Het Nieuws van den Dag voor Nederlandsch-Indië* (24 May 1913)).

[1233] "Viva la joya!", *Het Nieuws van den Dag voor Nederlandsch-Indië* (14 February 1912).

> First, it should be ensured that the visitors to the theatre, who represent the majority of those who will have to pay the tax, no longer run the risk of breaking their limbs on the horrendous roads leading to that place of amusements, and further meet the needs of taxpayers, who henceforth will be treated to some light in Tjekini on their way to retiring to the Zoo. With the busy vehicle traffic when there is "something to do" in the Garden, the Egyptian darkness that reigns there makes a tour through Tjekini perilous on such evenings. If those two issues are decently addressed, then income from the new tax will probably be going in the right direction.[1234]

Once again, the European community was expecting urban development to be mostly on the Weltevreden side, especially with what was perceived as a tax that would generally come from "European" spectators.

Others were less forgiving of the new initiative and predicting a deterioration in the quality of amusements to be offered to the public, as well as a decrease in the number of spectators.

> In the colony of any other country, art is encouraged and protected – not so in the Dutch colonies, where it is so difficult to go out for entertainment or distraction. Because such a tax will unquestionably raise more or less obstructive reactions to the theatre and concert life. Indies men line behind the growing struggle over everyday life, gradually becoming economical and now counting every dime […]. Suppose that the charge provided is ten per cent, then for a ticket of f 2.50 you would pay f 2.75. If your family numbers four persons, then for four tickets you can pay f 11, for which you would have usually sacrificed f 10. That is a lot, that is very much. Then the seat reservations, transport, and other supplementary purchases. The result: less theatre and concert visits, even though you already have so little in the Indies to resist an appropriate and useful opportunity.[1235]

Another newspaper commented: "Instead of giving a subsidy to the good-doers who come here with theatre groups or operetta troupes; instead of paving the way for magicians, reciters, circus directors, one makes it difficult for these brave businessmen. […] the public is going to pay for it, but not for long! The more expensive the seats are, the less people go somewhere, that makes perfect sense."[1236]

Operators of public amusements were also victims of the new taxation, yet another report claimed, since they will have to lower their prices.[1237] The new tax – added to the "mercilessly long list" of expenses, including income tax, tax on lighting, a flat fee for every performances, tax on free tickets, tax on programmes, and others – was further expected to deter foreign performers and entrepreneurs of public amusements from visiting the Indies.[1238] This was reportedly already happening in Medan, where such taxation had gone into

---

1234 "Belasting op openbare vermakelijkheden", *Het Nieuws van den Dag voor Nederlandsch-Indië* (10 January 1911).

1235 "Belasting op publieke Vermakelijkheden", *Bataviaasch Nieuwsblad* (21 January 1911).

1236 "Belasting op Vermaak", *Het Nieuws van den Dag voor Nederlandsch-Indië* (2 October 1911).

1237 "Belasting op publieke Vermakelijkheden", *Bataviaasch Nieuwsblad* (21 January 1911).

1238 Ibid.

effect just a month earlier (see further on Medan in Section 7.4).[1239] The report also drew attention to the terribly inefficient control method exercised by municipal controllers in Medan, who disrupted a moving picture show in the middle of a screening, causing a ten-minute break in the show. "The Medanese control method, dare we say without reservation, is used in every town where taxation of amusements exists. Imagine that such a thing took place during an opera or a *comedie* [*komedi*]. The gentlest people in the world would not tolerate this. It is to be hoped that the method of control outlined here will no longer be used. The tax itself is already unpopular enough."[1240]

Interestingly, the new legislation demanded a definition of what the concept "public amusements" actually entailed.[1241] Some targets of the legislation were the usual suspects: theatre shows and concerts (whether European operas or *komedi stambul*), circus and cinema tents, sporting events. Other cases were less clear-cut. European clubs, like Harmonie and Concordia, it was argued, had regular members who needed to be elected to join the club, and since they were holding private parties they should not be subject to the new tax. The Botanical and Zoological Garden, on the other hand, was open to practically anyone and should be taxed. While public lectures also fell under the new taxation initially, it was suddenly advocated that not all lectures should be taxed, for instance, lectures for public interest held by the union of women's suffrage, the physics society, or medical associations which held regular meetings and imposed no entrance fee. Shows held to collect money for charity were also exempt. Indigenous and Chinese traditional performance arts were initially to be included in the new taxation according to the initial draft; however, the authorities in Buitenzorg (Bogor) which were consulted to approve the regulations, claimed that these sorts of amusements were already covered by the so-called "*wayang* tax" collected by the government and, therefore, should not be double-taxed.[1242]

5.2.3 Implementation and Consequences of the Public Amusements Tax

Moving picture shows were clearly affected by the new legislation. Cinemas were to be taxed after deduction of ten free tickets that could be handed out by exhibitors, presumably offered to members of the press. Entrepreneurs of moving pictures therefore had to stop handing out free tickets to ordinary spectators. This practice was apparently common when weather conditions

1239 "Belasting op Vermaak", *Het Nieuws van den Dag voor Nederlandsch-Indië* (2 October 1911).

1240 Ibid., emphasis added.

1241 "Gemeenteraad van Batavia", *Bataviaasch Nieuwsblad* (25 January 1911).

1242 "De belasting op openbare vermakelijkheden", *Het Nieuws van den Dag voor Nederlandsch-Indië* (20 May 1911), emphasis added. The newspaper claimed that this was the wrong way of looking at it, and that the government should withdraw the "*wayang* tax" to allow the municipality to collect the profits from these performances. The revenue from the "*wayang* tax" in 1906 was 5,497 guilders, dropping to 4,525 in 1907, further down to 2,200 in 1908, and was projected to bring in an estimated 2,300 guilders in 1911 (ibid.). The "*wayang* tax" was unique to the Batavia residency, covering Chinese opera, all varieties of Javanese and Chinese puppet theatres, and popular theatre, like *wayang wong*. The Komedie Stamboel was exempted from paying the "*wayang* tax" (see Cohen, *The Komedie Stamboel*, 171–176).

were particularly rainy, in order to fill up the ranks of the cinema tent, or, as it turned out, in order to avoid complaints to the local authorities from neighbours living in close vicinity to the venue about the noise coming from the cinema. Indeed, as soon as free admittance to the cinema tent in Bungur (in Senen) was revoked, residents suddenly began to complain about the nuisance they encounter every evening from the cinema tent.[1243] Mr. J. C. Jacquet, the owner of the cinema tent, wrote in response to the newspaper:

> For years and years that moving picture shows have been given in Bungur, the neighbours never complained. The first ranks were as a rule well attended, not only by not paying neighbours, but also by the friends and acquaintances they brought with them. With such attendance a cinema entrepreneur cannot cover his expenses; with envious eyes, he sees his first ranks getting filled and for the seats, for which he still must pay rent, he sees not a penny going to his cash flow. The courtesy of the entrepreneur to provide the closest neighbours a free pass was grossly abused; people living far removed from Bungur sometimes came in with a free ticket. Furthermore, the residents demanded that not only close neighbours, but people who live within 1,000 meters or more from the tent receive free tickets. I have put an end to this provision of free tickets on 25 January this year in the cinema at Bungur, after the *stambul* moved its tents and began to operate. The shortly to be introduced municipal ordinance concerning the taxation of public amusements states that the cinema owner is liable for the free tickets he provides. The company must comply with the ten per cent surtax on the entrance fee. The entrepreneur must therefore pay the municipality the ten per cent in respect of every person who enters with a free ticket. Under these circumstances, it would be too crazy to continue the lavish distribution of free tickets.[1244]

The move by Mr. Jacquet, nevertheless, was somewhat premature. The Municipal Council was to discuss the details of the public amusements tax for the most part of 1911, ultimately agreeing on a final version in a meeting held on 11 October 1911.[1245] The draft regulation was approved by the Governor on 7 February 1912 and was to go into effect 30 days after 13 February – the date on which it was officially issued in the *Javasche Courant* – thus, on 15 March 1912.[1246] Meanwhile, several cinema entrepreneurs led by Tan Joe Hok, owner of the West-Java Bioscope at Flora Theatre in Pasar Senen, were trying to convince the Municipal Council to refrain from implementing the flat fee on public amusements that they were to be charged.[1247] The Municipal Council, however, was already deliberating the provisional formation of the control office staff for that tax: a controller with zero salary (probably an existing police inspector who was put in charge of this operation), a principal controller

---

1243 "De Ripograaf", *Het Nieuws van den Dag voor Nederlandsch-Indië* (14 March 1908); "'Overlast'", *Het Nieuws van den Dag voor Nederlandsch-Indië* (1 February 1911).

1244 Ibid., emphasis added.

1245 "Officieele Besluiten", *Het Nieuws van den Dag voor Nederlandsch-Indië* (12 February 1912).

1246 "Viva la joya!", *Het Nieuws van den Dag voor Nederlandsch-Indië* (14 February 1912).

1247 "Agenda", *Het Nieuws van den Dag voor Nederlandsch-Indië* (17 February 1912); "Bioscoop di Boijcot", *Pantjaran Warta* (30 January 1913). See further on West-Java Bioscope in section 5.3.4.

receiving a salary of ƒ 100 per month (transportation ƒ 25 per month) and three controllers at a salary of ƒ 50 per month (no transportation costs).[1248]

The new tax and more stringent regulations nevertheless proved to be beneficial, at least in the case of some exhibitors. For instance, it turned out that the employees of one cinema in Batavia were double selling the same tickets and pocketing the extra income. This was discovered thanks to the tax controller, who compared the number of tickets sold and free tickets handed out with the actual number of spectators, leading to the conclusion that there were more spectators than tickets issued. The entrepreneur immediately fired his entire staff, which were found responsible for the loss of approximately 900 guilders that month.[1249] However, the new regulations were generally considered a serious burden on entrepreneurs of public amusements, in all fields. The Batavia Theatre, for instance, was facing problems due to the new taxation and further planned changes to the leasing conditions. With the new fee for leasing of the theatre from the municipality set at 3,600 guilders per year, on top of which the flat fee and ten per cent tax per ticket were to be added, "in order to earn enough money", a concerned member of the Municipal Council cautioned, "the lessees would be forced to offer moving picture shows, organize beer evenings, etc., which would drop the artistic level down".[1250] Nevertheless, other members of the Municipal Council, including its Chairman, had no objection to moving picture shows at the venue, feeling that this would not detract from enjoying the theatre.

In June 1912, the first of seven rounds of tax collection for the year 1912 came in, with public amusements tax from 14 March to 4 May (52 days) bringing in 1,400 guilders from the flat fee paid by owners and another 7,775.63 guilders from the ten per cent added fee paid by ticket holders. Based on these figures, the income from the tax on public amusements for 1912 was estimated at 54,431.51 guilders for the entire year. This figure did not even take into account the pending opening of the Flora Theatre at Pasar Senen and the upcoming reopening of a cinema at Prapatan, both of which were to yield 300 guilders (150 guilders each) on the flat fee per month, i.e. 3,600 guilders per year. In addition, it was estimated that the two cinemas were to bring in another 40 guilders per day, i.e. 14,560 guilders per year, from the ten per cent added fee, thus "less than the proceeds of the Globe Bioscope at Pasar Baroe" which were not specified.[1251] Therefore, adding up the extra 13,450 guilders from flat fees and 68,991.51 from the ten per cent fee, public amusements tax for 1912 was expected to total 82,391.51 guilders.

Based on these projected figures, as well as on the fact that additional cinemas were to be opened, the Municipal Council now wished to modify the provi-

---

1248 "Gemeenteraad van Batavia", *Het Nieuws van den Dag voor Nederlandsch-Indië* (16 February 1912).

1249 "Een gezegende belasting", *Het Nieuws van den Dag voor Nederlandsch-Indië* (27 March 1912).

1250 "Gemeente van Batavia", *Het Nieuws van den Dag voor Nederlandsch-Indië* (22 February 1911).

1251 "De belasting op de publieke vermakelijkheden", *Het Nieuws van den Dag voor Nederlandsch-Indië* (10 June 1912). For more on Globe Bioscope, see Section 5.3.3.

sional framework of the controlling staff. The Chairman of the Board proposed a new scheme: a controller with zero salary, a main controller with a starting salary of 200 guilders per month, with a second- and third-year raise each in the sum of 50 guilders per month, once satisfactory diligence and suitability is proven, in addition to 50 guilders per month for travel expenses; three controllers with a salary of 60 guilders per month, in addition to 25 guilders per month for travel expenses, and a temporary controller with a salary of 60 guilders per month, in addition to 25 guilders per month for travel expenses. They were also to be provided with badges, to be able to identify themselves as controllers of public amusements tax.[1252] The formation of the public amusements tax control was changed once again in early 1913, when another controller was added to the team.[1253]

Even so, members of the Municipal Council were complaining about the high costs associated with the control of public amusements, which reportedly left the municipality with only twenty five per cent of the flat fee proceeds paid by the five permanent cinema theatres as well as several temporary venues of public amusements.[1254] Indeed, by October 1913, 8,832.50 guilders of flat fees were received that year, while the remuneration of the controlling staff for public amusements amounted to 6,678 guilders.[1255] Other unexpected expenses, which in 1912 totalled 300 guilders, spiked to 1,400 guilders in 1913, the report shockingly revealed. Nevertheless, as the figures for 1912 mentioned above indicate, the larger proportion of income from the public amusements tax came from the ten per cent paid by ticket holders, so the Municipal Council was still making significant profits from this scheme.

While the Municipal Council was celebrating its achievements and the new income, patrons and entrepreneurs of public amusements were less than jubilant. A commentator for the *Bataviaasch Nieuwsblad*, musing about whether the income from the public amusements tax was being spent wisely, described the following scene:

> In the evening in calm weather, when the moon shines brightly, it is particularly a pleasure to walk along Krekot, especially along the area two hundred meters to the right of the cinema. A scent of dead cats, of leftover food, mixed with mud, greets the stroller there. And all free of charge, not even tax on "Public Amusements" stamped on it.[1256]

New entrepreneurs wishing to start off on a cinema venture felt like they were being especially targeted. *Taman Sari* warned that, anybody who now wished to open a new cinema but did not own land of their own at Pasar Baru, Mangga Besar, Tanah Abang or Senen, would not be able to do so without a starting

---

1252 "Publieke vermakelijkheden!", *Het Nieuws van den Dag voor Nederlandsch-Indië* (29 November 1912).

1253 "Gemeenteraad van Batavia", *Het Nieuws van den Dag voor Nederlandsch-Indië* (11 March 1913).

1254 "Gemeenteraad van Batavia", *Het Nieuws van den Dag voor Nederlandsch-Indië* (29 October 1913). The five permanent venues were mentioned by name as Globe Bioscope, Cine Lumen, Elite Bioscope, Flora Theatre and Thalia Theatre, all of which will be elaborated on in Section 5.3.

1255 "De gemeentelijke dienst der Openbare Vermakelijkheden", *Het Nieuws van den Dag voor Nederlandsch-Indië* (20 February 1914).

1256 "Rozegeur en Maneschijn", *Bataviaasch Nieuwsblad* (20 March 1913).

capital of between 1,000 to 1,500 guilders. Rental of land from the Municipality was at least ƒ 1 per square meter per month, and therefore the smallest cinema tent would cost 275 guilders per month. On top of these, it was estimated that the price of setting up a tent was 400 guilders and another 275 guilders would be required for decoration. Other costs to be taken into account were the fees for film rental for seven nights per week and, obviously, the new municipal tax.[1257]

5.2.4 No more "murders, robberies, adulteries, and muggings"

Another issue that new and existing exhibitors of moving pictures had to consider was a new initiative by the assistant-resident of police in Batavia. In July 1912, the latter decided to take action against the unmonitored content of moving picture shows, communicating to cinema entrepreneurs directly that they would no longer be allowed to screen films showing "murders, robberies, adulteries, and muggings".[1258] The Batavia correspondent for *De Locomotief* noted a few days later that chances of cinemas in Batavia to make handsome profits had been greatly diminished by the recent circular, especially new ones to be opened such as the abovementioned Flora Theatre and Elite Bioscope.[1259] If "sensation films" were no longer to be shown, then spectators will be robbed of the big attraction that draws them to the cinema, the report claimed, and therefore income would drop. The article further expressed serious doubts about the logic behind this decree, arguing that if the crime shown in the film is punished, as happens in most cases, then one could argue that these films have a pedagogical value. The correspondent further questioned the notion that so-called "sensation films" had any effect on crime level:

> Now I can still remember very well the time when there were no cinemas, so no thrill movies existed in Java. And ever since, not much has changed in Java, at least not in Batavia. The general development of the natives and the other Orientals is largely unchanged, not significantly improved. The police remained virtually the same; until recently very few advancements can be found. The social conditions, the living conditions of people are almost the same. Therefore, one can safely conclude that if the sensation films were actually so dangerous, this would have necessarily expressed itself in an increased number of crimes, and overall everything has remained the same.[1260]

Moreover, the reporter emphasised the potential pedagogical value of cinema, especially for "Native" spectators: "[...] the little man [*kleine man*] can obtain a lot of knowledge which, under his circumstances, he would not be able to get in any other way. He sees other countries, other peoples, other customs and traditions. He is taken out of the small circle of his *kampoeng* and a large, new, never-thought of world is opened up to him."[1261]

1257 "Bioscoop", *Taman Sari* (9 April 1912).

1258 "Bioscoop-censuur", *De Locomotief* (5 July 1912).

1259 "Batavia", *De Locomotief* (10 July 1912). See further on Flora Theatre and Elite Bioscope in Sections 5.3.4 and 5.3.5.

1260 Ibid.

1261 Ibid., emphasis added.

5.2.5 New Regulations on Construction of Permanent Venues

The situation of entrepreneurs was soon to become even more complicated. In October 1912 the Municipal Council was in the process of writing up new regulations on the construction of facilities for public amusements, with the explicit intention being to put an end to "the cinema-building boom".[1262] Henceforth, no cinema was to receive a permit to be built without the watchful eye of the Council having looked over the building plans first. "If the rampant cinema competition continues, then the prices will be reduced as a result and a drop in the tax on public amusements will ensue", argued a member of the Municipal Council.[1263] The Municipal Council subsequently brushed off a request submitted on behalf of lieutenant of the Moors and Bengalese P. N. Kattan to set up a cinema theatre near the lock bridge (*Sluisbrug*), raising several objections and relying heavily on the proposal not meeting fire safety demands which were more seriously observed ever since the fire at Loa Soen Yang's Flying Bioscope in 1910.[1264] Cinema owners were now also expected to cover the costs of installing turnstiles at their venues, to facilitate the work of the tax controller.[1265]

At the same time, Municipal Council decisions arguably favoured Chinese cinema-owners, often finding roundabout solutions to licensing conundrums. Thus, in 1912, after Pathé Frères' application to build a cinema theatre at Glodok was turned down by the Municipal Council one year earlier, under the pretence that the Chairman of the Council guaranteed to the owner of the Thalia Theatre that no other cinema theatre would ever be built in the *benedenstad*, it turned out that the Council nevertheless approved the construction of two new cinemas in Glodok and Pancoran, one owned by Lie Kang Soeij and the other by Oeij Khoen.[1266] Yet another permit for constructing a cinema theatre in Pancoran was granted to Koh Tjing Bie in September 1913.[1267] "Why are there always unconventional decisions to mention here when it applies to awarding cinema licenses to Chinese?" *Het Nieuws van den Dag voor Nederlandsch-Indië* wondered out loud.[1268] Whether this was a justified claim or an unwarranted statement, Chinese-owned cinemas certainly blossomed in Batavia, presenting a challenge to some of the decisions that the Municipal Council initially insisted upon.[1269]

1262 "Gemeenteraad van Batavia", *Het Nieuws van den Dag voor Nederlandsch-Indië* (15 October 1912).

1263 Ibid.

1264 "Gemeenteraad van Batavia", *Bataviaasch Nieuwsblad* (14 January 1913). See further on Loa Soen Yang in Section 5.3.3.

1265 "Gemeenteraad van Batavia", *Het Nieuws van den Dag voor Nederlandsch-Indië* (16 September 1913).

1266 "Een zonderlinge belofte", *Het Nieuws van den Dag voor Nederlandsch-Indië* (3 April 1913). See further on Thalia Theatre in Section 5.3.2.

1267 "Gemeenteraad van Batavia", *Het Nieuws van den Dag voor Nederlandsch-Indië* (16 September 1913).

1268 Ibid.

1269 In addition to Tio Tek Kang and Loa Soen Yang, to be elaborated on further below, there were other Chinese entrepreneurs who either fully- or co-owned moving pictures exhibition companies, some of them setting up shop outside the Chinese quarters of Batavia. For instance, the Cynema Theatre was established in Batavia in 1908 as a public limited company under joint ownership of Mr. Isidore Henri

5.3 Permanent Venues
5.3.1 First-run of Pathé Frères: Cine Lumen at Manège Fuchs Tanah Abang, 1906–1914

Cine Lumen, under the management of Mr. S. M. Aidid and owned by the company Het Centrum from Noordwijk, occupied the Manège Fuchs more or less successively from November 1906 up to January 1915.[1270] Besides ownership of Cine Lumen, Het Centrum was the exclusive importer to the Indies of French automobiles Cottereau and Bayard, as well as of Fiat, a point that it did not fail to mention in the advertisements when a scene of the Circuit de la Sarthe was featured on one of Cine Lumen's programmes in early 1907 showing some of the vehicles the company was dealing in.[1271]

The building known as the Manège Fuchs was located at Tanah Abang, to the west of the Koningsplein. As of the eighteenth century this part of town served as the site of luxury homes of Dutch and Chinese alongside the homes of local residents who often worked on the fancier estates. Later in the nineteenth century many Arabs also lived in and around Tanah Abang. Originally owned by the carriage company of M. J. Fuchs, established in 1868 as a "small livery stable and farrier's shop", Manège Fuchs was first inaugurated as a stable and horseback riding school in January 1884.[1272] With its newly fitted easy chairs,

---

[1270] Pierre Ramier, salesmen, the Chinese Souw Sian Tjong, merchant, and Tje Hin To, merchant – all residents of Batavia (*Extra Bijvoegsel der Javasche Courant*, 6 November 1908, no. 89). Established for a period of seventy-five years, the company's purpose was to operate a cinema (*bioscope*) and related equipment and deal with the purchase of films, tools, appliances or parts required for the operation of such an endeavour. With a capital of 25,000 guilders divided into one hundred shares, only sixty per cent of the company were paid by the above shareholders (Ramier – 12 per cent, Souw Sian Tjong – 38 per cent, Tje To Hin – 10 per cent) and the remaining forty per cent were deposited with the Governor-General of the Netherlands Indies, to be paid in full within the coming ten years. Setting up its tent in the fashionable area of Prapatan – Kebon Sirih, in another *manège* formerly occupied by the Fuchs company, the device operated by the Cynema Theatre appears to have been a Gaumont Chronophone, which synchronised the Cinematographe with a disc Phonograph. Newspapers were excited about the new company, noting that the device is currently successfully exhibited in Paris and that Gaumont has effectively recorded entire operas, operettas and pantomimes, including "Mignon, Carmen, L'Enfant prodigue van Wormser, etc". "Cinéma-theater [sic]" (*De Locomotief* (14 May 1908)). Nevertheless, the phono numbers were found to be "a shrill dissonance", which "of course took away some of the charm" and the effect of simulating reality ("Cinéma-théâtre", *Java-Bode* (29 September 1908)). The venue itself was "well maintained, fully electrically lit and, with its conspicuous cleanliness, highly suitable to be visited with the ladies" (ibid.).

1270 Screenings of Cine Lumen at Manège Tanah Abang were suspended as of January 1915 (Advertisement, *Bataviaasch Nieuwsblad* (4 January 1915)). Aidid's name had earlier been associated with the Urban Bioscope in 1905, also at the Manège in Tanah Abang, with the Edison Bioscope Company in a tent at Jembatan Batu in 1905, with the Royal Optigraph at Prapatan in 1906, and at Kongsi Besar and Pasar Tanah Abang in 1907 (Advertisement, *Kabar Perniagaan* (21 June 1905); Advertisement, *Kabar Perniagaan* (28 February 1905); Advertisement, *Kabar Perniagaan* (24 November 1906); Advertisement, *Kabar Perniagaan* (9 February 1907); Advertisement, *Kabar Perniagaan* (28 February 1907)). In 1912, he also ran advertisements offering the Royal Optigraph for hire, including a device, engine and electric lamps, for screenings at private events (Advertisement, *Pantjaran Warta* (14 February 1912)). Although Aidid's name often appeared as the manager or owner of the above enterprises in advertisements in the Malay newspapers, this research has found no mention of Aidid in any Dutch language newspaper – either in advertisements or in reports.

1271 Advertisement, *Het Nieuws van den Dag voor Nederlandsch-Indië* (1 February 1907). Spectators were reportedly so scared by the furiously racing vehicles, to the extent that one even wanted to complain to the police ("Cine-Lumen", *Het Nieuws van den Dag voor Nederlandsch-Indië* (5 February 1907)).

1272 Wright, *Twentieth Century Impressions of Netherlands India*, 461.

"beautifully lit and tastefully decorated", it exuded comfort and was intended to operate as a members' club.[1273] Plans to install a carousel for the pleasure of ladies and gentlemen were also in place, and occasional free demonstrations were to be offered to the children of club members. This, nevertheless, appears to have been an unsuccessful endeavour. As of 1899 the Manège was converted into a venue for exhibiting moving pictures, with each new occupant making necessary adjustments to the space as they found fit.[1274]

It appears that moving pictures had found a home of their own in the converted building, and it is perhaps not surprising that in most previous writings on the history of cinema in Indonesia, the Manège was identified as the first venue in which moving pictures were screened.[1275] Ten Broeke's American Biograph was the first entrepreneur found in this research to use the Manège at Tanah Abang as an exhibition space for moving pictures in 1899 and 1900, followed by the Netherlands Bioscope Company in late 1900 and early 1901.[1276] Other major occupants of the Manège included Salzwedel's Java Biorama in 1901 and Abdulally Esoofally's Royal Bioscope during his many visits from 1903 to 1906.[1277] By 1907 the Manège was essentially perceived as a permanent venue, and the conversion of such a space was further suggested to other enterprising companies, for whom the Batavia Theatre was too expensive or too big.[1278]

As Cine Lumen, the "appropriately decorated permanent building" of the Manège pledged to "[...] excel in clarity and stability compared to other

[1273] "Nederlandsch-Indië", *Bataviaasch-Handelsblad* (8 January 1884). Charging a membership fee of ƒ 2.50 per month, in addition to the projected income from riding lessons and dressage, it was estimated that 200 members would be sufficient to cover the operating costs.

[1274] M. J. Fuchs and his company underwent several cycles. In 1885 it became a public limited company, with Mr. Fuchs staying on as managing director until 1895. In 1897 Fuchs became involved in the business of a competing carriage-building company, but this was unsuccessful and he ended up selling it to the company bearing his name (Wright, *Twentieth Century Impressions of Netherlands India*, 461).

[1275] See Biran, *Sejarah Film 1900–1950*, 27.

[1276] Advertisement, *Bintang Barat* (21 April 1899); Advertisement, *Bataviaasch Nieuwsblad* (2 April 1900); Advertisement, *Het Nieuws van den Dag voor Nederlandsch-Indië* (1 December 1900).

[1277] Advertisement, *Bataviaasch Nieuwsblad* (16 September 1901); Advertisement, *Bintang Betawi* (24 March 1903); Advertisement, *Het Nieuws van den Dag voor Nederlandsch-Indië* 20 December 1904); Advertisement, *Bintang Batavia* (18 July 1905); Advertisement, *Bataviaasch Nieuwsblad* (7 June 1906). Other less enduring dwellers in the Manège included the American Animatograph in 1904, Strauss's Oriental Amusements Company with a Cineograph in March 1905, the Urban Bioscope in June 1905; the Netherlands Indies Biograph Company in November 1905, the Chrono in March 1906 (Advertisement, *Bintang Betawi* (2 September 1904); Advertisement, *Het Nieuws van den Dag voor Nederlandsch-Indië* (17 March 1905); Advertisement, *Kabar Perniagaan* (13 June 1905); Advertisement, *Taman Sari* (30 October 1905); Advertisement, *Het Nieuws van den Dag voor Nederlandsch-Indië* (15 March 1906)). Others yet, like the Java Cineograph Company, chose to station their tent next to the Manège, leading to direct competition in close quarters ("Nederlandsch-Indië", *Bataviaasch Nieuwsblad* (23 September 1905)). The Royal Vio performed at the Manège on and off throughout 1906, in February–March, May–June, and September–October, while the Royal Bioscope and Cine Lumen filled the gaps in between (Advertisement, *Het Nieuws van den Dag voor Nederlandsch-Indië* (1 February 1906); Advertisement, *Bataviaasch Nieuwsblad* (11 May 1906); Advertisement, *Java-Bode* (13 September 1906)). The Royal Bioscope performed at the Manège from June to August (Advertisement, *Bataviaasch Nieuwsblad* (7 June 1906)). Cine Lumen was there in November and returned again at the beginning of 1907 (Advertisement, *Het Nieuws van den Dag voor Nederlandsch-Indië* (6 November 1906); Advertisement, *Het Nieuws van den Dag voor Nederlandsch-Indië* (1 February 1907)).

[1278] "Cine Lumen", *Het Nieuws van den Dag voor Nederlandsch-Indië* (5 February 1907).

cinemas, while the subjects, which the Cine Lumen has selected from Europe, [were to] consist of interesting views of nature and of funny, especially exciting, comical films".[1279] It offered two shows per night, the first from 7 pm to 8.30 pm and the second from 9.30 pm to 11 pm, with ticket prices ranging from $f\,2$ for box seats, $f\,1.50$ for first class, $f\,1$ for second class, $f\,0.50$ for third class, and $f\,0.25$ for fourth class (for "Natives").[1280] Ticket prices appear to have remained unchanged up until 1912, when the ten per cent tax on public entertainment went into effect.[1281] The film screenings were accompanied by a grand piano.[1282] Cine Lumen prided itself on its selection of Pathé films and on the fact that it functioned as a first-run cinema, with programme changes twice per week. All Pathé films were premiered at Cine Lumen and only after four days of screenings at the Manège were offered for sale at discounted prices to other cinema companies.[1283] According to the information provided in advertisements, effectively, this meant that for the first fourteen days of every month Cine Lumen showed exclusively Pathé films, after which they could be sold and sent to other moving picture companies in the Indies.[1284] Cine Lumen's programmes included "[...] images from Europe, America and Asia, but one can also see pictures of Java".[1285] Presumably not all films on the programme were Pathé productions, but those were certainly the ones highlighted. Not all pictures shown were moving pictures, either. In 1906, when the programme advertised pictures from the recent expedition to Bali, an article later clarified that "[...] in between the films, lantern plates with images of the latest Bali expedition will be exhibited".[1286]

Initially, entrepreneurs who were interested in acquiring Pathé Frères films were referred to Het Centrum for further details. As of August 1907, Pathé agent F. Dreyfus was located in Singapore, serving the entire region of Southeast Asia.[1287] He was immediately seeking an "Experienced Traveller for Java; must have good references and knowledge of travelling for business".[1288] In September 1908, an official Pathé agency was opened at no. 14 Rijswijkstraat in Weltevreden, advertising as follows: "In stock all types of Appliances, Components, Electric motors etc. With every new boat arriving supply of the

1279 Advertisement, *Het Nieuws van den Dag voor Nederlandsch-Indië* (30 January 1907).
1280 Advertisement, *Het Nieuws van den Dag voor Nederlandsch-Indië* (1 February 1907).
1281 Advertisement, *Het Nieuws van den Dag voor Nederlandsch-Indië* (27 April 1912).
1282 "Cine Lumen", *Java-Bode* (27 January 1910).
1283 Advertisement, *Het Nieuws van den Dag voor Nederlandsch-Indië* (30 January 1907).
1284 Advertisement, *Soerabaiasch-Handelsblad* (5 February 1907).
1285 "Cine Lumen", *Taman Sari* (26 April 1910).
1286 "Cine Lumen", *Het Nieuws van den Dag voor Nederlandsch-Indië* (7 November 1906).
1287 Advertisement, *Eastern Daily Mail* (8 August 1907).
1288 Advertisement, *Eastern Daily Mail* (12 August 1907). Dreyfus also placed advertisements for Pathé's film rentals and phonograph records in the local newspapers of the Indies, in both Dutch and Malay (Advertisement, *Soerabaiasch-Handelsblad* (26 August 1907); Advertisement, *Bintang Soerabaia* (25 August 1907)). He was possibly initially relying on the services of alcohol traders, J. Garreau Frères, which had offices in Buitenzorg (Bogor), Batavia, Semarang, and Surabaya, and were advertising Pathé films for sale as of early 1908 (Advertisement, *Nieuwe Soerabaja Courant* (3 February 1908)).

Latest Films (uncoloured). ƒ 60 per meter."[1289] Pathé's agent in Batavia, a man by the name L. Schwartz, was apparently rather proactive.[1290] When the *Java-Bode* wrote that the famous Pathé Frères was also the owner of Cine Lumen, he immediately contacted the editors, asking to clarify that Pathé was not the owner but only provided Cine Lumen with films.[1291] It was not beyond him to call newspaper editors in other cities, to protest unfavourable reviews of Pathé films.[1292] Beyond having the most immediate access to Pathé films in the Indies, Cine Lumen also boasted that it would benefit from the newest technologies introduced by Pathé, with new devices first being introduced at the Manège in Tanah Abang.[1293]

At the end of the first decade of the twentieth century, the Manège at Tanah Abang was ready for a face lift. "In terms of décor, furnishings and convenience, Surabaya still holds the crown, although performances there only take place in a tent. The owners of Cine Lumen have now realised this and will introduce [such upgrades] themselves, shortly reopening a restored building that meets competitive, modern demands for Europeans and natives. What we have heard of the plans sounds very good to us."[1294] The management of Cine Lumen circulated handbills to the public explaining the move:

> The growing interest in cinema performances in general has led us to the decision to introduce the most necessary renovations to the Manège building in Tanah Abang and to turn Cine Lumen into a venue that complies with the most modern demands. As is well known, Cine Lumen continues to screen the best and newest in the field of cinema and thanks to a contract we have signed with the famous firm Pathé Frères in Paris, the public can be assured that Cine Lumen does not stay behind.[1295]

In fact, during the renovation of Cine Lumen, the Globe Bioscope, yet another cinema theatre that underwent several rounds of renovations, was promoted to be the first to premiere new Pathé films.[1296]

When Cine Lumen reopened in late November, the responses were indeed enthusiastic. "The box seats have indeed become box seats, one is seated there easily and cosily, the entrances are much improved, etc. etc. To be convinced, go have a look yourself. No one expects so much convenience in any other

---

1289 Advertisement, *Java-Bode* (7 September 1908).

1290 L. Schwartz's name started appearing on Pathé advertisements as of the beginning of 1910, but it is not clear whether he served as agent already since 1908 (Advertisement, *Java-Bode* (29 January 1910)). He was so successful that his name was still mentioned as Pathé's agent for Java and the Netherlands Indies in a Pathé document from 1921 (see Stéphanie Salmon, *Pathé: À la conquête du cinéma 1896–1929* (Paris: Éditions Tallandier, 2014), 475). I would like to thank Sabine Lenk for pointing this out to me.

1291 "Cine Lumen", *Java-Bode* (27 May 1909); "Pathé Frères", *Java-Bode* (29 May 1909).

1292 "De Bende van Pathé", *Soerabaiasch-Handelsblad* (26 October 1909).

1293 "Alweer iets nieuws", *Java-Bode* (18 June 1909).

1294 "Cine-Lumen", *Java-Bode* (6 October 1910).

1295 "Cine Lumen", *Java-Bode* (19 November 1910).

1296 "Globe-bioscope", *Het Nieuws van den Dag voor Nederlandsch-Indië* (12 October 1910); "Globe-bioscoop", *Java-Bode* (18 October 1910). See further on Globe Bioscope in Section 5.3.3.

Indies cinema. Also the programme is such that the entrance fee to the Cine Lumen is more than justified."[1297] Nevertheless, the quality of the projection was not necessarily better. The *Bataviaasch Nieuwsblad* at first pointed out that the distance between the device and the screen was too big, so the images projected were not clear and not shown in full width.[1298] A repeat visit a few days later produced a better result and review: "The canvas is enlarged to 8x8 meters, so every image emerges in its entirety".[1299] Fire hazard was another concern addressed in the renovation, following the events at Pasar Baru's Flying Bioscope (see further in Section 5.3.3). The new setup of the device was placed outside the hall, whereas before the device was located inside, just above the door leading in and out of the hall, meaning that, if a film caught on fire, spectators were at grave risk when running for the exit.[1300]

5.3.2 Variety at Mangga Besar: The Oriental Bioscope at Tio Tek Kang's Thalia Theatre, 1910–1913

The case of the Oriental Bioscope at Thalia Theatre differs from other moving picture shows in Batavia in this period, since the venue was a *komedi* theatre which was not purely dedicated to screening films. It was in fact the kind of venue envisioned by Surabaya, Semarang and Medan as well, but which was never executed due to funding shortage. Thalia Theatre, the new variety theatre building in Mangga Besar, on the corner of Prinsenlaan and Molenvliet, was owned by the Chinese Tio Tek Kang and was intended as a venue for various types of popular entertainment forms: from *komedi stambul* and operetta troupes, through magicians and marionette companies, to moving picture shows.[1301] The original permit from the Municipal Council was for the construction of a permanent building for *bangsawan* shows, and the ground was to be leased for ten cents per square meter per year, subject to approval of the building plans by the Council.[1302] Construction ran over schedule, and Tio Tek Kang sought a permit extension for the building plans which was approved.[1303] He was simultaneously lobbying for further development of Glodok, wishing to attain a ten-year lease on the entire main square and be given a permit to rent it out to "natives and Indies-born Foreign Orientals" for opening shop houses.[1304] Despite the potential profit for the Municipality,

1297 "Cine Lumen", *Java-Bode* (21 November 1910).
1298 "Cine Lumen", *Bataviaasch Nieuwsblad* (26 November 1910).
1299 "Cine Lumen", *Bataviaasch Nieuwsblad* (30 November 1910).
1300 Ibid.
1301 "Thalia", *Bataviaasch Nieuwsblad* (9 February 1909).
1302 "Gemeenteraad van Batavia", *Bataviaasch Nieuwsblad* (21 September 1907); "Bataviaasche gemeenteraad", *Het Nieuws van den Dag voor Nederlandsch-Indië* (30 October 1907). The final agreement with Tio Tek Kang was signed in December 1907 ("Gemeenteraad van Batavia", *Het Nieuws van den Dag voor Nederlandsch-Indië* (24 December 1907)).
1303 "Gemeenteraad", *Het Nieuws van den Dag voor Nederlandsch-Indië* (26 September 1908).
1304 "Gemeenteraad van Batavia", *Bataviaasch Nieuwsblad* (19 October 1908).

there still seemed to be some consternation about leasing an entire square to one entrepreneur, and the request was never authorised.[1305]

Six weeks before Thalia Theatre opened to the public in February 1909, journalists were already invited to get a first glimpse of the facilities under advanced stages of construction. Some were dismissive of the choice of name, dubbed after the Greek muse of comedy, which was emblazoned on the façade of the Chinese venue in large colourful letters. "Is Chinese mythology so lacking in fair muses?" remarked the Batavia correspondent of *Soerabaiasch-Handelsblad*.[1306] Others were more supportive and, despite the fact that it was difficult to judge how the theatre would hold in terms of the acoustics, anything concerning safety and ventilation was rated highly.

A detailed report in *Het Nieuws van den Dag van Nederlandsch-Indië* provides a vivid image of what spectators were expected to find at the venue.[1307] Entering from the driveway through a large hall, eight stairs led to the foyer, which extended over the whole length of the first floor. To the left were large doors leading to the Prinsenlaan or to elevated seating for the fourth class seats. To the right were doors leading to the box close to the stage (*loge d'avant-scène*) for visitors of rank. The parterre, to be separated into two tiers of seating, was equipped with chairs and built at an incline, so even spectators in the rear would be able to see well. Bordering the sides of the stage was a smaller section of first class seats, while in the rear of the hall was a large elevated room with benches for the fourth class seats. On the remote side of the foyer on the first floor were another eight stairs, which led to a corridor at the back of the building and emergency exits, allowing for rapid egress from all sides.[1308] The space between the stage and seats was very deep, and a small area was reserved under the spectators' seats, for the use of a small orchestra if required for a performance. Eight dressing rooms were available behind the stage. The lighting was still provisionally gas-lit, until the Electricity Company could extend its coverage to the Prinsenlaan. The materials used for construction were mostly iron and stone: the crossbars of the floor of the parterre were made of steel, and pressed steel plates were used for the ceiling. A very large, airy space was created to make sure there was good ventilation, in addition to the use of several small vents, and although the roof was made out of galvanized iron, it remained pleasantly cool inside even during the hottest hours of the day. "In short, the new theatre is apparently not built 'on the cheap'", the report concluded.[1309] "A large, well-equipped building of this kind, where for instance moving picture shows can be given, magicians and variety theatres perform,

---

1305 "Raadsoverzicht", *Bataviaasch Nieuwsblad* (15 March 1909).

1306 "Uit Batavia", *Soerabaiasch-Handelsblad* (14 October 1908).

1307 "De Nieuwe Schouwburg", *Het Nieuws van den Dag voor Nederlandsch-Indië* (18 November 1908).

1308 The Municipal Council later expropriated an additional portion of 39 over 2 meters from the Public Native school bordering on the square at Mangga Besar, which enabled to broaden the road onto which the emergency exit from the theatre led out ("Gemeenteraad", *Het Nieuws van den Dag voor Nederlandsch-Indië* (21 November 1908)).

1309 "De Nieuwe Schouwburg", *Het Nieuws van den Dag voor Nederlandsch-Indië* (18 November 1908).

5 – Batavia: Capital of Chinese Cinema Venues

Figure 5–4. Interior of Thalia Theatre ca. 1920, picture postcard. Postcard publisher: Lie Tek Long [Greetings from Jakarta © Scott Merrillees and Equinox Publishing Jakarta.]

located in Batavia's middle [*middenstad*, i.e. between the *benedenstad* and *bovenstad*], as we may call it, has been required for a while."[1310]

The opening act at Thalia Theatre was a *komedi stambul* troupe, Indo's Komedie Vereeniging de "Eendracht", with the first show given for invited guests only. This did not stop non-invited residents of the surrounding area from showing up to marvel at the well-lit exterior. The large hall was completely full: "the elite of Batavia was there, and also Chinese and natives, from high finance and from the guild of dignitaries, respectively".[1311] The Dutch newspapers were not so convinced about the "content of this drama or comedy – we truly do not know what it was".[1312] The *Bataviaasch Nieuwsblad* wrote: "It was better than we expected. Of course, one does not go to see art as we understand it. Performances of *komedi stamboel* are only for the little man [*kleinen man*], for native and Chinese, who can easily understand and enjoy the at times dizzying complications, especially because of the gags and jokes of the indispensable clowns who know to keep the tone exactly."[1313] However, the report continued,

> [...] the main thing is the building; and that complies outstandingly. The big hall that offers space for up to 1,300 people is as airy as possible; the lighting is more than adequate; the stage meets all demands. For the Indies – a novelty: the inclined wooden floor can be lowered, to align with the couloir, for dance events. A

1310 Ibid.
1311 "Thalia", *Het Nieuws van den Dag voor Nederlandsch-Indië* (9 February 1909).
1312 Ibid., emphasis added.
1313 "Thalia", *Bataviaasch Nieuwsblad* (9 February 1909), emphases added.

building, as the designer Mr. Van der Tas intended, suited for various purposes: for the stage, for ballroom, to hold meetings, for moving picture shows, etc. etc. and all built with large pockets, tight and strong, neat, even tasteful. The owner, Mr. Tio Tek Kang, proved himself to be a generous host. A well-stocked buffet was available to the guests.[1314]

It was not long before the free drinks of the opening night and the initial excitement of local visitors subsided, permitting critique of the venue itself to rise to the surface:

> Since no one is actually concerned with what happens on the stage, it was barely noticed or entirely missed that the acoustics were very poor. But when the regular performances began – so far there have been only *stamboel* companies performing – the flaws of the new theatre quickly came to light. Besides for the fact that no one in the entire theatre could hear what was said on the stage, except for those seated in the front rows of the parterre, the inventiveness of the theatre's builder of covering the roof with zinc turned out to be less than clever! The rain made such an infernal rattle, that there was nothing at all one could understand anymore. These defects and the objection that the theatre is at least half an hour's drive outside the residential Weltevreden, have decreased the attendance at Thalia; and now the *Stamboel* troupe is scratching its head: the costs are not even covered. It has therefore already requested permission to be allowed to play again in a tent on the Koningsplein; that brings in more. This company could very well be regarded as a failure and the Chinese operator – who this time has not been so smart – will lose ƒ 500,000. But for all that, I dare say that even if the theatre had been flawless, it would not have drawn a crowd: here we have one theatre more than necessary.[1315]

As time went by, many of the glitches were ironed out, thanks to an alteration of the roof which very much improved the acoustics.[1316] There were some more success stories of performances, especially when gala events to benefit the Chinese schools or other charitable causes were held.[1317] Yet, the problem of drawing spectators from Weltevreden persisted. When the Thalia Theatre hosted a Dutch tenor singer, *Het Nieuws van den Dag voor Nederlandsch-Indië* remarked: "It is a pity that Thalia has the reputation of being so far away. This is not the case, the Zoo is at the same distance from the centre of Weltevreden, but the reputation is there. But visiting Thalia these days [...] can only be recommended."[1318]

Nevertheless, there were presumably "European" visitors to the Thalia Theatre, at times resulting in clashes with staff or other spectators. A spectator identified as "A. J. de W., resident of the Koningsplein", was enraged when one

---

1314 Ibid.

1315 "Van Java", *Sumatra Post* (16 April 1909), emphases added. Other scandals included a puppet theatre show that had to be discontinued after the first performance, much to the discontent of the raging spectators, when it turned out the impresario brought the marionettes to Batavia against the actual owner's consent ("Grand Theatre Guignol", *Het Nieuws van den Dag voor Nederlandsch-Indië* (9 May 1910)).

1316 "The Indra Zanzibar Royal Theatrical Coy", *Het Nieuws van den Dag voor Nederlandsch-Indië* (5 July 1909).

1317 "Chineesch Tooneelgezelschap", *Het Nieuws van den Dag voor Nederlandsch-Indië* (15 June 1909); "Oneenigheid", *Het Nieuws van den Dag voor Nederlandsch-Indië* (5 July 1909); "Chineesche Tooneelvereniging", *Het Nieuws van den Dag voor Nederlandsch-Indië* (1 August 1910).

1318 "Een Hollandsche tenor-zanger", *Het Nieuws van den Dag voor Nederlandsch-Indië* (6 June 1910).

of the Chinese employees pointed out he had taken the wrong seat. The "[...] art loving Koningsplein-resident was so furious, that he 'took off his coat' and slammed the Chinese against the ground. The latter sustained a serious head injury, and another employee was assaulted by the agitated opera visitor."[1319] The Chinese men subsequently filed a complaint against their assailant. Another incident involved young officers of the Royal Packet Navigation Company (KPM), who were reportedly showing increasingly bad habits and causing mischief during performances at Thalia Theatre.

> On Monday evening the actions of these gentlemen reached the height of impropriety. After first having made Noordwijk and the restaurants there unsafe, the group went to the Thalia Theatre. The way the drunken ship's officers behaved there is beneath all criticism. They disturbed the public, they interrupted the performance, they sat in seats not meant for them, yelling, screaming, drunk-male-play, anyway, one knows the pleasures to which the gentlemen surrender when they are 'off.' The police had more than its hands full in order to protect the audience against the 'gang,' and there is no softer word for it. One of the biggest troublemakers was dragged outside by the collar by two guardians, but he was released there, unfortunately. The police was on the streets all night seeking to maintain law and order. It seems to us that a few arrests, preferably handcuffed, would have served better. [...] It is high time to put an end to the inappropriate behaviour of these young people once and for all.[1320]

Moving picture shows were never intended to be a main fixture at the Thalia Theatre, and were only occasionally included on variety programmes in between other acts.[1321] This situation changed as of August 1910, when the Oriental Bioscope began to play "regularly" at Thalia Theatre.[1322] Later reports from 1912 claimed that the owner of the Oriental Bioscope was an Arab, but we cannot be sure that it was under the same ownership in 1910.[1323] The films on the Oriental Bioscope's programmes were advertised as originating from various companies, including Gaumont, Pathé Frères, and Éclair.[1324] *Het Nieuws van den Dag voor Nederlandsch-Indië* wrote in anticipation of the opening show: "The Oriental Bioscope begins a series of performances [at Thalia Theatre] and we know from experience that the films, which will be screened in Mangga Besar, are worth the trip over there".[1325]

1319 "Een aristocraat", *Het Nieuws van den Dag voor Nederlandsch-Indië* (1 March 1909).
1320 "Passagierende officieren der Paketvaart", *Het Nieuws van den Dag voor Nederlandsch-Indië* (20 April 1910).
1321 The first mention of moving pictures at Thalia found in this research was as part of a variety programme in June 1910 ("Een Hollandsche tenor-zanger", *Het Nieuws van den Dag voor Nederlandsch-Indië* (6 June 1910)).
1322 "Bioscopen", *Bataviaasch Nieuwsblad* (5 August 1910).
1323 "Bioscope Derma", *Taman Sari* (18 October 1912); "De liefdadigheids-bioscope", *Het Nieuws van den Dag voor Nederlandsch-Indië* (17 October 1912). According to these reports, the Arab entrepreneur performing at the Thalia Theatre requested an exemption from tax on public amusements for charity shows, which was refused when he did not name who would be the benefactor of the funds collected.
1324 Advertisement, *Bataviaasch Nieuwsblad* (5 August 1910). All films had recently arrived on board the steamship *Kawi*.
1325 "Oriental Bioscope", *Het Nieuws van den Dag voor Nederlandsch-Indië* (5 August 1910).

Nevertheless, its supposedly "regular" shows at Thalia Theatre came in intervals. The Oriental Bioscope initially took over the Thalia Theatre for a couple of weeks in August, offering shows three times a day – at 7.15 pm, 8.30 pm and 9.45 pm – with several programme changes. It returned again only at the end of November for a month of shows, once more, offered three times a day – at 7.15 pm, 8.45 pm and 10 pm.[1326] Another run of performances took place in March 1911, and then from September to December of that year.[1327] In 1912 the Oriental Bioscope was more prominent, but even then only for several months at a time: from March to June and from September to October.[1328] By 1913, it was only mentioned for a few shows in November, when it performed as part of the celebrations of the centenary of the Dutch regaining independence from the French (*Eeuwefeesten*).[1329]

By that point, it appears that there were better options for movie-going in the area, with more venues established during 1912 and 1913. Another variety theatre was planned to be built at Krekot by entrepreneur A. A. C. Abelain (sometimes spelled Abalain), owner of the Imperial Theatre in 1908–1909.[1330] The Walhalla Theatre was intended to rent out the space to moving picture companies, *stambul* troupes, and variety acts.[1331] Abelain was further considering forming an association of moving pictures entrepreneurs who had no building of their own, and offer them to give their performances at Walhalla for a small rental fee. The building plans looked promising: with a "[...] neat, spacious and airy [building], the nice façade makes a good impression".[1332] However, it seems that spectators of moving pictures ultimately preferred purpose-built cinema theatres for their movie-going experience, as may be inferred from the examples provided in the following sections.

5.3.3   Fire Hazard at Pasar Baru: Loa Soen Yang's Globe Bioscope, 1910-2009

The first mention of Chinese contractor Loa Soen Yang in connection with moving pictures appeared in the documents marking the formation of the Solar Bioscope Company Limited in 1908.[1333] He was one of no less than fourteen other Chinese shareholders in the company, including his brother Loa Soen

---

1326 Advertisement, *Het Nieuws van den Dag voor Nederlandsch-Indië* (28 November 1910).

1327 Advertisement, *Het Nieuws van den Dag voor Nederlandsch-Indië* (20 March 1911); Advertisement, *Pantjaran Warta* (9 September 1911); Advertisement, *Pantjaran Warta* (4 December 1911).

1328 Advertisement, *Bataviaasch Nieuwsblad* (25 March 1912); Advertisement, *Het Nieuws van den Dag voor Nederlandsch-Indië* (14 June 1912).

1329 Advertisement, *Het Nieuws van den Dag voor Nederlandsch-Indië* (14 September 1912); Advertisement, *Het Nieuws van den Dag voor Nederlandsch-Indië* (18 October 1912); Advertisement, *Bataviaasch Nieuwsblad* (5 November 1913). The awkwardness of these celebrations of Dutch liberation from the Napoleonic occupation, to be conducted on colonial soil itself under occupation by the Dutch, did not go unnoticed at the time. Particularly the expectation that Indonesians should partake in and even contribute funds to hold these festivities, drew outraged responses from various contemporary commentators. See Dijk, *The Netherlands Indies and the Great War*, 54–60; Anderson, *Imagined Communities*, 116–120.

1330 Advertisement, *Taman Sari* (26 January 1909).

1331 "Walhalla Theatre", *Het Nieuws van den Dag voor Nederlandsch-Indië* (10 July 1912).

1332 Ibid.

1333 *Extra Bijvoegsel der Javasche Courant* (18 September 1908), no. 75.

5 – Batavia: Capital of Chinese Cinema Venues

Tjoeij, all of them residents of Batavia.[1334] The company, established for a period of twenty-five years, aimed to deal in "Ordering and purchasing of a Bioscope [presumably referring to the device] with corresponding films and tools and to operate these".[1335] The Solar Bioscope did not have a fixed venue in Batavia but rather popped up at various locations in the period between July and December 1908: from Pasar Pisang Senen, through Pasar Baru, to Bungur.[1336] It also travelled to nearby Buitenzorg (Bogor) for sold-out shows, prompting the manager to extend the shed where the screenings took place by another six meters.[1337] The Solar Bioscope's programmes included "[...] very beautiful films, not only from Pathé, but also of English production".[1338] By early 1910 the Solar Bioscope appears to have been permanently stationed in a building at Meester Cornelis, where it was attended mostly by lower-ranked soldiers.[1339]

In 1910 Loa Soen Yang was also identified as the owner of the bamboo tent at Pasar Baru, which was referred to in advertisements and newspaper reports as the Flying Bioscope.[1340] As there was already one, if not more, active enterprises named "Flying Bioscope" travelling through Java, Sumatra and Celebes since 1907, it is not clear whether this was the same company that had now found a home in Pasar Baru, or whether this was simply the name chosen by Loa Soen Yang for the new cinema tent.[1341] Of "the otherwise well-equipped" venue, *Het Nieuws van den Dag voor Nederlandsch-Indië* wrote upon first visiting the Flying Bioscope in January 1910, the owner should consider slightly changing the staircase that leads to the box seats. At the moment, it was argued, "[...] it is almost impossible, particularly for the ladies, to climb down accident-free, especially if impatient visitors for the next show are already pushing to go upstairs".[1342]

1334 With a capital of 20,000 guilders and each share worth 500 guilders, the structure of shareholders upon establishment appeared to be split between members of various families: Hauw Tek Kong (two shares), Sie Tjeng Hong (two shares), Gouw Tjeng Soen (one share), Thong Kim Ho (two shares), Tio Tek Seng (one share), Loa Soen Yang (two shares), Khouw Keng Thaij (one share), Loa Soen Tjoei (one share), Tan Eng Soeij (one share), Tan Eng Siang (one share), Gouw Tjeng Tin (one share), Gouw Tjeng Soan (one share), Tan Tjan Soeij (one share), Gouw Tjeng Bie (one share). Ibid.

1335 Ibid.

1336 "Kabar Hindia", *Taman Sari* (15 July 1908); "Solar Bioscope", *Het Nieuws van den Dag voor Nederlandsch-Indië* (15 August 1908); Advertisement, *Het Nieuws van den Dag voor Nederlandsch-Indië* (18 December 1908).

1337 "Uit Buitenzorg", *Soerabaiasch-Handelsblad* (17 March 1909).

1338 Ibid.

1339 "Uit Meester Cornelis", *Het Nieuws van den Dag voor Nederlandsch-Indië* (21 February 1910).

1340 "De Brand in de Flying Bioscoop", *Java-Bode* (12 March 1910).

1341 I have found the Flying Bioscope in Batavia in December 1907 and in early 1908, in Kuta Raja in July 1908, back on Java a couple of months later for shows in Batavia, Buitenzorg (Bogor), Cilacap and Bandung, before heading out for a couple of months to Makassar in late 1909 (Advertisement, *Taman Sari* (23 December 1907); "Gambar Hidoep Flying Bioscope", *Sinar Atjeh* (27 July 1908); "Flijeng Bioscope", *Taman Sari* (28 October 1908); "Uit Buitenzorg", *Het Nieuws van den Dag voor Nederlandsch-Indië* (9 September 1908); "Tjilatjap", *De Locomotief* (25 January 1909); "Uit Bandoeng", *Soerabaiasch-Handelsblad* (5 July 1909); Advertisement, *Makasaarsche Courant* (4 August 1909)).

1342 "Flying Bioscope", *Het Nieuws van den Dag voor Nederlandsch-Indië* (24 January 1910).

This was not the only grievance that the Dutch newspapers had against the Flying Bioscope. When a month later the Flying Bioscope introduced on its programme a local view titled: "The Arrival of the new Governor-General and the departure of Mr. J. B. van Heutsz", it was reported that due to an error in the recording of the scenes, when the film was projected, the people, animals and objects on screen appeared to be moving approximately tenfold faster, leading to a highly comic result. For instance: "[...] the phlegmatic sheriff Heijnen flies with the speed of the first prize winner of the Marathon race at the Koningsplein. The advance of the Militia's guard of honour, with a band leading ahead, was executed at a pace which would reduce the Japanese storming Port Arthur to nothingness. The oncoming car of the Governor-General appears [...] as if blasted out of a cannon, and the first thought that goes through visitors' minds is: Why doesn't that driver immediately get a ticket? Also, the departure of Mr. Van Heutsz from Tanjong Priok made us all laugh with tears running down our cheeks. The former Viceroy flies out of the station, with nobody paying any attention, dashes across the runners to the stairs, which provide access to the mail steamer, leaping on board with a turkey's jump, almost without touching the stairs."[1343]

Another more serious gripe was voiced against the evening programmes "for gentlemen" offered by the Flying Bioscope, in which "[...] a few dozen decent people submit themselves to peeping pleasures: The bath of a *demi-mondaine* and what follows next, the pleasures of a hypnotist who compels a woman to undress, etc. And even more filth."[1344] The Assistant Resident should prohibit such obscene antics and revoke the exhibitors' license, the *Bataviaasch Nieuwsblad* commanded. The police claimed in response that no such obscene prints have been shown at the Flying Bioscope to date, suggesting the newspaper may have gotten false information from a competing cinema operator who was jealous of the Flying Bioscope's success.[1345] The newspaper nevertheless insisted that it had accurate information, suggesting that the Assistant Resident should also replace the chief of police.

It was not long before the state of affairs changed. In March 1910, a fire broke out at the Flying Bioscope's bamboo tent, quickly spreading to the adjacent *warungs* managed by Bio A Joen and Tji Siang Tan.[1346] All of these structures were in fact owned by Loa Soen Yang, the newspapers publicised, leading him to suffer a loss of approximately 5,000 guilders as a result.[1347] Reports in the newspapers believed that the fire was caused by a short circuit and, since it took

---

1343 "Flying Bioscope", *Het Nieuws van den Dag voor Nederlandsch-Indië* (24 February 1910).

1344 "Zedenbederf", *Bataviaasch Nieuwsblad* (2 March 1910), emphasis added.

1345 "De Politie helpt mee!", *Bataviaasch Nieuwsblad* (3 March 1910).

1346 "De Brand in de Flying Bioscoop", *Java-Bode* (12 March 1910); "Tenda bioscoop terbakar", *Pembrita Betawi* (12 March 1910).

1347 Loa Soen Yang owned various properties at Pasar Baru, and was seeking to acquire even more land ("Gemeenteraad van Batavia", *Het Nieuws van den Dag voor Nederlandsch-Indië* (13 June 1911) ("Gemeenteraad van Batavia", *Het Nieuws van den Dag voor Nederlandsch-Indië* (16 June 1911)).

place at 6.45 pm, the show had not yet commenced and luckily there were not many spectators in the tent.[1348] The exhibitor in his box was the first one to notice the fire breaking out, and he immediately exited and left everyone in the lurch. Thanks to the fact that the doors were still open, the few dozen spectators who were inside could step out quickly. "Not even five minutes later everything was ablaze; everything happened so fast, it can be said with absolute certainty that if the fire were caused during the performance, certainly some people would have been found dead."[1349] The tent was beyond saving, even with the fire-extinguishing equipment on hand in the tent, and it took another half an hour and extra help from passing by soldiers to put out the fire and prevent it from spreading further. "It is to be hoped that the necessary precautions will be taken in the future. We really must not wait until some people are burnt alive", was the grim conclusion of a Surabaya-based newspaper reporting about the incident.[1350] Newspapers continued to caution against hazardous sites, such as the sheds during the Pasar Malam of 1913, which still used palm leaves as covering, although an extra chamber was constructed to provide more protection. "That helps a little bit, but the danger remains. Oh, why not. Everything has been fine for so long, right?"[1351]

Newspapers, at least, were aware of the risk of fire even earlier: in 1908, after reporting about fire in a circus tent in Germany, during a moving picture show in Ludwigshafen, in which the spectators were resourceful and cut open the linen tent to escape, *Bataviaasch Nieuwsblad* suggested there was a lesson to be learned from this in the Indies, where tents are made of highly flammable materials. "Do not look for the exit; simply go through the wall to the outside. In case of fire in the theatre, that would be the best method as well. Do not run for the official exit, causing panic to occur, but simply leap out of the foyers, close enough to the ground."[1352]

Just a couple of weeks after the fire, the cinema at Pasar Baru had risen from the ashes and opened its doors to the public under the name Globe Bioscope.[1353] During the renovation, which took place under close municipal supervision, special care was taken to avoid the risk of fire. The material chosen for construction this time was zinc, but the building was still found to contain too much bamboo upon the final inspection. However, it was agreed that the utmost possible had been done to avoid danger by isolating the room where the projector and films were located.[1354] The box of the projectionist was

---

1348 "De Bioscoop-Brand te Batavia", *Soerabaiasch-Handelsblad* (14 March 1910).

1349 Ibid.

1350 Ibid. Reports about the fire at the Flying Bioscope were picked up by newspapers in Dutch and Malay across the archipelago, for example, in Semarang and in Medan: "Bioscoop Terbakar", *Selompret Melajoe* (15 March 1910); "De bioscoop brand te Batavia", *Sumatra Post* (30 March 1910).

1351 "Politionele Voorzorgen", *Bataviaasch Nieuwsblad* (1 February 1913).

1352 "Een goede les voor Indië", *Bataviaasch Nieuwsblad* (3 September 1908).

1353 "De Bioscoop op Pasar Baroe", *Java-Bode* (1 April 1910).

1354 "Bioscoop-tent", *Het Nieuws van den Dag voor Nederlandsch-Indië* (6 April 1910).

further covered with asbestos and, moreover, a large bucket of water was set next to the projector which could be used immediately in case of fire.

As a further public relations stunt, the Globe Bioscope hitched a ride on the just-arrived Dayaks, brought to Batavia by A. H. Lorentz after his explorations in New Guinea.[1355] The Dayak people are native to Borneo, but several dozen Dayaks were recruited as porters and trekkers to accompany the expedition. During the day the Dayaks were "drawn through the city to view various sights", *Bataviaasch Nieuwsblad* wrote. "Tonight they will attend a cinema screening at Pasar Baroe. There are many films shown which are understandable to them."[1356] *Het Nieuws van den Dag voor Nederlandsch-Indië* further expounded the point: "The notion of 'understandable' is flexible. Whether the men of nature [*natuurmenschen*], for instance, can 'learn' much from the Parisian theatre film, 'Conjugal cheating', we are quite doubtful. And also 'the exploits of Tartarin' will go past them. Dayaks are generally more men-of-action than sharp conversation-makers like Tartarin."[1357] Debating the Dayaks' capability to fully grasp the content of films and to appreciate this modern technology continued to preoccupy newspapers and residents of Batavia over the next few days.

The announcement that the Dayaks were going to attend the Globe Bioscope attracted many curious spectators to Pasar Baru who were hoping to catch a glimpse of the Dayaks for themselves.

> They probably fancied themselves to behold [the Dayaks] dressed in special attire, possibly armed with a bow and arrow and the compulsory head sash. But they did not have much of it. They were ordinary, calm natives in coolie clothing [*koeliepakje*], which looked pretty distasteful with their long hair under the scarf. They themselves, however, had a good time, as Mr. Lorentz, who accompanied them, told us. The most beautiful film they found was "to the heart of the past". The fanciful scenes with dragons and other treats went over their heads.[1358]

Other films on the programme, according to another report, included: "Planting and preparing tea, the state of affairs in a chicken-breeding facility, scenes from Burma, a few seascapes, with many warships [...]".[1359] It was especially the images of seascapes that reportedly fascinated the Dayaks. As "mountain people of the hinterland of Sintang", *Het Nieuws van den Dag voor Nederlandsch-Indië* speculated, they were probably drawn to these images, "for the same reason that Dutch people admire distinctive mountain landscapes: the unusual."[1360] The *Java-Bode*, however, found the chicken-breeding scene to have

---

1355 This 1909–1910 expedition to New Guinea was the second made by Dutch explorer and diplomat Hendrikus Albertus Lorentz, with a previous expedition preceding in 1907 and a third one to follow in 1913.

1356 "Dajaks in Batavia", *Bataviaasch Nieuwsblad* (5 April 1910).

1357 "De Dajaks naar de Bioscope!", *Het Nieuws van den Dag voor Nederlandsch-Indië* (5 April 1910). Possible title: LES EXPLOITS DU JEUNE TARTARIN (Pathé Frères, 1910).

1358 "De Dajaks in de Bioscoop", *Bataviaasch Nieuwsblad* (6 April 1910).

1359 "Dajaks in de bioscoop", *Het Nieuws van den Dag voor Nederlandsch-Indië* (6 April 1910). Possible film titles: LE THÉ: CULTURE, RÉCOLTE, PRÉPARATION INDUSTRIELLE (Pathé Frères, 1909), L'ÉLÉVAGE DES POULES DE RACES (Pathé Frères, 1909), INDIA: SCENES IN BURMAH aka SCENES IN BURMAH (Urban, 1909).

been an inappropriate choice because of the barbarous manner in which the fattening of chickens was represented on screen.[1361]

The Dayaks, *Het Nieuws van den Dag voor Nederlandsch-Indië* observed, were "gaping with admiration at all the beautiful and surprising things that were screened", which were explained with the help of a lecturer in Malay. In response to the moving images they were making "mostly naïve, often very witty remarks" amongst themselves.[1362] The reaction of one of the Dayaks was found to be particularly striking:

> For a while, like all the others, he enjoyed the moving, true to life coloured images on the canvas. The illusion that he was seeing reality proved to have bitten him as well. However, when he turned around, he wanted to see where all this was coming from, and it took a whole while before he stopped to gaze at the small, brightly lit opening of the projection device. The puzzle – how everything emerged from there, without him perceiving anything there, was too much for him.[1363]

While it appears that the content of the films selected seemed to strike a chord with the Dayaks, it was the encounter with the technology that proved to be incomprehensible. These kinds of comments were very much in line with racial conceptions of the day, suggesting that technology was beyond the "native" population's grasp, and several examples of this kind have been mentioned here in previous chapters.[1364] The fact that this screening occurred at a Chinese cinema house adds another layer of complexity to this highly racially coded situation.[1365] During the day, the Dayaks were taken around by their European "discoverer", showing them the wonders of big city life, just as much as they were themselves being put on display for the pleasure of urban residents. In the evening, it was the Asian exhibitor with an *explicateur* speaking Malay who was in charge of displaying the wonders of Western technology to the "Natives" from the jungles of Borneo. Another interesting aspect is the parallel spectatorial process at play in this screening situation: the Dayaks were being watched in the act of watching films, in a kind of live version of the so-called "rube films", which show the naïve, intuitive responses of a country bumpkin in the West to their first encounter with moving pictures.[1366] Finally, the journalist here, who was either Dutch or of ethnically mixed descent,

---

1360 Ibid.

1361 "De Dajaks in de Globe-Bioscoop", *Java-Bode* (6 April 1910).

1362 "Dajaks in de bioscoop", *Het Nieuws van den Dag voor Nederlandsch-Indië* (6 April 1910).

1363 Ibid.

1364 See Larkin's writing about the "colonial sublime" in Larkin, *Signal and Noise*, 38–39.

1365 See also Tofighian's discussion of "Native astonishment" and Western technology disseminated by Asian exhibitors in Southeast Asia in Tofighian, *Blurring the Colonial Binary*, 90–93.

1366 "Uncle Josh" films or "Rube" films were made since the emergence of cinema itself, showing a member of a cinema audience who confuses the representations on the screen within the screen for reality. See Thomas Elsaesser, "Discipline through Diegesis: The Rube Film between 'Attractions' and 'Narrative Integration', in Wanda Strauven (ed.), *The Cinema of Attractions Reloaded* (Amsterdam: Amsterdam University Press, 2006), 205–223.

appears to have been just as awed by the Dayaks' reactions as they were supposedly amazed by the attractions on and off screen.

Once the memories of the fire settled, and following the excitement presented by the Dayaks' visit, the Globe Bioscope quickly established a reputation for itself. Its performances took place no less than three times per day, at 7 pm, 8.30 pm and 10 pm, with ticket prices ranging from f 1 for a box seat, f 0.50 for first class, f 0.25 for second class, f 0.10 for third class ("Natives"), and children below age ten and military below the rank of officer were offered a half price discount in the box and first class, or a ticket at f 0.15 for second class. The wives of soldiers were nevertheless expected to pay full price.[1367] Lighting in the cinema tent was considered to be better than that of its competitors, and the selection of films, which included local views, such as a boat race, or the films of international stars such as Max Linder, were found to be very good and up to date.[1368]

When the tent of the Excelsior Bioscope, stationed at Defensielijn van den Bosch on the eastern edge of Weltevreden, prohibited the attendance of soldiers, the military men marched right over to Pasar Baru for shows at the Globe Bioscope.[1369] Other spectators patronising the Globe Bioscope appear to have been of higher socio-economic class, if to judge by the kinds of items found and/or reported as stolen. For example, a Chinese woman complained that, upon leaving the cinema theatre, her diamond pin was stolen by a "Native".[1370] In another case, a golden bracelet was found at the Globe Bioscope and the owner was invited to retrieve it at the police station.[1371]

As mentioned above, during the renovation of the Cine Lumen, the Globe Bioscope was promoted to be the first to premiere new films.[1372] The Globe Bioscope was itself upgraded in December 1910, but, in this case, the new building was constructed just behind the existing one, so it did not disrupt the continuation of shows. The new building, the *Bataviaasch Nieuwsblad* exclaimed, "now deserves to bear the name Cinema theatre".[1373] "The lighting is more than adequate; the distribution of seats was executed with care; the entrances and exits, a sore point in cinemas, are spacious and finally there is also a buffet where one can get refreshments. It is a building just as a cinema should be", the *Bataviaasch Nieuwsblad* continued to sing praises.[1374] When

1367 Advertisement, *Het Nieuws van den Dag voor Nederlandsch-Indië* (18 June 1910).

1368 "Globe Bioscope", *Het Nieuws van den Dag voor Nederlandsch-Indië* (16 August 1910); Advertisement, *Het Nieuws van den Dag voor Nederlandsch-Indië* (28 June 1910); "Globe Bioscope", *Pantjaran Warta* (22 June 1910).

1369 "Op den index!", *Het Nieuws van den Dag voor Nederlandsch-Indië* (15 April 1910).

1370 "Politie-nieuws", *Het Nieuws van den Dag voor Nederlandsch-Indië* (10 April 1909).

1371 "Gevonden Voorwerpen", *Het Nieuws van den Dag voor Nederlandsch-Indië* (14 August 1911). Bicycle theft outside the cinema tent was quite common as well ("Politie-Nieuws", *Het Nieuws van den Dag voor Nederlandsch-Indië* (14 December 1908)).

1372 "Globe-bioscope", *Het Nieuws van den Dag voor Nederlandsch-Indië* (12 October 1910); "Globe-bioscoop", *Java-Bode* (18 October 1910). See further on Cine Lumen in Section 5.3.1.

1373 "Nederlandsch-Indië", *Bataviaasch Nieuwsblad* (2 December 1910).

1374 Ibid.

approaching the cinema, the ticket counter was to be found on the left and the buffet – on the right. Inside, the different classes were "separated by neat wooden walls". [1375] The canvas was found to be "quite large" and very nice films were screened on the opening night.[1376] The Malay newspapers similarly drew their readers' attention to the opening of the new building, mentioning that journalists were invited for a first visit to the venue ahead of the public and were treated to a pre-screening of the programme.[1377] Beyond film screenings every night, there were occasionally other entertainment forms available at the Globe Bioscope, such as magic shows.[1378] At this time, Loa Soen Yang also entered a leasing agreement for the sum of 10,600 guilders per year for a piece of land at Pasar Baru which was intended by the Municipal Council to be the location of yet another cinema tent.[1379] It later transpired that he simply wanted to keep away any potential competition, and the land was left unutilized.

Nevertheless, Loa Soen Yang could not escape the risk of fire after all. One morning in October 1911, at about 8 am, when he was checking some new films in the front gallery of his home, also located in Pasar Baru, a servant who had assisted him accidentally dropped a film on a lit lamp, instantly igniting a large flame that spilled over to a nearby bottle of gasoline. Flames blazed high, especially since there were other gasoline bottles in the front gallery, and the house was soon up in flames. By nine o'clock, with the help of the fire engine squad, police and other passers-by who jumped in to help, the fire was put out. Everything in the front gallery was totally lost, but the rescuers still managed to drag out from the inside gallery a jumble of partially damaged and burned furniture, including some cabinets and a piano. All the salvaged goods were laid out in the garden, beside the nearly immobilised servant who had caused the accident. The damage to the house itself was estimated at 10,000 guilders, on top of which the films burned were reportedly worth 15,000 guilders in total. Nothing was insured as Loa Soen Yang had recently terminated his insurance.[1380] By contrast, the "Concurrent" restaurant next door, which also burned down in the incident, had been insured for the amount of 2,000 guilders just two days before the fire.[1381] This, and the fact that nobody had shown up from the restaurant to check on the damage immediately after, raised the police's suspicion, but no direct link to the fire incident was ever found. To add to Loa Soen Yang's strife, his recent application to the Municipal Council, requesting a permit to offer moving picture shows at the Batavia

---

1375 "Globe-bioscoop", *Java-Bode* (2 December 1910).
1376 Ibid.
1377 "Komedie", *Pantjaran Warta* (2 December 1910); "Globe Bioskop", *Taman Sari* (3 December 1910).
1378 Advertisement, *Het Nieuws van den Dag voor Nederlandsch-Indië* (18 December 1914).
1379 "Een voordeeltje voor de gemeentekas", *Het Nieuws van den Dag voor Nederlandsch-Indië* (17 February 1912).
1380 "Brand", *Bataviaasch Nieuwsblad* (11 October 1911).
1381 "Het brand te Passar Baroe", *Het Nieuws van den Dag voor Nederlandsch-Indië* (13 October 1911).

Figure 5–5. The Globe Bioscope, ca. 1930, picture postcard. [Greetings from Jakarta © Scott Merrillees and Equinox Publishing Jakarta.]

Theatre for a period of one year, was rejected, following an unfavourable opinion by the Theatre Commission.[1382] Not surprisingly perhaps, in light of these events, in 1912 "the famous Cinema Theatre" at Pasar Baru was transformed by Loa Soen Yang into a public limited company: the Company for Operation of Cinemas and Trade in Films Ltd. ("Naamlooze Vennootschap Maatschappij tot Exploitatie van Bioscopen en handel in films").[1383] Mr. J. Frank, who was also one of the owners of the Elite Bioscope, was appointed as company manager and Loa Soen Yang stayed on as member of the board of directors.[1384] In 1915 it was rumoured the Loa Soen Yang was going bankrupt; however, he quickly clarified that this was not the case but that he had to cover debts of his father-in-law.[1385] Nevertheless, this financial entanglement forced him to put up some of his property for sale in auction.[1386] Either way, the Globe Bioscope, in the various building forms and under several owners, continued to be a permanent fixture in the local movie-going scene for decades to come, closing down permanently only in 2009 (see Figures 5–5 and 5–6).[1387] In the mid-1910s it held the monopoly over Asta Nielsen films, and it was possibly the first to screen a "talking movie" in Batavia in 1929.[1388]

1382 "Gemeenteraad van Batavia", *Het Nieuws van den Dag voor Nederlandsch-Indië* (22 December 1911).
1383 "Een goede zaak", *Het Nieuws van den Dag voor Nederlandsch-Indië* (30 March 1912).
1384 For more on the Elite Bioscope, see Section 5.3.5.
1385 "Een opzienbarend faillissement", *Het Nieuws van den Dag voor Nederlandsch-Indië* (1 February 1915); "Onjuist Voorgesteld", *Het Nieuws van den Dag voor Nederlandsch-Indië* (3 February 1915).
1386 Advertisement, *Bataviaasch Nieuwsblad* (9 February 1915).
1387 Scott Merrillees, *Greetings from Jakarta: Postcards of a Capital 1900–1950* (Jakarta/Kuala Lumpur: Equinox Publishing, 2012), 204.
1388 See Dafna Ruppin, "Asta Nielsen, Cinema-going and Film Censorship in the Netherlands-Indies, 1912–1918", in Martin Loiperdinger and Uli Jung (eds.), *Importing Asta Nielsen: The International Film Star in the Making 1910–1914* (New Barnet: John Libbey, 2013), 299–307; Merrillees, *Greetings from Jakarta*, 204.

5 – Batavia: Capital of Chinese Cinema Venues

5.3.4 The Fear of Chinese Boycott: The West-Java Bioscope at Flora Theatre

The Flora Theatre, which opened to the public at Pasar Senen in May 1912 with shows by the West-Java Bioscope, was expected to provide "stiff competition" to the Globe Bioscope at Pasar Baru.[1389] Owned by Tan Joe Hok, the

Figure 5–6. Audience at the Globe Bioscope or Rex cinema house, ca. 1940. Courtesy of Leiden University Library, Image code 115145.

Figure 5–7. West-Java Bioscope at Flora Theatre, picture postcard, postmarked 21 January 1920. [Greetings from Jakarta © Scott Merrillees and Equinox Publishing Jakarta.]

1389 "Flora Bioscoop", *Pembrita Betawi* (12 April 1912). It is unclear if there was a direct connection between the Batavia company and the West-Java Bioscope, which performed in one of the semi-permanent cinema tents in Surabaya's Pasar Besar in late 1913 and early 1914 (Advertisement, *Soerabaiasch-Handelsblad* (31 October 1913)). Nor is it clear if either of these companies had any relation to the West-Java Film Rental and Sales company (*Het Filmverhuur- en Verkoopkantoor West-Java*), operating from the Apollo Theatre in Bandung. The company sold "second-hand copies of films of all types and lengths, from 10 to 25 cents per meter" with "regular supplies of the latest released films from Europe, America and the most reputable companies" (Advertisement, *De Locomotief* (24 November 1913)).

West-Java Bioscope was scheduled to give its first show in the newly completed building on 5 May.[1390] On 4 May, invited guests were summoned to admire the neatly decorated venue and get acquainted first-hand with the new cinema theatre.[1391]

On Saturday evening, on the opening night, the entire area surrounding the Flora Theatre, according to reports, was "[...] bathed in a sea of light; the West-Java Bioscope opened its doors to the public for the first time and numerous giant arc lamps transformed the dark night into clear day".[1392] The building made a strong impression as well: "spacious, airy, cosy and can accommodate many. The classification scheme of seats is similar to those in other cinemas".[1393] According to a surviving postcard showing the theatre's exterior, it appears that separate entrances were provided to spectators of the higher rank of seats and to spectators seated in second and third class (see Figure 5-7). A nice lounging area and a well-stocked buffet were available to visitors. "For lovers of cinema, the West-Java Bioscope is certainly an asset", the report continued, and since there was no other cinema in that part of town, it was suggested that the owner should be successful in his endeavour.[1394] *Taman Sari* expected that, from now on, many residents of Senen would prefer to stay in Senen itself to watch moving picture shows, rather than venture out to the Pasar Baru.[1395] The most successful films on the programme quickly proved to be Nordisk Films, especially the ones featuring Asta Nielsen.[1396] Occasionally, Flora Theatre could be used for performances of entertainments other than moving pictures, such as *wayang wong* performances during a special charity show.[1397]

The West-Java Bioscope provides an interesting insight into the politics behind Chinese exhibition and consumption of moving pictures. Its owner, Tan Joe Hok, was in fact one of the more outspoken cinema entrepreneurs against the taxation of public amusements introduced in 1912. His clashes with the Municipal Council did not end there. In early 1913, the West-Java Bioscope was interested in setting up a temporary tent at Glodok Square, to hold screenings to coincide with the celebrations of Chinese New Year (*Cap Go Meh*), undoubtedly the biggest festival on the Chinese calendar. Lasting for twelve days around January–February and enjoyed by all members of colonial society for its spectacles, *Cap Go Meh* involved Chinese opera shows and

---

1390 In August 1912, the brother of Tan Joe Hok apparently bought land on the corner of Kramat and Tanah Tinggi, with the intention of constructing another cinema theatre ("Nog een bioscope theatre", *Het Nieuws van den Dag voor Nederlandsch-Indië* (3 August 1912)).

1391 "Steeds meer Bioscopen", *Het Nieuws van den Dag voor Nederlandsch-Indië* (17 April 1912).

1392 "Opening der West-Java Bioscope", *Het Nieuws van den Dag voor Nederlandsch-Indië* (6 May 1912).

1393 Ibid.

1394 Ibid.

1395 "Flora Bioscoop", *Taman Sari* (7 May 1912).

1396 "Bioscopen", *Bataviaasch Nieuwsblad* (30 November 1912). On Asta Nielsen films in the Indies, see Ruppin, "Asta Nielsen, Cinema-going and Film Censorship", 299–307.

1397 "Voor Benkolen", *Bataviaasch Nieuwsblad* (25 July 1914).

processions through the streets with the *barongsai*, "[...] a dragon-like creature supported by a number of boys [... accompanied by] a barrage of fire-crackers intended to drive away devils".[1398] However, a license that was granted to Tan Joe Hok earlier for this purpose was suddenly revoked for reasons that remained unspecified. It then transpired that a license was given to another cinema entrepreneur, "an Indo-European", who was the owner of the Insulinde Bioscope.[1399]

A circular was subsequently distributed among the Chinese community on behalf of Tan Joe Hok, calling on them to boycott the cinema tent.[1400] The Chinese, who had a "boycott history", as *Bataviaasch Nieuwsblad* put it, aggressively distributed the circulars, even more outraged than usual because this was clearly a cultural Chinese celebration.[1401] Boycott out of racial solidarity, *Pantjaran Warta* exclaimed, "[...] is the ULTIMATE WEAPON that Chinese people use, and that scares [all people of] other ethnicities".[1402] Like earlier boycotts of other circus and cinema tents, this boycott reportedly also led the entrepreneur of the Insulinde Bioscope to suffer great losses.[1403]

5.3.5 Calls for Cinema Censorship: The Elite Bioscope by the Sluisbrug

Yet another cinema built in 1912 was the Elite Bioscope, located on the terrain of the Sluisbrug, opposite the Wilhelmina Park, next to the offices of the Royal Packet Company and in close vicinity to the main station at Noordwijk. "Negotiations for the sale of the land with the owner, the Arab [Ali bin Abdulla] bin On, are progressing well", *Het Nieuws van den Dag voor Nederlandsch-Indië* reported in May 1912, and "all the plans have already been completed. We were shown a sketch of the building; it makes an agreeable impression with its lean, white façade. Competition for Pasar Baru and Senen will be tough, this crossing being, *par excellence*, so conveniently located."[1404] The cinema was to take up a third of the plot of land occupied at the time by the firm Van Beem & Co., where a tobacconist was located. The tobacconist was not to be uprooted, *Bataviaasch Nieuwsblad* reassured its readers, but it would get a modern new home in the front of the cinema building.[1405] However, from now on, instead of the 75 guilders rent per month, it would have to add another 25 guilders due to the lighting that will be provided by the cinema all night long. Not "too exaggerated" a demand, *De Locomotief* considered the transaction.[1406]

1398 Abeyasekere, *Jakarta*, 63.
1399 "Een Boycot", *Bataviaasch Nieuwsblad* (1 February 1913).
1400 "Bioscoop di Boicot", *Pantjaran Warta* (30 January 1913).
1401 "Een Boycot", *Bataviaasch Nieuwsblad* (1 February 1913).
1402 "Bioscoop di boijcot", *Pantjaran Warta* (30 January 1913), emphasis in original.
1403 "Een Boycot", *Bataviaasch Nieuwsblad* (1 February 1913).
1404 "Een nieuwe bioscope", *Het Nieuws van den Dag voor Nederlandsch-Indië* (23 May 1912), emphasis added.
1405 "De Elite bioscoop", *Bataviaasch Nieuwsblad* (3 July 1912).
1406 "Bioscoop", *De Locomotief* (5 July 1912).

According to the same report in *De Locomotief*, the idea for a modern European designed and decorated cinema theatre apparently came from one of the entrepreneurs involved in the project, who had observed the local moving picture trade in the Indies and witnessed the huge profits raked in by the cinema tents.[1407] This unidentified man was probably Mr. J. Frank, who was also appointed as company manager of Loa Soen Yang's newly established Company for Operation of Cinemas and Trade in Films Ltd.[1408] Frank was an enterprising man in Batavia, simultaneously engaged in the construction of a new hotel on the eastern side of the Koningsplein.[1409] In 1913 he travelled to Amsterdam, to study filmmaking at the Dutch film company of Nöggerath. As reported in *Het Nieuws van den Dag voor Nederlandsch-Indië*, the intention behind this was

> [...] to produce scenes in Java of typical *Indische* things, landscapes and events. The films will be screened in Batavia, but the primary objective is to have them screened in Europe. A good idea! Thus some more knowledge about the Indies can be distributed in the Netherlands, more interest in the land of eternal summer will be awakened in Europe. And that is undoubtedly a good thing for the Indies! I asked Mr. Frank whether he was also planning on making comedies, for example, the police in Batavia detecting a criminal, with Ruempol-Rigadin, or a parade of a civic guard or a meeting of the Municipal Council, or a walking tour of Batavia's beautiful avenues, or a crime scene... We'll have to wait and see what he does. He did not provide his position in this matter.[1410]

As in many such cases, it is not clear if and what kinds of films were subsequently made, and if they were ever shipped to the Netherlands.[1411]

The company behind the Elite Bioscope raised a capital of 50,000 guilders from five partners, Chinese and European or Eurasian, with at least half of the sum to be spent on the construction of the building.[1412] And even before all the details of the contract were finalised, the plans and some of the subcontracts were already in place:

1407 Ibid.

1408 For more on Loa Soen Yang, see Section 5.3.3. In early 1914 it was rumoured that the Globe Bioscope was in negotiations for acquiring the Elite Bioscope, to be included under the Company for Operation of Cinemas and Trade in Films Ltd.; however, this rumour was denied by the Elite Bioscope ("Tegengespraak", *Het Nieuws van den Dag voor Nederlandsch-Indië* (23 January 1914)).

1409 "Een nieuw hôtel", *Het Nieuws van den Dag voor Nederlandsch-Indië* (25 January 1913).

1410 "Diederik Baltzerdt op Reis", *Het Nieuws van den Dag voor Nederlandsch-Indië* (11 September 1913), emphasis added.

1411 By this point, there were several institutional ventures by the Dutch into producing moving pictures of their colonies, for the benefit of people back in the Netherlands to be educated about their colonial possessions through film. One initiative came from Louis van Vuuren, a civil servant in Batavia heading the Encyclopaedisch Bureau, who in 1912 proposed to establish a government film company in order to supplement the kind of knowledge collected by the Bureau with moving images. Van Vuuren's proposal was rejected, but films were nevertheless made by a cameraman hired by the Bureau, as traced by Gerda Jansen Hendriks in Jansen Hendriks, *Een voorbeeldige kolonie*, 25–55. The same year that Van Vuuren made his proposal, J. C. Lamster arrived in the colony on behalf of the Colonial Institute for his first stint as cameraman. See further on Lamster in Dijk et al. (eds.), *J. C. Lamster, een vroege filmer*.

1412 "De Elite bioscoop", *Bataviaasch Nieuwsblad* (3 July 1912).

5 – Batavia: Capital of Chinese Cinema Venues

The building, to be constructed by a Chinese under European supervision, has been subcontracted, the machinery, to be delivered by the firm Lindeteves and Stokvis, has already been ordered by telegraph, 2,500 meters of films are in stock, while the device will be supplied by a European trade company here as soon as possible. If everything goes to plan as the entrepreneurs have proposed, then the first show will take place in December. The orchestra, which will consist entirely of European instruments, will be complemented by an [electric] pianoforte, which also produces flute and fiddle tones, a musical instrument that will cost 4,500 guilders. The advantage of this cinema is that one of its shareholders is an agent for one of the big American film companies, whose long films are currently exhibited by the Globe Bioscope, [and] his agency will transfer the company so that the films will first be shown at the Elite, as this cinema will be called. The seats will be arranged amphitheatre-like, so that the audience will have a good overview of the projection screen, and comfortable chairs await the visitor. Balcony, box and first class seats will include a large number of seats, as this cinema mainly wants to attract the European public. Soon our shopping area will be enriched with a cinema theatre, such as one finds in the great European cities.[1413]

The contract for the land at 12,000 guilders in rent per year was finally signed on 3 July 1912, 25 per cent of which had to be paid upon signing.[1414]

The Batavia correspondent for *De Locomotief* concurred that the location chosen for the new cinema theatre would be most advantageous for the European going-out public:

> [...] the cinema will be located in one of the busiest crossings of Weltevreden, in the same street as that in which the restaurants are located, where day in and day out the *beau monde* come to enjoy the calm of a comfortable armchair to observe the busy hustle and bustle along Noord- and Rijswijk. A ride home for dinner and then back to the dirty Chinese *kamp*[*ung*] is ruled out, while in the evening, when passing by, one can also benefit from a show. The plan is in any case to offer shows of only an hour long. It is reckoned here then that mainly Europeans will visit because the balcony is calculated at 80 [seats] while the box and first class have 200 seats each. The second class and those for natives are much smaller than in other cinemas.[1415]

The Dutch newspapers in Batavia and outside of it created such a hype around the Elite Bioscope that, even before construction was completed, as soon as the cinema was declared a public limited company, bids of 25 per cent above par were made, including a bid of 60 per cent above the company's initial valuation price. "Notwithstanding the great competition, it seems a cinema in Batavia will always be a goldmine still."[1416]

As promised earlier by the entrepreneurs, the Elite Bioscope (see Figure 5–8) was ready for its grand opening by December 1912:

1413 Ibid.
1414 "Bioscoop", *De Locomotief* (5 July 1912). In 1913, *De Kinematograaf* in Amsterdam reported that the Netherlands Indies Escompto Company (*Nederlandsch Indische Escompto Maatschappij*, later *Escomptobank*) confiscated shares of the Elite Bioscope in the value of 10,000 guilders, which were held by the embezzling Agent Gerth van Wijk ("Uit onze Koloniën", *De Kinematograaf*, no. 30 (15 August 1913): 197).
1415 "Bioscoop", *De Locomotief* (5 July 1912), emphasis added.
1416 "Een Goudmijnte", *Bataviaasch Nieuwsblad* (25 July 1912).

Figure 5–8. Elite Bioscope, ca. 1915, picture postcard. [*Greetings from Jakarta* © Scott Merrillees and Equinox Publishing Jakarta.]

Without exaggeration it may be said that the interior of this cinema surpasses that of other cinemas in this city. Of course the division [of the space] is essentially the same, but with the establishment of the Elite the small details were observed, that just make the stay in the hall pleasant. So it does not have the shed-like appearance of the other *Kientops*, but a clean, white ceiling, fitted with gold stars, on the ends of which are positioned electric lamps, increasing convenience. Three large electric fans provide the necessary coolness while attention was drawn to the comfort of the chairs. A huge electric pianola already adorns one corner. The decoration of the interior was accomplished by the firm Empting. Also from outside the building looks nice. The wooden veranda, with many squares of cathedral-glass, produces a nice effect; the front yard, with many plants is beautifully lit by five large incandescent lights.[1417]

The opening dates, Sunday for invited guests and Monday for the public, were also found to be well-chosen, since they coincided with the celebrations of Saint Nicholas.

Despite the unequivocal appeal to European spectators as laid out in the newspapers, with its cheapest tickets for third class offered at f 0.15 (after the added public amusements tax), the Elite Bioscope must have been attended by "Native" spectators as well.[1418] According to a report that appeared in *Taman Sari* by a journalist who visited the Elite Bioscope's late evening show as a spectator, all seating ranks were very full, and it was lucky that the electric fans

---

1417 "Elite Bioscope", *Het Nieuws van den Dag voor Nederlandsch-Indië* (29 November 1912), emphasis added.

1418 Ticket prices were f 2.20 for a balcony seat, f 1.65 for a box seat, f 0.825 for first class, f 0.425 for second class, and f 0.15 for third class. Advertisement, *Het Nieuws van den Dag voor Nederlandsch-Indië* (12 November 1913).

5 – Batavia: Capital of Chinese Cinema Venues

were installed, otherwise people would not have been able to watch the films properly due to the heat.[1419] It was so full that some people who arrived late were not admitted into the cinema. He was especially taken with the comic scenes on the programme, as well as a film about an "[...] Indian chief who wants to get married to a young European lady".[1420] This was probably exactly the kind of film that the Dutch authorities would have been anxious about. How European women were presented on screen and could be perceived by "eager Native and Chinese eyes" was already a concern, especially in films showing a "white beauty" intimately kissing and hugging, "reviving in front of the appraising eyes of *Kromo* and *John Chinaman* images that must give the Native a most peculiar peek at our civilised European life… of our European women".[1421] Many such comments in various cities were made specifically about Asta Nielsen films, which also featured on the Elite Bioscope's screen. However, the added interracial layer of the specific film highlighted by the *Taman Sari* journalist above likely made it an even more *risqué* item on the programme in the Indies at that time, from a European point of view.[1422]

The Elite Bioscope did not shy away from controversy, at times – at the cost of legal action against its owners. Thus, in March 1914 a police report was filed against the owners of the Elite Bioscope due to the screening of a banned film, Gaumont's L'AGONIE DE BYZANCE (1913).[1423] The primary reason for the ban was not based on the testimony of any police official watching the film, but rather on the film's description in the Malay cinema programmes, which included the phrase: "Women brought to be sold like beasts in the market [...]".[1424] According to the police's interpretation, since "women" was meant to be read as "Christian women", the combination of "Christian women" and "sold like beasts on the market" was inexcusable. Furthermore, *Het Nieuws van den Dag voor Nederlandsch-Indië* continued to relate

> [...] native spies of [police] commissioner Heynen informed that the natives, their countrymen, were aroused to go see the film thanks to the encouragement: *orang christen di telandjangin dan dipantatin oleh orang Turkij*, which means: 'naked Christian women being raped by Turks!' The joy which this communication gave the natives was too much to take. The further screening was then immediately banned. Everyone will agree with us that the attitude of the police can only be praised. If there were controlled film censorship here, then the film could have been banned before the screening [...].[1425]

Such overarching censorship would be introduced only in 1916, with the Bioscope Ordinance, and since Batavia was one of the main entry points for films to the Indies, it played a major role in the new control apparatus.[1426]

1419 "Elite-bioscope", *Taman Sari* (3 February 1913).

1420 Ibid.

1421 "De Inlander en de bioscoop", *De Locomotief* (12 April 1912), emphasis added.

1422 On control of film content introduced in 1912, see Section 4.6.

1423 "Verboden film", *Het Nieuws van den Dag voor Nederlandsch-Indië* (9 March 1914).

1424 "De verboden film 'Byzantium'", *Het Nieuws van den Dag voor Nederlandsch-Indië* (10 March 1914).

1425 Ibid.

5.4 Conclusion

This chapter traced the growth of moving picture venues in Batavia, from the earliest shows at theatre houses and clubs, through converted buildings and tents, to purpose-built modern cinema palaces. It paid particular attention to the contribution of Chinese entrepreneurs in this process. Emphasis was also placed on legislative proceedings, primarily the public amusements tax and its implementation. In light of the increasingly growing number of venues mushrooming around the city in the 1910s, it appears that the Municipal Council's concern about controlling and limiting the spread of such venues was finally assuaged by the revenue it was making on tax collected.

In 1914, the flat fees charged from cinema owners were expected to be considerably higher due to the impending opening of three new cinemas – Oey Boen Hoei's Cinema Palace in Krekot in May, Cinema Orion at Pollux Theatre in Glodok in August, and Excelsior Bioscope at Gloria Theatre in Pancoran in November – with each cinema paying a flat fee of 150 guilders per month, in addition to the ten per cent tax to be received from ticket sales.[1427] Nevertheless, the Municipality was in for a sore disappointment, as the tax on public amusements collected in 1914 was 50,000 guilders – 13,000 guilders less than in 1913 and far below the estimated 73,000 guilders. The "European war had a serious impact on the visit to entertainment venues", *Bataviaasch Nieuwsblad* interpreted the dismal results.[1428]

The year 1914 nevertheless proved to be a good time to take stock of what had passed in Batavia in the field of moving picture shows in the past decade. In May 1914, upon the opening of the new Cinema Palace in Krekot, *Het Nieuws van den Dag voor Nederlandsch-Indië* summarised the developments accordingly:

> It is not many years ago that people here had to speak of the bamboo-shed, a hideous shack, standing at Pasar Baru as the bioscope. Earlier there had already been bioscope exhibitions at the manège in Tanah Abang, but it was attended almost exclusively by residents of Tanah Abang and its surroundings. The majority of the population had only the "Cinema" at Pasar Baru.
>
> Up until five years ago no other [cinema] stood. Batavians streamed every night to that filthy building. Until the elements took care of it, and – in 1911 – the shed [likely, the Flying Bioscope] burned down to the ground. [...]
>
> The Globe Bioscope, the first permanent building, erected at Pasar Baru, was followed within a short time by the West-Java Bioscope at Senen and the Elite Bioscope by the Sluisbrug. Yesterday we also patronised the opening the Cinema Palace and soon the first cinema screenings [of Cinema Orion] in the new building [Pollux Theatre] at Glodok square will take place. Then we will have been

---

1426 See more on the Bioscope Ordinance in Concluding Remarks.

1427 "De gemeentelijke dienst der Openbare Vermakelijkheden", *Het Nieuws van den Dag voor Nederlandsch-Indië* (20 February 1914); "Cinema Palace", *Pantjaran Warta* (6 May 1914); "Pollux Theatre di Cinema Orion", *Sin Po* (6 August 1914); "Excelsior Bioscope di Gloria Theatre", *Sin Po* (5 November 1914).

1428 "Batavia's Gemeente-begrooting", *Bataviaasch Nieuwsblad* (30 September 1914).

enriched here in Batavia with five good cinemas, housed in neat and modern-equipped buildings. We have not even mentioned the many loose plans hanging in the air here in the cinematic field.[1429]

The above summary thus overlooked most of the early venues where moving picture shows took place. Furthermore, similarly to reports from the Municipal Council discussions of the public amusements tax, it shone a spotlight only on the more permanent venues and did not account for many of the non-permanent locations and touring entrepreneurs still active at this time, especially in the Indonesian *kampungs*. These included the Shahab Brothers' General Bioscope at Bungur in 1909 and at Kongsi Besar in 1910, London China Matograf and the Modern Bioscope at Jagal in 1908, Olympia Bioscope at Prapatan in 1910, an unnamed Chinese cinema at Jembatan Batu, Abdul Challik's Maltheser Bioscope at Prapatan, and Insulinde Bioscope at Kongsi Besar – all in 1913.[1430] Most of these companies did not advertise in the newspapers and there were surely many others performing shows that were never reported about.[1431] In fact, according to a report in *Pembrita Betawi* from 1908, there were eight or nine moving picture venues in Batavia, causing great confusion even for locals.[1432] For instance, a reporter who was supposed to attend a moving picture show in Salemba – a neighbourhood housing two venues at the time – was dropped off at the wrong one by his *sado* driver.[1433]

Finally, although it was obviously easier for audiences to attend screenings in their own neighbourhoods, as the 1914 report claimed, spectators did venture out beyond their comfort zones. Especially in the earlier period, when spectators were admitted free of charge, some of them supposedly travelled from far and wide for a chance to watch moving pictures. Batavia's modern electric tram system, the source of envy for Surabaya's residents, was one of the readily available modes of transport.[1434] Spectators from the higher end of society were transported to the Chinese and Indonesian *kampungs* to attend moving picture

1429 "Opening van de Cinema Palace", *Het Nieuws van den Dag voor Nederlandsch-Indië* (8 May 1914). One of these loose plans was possibly referring to a permit request by Tjio Tjong Hin for constructing a cinema at Palmerah, which had recently been approved ("Gemeenteraad van Batavia", *Het Nieuws van den Dag voor Nederlandsch-Indië* (18 March 1913)).

1430 Advertisement, *Taman Sari* (9 August 1909); "Generaal Bioscoop", *Taman Sari* (18 February 1910); "Kabar Hindia", *Taman Sari* (19 May 1908); "Kabar Hindia", *Taman Sari* (17 July 1908); "Nederlandsch-Indië", *Bataviaasch Nieuwsblad* (15 November 1910); "Een goed figuur!", *Het Nieuws van den Dag voor Nederlandsch-Indië* (14 February 1913); Advertisement, *Pantjaran Warta* (5 November 1913); "Bioscoop di boijcot", *Pantjaran Warta* (30 January 1913).

1431 Accidents or violent incidents occurring in or around the cinema sometimes got a brief mention in the section for "Police news". For example, in 1908 a "Chinese and a Native, both employees of the cinema at Sawah Besar", reportedly got into a brawl in the engine room, thus damaging the machine. "The owner delivered both to the police." However, like many other articles of this kind, the report did not identify the name of the cinema or its owner("Politie-nieuws", *Het Nieuws van den Dag voor Nederlandsch-Indië* (6 January 1908)). Another police-related report did mention the name of a Chinese cinema owner, Lim Pa Seng, when the latter refused to take down his tent at Kongsi Besar which subsequently became a shelter for homeless persons, and finally had to be removed by the police ("Politie-nieuws", *Het Nieuws van den Dag voor Nederlandsch-Indië* (22 April 1908)).

1432 "Komedi Gambar Hidoep", *Pembrita Betawi* (6 April 1908).

1433 "De Ripograaf", *Het Nieuws van den Dag voor Nederlandsch-Indië* (14 March 1908).

1434 "Wanneer krijgt Soerabaja electrisch licht?", *Soerabaiasch-Handelsblad* (3 October 1908).

shows using *sado*s or even taxi-autos which were reportedly available in significant numbers by 1913.[1435] As a reporter for *Het Nieuws van den Dag voor Nederlandsch-Indië*, who troubled himself to attend the opening of the Cinema Palace in Krekot, found: "During the drive to this part of town, which seems to lie so very far away, we took note that remoteness exists only in the imagination".[1436] Therefore, the modern state of facilities and the quality of films in the programmes were the main drivers in determining whether spectators find these venues worthwhile, and the hassle induced by the distance involved was tapered by the advent of increased urban mobility.

1435 "Taxi-auto's voor Soerabaja", *Soerabaiasch-Handelsblad* (23 January 1913).

1436 "Opening van de Cinema Palace", *Het Nieuws van den Dag voor Nederlandsch-Indië* (8 May 1914).

6

Semarang: The Battleground over the Permanent Fairground Town

We have said this more than once: it often happens that in our pathetic town months go by with nothing happening [...] to give one fresh air from the drudgery and tedium, and other months when we get everything at once, and you can go on one evening to three or more amusements. Now we find ourselves in the latter scenario since, besides the opera, we are now also graced by a cinematograph – which seem to be targeting Semarang in particular, because one [company] is not yet gone and the next one has already applied for a permit – while the Bengal circus is also coming here in a couple of days for about a fortnight. It's lucky for the opera that it secured the place first since, if they were both to offer a performance on the same evening, then the circus would have come up short for seats while in the theatre you would have found one person for every ten seats who call themselves a public.
"Brieven uit Semarang", Het Nieuws van den Dag voor Nederlandsch-Indië *(7 June 1904).*

Semarang, the capital of the district in Central Java by the same name, served as one of the three commercial centres of the island, along with Batavia and Surabaya. Historically, nearby Jepara was the main port of Central Java, yet the silting up of the harbour prevented larger ships from landing. The Dutch therefore decided to move their activities to nearby Semarang.[1437] The site was acquired by the VOC thanks to an arrangement with the Sultan of Mataram in 1708. Semarang's port primarily served for exporting agricultural products from Java's interior and for importing goods from abroad. As transportation and communication networks were improved, the city was able to process increasing quantities of goods. A connection with Solo (Surakarta) and Yogyakarta (known as the Principalities, or *Vorstenlanden*) was completed in 1873, subsequently turning Semarang into a depot for products ranging from coffee, tobacco, indigo dye, sugar and rice.[1438] Railway lines connecting with Juana to the east and with Cirebon to the west were completed only in the eighties and nineties.

1437 See Theo Stevens, "Semarang, Central Java and the World Market 1870–1900", in Peter J.M. Nas (ed.), *The Indonesian City: Studies in Urban Development and Planning* (Dordrecht-Holland/Cinnaminson-U.S.A.: Foris Publications, 1986), 56–70, here 57. The harbour problems of Jepara were common in all ports of the north coast ports and were, more or less, successfully resolved in each of them (ibid., 59).

1438 See A. Cabaton, *Java, Sumatra, and the other islands of the Dutch East Indies*, trans. by Bernard Miall (London: Unwin, 1911), 66.

Semarang was built on two sides of a river bank by the same name, which became ineffective due to the silting up problems. The city was generally divided into an old quarter, lying nearer to the sea and up until 1824 surrounded by ramparts and moats, and a new quarter with modern housing spreading further south.[1439] A travel guidebook from 1903 found the former to have "[...] some resemblance to a South-European seaport town: the houses are built right out into the street, and are not detached; many of them are two stories high; the streets are, for the greatest part, narrow, and without any trees, which consequently makes them close, hot, and dusty".[1440] A few years later, another guidebook from 1911 was even less forgiving:

> The old city, built by a natural and pathetic fallacy, in the Dutch manner – its two-story houses crowded together in the narrow streets, without the ventilation of large gardens – is so insupportably hot that all who have been able to desert it have done so; it is used now only for stores and warehouses, and, in the more habitable quarters, for barracks and orphan asylums. The Europeans have taken refuge on the road to Bondjong and Pontjol (two quarters of the new city [to the southwest of the old city]), which stand a little higher than the surrounding plain. There they have built their white villas, shaded by tall trees. A magnificent avenue of tamarind-trees connects Bondjong with the *aloun-aloun*, the central public square of every native town, where the Government offices, the Residency, the town hall, indeed all the official buildings, are grouped about its green expanse.[1441]

The nicest part to reside in was Candi, a suburb fifteen minutes ride south, on the slope of the mountain at 100 metres in altitude, which was dotted with ruins of Hindu temples, and drew further European construction in the 1910s due to its cooler climate. The Chinese quarter and the Arab and Javanese *kampungs* were considered to be especially intriguing. Tourists found the Chinese quarter, built on the river bank further to the south, to be "almost as picturesque as it is dirty".[1442] They were equally fascinated by the Arab and Javanese *kampungs*, located at a low point on the western end of town, which were prone to floods during the west monsoon season.[1443] Houses in these *kampungs* were "[...] scattered among the coco-palms, or along the roads, or on the banks of the canal, according to the occupations of the inhabitants".[1444]

Around the time of the arrival of moving pictures, Semarang experienced a population explosion. "Decline in rural economy, loss of land, drought and over population, as well as the attraction of work opportunities in the city" were all named as causes for the increase in the "Native" population of the city, which increased from 53,874 in 1890 to 126,629 in 1920 (135 per cent growth

---

1439 See Bemmelen et al., *Guide through Netherlands India*, 58.

1440 Ibid.

1441 Cabaton, *Java, Sumatra, and the other islands*, 66–67, emphasis added.

1442 Ibid., 67.

1443 See Bemmelen et al., *Guide through Netherlands India*, 60.

1444 Cabaton, *Java, Sumatra, and the other islands*, 67.

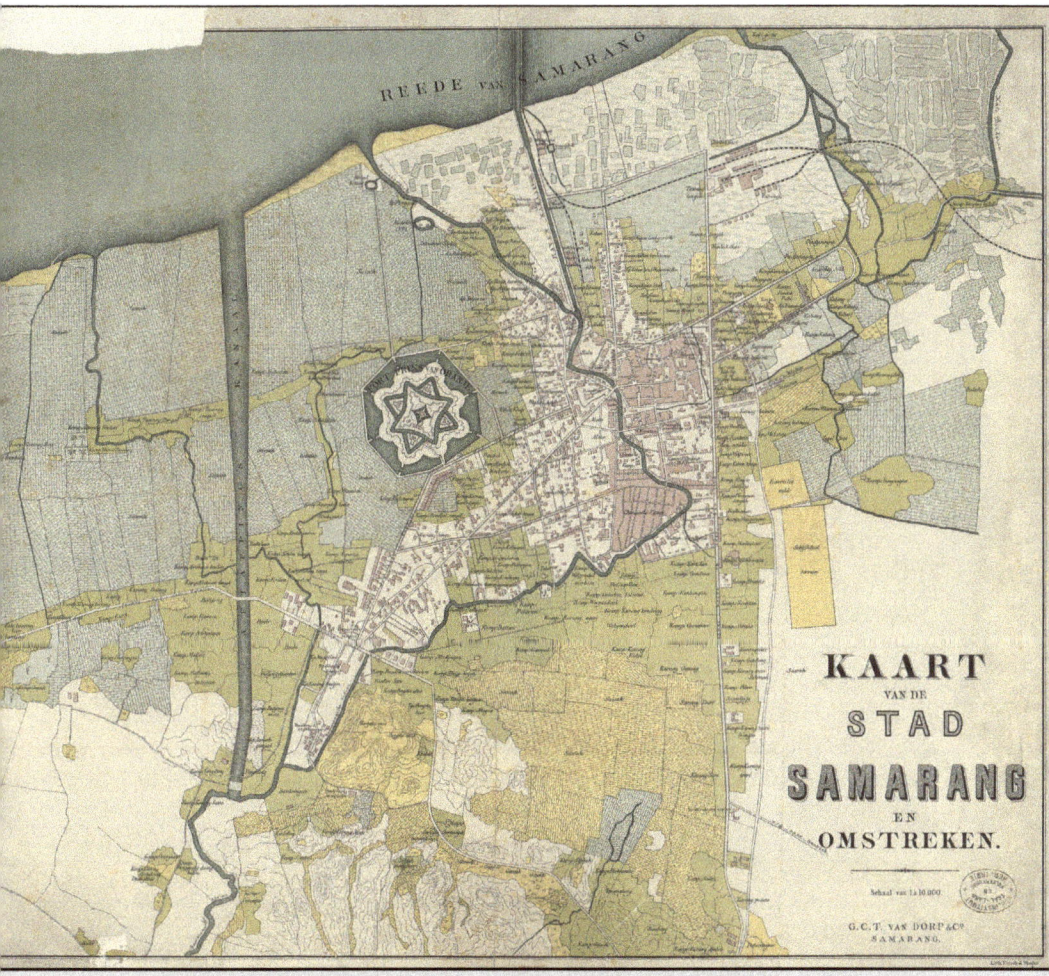

Figure 6–1. Map of Semarang and its surroundings, ca. 1880, G.C.T. van Dorp & Co. Courtesy of Leiden University Library, Image code D E 38,5.

in 30 years).[1445] The European population had grown from 8,402 in 1900 to 15,144 in 1920 (93,5 percent growth in 20 years), mostly consisting of newly-arrived Europeans from the Netherlands, and the Chinese community increased from 15,921 in 1890 to 32,701 in 1905 (105,4 per cent growth in 15 years). These demographics contributed to a significant history of epidemics: in 1910, thirty-five per cent of Semarang's Javanese population died of cholera and the mortality rate in the second decade of the twentieth century averaged around 50 to 60 per 1000 inhabitants.[1446] Following the establishment of the Semarang Municipal Council in 1906, the local authorities tried to address

---

[1445] Joost Coté, "Making the kampung modern: colonial planning in Semarang 1910–1925", *Review of Indonesian and Malaysian Affairs* 44, no. 2 (2010): 23.

[1446] Ibid., 24.

issues of hygiene and health improvement. Exhibitors of moving pictures, who were touring Central Java at the time, were also confronted with these challenging conditions.

While Semarang had far less entertainment on offer, compared with Batavia or Surabaya, the city was well-connected via roads, canals, railways, steam trams, and steamship lines.[1447] It thus proved to be an attractive destination for many itinerant show people who were already touring Java. Semarang had its own European-style theatre and several city squares where tents for public amusements, such as the circus, *komedi stambul* or moving pictures, were set up over the years. *De Locomotief*, one of the Dutch daily newspapers published in Semarang as of 1852, was a major publication read throughout Java, providing insight into goings-on in Semarang and beyond.[1448] Furthermore, although it was less of a modern city than Batavia or Surabaya, in 1914 Semarang served as the site of the much anticipated International Colonial Exhibition, in an effort to bring it up to par with the other major Javanese port cities. Therefore, while Semarang was by no means a small town or rural site of exhibition, it still provides a useful contrast to Batavia and Surabaya when studying the development of movie-going in Java.

After introducing the venues and locations for the early moving picture shows in Semarang, this chapter reflects on the weather conditions and flooding in Semarang, which wreaked havoc with many a cinema tent and had a detrimental effect on exhibitors' potential for profit-making. It then moves on to discuss the local legislation by the newly founded Municipal Council which, similarly to Surabaya and Batavia, was working towards extending more control over public amusements. With its shortage of possible venues and open city squares for housing tents, compared to the other two Javanese metropolises, and as an increasingly growing number of amusements lined up to offer shows, the municipal authorities would prove to be stringent when it came to allocating permits. They were also debating the opening of a new municipal multi-purpose theatre, envisioned to house theatre companies, *stambul* troupes, and moving picture shows, in a desperate attempt to halt what seemed to be an endless cycle of semi- and permanent tents defiling the *Alun Alun*. Finally, this chapter discusses the planning leading up to the 1914 International Colonial Exhibition in Semarang, and the role that cinema played in it.

6.1 Early Shows at Semarang Theatre

While it appears that Semarang was not the first to host projections of moving images, the earliest promise of such amusement in the Indies found in this research appeared in *Semarang-Courant* in September 1896:

> Shortly the Cinématographe will be on display here. Through this instrument one sees so to speak "living photographs" [*levende photografieën*]. The different parts, separately photographed by means of electricity, are quickly set in motion by this

---

1447 See Cabaton, *Java, Sumatra, and the other islands*, 67.

1448 See Adam, *The Vernacular Press*, 183.

Cinématographe, so that one sees all in such a manner as in real life, as if it were alive. In Europe this device is a big hit, so we have no doubt that much interest will also be shown here.[1449]

This report appeared a couple of weeks before Talbot's opening show with the Scenimatograph in Batavia in October 1896.[1450] It is likely to assume that, were his tour to continue at the time as planned, Semarang would have been one of the cities next in line. Otherwise, it might have been a reference to the upcoming visit of Harley's Kinetoscope to Semarang, which was to be installed at the Semarang Theatre.[1451] Nevertheless, this too ended up as an unfulfilled promise, since the Kinetoscope's batteries were totally depleted and could not be recharged on the spot. Therefore, beyond a sneak preview to local journalists, the Kinetoscope was not on display to the public in Semarang.[1452]

Talbot finally arrived in Semarang for a few days in April 1897, following shows in Batavia, Bandung, Solo (Surakarta) and Yogyakarta.[1453] Initially, only a couple of shows were planned to be given at the Semarang Theatre, for the price of ƒ 1 per person.[1454] The audience turnout was reportedly bigger than expected, especially attracting a large number of children for whom, *De Telefoon* found, the show was in fact better-suited than for the adults.[1455] Talbot also invited the children of the orphanage in Semarang, located just across the street from the Theatre, to attend his show.[1456] Semarang had the highest concentration of orphans in the entire archipelago, mostly "[...] the fruit of a union between a European man and an Asian woman, be it slave, concubine or spouse".[1457] Talbot further sought permission to hold a screening at the military canteen, but finally a third show was added at the Theatre itself and soldiers – a mix of Europeans and non-Europeans – were also invited to attend it for free.[1458]

Other moving picture shows over the next couple of years were mostly offered at the Semarang Theatre, including Miss Meranda's Kinematograph and Graphophone (and later again, as the Xylophone and Kinematograph), Carl

---

1449 "Cinématographe", *Semarang-Courant* (30 September 1896).

1450 See Section 1.2.

1451 Advertisement, *Semarang-Courant* (24 November 1896).

1452 "Kinetoscoop", *De Locomotief* (25 November 1896); "De Kinetoscoop en Phonograaf", *Semarang-Courant* (25 November 1896). See Section 1.1.

1453 Advertisement, *Semarang-Courant* (3 April 1897).

1454 Ibid.

1455 "De Scenimatograaf", *De Telefoon* (5 April 1897).

1456 "De Scénimatograaf", *De Locomotief* (5 April 1897).

1457 Bosma et al., *Being "Dutch" in the Indies*, 50. In fact, the number of these abandoned Mestizo children, which raised concern in the Dutch authorities as to the future of the Dutch race, almost tripled within forty years: from 900 in 1860 to 2,673 in 1900 (ibid., 240–241). Yet the number of orphans in Batavia remained relatively small, as many of them were "shipped off to the big orphanages in Semarang", which had the highest concentration of orphans in the entire archipelago (ibid., 242).

1458 "Scénimatograaf", *De Locomotief* (6 April 1897); "De Scénimatograaf", *De Locomotief* (7 April 1897). This free show for the soldiers was most likely funded to a certain extent by the military *Cantinefonds*. See further in Section 1.2.

Hertz's Cinematographe, a show by the Salvation Army with "the famous lime-light lantern and kinematograph", and Mr. J. E. Frans with his Kino vitagraph.[1459] Meanwhile, Mr. Holton's Cinematographe offered shows at the *Sociëteit Harmonie*.[1460] Mr. Ribaud's Giant Cinematograph initially performed a few shows at the theatre, and then moved for a couple of nights to the *Kong Koan*, or Council of Chinese Officers, which was the governing institution of Chinese community life in Javanese cities.[1461] Nevertheless, it is unclear how many spectators attended these early screenings. Even many of those who could afford the expensive tickets or were members of the Club house, reportedly chose to stay away. For instance, Carl Hertz's magic shows, with moving pictures as one of the items on the programme, remained poorly attended.[1462] Holton's Cinematographe at the *Sociëteit Harmonie* did not attract many visitors either, despite the fact that the show was offered free of charge to Club members.[1463] The future of moving pictures in Semarang looked rather grim from the start.

6.2 Weather and Hygiene: "The rain is a sworn enemy of the cinema tent"

Extending along the equator and lying mostly in the southern hemisphere, the Indonesian archipelago is marked by a tropical climate, which meant that touring entertainers (and their spectators) were often exposed to the elements. Enterpreneurs of moving pictures were faced with particular challenges of mantaining their cameras and projectors, which were made of wood that reacts strongly to water and damp conditions. During the wet season, roughly from November to March on Java, a contemporary report boasted:

> Water streams from the clouds often for twenty-four hours continuously, and then the splashing of rain overpowers the human voice, the brooks and rivers overflow their banks, the frogs croak day and night, and even the lizards and snakes leave their holes and creep into the houses for shelter. It is hardly possible to keep any place dry, for where the rain cannot penetrate the warm sultry air is so charged with humidity that everything quickly becomes covered with mildew.[1464]

1459 Advertisement, *Semarang-Courant* (13 August 1897); "Alweer wat nieuws", *De Locomotief* (26 July 1898); Advertisement, *De Locomotief* (9 August 1898); "Nederlandsch-Indië", *De Locomotief* (31 October 1900); Advertisement, *De Locomotief* (3 September 1900).

1460 Advertisement, *Semarang-Courant* (15 November 1897).

1461 Advertisement, *De Locomotief* (12 June 1897). For more on the *Kong Koan*, see Mary Somers Heidhues, "Chinese Voluntary and Involuntary Associations in Indonesia", in Khun Eng Kuah-Pearce and Evelyn Hu-Dehart (eds.), *Voluntary Organizations in the Chinese Diaspora* (Hong Kong: Hong Kong University Press, 2006), 77–97. The first show was well attended, and it was especially noted that many Chinese women were present ("Nederlandsch-Indië", *De Locomotief* (17 June 1897)). The second show was disrupted when an "inquisitive Chinese" decided to poke around the area where the unit was located and punctured a large bag laying on the ground with his cane. The show, which had only just begun, had to come to an end, and spectators were invited to return the following evening with the same ticket ("De Kinematograaf", *De Locomotief* (19 June 1897)).

1462 "Nederlandsch-Indië", *De Locomotief* (8 August 1898); "Nederlandsch-Indië", *De Locomotief* (9 August 1898).

1463 "Nederlandsch-Indië", *De Locomotief* (17 November 1897).

1464 Braak, "Climate of Netherlands India", 305. For more on Miss Meranda's Kinematograph and Carl Hertz's Cinematographe, see Sections 1.3.2 and 1.3.4, respectively.

6 – Semarang: The Battleground over the Permanent Fairground Town

The first tent shows in Semarang found in this research were given in a specially constructed "small building" (*gebouwtje*) by Mr. Salzwedel's Java Biorama in December 1900 and January 1901.[1465] No description of the construct is available in any of the reports at the time, but it was most likely some sort of temporary bamboo structure. Salzwedel initially offered two performances per evening, in order to attract children to the shows. However, since the direction of the wind and, resultantly, the intensity of rainfall was markedly different by day and night, he quickly had to cancel the early evening shows due to the increasingly poor weather conditions at that time.[1466]

The wet conditions continued to challenge exhibitors, who were increasingly in direct competition with one another, scattered in different locations throughout the city. In early 1904, for example, Abdulally Esoofally's Royal Bioscope stationed its tent at the *Alun Alun*, while another company, identified simply as N.V. Biograph, was screening films in an electrically lit, "neat, airy and waterproof tent" in Karang Tengah, the Chinese part of town.[1467] Ticket prices for the Royal Bioscope were: box ƒ 2, first class ƒ 1.50, second class ƒ 1, third class ƒ 0.50, and fourth class ƒ 0.25.[1468] The admission prices to the Biograph, by comparison were much cheaper and explicitly targeted non-European spectators: box ƒ 1.50, first class ƒ 1, second class ƒ 0.50, third class ƒ 0.25 (Foreign Orientals), and fourth class ƒ 0.10 (Natives).[1469] Yet, if patronisers expected better spectator comforts in the more expensive tent, they were in for a surprise:

> The biograph and the bioscope both attract reasonable audiences. As far as the first is concerned, it can boast of a spacious, airy and very clean tent […]. The tent of the latter is in desperate need of cleaning, especially seeing as the seats seem very dodgy. Now, it is true that people in the dark pay less attention, but it is still less pleasant […]. As I have overheard someone remarking last night, for instance, the pig's trotters that he had eaten for supper began to run; the man's words were paired with nauseous tampering and horrible bodily convolutions.[1470]

"The rain is a sworn enemy of the cinema tent", the report summarised, and "with just a little bit of rain the canvas has everyone from all seats running as if they were possessed by a demon". Shows often could not proceed as planned because, even before the shows would start, the tent was already "at least half a foot under water".[1471]

Dutch colonial engineers first attempted to address the flooding in Semarang with the construction of the Banjir canals between 1880 and 1900. From the end of the 1890s medical professionals were constantly advising on "[…]

1465 "Nederlandsch-Indië", *De Locomotief* (17 December 1900).
1466 "De Biograaf", *De Locomotief* (11 January 1901). See further on Salzwedel's Java Biorama in Section 2.2.
1467 Advertisement, *De Locomotief* (30 December 1903); "N.V. Biograaf", *De Locomotief* (8 January 1904).
1468 Advertisement, *De Locomotief* (2 January 1904).
1469 Advertisement, *De Locomotief* (21 January 1904).
1470 "Uit Semarang", *Het Nieuws van den Dag voor Nederlandsch-Indië* (4 February 1904).
1471 Ibid. See further on Esoofally's Royal Bioscope in Section 3.2.

protection against epidemics, recommending improved drainage and land reclamation, and widespread inoculation against cholera and typhoid were commenced".[1472] By the 1910s, urban over-population and crowding, along with what seemed like a constant threat of epidemics, including cholera, typhoid, dysentery, malaria and the plague, led to calls and initiatives for more action to improve the drainage, sanitation and the well-being of the urban *kampung* dwellers, which were not only Javanese but also poor Europeans and Eurasians.[1473]

During a public meeting called by the Resident in 1911, the board of the Semarang *Stadstuin* proposed to order from Europe a film about the pest, its causes, expansion and control.[1474] Expected to be received within 14 days, the 205-meter long "instructive, scientific film" was first screened to an invited audience comprised of the Resident and other European and Javanese officials, Captain of the Chinese and other Chinese officials, heads of the Arab community in Semarang, representatives of the military and police, all civilian and military doctors and pharmacists as well as Javanese doctors (*dokters djawa*).[1475] The film was later included in the regular programming of the Juliana Bioscope for the general public.[1476] *De Locomotief* noted that this film, in addition to its pedagogical qualities, also served as good "propaganda for the *Stadstuin*".[1477] The report further protested the fact that one had to be a paying member of the *Stadstuin* (at f 1.50 per month) in order to go to the cinema and watch this film, so it remains unclear who was able to watch it and what kind of public education outreach this initiative actually had.[1478]

6.3 Controlling the "permanent fairground": Permits and Public Amusements Tax

As tents of the circus, *komedi stambul*, "biograph, bioscope, cineograph, cinematograph, or whatever that beast [*bessie*] is called" continually occupied Semarang's *Alun Alun*, the local authorities were becoming increasingly apprehensive about controlling the local entertainment scene.[1479] By September

---

1472 Coté, "Making the kampung modern", 21.

1473 Ibid., 24. Coté writes: "A discourse of urban reform had emerged at the beginning of the second decade of the twentieth century from the interaction of engineers, doctors, architects and philanthropic polemicists. [...] Key strands of this discourse originated in Semarang, with the activities and publications of three key figures involved in Semarang's 'kampung reform movement': Hendrick Freek Tillema, Johan Anton Westerveld and Herman Thomas Karsten" (ibid., 25).

1474 "Pest-film", *De Locomotief* (17 June 1911).

1475 "Stadstuin", *De Locomotief* (6 July 1911).

1476 "Stadstuin", *De Locomotief* (15 July 1911).

1477 "Stadstuin", *De Locomotief* (11 July 1911). The *Stadstuin* was the city gardens. The outdoor grounds and indoor pavilion were partly accessible to all for a certain fee, while some events were reserved for subscribed members only.

1478 "Juliana-Bioscoop", *De Locomotief* (9 September 1911). Soon after this, certain screenings were supposedly for members only while other screenings were offered at a discount to members, suggesting that they were open to the non-member public too for a one-time fee. Membership fees were further reduced to 50 cents ("Stadstuin", *De Locomotief* (30 October 1911)).

1479 "Brieven uit Semarang", *Het Nieuws van den Dag voor Nederlandsch-Indië* (23 June 1904).

6 – Semarang: The Battleground over the Permanent Fairground Town

1906, the local administration (*plaatselijk bestuur*) decided to put an end to what was perceived as a "permanent fairground" of entertainments successively occupying the main city square: it would respect permits already granted to "tents, carousels and the likes" up to May 1907, but any new applications were to be rejected out of hand.[1480] In spite of, or perhaps due to, this warning, applicants seized the window of opportunity left by Mr. Hartmann's Wilhelmina Bioscope, which departed from Semarang for eight days in November 1906 in order to visit (and possibly film) the *Sekaten* celebrations in Klaten, submitting permit applications left, right and centre. "The *Alun Alun* will become a battleground", *De Locomotief* announced.[1481]

By the time May 1907 came around, the local administration most likely realised that it would neither be practical nor economically sensible to entirely ban public amusements. Thus, new provisions for setting up "tents, circuses, carousels etc." on public property within the recently-established municipality were drafted.[1482] The main clauses stipulated that a written authorisation from the head of the Municipal Council was required and that no entertainers were to be awarded a permit between the months of December and March (the wet season). Licenses were to be issued for a period of no more than eight weeks, and only one type of public amusement form would be permitted at a time. The rent of the premises was also regulated in this document, starting from two cents per square meter per day, and the highest bidder was to receive the permit. No performances of morally offensive or objectionable content would be tolerated and attendance of children below age 12 was forbidden.[1483] Finally, sale of alcohol in such tents was banned. It is unclear how many of these provisions made it to the final version of the decree, and if they were ever enforced effectively. Just a few months later, a Surabayan-newspaper reported that, while exhibitors in Semarang were given permits for shows valid for one month and up to six weeks at most, they tended to remain on site for months beyond the allotted time, much to the discontent of the other 35 odd cinemas touring Java who were awaiting their turn.[1484]

New regulations on public amusements in Semarang were released in early 1909, relating to "stationing tents, sheds, circuses, [and] carousels associated with fairs and exhibitions, restaurants, beer halls and such establishments intended for public amusements" located on publicly- or privately-owned property.[1485] A permit for setting up a tent on public property could be awarded

---

1480 "De permanente kermis in den ban", *De Locomotief* (14 September 1906).
1481 "Wilhelmina Bioscope", *De Locomotief* (6 November 1906), emphasis added.
1482 "Publieke vermakelijkheden", *De Locomotief* (15 May 1907).
1483 This particular attention to banning children from attending shows might have been due to the fact that Semarang was home to many orphaned and abandoned children. It was home to the biggest orphanages on Java (one Protestant and one Catholic). For more on orphans and orphanages on Java, see Bosma et al., *Being "Dutch" in the Indies*, 236–244. In the early years of moving picture shows, orphans in Semarang were often invited for free shows.
1484 "Bioscoopconcurrentie", *Nieuwe Soerabaja Courant* (16 August 1907).
1485 "Gemeentezaken", *De Locomotief* (19 January 1909).

by the Municipal Council for a maximum period of one month, with only one extension of up to 14 days permitted. No more than three amusements were to be granted permits to perform at the same time, and it was not possible to operate two entertainments of the same kind simultaneously. In order to ensure this, the licensee was forbidden from handing over the permit granted to a third party. They were also required to leave a deposit with the municipality in respect of the permit. Moreover, the construction and maintenance of tents were now to be subject to control: if tents were not kept in good condition, to the satisfaction of the head of the council, they could be shut down and removed by the municipality without advance notice.[1486] But, at least, once a tent was up and running, the manager was not required to remove it at the conclusion of the period, but could leave it standing to be bought by his successor on the same site. This was a good incentive for managers to invest in their venues, countering the effect of the one-month limitation. Nevertheless, during outbreaks of epidemics, the tents had to be removed no later than two days after a notification given.[1487] Interestingly, *komedi stambul* and carousels were to be charged half a cent per day per square meter, while cinemas, circuses and other amusements had to pay two cents per day per square meter, possibly reflecting their higher ticket pricing and potential for profit. Finally, any shows deemed morally offensive by the head of the council could lead to penalty and immediate revocation of the license. In spite of these legislative efforts, at least some of the stipulations remained on paper only. For instance, although regulations stated that it would not be possible to operate two amusements of the same type simultaneously, there were often two cinema companies active alongside each other in Semarang – one on the *Alun Alun* and the other at the *Stadstuin*, whether as open-air screenings or in the *Stadstuin*'s theatre space.[1488]

The local authorities were in fact suffering from an internal clash of interests: between their wish to have a more balanced and controlled popular entertainment scene, and the potential profits to be raked in from their constant presence. A tax on public amusements, based on the similar taxation scheme introduced in Surabaya six months earlier, was thus being drafted in the beginning of 1910, expected to yield the municipality some 10,000 guilders per year.[1489] This was not much, the *Soerabaiasch-Handelsblad* claimed, if one considers that the tax on public amusements in Surabaya brought in more than 11,000 guilders in respect of activities in the months of June to December 1909

1486 This indeed occurred to the Excelsior Bioscope, which was performing on the *Alun Alun* in May 1909, and was ordered by the Assistant Resident to replace some of the bamboo since the strength of the long-standing structure was found lacking ("Stadsnieuws", *De Locomotief* (18 January 1909)).

1487 The latter option was used, for example, during the major cholera outbreaks of 1910, when the cinema and *komedi stambul* were banned ("Koempoelan perlombahan Koeda di Semarang", *Selompret Melajoe* (13 June 1910); "De Cholera", *Sumatra Post* (29 July 1910)).

1488 For example, in May 1909 Bioscope Artistique was showing at the *Stadstuin* while Johannes Bioscope was stationed at the *Alun Alun* (Advertisements, *De Locomotief* (28 May 1909)).

1489 "Belasting op Publieke Vermakelijkheden", *Soerabaiasch-Handelsblad* (29 January 1910).

Figure 6–2. "Native" *warung* in Semarang, ca. 1900. Courtesy of Leiden University Library, Image code 6039.

alone, but it could still boost the municipal income in Semarang.[1490] Nevertheless, the draft that was put forward and voted on at the Municipal Council meeting in March was rejected for undisclosed reasons, and no distribution of the votes was made available.[1491] The "native members as a rule vote haphazardly" in every city council, the report further claimed; therefore, surprises are always possible. It was further suggesting that a written ballot might prevent a situation of the "native members simply parroting the vote made by the European" members preceding them.[1492]

It was only at the end of November 1911 that an official regulation on levying and collection of taxes on public amusements came into effect in Semarang, defining the following activities as public amusements: "[...] exhibitions, fairs, fancy fairs, sports competitions, dances, operas, plays, lectures, songs and musical performances [...] to which access is granted to the public for a fee".[1493] A special controller was appointed to check that spectators at the theatre and *Stadstuin* paid the additional tax in respect of their entry tickets and that they were seated in the rank paid for, after a couple of weeks in which a policeman filled this job.[1494] About a year after levying the new tax on public amusements, the income from this scheme apparently far exceeded expecta-

---

1490 Ibid. The report noted though that what was included under the heading of "public amusements" might be debatable, since even a recent public reading about the Bataks apparently fell under this category.

1491 "Semarangsche Amusementen", *Soerabaiasch-Handelsblad* (21 March 1910).

1492 Ibid.

1493 "Belasting op de openbare vermakelijkheden", *De Locomotief* (24 November 1911).

1494 "Meer passende contrôle", *De Locomotief* (19 November 1911). It is curious that this list did not explicitly include cinema, whereas in Surabaya cinemas were particularly targeted by the new taxation scheme ("De Belasting of Publieke Vermakelijkheden", *Soerabaiasch-Handelsblad* (3 June 1909)).

tions, although an exact sum was not specified. As complaints were heard about the poor condition of roads in Semarang, *De Locomotief* proposed that this money should be put towards improving the city: "The very least that can be expected is decent paving and some sanitation".[1495]

Nevertheless, for the most part, it appears that nothing much had changed, in terms of the perceived blemish caused by cinema tents to the city's landscape. Echoing voices from the not too distant past, Semarangers were still complaining that the *Alun Alun* was an absolute dump, "[...] especially around the cinema tent, where all kinds of night soils are simply deposited on the ground [...]. The *Alun Alun* is a jack of all trades: constantly occupied by a large bamboo tent, [serving as] a parade ground for soldiers, a parking place for dogcarts, an auction place for horses – otherwise it could have been the nicest part of the city."[1496] Native- and Chinese-owned *warungs* selling their wares on the street (see Figure 6–2) were similarly deemed to be spoiling and littering the streets and sidewalks, with calls for more organised *pasar* spaces to be set up for them.[1497]

6.4 Municipal Council Resists "Cinema Fever"

By 1912, as part of what was branded a genuine "cinema fever" in Semarang, there were at least seven cinema companies, either active or in the process of permit application.[1498] Two of them, the Juliana Bioscope and the East Java Bioscope, were operating at the usual spots occupied by moving picture shows: the *Stadstuin* and the *Alun Alun*, respectively.[1499] Since the space at the *Alun Alun* was proving to be too small to accommodate all its spectators, the East Java Bioscope was offering to pay 150 guilders per month towards renting the square in front of the town hall, located next to the clubhouse on Bojong road.[1500] However, some council members deemed the operation of such an apparatus for public entertainment under the auspices of the town hall to be undignified, and the permit was never granted.[1501] Another request by the Central-Java Bioscope to hold performances at the *Alun Alun*, in a tent formerly occupied by the *wayang wong* company, was also refused.[1502] A fourth uniden-

---

1495 "De wegen", *De Locomotief* (12 August 1912).

1496 "De Aloen-Aloen", *De Locomotief* (6 July 1911), emphases added.

1497 "De Warongs langs den Weg", *De Locomotief* (11 August 1911).

1498 "Bioscopen-koorts", *De Locomotief* (25 March 1912).

1499 Advertisement, *De Locomotief* (22 March 1912).

1500 "Semarangsche Causerie", *Soerabaiasch-Handelsblad* (16 April 1913); "Bioscopen-koorts", *De Locomotief* (25 March 1912). By comparison, in 1913 the East Java Bioscope paid 250 guilders per month for renting the land at the *Alun Alun* in Pekalongan for setting up its bamboo tent ("Pekalongan", *De Locomotief* (1 April 1913)). Mr. Cooper, who was the manager of the East Java Bioscope in Pekalongan, then proposed to the municipal council to pay 400 guilders per month in rent (for a space the size of 36 by 14 meters), provided that no other cinemas would be awarded a permit to set up their tent on municipal land during this time. The municipal council refused to allow such a monopoly, and stated in response that it had its own plans of constructing a permanent building to be rented for the purpose of moving picture shows ("Gemeenteraad van Pekalongan", *Soerabaiasch-Handelsblad* (3 April 1913)). See further on the cinema monopoly in Medan in Chapter 7.

1501 "Bioscopen-koorts", *De Locomotief* (25 March 1912).

6 – Semarang: The Battleground over the Permanent Fairground Town

tified company was stationed at Karangturi, to the southeast of the Chinese *kampung*.[1503] Another unidentified company was not exhibiting at the time, but reportedly in the process of shooting a film in Semarang.[1504]

On top of these, there were permits pending for constructing two more cinema tents at the *Alun Alun*: "one 'permanent' and one of a 'more permanent' character", although the report did not specify what kind of materials were to be used for these purposes.[1505] Mr. Golfman applied for a five-year permit to build a cinema theatre ("*bioscooptheater*") on a piece of land of 50 meters by 20 meters.[1506] He offered to pay 600 guilders per month for the construction permit, on top of the rent for the land use which was not specified. After five years, the municipality would have had the right to acquire the building at two thirds the cost of its construction. The other applicant seeking to construct a cinema tent "of a more permanent character than the other bamboo sheds on the *Alun Alun*" was the Chinese Kwa Wan Hong.[1507] Similarly to Golfman, he was interested in obtaining a permit for a minimum period of at least five years.[1508]

Tan Tiong Tie, owner of the Juliana Bioscope, had another proposition in mind.[1509] The three cinema tents in operation on the *Alun Alun* at the time, he gathered, were apparently paying only f 0.01 per square metre, which brought in a maximum sum of 600 guilders per month. By comparison, the much smaller municipality of Magelang, to the southwest of Semarang, was reportedly earning 1,650 guilders in respect of three months of its *Alun Alun*. Tan Tiong Tie was therefore offering the Semarang Municipal Council to rent the *Alun Alun* for 12,000 guilders per year and become the sole permanent venue at the site. This, *De Locomotief* argued, would help to get rid of the proliferation of ugly cinema tents, and would also ensure a regular cash flow, since the municipality sometimes needed the *Alun Alun* for other purposes and had to clear out the more temporary tents taking up the entire square, thus leading to loss of income.[1510]

1502 "Midden-Java Bioscoop", *De Locomotief* (23 March 1912).

1503 "Bioscopen-koorts", *De Locomotief* (25 March 1912).

1504 Ibid.

1505 Ibid. In addition to these, film screenings were sometimes offered at the Harmonie Club for members, their wives and children, for instance, to mark the birthday of Princess Royal Juliana (Advertisement, *De Locomotief* (27 April 1912)). In order to secure a bioscope performance, the club advertised a "wanted ad" in several newspapers (Advertisement, *De Locomotief* (6 April 1912); Advertisement, *Soerabaiasch-Handelsblad* (15 April 1912)).

1506 "Bioscooptenten", *De Locomotief* (22 March 1912).

1507 Ibid.

1508 During this "cinema fever" period, there was also a "good as new Bioscope [*Bioscoop*]" offered for sale, due to the departure of its owner, along with around "1,500 meters of beautiful films and a harmonious piano" (Advertisement, *De Locomotief* (22 March 1913)). Another cinema "in a cool climate and with favourable conditions" placed an advertisement in the newspapers, seeking to hire a "violinist, flutist and clarinettist" (Advertisement, *De Locomotief* (25 March 1913)). Piano-playing skills were considered an advantage.

1509 "Om de aloon-aloon", *De Locomotief* (23 April 1912).

1510 Ibid.

Although the Municipal Council did not view this idea in a favourable light, it did seem to realise that it was under-pricing its land. While the Juliana Bioscope was paying 600 guilders per month for performing at the *Stadstuin* at the time, F. van Vianen's Venus Bioscope from Tegal that followed in its place in late 1912 was now asked to pay 1,000 guilders per month for screenings at the venue, which could seat about 1,500 spectators.[1511] Offering two shows per day, one in the afternoon for children and another in the evening for adults, ticket prices for members of the *Stadstuin* were advertised at f 0.50 for regular shows, while non-members were required to pay f 1 for a box seat, f 0.75 for first class, f 0.60 for second class, f 0.30 for third class, f 0.15 for fourth class, and children in all classes were admitted at half price. Another category reserved for Javanese only was offered at f 0.05, and none of the tickets were apparently subject to the additional municipal tax.[1512] Special late night screenings of films that were forbidden for screening elsewhere on Java, such as detective films, were occasionally offered to members only, at f 1 for adults and f 0.50 for children.[1513] Since attendance figures were apparently climbing, as of 1 January 1913, the Venus Bioscope was required to offer two free shows per month to subscribed members of the *Stadstuin* rather than just once a month.[1514] To make up for its expected loss of income, the Venus Bioscope immediately began to offer companies to hang advertising posters in the cinema space, but the fee charged for this is not known.[1515]

The future of the *Alun Alun*, meanwhile, continued to be the subject of stubborn debates between the Municipal Council and the government which, despite the decentralisation in place, apparently still held sway over certain aspects of urban administrative processes in Semarang. A lengthy report in April 1913 revealed some of the background of the situation and ongoing power struggles between the two authorities. In 1912, when the first proposal for a permanent tent was submitted, the former Municipal Council chairman apparently conveyed to the government that he was of the opinion that placement of a permanent tent for a significant time of five years would detract from the "preservation of [what he perceived as] the historic character of the *Alun Alun* and therefore be in breach of article 5 of the institution ordinance of the municipality", relating to the conservation of the site.[1516] By the time two more requests for setting up permanent cinema tents on the *Alun Alun* came in, alongside a permit application for a lemonade stand, the new council

---

1511 "De Stadstuin", *De Locomotief* (16 November 1912).

1512 Advertisement, *De Locomotief* (13 December 1912).

1513 Advertisement, *De Locomotief* (14 December 1912). Since the orders by the Assistant-Resident of Police from Batavia regarding the ban of films were already in place at the time, and as Semarang reportedly had its own inspection commission in place, *De Locomotief* suggested that the police chief in charge was getting some incentives to allow such screenings to go ahead ("De keuring van de bioscoop-films", *De Locomotief* (4 September 1912)).

1514 "De Stadstuin", *De Locomotief* (16 November 1912).

1515 Advertisement, *De Locomotief* (23 December 1912).

1516 "De Aloon Aloon", *De Locomotief* (18 April 1913).

6 – Semarang: The Battleground over the Permanent Fairground Town

chairman pointed out that any such long-term permit should stipulate that the municipality was entitled to terminate the contract at any point.[1517] The *Alun Alun* was intended to provide relaxation for the people, he argued, and "the cinema was now indeed a popular leisure activity and – since the supervision set in place – a form of relaxation with an educative effect. Had the cinema previously existed, [such permanent tents] would have surely been an inseparable part of the historical character of the *Alun Alun*", he concluded.[1518] It was further argued that a third of the *Alun Alun* was already ceded for the construction of the *Stadstuin* and other municipal buildings, so the authorities themselves had already infringed the original use of the site.

Nevertheless, the government remained firm in its convictions: permanent cinema tents on the *Alun Alun* were considered to be "inconsistent with the purpose of the site". The "unsightly temporary tents, in which the cinema and other amusements are shown, should be warded off the *Alun Alun* as soon as possible", the council chairman then wrote, maintaining the official line, in order to enable the municipality to recover the communal lawn space.[1519] Finally, while the chairman was in support of authorising the permanent lemonade kiosk, since the presence of the mobile *warungs* at the *Alun Alun* signalled that such an establishment was indispensable, the government still considered it to be at odds with the historical character of the site. The government had no problem with the portable *warungs* occupying the *Alun Alun* for a few hours a day, it said, but objected to anything of a more permanent nature. Finally then, all requests submitted to the council were rejected.[1520]

Tan Tiong Tie gave up on the endeavour long before these discussions were finally laid to rest. By the end of 1912, when his contract at the *Stadstuin* was about to expire and Vianen was to replace him with the Venus Bioscope, Tan put his device up for sale for 12,000 guilders in cash, in addition to a piano and 40,000 meters of films "in good condition" for an unspecified amount.[1521]

1517 The concept of the Javanese "*alun-alun*" carries symbolic significance, going back to the royal kraton culture. Traditionally serving as a large space in front of the residence of the Regent, the *alun-alun*, according to Basundoro, was a "formal space closely related to official (royal) ceremonies, […] a meeting ground for a ruler and his subjects […] where] the king's guests had to wait before being admitted into his presence" (Purnawan Basundoro, "The Two *alun-alun* in Malang (1930–1950)", in Freek Colombijn and Joost Coté (eds.), *Cars, Conduits, and Kampongs: The Modernization of the Indonesian City, 1920–1960* (Leiden: Brill, 2015), 272–299, here 273). As a symbol of power, the Dutch colonial government was drawn to the *alun-alun*, often erecting the accommodation of colonial officials or staging military parades at such sites. Nevertheless, during the colonial period, as the powers of the traditional Regents waned, the interpretation of the *alun-alun* was also shifting: "It was no longer regarded with respect as an official space belonging to the government, but was transposed into a public space, which was accessible to anyone, high or low. Relegated to the secular sphere, the *alun-alun* also functioned as an urban park whose subsequent development was inextricably linked to the growth of the town as a whole" (ibid., 273–274). Cinema tents played a part in these transformations of the *Alun Alun*, in Semarang and in other cities.

1518 "De Aloon Aloon", *De Locomotief* (18 April 1913), emphasis added.

1519 Ibid., emphasis added. Bamboo tents or sheds on the *Alun Alun* were occupied by different performers who followed each other in the same tent, possibly after making some stylistic adjustments.

1520 Ibid.

1521 Advertisement, *De Locomotief* (25 November 1912).

6.5 Plans for a New Multi-Purpose Semarang Theatre Building

In 1913, against the backdrop of the municipality's continued refusals of applications for constructing permanent cinema buildings, and with the preparations for the Semarang International Colonial Exhibition in 1914 underway, another initiative to construct a new European-style theatre building was taking shape. The existing Semarang theatre building, which was opened in 1877, was still satisfactory to some: "There is a hall and there is a stage and both are tolerable."[1522] At the same time, it was an "inhospitable, shabby building, where the entrance also serves as the exit, everything is just good enough to sit in, to watch and to applaud. Any improvement of the old hovel would be a waste of money; a waste of money which is not there", proponents for keeping the existing theatre argued.[1523] Others found it to be poorly painted, susceptible to interruptions due to rainy conditions, and lacking separate seats and access ways for "natives and native women".[1524] The absence of separate seats for less well-off Europeans was further considered a shortcoming of the existing theatre. Since the new theatre was projected to be used for theatrical shows during 300 nights per year as well as to be rented out to "a good cinema company" and *stambul* troupes for the remaining 65 nights, such facilities were thought to be indispensable.[1525] This was considered to be the opportune moment to construct a new theatre, with a new harbour about to open in Semarang and the Exhibition looming ahead.

Due to shortage of funds, some members of the theatre association were even proposing to ride on the back of the upcoming Exhibition for the construction of the new theatre. Most of the pavilions for the Exhibition were to be constructed as temporary structures, to be taken down once the event was concluded. Nevertheless, as the Exhibition plans were coming into full swing, it was suggested that the main hall for the festivities could potentially double up as the future theatre building.[1526] The building plans incorporated an attractive design for the Exhibition hall and subsequent theatre, serving as a monument to commemorate the Exhibition.[1527] Yet, there were a couple of problems with this plan. Firstly, the Exhibition's main hall was to be built in an area that was virtually a deserted part of the city, while it was recognised that a theatre should ideally be located in the most central spot. Secondly, with just over a year to go until the Exhibition's opening, time was quickly running out

---

1522 "De Schouwburg-komedie", *De Locomotief* (16 August 1913).

1523 Ibid.

1524 "Een Nieuwe Schouwburg", *De Locomotief* (17 May 1913).

1525 "Het geheim van den schouwburg", *De Locomotief* (14 May 1913).

1526 A similar scheme was planned for a museum of "Native arts and crafts", to be constructed for the Exhibition and to remain in place after its conclusion ("Een museum voor Semarang", *De Locomotief* (18 September 1913)). Five thousand and five hundred guilders out of the 20,000 guilders were already raised by the Exhibition's committee in order to construct the Semarang pavilion in the "Javanese style". The financial logic of constructing the pavilion-museum continued to be subject of debate ("Het Museumplan", *De Locomotief* (15 October 1913)).

1527 "Schouwburgplannen", *De Locomotief* (31 May 1913).

and the risk of failing to execute the construction as planned was high.[1528] The *Alun Alun* was again raised as an optional location but quickly rejected, finally resorting, once again, to the site next to the Clubhouse, on the corner of Karang Tengah.[1529] A new shop building was also in the process of construction along Bojong road, and land on the corner of Depok next to the Club, with the *kampung* land lying behind it, was being offered up for sale. "A theatre there can be more than a rent-free city monument", *De Locomotief* purported, and would make for a nice town square leading to an improvement in urban life.[1530]

In terms of its profitability, as a theatre that could also serve as a cinema, well-located and functional, the new building was expected to quickly cover the costs of construction. Operating it as a theatre and a cinema harnessed potential for financial gains, based on the following rough approximations provided: the cost of the land was estimated at 50,000 guilders and the construction of the theatre building and cinema at another 150,000 guilders, while the projected revenues were 50,000 guilders (presumably, per year), meaning that a capital of 150,000 guilders would have had to be sustained, possibly via mortgage. These were considered to be the worst case predictions.[1531] The cinema would in principle be able to be in operation every night, except for nights when the theatre was to be used by other companies and, if the need occurred, a separate cinema tent could be set up. While the report was unable to quantify the feasible operating costs, the net profit was nevertheless estimated as at least 40 guilders per night on average. "For 300 nights this would represent a net profit of *f* 12,000 per annum."[1532] This did not even take into account the potential income from rental to other performing troupes. Based on these modest figures, the capital of 150,000 guilders was to yield a respectable interest rate of eight per cent, according to *De Locomotief*.[1533] Despite this optimistic projection, there still appeared to be hesitation about delving into such an investment, and no decision was made in the matter before the Colonial Exhibition was underway.

6.6 The Semarang International Colonial Exhibition, 1914

6.6.1 *Lead Up to the Exhibition*

By 1913 the Municipal Council was heavily preoccupied with preparations for the Semarang International Colonial Exhibition, which was to take place from August to November 1914. Conceptually based on the international exhibitions held in the West, the International Colonial Exhibition of Semarang was

---

1528 "De schouwburg", *De Locomotief* (13 June 1913).

1529 "Schouwburgplannen", *De Locomotief* (31 May 1913).

1530 Ibid.

1531 "De Schouwburg", *De Locomotief* (13 June 1913).

1532 Ibid.

1533 Ibid.

intended to display Dutch colonial achievements.[1534] Such exhibitions often served as a setting for demonstrating modernity and progress, in the content of the displays as well as in the form of the exhibition grounds through the employment of architecture and technologies like electricity or new construction materials. These kinds of exhibitions held in colonial settings fulfilled equivalent roles towards a different target audience. Thus, rather than nationalistic celebrations showing residents in Europe their colonial achievements, exhibitions in the colonies with many "Native" visitors were often even more didactic and pedagogical in their approach.[1535]

The Semarang Colonial Exhibition was proposed to be the biggest exhibition ever displayed in the Netherlands Indies: "It covered 26 hectares, included 600 meters of roadway, 1,067 meters of railway, 105 specially built buildings covering 39,260 square meters, featured extensive electric and gas lighting and power generation and employed hundreds of Indonesian 'helpers' and 'coolies' to establish and maintain it. Modernity and progress were embedded into its very design, construction and operation."[1536] The exhibition was essentially intended to promote Semarang as a commercial hub and centre of culture. Initial planning began already in 1912 with the goal of opening in 1913, to coincide with the centenary of Dutch independence from France. However, since financing proved to be difficult to raise, the exhibition had to be postponed to 1914. This was, nevertheless, rationalised as an occasion to mark the Post-Napoleonic restoration of Java to the Dutch. Postponing it unfortunately meant that the exhibition now coincided with the outbreak of the First World War, therefore restricting the event to a more muted tone than originally intended, to maintain a low profile and in keeping with Dutch neutrality. The exhibition was nevertheless international, thanks to its representation of regional interests, including Japan, China, some exhibiters from British India, and official exhibits from New South Wales and Western Australia.[1537]

The Exhibition included industrial and agricultural displays, with the sugar industry taking a prime spot, and the principle aim of showing European colonial progress. The "Native" section of the exhibition included all major administrative and ethnic regions of the archipelago, represented by arts and

---

1534 The tradition of international exhibitions, also known as world fairs, dates back to the 1851 Great Exhibition of the Works of Industry of All Nations in London and continued over the next century at different locations. While the colonies were present in all such exhibitions through the display of goods, they would become expressly on display as of the first (and only) world exhibition held in the Netherlands: the 1883 International Colonial and Export Trade Exhibition in Amsterdam. On the history of the Dutch colonial entries to world exhibitions in the West from 1880 to 1931, especially the ethnographic displays of indigenous people's everyday lives and crafts, see Marieke Bloembergen, *Colonial Spectacles: The Netherlands and the Dutch East Indies at the World Exhibitions, 1880–1931*, trans. Beverley Jackson (Singapore: Singapore University Press, 2006).

1535 Joost Coté, "Staging modernity: the Semarang International Colonial Exhibition, 1914", *Review of Indonesian and Malaysian Affairs* 40, no. 1 (2006): 2.

1536 Ibid., 3.

1537 Ibid., 4.

6 – Semarang: The Battleground over the Permanent Fairground Town

Figure 6–3. The Luna Park at the Semarang Colonial Exhibition, 1913. Reproduced from Heel, *Gedenkboek van de Koloniale Tentoonstelling. Tweede Deel*.

crafts displays, dance and music performances, or even traditional housing.[1538] Special attention was also paid to entertainment for the visitors. Four restaurants (including one Chinese), six bars, and three other rooms where tea and coffee could be purchased were available on the premises, alongside several *warungs* in the "Native" section.[1539] Three permanent music tents were stationed in front of the terrace of the main exhibition hall, and next to the football and hockey fields, alongside open-air concerts given by the music corps of the fifth infantry battalion of Semarang. Moreover, each bar and restaurant offered live musical accompaniment of its own, whether in the form of a string orchestra, operetta company, or ladies' choir.[1540] On top of these, there were piano concerts, opera performances, operetta and cabaret shows, and ballroom dancing. The "Native Amusements" included *gamelan* music in several of the pavilions, ceremonial Javanese dances, and *wayang wong* performances.[1541] Initially, there was one fireworks display during the day and two at night; however, while these attracted much attention, it was decided to put an end to them due to the risk of fire.[1542] Spectators were invited to watch football, hockey and tennis matches, as well as horse and car races.[1543] According to Coté, "Native attendance had been a principle issue for the organising committee, if only in financial terms. The erection of a Luna Park [see Figure 6–3],

---

[1538] Ibid., 21.

[1539] M. van Heel (ed.), *Gedenkboek van de Koloniale Tentoonstelling Semarang, 20 Augustus–22 November 1914. Eerste Deel* (Batavia: Mercurius, 1916), 67–68.

[1540] Ibid., 68–69.

[1541] Ibid., 71.

[1542] Ibid., 73.

[1543] Ibid., 73–74.

of native entertainments and *warung* were expressly aimed at improving 'the gate': the Javanese were to provide the crowd."[1544]

6.6.2 Cinema at the Exhibition

By the time the Colonial Exhibition was held in 1914, cinema was rather well-established in the Indies as a form of popular entertainment and a regular feature at any kind of *pasar malam* held in the main towns and cities. Moreover, since cinema was also present at international exhibitions in the West on which the Semarang initiative was modelled, it was bound to be included at the Colonial Exhibition in Semarang as well.[1545] In fact, the cinema was to fulfil three different functions, as conceptualised in advance by the Exhibition's organising committee. The first function was to serve as part of the forms of popular entertainment available to visitors to the Exhibition. Already about a year before the Exhibition's opening, advertisements were placed in the local newspapers across the Indies, calling on operators of cinemas and other amusements to urgently contact the Secretariat of the Colonial Exhibition directly for all the information on the application procedures for a permit to perform on the Exhibition grounds.[1546] The second function was to use films as illustrative or pedagogical tools, side by side with the various objects and peoples on display at the Exhibition.[1547] Finally, the third function of the cinema was to capture scenes from the Exhibition itself on film, in order to disseminate them and reach people who could not physically attend the Exhibition in person. Since Umbgrove's East Java Bioscope was put in charge of this, it is likely that the plan was to keep the films in the archive he was compiling which, as may be recalled, burned down in 1918.

Yet, as the 1916 souvenir book of the Exhibition suggests, many of the original plans conceived on paper by the organisers never took shape in reality. For instance, the initial proposal for the Luna Park, in the context of which at least

---

[1544] Coté, "Staging modernity", 30, italics in original. The range of ticket prices reflected this: subscription tickets for the entire period of the Exhibition, providing unlimited access between 20 August and 22 November, cost 30 guilders for a main ticket (*hoofdkaart*) for Europeans and Foreign Orientals and ten guilders for a minor ticket (*bijkaart*) "for female and minor-aged male members of a family" accompanying. In addition, a subscription specifically for "Natives" was priced at a flat fee of 6 guilders. Single entry tickets were also available, similarly differentiating between the categories of European and Foreign Oriental visitors and "Native" visitors: daytime tickets for Europeans and Foreign Orientals at f 0.50 and f 0.25 for their children below ten years old, evening tickets for Europeans and Foreign Orientals at f 0.75 and f 0.40 for their children. Daytime tickets for "Natives" were offered at f 0.10, while evening tickets were sold for f 0.15. The prices of tickets for "Natives" were lowered near the end of October, in a further attempt to attract more Javanese visitors. When it was realised that the price cut did not provide enough stimulus, the prices were raised back (see Heel, *Gedenkboek van de Koloniale Tentoonstelling*, 117–118).

[1545] On moving pictures at World Fairs in the West, see Emmanuelle Toulet, "Le cinéma à l'Éxposition universelle de 1900", *Revue d'histoire moderne et contemporaine* 33, no. 2 (April–June 1986): 179–209; Tom Gunning, "The World as Object Lesson: Cinema Audiences, Visual Culture and the St. Louis World's Fair, 1904", *Film History* 6, no. 4, Audiences and Fans (Winter 1994), 422–444.

[1546] Advertisement, *Soerabaiasch-Handelsblad* (2 September 1913).

[1547] On the pedagogical uses of objects and still images at the Semarang Colonial Exhibition, see Joost Coté, "'To See is to Know': the Pedagogy of the Colonial Exhibition, Semarang, 1914", *Paedagogica Historica* 36, no. 1 (2000): 341–366.

one cinema show was to be embedded, had proposed the attraction in the style and scale made available at exhibitions in Europe, at a projected investment of 40,000 guilders.[1548] Nevertheless, based on information obtained from British India regarding the operation of a Luna Park in densely populated areas, doubts were raised about the feasibility of success of a European-style Luna Park in the tropics. The risks involved finally appeared too great for the organising committee to take upon itself, leading to the construction of a Luna Park of a much more modest scale. Covering 5,120 square-meters, the Luna Park was not paved but at least was provided with a good drainage system. Moreover, the ground was raised where deemed necessary, to help prevent flooding. Mr. Bennis, Director of The Carnival Show, paid 5,000 guilders for a permit – although without guaranteeing monopoly – to set up and operate various attractions, including a movie theatre, a steam carousel, an aerial tramway, various tents for shooting and throwing games and other such amusements.[1549] The Exhibition's management set up a 585-square-meter hangar used by alternating theatre and dance companies, as well as by film exhibitors. Film screenings were thus not necessarily a regular fixture on the Luna Park grounds, but rather one of various popular entertainment forms. During the month of October, a circus performed at the Luna Park as well.

Access to the Luna Park was free of charge, as were at least some film screenings, such as those offered in early September. A notice for these free shows appeared in the Exhibition's weekly journal, printed and distributed by *De Locomotief*, providing the time and location of the shows in Malay and Dutch, the only difference being that the Malay text omitted the final statement included in the Dutch version: "An attraction, especially for the native visitors".[1550] No information was found about the film programmes that were screened at the Exhibition, so it is unclear what kind of special "attraction" these shows should have constituted for "Native" spectators, who had been flocking to cinema tents for years by that time. Dedicated film screening venues remained operational concurrently with the Exhibition, in the regular locations for cinema shows, such as the Venus Bioscope at the *Stadstuin* and the East Java Bioscope behind the *Stadstuin*.[1551]

Another hall, built for the exhibition section of the sugar industry, was designated especially for screenings of films captured by Umbgrove's East Java Bioscope, in collaboration with several managers of sugar companies and other agricultural enterprises in the Indies. The back wall of the hall was decorated with a neatly-executed painting of the map of Java, 13 meters long and 4.80 feet high. It was intended that these educational films would be screened in rotation, as popular science illustrations of the sugar industry. However, shortly before the Exhibition's opening, and much to the disappointment of

1548 Heel, *Gedenkboek van de Koloniale Tentoonstelling, Eerste Deel*, 72.
1549 Ibid.
1550 "Bioscoop", *Tentoonstellings-Courant* (5 September 1914).
1551 Advertisements, *De Locomotief* (25 August 1914).

all those involved, it was revealed that none of the scenes shot especially for the occasion could be used. This was probably linked to problems with film development that Umbgrove later admitted to have experienced.[1552] Unable to fulfil its original designation, the hall was handed over to the sugar company Lindeteves & Stokvis, which used it to display tools related to the sugar industry.[1553]

Despite the failure to deliver the films for the Exhibition, Umbgrove's East Java Bioscope was still welcomed to film at the Exhibition itself (see Figure 4–5). The motivation for capturing these scenes was equally about entertainment, education and keeping an archival record "[...] for posterity [...] beyond the purpose and demands of an exhibition in the tropics".[1554] In the meantime, the East Java Bioscope's films from the Exhibition were quickly capturing headlines in Surabaya. "The Colonial exhibition can be visited from tomorrow at the East Java Bioscope", the *Soerabaiasch-Handelsblad* read. "The industrious management has 'recorded' the entire show."[1555] Another report noted that the Exhibition opening could now be experienced in Surabaya, without having to spend anything on costly travel and accommodation in Semarang itself. "The exhibition opened yesterday and tomorrow we already get to see everything on screen."[1556]

The footage from the Exhibition was split into two programmes and offered on different evenings. The first included around twenty glimpses from the Semarang Colonial Exhibition, covering the pavilions representing Japan, China, the Toba Batak and Celebes (Sulawesi), in addition to Acehnese amusements and views of a Dayak war dance.[1557] It further included records of the transportation modes on the Exhibition grounds.[1558] The second programme was comprised of scenes captured at the *kampung tukang* of "native industry and crafts in the Netherlands Indies", providing an "interesting recording" of, among others, Balinese sculptors at work, a *batik* workshop, production of copper pots and other objects, and manufacturing of *pajongs* (Indonesian sun or rain shades).[1559]

6.6.3 Aftermath of the Exhibition
In the final analysis, while the number of visitors to the Exhibition was initially satisfactory, the Luna Park's attractions and the Exhibition in general did not

---

[1552] See Section 4.5.

[1553] M. van Heel (ed.), *Gedenkboek van de Koloniale Tentoonstelling Semarang, 20 Augustus–22 November 1914. Tweede Deel* (Batavia: Mercurius, 1916), 94.

[1554] "De Koloniale tentoonstelling op de film", *Soerabaiasch-Handelsblad* (23 October 1914).

[1555] Ibid.

[1556] "Bioscopen", *Nieuwe Soerabaja Courant* (21 August 1914).

[1557] "Film-nieuws", *Nieuwe Soerabaja Courant* (23 October 1914).

[1558] Ibid.

[1559] "Amusementen", *Soerabaiasch-Handelsblad* (30 October 1914); "Film-nieuws", *Nieuwe Soerabaja Courant* (30 October 1914).

6 – Semarang: The Battleground over the Permanent Fairground Town

Figure 6–4. The Main Hall of the Semarang Colonial Exhibition with its garden terrace, 1913. Reproduced from Heel, *Gedenkboek van de Koloniale Tentoonstelling, Tweede Deel*.

prove to be big draws for "Native" visitors, leading to considerable losses to the different operators. The Luna Park, the souvenir book concluded, "by and large did not serve as a special attraction" able to draw visitors to the Exhibition, as the organisers had hoped.[1560] "In fact, in the three months between 20 August and 22 November", Coté recaps, "the exhibition was attended by slightly less ["Natives"] than Europeans, 306,795 compared with 370,472. The lower than expected native attendance – and the non-arrival of foreign tourists due to the war – meant that the exhibition was a financial failure."[1561] Several reasons were advanced as to why "Natives" failed to attend the Exhibition: intimidation because the exhibition was "too modern for the 'ordinary native'", fantastic stories disseminated of visitors either disappearing at the Exhibition or dying subsequently after, the influence of the growing opposition to the colonial regime, and the simple admission that perhaps there was merely nothing interesting for them to see.[1562]

Following the conclusion of the Semarang International Colonial Exhibition, and since the building plans for a new multi-purpose Semarang theatre building were still hanging in the air, discussions returned to revolve around using the Exhibition's main hall with garden terrace (see Figure 6–4) as a temporary theatre, at least until the dust of war settled and a new theatre could be built. "We would find it very unfortunate", wrote *De Locomotief*, "if this

---

1560 Heel, *Gedenkboek van de Koloniale Tentoonstelling, Eerste Deel*, 72. The Diorama of Central Java, on display as part of the "Native" section of the exhibition, presented as a gift of the Netherlands-Indies Railway Company, was similarly a disappointment, with merely 8,423 visitors, most of whom were non-Natives. The diorama was displayed in an iron shed, 460 square meters in size. Entrance prices for Natives was ƒ0.05 and ƒ0.25 for non-Natives (ibid., 73).

1561 Coté, "Staging modernity", 30.

1562 Ibid., 30–32.

opportunity to acquire a new theatre building were neglected. A better chance than this will not recur."[1563] In order for the theatre union to take over the former exhibition hall, Oei Tiong Ham, one of the wealthiest men in Semarang and the owner of the land on which it was built, still needed to agree to lease the land for fifty years, the first twenty-five of them – free of charge. Calculating a cost of 1,000 guilders per year on leasing the land, this would have already represented a saving of twenty thousand guilders for the theatre union, compared to the earlier construction plans drawn up in 1913. While the Netherlands Indies Railway Company (NIS) was ready to make an offer to acquire the old theatre, there was still foot-dragging with the decision making. Some nostalgically maintained that the old theatre was "so nice", had "such beautiful acoustics" and that it was, after all, "well located".[1564] No further evidence of what occurred to the celebration hall, or to the plans for a multi-purpose new theatre, have been found in this research.

6.7 Conclusion

This chapter examined the state of moving picture exhibition in Semarang, from the earliest promises of moving picture shows, through temporary structures washed away by the monsoons, to the later flood of exhibitors wishing to set up more permanent venues, only to be exasperated and dismissed by the local authorities. As opposed to the lively movie-going scene we have previously witnessed on the sprawling urban landscapes of Surabaya and Batavia, by the end of the period studied here and at the conclusion the International Colonial Exhibition in 1914, the status of cinema in Semarang, a circular-shaped city with a distinct centre, was mixed. On the one hand, the Japanese firm Choya & Co. on Pekojan Street, which normally traded in Japanese products including beer and cigarettes, began offering rental of films that were acquired in Singapore.[1565] This meant that Semarang was officially becoming a trading point for films, which would be enough to make the city one of the four locations singled out by the Cinema Ordinance of 1916 for closer inspection of films.

On the other hand, the state of infrastructure of cinema houses was rather dire, compared to Surabaya and Batavia. For example, while the East Java Bioscope offered shows in Semarang in its own "spacious, clean, ventilated" permanent tent, with several emergency exit doors and "well-arranged seating", it was far too small to accommodate all spectators wishing to attend shows.[1566] However, since the land that it was occupying was situated between a hotel and a mosque, it had no room to expand, and the Municipal Council was not showing any

---

1563 "De Schouwburg", *De Locomotief* (18 December 1914).

1564 Ibid.

1565 Advertisement, *De Locomotief* (1 May 1914). The advertisement included a recommendation for the films from Singapore's Harima Cinematograph.

1566 "De Openingsvoorstelling van de Oost-Java Bioscoop", *De Locomotief* (23 September 1912).

6 – Semarang: The Battleground over the Permanent Fairground Town

signs of relenting in matters of permits anytime soon.[1567] The well-ventilated hall at the *Stadstuin* was often used for film screenings by some of the prominent companies touring Java at the time, and by 1914 was regularly occupied by the Venus Bioscope. Yet, cinema was only one occupant of this building and it therefore had to share the space with other entertainments, not to mention – to offer a certain amount of shows per month free of charge to members of the *Stadstuin*.[1568] We might conclude, then, that the municipality's incessant efforts to control the landscape of popular entertainment, seemingly driven by a more puritanical approach, was a success. And although it appears Semarang did not get to boast of its own modern cinema palace that other towns and cities already had by this point, in the coming years this capital of Central Java was about to undergo some major changes and set the tone in town planning, redevelopment of the *kampung* and urban architecture.[1569]

[1567] "Semarangsche Causerie", *Soerabaiasch-Handelsblad* (16 April 1913).

[1568] Advertisement, *De Locomotief* (16 November 1912).

[1569] The work of architect Thomas Karsten, philanthropist and entrepreneur Henry Freek Tillema, and civil servant Dirk Johan Anton Westerveld are often underlined in this regard, even if their modernising initiatives were not always welcomed by *kampung* dwellers. See further in Erica Bogaers and Peter de Ruijter, "Ir. Thomas Karsten and Indonesian Town Planning, 1915–1940", in Peter J. M. Nas (ed.), *The Indonesian City: Studies in Urban Development and Planning* (Dordrecht-Holland/Cinnaminson-U.S.A.: Foris Publications, 1986), 71–88; Joost Coté, "Towards an Architecture of Association: H. F. Tillema, Semarang and the discourse on the colonial 'slum'", in Peter J. M. Nas (ed.), *The Indonesian Town Revisited* (Münster: LIT Verlag, 2002), 319–347.

7

Medan: The Making and Breaking of a Monopoly

*Deli is advancing at an incredible pace. For some years now, one can stand on the street looking out for the happy owner of a bicycle pedalling by, the vehicle having been stolen from under the veranda of a European household, without being able to identify the offender. People of all ranks and classes cycle here. Natives and Chinese, who in an entire year do not make enough money to cover the cost of a mediocre bicycle [*fiets*], can be seen on a bike [*karetta angin*]. [...]*

*The fact that, before proceeding with business, murderers, burglars and thieves like [to consult] spirit séances and through a medium determine a good day [...] also testifies to the progress [*vooruitgang*] and modern [*moderne*] pursuit of the mystical elements in Deli.*

Luckily, we can also speak of changes in the right direction here. We have been promised an improvement in the street and city cleaning; Medan's bridges have been repaired and restored, and the narrow [...] perilous road from the Benting to Polonia was made sufficiently wide. On the crossroads by the office of Mr. Opry a new building is being erected, the purpose of which is not yet known to me. Judging by the foundations, it could be the construction of an observatory.

Also, in amusements, Medan is provided for: one night we go to the Bioscope and the other – to the Bangsawan *opera; at least we can do that.*

"Deli-Nieuws", Sumatra Post *(6 November 1901).*

Medan, capital of the Deli region on the island of Sumatra, served as the seat of the Resident of East Sumatra and of the Sultan of Deli. Since 1862, when the treaty between the Sultan and the Dutch was signed, Deli was opened up to colonial exploitation and Medan became the centre of the region.[1570] Unlike the Javanese experience of more than 300 years of foreign control, the "international 'pioneering' of Sumatra" was a relatively new development, with the local leaders being the Sultans of each region.[1571] During the second half of the nineteenth century the Deli region became known for its tobacco industry, developed with Dutch and later foreign

---

1570 The Agrarian Land Act of 1870, which opened the door to private entrepreneurs, may have only applied to areas under direct Dutch rule, thus, Java, but local rulers on the east coast of Sumatra also began granting long-term concessions of questionable legality to foreign companies at this time (see Ann Laura Stoler, *Capitalism and Confrontation in Sumatra's Plantation Belt, 1870–1989* (New Haven/London: Yale University Press, 1985), 16).

1571 Ibid., vii.

investment.[1572] By the 1890s, plantations specialising in cultivating tobacco, primarily intended for the European and American markets, had transformed the region: "Plantation systems based on careful demarcation of planted areas, a reliance on imported, largely Chinese, labour and the development of an infrastructure of small railways and linking roads dramatically altered the appearance and social structure of large parts of East Sumatra".[1573] At the turn of the century new industries, namely, rubber and palm oil, became even bigger businesses.[1574] Railway building on Sumatra, as opposed to Java, nevertheless struggled to connect the three distinct regions of East, West and South Sumatra (see further discussion in the Introduction).

Travellers arriving at the port of Belawan-Deli would have been transported by railway into town, gaining an impression of the characteristic Deli scenery: "[...] a large, bare, monotonous surface, for the most part covered with high alang-alang grass [...] or with wild, tangled shrubs; little inhabited, except where here and there a tobacco plantation lies in the midst of the fields".[1575] Upon arriving in "electrically lighted" Medan, the city's attractions and character would have stood out immediatel:

> As soon as we exit the station into the spacious *alun-alun* [Esplanade], we perceive at first glance that we have arrived at a new, busy, and flourishing place. In 1869 it was chosen by NIENHUYS, the originator of the Deli Company [the largest and oldest of the many tobacco-cultivating companies], as the seat of their chief administration, on account of its adaptability for import and export. Before that time it was a wretched *campong*, surrounded by a double wall, traces of which still remain. It was not till 1871 that Medan had a doctor of its own. Now we find "*De Witte Sociëteit*" (club), next to which stands the post and telegraph-office, the barracks, the fort, large Chinese and other shops, a couple of hotels (the "Orange"- and "Medan"-hotel), the racecourse, the Resident's house, with offices, prisons, etc., and the establishments of the Deli Company.[1576]

What was found to be particularly striking for anyone coming to Medan after visiting Java was apparently "the more modern Western character in the laying out of the grounds and buildings, the greater variety in architecture, adapted to the mixed population", as compared to Java and sharing more features with nearby Singapore.[1577] With some two thousand Europeans, fourteen thousand Chinese, and seventeen thousand "Natives" in Medan in 1915, it was a hub for people of various ethnicities from the region (Malays, Toba Batak, Karo, Mandailing, Simalungun, Acehnese, Chinese, Arabs), different Western nationalities (American, Belgian, Dutch, English, French, German, Poles, Scandinavians, Swiss), and various religious affinities (Muslim majority, Christian

---

1572 See Mark Cleary and Goh Kim Chuan, *Environment and Development in the Straits of Malacca (Routledge Studies in Development and Society)* (London: Routledge, 2000), 73.

1573 Ibid.

1574 Ibid., 74.

1575 Bemmelen et al., *Guide through Netherlands India*, 130.

1576 Ibid., 131–132, emphases added.

1577 Ibid.

7 – Medan: The Making and Breaking of a Monopoly

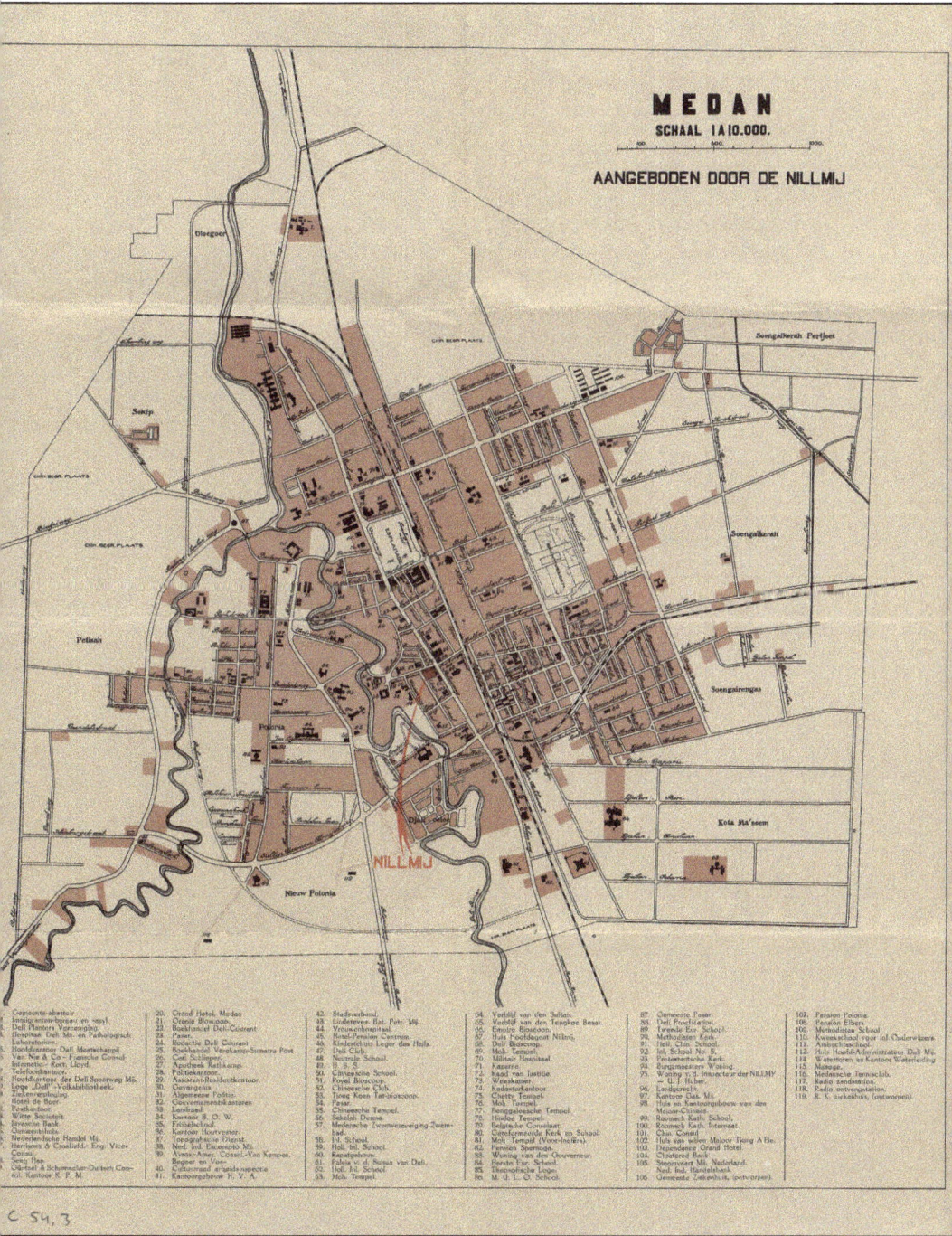

Figure 7-1. Map of Medan, offered by the Nederlandsch-Indische Levensverzekering- en Lijfrente-Maatschappij (NILLMIJ), ca. 1915. Courtesy of Leiden University Library, Image code D C 54,3.

minority – consisting of European and others, like many Toba Bataks, and small percentages of Buddhist and Hindu).[1578] Another guidebook from around 1925 noted:

> Deli is the most flourishing district of entire Sumatra and Medan, its capital, is a thriving and busy city of more than 45.200 inhabitants. Modern hotels, beautiful homes in spacious garden grounds, smooth automobile roads, good stores, and tidy, well-policed streets give the place a general aspect of prosperity and wealth. On weekends Medan is at its best and brightest. Then the employees of the various estates up-country motor into town to partake its pleasures, and by escaping, once in a while, from their solitude to the dance floor of Hotel De Boer or the Medan Hotel they keep free from depression and fit for their work.[1579]

The modern, cosmopolitan character of Medan, as well as its advantageous location – in close proximity to the British settlements of Singapore and Penang, and its connection via a major port – made it an attractive spot for travelling entertainers in the late nineteenth century and early twentieth century. At the turn of the century the *Koninklijke Paketvaart Maatschappij* operated a line from Singapore to Belawan-Deli fortnightly, a service from Batavia every four weeks (in addition to weekly communication services available during the first four months of the year), and from Penang around every five days.[1580] Indeed, many of the early travelling moving picture shows, even when first performing on Java or in Makassar, kept Medan in their itineraries with access via Singapore, and then would typically either continue to Penang or return to Singapore. At times, Medan was the first to receive some new technologies via Singapore, as journalists noted in January 1914:

> It may be a great peculiarity that the Netherlands Indies, Deli at least, is provided with the latest gadget in the cinematographic field, while Europe, not counting the very rare exception, is still waiting. This is the case with Edison's latest invention, the kinetophone [*kinetofoon*]: the talking and singing film has arrived in Deli [at the Orange Bioscope] via the Straits from America, while only barely a month ago it was shown in the renowned Berlin.[1581]

At the same time, Medan, and Sumatra in general, was also a somewhat limiting destination for touring companies. Compared with the comprehensive railway network in Java, Sumatra was fragmented, with three distinct and unlinked lines: "The northern Sumatra network, begun at different ends in the 1880s, finally joined Aceh with Medan, Belawan, and Asahan only in 1916. Similarly in the South, the Lampung line and the Palembang-Lahat line joined in 1927. Meanwhile a third, smaller network developed in West Sumatra from the 1880s."[1582] Roads were difficult to travel on in the hilly terrain of Sumatra and,

---

1578 See Rudolf Mràzek, *Sjahrir: Politics and Exile in Indonesia* (Ithaca: SEAP Publications, 1994), 27; M. A. Loderichs, *Medan: Beeld van een Stad* (Purmerend: Asia Maior, 1997), 11.

1579 Adriaan Jacob Barnouw, *A Trip Through the Dutch East Indies* (Gouda: Koch & Knuttel, ca. 1920), 12–13.

1580 See Bemmelen et al., *Guide through Netherlands India*, 192–194.

1581 "In de Oranje bioscoop", *Sumatra Post* (26 January 1914). As Sabine Lenk has pointed out to me, it was in fact not the "latest gadget" but rather an old system that was totally out of fashion in Europe and the US after 1910.

1582 Reid, *An Indonesian Frontier*, 29.

7 – Medan: The Making and Breaking of a Monopoly

while a road might run "most of the time through cultivated land", a tourist guide commented, "now and then it cuts through the primeval jungle where one guesses, but never sees or hears, the existence of wild animal life behind the impenetrable undergrowth of giant ferns".[1583]

Medan was not reputed for its vibrant entertainment scene at the turn of the century, compared with Surabaya or Batavia, and did not have its own European-style theatre, like the Batavia-, Semarang- or Surabaya- Theatre. In fact, the entrepreneur behind the Kinetophone in Singapore initially turned down a Deli planter trying to persuade him to bring the device for shows in Deli, due to its reputation of not being conducive for business, which apparently held sway in the field.[1584] Musical *soirées* and amateur theatrical events were held at the European clubs, performances of the Manila Band were staged at the Medan Hotel for the pleasure of guests, and *komedi stambul* or *bangsawan* troupes propped up their tents on the main city square (known in Medan as the Esplanade).[1585] Some popular entertainment shows were attended by residents from Medan's surroundings, in which case extra night trains were added to the schedule, in order to enable spectators to enjoy the entire programme before heading back home.[1586] There were periods when options were severely lacking, and times when audiences were spoiled for choice:

> "Nothing is harder to bear than a succession of ordinary days", says Goethe, and I realised the truth of these words last week. Three Race days preceding three lotteries, [in the] evenings – performance of *Gezelligheid* [*in Deli*, an amateur music and theatre society…], football match and bioscope – all enjoyed in a single week. Those were beautiful days, but now our nerves and coffers can take a rest – especially with regards to the latter, which has become very empty for me.[1587]

Furthermore, there appears to have been a hierarchy between Javanese and Sumatran cities, when it came to professional, popular entertainment options. For instance, when the Japanese Cinematograph visited Medan in 1905 and gave a series of disappointing shows, the *Sumatra Post* exclaimed: "We guarantee to the owner that, if he had had the nerve to give such a show in one of the great cities of Java, he would have bitterly regretted it. 'Money back or a beating', that would be the slogan of the public."[1588]

This chapter focuses on the case study of Medan as an important city outside the main island of Java, with its own particular rules of operation and target

---

1583 Barnouw, *A Trip Through the Dutch East Indies*, 14.
1584 "De Kinetofoon naar Deli", *Sumatra Post* (21 January 1914).
1585 "De afgeloopen week", *Deli-Courant* (12 October 1901). In fact, it was rumoured that the Medan Hotel decided to hire the Manila Band after Abdullally Esoofally hired Manilan musicians to accompany his New Bioscope shows in 1901, and hotel guests mentioned they enjoyed the music coming from the tent. The Manila Band later accompanied various moving picture shows on the Esplanade ("Op den Uitkijk", *Sumatra Post* (12 October 1901); "Internationale Bioscoop", *Sumatra Post* (18 October 1909)).
1586 For instance, when Harmston's Circus visited in 1897, an extra train ran from Medan to Sunggal, Diski and Timbang-Langkat at 11.45 pm, in order to allow non-residents to enjoy the show (Advertisement, *Deli Courant* (30 April 1897)).
1587 "Deli-Nieuws", *Sumatra Post* (8 October 1901), emphasis added.
1588 "De Kinematograaf", *Sumatra Post* (28 August 1905).

audiences for popular amusements. It first examines the earliest shows, and the issues they encountered with respect to lighting and electricity. It then discusses the tent shows on the Esplanade, which was the main site for setting up tents for all kinds of entertainments at the time. As we shall see, the concerns about the state of affairs in the city, in terms of film control and city maintenance, led to the creation of a "cinema monopoly", with only one permanent tent operated by the same exhibitor from 1910 to 1913. In parallel, Medan's Municipal Council initiated construction of a municipal cinema theatre into which the said exhibitor was to move once completed, hinting at a certain degree of corruption or dodgy decision-making and misconduct behind the scenes that might have also played into these decisions. Finally, this chapter examines the building boom of cinema venues as soon as the "cinema monopoly" was finally lifted in 1913.

7.1   Direct Current: The Arrival of Moving Pictures in Medan

The earliest screenings of moving pictures in Medan found in this research were performed by Louis Talbot's Scenimatograph in November 1897, after he had completed his tour of Java and the Straits.[1589] Arriving on board the *Calypso* from Singapore with his manager J. von Geyer on 16 November, the opening show at the *Witte Sociëteit* took place immediately the next day at 7 pm.[1590] Entrance fee was set at *f* 1.50 for adults and *f* 1 for children.[1591] The scenes displayed by "artificial light", including the local views of Batavia shot by Talbot himself, received great applause.[1592] Yet, the technology was still found to be lacking: "It is not entirely free of vibration. One must remember that the images, which are not larger than 1½ x 2 centimetres, are enlarged to nearly life-size as a result of which the slightest vibration of the rotary device itself is colossally amplified when transferred onto the canvas. But this too will soon disappear through new developments, meanwhile the invention itself is already interesting, so every learned man must not fail to make its acquaintance."[1593] After merely a few nights, Talbot left for nearby Binjai, and from there continued to other locations on Sumatra, such as the Sultanate of Serdang and possibly Padang, before leaving from Medan for Penang on board the steamship *Avagyee* on 19 December.[1594]

[1589] "De Scènimatograaf", *Deli Courant* (17 November 1897). See further on Talbot in Section 1.2.

[1590] "Aangekomen en vertrokken passagiers", *Deli Courant* (17 November 1897).

[1591] "De Scènimatograaf", *Deli Courant* (17 November 1897). Prices in Medan were usually stated in Mexican dollars during this period, so the pricing in guilders was an anomaly.

[1592] "De Scènimatograaf", *Deli Courant* (20 November 1897).

[1593] Ibid. The kind of language used in this report suggests that there may have been an earlier device exhibited to the public in Medan, but this research was not able to find any earlier shows. It could also be that the reporter for the *Deli Courant* was simply picking up on some of the issues previously discussed in earlier newspapers reports from Java and the Straits, or as presented by Talbot during the show or as promotional information to be used by the newspaper.

[1594] Advertisement, *Deli Courant* (24 November 1897); "Bobonganfeest", *De Locomotief* (4 January 1898); "Aangekomen en vertrokken passagiers", *Deli Courant* (22 December 1897). Another device showing in Padang, western Sumatra, in December 1897 was Miss Meranda's Kinematograph and Graphophone, which was promoted as "an improved Scenimatograph [*Scenematograaf*]", which could suggest that Talbot

7 – Medan: The Making and Breaking of a Monopoly

Later exhibitors often relied on the local electricity company to provide them with alternating current (AC).[1595] Medan's electricity company (*Electriciteit-Maatschappij Medan*), founded in 1898 and equipped with four diesel engines of 100 horse-power each, was awarded a Medan street-lighting contract in March 1900.[1596] The electric power was "[...] carried through the town on overhead wires as a high-tension single-phase alternating current of 110 volts at 44 stations situated at different points. There [were] 167 private consumers [in 1909], the largest being the Medan Hotel with 523 lamps, the residence of the Captain of the Chinese with 425, the 'Witte' Club with 354, Hotel de Boer with 352, and the Sultan's Temple with 317."[1597] It further provided power to industrial companies, such as the ice factory, offices of the newspapers *Deli Courant* and *Sumatra Post* (Dutch) and *Pertja Timor* (Malay) which were printed in Medan and Binjai, and other branches of industry. The availability of electricity from the local company was a handy solution, which freed up some exhibitors from transporting and carrying around additional heavy equipment. As mentioned earlier, before travelling from Singapore to Medan, Ten Broeke's American Biograph offered up for sale in auction its portable engine and a dynamo.[1598] Nevertheless, it also caused problems for some exhibitors, such as Abdulaly Esoofally's New Bioscope, who struggled with optimising his device to fit the technical conditions on site.[1599]

Interestingly, it appears that most of these early exhibitors chose to offer their shows in pre-existing buildings and structures rather than travelling with a tent of their own. Talbot's Scenimatograph, for example, was screened at European Clubhouses in Medan and Binjai, similarly to the type of locations he played in on Java.[1600] Ten Broeke's American Biograph screenings, which on Java were mostly displayed in a tent, were initially held at the building of the Gymnastics Club and later, when facing direct competition from the tent of Wirth's Circus, in an existing *bangsawan* tent.[1601] This may have been a function of easier railway transport on Java than on Sumatra, as mentioned earlier, or possibly to do with the sorts of permits issued at the time. Either way, the clear advantages of using existing structures for their shows were the lower travel costs entailed, no time spent on building a big tent, and the potential audience already lured to these sites for other entertainments.

was there earlier with his Scenimatograph ("Mme. Meranda's Variety & Novelty Company", *Sumatra-Courant* (24 December 1897)). Yet another Scenimatograph (*Scènimatograaf*) was advertised in Padang in March 1898, with the exhibitor identified as Mr L. Rosenberg and the director as J. Schvartz (Advertisement, *Sumatra-Courant* (25 March 1898)).

1595 "Plaatselijk Nieuws", *Sumatra Post* (21 February 1900).

1596 See Wright, *Twentieth Century Impressions of Netherlands India*, 569–570.

1597 Ibid., 569.

1598 Advertisements, *The Straits Times* and *The Singapore Free Press* (22 January 1899). See further on the American Biograph in Section 2.1.

1599 "Het licht in de bioskoop", *Sumatra Post* (9 October 1901). See further in Section 3.2.1.

1600 "De Scènimatograaf", *Deli Courant* (17 November 1897).

1601 Advertisement, *Deli Courant* (24 November 1897); "Een Zaterdagsche Praatje", *Sumatra Post* (10 March 1900).

7.2 Tent Shows on the Esplanade

The Esplanade, the main city square serving as the site for most tent shows in Medan, was a convenient site for popular entertainment performances, being centrally located on a wide open space that was ideal for setting up a large tent (see Figures 7-2 and 7-3). Formerly a fallow tobacco field east of the Deli Company headquarters, in around 1880 roads were paved surrounding it to create the Esplanade, with other European buildings to follow.[1602] There were several hotels bordering on the Esplanade, chief among them – the Medan Hotel, but also hotel De Vink (later Grand Hotel Medan) which opened in 1884 and hosted theatrical and musical performances organised by the association *Gezelligheid in Deli*. The *Witte Sociëteit* stood in a temporary building next-door since 1882, until it moved to its new building across the street from the Esplanade in 1887. Hotel de Boer was opened in 1898. The railway station was located on the east side of the Esplanade, and as more and more companies and institutions (including, the Chartered Bank of India, Australia and China, and the Netherlands Trading Society) chose the Esplanade as the place to establish themselves in Medan, it became the "undisputed centre of the young city".[1603]

Abdulally Esoofally's New Bioscope tent, which was one of the first to be propped up for moving picture shows on the Esplanade in October 1901, was described as "[...] the Flying Dutchman [that] crashed here from the delirious skies and was stranded on Medan's land, but inside it is clean and proper".[1604] The Medan Hotel served as the foyer for the higher ranks of spectators, who retired there during the break in the show. The dearth of entertainment in Medan meant that the erection of a tent was often an attraction in and of itself. In July 1902, as the Java Biorama's "oddly shaped tent" was being erected on the Esplanade, throngs of curious "Natives" were reportedly constantly surrounding it, "trying to peek inside but seeing little".[1605] The review of the opening night made sure to satisfy the craving for information on the tent's interior: "As neat as the tent looks from the outside, so it is also inside; everything is convenient, everything looks just right and the notion of a 'tent' is lost, once one has taken a seat in one of the comfortable chairs".[1606] Another review a couple of days later noted that, despite the terrible rains, the tent remained dry.[1607]

Setting up a tent was not always a straightforward task. The Japanese Cinematograph's tent took a while to erect in August 1905, and reportedly involved a

1602 See Loderichs, *Medan*, 16.

1603 Ibid.

1604 "De afgeloopen week", *Deli Courant* (12 October 1901).

1605 "Java Biorama", *Sumatra Post* (12 July 1902).

1606 "Java Biorama", *Sumatra Post* (14 July 1902).

1607 "Het Java Biorama", *Sumatra Post* (17 July 1902). Salzwedel apparently continued travelling with this tent in Sumatra, turning up for shows on the Esplanade in Binjai at the end of August (Advertisement, *Sumatra Post* (22 August 1902)). See further on Salzwedel's Java Biorama shows in Section 2.2.

7 – Medan: The Making and Breaking of a Monopoly

Figure 7–2. The Esplanade, ca. 1890. Stafhell & Kleingrothe / Medan-Deli. Courtesy of Leiden University Library, Image code 100574.
[Credit http://www.asia-pacific-photography.com/towardindependence/Kleingrothe/index.htm]

Figure 7–3. The Esplanade lane, showing offices, Chartered Bank and the Medan Hotel, undated postcard. Courtesy of Leiden University Library, Image code 1407217.

lot of sweat, exasperation, and "even worse than usual" maltreatment of the coolies employed for the job.[1608] Unfortunately, the anticipation was met with an opening night disappointment, for spectators and owners alike. While the audience turnout was quite high, with the Japanese community present in full force, as well as some thirty Europeans and a mass of "Natives", the tent was steaming hot. A "furnace is nothing in comparison", *Sumatra Post* grumbled.[1609] Moreover, the show could not begin on time due to technical problems, and even after several attempts to get the device to operate properly and asking spectators to move closer to the screen, the result was still "a long whirl of colours, a chaos of figures".[1610] "A spiteful growl rose from the ranks of the spectators, even the Japanese did not hold back their dissatisfaction", the report continued.[1611] Finally, at the suggestion of one of the spectators, the owner gave money back to ticket holders or issued a ticket for the next show, for those who were still interested in coming back.

The following shows were fully packed, but the result was still lacking, according to *Sumatra Post*, leading the journalist to regret having spent two dollars on the entrance fee:

> Firstly, most of the films were so obscure that it is absolutely impossible to distinguish what is happening on the canvas. Secondly, it is so shiny that the eyes begin to ache. Thirdly, the films, with the exception of the last one, which allowed to behold the "wonders of the sea" and was clear, are not worth much and were poorly suited to provide an idea of the Russo-Japanese War. Fourthly, the pauses in between the display of the different films were too long. Fifthly, the public was grievously vexed by a temperature of around 100 ° [Fahrenheit] in the tent. Sixthly... well, we'll just stop, it's too sad.[1612]

As a final point, the article resolved, it would be better if people were to give their money to a pauper, rather than spend it on a ticket for this show.

Other tent shows were supposedly more successful, such as the General Bioscope Company, owned by the Shahab Brothers and managed on its tour of Sumatra by M. Lewis.[1613] A lengthy review of one of their first shows in

---

1608 "Langs den Weg", *Sumatra Post* (24 August 1905).

1609 "De Kinematograaf", *Sumatra Post* (26 August 1905).

1610 Ibid.

1611 Ibid.

1612 "De Kinematograaf", *Sumatra Post* (28 August 1905).

1613 Advertisement, *Sumatra Post* (17 October 1906). According to Tofighian, "the Shahab brothers (two Arabs, in Batavia in November 1905 for General Bioscope) were the owners of the Central Bioscope and the General Bioscope in Medan (and later the owners of the Alhambra Theatre in Batavia)" (Tofighian, *Blurring the Colonial Binary*, 92, footnote 139). I have further found they previously offered shows with the General Bioscope in Padang in April 1906 ("Uit Padang", *Het Nieuws van den Dag voor Nederlandsch-Indië* (10 April 1906)). An advertisement from shows in 1907 in Batavia claimed that following "a successful tour in Sumatra, British India, the Straits, China and Japan, the [General] Bioscope on its way to Australia will give a series of shows during the Pasar Gambir Celebrations" (Advertisement, *Het Nieuws van den Dag voor Nederlandsch-Indië* (23 August 1907)). In 1912 they were again operating a cinema in Padang, possibly a more permanent venue, next to which they opened a car rental service company ("Uit Padang", *Soerabaiasch-Handelsblad* (2 February 1912)).

Medan in October 1906 provides a detailed description of the scene around the Esplanade:

> In recent days the avenue of the Esplanade, which runs parallel to the railway, provides quite the busy sight once it has become dark. There stands a tent for the bioscope and three beautiful arc lamps illuminate the whole avenue as if it were daytime. Compare this to the candles that our power station calls arc lights!
>
> On the edge of the avenue are the countless Chinese food- and drink- salesmen, offering to the people a great variety of everything that seems to be tasty to them. And particularly now, when it is Ramadan and [during] the days before, it was not especially busy with buyers [...][1614]

Inside the tent was also full to the brim, with the audience comprised almost entirely of Chinese spectators, "the long-tailed brethren", as described in the report, but a fan running managed to provide some coolness in the oppressive heat. "The bioscope man makes business here!" the article concluded.[1615]

7.3 Restaurant Shows and Screenings at Plantations

In 1909 another kind of venue for moving picture shows emerged in Medan, as films were being screened in Mr. Berlijn's Café Restaurant Bodega. Initially, it was a man by the name Haji Ibrahim who made an operating agreement with the café's proprietor, according to which he had the right to operate moving picture shows in the venue for one year while Mr. Berlijn was to reap the profits from running the buffet.[1616] Haji Ibrahim apparently also had documents from Pathé Frères, proving that he was the exclusive proprietor of a device advertised as the Pathéscope ("*Pathescope*") in Medan. Nevertheless, following a debt of $500 to Chinese tradesman Khoe Guan Chuan, the Pathéscope and films had to be handed over. As of June 1909, Mr. K. H. Tann operated the shows at the venue.[1617] Under his management, the Pathescope continued to receive regular shipments of Pathé films from Singapore, offered free screenings to schoolchildren and soldiers, and distributed ice cubes to the ladies during the break in the show.[1618]

A few months later, the International Bioscope (*Internationale Bioscope*) also performed at Bodega Café. However, the exhibitor was permitted to exhibit films only to Europeans, with the exception of the elite and wealthy members of the "Native" and Chinese communities.[1619] The local authorities explained

---

1614 "Bioscoop", *Sumatra Post* (19 October 1906).

1615 Ibid.

1616 "Beslaglegging op een bioscoop", *Sumatra Post* (17 June 1909).

1617 Ibid. The shows were at least temporarily halted, as Haji Ibrahim sued Khoe Guan Chuan for unlawful seizure, demanding damages in the sum of ƒ 10,000. The dispute was even covered by the Malay press in Batavia ("Penarohan beslag atas komidi bioscoop", *Taman Sari* (29 June 1909)). It appears that the dispute was resolved favouring the position of Khoe Guan Chuan, as shows were resumed under Tann's name and continued until the end of July (Advertisement, *Deli Courant* (31 July 1909)).

1618 "De Pathescoop", *Sumatra Post* (19 July 1909); "Gratis bioscoopvoorstellingen", *Sumatra Post* (17 July 1909); "De Pathescoop", *Sumatra Post* (19 July 1909). In November, for instance, Tann announced that he received 45 new films ("De bioscopen", *Sumatra Post* (1 November 1909)).

1619 "Internationale Bioscope", *Deli Courant* (4 August 1909); "De Bioscoop en de Inlanders", *Sumatra Post* (5 August 1909).

their decision was based on statistics showing a rise in theft following the last visit of a moving picture show (possibly referring to the Pathescope), linking this to the harmful influence of the cinema.[1620] "Recently complaints flowed in regarding thefts, in Medan as well as in the *kampong*, and the pawnshop made extra good business!" *Sumatra Post* reported.[1621] Another article from a newspaper published in 's Hertogenbosch in the Netherlands wrote about the case of the International Bioscope and its permit problems in Medan, and made similar claims based on comparisons with Java: "As in Java, the *wayang orang* or *wayang wong*, and it seems the *"gambar hidoep"* (that is, living pictures), exercise a particular appeal on the Native. In order to have money to be able to pay the entrance fee, he brings his [and presumably others'] goods to the pawnshop."[1622] In some parts of Java, it further claimed, even the "Native" police officers forbid *wayang wong* shows from taking place because of thefts. It is not clear what kind of figures this report was basing itself on, but it is nevertheless noteworthy that moving pictures were identified on the same plane as *wayang wong* shows, performed on stage by live actors.

Remarkably, the review of the International Bioscope's opening show clearly found the absence of "Native" spectators took away from the movie-going experience:

> The largest contingent of spectators, the Native element, has been expelled [from the cinema]. Only the European bourgeoisie sits in the hall. A certain attraction is thereby lost.
>
> The huddled masses, men and women separately, seated amphitheatre-like along the two side walls of the sitting room in front of the screen […] the colourful headwear, the cheers, laughter […] were part of the bioscope show. The brown sisters may have had a certain charm for some of the visitors as well.[1623]

Moreover, this constraint clearly diminished the viability of the commercial enterprise, and the local authorities soon changed their decision, no doubt following remonstrations from the owner.[1624] The tariff for the lowest ranks was cut to 50 cents[1625] and, in the only example of its kind found in this research, "Native" spectators were explicitly denied access to the box seats.[1626] The change of approach nevertheless did not bolster attendances much.[1627] In fact, one night was so weak that only about fifty "Europeans" filled the box

---

1620 It is not clear whether this was already a decision made by the newly founded Municipal Council.

1621 "De Bioscoop en de Inlanders", *Sumatra Post* (5 August 1909), emphasis added.

1622 "De bioscoop en de inboorlingen", *De Tijd* (7 September 1909), emphasis added.

1623 "Internationale Bioscope", *Deli Courant* (6 August 1909).

1624 De Bioscoop en de Inlanders", *Sumatra Post* (7 August 1909).

1625 While the currency system on Sumatra was changing around this time to guilders, cents here probably still refers to the Mexican dollar. This price would have been in agreement with earlier shows which were in Mexican dollar.

1626 Ibid.

1627 "Internationale Bioscope", *Sumatra Post* (10 August 1909).

seats and the third class was dotted with "Natives", but, between these, it was "as good as empty".[1628]

The Pathéscope returned to the Bodega Café in October, still under the management of K. H. Tann and continued to screen films with the Pathéscope.[1629] The shows at times included a variety act as well, in the form of song, dance and sketches.[1630] Tann was actually operating more than one device simultaneously, offering to give special shows on private estates as entertainment for the working coolies with the "Pathescope No. 1 and 2".[1631] Providing amusement for the coolies on site was a common practice also before moving picture shows, as many estates had "a festival fund for the coolies", meaning a certain sum of money was set aside to be spent "on their recreation, providing for musical instruments and paying for travelling shows, etc.". [1632] Reservations for the Pathescope were to be made with Tann, identified now as agent of the Grand Eastern Life Insurance Company Ltd.

There was a considerable difference between the two screening situations. Unfortunately, no numbers are available for the screenings at Bodega Café and this research has not found any detailed description of the layout of the space. It was, in any case, undoubtedly on a smaller scale of attendance than at the private estates, where the Pathescope played to thousands of spectators, presumably in an open-air setting. Thus, 2,000 coolies attended the show at Saint Cyr Estate and, a few days later, the Pathescope screened films to 1,500 "awe-struck" coolies at Batang Kwis.[1633] Tann subsequently boasted that he was invited by the Sultan of Deli for a screening with the Pathescope at his palace.[1634]

To summarize, despite the shortage of other entertainment options, compared to Batavia or Surabaya, Medan was a difficult market for moving picture exhibitors, who were thus constantly looking for business opportunities outside the city, and possibly also second lines of work alongside their cinema endeavours. Unlike in the big cities of Java where shows were often given two or even three times per day, most exhibitors in Medan played only one show per night, and programming had to be attractive enough to draw spectators to make repeat visits.[1635] As a report at the time claimed, a bioscope manager should not expect an entirely new audience to turn out in Medan every night.

1628 "Internationale Bioscope", *Sumatra Post* (18 August 1909).
1629 "De bioscoop op de kebon", *Sumatra Post* (21 October 1909).
1630 "De Pathescope", *Sumatra Post* (19 January 1910). When not used by film exhibitors, the Bodega Café would also host *bangsawan* troupes ("Vergaderingen, Vermakelijkheden Enz", *Sumatra Post* (2 April 1910)).
1631 Advertisement, *Sumatra Post* (22 October 1909). The advertisement mentioned that such shows were already given in Tandem – St Cyr and Wampoe Estate.
1632 Keyser, *From Jungle to Java*, 75.
1633 "De bioscopen", *Sumatra Post* (1 November 1909); "Bioscoopgenot", *Sumatra Post* (4 November 1909).
1634 Ibid.
1635 See also Tofighian's discussion of programming in Southeast Asia in this period (Tofighian, *Blurring the Colonial Binary*, 102–109).

Therefore, the journalist advised, more frequent changes of programme were required to ensure success.[1636] Yet, having a larger selection of films was becoming increasingly more costly, as the industry was moving from sale to rental of films, with some of the most attractive longer films available only at very high rates (see further discussion in Section 3.3.7). As we shall see, Medan, some felt, did not require more than one venue for moving pictures to cater to residents' needs.

7.4 Municipal Cinema Theatre and Medan's Cinema Monopoly: The Case of the Orange Bioscope

7.4.1 "Monstrous Cinema Sheds" to be Replaced by "Native Cinema and Bangsawan Theatre"

The Orange Bioscope (*Oranje Bioscoop*) was managed by an entrepreneur identified as an Armenian, probably a local of the Indies, by the name Martherus Sarkies Michaël, referred to simply as M. S. Michael or Michaël in various reports.[1637] Michaël was earlier the owner of the Netherlands Indies Electro-Bioscope (*Ned. Ind. Electro-Bioscoop* or *N. I. Electro-Bioscoop*) which performed moving picture shows on Java and Celebes from 1904 to 1913.[1638] After setting up a tent on the Esplanade in September 1909, the first shows of the Orange Bioscope in Medan were given in mid-October, alongside the Pathéscope at Bodega Café mentioned above.[1639] His shows immediately drew the attention of the authorities since the orchestrion, used to accompany the films, reportedly drew complaints from neighbours around the Esplanade. It was therefore forbidden to use the orchestrion after 8.30 pm and, from then on, Michaël could only rely on piano accompaniment, to which no objections were presented.[1640]

No detailed descriptions of the tent were found, but it was most likely built out of similar materials to the ones used for the permanent bamboo tents on

---

1636 "Bioscoop", *Sumatra Post* (20 August 1909).

1637 "Ingezonden stukken", *Sumatra Post* (8 January 1913); "Familiebericht", *Sumatra Post* (23 March 1938).

1638 The earliest shows of the Netherlands Indies Electro-Bioscope identified in this research were given in Malang, eastern Java, in July 1904 ("Malang", *De Locomotief* (21 July 1904)). That same year, the company travelled to Makassar on Celebes, before returning for shows in towns across Eastern, Central and western Java in 1905 ("India Ollanda", *Bintang Soerabaia* (7 December 1904); "Nederlandsch-Indië", *Het Nieuws van den Dag voor Nederlandsch-Indië* (23 August 1905)). The last shows of the Netherlands Indies Electro-Bioscoop found in this research were performed in Solo, Central Java, in early 1913 ("Solo", *De Locomotief* (19 February 1913)). Since late 1908, G. Gabriel, presumably another Armenian, was mentioned in the company's advertisements as the owner (Advertisement, *Bintang Soerabaia* (24 September 1908)). Gabriel, or possibly a relative of his, would later be the owner of the Parisian Cinema (*Cinema Parissien* [sic]) in Kuta Raja, in the Aceh region on the northwestern coast of Sumatra ("Brieven van een bioscoopman", *Sumatra Post* (3 March 1913)).

1639 "Bouwplannen aan de esplanade", *Sumatra Post* (22 September 1909); Advertisement, *Sumatra Post* (20 October 1909). Earlier shows advertised under the name "Oranje Bioscoop" were found in Buitenzorg (Bogor), Magelang and Makasar in 1908 ("Uit Buitenzorg", *Soerabaiasch-Handelsblad* (2 March 1908); "Oranje-Bioscoop", *Makasaarsche Courant* (15 May 1908)). Another show was found in Kudus in 1911; however, it remains unclear whether this was the same company and whether there was any connection between all the abovementioned companies ("Oranje Bioscoop", *De Locomotief* (6 December 1911)).

1640 "De bioscopen," *Sumatra Post* (1 November 1909).

Java, considering that during later discussions at the Municipal Council in August 1910, the deliberations revolved around the "ugly cinema tent which has been stationed at the Esplanade for almost a year now".[1641] While some members of the Council preferred that the poorly maintained tent would move to another site, the Chairman, Assistant Resident Maier, explained that the Esplanade was private land owned and managed by the Deli Company, and therefore the Council had no right to evacuate the tent. Another Council member proposed that the tent could be relocated to a piece of land across from the Deli Riding Club, which was also owned by the Deli Company. However, most Council members found that site to be unsuitably located. They could have potentially had the local government revoke the Orange Bioscope's operating permit, but this solution was not deemed desirable either since the cinema tent, it was argued, was very profitable for the municipality coffers.[1642]

A couple of months later, the Municipal Council began mulling the option of establishing a permanent building out of brick and stone to house moving pictures and *bangsawan* shows, which would be operated by the municipality and rented out to private exhibitors.[1643] Mr. Stecher, the same Council member who earlier proposed to relocate the Orange Bioscope's tent, examined the feasibility of using Deli Company-owned land for this purpose. He already had a builder on hand, Law A Yok, who claimed that he could obtain agreement from the Deli Company to lease the land next to the race tracks for a period of 75 years, and even presented building plans and sketches. However, further inquiry revealed that the ground could be used only for the construction of tents, since there was no license to construct a permanent building on site.[1644]

Captain of the Chinese, Tjong A Fie, then proposed that, if the municipality were interested in constructing a theatre for "Natives", he would put down "*f* 15,000 as an interest-free advance or as a loan at four per cent" interest.[1645] This sum, it was estimated, could be paid back within a few years, based on the current proceeds from the rental of land for moving picture shows and *bangsawan* acts. One Council member objected on the grounds that *f* 15,000 would not produce much of a theatre, on top of which he did not consider it appropriate for the municipality to get into competition with private individuals or with the *Witte Sociëteit*. To this, the Chairman replied that the theatre was intended "for Orientals", and while naturally there would be seats allocated to

---

1641 "Gemeenteraad van Medan", *Sumatra Post* (12 August 1910). The Medan Municipal Council had been established in 1909.

1642 The cinema tent was about to become even more profitable for the municipality upon the introduction of municipal tax on public amusements in Medan, as detailed below.

1643 "Permanent bioscoop-gebouw", *Sumatra Post* (31 October 1910).

1644 Ibid. Changing land zoning regulations was probably not fully within the authority of the Municipal Council, and demanded the sanction of a higher stratum of government. Another option proposed at the meeting was to convert the Gymnastics Club building, due to its suitable location in the centre of town, but the municipality's offer was rejected by Club members.

1645 Ibid. In 1912, the Captain of the Chinese donated the bell tower for the town hall (see Loderichs, *Medan: Beeld van een Stad*, 16).

"Europeans", it should not pose any danger to the *Witte Sociëteit*.[1646] Another Council member pushed for levying municipal tax on public amusements rather than operating a municipal cinema, while yet another member suggested that the two schemes might work well together. The decision to go ahead with the plan to operate a "native cinema and *bangsawan* theatre" was finally passed (nine votes in support, one against), as was the proposal for the loan by Captain of the Chinese, who left the room while voting was in progress.[1647]

These developments were closely observed by other cities on Java, which were also tired of the "monstrous cinema sheds" hogging their main squares, as we have seen in previous chapters.[1648] Nevertheless, the construction of the municipal cinema theatre would take a couple of more years to accomplish. In the meantime, a recently introduced ten per cent tax on public amusements was employed in Medan in 1911, emulating the taxes introduced on Java.[1649] Some estimated that many entertainers, particularly those targeting "European" audiences, which were supposedly already operating on a low profit margin, would shy away from Medan from now on. Therefore, the municipality, which was banking on this extra money, would receive neither income tax nor the public amusements tax, not to mention other auxiliary institutions like *warungs* that popped up around such amusements and would now lose potential business, and Medan's residents who would have less entertainment on offer.[1650] Indeed, several companies, including the popular Bandmanns opera troupe, as well as various magicians and circus outfits, refrained from visiting Medan following the new tax.[1651]

The Orange Bioscope, which earlier that year entirely removed and rebuilt its tent on the same spot on the Esplanade, raised its admission prices by ten per cent as of 1 October 1911.[1652] The method of controlling the implementation of the new tax proved to be just as unpopular as the tax itself, since not only were tickets checked at the entrance to the tent, but police officers further inspected inside, leading to delays in the show as spectators who did not hold on to their ticket stubs (or did not buy a ticket to begin with) were sent to buy a new one.[1653] Moreover, it was claimed, the control was not even effective and people were constantly sneaking in without a ticket.

At the same time, doubts began to be raised about the nature of the planned municipal cinema theatre. Some members of the Municipal Council began to

---

1646 Ibid.

1647 Ibid., emphasis added.

1648 Ibid. "Een gemeentelijke bioscoopgebouw", *De Locomotief* (30 August 1911).

1649 "Vermakelijkhedenbelasting", *Sumatra Post* (11 February 1911).

1650 "Ingezonden stukken", *Sumatra Post* (13 February 1911).

1651 "De Bandmanns komen niet", *Sumatra Post* (11 September 1911).

1652 "De bioscoop-tent", *Sumatra Post* (27 February 1911); Advertisement, *Sumatra Post* (28 September 1911). There was some talk about moving the tent away from the row of trees on the Esplanade to the grassy field of Stationweg; however, due to complaints against the new location, it ended up reconstructed on the same spot ("De bioscoop", *Sumatra Post* (20 March 1911)).

1653 "Belasting op Vermaak", *Sumatra Post* (2 November 1911), emphasis added.

question whether it would not be preferable to construct "a building for general application, a *'Town Hall'* [in English in the original], which everyone can benefit from" and contributes to the community, rather than a cinema theatre that houses only commercial enterprises.[1654] However, *Sumatra Post* readers were reminded, the decision on the construction of a municipal cinema was already approved by the Municipal Council in January 1912, which subsequently entered into a contractual agreement with the Orange Bioscope's owner approved by the Council in its meeting on 21 March of that year, so it was doubted whether any changes could now be made without suffering damages.[1655] In fact, the plan of eventually moving the Orange Bioscope to the completed municipal cinema building was first mentioned as early as in February 1911, before any steps towards construction or even a tender were taken.[1656] Thus, presumably, a previously unapproved arrangement had been reached before. Even though a petition was presented, calling on the Council to make the building more open to general public usage, the Council turned down the request arguing that the construction of a "town hall" would be too expensive.[1657] Surely, the Council's refusal to change or even discuss these issues was due to the fact that other arrangements had been made and agreed upon behind closed doors, either due to corrupt payments made, or freely entered into by the municipality – to ensure there was an occupant once the building would be completed.

A public tender for the "construction of a cinema theatre with a machine room" on the corner of Bali Street and Kling Street, was finally released in late May 1912, with the auction to take place at city hall on 7 June at 11 am.[1658] The Deli Company, again – the owner of the land, proclaimed that the land would be leased for a period of 30 years under the customary conditions: only an annual honourary fee of one guilder had to be paid by the municipality.[1659] The cost of construction soon ran over budget by an estimated 3,000 guilders, which was approved by the Municipal Council since it represented less than ten per cent of the total cost, estimated finally at 35,000 guilders.[1660] The projected income from renting out the new space in 1913 was 9,200 guilders, on top of which was to be added the ten per cent tax to be collected.[1661]

1654 "Voor de Verkiezingen", *Sumatra Post* (19 April 1912).
1655 "Het bioscooptheater-rekest", *Sumatra Post* (22 April 1912).
1656 "De bioscoop-tent", *Sumatra Post* (27 February 1911).
1657 "Gemeentelijk bioscooptheater", *Sumatra Post* (1 June 1912).
1658 Advertisement, *Sumatra Post* (24 May 1912).
1659 "Gemeenteraad van Medan", *Sumatra Post* (1 June 1912).
1660 "Begrootings-wijziging", *Sumatra Post* (3 August 1912); "Gemeentebegroting 1913", *Sumatra Post* (27 August 1912); "Ingezonden stukken", *Sumatra Post* (8 January 1913).
1661 "Gemeentebegroting 1913", *Sumatra Post* (27 August 1912). The income on rent was estimated according to eight months of activity in 1913, since the construction was expected to continue into 1913. Another report two months later estimated that the income on rent of the municipal cinema theatre would total 8,000 guilders in 1913 ("De gemeentebegroting voor 1913", *Sumatra Post* (9 September 1912)). A further estimate claimed that Mr. Michaël would rent the cinema theatre from the municipality for 800 guilders per month, meaning 9,600 guilders per year ("Ingezonden stukken", *Sumatra Post* (8 January 1913)).

7.4.2 Cinema Monopoly Comes to Light

Throughout this process, as the municipality was pressing ahead with the construction of the cinema theatre, potential competition was effectively nipped in the bud. Already in early 1911 the municipality refused P.A.C. Abalain, a cinema entrepreneur from Batavia, who sought to obtain a permit for a ten year land lease to construct his own permanent cinema theatre, with an investment of 27,000 guilders.[1662] The municipality explained that it, in fact, did not own land. Moreover, even in the case of using privately owned land, as was the case of the Orange Bioscope on the Esplanade, permits for operating shows in Medan were given by the local government (*plaatselijk bestuur*) for periods of one month, and exhibitors had to take the risk that their tent might be dismantled at any time.[1663] As the prospect of the municipal cinema theatre neared reality, the local government continually refused the permit requests of one applicant after another.

The latest applicant to be refused in 1913, Mr. D.A. van Kaathoven, initially received assurances that he would obtain a permit, but then was suddenly told he had to wait at least until April, when the Orange Bioscope was scheduled to move to the newly completed cinema theatre.[1664] Van Kaathoven protested the decision to several officials, and reportedly even sailed off to Batavia, to present his case to the Governor General. When the *Sumatra Post* appealed to the local government for an explanation, the latter laid out its reasoning as follows:

> Firstly, the revenue of the Orange Bioscope company proves the unfeasibility of having two cinemas in Medan; secondly, there is considered to be a certain moral obligation towards the owner of the Orange Bioscope, who had a contractual agreement to rent the municipal [cinema] building; thirdly, a deterioration in the quality of the films is feared due to competition, which is to the detriment of the Native population.[1665]

The newspaper found these to be ludicrous arguments and a few days later published a letter to the editor written by Van Kaathoven. Van Kaathoven revealed that the Municipal Council allegedly sought the advice of Mr. Michaël when making their decision in his case. He blamed the municipality for creating a monopoly, outed Michaël as "an Armenian", and wondered out loud whether on Java, too, "[...] the interests of Foreign Orientals are preferred over those of Europeans".[1666] Armenians in the Indies were rather classified under the "European" group, but this clearly did not stop Van Kaathoven from othering his competition. Another Armenian cinema entrepreneur in Sumatra,

---

1662 "Ingezonden stukken", *Sumatra Post* (13 February 1911).

1663 "Gemeenteraad van Medan", *Sumatra Post* (7 April 1911). The issue of land ownership was finally resolved later that year, when the municipality received control of land from the Sultan of Deli and from the Deli Company as of mid-August 1911 ("De grondkwestie te Medan", *Sumatra Post* (14 August 1911)).

1664 "De gemeente en de vrije concurrentie", *Sumatra Post* (7 January 1913).

1665 Ibid.

1666 "Ingezonden stukken", *Sumatra Post* (8 January 1913).

7 – Medan: The Making and Breaking of a Monopoly

Mr. Gabriel of the Cinema Parissien [sic] in Kuta Raja, was outraged by this and other statements made against Armenians by the Dutch, whom, he claimed, were suddenly encroaching on what Armenians have built up in the Indies in this field.[1667] He went out in Michaël's defence, pointing out that there used to be two cinemas in Medan before, but the prices of the Chinese-operated cinema (presumably, the Pathescope) were more expensive and the Chinese was subsequently crushed by the competition with the Orange Bioscope, resorting to travelling with *bangsawan* and *ronggeng* troupes.

Despite the promises made, even in April, after having received the consent of the *Witte Sociëteit* to screen films three times a week, Van Kaathoven was still not granted a permit.[1668] All fingers were now being pointed at head of the local government, Mr. S. van der Plas, who persistently maintained that a cinema monopoly was "[...] in the interest of the public, [and] that there [should be] only one cinema in Medan".[1669] The reasons he provided for this ranged in scope: from arguing that too much competition between cinemas, which were already facing more competition over "Native" and "Foreign Oriental" spectators from travelling circuses, *bangsawan* and other touring shows, would lead to deterioration in the quality of films on offer; to claiming that the Orange Bioscope itself was not very profitable and, based on the experience about three years earlier with a cinema which went into administration (referring to Mr. Berlijn's Bodega Café), he deemed it better to have one decently-running cinema house than two or more lesser cinemas.[1670]

Nevertheless, a meeting of the Municipal Interest electoral union (*kiesvereeniging "Gemeentebelang"*) at the Medan Hotel on 9 April 1913, attended by eighty to a hundred residents who showed up in defence of citizens' rights, was held up as proof that the people of Medan were not interested in a cinema monopoly.[1671] Discussions focused on the risks of the autocratic decision-making style of Van der Plas, zooming in particularly on a "secret Council meeting" initiated by him, and thus "held in violation of Art. 35 and 36 of the Local Governments Ordinance [*Lokale Raden Ordonnantie*]".[1672] All decisions taken at that meeting were therefore rendered null and void. The *Deli Courant*

1667 "Ingezonden stukken", *Sumatra Post* (3 March 1913).

1668 "Het Medansch Bioscope-Monopolie", *Soerabaiasch-Handelsblad* (15 April 1913). Van Kaathoven's plan to screen films at the *Witte Sociëteit* to "Europeans and their equals" led to a fierce debate in the "letters to the editor" section of the *Sumatra Post*. The "Wife of a *Soos* member" pointed out that "equals to European" were the Japanese, which in Medan meant mostly prostitutes, arguing that there should be at least one establishment in the city where these women should not be welcome ("Ingezonden stukken", *Sumatra Post* (10 April 1913), emphasis added). A "Planter woman" quickly sided with Japanese women in the name of womanly sisterhood and advancement of society's poor individuals ("Ingezonden stukken", *Sumatra Post* (15 April 1913)).

1669 "Bioscoop kwestie", *Het Nieuws van den Dag voor Nederlandsch-Indië* (11 April 1913).

1670 "De Bioscoop-kwestie", *Sumatra Post* (16 April 1913).

1671 "Het geval-Kaathoven", *Sumatra Post* (10 April 1913); "Gemeente-kwestie", *Bataviaasch Nieuwsblad* (11 April 1913); "Het Medansch Bioscope-Monopolie", *Soerabaiasch-Handelsblad* (15 April 1913).

1672 "Gemeente-kwestie", *Bataviaasch Nieuwsblad* (11 April 1913); "Gemeenteraad van Medan", *Sumatra Post* (16 April 1913); "Uit de Indische Bladen", *Het Nieuws van den Dag voor Nederlandsch-Indië* (21 April 1913).

claimed that Van der Plas was abusing the spirit of the law which granted him absolute authority over granting permits for public performances.[1673] Clearly, the newspaper argued, he was only to refuse performances "which are contrary to public order or morality", not simply to act on his own "whims and sympathies in bestowing or denying permits".[1674] This time, Van Kaathoven further decided to launch a petition to end the Medan cinema monopoly, circulated at the *Witte Sociëteit* and the two Medan hotels, stating that "women's signatures were also welcomed".[1675] The petition presented to the Governor-General included 183 signatures from Medan and 25 from Binjai, but no gender distribution was provided in the newspaper.[1676]

During a Council meeting held in mid-April, Van der Plas argued, in his own defence, that his policy had been practiced openly and consistently over the course of several years. He claimed that he was surprised that, while his decisions were previously implemented by the Municipal Council without any objections, now "all of a sudden" so much criticism was being voiced.[1677] He further explained that he never guaranteed any sort of monopoly over cinema shows to Mr. Michaël, who was still required to renew his license on a monthly basis. Rather, he simply told the Orange Bioscope's manager that, as long as he remained head of the local government, there was "little chance that more licenses would be issued".[1678] Clearly, he did not view this as a problematic stance. We do not know what kind of wheeling and dealing may have gone on behind the scenes, but several exhibitors on Java at the time were trying to convince Municipal Councils of a similar scale to award them sole rights to set up a permanent tent and shun other competitors.[1679] Although nothing as blatant turned up here, one can only assume there were considerations hidden from sight. Nevertheless, in light of the new developments, Van der Plas, agreed to reconsider his refusals of no less than twenty applications for permits from cinema companies, submitted over the course of just the last five months. The Council unanimously approved the motion concluding the meeting, which read as follows: "The Municipal Council declares that it does not support monopoly, but rather a healthy competition in the field of cinemas [*bioscopen*]".[1680]

7.4.3 Orange Bioscope Moves into the Municipal Cinema Theatre, 1913

While the plan was to open the municipal cinema at the beginning of April 1913, by mid-April, when the *Sumatra Post* got a sneak peek of the new cinema

1673 *Deli-Courant* quoted in "Uit de Indische Bladen", *Het Nieuws van den Dag voor Nederlandsch-Indië* (21 April 1913).
1674 Ibid.
1675 "Het Medansch bioscoop-monopolie", *Sumatra Post* (11 April 1913).
1676 "Het Nieuwe rekest-Van Kaathoven", *Sumatra Post* (15 April 1913).
1677 "De Medansche bioscoop-kwestie", *Het Nieuws van den Dag voor Nederlandsch-Indië* (23 April 1913).
1678 "De Bioscoop-kwestie", *Sumatra Post* (16 April 1913).
1679 See Section 6.4.
1680 "De Medansche bioscoop-kwestie", *Het Nieuws van den Dag voor Nederlandsch-Indië* (23 April 1913).

7 – Medan: The Making and Breaking of a Monopoly

Figure 7–4. The Orange Bioscope, ca. 1913, C. J. Kleingrothe. Courtesy National Museum for World Cultures. Coll.nr. TM–60039322.

theatre, the building was still under construction. Located just east of the Esplanade, on the other side of the railroad track and behind the viaduct, on the corner of Bali Street and Klingen Street, the front of the building was found to be "tasteless and ungainly, but this can be fixed with some simple relief decoration and some cheerful colours", the journalist proposed.[1681] The interior, although still far from ready, made quite an impression with its "[...] imposing hall space, tall ceilings and sleek great walls dotted with simple, tasteful relief decorations".[1682] At the front of the hall were the second- and third-class seats, carefully separated from the first rank seats and provided with their own entrance. At the back of the hall was the space for the operator and projection unit, located in a completely separate room, to prevent any potential fire hazard. A space was especially prepared to hold an orchestrion, opposite the entrance, in the middle of the right-hand wall, with sufficient space left for a string quartet which, "like at circuses, is raised a few feet above the heads of the spectators".[1683] In order to keep a cool temperature in the hall, several electric fans were provided, alongside many windows and side openings near the ceiling. A stand-alone shed outside was set up to house the engine. A cloakroom and a buffet, with some chairs and tables to be enjoyed during the break, were to be put in place. "Now if only those grimy little *warongs* on the opposite Kling Street could be knocked down, one would get a neat complex", the report concluded.[1684] Once the cinema was to be opened in mid-May, it

---

1681 "Het gemeentelijk bioscoop-theater", *Sumatra Post* (12 April 1913).

1682 Ibid.

1683 Ibid.

1684 Ibid.

was expected that the enticing glowing letters on the side of the massive building would be visible from afar.

At the end of May 1913 the Orange Bioscope moved into the municipal cinema building (see Figure 7–4).[1685] All profits from the two shows on opening night on 31 May, totalling 800 guilders, were to be donated to charity.[1686] The *Sumatra Post* noted that, unlike a town in the Netherlands of similar scale to Medan, where such an event would have been seized as an opportunity for a nice ceremony accompanied by speeches from council members and various representatives, the opening of this municipal building in Medan went by without much pomp and circumstance.[1687] The hall itself was still deemed to be not cosy enough, its austerity deriving from the bright glare of strong lights. It was suggested that Mr. Michaël might liven things up by placing flower pots hanging from the walls and palm trees in the corners, but it was advised that no more advertisements should be hung in the hall. In fact, just a few days before the opening, the Municipal Council accepted a proposal for displaying advertisements on the backs of the seats at the new municipal cinema.[1688] Some argued that it should be up to Mr. Michaël to decide, while others claimed this was a disfigurement of the city and set a precedent, since a similar proposal for advertising in the municipal urinary was previously rejected. The proposal was finally passed, pending Mr. Michaël's agreement which, apparently, was granted.

Other complaints were related to the seating and viewing conditions. The raised seats in the back for European spectators did not guarantee that every spectator got a good view of the screen, especially considering the fashionable coquette hats in vogue with the ladies, requiring many to stretch their necks. "If a high amphitheatre is not installed, after a few times of repeat visits many people will not return", the newspaper cautioned.[1689] Some people, it was further pointed out, found that the electric fans made the hall feel too drafty. Despite these apparent shortcomings, a throng of people, "European as well as Natives", gathered in front of the cinema all night long, flowing in as soon as the bell announcing the second show rang.[1690] The temperature in the hall indeed remained cool, despite the fact that the hall was packed full with more than 800 spectators, 50 of whom having to settle for standing-room. "All in all we have gone forward with the new cinema building in all respects", was the conceded conclusion.[1691]

Incidentally, the dream of having a tent-free Esplanade was unfortunately not fulfilled upon the opening of the municipal cinema building. The former

1685 Advertisement, *Sumatra Post* (28 May 1913).
1686 "Een Première", *Sumatra Post* (2 June 1913).
1687 Ibid.
1688 "Reclame in gemeente-bioscoop", *Sumatra Post* (24 May 1913).
1689 "Een Première", *Sumatra Post* (2 June 1913).
1690 "De bioscoopvoorstelling ten bate van het Instituut van der Steur", *Deli Courant* (2 June 1913).
1691 Ibid.

cinema tent of Mr. Michaël was sold to a Chinese entrepreneur and remained in place, where it served as a suitable space for stabling the elephants and horses of travelling circuses, which still set up shop on the Esplanade. Alternative locations for circus shows were now being suggested, including the race tracks, the land behind Hüttenbach, or land in the vicinity of the opium office, but it seems the tent persisted.[1692]

7.5 End of Medan's Cinema Monopoly

In July 1913, two other cinemas opened simultaneously in Medan, finally providing competition to the Orange Bioscope. "We are a city", proudly pronounced the *Sumatra Post*.[1693] Van Kaathoven finally received his long-awaited permit in May 1913 and began construction of a wood and zinc-covered tent, approximately the same size as the old Orange Bioscope, intended to open in mid-June, "wind and weather permitting".[1694] He planned to offer comfortable seats, musical accompaniment by a *clavimonium* (a combination piano-harmonium) and top quality films.[1695] Named the Deli Bioscope (*Deli Bioscoop*), it was located on the corner of Hindoe Street and Hüttenbach Street, just southwest of the Esplanade.[1696] The *Sumatra Post* got to visit the venue under construction and duly reported that "this tent indeed promises to be especially snug and cosy":

> No plank or beam remains hanging over. All along the walls and heavy wooden struts a dark grey cloth is stretched, trimmed with Bordeaux-red edges, and, moreover, where this was possible it features a neat wooden panelling of green and white, simple design.
>
> [...] tasteful flower pots [are placed] along the high walls, [... which] here and there will be lit by green-coloured incandescent bulbs. [...] The corners of the tent are further decorated with beautiful palm trees, especially in the box seats section, in the back of the room, against the broad, lofty wall, where the spotlight will cast its beam of light onto the screen through a small opening.
>
> The screen on which the films will be projected also deserves special mention. To attenuate the rigidity of the white screen there will be some ornaments and plants at the bottom [...lit with] footlights. During the projection of films these lights will obviously be switched off. So they only serve as further decoration of the plants during the pauses in order to mask the uninviting white screen.
>
> Particular attention was also paid to the seats. Even the third and second class spectators have comfortable chairs, while the box and first class all have very convenient rattan chairs [...].

1692 "Voor een gebouwen-vrije Esplanade", *Sumatra Post* (17 June 1913).

1693 "Bioscopen", *Sumatra Post* (21 July 1913).

1694 "De bioscoop-van Kaathoven", *Deli Courant* (20 May 1913); "Nieuwe bioscopen", *Sumatra Post* (20 May 1913).

1695 Ibid.

1696 "De Deli-bioscoop", *Sumatra Post* (14 July 1913). Another entrepreneur by the name Leyten was also mentioned, possibly Van Kaathoven's partner. Van Kaathoven further received a permit to operate another cinema in Tebing-Tinggi which, taking a leaf out of Medan's book, was going to have two moving picture shows playing at the same time ("Tweede bioscoop in Tebing-Tinggi", *Sumatra Post* (26 July 1913)).

The entrance to the tent will be on the edge of the Hüttenbach Street. The ticket booths are also located there as well as high arc lamps, which undoubtedly will lure many visitors in the evening.[1697]

Another report from the grand opening night on 22 July 1913 claimed that, despite the fact that you had to buy a ticket to enter the cinema, thanks to the warm furnishings of the tent and the hustle and bustle around, one felt immediately

> [...] like a sort of guest who, along with many others, was invited for a nice intimate cinema evening. [...] People imagined themselves to be at Pathé Frères on one of the boulevards of Brussels or Paris, so astonishing and tasteful was the decoration of this simple, timber-framed tent.[1698]

The Indian (*Klingaleesche*) cinema attendants, clad in white uniforms with red trimmings, handed out programmes in the different seating classes. The first two shows were packed full of residents of Medan as well as of surrounding areas, some of whom have "never before seen a cinema tent".[1699] "But not only the European, but also the Oriental" spectators were delighted with what they saw, seated in the front while the Europeans were sitting in the back of the hall, restlessly looking around, "feasting on all that light and that red and green all around".[1700] The programme itself was found to be well balanced and varied, and the pauses in between films were short, so spectators got good value for their tickets. The only suggestion for improvement was that perhaps there should also be a ticket booth on the other end of the tent, next to where the engine was installed, which could serve as an entrance for the lower ranks of the tent.[1701]

The opening show of Mr. Samson's Orion Bioscope (*Orion Bioscoop*), on Lieutenant Street, just a couple of days later, was also reviewed in the local press.[1702] The tent was located in *kampung* Kesawan, southeast of the Esplanade and railway station, which was originally mainly inhabited by Malays, but due to the large influx of Chinese from Malacca and later from China itself, the former dominated the neighbourhood after about 1880. The neighbourhood was characterised by its proliferation of Chinese shops.[1703] Nevertheless, the Orion Bioscope was reportedly not nearly as well-attended as the Deli Bioscoop: "The upper grades were as good as unoccupied; in the later evening show, we counted a dozen Europeans and one or two Chinese. The lower

1697 "De Deli-Bioscoop", *Sumatra Post* (14 July 1913).
1698 "De Deli-Bioscoop", *Sumatra Post* (23 July 1913).
1699 Ibid.
1700 Ibid.
1701 Ibid.
1702 "De Orion-Bioscoop", *Sumatra Post* (24 July 1913).
1703 See Loderichs, *Medan*, 18. After a fire in early 1899 which burned down a large part of the southern town since buildings were more or less improvised and built out of wood, only stone constructs were allowed. The reconstruction introduced the characteristically Chinese building with a shop gallery downstairs and living quarters upstairs.

grades, however, were nearly full during both shows."[1704] This should have come as no surprise, the report claimed, since this cinema was located in the Chinese quarter of Medan and was "meant to be primarily an attraction for Chinese men and women", for whom the other two cinemas were deemed too far to walk to. Its selection of films did not include current events ("unless 'the siege of Adrianople'[1705] may be regarded as such once again"), and most were "more or less old films, although often very interesting".[1706] Furthermore:

> As concerns the decoration of the room, that is all very simple. The wooden walls of the construct are only covered with brightly-coloured "dragons" – posters, as we are familiar with from the construct of the old Orange Bioscope. At the entrance to the hall are only a couple of dark-coloured *portières* and further fitted with red fabric with a floral motif conveying some atmosphere.
>
> The seating ranks are each arranged amphitheatre-like, so that people in the box seats can barely see the public "downstairs". In the higher seating ranks are placed beautiful teak solid wood chairs, but in our opinion they are a bit uncomfortable. In the lower ranks seating is on simple mats.
>
> The projection screen contrasts well against the broad frame of wine-red fabric. Additionally, a phonola is placed in one of the two side galleries.[1707]

Attendance figures improved for the following shows, and "even many Europeans" were spotted in the audience.[1708] However, the entrance fee of ƒ 2.20 guilders, which was likely for the high-paying seats, was not deemed worthwhile. The quality of the projection was also subject of criticism. The Orion Bioscope, one journalist wrote, made one "[...] reminiscent of the days of old, when the *kinos* on the fairgrounds were still new attractions and you would [...] sit there for a whole evening, and finally go home with a headache and tired eyes".[1709] It seems that the quality and success of the shows did not pick up. Just several months later, the operator of the Orion Bioscope "temporarily suspended" his shows in Medan and set off to Perbaungan, to offer film screenings to Sultans and their courts.[1710] Mr. Samson's (permanent) tent appears to have stayed in place, and was soon taken up by another entrepreneur identified as an Englishman, although this research has not found further details on his cinema.[1711]

As more cinema companies were coming and going over the next few months, usually with three active shows simultaneously in Medan, newspapers were excited about the potential of the new competition between cinemas in the

---

1704 "De Orion-Bioscoop", *Sumatra Post* (24 July 1913).

1705 The Siege of Adrianople was fought during the First Balkan War, from November 1912 to March 1913.

1706 "De Orion-Bioscoop", *Sumatra Post* (24 July 1913).

1707 "De Orion-Bioscoop", *Sumatra Post* (24 July 1913), emphasis added.

1708 "Orion Bioscoop", *Sumatra Post* (26 July 1913).

1709 Ibid., emphasis added.

1710 "Ned. Oost-Indië", *De Kinematograaf*, no. 37 (3 October 1913): 273.

1711 "Nieuwe bioscoop", *Sumatra Post* (25 September 1913).

city. "More than once the complaint has been heard that good money is not always well rewarded. Out of the competition, which has now started over the public's favour, it can be expected that they will endeavour to provide the public of the cinematographic field with what is reasonably required."[1712] Others had even greater expectations: "Only when the cinema sector [*bioscoopwezen*] is going to stand out here in pursuit of the best, it will be able to justify the lofty entrance prices which are demanded here, in distinction from other places in the Indies – like Batavia".[1713]

A letter to the editor in response to this article from a spectator, signed as Samber Malam, suggested that the ticket prices should be lowered, but that exhibitors ought to still strive for the best. Taking up the example of Batavia, the spectator mentioned the Globe Bioscope which apparently halved its prices, with its operator being quoted as saying: "I would rather screen my films to full houses [every evening, every performance] than five times per week to empty seats and twice per week to full houses".[1714] Indeed, even some higher-earning European spectators reportedly found it difficult to afford cinema shows. According to information on the salaries of European assistants on Sumatran plantations in 1910, the starting salary was 175 guilders in the first year. This sum, one newspaper noted, providing a full account of the projected spending of an assistant in one year, did not even leave employees with enough money to go to a movie.[1715]

Medan cinemas did follow in the footsteps of the Globe Bioscope in at least one respect, which was less warmly welcomed. The Globe Bioscope was reportedly quite liberally misleading its spectators about their programmes by re-titling and re-appropriating films, at least until this was declared a "press offense".[1716] "Orange-, Deli-, and Orion-cinema men, keep this in mind", the *Sumatra Post* warned. "You announce: The coolie row – but it is a strike scene from the Belgian mines. You put 'The campaign of the *Jong Indiërs*'[1717] on the programme – and it's a riot in Bengal; 'The tenders' – a workers' trade fair in Paris'; 'Arrest at the police station of the Express' – a robbery on the Canadian Pacific."[1718] Some of these titles would have instantly sounded the alarm bells of the authorities in Java, which by 1913 were increasingly clamping down on film contents of violent or political disruptive potential.

1712 "De Orion-Bioscoop", *Sumatra Post* (24 July 1913).

1713 "Dingen van den Dag", *Sumatra Post* (28 July 1913).

1714 "Ingezonden stukken", *Sumatra Post* (29 July 1913). Text in square brackets in the original. For more on the Globe Bioscope, see Section 5.3.3.

1715 "Assistenten-Salarissen", *Sumatra Post* (4 May 1910).

1716 "Ter zijde", *Sumatra Post* (6 August 1913).

1717 This title appears to have been in reference to the recent arrests of two leading figures of the *Indische Partij*, Tjipto Magoenkoesoemo and Raden Mas Soewardi, who in July 1913 founded a Native Committee for the Commemoration of the Netherlands Centenary of Freedom in response to the upcoming celebrations of Dutch independence from the French, as discussed in the previous chapter. Their goal was to draw public attention to the undemocratic colonial system and make a plea for political reform. See Dijk, *The Netherlands Indies and the Great War*, 53–60.

1718 "Ter zijde", *Sumatra Post* (6 August 1913).

7.6 Conclusion

This chapter examined the movie-going scene in Medan on Sumatra, to serve in contrast to the Javanese cities discussed in the previous three chapters (Surabaya, Batavia and Semarang). While it was a modern, cosmopolitan port town with electric current and lit streets, Medan was a smaller city in terms of its population and far less favourably connected by railway to other locations on the island, compared to the cities and towns of Java. Thus, although touring companies travelled back and forth, from town to plantation and back, they had limited options of venues and locations to offer their shows in and a small amount of potential spectators to cater to. More so than in the urban centres of Java, their financial success depended on repeat visitors. They were also faced with other methods for control of the local entertainment landscape. The Municipal Council in Medan may have been unable to forbid the rent of private land to cinema tents, but that did not stop it from banning the attendance of "Native" spectators, or from creating a "cinema monopoly" from 1910 to 1913, broken only by increasing pressures from entrepreneurs and local spectators.

Yet, while newspapers and spectators in Medan were calling for more open competition, the same sources were soon decrying the dearth of other entertainment options in Medan as moving picture shows were taking over the city:

> Our public life has large gaps. A newcomer sees that at first glance. The first night of his stay here, he asks if he can go to a concert, a theatre, a lecture or some other uplifting gathering. No, will be the answer; – but you can go to the... cinema [*bioscoop*]. And disappointed, because he is in need of a distraction, he goes to the cinema. The first time he mulls it over, how dreary [...] is his new home. But finally he accepts it.[1719]

A letter to the editor from a spectator further claimed: "Were there something else to do in Medan on a Saturday night, then the operators of the two cinemas still active in our city would never see me among their visitors again".[1720] Indeed, while the map of Medan reproduced here (see Figure 7–1), dated circa 1915, provides the location of several Clubhouses and hotels, as well as five (bamboo or stone-built) cinema houses, including the Orange Bioscope and Deli Bioscope, no other theatre building of any kind was available in the city. Cinema theatres appear to have effectively taken over the Medanese entertainment landscape, leaving amusement-seeking spectators no choice but to make repeat visits to their venues, even if somewhat reluctantly.

1719 "Het openbare leven in Medan", *Sumatra Post* (17 September 1913).

1720 "Bioscoop-genot", *Sumatra Post* (8 September 1913).

Concluding Remarks

The cinemas [bioscopen...] become more and more beautiful from one year to the next, and they invent all kinds of new names, such as the "Monarch" and others like "Flying" and "Electro" – both have been here [in Bandung] – the latter (which has since burned down) indeed showed very beautiful films. Yes, coming up with a new company name, in order to impress the public, requires ingenuity and sharp thinking due to the abundance of existing titles. A new title is a lucky find.

It is sometimes claimed that there are among the films screened some that show too much to the youth and to the people, and therefore leave an immoral or poor impression on the prospective spectators. On the other hand, there are also many (most of them) that can be regarded as a living newspaper [levende courant] which bring forth all the news and modern things in the fields of industry, art and ethnography. People of this land who may never witness Western conditions, are imparted here with an idea of European and American life. In this respect, the cinemas are very educational and useful.

A remarkable phenomenon in this city is that one always sees the same spectators at cinema screenings. They faithfully visit every cinema and love it; their emotions are aroused by the representation, and they are granted a pleasant distraction from the monotonous life in the Indies.

"Bandoengsche causerie", De Locomotief *(14 August 1909).*

This book outlined the emergence of the popular practice of movie-going in turn-of-the-century colonial Indonesia, from 1896 to the outbreak of the First World War. By covering a broad spectrum of locations and source materials over time, it was able to observe the arrival of the technology, the development of the market for films, the embedding of moving picture shows within the local popular entertainment landscape, and the institutionalisation of cinema venues on the urban landscapes of the Netherlands Indies. In the first three chapters (Part I), this strategy enabled to sketch out detailed tour routes of several itinerant exhibitors, the distribution of films throughout the archipelago, in addition to efforts in the field of local production. In the last four chapters (Part II), the focus on four different cities allowed to compare and contrast the development of more permanent cinema venues, techniques for control of moving pictures on the newly established municipal level, as well as to highlight aspects of film exhibition that became central in each location.

The aim throughout was to focus on moving picture entrepreneurs and their spectators, studying the history of cinema exhibition and consumption in the

Indies as a point of intersection for colonialism, race and technology. Thus, we have seen that entrepreneurs, as commercial agents, had to balance the concerns of colonial authorities – in order to gain permits to hold their shows – against the need to appeal to as wide an audience as possible, to meet their own profitmaking objectives. When repeatedly choosing to spend their leisure time and money at moving picture shows, spectators, as social agents coming from the entire spectrum of colonial society, were engaged in negotiations on various levels. They encountered authority at the cinema in the form of the exhibitor, *explicateur* or policeman. They were invited to engage in interchange with their fellow spectators, sometimes numbering several thousands, who may have been of a different social class, racial category and seating rank. Finally, they were experiencing all things new and modern, be it the technology itself, the projected images on screen, or the venue in which they were shown.

The cinema was neither the first nor only form of turn-of-the-century entertainment to offer Indies urbanites a place of leisure. As shown here, itinerant exhibitors of moving pictures in colonial Indonesia followed in the footsteps of circus and *stambul* tents, magicians and acrobats, and a melange of indigenous and Western forms of entertainment in terms of their tour routes, highly mixed spectatorship base, and, to a certain extent, the content of their programmes. Many of the semi- or permanent venues – whether bamboo-, iron- or stone-built – were intended to house moving pictures but could also be used for variety shows, *stambul*, magic and other entertainments, either in the same hall or in a specially built extra theatre space, invested capital permitting. And while cinema outlasted or even entirely replaced some of these attractions, it was constantly in competition with others.

Faced with stiff competition from existing indigenous and Western entertainment forms and catering to audiences of such diverse ethnic, social and cultural backgrounds, we cannot underestimate the professional risks taken by these showmen and women. The early itinerant exhibitors had to endure challenging tropical weather conditions and life-risking health threats. And while Java was well connected by steamship and railway, travel was expensive and train and steamer schedules often proved unreliable. Entrepreneurs of fixed cinema houses a decade later faced increasing regulation by the colonial authorities, in the form of ticket control, taxation and growing censorship. They were serving ever more demanding audiences against the backdrop of rising tensions between the different groups making up colonial society. Yet, remarkably, although most of the films on the programmes were presumably made with a Western audience in mind, exhibitors were able to tailor their shows to local audiences in a way that quickly embedded the new medium of moving pictures within the rich intermedial landscape of popular entertainments.

The micro-historical studies of the four port cities making up Part II have been particularly revealing of the place the new medium gradually came to occupy in the everyday lives of urban inhabitants and on the agendas of the newly established Municipal Councils. The comparison between the four cities provides location specific conclusions relating to the particular circumstances in each setting, yet also allows to draw more general understandings of how the cinema developed as a commercial entertainment form in urban colonial Indonesia. As the two largest cities, Surabaya and Batavia had more potential locations in which to hold moving picture shows and to eventually construct permanent cinema houses, as compared to Semarang and Medan, where most of the activity was centred on the main town square (the *Alun Alun* and the *Esplanade*, respectively). Looking more closely at the sprawling city maps of Surabaya and Batavia while projecting the locations of cinema houses onto them shows that, whereas in Surabaya cinema houses spread to the south as the city was progressively growing southwards, venues in Batavia dotted the map in all directions, with the building boom encompassing the newer part of town in Weltevreden to the south, as well as the northern *bovenstad*, especially its Chinese neighbourhoods. Although many spectators used public or private modes of transport (whether bicycles, horse-drawn, or motorised vehicles) to attend the cinema, most presumably came from neighbouring surroundings. These may not have necessarily been people living in the vicinity of each venue, but possibly working nearby – as in the case of port workers and navy personnel in Batavia's *bovenstad*, or soldiers stationed in town, as in the case of cinemas on or next to military grounds in Surabaya. By comparison, Semarang and Medan, with their more circular shape, appeared to be content with keeping cinemas centralised, thus requiring potential spectators to flock to a singular hub. Despite the difference in the number and geographical spread of cinema houses as dictated by each administrative authority, all Municipal Councils, in dire need of cash in their coffers, identified the potential income from the increasingly popular medium. Following Surabaya's lead, new taxation schemes based on a similar model were introduced in each city, thus beginning to standardise the regulation mechanisms of moving picture exhibition.

One of the most striking findings of this research is how cutting edge colonial Indonesia was from a global perspective when it came to the introduction and exhibition of moving pictures.[1721] New technologies for projecting moving images, along with the latest films on offer, often arrived in far flung locations within just a matter of weeks from their first appearance on screens in the West. This is in line with other research examining modernity and popular culture in Southeast Asia in specific, and in Asia in general, claiming that we should consider these processes as parallel rather than belated or derivative (see further discussion in the Introduction). Therefore, while it was previously accepted that the Netherlands Indies served in the early 1910s as a market for handed down degraded film copies from the Netherlands, this now appears to have

---

[1721] According to Tofighian's findings, the Netherlands Indies was also ahead of many of the other countries in the region and, along with the Straits Settlements and the Federated Malay States, were the most highly frequented in Southeast Asia by touring entertainers around the turn-of-the-century (see Tofighian, *Blurring the Colonial Binary*, 248).

been an aberration from its earlier status as a rife market for current films originating from distributors in London and Paris.[1722]

Although scenes of Western origin certainly dominated the screens, another surprising discovery was the scope of local production for the local market, nearly from the moment of arrival of the technology in the Indies (see Appendix II for full list of local views screened in the Indies). Moreover, many of the early scenes of modern life captured by filmmakers in the West were in fact easily reproduced by Louis Talbot and other local filmmakers in the Indies. Such local views depicting development and progress, along with the advanced state of infrastructure at many urban cinema theatres, gave especially city dwellers in the Indies a sense that they were on par with the great metropoles of Europe. It was in this setting that Bandung could be conceived of as the "Paris of Java", or that the "Crocodile City" of Surabaya could be dubbed a *"Ville Lumière"*.

Contemporary commentators in the Indies certainly realised that they were witnessing, and actively participating in, the international advent of (early) cinema, often framed within the discourse of the Ethical Policy as a modern tool for education. As a 1913 report from Medan presented it:

> If there is an invention that has become popular in a short time, that is the cinema [*cinema*], thanks especially to the great leaps in development made in this area of technology, particularly in perfecting the manner in which the bioscope [*bioscoop*] projects images. It shows images in the highlands. It shows our tropical life in the far north, it brings us memories of Europe to our region, it makes us feel at home in places where we have never been, teaches manners and customs of all nations. It gives us, aside for images of nature, also comedies and tragedies, which teach us about life, farces which function hygienically, since laughter is good for health. And all in an entertaining manner. We need not argue in any more detail. The fact that around the world cinema establishments [*bioscoopinrichtingen*] are erected everywhere and attract visitors speaks for itself.[1723]

Thus, by going to the movies, cinema spectators in the Netherlands Indies were not only invited to recognise themselves and their engagements with the modern on screen, but were also to be taught about other places and cultures, as suggested in the opening quote from Bandung which, as may be recalled, was also the setting of Boong Indri's first cinema screening (see Prologue). Similarly to the "cultural citizens" who were the target audiences of advertisements in Schulte Nordholt's work, cinema spectators were exposed to "modern things" and desirable lifestyles on screen. At Indies cinema theatres,

1722 As Sabine Lenk has pointed out to me, as soon as cinemas in Europe began renewing their programmes once a week, one week old prints would have been available on the market. It is therefore likely that many films were obtained second hand also earlier on, as this certainly reduced the financial risks entailed. However, as opposed to previous research that identified the Indies as a veritable junk market for dumping films that have finished their runs in the Netherlands, findings in this research suggest that the main exhibition companies in the Indies were more up to date.

1723 "De Deli-Bioscoop", *Deli Courant* (23 July 1913).

"cultural citizenship" as an invitation to abandon traditional ways of life was not the sole preserve of "Europeans" or indigenous elites, but open to moviegoers from all levels of colonial society. The ability to purchase a movie ticket and spend one's leisure time at the cinema gave spectators an illusion of equality and, in turn, served to reinforce the objectives of colonial authorities in executing the Ethical Policy: educating and uplifting the "Natives" from their present conditions by exposing them to scenes depicting European and American living through the medium of moving images. Seen in this light, the free shows offered to orphans or soldiers alongside the charity shows pledging to various causes, thus tapping into the Ethical Policy's discourses of education and progress, were part of entrepreneurs' strategy of appealing to their spectators, at the same time as pacifying the authorities.

At the same time, "cultural citizenship" in the cinema literally set in stone the class and racial hierarchies of colonial society, through the separation between the different classes of spectators: whether by relegating the so-called "Native" section to the space behind the screen or locating it in the front rows known as the *kambing* (goat) class. At times, separation along gender lines also occurred at certain cinemas. And while spectators of the *komedi stambul*, circus, or earlier tent shows for moving pictures could jump seats to secure a better viewing spot and mix with other sections of the audience, it is difficult to imagine how "Native" spectators at Surabaya's East Java Bioscope could emerge from behind the screen. Nevertheless, as Rudolf Mrázek writes about the experience of riding the trains in the Indies, even though there were separate cars for each class of passengers, "[…] the rhythm of the train, the shaking, and the machine were the same. All the passengers were (travelling) humans, and their uncomfortable sameness could nowhere be seen, felt, and smelled as strongly as in the train."[1724] While the comfort level in the cinema was similarly stratified – in terms of access and seating comfort – all spectators, seated in the dark, could be transported together to another world thanks to the images they were watching on screen, projected from the same flickering device. Spectators' engagement with modernity at the cinema in colonial Indonesia was thus often classed, racialized, and gendered; yet, despite the fact that they often could not see each other, they could presumably still hear and smell each other.

Moreover, as soon as education at the cinema was perceived by the authorities as instruction in the wrong kind of "modernity", such as in detective films and violent themes, often with strong racial under- and overtones, the pendulum swung towards anxieties about cinema's negative effects on "Native" spectators.[1725] Questions of morality, alcohol abuse, and crime in the cinema were

---

1724 Mrázek, *Engineers of Happy Land*, 13.

1725 The opening quote echoes similar concerns in the West about cinema's potential negative effects on youth, although in the Indies the emphasis is clearly placed more urgently on "Native" spectators. For an overview of work on moral panics and regulation initiatives of early cinema, see William Uricchio, "Law and the Cinema: Regulating Exhibition", in Abel (ed.), *Encyclopedia of Early Cinema*, 374–377.

raised over the years, but often were laid to rest just as quickly, with the colonial authorities exhibiting a *laissez-faire* attitude as long as films' educational value outweighed their disruptive potential of the colonial *status quo*. Control of moving picture shows, which was initially left at the hands of the local police in each province and municipal authority, leaving an opening for many dissenters, was becoming tighter with more directives emanating from the Governor General as of 1912.[1726] With a growing focus on prescribing what should not be screened rather than what could be of instructive value, it appears that the colonial authorities had a sense they were losing control over a medium they neither seemed to have a grip on, nor appeared to take an interest in up to the point when it was finally perceived as potentially dangeours.

The next phase in cinema's institutionalisation in the Netherlands Indies came during the period of the First World War, upon the exertion of more consolidated regulation over the cinema. A conscious decision was made in marking the onset of the First World War as the end point of this dissertation, due to changes in the way films were being traded and the shipping restrictions experienced in the Indies. Nevertheless, it is important to provide a short overview of the way in which film censorship and control developed from its earlier manifestations observed in this study, especially since the Cinema Ordinance (*Bioscoopordonnantie*) of 1916 was used in order to single out the four cities focused on in Part II. Maintaining neutrality in the Indies, on the ground and on the maritime front, as well as in public opinion, had proven to be a problematic ambition already in earlier global conflicts, such as the Boer War and Russo-Japanese War, and nobody was willing to risk potentially disruptive content at this time.[1727] Nevertheless, there appeared to be even more at stake in the Indies, at this time of a maturing popular nationalist movement, and the issue of the "cinema danger" (*bioscoopgevaar*) in the Indies was quickly gaining ground in the halls of government in the Indies and back in the Netherlands.[1728]

The public in the Indies "loves *wayang* and sees the cinema as a modern *wayang*", J.G. Scheurer, a Member of Dutch Parliament on behalf of the Anti-Revolutionary Party who was formerly a missionary doctor in the Indies, told the House of Representatives (*Tweede Kamer*) in 1915, advocating for more

---

[1726] This process took place almost in parallel with the establishment of municipal cinema commissions in the Netherlands (see Berg, "Notabele ingezetenen en goedwillende ambtenaren", 148).

[1727] For more on the problems of retaining neutrality in the Indies at these times of conflict, see Dijk, *The Netherlands Indies and the Great War*, 12–18, 100–104, 165–200. On "neutrality" on Dutch cinema screens in the Netherlands, see Klaas de Zwaan, *A cinema in between. Nationalizing foreign propaganda film in Dutch cinema culture (1914–1919)* [working title], PhD Dissertation (Utrecht University, forthcoming 2016).

[1728] For more on the development of the nationalist movement in the Indies within the context of the First World War, see Dijk, *The Netherlands Indies and the Great War*, 45–71 (on the *Indische Partij*), 621–622 (on the advance of communist leaders).

control of moving pictures in the Indies.[1729] Discussions in the Senate (*Eerste Kamer*) similarly mentioned with alarm the "[...] extremely large and still growing number of cinemas in Java, of which the Native population makes ample use".[1730] More supervision, beyond the local initiatives, was deemed necessary "[...] because some of the performances in the abovementioned cinemas not only pose a danger to public morality, but their injurious impact, also from a political standpoint, should not be underestimated. In many of these movie theatres, the European population in the Indies is presented in a ridiculous light."[1731] As soon as the content of films was perceived as endangering political tranquillity and colonial sovereignty, there was no holding back.

In 1916 the Governor-General of the Indies finally drafted the Cinema Ordinance, which touched on issues of copyright, taxation and film censorship, on both moral and political grounds, to be implemented across the entire archipelago as of March 1917.[1732] The Cinema Ordinance – made available in Dutch, Malay and Chinese, in order to avoid any potential misunderstandings – placed an emphasis on Batavia, Surabaya, Semarang and Medan as local hubs of the cinema trade. Cinema operators and local film distributors heavily opposed this initiative from the get-go because it would have led to taxes being levied on all purchased films, regardless of whether or not they would be authorised for exhibition. Even after the Cinema Ordinance was amended in 1917 in an attempt to appease them somewhat, they were still charged quite a significant tax for submitting a film to the censorship committee, therefore placing them at risk.[1733]

By 1918 the police was still struggling to implement the Cinema Ordinance in full and to keep up with the flow of films, which would have required 48 viewing hours per week just for the twelve cinema houses in Batavia, according to a calculation by the local police commissioner.[1734] This meant that censorship decisions in some cities were being made based on reviewing film titles alone.[1735] However, this quickly proved to be an unsatisfying solution since

---

1729 *Handelingen Tweede Kamer*, *Handelingen der Staten Generaal* ('s-Gravenhage: Algemeene Landsdrukkerij, 18 November 1915), 189. It is worth noting that this connection drawn by the former missionary turned politician between *wayang* and the cinema was probably grounded in reality, as Claire Holt similarly notes that "before the Dutch word *bioskop* [sic]was thoroughly entrenched in Indonesian usage, the cinema was called by villagers *wayang gambar hidup*, 'living pictures *wayang* or *wayang gelap*, 'dark *wayang*'" (Claire Holt, *Art in Indonesia: Continuities and Change* (Ithaca: Cornell University Press, 1967), 123, italics in original).

1730 *Handelingen Eerste Kamer*, *Handelingen der Staten Generaal* ('s-Gravenhage: Algemeene Landsdrukkerij, 1914–1915), 5.

1731 Ibid.

1732 Besluit van den Gouverneur-Generaal 18 March 1916, no. 47, in *Staatsblad van Nederlandsch-Indië 1916* (Batavia: Landsdrukkerij, 1916), no. 276 and 277. The ordinance was made available in Dutch, Malay and Chinese, in order to avoid any potential misunderstandings.

1733 "De bioscoop-censuur", *Sumatra Post* (29 April 1918).

1734 "De Film-censuur", *Sumatra Post* (25 September 1918).

1735 "Plaatselijke commissies tot het keuren van films", *Het Nieuws van den Dag voor Nederlandsch-Indië* (27 February 1918).

some suitable films might have been dismissed out of hand, while others could have simply been re-titled by savvy exhibitors in order to sneak forbidden films through the system.[1736] The police was then discussing the possibility of waiving films previously approved by censorship committees in other countries directly to cinemas. Britain was brought up as an example, since it also had indigenous populations under its rule which had to be taken into consideration in its decision-making. This was also believed to potentially solve the problem of exhibitors and distributors, who could then instruct their agents to ship only films which had already received the seal of approval in their respective production countries.[1737] Moreover, it was proposed to establish censorship committees based on volunteers, preferably consisting of retired policemen and European women. The latter, having enough free time on their hands and perceived to be strict and meticulous, were particularly expected to benefit the censorship process.[1738]

By the time the next amendment to the Cinema Ordinance was released in 1919, it was clear that the four commissions were a waste of resources and a single control body was conceived: the Central Cinema Commission (*Centrale Bioscoop Commissie*), located in Batavia.[1739] Local exhibitors and the films they were able to show movie-goers across the Netherlands Indies were finally fully subject to one centralised regulatory system, eliminating – although most likely not crushing entirely – the whims and fancies of local controllers and committees or the potential subversiveness of film contents.

★★★

While this research endeavoured to be as comprehensive as possible, more work is still required to fully map out the routes of exhibitors and the distribution of films in the Netherlands Indies. This research focused on Java and Sumatra, and therefore more work is needed to be carried out on other islands of the archipelago. The initial plan for this research was to include further investigation of newspapers from Makassar and Padang, which operated two other major ports; however, since the Cinema Ordinance identified Batavia, Surabaya, Semarang and Medan as sites for film control, I finally chose to limit the coverage of materials from other cities and to zoom in on the latter

---

1736 For instance, a screening of the Asta Nielsen film NACHTFALTER (in English "The Moth" aka "Retribution") in August 1912 at the Oranje Bioscoop in Medan sparked the concerns of the recently-instated film censor in Sumatra. Apparently the film's title, which in German and Dutch ("Nachtvlinder") could have been interpreted as insinuating unseemly nocturnal activities, aroused suspicion that this might be a spectacle of questionable morality. The film was subsequently "tested, tried, weighed and approved" for screening by the police commissioner ("Bioscoop-censuur", *Sumatra Post* (16 August 1912)).

1737 "De Film-censuur", *Sumatra Post* (25 September 1918).

1738 Ibid. Another report cautioned against employing too many "old spinsters" to perform the task, thus running the risk of ending up with a far too scrupulous censorship system ("De bioscoop-censuur", *Sumatra Post* (24 April 1918)).

1739 See Berg, "Notabele ingezetenen en goedwillende ambtenaren", 151. Fast-forward to 1931, and 2.28 million meters of film were inspected by the Commission in the Indies in that year, compared with 1.66 million meters in the Netherlands at the same time (ibid., 146). For more on censorship in the Indies in the 1910s up to the 1940s, see Arief, *Politik Film di Hindia Belanda* and Berg, *Film en filmkeuring in Nederlands-Indië*.

four hubs of the film trade here. Further research on other cities and more rural areas on Java and Sumatra is also required. Eastern Java, thanks to the efforts of Umbgrove's East Java Bioscope Company, would be potentially the most fruitful avenue to explore in respect of rural film exhibition and movie-going. Yogyakarta, the city where Helant, who traded with Jean Desmet, finally settled for his permanent venue, would be another interesting town in Central Java to research, especially with its rich history of *wayang kulit*.

While the only female exhibitor identified in this research was Miss Meranda (Section 1.3.2.), I take this as a sign that there must have been other women involved in exhibition of moving images. Some exhibitors travelled with their wives, who were also incorporated into the shows as in the case of Emily D'Alton, the wife of Carl Hertz (see Section 1.3.4.). Other women were involved on the management side, for instance, after the death of her husband in 1893, Jane Harmston Love managed Harmston's Circus together with her second husband, Robert Love.[1740] According to the establishment documents of the Venus Cinema Theater in Tegal in 1913, another widow by the name Emelie Anna Damme (*née* Straub) from Semarang was the co-founder and co-owner of the cinema, alongside Mr. Dirk van Vianen.[1741] These findings may open up another avenue for further research on the role of women in turn-of-the-century popular entertainment and early cinema exhibition, in colonial Indonesia and beyond.

Although the minutes and decisions of the local authorities were brought in full over the pages of the newspapers, there are surely more documents to be explored at the National Archives of Indonesia (ANRI) in Jakarta, which this researcher had limited access to. Further reading of contemporary popular Chinese-Malay novels may also yield some intriguing anecdotes on cinema excursions. Finally, although I have attempted to capture some of the regional flows, the micro-level has been the dominant mode of research here. More connections can be drawn with the rest of Southeast Asia, as Tofighian and I have begun to do, but also with networks of entertainment and film distribution in the rest of Asia, Australia and the Pacific.[1742] The period of the First World War may provide links between movie-going and budding Indonesian nationalism, hints of which were already registered here. Hopefully more researchers will follow in exploring other aspects and later periods, especially considering that many spectators in present-day Indonesia today are still exposed to cinema via the work of touring operators.

1740 See Tofighian, *Blurring the Colonial Binary*, 121.

1741 See *Extra-Bijvoegsel der Javasche Courant van* 18/4–1913, no. 31.

1742 See Tofighian, *Blurring the Colonial Binary* and Dafna Ruppin et al., "Moving Pictures across Colonial Boundaries".

Bibliography

Archives, Collections, and Libraries

Indonesia:
National Archives of Indonesia (Arsip Nasional Republik Indonesia, ANRI), Jakarta
National Library of Indonesia (Perpustakaan Nasional Republik Indonesia, PNRI), Sinematek Indonesia, Jakarta

The Netherlands:
Amsterdam University Library (Universiteitsbibliotheek Amsterdam), Amsterdam
EYE Film Institute Netherlands (EYE Filminstituut Nederland), Amsterdam
Leiden University Library (Universiteitsbibliotheek Leiden), Leiden
National Archives of the Netherlands (Nationaal Archief, NA), The Hague
National Library of the Netherlands (Koninklijke Bibliotheek, KB), The Hague
Royal Tropical Institute (Koninklijk Instituut voor de Tropen, KIT), Amsterdam
Royal Netherlands Institute for Southeast Asian and Caribbean Studies (Koninklijk Instituut voor Taal-, Land- en Volkenkunde, KITLV), Leiden
Utrecht University Library (Universiteitsbibliotheek Utrecht), Utrecht

United Kingdom:
Bodleian Library, Oxford University

United States:
The John M. Echols Collection on Southeast Asia and the Rare and Manuscript Collection, Carl A. Kroch Library, Cornell University, Ithaca, NY

Journals

De Bioscoop-Courant 1912–1913, 1915–1916, 1918
Filmwereld 1917–1918
Indië: Geïllustreerd Tijdschrift voor Nederland en Koloniën★
Indisch Bouwkundig Tijdschrift 1898–1907
De Kinematograaf 1913–1919

★ Digitized by KIT and available as the Colonial Collection (KIT) of Universiteit Leiden at http://colonial.library.leiden.edu/cgi-bin/ubl.exe

Newspapers

Advertentieblad voor Tegal en Omstreken 1896–1897
Albrecht's Zondagsblad 1899
Andalas 1917–1918
Bataviaasch-Handelsblad 1895–1898, 1908
Bataviaasch Nieuwsblad 1895–1914★
Bintang Barat 1896–1899
Bintang Betawi/Batavia 1900–1901, 1903–1906
Bintang Soerabaia 1896–1912, 1914–1918
Bintang Tionghoa 1914–1915
Dagblad van Celebes 1914
Deli Courant 1896, 1898
Het Centrum 1897–1898, 1901–1902
Chabar Hindia Belanda 1896
Deminggoe Daripada Bintang Barat Courant 1896–1898
Djawa Tengah 1913–1916
Ik Po 1905–1906
De Indische Handelscourant 1897
De Indische Kinder Courant 1902–1905
Java-Bode 1896–1897★, 1898–1899, 1904–1910
Javasche Courant 1896–1914
Kabar Perniagaan 1904–1907
Kaoem Moeda 1915, 1918
Li Po 1903–1907
De Locomotief 1895–1903★, 1904–1914
Makasaarsche Courant 1908–1910
De Makassar 1901–1903
De Nieuwe Soerabaja Courant 1896–1914
De Nieuwe Vorstenlanden 1896, 1906
Het Nieuws van den Dag voor Nederlandsch-Indië 1900–1914★
Oetoesan Hindia 1914–1918
Pantjaran Warta 1910–1914
Pembrita Betawi 1896–1916
Pembrita Makassar 1914–1918
Penghetar 1897–1901
Prange's Nieuws en Advertentie Blad 1896–1897
De Preanger Bode 1896–1897, 1902, 1906
Primbon Soerabaia 1900–1901
Selompret Melajoe 1896–1911
Semarangsche Courant 1896–1897, 1906
Sin Po 1914–1918
Sinar Atjeh 1907–1908
Sinar Djawa 1914–1918
Sinar Matahari 1914–1919

Sinar Sumatra 1914
The Singapore Free Press 1896–1905★★
Soerabaiasch-Handelsblad 1895–1896★, 1897, 1898★, 1899–1901, 1902–1908★, 1909–1914
Soerabaiasch Nieuwsblad 1909–1914
The Straits Times 1896–1899★★, 1902–1907★★
Sumatra Courant 1895–1900★
Sumatra Post 1900–1914★
Taman Sari 1904–1914
De Telefoon 1896–1897
Warta Perniagaan 1914

★ Fully or partially digitized at the time this research was conducted by the National Library of the Netherlands (KB), available at http://www.delpher.nl/nl/kranten
★★ Digitized by the National Library Board, Singapore, available at http://eresources.nlb.gov.sg/newspapers/

Published Sources

Handelingen Eerste Kamer. Handelingen der Staten Generaal. 's-Gravenhage: Algemeene Landsdrukkerij, 1914–1915.

Handeligen Tweede Kamer. Verslag der handelingen van de Tweede Kamer der Staten Generaal met verschillende supplementen. 's-Gravenhage: Algemeene Landsdrukkerij, 18 November 1915.

Koloniaal Verslag 1900. 's-Gravenhage: Algemeene Landsdrukkerij, 1900.

Koloniaal Verslag 1907–1908. 's-Gravenhage: Algemeene Landsdrukkerij, 1908.

Secondary Sources

Abeyasekere, Susan. *Jakarta: A History*. Singapore: Oxford University Press, 1989 [1987].

Abdullah, Taufik, Misbach Yusa Biran and S. M. Ardan. *Film Indonesia. Bagian I (1900–1950)*. Jakarta: Perum Percetakan Negara Ri, 1993.

Abel, Richard. "Early Film Programs: An Overture, Five Acts, and an Interlude". In *A Companion to Early Cinema*, edited by André Gaudreault, Nicholas Dulac and Hidalgo Santiago, 334–359. Malden, MA/Oxford: Wiley-Blackwell, 2012.

———, (ed.). *The Encyclopedia of Early Cinema*. London: Routledge, 2005.

Adam, Ahmat B. *The Vernacular Press and the Emergence of Modern Indonesian Consciousness (1855–1913)*. Ithaca: Cornell Southeast Asia Program, 1995.

Ahmad, Aijaz. *In Theory: Classes, Nations, Literatures*. London: Verso, 1992.

Allen, Robert C. "Decentering Historical Audience Studies. A Modest Proposal". In *Hollywood in the Neighborhood: Case Studies of Local Moviegoing*, edited by Kathryn H. Fuller-Seeley, 20–33. Berkeley: University of California Press, 2008.

———, "From Exhibition to Reception: Reflections on the Audience in Film History". *Screen* 31, no. 4 (1990): 347–356.

Ardan, S. M. "Indonesia", translated by Raymond Edmondson. In *Encyclopedia of Early Cinema*, edited by Richard Abel, 320. London: Routledge, 2005.

———, *Njai Dasima*. Jakarta: Pustaka Jaya, 1965.

Arief, M. Sarief. *Politik Film di Hindia Belanda*. Depok: Komunitas Bambu, 2010.

Arrighi, Gillian. "The Circus and Modernity: A Commitment to 'the Newer' and 'the Newest'". *Early Popular Visual Culture* 10, no. 2 (2012): 169–185.

Anderson, Benedict. *Imagined Communities: Reflections on the Origin and Spread of Nationalism*.

Revised edition, London/New York: see footnote 649London and New York: Verso, 2006 [1983].
Barendregt, Bart. "Sonic Histories in Southeast Asia". In *Sonic Modernities in the Malay World: A History of Popular Music, Social Distinction and Novel Lifestyles (1930s–2000s)*, edited by Bart Barendregt, 1–43. Leiden: Brill, 2014.
——, (ed.). *Sonic Modernities in the Malay World: A History of Popular Music, Social Distinction and Novel Lifestyles (1930s–2000s)*. Leiden: Brill, 2014.
Barnouw, Adriaan Jacob. *A Trip Through the Dutch East Indies*. Gouda: Koch & Knuttel, ca. 1920.
Barnouw, Erik and S. Krishnaswamy. *Indian Film*. New York/London: Columbia University Press, 1963.
Basundoro, Purnawan. "The Two alun-alun in Malang (1930–1950)". In *Cars, Conduits, and Kampongs: The Modernization of the Indonesian City, 1920–1960*, edited by Freek Colombijn and Joost Coté, 272–299. Leiden: Brill, 2015.
Baudelaire, Charles. "The Painter of Modern Life (1863)". In *The Nineteenth-Century Visual Culture Reader*, edited by Vanessa R. Schwartz and J.M. Przyblyski, 37–42. New York: Routledge, 2004.
Bemmelen, J. F. van and G. B. Hooyer. *Guide to the Dutch East Indies, Compiled by order of the Koninklijke Paketvaart Maatschappij (Royal Packet Company)*, translated by B. J. Berrington. New Edition revised by Otto Knaap. London/Amsterdam: Thos. Cook & Son/J. H. de Bussy, 1903 [1897].
Benjamin, Walter. "The Work of Art in the Age of Mechanical Reproduction (1936)". In *The Nineteenth-Century Visual Culture Reader*, edited by Vanessa R. Schwartz and J.M. Przyblyski, 63–70. New York: Routledge, 2004.
Berg, Rob van den. "De koloniale maatstaf: filmkeuring in Nederlands-Indië". *Jambatan: Tijdschrift voor de geschiedenis van Indonesië* 9, no. 3 (1991): 91–107.
Berg, Robert van den. *Film en filmkeuring in Nederlands-Indië 1910–1925*, PhD Dissertation. Radboud University Nijmegen, 1988.
Berg, Soeluh van den. "Notabele ingezetenen en goedwillende ambtenaren: De Nederlands-Indische filmkeuring, 1912–1942". In *Jaarboek Mediageschiedenis 4: Nederlands-Indië*, edited by Soeluh van den Berg and René Witte, 145–171. Amsterdam: Stichting Mediageschiedenis, 1992.
Beusekom, Ansje van. "Ivens, Cees A. P.". In *Encyclopedia of Early Cinema*, edited by Richard Abel, 342. London: Routledge, 2005.
Bhabha, Homi K. *The Location of Culture*. London: Routledge, 1994.
Biltereyst, Daniel, Richard Maltby and Philippe Meers. "Cinema, Audiences and Modernity: An Introduction". In *Cinema, Audiences and Modernity: New Perspectives on European Cinema History*, edited by Daniel Biltereyst, Richard Maltby and Philippe Meers, 1–16. London: Routledge, 2012.
——, eds. *Cinema, Audiences and Modernity: New Perspectives on European Cinema History*. London: Routledge, 2012.
Biran, Misbach Yusa. *Sejarah Film 1900–1950: Bikin Film di Jawa*. Jakarta: Komunitas Bambu, 2009.
Bloembergen, Marieke. *De geschiedenis van de politie in Nederlands-Indië. Uit zorg en angst*. Amsterdam: Boom, Leiden: KITLV Uitgeverij, 2009.
——, *Colonial Spectacles: The Netherlands and the Dutch East Indies at the World Exhibitions, 1880–1931*, translated by Beverley Jackson. Singapore: Singapore University Press, 2006.
Blom, Ivo. *Jean Desmet and the Early Dutch Film Trade*. Amsterdam: Amsterdam University Press, 2003.
Bogaers, Erica and Peter de Ruijter. "Ir. Thomas Karsten and Indonesian Town Planning, 1915–1940". In *The Indonesian City: Studies in Urban Development and Planning*, edited by Peter J. M. Nas, 71–88. Dordrecht-Holland/Cinnaminson-U.S.A.: Foris Publications, 1986.
Bordwell, David. *Figures Traced in Light: On Cinematic Staging*. Berkeley: University of California Press, 2005.

———, *On the History of Film Style*. Cambridge, MA: Harvard University Press, 1997.

Bosma, Ulbe and Remco Raben. *Being "Dutch" in the Indies: A History of Creolisation and Empire, 1500–1920*, translated by Wendie Shaffer. Singapore: NUS Press, 2008.

Bottomore, Stephen. *Filming, Faking and Propaganda: The Origins of the War Film, 1897–1902*, PhD Dissertation. Utrecht University, 2007.

———, "Malaya". In *Encyclopedia of Early Cinema*, edited by Richard Abel, 590–591. London: Routledge, 2005.

———, "The Panicking Audience?: Early Cinema and the 'Train Effect'". *Historical Journal of Film, Radio and Television* 19, no. 2 (1999): 177–216.

———, "'Zischen und Murren': Die Dreyfus-Affäre und das frühe Kino", *KINtop* 2 (1993): 69–82.

Bousquet, Henri (ed.). *Catalogue Pathé des années 1896 à 1914*. S.l. [Bures-sur-Yvette]: Henri Bousquet, 1993–1996.

Braak, C. "Climate of Netherlands India". In *Twentieth Century Impressions of Netherlands India: Its History, People, Commerce, Industries and Resources*, edited by Arnold Wright, 303–308. London: Lloyd's Greater Britain Publishing Company, 1909.

Buitenweg, Hein. *Krokodillenstad*. Katwijk aan Zee: Servire, 1980.

Burke, Peter. *Cultural Hybridity*. Cambridge: Polity Press, 2009.

Cabaton, A. *Java, Sumatra, and the other islands of the Dutch East Indies*, translated by Bernard Miall. London: Unwin, 1911.

Chabria, Suresh. "Royal Bioscope". In *Encyclopedia of Early Cinema*, edited by Richard Abel, 555. London: Routledge, 2005.

Chandra, Elizabeth. "Women and Modernity: Reading the Femme Fatale in Early Twentieth-Century Indies Novels". *Indonesia* 92 (October 2011): 157–182.

Claver, Alexander. *Dutch Commerce and Chinese Merchants in Java: Colonial Relationships in Trade and Finance, 1800–1942*. Leiden: Brill, 2014.

Cleary, Mark and Goh Kim Chuan. *Environment and Development in the Straits of Malacca (Routledge Studies in Development and Society)*. London: Routledge, 2000.

Clifford, James. "On Orientalism". In *The Predicament of Culture: Twentieth Century Ethnography, Literature and Art*, 255–276. Cambridge, MA: Harvard University Press, 1988.

Cohen, Matthew Isaac. *The Komedie Stamboel: Popular Theater in Colonial Indonesia, 1891–1903*. Leiden: KITLV Press, 2006.

———, "Border Crossings: Bangsawan in the Netherlands Indies in the Nineteenth and Early Twentieth Centuries". *Indonesia and the Malay World* 30, no. 87 (2002): 101–115.

———, "On the Origins of the Komedi Stamboel: Popular Culture, Colonial Society, and the Parsi Theatre Movement". *Bijdragen tot de Taal-, Land- en Volkenkunde* 157, no. 2 (2001): 313–357.

Colombijn, Freek and Joost Coté (eds.). *Cars, Conduits, and Kampongs: The Modernization of the Indonesian City, 1920–1960*. Leiden: Brill, 2015.

Cooper, Frederick. *Colonialism in Question: Theory, Knowledge, History*. Berkeley: University of California Press, 2005.

Coté, Joost. "Making the kampung modern: colonial planning in Semarang 1910–1925". *Review of Indonesian and Malaysian Affairs* 44, no. 2 (2010): 15–48.

———, "Staging modernity: the Semarang International Colonial Exhibition, 1914". *Review of Indonesian and Malaysian Affairs* 40, no. 1 (2006): 1–44.

———, "Towards an Architecture of Association: H. F. Tillema, Semarang and the discourse on the colonial 'slum'". In *The Indonesian Town Revisited*, edited by Peter J. M. Nas, 319–347. Münster: LIT Verlag, 2002.

———, "'To See is to Know': the Pedagogy of the Colonial Exhibition, Semarang, 1914". *Paedagogica Historica* 36, no. 1 (2000): 341–366.

Coulter, Harold G. "The Kinematograph in the East". *The Kinematograph & Lantern Weekly* (4 February 1909): 1039.

Bibliography

Cribb, Robert (ed.). *The Late Colonial State in Indonesia: Political and Economic Foundations of the Netherlands Indies 1880–1942*. Leiden: KITLV Press, 1994.

——, "Introduction: The Late Colonial State in Indonesia". In *The Late Colonial State in Indonesia: Political and Economic Foundations of the Netherlands Indies 1880–1942*, edited by Robert Cribb, 1–9. Leiden: KITLV Press, 1994.

Dick, Howard and Peter J. Rimmer. *Cities, Transport and Communications: The Integration of Southeast Asia since 1850*. Houndmills: Palgrave Macmillan, 2003.

Dick, H. W. *Surabaya: City of Work: A Socioeconomic History*. Athens: Ohio University Press, 2002.

Diessen, J.R. van. *Soerabaja 1900–1950. Havens, Marine, Stadsbeeld*. Zierikzee: Asia Maior, 2004.

Dijk, Janneke van, Jaap de Jonge and Nico de Klerk (eds.). *J. C. Lamster, een vroege filmer in Nederlands-Indië*. Amsterdam: KIT Publishers, 2010.

Dijk, Kees van. *The Netherlands Indies and the Great War 1914–1918*. Leiden: KITLV Press, 2007.

Edgerton, David. *The Shock of the Old: Technology and global history since 1900*. London: Profile Books, 2008 [2006].

Elsaesser, Thomas. "Discipline through Diegesis: The Rube Film between 'Attractions' and 'Narrative Integration', in *The Cinema of Attractions Reloaded*, edited by Wanda Strauven, 205–223. Amsterdam: Amsterdam University Press, 2006.

Faber, G. H. von. *Nieuw Soerabaia: De Geschiedenis van Indië's voornaamste Koopstad in de Eerste Kwarteeuw Sedert hare Instelling 1906–1931*. Bussum/Soerabaia: N.V. Boekhandel en Drukkerij H. van Ingen, 1936.

Fasseur, C. "Cornerstone and stumbling block: Racial classification and the late colonial state in Indonesia". In *The Late Colonial State in Indonesia: Political and Economic Foundations of the Netherlands Indies 1880–1942*, edited by Robert Cribb, 31–56. Leiden: KITLV Press, 1994.

Fernando, M. R. "The Trumpet Shall Sound for Rich Peasants: Kasam Mukmin's Uprising in Gedangan, East Java, 1904". *Journal of Southeast Asian Studies* 26, no. 2 (September 1995): 242–262.

Fossati, Giovanna. "Multiple Originals: The (Digital) Restoration and Exhibition of Early Films". In *A Companion to Early Cinema*, edited by André Gaudreault, Nicolas Dulac and Santiago Hidalgo, 550–567. Malden, MA/Oxford: Wiley-Blackwell, 2012.

Francis, G. *Nyai Dasima*, Working Paper no. 46, translated by Harry Aveling. Clayton, Australia: Monash University, 1988.

——, *Tjerita Njai Dasima*. Batavia, 1896.

Frederick, William Hayward. *Visions and Heat: The Making of the Indonesian Revolution*. Athens: Ohio University Press, 1989.

——, *Indonesian Urban Society in Transition: Surabaya, 1926–1946*, PhD Dissertation. University of Hawaii, 1978.

Fuhrmann, Wolfgang. *Imperial Projections. Screening the German Colonies*. New York/Oxford: Berghahn, 2015.

Fuller-Seeley, Kathryn H. and George Potamianos. "Introduction: Researching and Writing the History of Local Moviegoing". In *Hollywood in the Neighbourhood: Historical Case Studies of Local Moviegoing*, edited by Kathryn H. Fuller-Seeley, 3–19. Berkeley: University of California Press, 2008.

Fuller-Seeley, Kathryn H. (ed.). *Hollywood in the Neighbourhood: Historical Case Studies of Local Moviegoing*. Berkeley: University of California Press, 2008.

Furnivall, J. S. *Netherlands India: A Study of Plural Economy*. Cambridge: Cambridge University Press, 2010 [1967].

Gaudreault, André, Nicolas Dulac and Santiago Hidalgo (eds.) *A Companion to Early Cinema*. Malden, MA/Oxford: Wiley-Blackwell, 2012.

Gaudreault, André. "The Culture Broth and the Froth of Cultures of So-called Early

Cinema". In *A Companion to Early Cinema*, edited by André Gaudreault, Nicolas Dulac and Santiago Hidalgo, 15–31. Malden, MA/Oxford: Wiley-Blackwell, 2012.

Gaudreault, André and Philippe Marion. "A medium is always born twice…". *Early Popular Visual Culture* 3, no. 1 (2005), 3–15.

Gildemijer, Johan. *Koningin Kino*. Amsterdam: De Nieuwe Tijd, ca. 1914.

Goss, Andrew. "From *Tong-Tong* to Tempo Doeloe: Eurasian Memory Work and the Bracketing of Dutch Colonial History, 1957–1961". *Indonesia* 70 (October 2000): 9–36.

Grieveson, Lee. "Audiences: Surveys and Debates". In *The Encyclopedia of Early Cinema*, edited by Richard Abel, 64–69. London: Routledge, 2005.

——, *Policing Cinema: Movies and Censorship in Early-Twentieth-Century America*. Berkeley: University of California Press, 2004.

Griffiths, Alison. *Wondrous Difference: Cinema, Anthropology, and Turn-of-the-Century Visual Culture*. New York: Columbia University Press, 2003.

Gunning, Tom. "An Aesthetic of Astonishment: Early Film and the (In)Credulous Spectator". In *Viewing Positions: Ways of Seeing Film*, edited by Linda Williams, 114–133. New Brunswick: Rutgers University Press, 1995.

——, "The World as Object Lesson: Cinema Audiences, Visual Culture and the St. Louis World's Fair, 1904". *Film History* 6, no. 4, Audiences and Fans (Winter 1994), 422–444.

Hansen, Kathryn. *Stages of Life: Indian Theatre Autobiographies*. London: Anthem Press, 2011.

Headrick, Daniel R. *The Tools of Empire: Technology and European Imperialism in the Nineteenth Century*. New York: Oxford University Press, 1981.

Heel, M. van (ed.). *Gedenkboek van de Koloniale Tentoonstelling Semarang, 20 Augustus–22 November 1914. Eerste en Tweede Deel*. Mercurius: Batavia, 1916.

Hertz, Carl. *A Modern Mystery Merchant: The Trials, Tricks and Travels of Carl Hertz, the Famous American Illusionist*. London: Hutchinson & Co., 1924.

Hesselink, Liesbeth. *Healers on the colonial market: Native doctors and midwives in the Dutch East Indies*. Leiden: KITLV Press, 2011.

Holt, Claire. *Art in Indonesia: Continuities and Change*. Ithaca: Cornell University Press, 1967.

Huisman, Frank. "Struggling for the Market: Strategies of Dutch pharmaceutical companies, 1880–1940". In *Perspectives on Twentieth-century Pharmaceuticals*, edited by Viviane Quirke and Judy Slinn, 63–89. Bern: Peter Lang, 2010.

Indian Talkie. 1931–56: Silver Jubilee Souvenir. Bombay: Film Federation of India, 1956.

Jansen Hendriks, Gerda. *Een voorbeeldige kolonie: Nederlands-Indië in 50 jaar overheidsfilms, 1912–1962*, PhD Dissertation. University of Amsterdam, 2014.

Java, The Wonderland. Weltevreden/Batavia: The Official Tourist Bureau, ca. 1900.

Jedamski, Doris. "The Vanishing-Act of Sherlock Holmes in Indonesia's National Awakening". In *Chewing Over the West: Occidental Narratives in Non-Western Readings*, edited by Doris Jedamski, 383–413. Amsterdam/New York: Rodopi, 2009.

——, "…and then the lights went out: From Stamboel to Tonil – Theatre and the Transformation of Perceptions". *South East Asia Research* 16, no. 3 (2008): 481–511.

Jongmans, Rob and Janneke van Dijk, "From colonial topicality to cultural heritage: the history of the photograph collection". In *Photographs of the Netherlands East Indies*, edited by Janneke van Dijk, Rob Jongmans, Anouk Mansfeld, Steven Vink and Pim Westerkamp, 15–37. Amsterdam: KIT Publishers, 2012.

Kahn, Joel S. *Modernity and Exclusion*. London: SAGE Publications, 2001.

Kember, Joe. *Marketing Modernity: Victorian Popular Shows and Early Cinema*. Exeter: University of Exeter Press, 2009.

Keppy, Peter. "Southeast Asia in the Age of Jazz: Locating Popular Culture in the Colonial Philippines and Indonesia". *Journal of Southeast Asian Studies* 44, no. 3 (October 2013): 444–464.

Kessler, Frank. "Viewing Change, Changing Views: The 'History of Vision'-Debate". In *Film 1900: Technology, Perception, Culture*, edited by Annemone Ligensa and Klaus Kreimeier, 23–35. New Barnet: John Libbey, 2009.

Keyser, Arthur. *From Jungle to Java. The Trivial Impressions of a Short Excursion to Netherlands India*. Westminster: The Roxburghe Press, 1897.

Klerk, Nico de. "Een onmogelijke opdracht: J. C. Lamster filmopnamen voor het Koloniaal Instituut". In *J. C. Lamster, een vroege filmer in Nederlands-Indië*, edited by Janneke van Dijk, Jaap de Jong and Nico de Klerk, 79–114. Amsterdam: KIT Publishers, 2010.

———, "'The Transport of Audiences': Making Cinema 'National'". In *Early Cinema and the "National"*, edited by Richard Abel, Giorgio Bertellini and Rob King, 101–108. New Barnet: John Libbey, 2008.

———, "Volgt het voorbeeld van John Wayne: Over onze grenzeloze nationale cinema". In *Film in Nederland*, edited by Rommy Albers, Jan Baeke and Rob Zeeman, 414–421. Gent/Amsterdam: Ludion/Filmmuseum, 2004.

Kowner, Rotem (ed.). *The Impact of the Russo-Japanese War*. London: Routledge, 2007.

Kuitenbrouwer, Maarten. *The Netherlands and the Rise of Modern Imperialism: Colonies and Foreign Policy, 1870–1902*, translated by Hugh Beyer. New York: Berg, 1991.

Kumar, Ann. *Java and Modern Europe*. Surrey: Curzon Press, 1997.

Kuntowijoyo. "Making an Old City a Pleasant Place to Stay for *Meneer* and *Mevrouw*: Solo, 1900–1915". *Humaniora* XII, no. 2 (2000): 139–146.

Laffan, Michael. "Tokyo as a shared Mecca of modernity: War echoes in the colonial Malay world". In *The Impact of the Russo-Japanese War*, edited by Rotem Kowner, 219–238. London: Routledge, 2007.

Laffan, Michael Francis. *Islamic Nationhood and Colonial Indonesia: The* umma *Below the Winds*. London: RoutledgeCurzon, 2003.

Larkin, Brian. *Signal and Noise: Media, Infrastructure, and Urban Culture in Nigeria*. Durham: Duke University Press, 2008.

Locher-Scholten, Elsbeth. *Women and the Colonial State: Essays on Gender and Modernity in the Netherlands Indies 1900–1942*. Amsterdam: Amsterdam University Press, 2000.

Loderichs, M. A. *Medan: Beeld van een Stad*. Purmerend: Asia Maior, 1997.

Loiperdinger, Martin. "Lumière's Arrival of the Train: Cinema's Founding Myth", translated by Bernd Elzer. *The Moving Image* 4, no. 1 (Spring 2004): 89–118.

Lombard-Salmon, Claudine. "Le voyage du marchand Tan Hoe Lo à Paris (1889)". *Archipel* 54, No. 1 (1997), 177–188.

Mackenzie, John M. (ed.). *Imperialism and Popular Culture*. Manchester: Manchester University Press, 1986.

Maier, Henk. "Explosions in Semarang: Reading Malay tales in 1895". *Bijdragen tot de Taal-, Land- en Volkenkunde (BKI)* 162, no. 1 (2006): 1–34.

Maltby, Richard, Philippe Meers and Daniel Biltereyst, (eds.), *Explorations in New Cinema History: Approaches and Case Studies*. Oxford: Wiley-Blackwell, 2011.

Maltby, Richard. "New Cinema Histories". In *Explorations in New Cinema History: Approaches and Case Studies*, edited by Richard Maltby, Philippe Meers and Daniel Biltereyst, 3–40. Oxford: Wiley-Blackwell, 2011.

———, "On the Prospect of Writing Cinema History from Below". *Tijdschrift voor Mediageschiedenis* 9, no. 2 (2006): 74–96.

M., K. "Reisherinneringen uit Indië. Soerabaja". *Indië: geïllustreerd weekblad voor Nederland en koloniën* 3, no. 44 (28 January 1920): 708–712.

Mandere, H.Ch.G.J. van der. "De Cultuurmaatschappij Wonolangan (1895–1925)". In *Indië: Geïllustreerd Tijdschrift voor Nederland en Koloniën* 9, no. 19 (9 December 1925): 306–340.

Mannoni, Laurent. *Le grand art de la lumière et de l'ombre: archéologie du cinema*. Paris: Nathan, 1994.

Manusama, A. Th. *Njai Dasima, Het Slachtoffer van bedrog en misleiding, een historische zedenroman van Batavia*. Batavia, 1926.

Martin, Michèle. *Images at War: Illustrated Periodicals and Constructed Nations*. Toronto: University of Toronto Press, 2006.

Masak, Tanete A. Pong. *Le cinéma indonésien (1926–1967): Études d'Histoire Sociale*, PhD Dissertation. L'École des Hautes Études en Sciences Sociales, Paris, 1989.

McClintock, Anne. *Imperial Leather: Race, Gender, and Sexuality in the Colonial Contest*. London: Routledge, 1995.

McKernan, Luke. *The Boer War (1899–1902): Films in BFI Collections, National Film and Television Archive*, Second Edition. London: National Film and Television Archive, 1999 [1997].

Merrillees, Scott. *Greetings from Jakarta: Postcards of a Capital 1900–1950*. Jakarta/Kuala Lumpur: Equinox Publishing, 2012.

———, *Batavia in Nineteenth Century Photographs*. Richmond (Surrey): Curzon, 2000.

Miller, Elizabeth Carolyn. *Framed: The New Woman Criminal in British Culture at the Fin de Siècle*. Ann Arbor: University of Michigan Press, 2008.

Miller, Michael B. *Europe and the Maritime World: A Twentieth-Century History*. New York: Cambridge University Press, 2012.

Milone, Pauline Dublin. "Indische Culture and Its Relationship to Urban Life". *Comparative Studies in Society and History* 9 (1967): 407–26.

———, *Queen City of the East: The Metamorphosis of a Colonial Capital*, PhD Dissertation. Berkeley: University of California, 1966.

Moon, Suzanne. *Technology and Ethical Idealism: A History of Development in the Netherlands East Indies*. Leiden: CNWS Publications, 2007.

Mrázek, Jan. *Phenomenology of a Puppet Theatre: Contemplations on the Art of Javanese Wayang Kulit*. Leiden: KITLV Press, 2005.

Mrázek, Rudolf. *A Certain Age: Colonial Jakarta through the Memories of its Intellectuals*. Durham: Duke University Press, 2010.

———, *Engineers of Happy Land: Technology and Nationalism in a Colony*. Princeton: Princeton University Press, 2002.

———, *Sjahrir: Politics and Exile in Indonesia*. Ithaca: SEAP Publications, 1994.

Musser, Charles. *Edison Motion Pictures, 1896–1900. An Annotated Filmography*. Gemona: Le Giornate del Cinema Muto, 1997.

Musser, Charles. "Passions and the Passion Play: Theatre, Film and Religion in America 1880–1900". *Film History* 5, no. 4 (1993): 419–456.

———, *Before the Nickelodeon: Edwin S. Porter and the Edison Manufacturing Company*. Berkeley: University of California Press, 1991.

———, *The Emergence of Cinema: The American Screen to 1907*. New York: Scribner, 1990.

Nas, Peter J.M. (ed.). *The Indonesian Town Revisited*. Münster: LIT Verlag, 2002.

———, (ed.). *The Indonesian City: Studies in Urban Development and Planning*. Dordrecht-Holland/Cinnaminson-U.S.A.:: Foris Publications, 1986.

Neys, A. F. "Bioscopische ervaringen in de tropen", *De Kinematograaf* 31 (22 August 1913): 205.

———, "Bioscopische ervaringen in de tropen", *De Kinematograaf* 32 (29 August 1913): 214–215.

———, "Bioscopische ervaringen in de tropen", *De Kinematograaf* 33 (5 September 1913): 224–225.

Niel, Robert van. *The Emergence of the Modern Indonesian Elite*. Dordrecht-Holland/Cinnaminson-U.S.A.: Foris Publications, 1984.

Norindr, Panivong. "Enlisting Early Cinema in the Service of 'la plus grande France'". In *Early Cinema and the "National"*, edited by Richard Abel, Giorgio Bertellini and Rob King, 109–117. New Barnet: John Libbey, 2008.

Pleyte, Cornelis Marinus. *Verslag Nopens de Pasar Gambir Gehouden op het Koningsplein te Weltevreden van 28 Augustus–2 September, 1906*. Batavia: Landsdrukkerij, 1907.

Oort, Thunnis van. "'That pleasant feeling of peaceful coziness': Cinema Exhibition in a Dutch Mining District during the Inter-war Period". *Film History* 17, no. 1 (2005): 148–159.

Pratt, Mary Louise. *Imperial Eyes: Travel Writing and Transculturation*. London: Routledge, 1992.

Ray, Sandeep. *Celluloid Colony: The Inadvertent Ethnography in Propaganda Films from the Dutch East Indies (1912–1930)*. PhD Dissertation. National University of Singapore, 2015.

Reid, Anthony. *An Indonesian Frontier: Acehnese & Other Histories of Sumatra*. Singapore: Singapore University Press, 2005.

Ricklefs, M. C. *A History of Modern Indonesia since c. 1200*, Third Edition. Houndmills: Palgrave Macmillan, 2001 [1981].

Rosaldo, Renato. "Introduction: The Borders of Belonging". In *Cultural Citizenship in Island Southeast Asia: Nation and Belonging in the Hinterlands*, edited by Renato Rosaldo, 1–15. Berkeley: University of California Press, 2003.

Rossell, Deac. *Living Pictures. The Origins of the Movies*. New York: SUNY, 1998.

Ruppin, Dafna and Nadi Tofighian. "Moving Pictures across Colonial Boundaries: The Multiple Nationalities of the American Biograph in Southeast Asia". *Early Popular Visual Culture* 14, No. 2 (2016): 188–207.

Ruppin, Dafna. "From 'Crocodile City' to '*Ville Lumière*': Cinema Spaces on the Urban Landscape of Colonial Surabaya". *SOJOURN: Journal of Social Issues in Southeast Asia* 29, no. 1 (2014): 1–30.

———, "Asta Nielsen, Cinema-going and Film Censorship in the Netherlands-Indies, 1912–1918". In *Importing Asta Nielsen: The International Film Star in the Making 1910–1914*, edited by Martin Loiperdinger and Uli Jung, 299–307. New Barnet: John Libbey, 2013.

———, "'Views from the Japanese-Russian War': Re-titling Russo-Japanese War Film Programmes in the Netherlands and Netherlands Indies". In *The Construction of News in Early Cinema*, edited by Angel Quintana and Jordi Pons, 191–202. Girona: Fundació Museu del Cinema & Ajuntament de Girona, 2011.

Ryan, James R. *Picturing Empire: Photography and the Visualization of the British Empire*. Chicago: The University of Chicago Press, 1998.

Sadoul, Georges. *Histoire générale du cinéma. Tome 2: Les Pionniers du cinéma, 1897–1909*. Paris: Denoël, 1973.

Said, Edward W. *Orientalism*. New York: Vintage Books, 1979.

Salmon, Claudine. *Literature in Malay by the Chinese of Indonesia: A Provisional Annotated Bibliography*. Paris: Éditions de la Maison des Sciences de l'Homme, 1981.

Salmon, Stéphanie. *Pathé: À la conquète du cinema 1896–1929*. Paris: Éditions Tallandier, 2014.

Sarkissian, Margaret. "Armenians in South-East Asia". *Crossroads: An Interdisciplinary Journal of Southeast Asian Studies* 3, no. 2/3 (1987): 1–33.

Schulte Nordholt, Henk. "Modernity and middle classes in the Netherlands Indies: Cultivating cultural citizenship". In *Photography, Modernity and the Governed in Late-colonial Indonesia*, edited by Susie Protschky, 223-254. Amsterdam: Amsterdam University Press, 2015.

———, "Modernity and Cultural Citizenship in the Netherlands Indies", *Journal of Southeast Asian Studies* 42, no. 3 (October 2011): 435–457.

———, "Introduction". In *Outward Appearances: Dressing State and Society in Indonesia*, edited by Henk Schulte Nordholt, 1–37. Leiden: KITLV Press, 1997.

———, (ed.). *Outward Appearances: Dressing State and Society in Indonesia*. Leiden: KITLV Press, 1997.

Schwartz, Vanessa R. and J.M. Przyblyski (eds.), *The Nineteenth-Century Visual Culture Reader*. New York: Routledge, 2004.

Scidmore, Eliza Ruhamah. *Java, The Garden of the East*. New York: The Century Co., 1897.

Sears, Laurie J. "Modernity and Decadence in *Fin-de-Siècle* Fiction of the Dutch Empire". *Indonesia* 90 (October 2010): 97–201.

See Java: Garden of the East. Issued by Michael's Java Motor Touring Co. Sourabaya: J. M. Chs. Nijland Ltd., ca. 1920.

Setijadi-Dunn, Charlotte and Thomas Barker. "Imagining 'Indonesia': Ethnic Chinese film producers in pre-independence cinema". *Asian Cinema* 21, no. 2 (2010): 7–24.

Shail, Andrew. "Intermediality: Disciplinary flux or formalist retrenchment?". *Early Popular Visual Culture* 8, no. 1 (2010): 3–15.

——, "'A distinct advance in society': Early cinema's 'proletarian public sphere' and isolated spectatorship in the UK, 1911–18". *Journal of British Cinema and Television* 3, no. 2 (2006): 209–228.

Shiraishi, Takashi. *An Age in Motion: Popular Radicalism in Java, 1912–1926*. Ithaca: Cornell University Press, 1990.

Simmel, Georg. "The Metropolis and Mental Life (1903)". In *The Nineteenth-Century Visual Culture Reader*, edited by Vanessa R. Schwartz and J.M. Przyblyski, 51–55. New York: Routledge, 2004.

Singer, Ben. *Melodrama and Modernity: Early Sensational Cinema and Its Contexts*. New York: Columbia University Press, 2001.

Somers Heidhues, Mary. "Chinese Voluntary and Involuntary Associations in Indonesia". In *Voluntary Organizations in the Chinese Diaspora*, edited by Khun Eng Kuah-Pearce and Evelyn Hu-Dehart, 77–97. Hong Kong: Hong Kong University Press, 2006.

Stein, Eric A. "Colonial Theatres of Proof: Representation and Laughter in 1930s Rockefeller Foundation Hygiene Cinema in Java". *Health & History*, 8 no. 2 (2006): 14–44.

Stevens, Theo. "Semarang, Central Java and the World Market 1870–1900". In *The Indonesian City: Studies in Urban Development and Planning*, edited by Peter J.M. Nas, 56–70. Dordrecht-Holland/Cinnaminson-U.S.A.: Foris Publications, 1986.

Stoler, Ann Laura. *Carnal Knowledge and Imperial Power: Race and the Intimate in Colonial Rule*. Berkeley: University of California Press, 2002.

——, "Making Empire Respectable: The Politics of Race and Sexual Morality in 20th-Century Colonial Cultures". *American Ethnologist* 16, no. 4 (November 1989): 634–660.

——, *Capitalism and Confrontation in Sumatra's Plantation Belt, 1870–1989*. New Haven/London: Yale University Press, 1985.

Suryadi. "The 'talking machine' comes to the Dutch East Indies: The arrival of Western media technology in Southeast Asia". *Bijdragen tot de Taal-, Land- en Volkenkunde (BKI)* 162, no. 2/3 (2006): 269–305.

Tan Sooi Beng. *Bangsawan, A Social and Stylistic History of Popular Malay Opera*. Singapore: Oxford University Press, 1993.

Taylor, Jean Gelman. *Global Indonesia (Routledge Contemporary Southeast Asia Series)*. London: Routledge, 2013.

——, *The Social World of Batavia: Europeans and Eurasians in Colonial Indonesia*, Second Edition. Madison: The University of Wisconsin Press, 2009 [1983].

——, "Nyai Dasima: Portrait of a Mistress in Literature and Film". In *Fantasizing the Feminine in Indonesia*, edited by Laurie J. Sears, 225–248. Durham/London: Duke University Press, 1996.

Thompson, Kristin. *Exporting Entertainment: America in the World Film Market, 1907–34*. London: BFI Publishing, 1985.

Tjasmadi, H. M. Johan. *100 tahun sejarah bioskop di Indonesia*. Bandung: Megindo Tunggal Sejahtera, 2008.

Tjiang, O. S. *Sair Tjerita di tempo tahoen 1813 Jang Belom Brapa Lama Soeda kadjadian di Betawi Terpoengoet Dari Boekoe: Njaie Dasima*. Batavia: Ijap Goan Ho, 1897.

Toer, Pramoedya Ananta. *This Earth of Mankind [Bumi Manusia]*, translated by Max Lane. New York: Penguin, 1990 [1975].

Tofighian, Nadi. *Blurring the Colonial Binary: Turn-of-the-Century Transnational Entertainment in Southeast Asia*, PhD Dissertation. Stockholm University, 2013.

Toulet, Emmanuelle. "Le cinéma à l'Éxposition universelle de 1900". *Revue d'histoire moderne et contemporaine (1954-)* 33, no. 2 (April–June 1986): 179–209.

Tsuchiya, Kenji. "Popular Literature and Colonial Society in Late-Nineteenth-Century Java – Cerita Nyai Dasima, the Macabre Story of an Englishman's Concubine". *Southeast Asian Studies* 28, no. 4 (1991): 467–480.

Urban, Charles. *A Yank in Britain: The Lost Memoirs of Charles Urban, Film Pioneer*, edited by Luke McKernan. Hastings (East Sussex): The Projection Box, 1999.

Uricchio, William. "Law and the Cinema: Regulating Exhibition". In *Encyclopedia of Early Cinema*, edited by Richard Abel, 374–377. London: Routledge, 2005.

Velden, André van der and Judith Thissen. "Spectacles of Conspicuous Consumption: Picture Palaces, War Profiteers and the Social Dynamics of Moviegoing in the Netherlands, 1914–1922". *Film History* 22 (2010): 453–462.

Veth, Bas. *Het Leven in Nederlandsch-Indië*. Amsterdam: P.N. van Kampen & Zoon, 1900.

Vickers, Adrian. *A History of Modern Indonesia*. Cambridge: Cambridge University Press, 2005.

——, "Modernity and Being *Moderen*: An Introduction". In *Being Modern in Bali: Image and Change*, edited by Adrian Vickers, 1–36. New Haven: Yale University Southeast Asia Studies, 1996.

Wachlin, Steven. "Salzwedel". In *In het Voetspoor van Louis Couperus*, edited by Karin Peterson and Steven Wachlin, 112–118. Amsterdam, KIT Publishers, 2009.

Watson, C. "Some preliminary remarks on the antecedents of modern Indonesian literature". *Bijdragen tot de Taal-, Land- en Volkenkunde (BKI)* 127, no. 4 (1971): 417–433.

Wellenstein, E. "Means of Communication". In *Twentieth Century Impressions of Netherlands India: Its History, People, Commerce, Industries and Resources*, edited by Arnold Wright, 189–204. London: Lloyd's Greater Britain Publishing Company, 1909.

Wertheim, W. F. *Indonesian Society in Transition: A Study of Social Change*, Second Revised Edition. The Hague: W. van Hoeve Ltd., 1959 [1956].

Williams, Lea E. *Overseas Chinese Nationalism: The Genesis of the Pan-Chinese Movement in Indonesia, 1900–1916*. Glencoe: The Free Press, 1960.

Worsfold, W. Basil. *A Visit to Java. With An Account of The Founding of Singapore*. London: Richard Bentley and Son, 1893.

Wright, Arnold (ed.). *Twentieth Century Impressions of Netherlands India: Its History, People, Commerce, Industries and Resources*. London: Lloyd's Greater Britain Publishing Company, 1909.

Wright, Nadia H. *Respected Citizens: The History of Armenians in Singapore and Malaysia*. Melbourne: Amassia Publishing, 2003.

Young, Robert J. C. *White Mythologies: Writing History and the West*. London: Verso, 1990.

Zwaan, Klaas de. *A cinema in between. Nationalizing foreign propaganda film in Dutch cinema culture (1914–1919)* [working title], PhD Dissertation. Utrecht University, forthcoming 2016.

Websites

The Bioscope, Luke McKernan. "Lives in Film no. 1: Alfred Dreyfus – Part 2". Accessed on 2 February 2016. http://thebioscope.net/2010/03/11/lives-in-film-no-1-alfred-dreyfus-part-2/.

Cinema Context. "Boer War Films". Accessed on 2 February 2016, http://www.cinemacontext.nl/id/F032064.

La Cineteca del Friuli. "The Wonders of the Biograph". Accessed on 2 February 2016. http://www.cinetecadelfriuli.org/gcm/ed_precedenti/edizione2000/biograph2000.html.

Colonial Film: Moving Images of the British Empire. "Battle of Spion Kop: Ambulance Corps Crossing the Tugela River". Accessed on 2 February 2016. http://www.colonialfilm.org.uk/node/1943.

——, "Field Ambulances Crossing the Vaal River". Accessed on 2 February 2016. http://www.colonialfilm.org.uk/node/1950.

Eye Film Institute Netherlands. "The Coronation of Queen Wilhelmina of Holland at Amsterdam". Accessed on 2 February 2016. https://www.eyefilm.nl/en/collection/film-history/film/the-coronation-of-queen-wilhelmina-of-holland-at-amsterdam.

——, "Feestelijke ontvangst van H.M. Koningin Wilhelmina en den Prins-Gemaal te

Schwerin". Accessed on 2 February 2016. https://www.eyefilm.nl/en/collection/film-history/film/feestelijke-ontvangst-van-hm-koningin-wilhelmina-en-den-prins-gemaal-te.

———, "Hoek van Holland nach der Katastrophe. Der Schiffbruch des Dampfers Berlin". Accessed on 2 February 2016. https://www.eyefilm.nl/en/collection/film-history/film/hoek-van-holland-nach-der-katastrophe-der-schiffbruch-des-dampfers.

———, "De Huwelijksplechtigheden te 's-Gravenhave". Accessed on 2 February 2016. https://www.eyefilm.nl/en/collection/film-history/film/de-huwelijksplechtigheden-te-s-gravenhage.

———, "Huwelijksstoet ter gelegenheid van het huwelijk van Wilhelmina en Hendrik". Accessed on 2 February 2016. https://www.eyefilm.nl/en/collection/film-history/film/huwelijksstoet-ter-gelegenheid-van-het-huwelijk-van-wilhelmina-en.

https://www.eyefilm.nl/collectie/filmgeschiedenis/film/huwelijksstoet-ter-gelegenheid-van-het-huwelijk-van-wilhelmina-en.

———, "Inhuldiging Koningin Wilhelmina te Amsterdam". Accessed on 2 February 2016. https://www.eyefilm.nl/en/collection/film-history/film/inhuldiging-koningin-wilhelmina-te-amsterdam).

———, "Nederlandsche Biograaf- en Mutoscope Maatschappij". Accessed on 2 February 2016. https://www.eyefilm.nl/en/collection/film-history/company/nederlandsche-biograaf-en-mutoscope-maatschappij.

———, "Plechtige Intocht van H. M. Koningin Wilhelmina in Amsterdam". Accessed on 2 February 2016. https://www.eyefilm.nl/en/collection/film-history/film/plechtige-intocht-van-hm-koningin-wilhelmina-in-amsterdam.

Film Indonesia. "Njai Dasima". Accessed on 2 February 2016. http://catalogue.filmindonesia.or.id/movie/title/lf-n011-29-352520_njai-dasima-i.

Fondation Jérôme Seydoux-Pathé. "Java pittoresque". Accessed on 2 February 2016. http://filmographie.fondation-jeromeseydoux-pathe.com/453-java-pittoresque.

Gaumont-Pathé Archives. "Gaumont (Boites Vertes) Actualité". Accessed on 2 February 2016. http://www.gaumontpathearchives.com/indexPopup.php?urlaction=doc&id_doc=158645&rang=4.

Geheugen van Nederland, ReclameArsenaal. "Pink Pillen". Accessed on 2 February 2016. http://www.geheugenvannederland.nl/?/nl/items/RA01:30051001526331.

Genelogie Online. "Charles Jacob Umbgrove". Accessed on 2 February 2016. http://www.genealogieonline.nl/genealogie-baert-cornelis-kalshoven/I10231.php.

Indonesian Film Center. "Soerabaia, het straatverkeer op pasar-besar 15 juli 1929". Accessed on 2 February 2016. http://www.indonesianfilmcenter.com/pages/filmbox/filmbox.php?bid=6059.

———, "Stadsgemeente Soerabaja mei 1930 haven en reede van Soerabaja". Accessed on 2 February 2016. http://www.indonesianfilmcenter.com/pages/archive/watch.arcv.php?v=5620.

———, "Rondvaart in het basin van het Marine Etablissement te Soerabaja 9 mei 1932". Accessed on 2 February 2016. http://www.indonesianfilmcenter.com/pages/archive/watch.arcv.php?v=5650.

Koninklijk Instituut voor de Tropen. "Programma [van de] Nederlandsch-Indische Electro Bioscoop in den Soloschen Schouwburg", ca. 1930. No longer available. http://search.kit.nl/vivisimo/cgi-bin/query-meta.exe?v%3Aproject=kit-da&query=nederlandsch-indische+electro+bioscoop.

Library of Congress. "History of Edison Motion Pictures". Accessed on 2 February 2016. http://www.loc.gov/collections/edison-company-motion-pictures-and-sound-recordings/articles-and-essays/history-of-edison-motion-pictures/.

Rutgers University Community Repository. "Films of the Passion Play". Accessed on 2 February 2016. http://dx.doi.org/doi:10.7282/T3X92BMJ.

Swiss Camera Museum. "Le cocher et le mauvais payeur". Accessed on 2 February 2016. http://www.cameramuseum.ch/fr/N2071/le-cocher-et-le-mauvais-payeur.html.

Appendix

Local Views as Screened by Exhibitors

Talbot's Scenimatograph
- "Four Acehnese in combat with a sergeant", or "A sergeant attacked by four Acehnese", or "an Attack on a sergeant in Acheen" (1897)
- "A tram on Rijswijk", or "The departure of the tram at Batavia" (1897)
- "A scene from the Zoo in Batavia", or "The [bicycle] ride to the pond at the Zoo" (1897)
- "The departure of a mail boat from Tandjong Priok" (1897)
- "Bathing natives", or "A troop of natives bathing", or "Bathing and clothes washing women in the Kali river at Noordwijk", or "A number of boys bathing in the Kali at Batavia", or "Malays bathing in a river" (1897)
- "Javanese dancing girl" (1897)

Netherlands Indies Biograph (later Johannes Biograph and Vardon Biograph)
- "Uprising in Gedangan" (1904)
- "Javanese folk games [*volksspelen*]" (1906)
- "*Sedekah* [giving alms]" (1906)
- "*Topang* [masquerade]" (1906)
- "*Tandak* [Javanese dancers in] Bandung" (1906)
- "Native wedding ceremonies" (1906)
- "Marriage of the Crown Prince of Jogja (Own recording)" (1907)
- "The zest of Surabaya", or "Surabaya's zest on Pasar Besar" filmed by Van der Kloet and Verder (1908)
- "Two Chinese cruisers the Haij Kie and Haij Yong", or "Chinese warships in Surabaya" (1908)
- "The celebration at [Semarang's] City Garden" (1908)
- "The great Football match in Surabaya between Thor and E.C.A. (Own recording)" filmed by Van der Kloet and Verder (1908)
- "Own recording of the recent *Sekaten* celebrations in Solo", filmed by Van der Kloet and Verder (1908), or "The *Sekaten* celebrations in Solo (in several tableaux, own recording)"
- "The parades etc. at the *Pasar Malam* [Night Market in Surabaya]" in 35 tableaux (1908), including:
  - A beautifully lit picture of the influx of the public to the main gate, seen from the "Tobacco Plant"
  - A series of images, particularly clear, from the exhibition's opening, seen from the inside, such as: the flow of people inside, curiosities of every nationality; women in neat frocks; and dignified committee members
  - An overview of what was on display at the exhibition, such as: along the attractive rows of sheds; along the restaurants, along the dancers and swordsmen, along the *gamelan* and the *kampung tukang*; an incubator where eggs are hatched
  - Other events immortalised on film include: the parades, the cattle exhibition, "Native" competitions
- "A peek into the *ateliers* of construction shop der Vorstenlanden" (1908)

- "Mr. Watson's iron factory in Yogyakarta" (1908)
- "Borobudur [famous Buddhist temple] in Magelang, Central Java" (1908)
- "Own recordings of the celebrations [in Semarang]" (1908), or "Pasar Malam [Night Market] in Semarang (own recording)"
- "Nature views from the Tenger mountain range (own recording)", or "Nature scenes from the Tenger [mountains]" (1909)
- "Crocodile hunt" (1909), or "The crocodile hunt on Java" (screened in Makassar in 1911)
- "Catching snakes in the caves of Pasuruan [in Eastern Java]" (1909)
- "The Chinese Fancy Fair, in the city gardens here [Surabaya]" in 25 tableaux, and possibly shown with the addition of other scenes as "Fancy Fair in Surabaya (32 tableaux) (own recording)" (1909)
- "Javanese pleasures" (1909)
- "The *Oranje* celebrations in Surabaya" (1909), including:

    - "The gun salute with cannons"
    - "The heavy traffic at Pasar Besar"
    - "The parade at *alun alun* Kemajoran"
    - "The arrival of 8,000 schoolchildren at the Stadstuin"
    - "Children's singing directed by Mr. Stoel"
    - "The resident thanking Mr. Stoel for his direction"
    - "The Chinese schoolchildren"
    - "The Javanese amusements"
    - "Awarding of the prizes at the *alun alun* Kemajoran"
    - "*Tonnetje steken* [Dutch folklore game]"
    - "Blindfolded bottle game"
    - "Climbing the mast"
    - "Bicycle riding"
    - "Running on smooth tree trunks"
    - "Procession of different peoples, coloured"

- "Hunting wild animals on Java" (1909)
- "Surabaya at every hour of the day" (1913), probably from East Java Bioscope

Esoofally's Royal Bioscope

- "Njai Dasima. Specially recorded by the Royal Bioscope Cy." (1906)
- "The *Sekaten* festival in Yogyakarta. Filmed by the Royal Bioscope Cy." (1906)
- "Panoramas of the whole of Java. Recorded by the Royal Bioscope Cy." (1906)
- "Surabaya. Pasar Besar at Wonokromo. Filmed by the Royal Bioscope Cy." (1906)

Phono Animatograph

- "The trip from Marseille to Batavia, coloured film" (1906)

Royal Vio

- "Shots of nature of Batavia and Java" (1906)
- "*Tandak* and *topeng* festival in Batavia" (1906)
- "Opium den in Senen" (1906)

Loa Soen Yang's Flying Bioscope

- "Idyll in the Indies. (a very beautiful film)" (1907) – possibly Pathé Frères

Alhambra Bioscope

- "A turtle capture in Surabaya" (1908)

Appendix – Local Views as Screened by Exhibitor

Emma Ripograph
- "*Karapan* [bull racing festival] held at Bangkalan, recorded by the Emma Ripograph" (1908)

Artiestieke Bioscope
- "A peek at Sunda. Recording from nature" (1909)
- "Great *Garebeg Moeloed* [Javanese celebration marking the birthdate of the Prophet Muhammad] in Yogyakarta 1909" (1909)

Excelsior Bioscope
- "Wedding celebrations in Solo" (1909) – possibly Pathé Frères
- "Second part of Wedding celebrations in Solo" (1909)

Flying Bioscope
- "The Batavia races" filmed by Demmeni, 300 meters long (1909)
- "*Oranje* celebrations in Batavia" filmed by Demmeni (1909), among the tableaux:

> "1.The entire parade: arrival, inspection by and honouring of the Governor General.
> 2.The children's festival (for 4,000 children) at the Wilhelminapark.
> 3.The folklore games at Koningsplein; one sees here the gentlemen's race carrying women in a *dos-à-dos*, races of "Natives", *boegsprietlopen* [walking the greasy pole], *ringsteken* [ring stabbing, i.e. tilt at the ring], etc.
> 4.The children's festival at the Zoo, boys sack racing and parade to the bust of H. M. Queen Wilhelmina (this recording is very nice).
> 5.The celebration at the Zoo by "Natives" and Foreign Orientals, flying hot air balloons, parades, *wayang wong* dance, etc.
> 6.Military cyclists festival at Waterlooplein. The festivities at the Zoo and the military celebrations especially excel in action."

Helios Bioscoop
- "A tea plantation in the Preanger. One saw on screen how the tea is planted, pruned, plucked and prepared, and finally how you can enjoy afternoon tea in Europe. If the pickers in the Preanger looked as dainty as the tea drinkers in Europe, nothing much would come out of the tea crop!" (1909) – possibly Pathé Frères

Nationaal Bioscoop
- "The *Oranje* celebrations in Yogyakarta: Children's parade and planting the Juliana-tree at the Residence yard" (1909)

Hartman Bioscoop, by Umbgrove
- "New films of the *Oranje* celebrations" filmed by C. J. Umbgrove (1909), including:

> ᵒ"For instance, it is in no part undesirable that one in Holland learns to realize that our militia is a brave gang willing and able, like Van der Werft, to let one hand devour and fight with the other one, and flannering in the ranks as if they never had anything else in hand."
> ᵒ"A representation of a pottery workshop company near Surabaya. One sees the work at the familiar turntable, the colouring, and baking of the pots and pans, all recorded with a sharpness that leaves no doubt about what is happening."

Sirene Bioscope
- "A panther hunt in Java (beautifully coloured nature scene)" (1909)

Apollo Modern Biograph
- "The flying foxes (*kalongs* [fruit bats]) hunt on Sumatra" (1910)

Cine Lumen, S. M. Aidid
- "A trip to the volcanoes and craters in Java" (1910)

  º"Tangkuban Perahu in action, one can form a clear image of the great volcanic dead and living world. The Bromo and Semeru are not to be forgotten either".

Globe Bioscope, Loa Soen Yang
- "The sailing and motorboat races of the B. J. C. [Batavia Yacht Club]" (1910)
  º"The recording is a bit blurry and grey which, considering the weather that day, is not surprising. On the screen are successively brought forth: the start of the sailing boats race, the two motor boats steaming ahead towards the tribune, the arrival of *Sri Tadjau* from the sea and the departure of motor boats from Tanjung Priok port."

East-Java Bioscope, C. J. Umbgrove
- "The collapsed structure of the Mutual Interest [Onderling Belang] Company, O. J. B. recording", or "The collapsed plot of the Mutual Interest Limited Company" (1911)
- "The arrival of the Governor General in Surabaya" (1911)
- "The opening of the port construction work" (1911)
- "With a cinema device on board the *Willem I* to Magelang with the aim of capturing the cog railway outbound and return journey", filmed by R. W. Badenbreek (1912)
- "Bull contest in Bangkalan (Madura)" (1913)
- "Surabaya at every hour of the day" (1913), screened by Vardon and the Imperial
- "A Dayak village on the island of Borneo" (1913)
- "Surabaya news" (1913)

ºThe collapsed warehouse on West Kalimas
ºThe propaganda meeting of the Sarekat Islam
ºThe assembly of a glider in the A.C.W.
- "Independence celebrations [probably a recording of the celebrations held in Surabaya to mark Dutch independence from the French" (1913)

Stella Ripograph, Hartman
- "The sugar industry in Java, a rare beautifully coloured recording from reality of one of the sugar factories in Pasuruan" (1911), probably a Pathé Frères recording

Transvalia Theater, owner: J. G. C. Droste (also owner of Walhalla Bioscoop)
- "The sugar industry on Java" (1911) – Probably a Pathé Frères recording
- "Mouse deer hunting on Java, beautifully coloured recording from nature. An opportunity for hunting enthusiasts to enjoy" (1911)

Imperial Bioscoop
- "Interesting Javanese nature" (1913)

Modjo-Pahit Bioscoop
- "A crocodile hunt" (1913)
- "Dancing girls in Bali" (1913)
- "Plough Monday [traditional start of the agricultural year] on Java" (1913)

www.ingramcontent.com/pod-product-compliance
Lightning Source LLC
Chambersburg PA
CBHW061250230426

43664CB00024B/2909